Computational Social Sciences

Computational Social Sciences

A series of authored and edited monographs that utilize quantitative and computational methods to model, analyze and interpret large-scale social phenomena. Titles within the series contain methods and practices that test and develop theories of complex social processes through bottom-up modeling of social interactions. Of particular interest is the study of the co-evolution of modern communication technology and social behavior and norms, in connection with emerging issues such as trust, risk, security and privacy in novel socio-technical environments.

Computational Social Sciences is explicitly transdisciplinary: quantitative methods from fields such as dynamical systems, artificial intelligence, network theory, agent based modeling, and statistical mechanics are invoked and combined with state-of the-art mining and analysis of large data sets to help us understand social agents, their interactions on and offline, and the effect of these interactions at the macro level. Topics include, but are not limited to social networks and media, dynamics of opinions, cultures and conflicts, socio-technical co-evolution and social psychology. Computational Social Sciences will also publish monographs and selected edited contributions from specialized conferences and workshops specifically aimed at communicating new findings to a large transdisciplinary audience. A fundamental goal of the series is to provide a single forum within which commonalities and differences in the workings of this field may be discerned, hence leading to deeper insight and understanding.

More information about this series at http://www.springer.com/series/11784

Juan A. Barceló · Florencia Del Castillo
Editors

Simulating Prehistoric and Ancient Worlds

Springer

Editors
Juan A. Barceló
Department of Prehistory
Universitat Autònoma de Barcelona
Bellaterra
Spain

Florencia Del Castillo
Patagonia National Research Center (CENPAT) National Scientific and Technical Research Council (CONICET)
Puerto Madryn
Argentina

ISSN 2509-9574 ISSN 2509-9582 (electronic)
Computational Social Sciences
ISBN 978-3-319-31479-2 ISBN 978-3-319-31481-5 (eBook)
DOI 10.1007/978-3-319-31481-5

Library of Congress Control Number: 2016948617

Printed on acid-free paper

This Springer imprint is published by Springer Nature
The registered company is Springer International Publishing AG
The registered company address is: Gewerbestrasse 11, 6330 Cham, Switzerland

Contents

1 **Simulating the Past for Understanding the Present. A Critical Review** 1
Juan A. Barceló and Florencia Del Castillo

2 **Multi-scale Agent-Based Simulation of Long-Term Dispersal Processes: Towards a Sophisticated Simulation Model of Hominin Dispersal** 141
Ingo J. Timm, Fabian Lorig, Ericson Hölzchen and Christine Hertler

3 **An Agent-Based Model of Resource Distribution on Hunter-Gatherer Foraging Strategies: Clumped Habitats Favor Lower Mobility, but Result in Higher Foraging Returns** 159
Marco A. Janssen and Kim Hill

4 **Testing Brantingham's Neutral Model: The Effect of Spatial Clustering on Stone Raw Material Procurement** 175
Simen Oestmo, Marco A. Janssen and Curtis W. Marean

5 **Population Spread and Cultural Transmission in Neolithic Transitions** 189
Joaquim Fort, Neus Isern, Antonieta Jerardino and Bernardo Rondelli

6 **Modelling Routeways in a Landscape of Esker and Bog** 199
Yolande O'Brien and Stefan Bergh

7 **Modelling Cultural Shift: Application to Processes of Language Displacement** 219
Neus Isern and Joaquim Fort

8 **Pathways for Scale and Discipline Reconciliation: Current Socio-Ecological Modelling Methodologies to Explore and Reconstitute Human Prehistoric Dynamics** 233
Mehdi Saqalli and Tilman Baum

9 Simulating Land Use of Prehistoric Wetland Settlements: Did Excessive Resource Use Necessitate a Highly Dynamic Settlement System? 255
Tilman Baum

10 Revisiting the Dynamics Between Two Ancient Japanese Descent Groups: What Happened from the Jomon to the Yayoi Periods in Japan 281
Fumihiro Sakahira and Takao Terano

11 Cultural and Genetic Transmission in the Jomon–Yayoi Transition Examined in an Agent-Based Demographic Simulation 311
Naoko Matsumoto and Mariko Sasakura

12 Economic Sustainability in Relation to Demographic Decline of Celtic Agglomerations in Central Europe: Multiple-Scenario Approach 335
Kamila Štekerová and Alžběta Danielisová

13 ZambeziLand: A Canonical Theory and Agent-Based Model of Polity Cycling in the Zambezi Plateau, Southern Africa 359
Gary Bogle and Claudio Cioffi-Revilla

14 Personalities, Physiology, Institutions and Genetics: Simulating Ancient Societies with Intelligent Virtual Agents 377
Tomas Trescak, Anton Bogdanovych and Simeon Simoff

Chapter 1
Simulating the Past for Understanding the Present. A Critical Review

Juan A. Barceló and Florencia Del Castillo

1.1 Introduction to an Introduction

This book has been edited with the explicit idea of allowing the reader to imagine that virtual histories can be generated in a computer in the same way as in her/his mind. This is not a literary exercise, however, but an example of a radical revolution in the way of doing History as a social science. While computational models can be used to simulate real-world processes in great detail (e.g., some manufacturing processes), their greatest potential for historical explanation lies in using them as environments of systematic, controlled, virtual experiments in human social and socio-ecological dynamics (Bankes et al. 2002; Diamond and Robinson 2010; Barton et al. 2012; Barton 2013, 2014; Hmeljak and Goldstone 2016; Nakoinz and Knitter 2016; Cegielski and Rogers 2016). Importantly, such models are constructed from the bottom up, requiring the integration of knowledge about human social processes and theory about the relationships among individual actors and groups at multiple scales to create the algorithms which drive agent perception, decision-making, and action. Used in this way, building computational models can help refine our concepts about the operation of societies, and the models can serve as complex hypotheses that can be tested against the empirical record of archaeological, ethnological or historical research (Barton 2014).

The essays present in this book are the result of a special session organized during the annual conference of the European Social Simulation Association (ESSA) held at the Autonomous University of Barcelona (Spain) on September 2014. "Simulating the Past to Understand Human History"—SPUHH—for the first time in an ESSA con-

J.A. Barceló (✉)
Department of Prehistory, Universitat Autònoma de Barcelona, Bellaterra, Spain
e-mail: juanantonio.barcelo@uab.cat

F. Del Castillo
National Scientific and Technical Research Council (CONICET), Puerto Madryn, Argentina
e-mail: delcastillo@cenpat-conicet.gob.ar

J.A. Barceló and F. Del Castillo (eds.), *Simulating Prehistoric and Ancient Worlds*, Computational Social Sciences, DOI 10.1007/978-3-319-31481-5_1

ference gathered a multidisciplinary group of researchers interested in different developments of computer simulation in the archaeological and historical sciences. The most interesting part of this session was the increasing interest of a multidisciplinary community to implement computer simulations to solve historical problems. Not only archaeologists and historians are now interested on long term simulations, the presence of physicists, economists, computer scientists, historians, sociologists, geographers and anthropologists reflects the transdisciplinarity of this way of research. The papers selected to be published in this book express some of this excitement.

Most contributions are studies of the most remote past: prehistory and archaeology. But it does not mean that other historical periods cannot be made understandable recreating what people did and believed within a computer. In practice, then, the virtual pasts we can recreate within a computer are accessible in the sense that they tend to realign this paradigmatic new way of understanding the past with both the commonsense trivial idea that history is about what people did in the past (Düring 2014; Lake 2015; Lercari 2016; Cegielski and Rogers 2016; Marwick 2016).

1.1.1 A "New" Way of Understanding Human History?

History is a science that should look for causal affirmations about the formation processes of society. Therefore, the startpoint of historical research should be explaining past social events by showing how human behavior fit into a causal structure, that is to say, a vast network of interacting actions and entities, where a change in a property of an entity dialectically produces a change in a property of another entity (transformation).

This focus on the causal understanding of historical processes fits well with the notion that archaeology and history should offer something to contemporary society as an integrated science of long-term societal change and human-environment interaction (Rashevsky 1968; Abbott 1983; Turchin 2008, 2011; Hurley 2012; Gavin 2014; Lake 2015; Cegielski and Rogers 2016). History is not the identification of who did what in the past, but the quest for what produced a social action whose effects and consequences may be discerned in the present. Moreover, what generated those consequences was the interaction of a number of actions and entities, characterized by direct, invariant and change-relating generalizations. History as an explicitly scientific discipline should evolve from a subjective description of what we believe happened in the past, to an investigation of the causes of the present.

Descriptive chains of events, even if true, are not explanations but they are something to be explained. Clearly, nothing is gained if we introduce as an explanation of why some x occured, an indicator that some y occurred before or after (where x and y refer to different acts, events or processes). In some sense, causal interactions are the factors explaining why a social action was performed at a specific time and place, which is, its motivation or reason.

We can understand social action in the past only in terms of how humans did it. It is easy to see then that the concept of mechanism becomes the heart of this kind of causal explanation. Obviously, the word "mechanism" is here a parable of how social intentions, goals and behaviors are causally connected. A "social mechanism" should then explain how social activity worked, rather than why the traits contributing to these activities or workings are there (Bechtel and Richardson 1993; Machamer 2002; Craver 2001; Darden 2002; Glennan 2002; Gerring 2008; Ylikoski 2011; Maurer 2016). "Mechanisms are entities and activities organized such that they are productive of regular changes from start or set-up to finish or termination conditions" (Machamer et al. 2000, p. 3). No matter how long or complicated the causal process is, it can be called a mechanism if its description answers the question how did the cause bring about the effect.

We are adopting an analytical approach in which "social facts" are seen as generated, triggered, produced, brought about or "caused" by actions which themselves are in some sense "caused," or at least partly determined by the constraints presented by the social environments and situations in which such actions take place (Elster 1989). To explain a social event therefore means to describe the various causal chains linking all the elements involved (once those elements have been appropriately described and separated) in constituting a social fact.

These prospective for a new way of understanding human history are strongly related with current developments in Analytical Sociology. Such a term officially entered the sociological vocabulary with Hedström's *Dissecting the Social* (Hedström 2005) to denote the sociological perspective that seeks systematically to formulate and empirically test micro-founded, mechanism-based explanations of complex macro-level patterns and dynamics (see also: Bortolini 2007; Hedström and Bearman 2009a, b; Racko 2011; Raub et al. 2011; Bearman 2012; Edling 2012; Wan 2012; Opp 2013; Manzo 2010; 2014; Lombardo 2015). According to such definition, we can envisage a kind of "Analytical history" when trying to understand complex chains of change in terms of the discovery of patterns in transitions. To build such a discipline, and paraphrasing Manzo (2014), we should modify the actual way of describing the past and:

1. using concepts that are as clear and precise as possible to describe both the facts to be explained and the explanatory hypotheses/facts mobilized to explain them, while avoiding all linguistic obscurity and convolutedness (Pomeranz 2011),
2. mobilizing the best quantitative and qualitative empirical information available and use the technical tools best suited to describing the facts to be explained,
3. making emphasis on the social outcome(s) evidenced somewhere and somewhen to understand what happened and why. This can be done by first formulating a "generative model" that is, a model of a set of mechanisms, where a mechanism is a set of entities and activities likely to trigger a sequence of events (i.e., a process) likely to bring about the outcome(s),
4. providing a realistic description of the relevant micro-level entities and activities assumed to be at work, as well as the structural interdependencies in which these entities are embedded and their activities unfold,
5. translating our hypothesis of the social mechanism implied in the causal connections between events into a "generative model" in order to rigorously assess

the internal consistency of the hypothesis and to determine its high-level consequences,

6. comparing the predictions made by the generative model with the empirical description of the historical facts to be explained in order to assess the generative sufficiency of the mechanisms postulated,
7. injecting as much empirical data as possible into the generative model in order to prove that the hypothesized assumptions are not only generative sufficient but also empirically grounded, and reanalyze its behavior and high-level consequences.

A common objection to employing mathematical and formal models in the study of historical dynamics is that social systems are so complex that any mathematical model would be a hopeless oversimplification without any chance of telling us interesting things about these systems. As Turchin (2008, 2011) has argued, this argument is wrong: when any model appears to be "complex" then, the only way to analyze its behavior is through objective measuring and using mathematical language. "Naked" human brain is not a bad tool for extrapolating linear trends, but it fails abysmally when confronted with systems of multiple parts interconnected with nonlinear feedback loops. We need mathematical formalism to express our ideas unambiguously, and both analytical methods and fast computers to determine the implications of the assumptions we made (West 2011).

The advantage of formal modeling is that, by making explicit and unambiguous the relationships between events and also the intended scope, it is easier to determine whether the model is supposed to be applicable to some observed phenomenon and, if so, whether it adequately fits it (Lake 2015; Nakoinz and Knitter 2016).

1.1.2 The Past as a Virtual Model

The past is only accessible through the filter of a "model" built indirectly from personal narratives, written in the past and preserved in our present. It is then an artificial world, more or less imaginary, more or less reliable: a replica of what really happened. There is no doubt that historians have been creating virtual surrogates of the past since the early days of Herodotus and Thucydides. Such virtual worlds are expressed narratively, using verbal language. In them, the historian places herself in the context in which the action took place, but she is situated in a virtual world extracted from a narration—supposed to be true—by an individual having seen someone doing something in the past, or explaining her intentions when acting (Bouissac 2015; Lercari 2016).

In any case, virtual worlds that can be narrated using verbal language can also be expressed using computer languages (Mayfield 2007; Millington et al. 2012). In that sense, an Artificial Society can be seen as a set of autonomous software entities (the agents) having autonomy to "act", thus taking their own decisions based on computer instructions that "simulate" the goals of the humans they "imitate" and the state of the world in which they are supposed to be. Computationally speaking, virtual agents will consist of a body that contains a set of state variables and behavioral instructions.

As the real world constrains the structure and behavior of the real agents, the simulated historical context plays that role for the simulated agent system. The perceptions of the simulated agents need to have some origin in all factors external to that agent, and it has to be represented in a specific environmental model. Thus, complex agent models require rich contextual information that should be transferred to a virtual model of the "landscape". This global entity may carry some global state variables like its own dynamics. These dynamics also can be so complex, e.g., containing production of new entities, that one may assign some form of behavior with the simulated environment.

The successful completion of virtual agents' tasks should be subject to the decision and actions of others, and on the specific way the environment constrains or determines the performance of social action. These models as well as real phenomena, for example, the societies, are dynamic because they change in time; therefore, a model will consist not only of structure but also of behavior. To observe a model's behavior the passage of time on it is necessary and it is here where computer simulation functionality is required (Sansores 2007).

In this way, we can move the unit of analysis to the social system of situated agents, whose center of gravity lies in the functioning of the relationships between social activities, social action, operations, and social actors. The unit of analysis is thus not the individual, nor the context, but a relation between the two. Questions of scale are relevant to understand the advantages of computer simulation of historical events and processes. In a computer model of a remote past, the historian can disaggregate in reverse order to the way social organization has evolved: the highest level groups become independent systems, disassociated from other groups, and which can subsequently disaggregate into their respective subgroups. Because in a virtual past, agents, processes and environment interact with other components in multiple dynamic ways, in variable frequency and intensity across the nested hierarchical organization, the scale and direction of change at the system level is not necessarily proportional to the scale and direction of the phenomena that trigger it. Additionally, it is more the character of the interactions among components rather than their inherent characteristics that determines the behavior of a simulation at the system level.

This way of building "artificial societies" from individual building blocks representing the lowest units of analysis may be contrasted to macro simulation approaches that are typically based on generalized models where the characteristics of a population are averaged together and the model attempts to simulate changes in these averaged characteristics for the whole population. Thus, in macro simulations, the set of individuals is viewed as a single entity that can be characterized by a number of variables, whereas in micro simulations the structure is viewed as emergent from the interactions between low-level entities—the individuals.

In this framework, time is defined in terms of steps, and steps are defined by a transition system that has a recursive structure. History is then computable to the extent that it can be represented algorithmically as the successive states of some determined input → output function (Abbott 1983; Ponse 1996; Moschovakis 2001; Moschovakis and Paschalis 2008; Mahoney 2015). Such a computable system should consist of a set of states, a set of labels representing the agents and the actions, and a transition relation, prescribing for each state the possible 'next steps', i.e., what actions can be performed, and (per action) what state results. Selecting one state as the root (the initial state) then yields a formal representation of a process. In this framework, time is defined in terms of steps, and steps are defined by the computational process (Mayfield 2007). However, it is not useful to call "computation" just any non-trivial yet somewhat disciplined coupling between state variables. We also want this coupling to be intentionally set up for the purpose of predicting or manipulating, in other words, from knowing or doing something (Toffoli 2005).

This way of considering the particular—causal—relationship between successive steps in an evolving social system of agents, activities and products (both people, things or other actions) brings about the vocabulary of complex systems and chaos theory into the domain of social science and history. Complexity social science is not a radically new domain, but in the recent years, it has changed its emphasis dealing with the unpredictability and non-linearity of many real world social mechanisms (Ball 2003; Dendrinos and Sonis 2012; Guastello 2013; Schieve and Allen 2014; Youngman and Hadzikadic 2014; Wright-Maley 2015). Complex adaptive systems (CAS) represent systems which are dynamic in space, time, organization, and membership and which are characterized by information transmission and processing that allow them to adjust to changing external and internal conditions (Barton 2014). Complex systems approaches offer the potential for new insights into processes of social change, linkages between the actions of individual human agents and societal-level characteristics, interactions between societies and their environment, and allometric relationships between size and organizational complexity.

1.1.3 Testing the Virtual Model

This emphasis on computability and algorithms implies a correlated emphasis in formalization, on objectivity, but not necessary on "truth". Simulating the past is just a way of increasing the explanatory power of historical explanatory models and not necessarily their "truth likeness".

We never know for sure whether the generated computer model of historical transitions and changes actually describes what happened really in the past. It is important to take into account, however, that the mechanical generation of "hypotheses" is no end in itself. A simulation can be "suggestive", "imaginative", "relevant", "probable", "plausible", "credible" (Bankes et al. 2002; Garson 2009;

Reynolds et al. 2013; Whitley 2016; Balzer 2015; Stettiner 2016). A generative model of the past that we belive existed is just a formal device to generate explanatory arguments that can be fitted to reality or not. As such, an "historical model" is just a deductive system as valid as its initial axioms. The only we can check is the deductive coherence, that is, that explanatory arguments are expressions generated by the system and hence coherent with the embedded assumptions. The degree to which that potential is realized is a function of the empirical validity of substantive models and the degree to which these theoretical ideas have been implemented clearly and accurately (Cederman 2002; Lustick and Miodownik 2009; Peeters and Romeijn 2016; Marwick 2016).

If virtual explanatory models cannot be tested, they can be explored. When exploring the resulting computable model of a causal trajectory of "events", where each event is just a momentaneous state of the evolving system of agents, and all events within a trajectory constitute a "history", we can generate large numbers of virtual histories by perturbing the chain of events randomly or introducing randomized adjustments in initial conditions. Each one of these alternative "histories" can be used both to experiment with a theory of historical transition and social change (parameters are manipulated to test for predicted differences) and as a demonstration tool (parameters are manipulated to test for predicted robustness). When used experimentally, manipulations are allowed for agent-level parameters to test the global implications of behavioral assumptions, but also it is allowed to manipulate global parameters to test a macro theory about their implications at the micro scales.

Three methods of evaluating the validity of simulation models, over and above reliability, have been delineated by Taber and Timpone (1996):

- Outcome validity: demonstrating that outcomes in a simulation correspond to outcomes in the real world. Outcome validity corresponds to what can also be called "predictive validity" (Sterman 1984).
- Process validity: demonstrating that the process that leads to outcomes in a simulation corresponds to processes in the real world by calibrating initial parameters to empirically known historical data, in the sense proposed by Epstein (2006). Conversely, if the model omits real-world processes thought to be important in outcomes, the validity of model predictions is undermined even when those predictions have outcome validity. In some sense, it can also be considered a form of "predictive validity".
- Internal validity: demonstrating that simulation software validly represents the process being modeled. Put another way, has the model been fully debugged so that a researcher can be sure that only explicit model assumptions are modeled without unintended effects due to software artifacts? This is similar to what others have called "structural validity".

Turchin (2011) has advocated the use of historical experiments, meaning a planned comparison between predictions derived from two or more theories and data. In this way, we may focus on making predictions about the state of a certain variable for a certain past society, which is not known at the time when the predictions are made. For example, Model #1 says that the variable should be decreasing, while Model #2 says, no, it should be increasing. We then ask historians to look for ancient narratives, documents or archaeological data sets, and determine which of the theories is closer to the truth. As more such experiments are conducted, and if one of the theories consistently yields predictions that are in better agreement with empirical patterns than the other(s), our degree of belief into the better performing theory is consequently enhanced.

Precise historical case studies offer an opportunity to examine the internal logic posited by a theory of transitions between different events. A good case study will trace the causal processes observed in situ and determine whether they are consistent with a specific theory or challenge it. Historical case studies frequently focus on a specific spatial and temporal scale, varying from small settlements in the past, to regional land-use changes. They are particularly well suited for testing theories that predict that some event or process will never occur. Many different methods can be used to observe the case, including archaeological data, historical documents, ethnographical observations, remote sensing, surveys, censuses, interviews, etc. The various ways the system is measured may lead to some challenges when comparing cases with somewhat different observation procedures (Janssen and Ostrom 2006; Marwik 2016; Rubio-Campillo 2016; Heppenstall et al. 2016).

Therefore, empirical information, both qualitative and quantitative, can be used in a variety of ways. It can be used as input data to the computable model or as a means to falsify and test if not the model itself, its explanatory predictions. When historical data are used as an input, the focus might be to study a particular scenario, i.e., the proper historical circumstances from which the data is derived. By carefully calibrating start-up conditions to what is known from the past, crucial experiments can be designed to generate particular trajectories whose final states can be considered as "predictions", and then individually compared with what we know from the real past and measure its fitness. The more fitted are those latter states with equivalently dated historical data, the better the predictive power of the model. The revolutionary potential of this technique is associated with the fact that alternatively possible "futures" (or "histories") can be produced by varying initial conditions or a specific parameter setting of interest or by subjecting the theoretically specified model to random perturbations.

1.2 Recreating the Past in the Computer

1.2.1 From Animality to Humanity

Humans are animals. We have evolved from beings that were similar to modern apes, and those antecessors evolved from previous antecessors with features and behavior similar to modern squirrels, modern reptiles, modern amphibians, modern fishes, and modern bacteria. Animal behavior is a good example of social mechanism (without abstract beliefs nor complex motivations, nor desires and only simple instinctive intentions), and therefore it has been studied in formal terms since the times of Lotka (1910) and Volterra (1926). Those early works have been later implemented as computer simulations; see: Bryson et al. (2007), Petersen (2012), Bak (2013), Dow and Lea (2013), Lei et al. (2013), Boumans et al. (2014), Ma (2015), Topa et al. (2016) among many others.

There is a lot of "animality" within us, and if we want to know why we do what we are doing in the present, the only way is to understand our "degree of animality" and the historical process of differentiation from our "original" animality. This is not a defense of sociobiological approaches, but just the plain observation that we act as complex animals, and there is some kind of relationship—probably non-linear and non-monotonic—from animality to humanity. In any case, the most important aspect of investigation will not be the animal basis of human behavior, but the specific process of progressive differentiation in the way we take decisions —more or less rational—from the original animal instincts. There is no magic in this historical (prehistorical) process, but a series of explicitly mechanical biological processes that have historically constrained and determined human behavior: evolution and natural selection. Human evolution is a complex temporal trajectory of changes, transformations and modifications, some of which emerged slowly, and others very quickly. Complex phenomena in the present can be interpreted as the cumulative products of relatively simple processes acting over time. It is a domain where computational simulation tools and methods show their idoneity. Among recent essays in this direction, we can mention: Arenas (2012), Hoban et al. (2012), Kawecki et al. (2012), Ma et al. (2012), Kutsukake and Innan (2013), Messer (2013), Mode et al. (2013), Villmoare (2013), Schlötterer et al. (2014), Smaldino et al. (2013), Acevedo-Rocha et al. (2014), Hunemann (2014), Lehman and Stanley (2014), Vevgari and Fioley (2014), Roseman et al. (2015), Peart (2015), Shamrani et al. (2015), Smith et al. (2015), Hatala et al. (2016), Lieberman (2016), Polly et al. (2016). An interesting related approach is that of considering the analogy of robot evolution to understand what may be going on human evolution (Wischman et al. 2012; Bongard 2013; Mitri et al. 2013; Eiben 2014; Muscolo et al. 2014).

In any case, natural selection and evolutionary mechanisms have affected animals and humans not only in morphology but in the development of pre-human behavior (Premo 2005; Barton and Riel-Salvatore 2012; Pradhan et al. 2012; Witt and Schwesinger 2013; Kramer and Otárola-Castillo 2015; Tang and Ye 2016). It is also the question of the origins of "intelligence" and complex decision making (Gabora and Russon 2011; Gabora and DiPaola 2012; Kurzweil and Ray 2012; Chandrasekaran 2013; Pringle 2013; Guddemi 2014; Ross and Richerson 2014; Geary 2015; Cowley 2016) and also culture. This is not the place to define what is culture, but recent work suggests its computable basis (Belew 1990; Goodhall 2002; Richardson 2003; Bentley et al. 2004; Henrich 2004; Harton and Bullock 2007; Enquist et al. 2011; Gabora and Saberi 2011; Premo 2012, 2015; Premo and Kuhn 2010; Gabora et al. 2013; Messoudi 2011; Crema et al. 2014a, b; Acerbi et al. 2014; Cowley 2016; Gong and Shuai 2016).

An interesting example of how computer simulation may be used to test hypothesis about human evolutionary history is Agustí and Rubio-Campillo (2016). These authors deal with Neanderthals fast extinction between 40,000 and 30,000 years ago. The authors suggest a much simpler scenario, in which the cannibalistic behaviour of Neanderthals may have played a major role in their eventual extinction. They show that this trait was selected as a common behaviour at moments of environmental or population stress. However, as soon as Neanderthals had to compete with another species that consumed the same resources cannibalism had a negative impact, leading, in the end, to their extinction. To test this hypothesis, Agustí and Rubio-Campillo have used an agent-based model computer simulation. The model is simple, with only traits, behaviours and landscape features defined and with no attempt to re-create the exact landscape in which Neanderthals lived or their cultural characteristics. The basic agent is a group of individuals that form a community. The most important state variable in the model is the location of the group, coupled with a defined home range and two additional factors: cannibalism and the chance of fission. The result of the simulation shows that cannibalistic behaviour is always selected when resources are scarce and clustered. However, when a non-cannibalistic species is introduced into the same environment, the cannibalistic species retreats and the new species grows until it has reached the carrying capacity of the system. The cannibalistic populations that still survive are displaced from the richest areas, and live on the borders with arid zones, a situation which is remarkably similar to what we know about the end of the Neanderthals.

In this book, Ingo Timm et al. (Chap. 2) explore the possibility of simulating some aspects of hominine prehistoric behavior, notably dispersal and migration. This subject has also been approached by Mithen and Reed (2002), Beyin (2011), Eriksson et al. (2012), Wren (2014), Wren et al. (2014), Thompson et al. (2015), Hölzchen et al. (2015), Kealy et al. (2015), Romanowska et al. (2016), Vahia et al. (2016). Timm et al. suggest a series of reflections for a future simulation, and not a current implementation. It is very instructive the way they approach the implied mechanism. Among other things, authors suggest that ecological variations and demographic pressure likely influenced the dispersal of hominins. The increasing number of members may have required band ("tribes"?) to split up into smaller groups in order to keep group sizes manageable. Furthermore, changes in climatic, geographical or sea-level conditions may have been responsible for hominins to move towards Eurasia, too. But also changes of physical abilities increasing the hominin's stamina as well as the absence or occurrence of diseases outside their former habitat may have caused migration.

Timm and co-authors have programmed their virtual human antecessors with a concrete reason to leave their original habitat, and detailed consideration of potential influencing factors. Although "animals" in the biological sense, these virtual hominins are seen as utility-based agents, considering changes in their environment and evaluating the consequences of their actions in advance. Furthermore, the "happiness" regarding new states created by performing an action is considered as well. Transferred to the challenges hominins faced when crossing

Africa towards Eurasia, this happiness can be equated with the sufficient availability of food and other resources of vital importance. However, hominins are not the only actors which are part of the Out-of-Africa-Hypothesis that deliberate their behavior in regard to their actions. The behavior of carnivores might for example be modeled by using a similar approach as well. Choosing appropriate prey as well as selecting, defending and marking their territory are processes which can be modeled using intelligent software agents. But not all aspects of the Out-of-Africa-Hypothesis can and should be modeled as decision-making mechanisms. There are also other factors affecting the dispersal processes such as outside influences (weather or climatic changes) or the condition of the landscape (vegetation or geological formation). These factors are modeled by Timm et al. as part of the environment the agents are located in. All of these factors influence the land's potential for hominin dispersal. Yet, the potential is not a constant value but it may change over time.

It can be of interest to compare the dispersal mechanism of pre-humans, to the motivations and intentionality of movement and dispersal by modern humans of "prehistoric" times, with motivations different from modern humans of present times, and even our antecessors from a more recent past with motivations assumed to be like ours (Young 2002). Janssen and Hill (Chap. 3), Oestmo et al. (Chap. 4), Fort et al. (Chap. 5) and O'Brien and Bergh (Chap. 6) deal with this issue in different historical contexts. Jansen and Hill begin their analysis with the assumption that among early humans it may have existed a relationship between group size and movement and whether resources are dispersed or clumped in space, because this relationship exists and it is well attested in animal behavior. The general prediction is that movement should be less frequent in patchy environments because foragers should stay within a patch until foraging gain rates drop below some critical value before moving on. The authors explore different resource distributions and how they affect optimal group size, movement frequency and average daily return rate per hunter. They also examine the effect of targeted camp movement (vs. random) on the return rate that can be obtained in more patchy environment.

Janssen and Hill (Chap. 3) consider the ecological parameters of the environment and prey characteristics measured in the Mbaracayu Reserve, Paraguay. They have actually measured the ethnographically known Ache hunter-gatherers moving in the real world while searching for prey and other resources in any of the seven vegetation types' landscapes. Therefore, the probability of encountering a prey or a resource of a specific type can be estimated, a value that it is unknown for hominins, and it depends on very general assumptions. Virtual hunter and gatherers in Janssen and Hill model have no explicit beliefs or desires, but a very general intention to survive by hunting and gathering. They are also implied in more social activities, like cooperative pursuits that impose on hunters the need to move though the landscape in a semi coordinated fashion. Instead of assuming that any human decision should be rational, and social processes are the consequence of plain and linear mechanisms, Janssen and Hill investigate the most probable way the agents residing in a camp together determine whether the average weight of meat hunted over the last few days is above a certain threshold. If so, people decide not to move and the camp remains in its location for another day, if not, agents migrate and the campsite is moved to a new. These two decision criteria define four broad strategies for a camp: whether it is adaptive or not, and whether new locations are targeted or not.

Oestmo et al. (Chap. 4) analyze how the actual placement of resources affects hunter-gatherer movements. The authors compare random walk behavior of virtual hunter-gatherers from prehistoric times with two other walk behaviors. The first one is called “seeking walk”. During seeking walk simulations, the forager will move towards the nearest material source if the level of the materials in the toolkit is lower than a certain number. This means that at any moment when a foragers' toolkit is empty it will seek to acquire new material. The second alternative walk model is termed the “wiggle walk” where it is assumed that a forager has a direction and moves forward one cell each time step. At each time step, the forager changes the direction by taking a left turn with a degree drawn from a uniform distribution between 0° and 90°. Both the seeking walk, which is a simplified analogy for a forager that returns to a stone cache, and the random walk behavior show that increased clustering of the raw material sources leads to increased time without raw materials in the tool kit. However, time between procurement instances and time without materials in the tool kit have different implications. If a forager can stockpile a cache at a central location and can return to such a place then the forager can go extended periods without procuring because it could return to the cache to fill up on raw materials. On the other hand, these results suggest that if random walk takes the forager away from the central location and never or very seldom returns directly to a stone.

O'Brien and Bergh (Chap. 6) go forward in the investigation of the rationality of people moving. Instead of considering dispersal in a macro scale, they opt for investigating local movement in particular well known geographical areas. Strong rationality is here equated with analytically calculated Least Cost Path, as the values assigned to these models are derived from legitimate factors which influence movement, such as distaste for steep slopes, the relative difficulties of traversing different soil types, and absolute obstacles. However, these authors go well beyond the logic of “animal” movement, and they consider that social factors should not be ignored for understanding human movement, and taboos, traditions, exclusivity can be incorporated into such models. In their case study, the aim of navigating to a known settlement presupposes a minimum pre-existing cognitive map, which may be constructed from personal experience, third-party knowledge and topographical gossip. They also consider the need to include the role of a leader, and some followers. Nevertheless, they do not consider the mechanisms underlying the emergence of such differentiation. In this way, the computer simulates how route ways are established through a series of discrete actions around those natural features, acted out by individual agents over time. Modelling allows the investigation of the overall evolution of a route way as individual agents have access only to local information, allowing them to approach the optimal path over time through a process of iterative attempts to traverse a landscape. The environment of North Offaly in the Irish Midlands is used as the study area, as it is a landscape of natural route ways and obstacles for which we have rich archaeological and documentary evidence supporting interpretation of movement.

Fort et al. (Chap. 5) consider a different way to analyze human motivated movement. These authors emphasize long run movements of people at a spatial macro scale as a consequence of population increase. They consider the case study of Neolithic times, when farmers go away from their birth place when available land saturates. At a global scale the set of individual migrations can be compared with a single wave or front, advancing to neighboring areas. In this contribution, the mechanism is entirely adaptive, and no rationality, except for the intention derived from recognizing the "need" of suitable land for farming once there are no empty places in the immediate vicinity due to population increase. At this macro scale, the rationality of individual decisions can be studied in terms of the central tendency of the accumulation of individual decisions. In that way, the dispersal behavior of the population can be probabilistically based on the mean age difference between parents and their children, and a set of dispersal distances per generation and their respective probabilities.

Fort et al. contribution vindicates the mechanical nature of some apparently intrinsically human decisions: migration. At first sight, it would not be an example of the evolution of human intelligence, but a kind of animal behavior, that is, instinctive. However, in homogeneous environments it is reasonable to expect that, on average, intelligent beings will not prefer any specific direction. Obviously, this is not the single possibility. As the comparison between the different contributions on human movement in pre-industrial societies show, the intrinsic human definition lies in the historical variability of such decisions. Other authors have addressed the same subject from different perspectives (Hazelwood and Steele 2004; Goldstone and Roberts 2006; Fitzpatrick and Callaghan 2008; Bevan 2011; Callegari et al. 2013; Reynolds et al. 2013; Silva and Steele 2015; Wren 2014; Lanen et al. 2015; Sanders 2015). It is interesting to compare Fort's results with Wren's (2014) hypothesis combining a model of cognitive dispersal with the wave of advance mechanism. Wren's experiments quantify the impact of cognition on dispersal velocity and wave pattern. The results show that the greater the level of cognitive complexity, the slower the wave of advance. Increased heterogeneity of the environment further decreases wave velocity when cognition is involved in mobility. Random movement, i.e., non-cognitive mobility, provides the highest velocity across almost all landscapes. This suggests that previous research may have either overestimated the importance of cognition in facilitating dispersal events, or has underestimated the rate of population growth and per generation dispersal distance of populations. If this is a distinctive feature of pre-human populations or even Paleolithic hunter-gatherers is something that should be analyzed further, by exploring the close relationship between cognitive complexity, the spatial heterogeneity of the landscape, and dispersal potential and velocity.

In this way we can approach the behavioral, cognitive and social consequences of evolutionary processes over the human lineages (see more discussion about those issues in Janssen et al. 2005; Griffith et al. 2010; Kempe et al. 2014; and Ackland et al. 2014; Kovacevic et al. 2015; Romanowska et al. 2016). Through the comparison of the mechanics of dispersal movements in animals, pre-humans, and humans we can arrive to understand the real impact of "intelligence" on mobility and survival in terms of an evolutionary trajectory of historically contextualized motivations and intentions.

1.2.2 Hunting-and-Gathering in the Past Explains How We Have Survived Until the Present

Previous discussion on simulating movement and dispersal among pre-humans and humans at different periods of history reveal the strong naturalistic character of many human decisions, and the constraints imposed by environment. Many modern historical simulations concentrate on that aspect of human behavior in the past.

Prehistoric hunter-gatherers have been studied many times from the point of view of animal foraging behavior, stating that human agents also forage in such a way as to maximize their net energy intake per unit time. In other words, it is assumed they should find, capture and consume food containing the most calories while expending the least amount of time possible in doing so. This is the old Malthusian view on population increasing exponentially while food production would have increased only linearly, in constant increments (Portugali 1999; Read and LeBlanc 2003; Lane 2010; Cai 2012; Schlueter et al. 2012; Levin et al. 2013; Hritonenko and Yatsenko 2013; Ribeiro 2015). Consequently, population growth would have generated on the long term the depletion of "natural capital", and declining biodiversity. Since these trends undermine the probabilities for survival, when "human load" exceeds local carrying capacity it erodes environmental potential. These concerns were the first to attract the interest of archaeologists who found the possibility of the computer modelling of hunter and gatherer survival (Zubrow 1971; Thomas 1972; Wobst 1974; Joachim 1976). The understanding of many ecological concepts such as adaptation, energy flow and competition hinges on the ability to comprehend what food items such human agents selected, and why. Nevertheless, it is obvious that if humans were in the past just like any other animal forager or predator, we would say that prehistoric hunter-gatherers survival would have depended just on the availability of edible resources. Given what we know about the natural irregularity of natural resources yield, *Homo sapiens* would have extinguished many times since their African origins!

The hypothetical explanation of "adaptive" mechanisms in human prehistory should be much deeper than that. For instance, in the case of gathering, we can assume that posterior probabilities for gathering success, and hence of survival, may be completely defined by the probability of plants availability. In case the environment is full of available resources ("rich world hypothesis"), the probability of finding enough plants to eat and make instruments is very high, and prior probabilities for survival are also high; in the case of low availability, prior probabilities for survival would be lower. Hunting seems to be a much more complex activity, whose success and hence the posterior probabilities of survival are less deterministically affected by the availability of animals in the area. If a social agent cooperates with another agent, the chances of hunting success are higher, even in the case of low animal availability, and so on. Availability of technology can also increase posterior probabilities of survival even in the case of low prior priors due to scarcity. Therefore, a successful explanation of hunting and gathering survival in prehistory needs additional factors and dependencies to be able to calculate posterior probabilities of survival (Del Castillo and Barceló 2013; Barceló et al. 2015).

The single most obvious constraint of human action in a particular environment is population size, especially when the means of production seem to be underdeveloped (hunting-and-gathering). Many modern computer simulations on human demography are centered on modeling the particular dependence on annual fertility tables and adopt a fecundity based model. The odds of conception for any one mating event can be kept constant for a female agent of a given age, and the probability of reproduction therefore becomes dependent on the frequency and timing of the female agent's mating activity. This allows for realistic fertility variations as a function of mating behavior frequency (and thus contextual opportunity in the form of access to male sexual resources) and the variations of individual agent fecundity over time. An important source of artificial structure (imposed annual fertility rates) is thus removed from the model, allowing the simulation's results to emerge more freely, especially in the very long term. Long term variations in access to reproductive partners can now have their full effect on fertility rates. This also opens the door to a much closer modeling of environmental and social factors affecting fecundity on an individual agent level (Stajich and Hahn 2005; Fletcher et al. 2011; Billari and Prskawetz 2012; Brandenburg et al. 2012; Eriksson and Manica 2012; Rogers and Kohler 2012; Santow 2012; Koenig et al. 2013; Dyke and MacCluer 2014; Dyble et al. 2015; Guillot et al. 2015; Kaur and Kaur 2015; Pastor et al. 2015; Bentley et al. 2016; Moya et al. 2016; Bauch and McElreath 2016; Chan et al. 2016; Rodríguez et al. 2016).

How simple and well adapted to the local carrying capacity is population growth in a hunting gathering economic system? Whereas the demands of non-human species on their habitats are fixed and limited, human demands, even during the most remote period of our past, have been hardly simple and are constantly evolving. Chapman (1980), Samuels (1982), Read (1998), Costopoulos (2002) have created social reproduction models based on modern ethnography of hunters and foragers groups, taking into account the social and political aspects of marriage and complex way of reproductive tasks scheduling influenced by political and ideological goals.

Smaldino et al. (2013) investigate the evolution of a population under conditions of different environmental harshness and in which selection can occur at the level of the group as well as the level of the individual. The authors focus on the evolution of a socially learned characteristic related to individuals' willingness to contribute to raising the offspring of others within their family group. They find that environmental harshness increases the frequency of individuals who make such contributions. However, under the conditions the simulation stipulates, the authors also find that environmental variability can allow groups to survive with lower frequencies of helpers.

White (2013, 2014, 2016) has built an Agent Based Model representing a hunter–gatherer system taking into account parameters such as mortality, fertility, and mean age. The demographic characteristics of a living population are the result of numerous human-level interactions and behaviors: persons and households make decisions about marriage and reproduction based on their individual circumstances within the context of "global" conditions that exert effects and constraints on all members of the population (e.g., the physiological factors that govern the length of the female reproductive span, ecological circumstances that affect the contributions of children to subsistence, cultural rules affecting marriage behaviors, etc.). The demographic characteristics of these systems (e.g., population age structure, mean fertility, mean mortality) emerge through a large number of human level interactions and behaviors related to marriage, reproduction, and mortality. The model has three main "levels": person, household, and system. Each agent in the model represents an individual person who is a discrete entity with a unique identity. Households are co-residential groupings of persons that form through marriage and change in size and composition primarily through marriage, reproduction, and mortality. Social links define relationships between pairs of living persons and are used to enforce marriage prohibitions. The system of the model is composed of all persons and households in existence at a given point in time. Methods representing marriage, reproduction, and death operate at the person and household levels in this model. Individual persons and households make probabilistic decisions about reproduction, marriage, and infanticide based on the current dependency ratio of the household (the ratio of the number of consumers to the number of producers in the household). Although the base probabilities affecting reproduction and mortality are set by model-level parameters (i.e., they are the same across the population), the economic circumstances of individual households affect the behavior of individuals in those households on a case-by-case, step-by-step basis. The households that form within the model systems are verifiably consistent with those documented among ethnographic hunter–gatherers in terms of their size, composition, and developmental cycles. Results of the computational implementation of the model suggest that changes in family-level economics can be coincident with subsistence intensification contributing to the emergence of social complexity among prehistoric hunter–gatherers by creating the conditions for a "rich get richer" scenario. Lowering the age at which children make a significant contribution to subsistence (e.g., through the broadening of the diet to include mass-harvested and "low quality" foods). This practice could have relaxed constraints on family size polygynous families economically viable. Positive feedbacks between the productive and reproductive potentials of larger families produce right-tailed distributions of family size and "wealth" when the productive age of children is low and polygyny is incentivized, permitting the emergence of hereditary social distinctions.

Crema (2014) assumes that human groups are characterized by a non-linear relationship between size and per-capita fitness. Increasing group size has beneficial effects, but once a certain threshold is exceeded, negative frequency dependence will start to predominate leading to a decline in the per-capita fitness. Such a relationship can potentially have long-term implications in the spatial structure of human settlements if individuals have the possibility to modify their fitness through group fission-fusion dynamics. He illustrates the equilibrium properties of these dynamics by means of an abstract agent-based simulation and discusses its implication for understanding long-term changes in human settlement pattern. Results suggest that changes in settlement pattern can originate from internal dynamics alone if the system is highly integrated and interconnected.

The second part of the problem when trying to couple the social and the environmental lies in modeling carrying capacity and the capability of prehistoric humans, even with inefficient technology to alter and modify it. Demographic and expansion behaviours of groups are largely influenced by the distribution and availability of resources. This has been an important domain for research on computer modeling and much effort is still being invested (Keane et al. 2002; Sept 2007; Seth 2007; Wainwright 2008; Garfinkel et al. 2010; Janssen 2010; Dearing et al. 2012; Van der Bergh et al. 2013; Ch'ng et al. 2013; Marean et al. 2015; Millington et al. 2013; Burch et al. 2014; Jones and Richter 2014; Balbo et al. 2014; Barton et al. 2014; Feola 2014; Bentley and O'Brien 2015; Codding and Bird 2015; Rammer and Seidl 2015; Rodriguez et al. 2015; Wood et al. 2015; Iwamura et al. 2016; Boumans et al. 2015; Polhill et al. 2016; Sarjoughian et al. 2016). The problem is that human–nature systems have been traditionally studied separately, either as human systems constrained by or with input from/output to natural systems (usually including the physical environment and the corresponding ecosystem), or as natural systems subject to human disturbance. This chasm between natural and social sciences, along with such unidirectional connections between natural and human systems, has hindered better understanding of complexity (e.g., feedback, nonlinearity and thresholds, heterogeneity, time lags). In the process of truly coupling human activity and natural environment, computer simulation approaches allow understanding how human decisions and subsequent actions would change (at least affect) the structure and function of many natural systems. Such structural and functional changes would in turn exert influence on human decisions and actions (An 2012; Widlock et al. 2012; Sarjoughian et al. 2015). In this sense, Dorward (2014) proposes a 'livelisystems' framework of multi-scale, dynamic change across social and biological systems. This describes how material, informational and relational assets, asset services and asset pathways interact in systems with embedded and emergent properties undergoing a variety of structural transformations. Related characteristics of 'higher' (notably human) "livelisystems" and change processes are identified as the greater relative importance of (a) informational, relational and extrinsic (as opposed to material and intrinsic) assets, (b) teleological (as opposed to natural) selection, and (c) innovational (as opposed to mutational) change. This suggestion provides valuable insights into the real understanding of 99 % of human history, when survival was only possible through hunting and gathering.

We may wonder about the unbalanced application of simulation, where the biological side (as in human evolution) has greatly benefitted from simulation while the more "sociological" aspect of archaeological simulation remains a challenge (Lake 2014; Cegielski and Rogers 2016). To understand the coupling between human and environmental systems in prehistory, researchers should study human collective behavior as a consequence of the indirect influence individual agents and organized populations of agents may have had on other hunter gatherers given that each one responds to an environment altered by the behavior of other agents. The general purpose of this way of studying prehistory seems to be the simulation of potential historical situations in which agents periodically may have modified their output behavior when they were able to learn to predict how the action at a previous step modifies the input at the next step. Many individuals can end up near each other simply because they tend to approach the same localized resource such as food or a water source. In these circumstances too, the agents' behavior resulting in social aggregation has not evolved for that function. Each individual approaches food or water for eating or drinking, not for social purposes. However, even if it is a simple by-product of learning nonsocial behaviors, social aggregation can be a favorable pre-condition for the emergence of social behaviors such as communication and economic exchange among individuals that happen to find themselves near each other. In other circumstances, however, social aggregation may not be simply a by-product of behavior emerged for other purposes but is the result of behavior which has emerged exactly because it produces spatial aggregation (Lake 2000; Costopoulos 2001; Berman et al. 2004; Goldstone and Ashpole 2004; Goldstone et al. 2005a, b; Parisi and Nolfi 2005; Janssen and Ostrom 2006; Kalff et al. 2010; Barton et al. 2011; An 2012; Rounsevell et al. 2012; Ch'ng and Gaffney 2013; Boone and Galvin 2014; Messoudi 2014; Clark and Crabtree 2015).

Related to this debate, in the present book, Saqalli and Baum (Chap. 8) consider that humans have historically formed complex groups and societies that are bound to their environment in more or less intense interactions, the imprint of which are found in landscapes. A society and its evolution can be studied as driven by their calorie and resource demand and constrained by environmental parameters. Thus, archaeological/paleo-environmental models can either directly analyze the social interactions between agents, or use the landscape as a reference plane. In any case, it is the mutual interdependence of humans and their environment that is in the focus: environment and natural resources are quickly and directly affected by human activities and at the same time, humans are directly and rapidly affected by the availability of natural resources.

However, it is important to take into account that not any measured differences in survival between individuals through time reflect necessary differences in fitness Brookfield (2001). Fitness represents an expected outcome, and what actually happens in small populations differs from expectation because each generation represents a sample, with an attendant sampling error, of the individuals produced by the previous generation. The fitness of a population is related only probabilistically to real events; sudden advantageous changes and transformations are usually lost by chance.

Janssen and Hill (Chap. 3), and Oestmo et al. (Chap. 4) have modelled the particular way in which human prehistoric behavior can be considered as "adapted" to environmental conditions (see also Read 2008; Kline and Boyd 2010; Collard et al. 2011; Kuhn 2012; Wood et al. 2015; Caiado et al. 2016; Martin and Fahrig 2016). In the first case, Janssen and Hill examine how optimal group sizes and movement frequency are affected by more dispersed or more clumped resource distributions, when the absolute number of resources in the environment is held constant. They also examine the effect of targeted camp movement (vs. random) on the return rate that can be obtained in more patchy environment. The model uses real measured parameters from a modern foraging society to create an agent-based model, which subsequently allows simulating a more or less patchy environment in order to determine how those changes affect optimal group size and mobility. They conclude that human foragers, by knowing the landscape and the spatial location of better habitats, and moving to facilitate hunting in those areas, can gain a substantial advantage from that knowledge. In the other contribution, Oestmo et al., investigate whether changes in stone tool raw material frequencies in an archaeological assemblage could be considered a reliable proxy for human forager adaptive variability. Two different patterns are obtained in their simulated model. First, when a forager engages in random or wiggle walk, a more clustered environment leads to lower average raw material richness in the toolkit. As clustering increases, the forager will on average move longer periods without encountering a source. Due to this and the fact that the forager use a material at every step, the forager will then when encountering a source fill up the tool kit to the maximum capacity resulting in one raw material dominating the make-up of the tool kit in terms of frequency. In the other pattern, the forager engages in a seeking walk and seeks the closest raw material sources when the tool kit is empty. In this case, the increased clustering of raw material sources leads to increased raw material richness. The richness increases because when the forager seeks the nearest raw material source, and this nearest raw material source is clustered with other sources, it increases the chance of encountering other sources in close proximity that in turn could lead to increased richness.

1.2.3 Rationality Within the Computer. The Myth of the Stupid Prehistoric Savages

Socio-ecological models make emphasis on physiological motivation, such as hunger, thirst, fatigue and comfort. In this case agents generate their goals around some physiological trigger, e.g., getting hungry. If needed, other types of motivation can be employed, such as safety. This is the case in some of the simulations presented in this book (notably Virtual Hominines in Chap. 2, and Virtual Hunter Gatherers in Chaps. 3 and 4) whose intelligence is expressed in the way they look for the satisfaction of their full stomachs. However, if physiological motivation is the only source of directness in the computer simulation of human behavior we may end with undesired, uniform behavior. Trescak et al. (Chap. 14) propose to configure motivational modifiers, which affect the decay rate of a given motivation. For example, a hunger modifier affects the pace in which an agent gets hungry. If such modifiers are different for every agent—then every individual follows its own circadian rhythm, executing goals at various time intervals, increasing believability of the simulated population.

In a sense, even computational agents implemented as biped stomachs can be considered "rational agents" because they make optimal decisions: they "want" to survive, and then they need to look for accessible resources. They have been programmed with the instinctive knowledge that they should hunt animals and gather for vegetables to acquire food, and therefore they hunt, gather and move looking for preys and resources. Janssen and Hill (Chap. 3, see also Janssen and Hill 2014) assume human hunting behavior is consistent with Optimal Foraging Theory, which is a model of animal behavior. In this way, hunter-gatherer foraging strategies—optimal group size, movement frequency and average daily return rate per hunter—are examined as the consequence of environmental factors—differences in resource distributions—and not because of social or political dispositions. Rationality here is approached in the sense of biological survival and not in terms of social reproduction. According to that, there is no difference in the programmed mind of hominid antecessors and Homo sapiens sapiens!

Human (and even animal) rationality is much more complex than expected and therefore, it is easy to conclude that deterministic relationships between environmental stress and social change are inadequate (Mithen 1991; Costanza et al. 2007; Gardner 2012; Polechová and Barton 2015; Bryson 2015). The challenge of a computer simulation of human behavior is them to assess the impact of culture and knowledge on decision making behavior (An 2012).

We need to implement a form of intelligence beyond literal rationality if we want our historical models be credible. Socially intelligent agents (SIAs) should be defined as agents that do not only from an observer point of view behave socially but that are able to recognize and identify other agents and establish and maintain relationships to other agents (Dautenhahn 1998). The process of building SIAs will always been influenced by what the human as the designer considers "social," and conversely, agent tools that are behaving socially can influence human conceptions of sociality. A cognitive technology (CT) approach toward designing SIAs would afford an opportunity to study the process of (1) how social agents can constrain their cognitive and social potential, and (2) how social agent technology and human (social) cognition can co-evolve and co-adapt and result in new forms of sociality. Aspects of human social psychology, e.g., storytelling, empathy, embodiment, and historical and ecological grounding, can contribute to a believable and cognitively well-balanced design of SIA technology in order to further the relationship between humans and agent tools.

One of the very first computer simulations of prehistoric hunter gatherers was that of Robert Reynolds (1986). He explicitly approached the problem of rationality in hunter-gatherer decision-making in terms of:

- the ability of each member to collect and process information about the resource distribution,
- the extent to which information is shared among members,
- the specific sets of decision available to each member, and
- the way in which the individual decisions are integrated to produce a group decision.

On that basis, Reynolds defined a general approach to programing that can also be considered as a general program for rationality in social evolution studies. He calls Cultural algorithm (CA) a specific kind of evolutionary computation framework where there is a knowledge component that is called the belief space in addition to the population component. The belief space of a cultural algorithm is divided into distinct categories representing different domains of knowledge that the population has of the search space. The belief space is updated after each iteration by the best individuals of the population. The best individuals can be selected using a fitness function that assesses the performance of each individual in population much like in genetic algorithms.

Reynolds lists different belief space categories:

- Normative knowledge: A collection of desirable value ranges for the individuals in the population component—e.g., acceptable behavior for the agents in population.
- Situational knowledge: Specific examples of important events—e.g., successful/unsuccessful solutions
- Temporal knowledge History of the search space—e.g., the temporal patterns of the search process
- Spatial knowledge Information about the topography of the search space

The "best-fitted" individuals of the population can update the belief space via an update function. Also, the knowledge categories of the belief space can affect the population component via an influence function. The influence function can affect population by altering the genome or the actions of the individuals.

The algorithm has been applied to find the optimum in a dynamic environment composed of mobile resources. The aim of this approach is to combine different knowledge sources to direct the decisions of the individual agents in solving optimization problems. Reynolds and collaborators developed an approach based on an analogy to the marginal value theorem in foraging theory to guide the integration of these different knowledge sources to direct the agent population (Reynolds et al. 2006a, b, c, 2008; Reynolds and Peng 2005; Stanley et al. 2014).

Cultural Algorithms were developed by Reynolds as a computational framework in which to embed social learning in an evolutionary context. Unlike traditional learning approaches, Cultural Algorithms derive their power from large collections of interacting agents. Within virtual worlds it is often the case that we wish to coordinate the behavior of large groups of intelligent agents in an efficient fashion. Cultural Algorithms are able to perform large-scale group learning within these virtual worlds. They have been used to generate socially intelligent controllers and group social behavior in various simulated environments, both serious and fun.

Given that the study of differences between animal and human behavior emphasizes human motivation and purposefulness and it affirms that human behavior is shaped first and foremost by an intention held by the subject, any historical explanation based only on the idea of "adaptation" seems to be limited (Stutz 2012). The same criticism is applicable to traditional "rational-choice" explanation where each agent individually assesses its situation and makes decisions based on a fixed set of condition-action rules (Gulyas 2002). That makes many agent-based models nothing more than a discrete planning for expressing descriptions of intended courses of action. It seems as if some designer (be a computer scientist or a god) needs to know the society before modeling it (Grand 2012).

Humans act supposedly on the grounds of beliefs about world-states that they contribute to modify, and which will be modified by their actions. Consequently, the "cause" of any social action that may have occurred in the past lies in the agent motivations for performing it. Social actions have been defined in terms of purposeful changing of natural and social reality (Leont'ev 1974; Engeström 1987; Wobcke 1998; Davydov 1999; Edwards 2000; Bedny and Karwowski 2004; Feldman and Orlikowski 2011; Thornton et al. 2012). Social actions are goal-directed processes that must be undertaken to fulfill some need or motivation. Therefore, they cannot be understood without a frame of reference created by the corresponding social motivation or intention. Leont'ev, one of the chief architects of activity theory, described social activity as being composed of subjects, needs, motivations, goals, actions and operations (or behavior), together with mediating artifacts (signs, tools, rules, community, and division of labor) (Leont'ev 1974). A subject is a person or group engaged in an activity. An intention or motivation is held by the subject and explains activity, giving it a specific direction. Activities are realized as individual and cooperative actions, and chains and networks of such actions that are related to each other by the same overall goal and motivation, which should not be considered as a mere condition for developing activity, but as a real factor influencing the actual performance of the action itself. A goal-directed action is under an agent's control if (1) the goal normally comes about as the result of the agent's attempt to perform the action, (2) the goal does not normally come about except as the result of the agent's action, and (3) the agent could have not performed the action (Wobcke 1998). For their part, actions consists of chains of operations, which are well-defined behaviors used as answers to conditions faced during the performing of an action. Activities are oriented to motivations, that is, the reasons that are impelling by themselves. Each motivation is an object, material or ideal, that satisfies a need. Actions are the processes functionally subordinated to activities; they are directed at specific conscious goals. Actions are realized through operations that are the result of knowledge or skill, and depend on the conditions under which the action is being carried out.

Goals, beliefs and intentions are in fact arbitrary interpretations of particular events (Bratman 1987). A particular course of action may be motivated in many cases in beliefs, represent the informational state of the agent. Using the term belief rather than knowledge recognizes that what an agent believes may not necessarily be true (and in fact may change in the future). These beliefs rest upon theories and these theories rest in turn on assumptions. Beliefs, the theories on which beliefs rest and the assumptions upon which theories rest must be valid if the means is to be considered right. Valid here means true if the belief bears on a representation of the world; and fair, good, legitimate in the case of should-be beliefs. Determining which means is right is not a trivial operation. Any belief is associated with reasons, but these reasons are often invalid for lack of access to relevant information, or because influenced by cognitive incompetence or of cognitive strategies, or due to the interference of conflicting goals (Boudon 2003). Correct beliefs result in sensible behavior; incorrect beliefs can cause unpredictable consequence actions. When we analyze our own behavior we are creating beliefs about our own goals. Desires represent the motivational state of the agent. They represent objectives or situations that the agent would like to accomplish or bring about. A goal can be described as a desire that has been adopted for active pursuit by the agent. Intentions represent the deliberative state of the agent—what the agent has chosen to do. Intentions are desires to which the agent has to some extent committed.

Nevertheless, the frontier between intentional activity and operational behavior is blurred, and movements are possible in all directions. Intentions can be transformed in the course of an activity; they are not immutable structures. An activity can lose its motivation and become an action, and an action can become an operation when the goal changes. The motivation of some activity may become the goal of an activity, as a result of which the latter is transformed into some integral activity. Therefore, it is impossible to make a general classification of what an activity is, what an action is and so forth, because the definition depends on what the subject or object in a particular real situation is. The constitutive elements of a belief cannot be precisely separated in the same way that two actors can be isolated from one another. Even when we separate one actor from another, the fact that his or her beliefs depend to a great extent on previously acquired knowledge means that he/she cannot be completely separated from the environment in which such knowledge has been acquired.

An additional trouble is that social motivations have their own dynamics, often contradictory. In other words, social activities are not isolated entities; they are influenced by other activities and other changes in the environment. People interact, influence others, reinforce some actions, interfere with others, and even sometimes prevent the action of other people (Creary 1981). The term contradiction is used to indicate a misfit within the components of social action, that is, among subjects, needs, motivations, goals, actions and operations, and even mediating artifacts (division of labor, rules, institutions, etc.), and produces internal tensions in apparently irregular qualitative changes, due to the changing predominance of ones over others. Activities are virtually always in the process of working through contradictions, which manifest themselves as problems, ruptures, breakdowns, clashes, etc. They are accentuated by continuous transitions and transformations between subjects, needs, motivations, goals, behavior, signs, tools, rules, community, division of labor, and between the embedded hierarchical levels of collective motivation-driven activity, individual goal-driven action, and mechanical behavior driven by the tools and conditions of action. Here lies the true nature of social causality and the motivation force of change and development: there is a global tendency to resolve underlying tension and contradictions by means of change and transformation. Since social activity is not relative to one individual but to a distributed collection of interacting people and the consequences of their actions, we cannot study how social activities took place by understanding the intentions or motivations of individual agents alone, no matter how detailed the knowledge of those individuals might be. To capture the teleological or purposive aspect of behavior, we should investigate collective action, that is, why different people made the same action, or different actions at the same place and at the same time. Its research goal should be to explain the sources or causes of that variability, and not exactly the inner intentions of individual action.

What we need to study is the constant interaction between agent and context. Consequently, the basic unit of motivation is not the discovery of some verbal proposition such as "*x* believes that *P*", "*x* desires that *P*", "*x* knows that *P*", and so forth. Rather, we are aware of those things that are playing a prominent role in constraining the global constraint satisfaction settling process in our minds (O'Reilly and Munakata 2002, p. 218). What constitutes "causality" is not just the "consciousness" of the reasoning system itself, but also the rich matrix of relations it bears to other agents, practices and institutions.

Beliefs, desires and intentions may change according to the variation in the local conditions, and according to what the agent may "learn" from its environment and from other agents interacting with it. To a certain extent, this is just giving the agents another level of rules. However, the nature of these rules is different, in that they are meta-rules about how to form rules (Lee and Lacey 2003). Such meta-rules allow for the type of self-reference that is key to the historical explanation. Individual social actors, in going about their various interactions, form representations of those interactions. Moreover, they abstract away from the details of individual interactions to formulate underlying rules that describe these interactions. In the case of societies, these rules are usually called norms or institutions. When individuals form abstractions about what the normative behaviors are in their society, they begin to act on them, either by behaving differently themselves or by reacting differently to the behavior of others. Thus, the abstractions the individuals make drive the behavior that emerges from their interactions. But the loop does not end here. As the individuals continue to interact based on the abstractions they have made and new societal patterns emerge, the individuals will make abstractions about those new patterns, which in turn will give rise to a new set of emergent behavior, ad infinitum (Baumer and Tomlinson 2006). Computational agents should be designed as learning entities, gaining ever more accurate information from the effects of their actions or more successful strategies from observing others' behaviors. In substance, reinforcement learning is shaped on the model of evolution, a fitness formula being always implied. This essentially has led to implement agents' capacity to gain more accurate information. But this is only part of the job required by a dynamic model of agent-hood. Agents undergo social influence, come to share the same beliefs and expectations, squeeze into the same practices, and this type of social influence sometimes leads them to form inaccurate, even wrong beliefs.

As a result of this focus on social actions as practiced by human actors in reference to other human actors, the idea of "agency" appears to be synonymous with an agent's way of being, seeing and responding in the world. It is an embedded and interpreting agency that draws on its funds of knowledge to both interpret and respond to the environment (Edwards 2000). The agent interprets and responds to the contexts of action and exploits the opportunities for effective action within them. It is an outward-looking mind which seeks local scaffolding to enhance its purposive action. However, it is not possible to fully understand how people act and work if the unit of study is the unaided individual with no access to other people. The unit of analysis is object-oriented action mediated by human produced tools and signs. Thus, we are constrained to study context to understand relations among agents, actions and goals. This is the reason of emphasizing the use of invariant change-relating capabilities to characterize historical events. What humans did and the way they did it is firmly and inextricably embedded in the social matrix of which every person is a member.

The obvious conclusion is that we are far from being perfect rational agents. And our ancestors even less, given the poor access to information at real time to take decisions (Leaf 2008). Nevertheless, we are very far from the current "stupidity" of usual computational agents in their eternal search for optimal but simple solutions.

Oestmo et al. agents' (Chap. 4) appear to be a bit more rational and less "adaptive" than traditional "optimal foragers". They know that they should produce tools to increase the possibilities of having success in hunting and gathering. This awareness on the necessity of technology is what makes them more "human" than strictly animal. They look for explanations of the changing raw material preferences when deciding to make tools. From a naturalistic point of view explanations for change in human raw material usage frequency would only include climate/environmental change and its co-variability with mobility and procurement strategies, the selection of certain raw materials for their physical properties, changes in demography, etc. All these parameters are well within a strong and limited rationality hypothesis, where prehistoric people, made optimal choices. But Oestmo et al. also consider the preference for appearance or color, symbolic value, and style. The authors have created a simple model of one forager with a mobile toolkit of fixed capacity that is randomly placed on the environment. The simulation is based on a previous model by Brantingham (2003). This "stupid but rational" behavior is compared to archaeological data from prehistoric settlements around the town of Mossel Bay, Western Cape, South Africa, offering a long sequence of change in raw material selection. Here, optimal decisions are not assumed, but tested against relevant prehistoric data. They think this is the right approach, instead of assuming the truth likeness of a particular theory of the way people made choices in a world with low developed means of production; we should look for particular tests of the explanatory power of the hypothesis. Oestmo et al. results should be compared with similar work by Davies et al. (2015), Clarkson et al. (2015), Pop (2015).

O'Brien and Bergh's agents (Chap. 6) are apparently even more "human", in the sense that the agents in their virtual world can build their own complex cognitive map of the environment around them, and they can make reference to ideological, social and political factor to motivate their decisions.

There is a growing interest in the computer science and artificial intelligence community to build more credible virtual agents that may act in a simulated world in the same way we believe humans would have acted. The belief–desire–intention software model (usually referred to simply, but ambiguously, as BDI, see Rao and Georgeff 1998; Wooldridge 2000; Luck et al. 2004; Bosse et al. 2011; Caballero et al. 2011; Taillandier et al. 2012; Kennedy 2012; Kim et al. 2013; Gelfond and Kahl 2014; Blount et al. 2014; Pantelis et al. 2016) is a software model developed for programming intelligent agents. In essence, it provides a mechanism for separating the activity of selecting a plan (from a plan library or an external planner application) from the execution of currently active plans. Consequently, BDI agents are able to balance the time spent on deliberating about plans (choosing what to do) and executing those plans (doing it). A third activity, creating the plans in the first place (planning), is not within the scope of the model, and is left to the system designer and programmer.

Alternative virtual agent architecture is "PECS" (Urban and Schmidt 2001; Malleson 2012) which stands for "Physical conditions, Emotional states, Cognitive capabilities and Social status". The authors of the architecture propose that it is possible to model the entire range of human behavior by modelling those four factors. PECS is seen as an improvement over BDI because it does not assume rational decision making and is not restricted to the factors of beliefs, desires and intentions (Schmidt 2000). Instead, an agent has a number of competing motives (such as "clean the house", "eat food", "raise children", "sleep" etc.) of which the strongest ultimately drives the agent's current behavior. Motives depend on the agent's internal state (an agent with a low energy level might feel hungry) as well as other external factors (an agent who smells cooking food might become hungry even if they do not have low energy levels). Personal preferences can also come into play, where some people feel a need more strongly than others even though their internal state variable levels are the same (Balke and Gilbert 2014). In this sense, Ho et al. (2006) have proposed a Categorized Long-term Autobiographic Memory (CLTM) architecture, utilizing abstracted notions of human autobiographic memory and narrative structure humans apply to their life stories (see also Pointeau et al. 2013; Lei et al. 2013; Bölöni 2014). El-Nasr et al. (2000) and Resisenzein et al. (2013) have explored the simulation of human emotions.

H-CogAFF cognitive architecture gives place to emotions and other high level cognitive layers integrating "fuzzy" boundaries between different levels of functionality, and allowing for some of the information-processing mechanisms to straddle two or more layers (Sloman and Christel 2003; Sloman 2011; Petters 2014; Goertzel et al. 2014).

Other recent essays in this direction are Goertzel et al. (2013), McRorie et al. (2012), Gratch et al. (2013), Faur et al. (2013), Kang and Tan (2013), Anastassakis and Panayiotopoulos (2014), Haubrich et al. (2015). For more advanced issues, see

Bostrom (2012), Hughes et al. (2012), Schönbrodt and Asendorpf (2011). Current work on cognition and artificial intelligence will allow the proper understanding of motivation in social action (Pollock 1995; Friedenberg 2011; Tenenbaum et al. 2011; Chella and Manzotti 2013; Diettrich 2014; Bryson 2015; Campennì 2016).

1.2.4 What Made Humans Really Human? Cooperation and "Collective" Action at the Dawn of Humanity

Certainly actual computational simulations of human behavior in the most remote past lack cognitive complexity. But this is not a source of troubles and problems, but a consequence of the emphasis on the generality and simplicity of human behavior and how the apparently unconscious repetition of simple actions produces the self-organized emergence of complex organization properties. This perspective should make us aware of the relevance of null models as a starting point of historical enquiry (Bocinsky 2014; Lake 2015; Cegielski and Rogers 2016). Bentley and Ormerod (2012) have argued for the utility of models which assume "zero-intelligence" on the part of agents to understand how far we can get with extremely simple social mechanisms and what must be added to them to explain social phenomena.

In any case, we do not think that the real problem of "intelligence" and "rationality" lies in the cognitive explicit content in the "mind" of each agent within the simulation. Obviously, we do not have in the present data about what men and women believed in ancient times. It is important to remember that we do not need to "recreate" the past as believed by people that lived then. It is the distance between our present problems and what happened in the past that motivates our emphasis on long term process and collective action instead of individual motivations. Probably this is not the case when studying a past situation that is relatively near to our present experience: the past desires of our grandparents and grandmothers may still constraint our decisions here and now. But there is no way that the desires of one person having lived more than 200 years ago can constrain what we want to do here and now. Therefore, when investigating the most remote past we are interested not in the individual but in collective action: what a population of a particular size made in the past can affect still what a new population that is a reproduction of the former one is able to do today (Oliver et al. 1985; Oliver 1993; Ball 2004; Iwanaga and Namatame 2002; Goldstone and Janssen 2005a, b; Miller and David 2013; Czaczkes et al. 2015; Will 2016). The negative side of this approach is that there is no possibility of knowing why an individual person made something somewhere at some moment. However, it does not presuppose the implicit randomness, subjectivity, or indeterminism of social action. The goal should be to explain the sources or causes of that variability, and not exactly the inner intentions of individual action.

The real issue is precisely that intentional actions of the individual agents give rise to functional, unaware collective phenomena. It is not that actual computer simulations ignore the basis of individual agency and that prehistoric people nor their computational surrogates were deprived of believes, desires and intentions beyond their direct survival (acquiring food), but social scientists are making emphasis on the analytical importance of understanding the roots of social self-organization before taking into account the role of the creative individual in a world constrained by unaware collective action. The fact that some characteristically human attributes are "mechanically" simple has been argued during the last 40 years. We do not need to affirm that prehistoric people were underdeveloped stupid people that acted like animals. Supposedly "modern" behavior like cooperation, alliance, technological innovations, etc. seems to be in fact the consequence of relative simple and plain mechanisms.

In this way, Janssen and Hill (Chap. 3) show how cooperation has a mechanical nature and, in some cases, it can be seen as adaptive. Fort et al. (Chap. 5) incorporate cultural transmission, that is, learning, to understand the speed of change in human populations during the Neolithic. They also argue that cultural transmission and economic change can be analyzed in adaptive and mechanical terms (although explicitly non-linear and non-monotonic) and not necessary the result of rational decisions nor cognitive states in the mind of agents.

Distributed computer simulation is one of the hallmarks for investigating this subjects given their ability to generate macro level behaviors caused by micro-level decisions of individual agents characterized by bounded rationality, decision-making autonomy, sociality, and dynamic interactions among them. According to that view the output of the social mechanism is a pattern of emergent behavior (self-organizing, collective behavior) which is difficult to anticipate from knowledge of the individual agents' behavior (Shoham and Tennenholtz 1997; Bedau 2003; Sawyer 2005; Neumann 2009; Helbing 2012; Helbing and Balietti 2013; Jennings et al. 2014; Schieve and Allen 2014; McHugh et al. 2016). For instance, any emergence of sociopolitical complexity should be considered as the resulting long and slow process produced by the model is generative, not deterministically hard-wired or causally pre-determined in any way (see Cioffi-Revilla and Bogle's contribution to this volume, Chap. 13). This reflection points to the necessary distinction between individual activity and their aggregated consequences, that is, between micro-motives and macro-behavior (Schelling 1978; Mella 2008). It is the same as distinguishing between agency and structure. In macro explanations, the set of individuals is viewed as a structure that can be characterized by a number of variables, whereas in micro motive explanation the structure is viewed as emergent from the interactions between the individuals. These models as well as real phenomena, for example, the societies, are dynamic because they change in time; therefore, a model will consist not only of structure but also of agency.

A good example of the way of taking into consideration intelligence as a collective phenomenon rather than as the simple summation of individual abilities was Jim Doran's EOS system, probably the first computer simulation of historical events in the true sense of word (Doran and Palmer 1995a, b, Doran et al. 1994).

The idea was to explore a computational interpretation of growth of social complexity in the Upper Paleolithic period (around the time of the last glacial maximum) relating changing features of the natural environment to the emergence in the prehistoric past of centralized decision making, hierarchy and related social phenomena. The computational model investigated what could happen when "artificial" social agents with elements of human-like cognition shared a common environment, were strongly aware of one another and collectively performed hunting and gathering tasks to survive. Although very simple in their contents, the collective execution of agent plans implied that each individual plan affected the plans of other agents, and was affected by them in a recursive way. Then, by "observation" of which agent first acquired each resource, agents came to recognize particular resources as "owned" by particular agents or groups, and a form of territoriality could be displayed.

Doran's model shows the consequences of cooperation at work and cultural transmission among hunter-gatherer systems. "Cooperation" is among the most analyzed causal factors for the modern understanding of "intelligent" decision-making in prehistory (Salgado et al. 2014). Current studies on cooperation as a social mechanism with relevant consequences for decision making are based on the effects of kinship and/or territoriality to reinforce the existence of social ties within clusters and to maintain group identity and shared practices. People have a preference for interacting with others who share similar traits and practices, which "naturally" diversifies the population into emergent social clusters. In the real world, as well as in a simulated world, individuals may display "in-group favoritism" (Hammond and Axelrod 2006), also called "parochialism" (Bowles and Gintis 2004; Koopmans and Rebers 2009; Fernández-Márquez and Vázquez 2014; Gintis et al. 2015; Santos et al. 2015; Salas-Fumás et al. 2016), in choosing how to interact, based on the advantages when interacting with "others" (according to individual or global beliefs). Especially relevant for this research is the possibility of simulating the social mechanism of Cultural Transmission as a form of social interaction (Reynolds et al. 2001; Mesoudi 2007; Roberts and Vander Linden 2011; Eerkens et al. 2013; Rorabaugh 2014, 2015; Clark and Crabtree 2015; Fort et al. 2015; Grüne-Yanoff 2015).

Analytically defining the consequences of cooperation according to the principle that "connected attracts" we make an important advance towards the explanation of apparently complex social behavior among small scale societies. More precisely, current simulations show that ethnicity can be understood in terms of the tendency of people with connected (or similar) traits (including physical, cultural, and attitudinal characteristics) to interact with one another more than with people unconnected (or dissimilar features). In addition, we can introduce the principle of social influence (i.e., the more that people interact with one another, the more similar they become) which runs at the level of communication and the formation of a socio-cognitive level. This influence process produces induced ethnicity, in which the disproportionate interaction of likes with likes may not be the result of a psychological tendency but rather the result of continuous interaction.

Computer simulation has allowed the discovery that social mechanisms that normally lead to cultural convergence—cooperation, influence and transmission—can also explain how population have diversified culturally through the ages (Read 2003, 2010). This conclusion is based on pioneer research by Axelrod (1997a, b). He proposed an abstract model based on the fundamental principle that the transfer of ideas occurs most frequently between individuals who are similar in certain attributes such as beliefs, education, social status, and the like. This study draws some interesting conclusions experimenting with different parameter configurations, including the non-intuitive result that the average number of stable regions formed decreases as the size of the territory increases. The resulting dynamics converges to a global monocultural macroscopic state when the initial cultural diversity is below a critical value, while above it ethnicity is unable to inforce cultural homogeneity, and multiethnic patterns persist asymptotically. This change of macroscopic behavior has been characterized as a non-equilibrium phase transition.

In any case, Axelrod's model is too simple to be used as an effective model of ethnogenesis. For instance, it has been proved (Klemm et al. 2003, 2005; San Miguel et al. 2005; Gracia-Lázaro et al. 2009) that if random noise is introduced at a low rate (allowing cultural traits to change randomly with a small probability), the basic dynamics of the ethnicity and influence model will drive the population away from cultural diversity and toward cultural homogeneity. This may happen because the introduction of random shocks perturbs the stability of cultural regions, eroding the borders between the groups. This allows the system to find a dynamical path away from the metastable configuration of coexisting cultural domains, toward the stable configuration of ethnogenesis.

Cultural drift raises the question of whether the above explanation of cultural diversity will hold if agents were permitted to make errors or develop innovations. Parisi et al. (2003), working also on the lineage of Axelrod's assumptions, have simulated a process of expansion of a single human group in an empty territory and looking at what happens to this group's previous culture when during the expansion process both cultural assimilation between neighboring sub-groups and random internal changes in the culture of each subgroup took place. By allowing multiplex influence, it is no longer possible for a deviant to lure its neighbors by influencing them one at a time. This strengthens the effects of ethnical homogeneity by insuring that agents can never be influenced in a direction that leaves them with less in common with their neighbors overall. If within-group interaction preference is the mechanism by which global convergence generates local diversity, then strengthening the tendency toward convergence might have the counterintuitive effect of allowing stable diversity to emerge. Parisi et al. show that Axelrod's result of no complete cultural homogenization is obtained even if we abandon the assumption that neighboring groups with completely different cultures cannot influence each other. In this expanded model not only assimilation is with the dominating culture of a site's entire neighborhood but, most importantly, there is no role of pre-existing cultural similarity as a determinant of cultural assimilation.

Instead of the exploration of a new territory by an ethnically homogenous population, Matthews (2008) has simulated the sudden arrival of a different ethnic group, and how it behaves with local populations. One might expect that in a culture with a very high rate of drift, new cultural regions may be absorbed very rapidly as common features may appear regularly by chance, facilitating interaction across boundaries. The results of this experiment suggest that despite such high levels of drift, distinct regions may persist for significant periods of time. In general though, it is possible to conclude that in relatively homogeneous cultures with low rates of cultural drift (as may be expected to be found in isolated, monoculture regions), any distinct cultures which do form are likely to persist for significant periods of time before being assimilated into the surrounding culture. These distinct cultures may appear through a number of possible mechanisms (including perhaps Axelrod's suggested local-interaction model), but an obvious example might be an invading or migrating group of people from a distant region with a very different culture. Finding aspects of culture in common with the invaders may be difficult, reducing the chances of further interaction and absorption. The second result suggests that even in a culture with a high rate of drift (such as a modern, fast-changing multicultural society) it may take a considerable amount of time for a new cultural group to integrate into its surroundings (Matthews 2008).

As ethnogenesis increases and activity restricts within the ethnically homogenous group, agents converge on their cultural characteristics; yet if there is enough heterogeneity in the population, this similarity among group members can also make them even more dissimilar from the members of other groups (Barceló et al. 2013a, b and 2015). Ultimately, this can produce cultural groups that are so dissimilar from one another that their members cannot interact across group boundaries. If cultural influence processes create differentiation between two neighbors such that they have no cultural traits in common, we should allow these individuals to alter the structure of the social network by dropping their tie and forming new ties to other individuals. Centola et al. (2007) have proposed a model where the network of social interactions is not fixed but rather evolves in tandem with the actions of the individuals as a function of changing cultural similarities and differences. The use of the level of heterogeneity in the population as a control parameter, allows to map the space of possible co-evolutionary outcomes and thereby show how network structure and cultural group formation depend on one another. These results address the question of how stable cultural groups can be maintained in the presence of cultural drift.

Contrary to Axelrod's claim, the effect of one cultural feature does not inherently depend on the presence or absence of others, but only so in dyadic relations where similarity matters. Boyd and Richerson (1987), McElreath et al. (2003), Heinrich and Heinrich (2007) have proved that if people preferentially interact in with people who have the same culture as they do, and if they acquire their markers and coordination behaviors by imitating successful individuals, groups distinguished by both norm and marker differences may emerge and remain stable despite significant mixing between them. Under such rules, within a group the behavior which is initially most common will reach fixation, as individuals with the less common behavior are less likely to receive the payoff. The successful behavior will also develop a marker associated with it as individuals sharing this marker will also be more likely to interact with each other and receive the higher payoff. These ethnically marked positions are examples of attractors within the model.

Some other important enhancements of Axelrod's model of the dissemination of culture includes: Barbosa and Fontanari (2009), Kim (2010), Bednar et al. (2010), Dutton et al. (2010), Lanchier (2012), Valori et al. (2012), Hawick (2013), Pfau et al. (2013), Kang et al. (2014), Gowdy and Krall (2015), Roos et al. (2015), Kovacevic et al. (2015), Upal (2015). Those research teams have constructed a diversity of computer models that allows the dynamic understanding of four hallmarks of culture: coordinated behavior, coherent cultural signatures, substantial within culture diversity, and cross cultural differences. In general, these approaches combine a social drive to coordinate with an individual desire for internal consistency. As a result, the formation of in-group favoritism in terms of the developing of a meaningful cultural signature implies that individuals within a community conform their behavior to match one another's, and also that there is some relationship that ties their behaviors and beliefs together from one activity or domain to the next, creating consistency across behaviors. In addition to conforming, people also choose to be around those who act as they do, what curbs group mergers because people avoid interacting with others who are not like themselves. Adding social influence to ethnogenesis exacerbates these effects: when individuals interact with others like themselves, and also actively become more similar to them, polarization between groups is even more pronounced. If individuals can use social markers to increase the likelihood of acquiring the behaviors adaptive in their context, markers and behaviors can become associated, and markers can in fact become exaggerated beyond initial differences between the populations.

A parallel approach has been Skyrms's study that patterns of coordinated behavior can best be explained from an adaptive dynamic perspective where the agents are only boundedly rational (Skyrms 2001). Skyrms concentrates on three mechanisms that can divert an abstract population of hunters from hunting hare on an individual disorganized basis to hunting stag and achieve a kind of collective equilibrium. The solutions are built on various *correlation* and *anti-correlation devices*. First, spatial and network embeddedness offer a correlation device that allows for the clustering of stag hunters (local interaction) and for efficient imitation, learning, and reproduction that all take place in the spatial or network locality. Second, these interactions change endogenously over time, such that network dynamics (due to partner selection) favors cooperation at the end. Adaptive dynamics operate on both strategy and interaction structure, which quickly shifts the balance in favor of cliques of stag hunters, without any kind of rationality assumed. Third, signaling and in particular signaling systems in which signals are not cheated and correctly interpreted can evolve and provide the solution towards equilibrium as collect ive action. Reinforcement learning helps to move coordination games to a signaling system in which signals are unambiguous (meaningful) with probability equal to one.

In this model rationality and common knowledge still play a role, although much less of it is required to explain game theoretical equilibria concepts than in standard motivations. The main problem is to give a convincing story of why agents will coordinate their behavior so as to establish a collective good. At first sight, social cooperation seems to be a prisoner's dilemma, or in the n-player case, a public goods game. In this game, by cooperating an individual helps all the other members of the group, but at a cost to himself. Therefore, a self-regarding player will never cooperate. It follows that social cooperation requires altruistic players—people must cooperate even though this is personally costly and the others alone benefit from one's prosocial behavior. It is easy to see why the public goods game is an allegory for social cooperation among humans. For instance, if we all hunt, if hunting is dangerous and exhausting, and we must share the kill equally, then a self-regarding hunter will prefer to shirk rather than hunt. Cooperation in this case requires altruistic hunters. Skyrms' point, however, is that if the game is repeated indefinitely, then cooperation among self-regarding agents is possible using what are known as "trigger strategies." A trigger strategy for a player is to cooperate as long as all other players cooperate as well. However, the first time one player defects, the trigger strategy dictates that all players defect on every succeeding round. It is easy to see that in this case, even selfish players will cooperate on all rounds, because the gains they have from defecting on one rounds may be swamped by the losses incurred by not benefiting from others' efforts on the succeeding rounds. The implication of Skyrms' position for social theory is quite dramatic. If he were correct, it would follow that humans could cooperate very effectively even if they were perfectly self-regarding, with absolutely no need for altruistic preferences, empathy, no predisposition for cooperating and sharing, nor any other prosocial behavior that goes beyond simple mutualism: An individual would help the group only as a byproduct of helping himself.

This is not the proper place to discuss the empirical validity of such ideas, but to insist in what can be done to understand the mechanical basis of collective action in terms of agent interaction. The model has been enhanced by Skirms and colleagues (Skyrms 2004, 2010, 2013; Huttegger and Skyrms 2013; Santos et al. 2008; Pacheco et al. 2011), and discussed critically by other authors (Bulbulia 2011; Starnini et al. 2011; Moreira et al. 2012; Tomasello et al. 2012; Wagner 2012; deBoer 2013; Song and Feldman 2013; Shaw 2015; Riebling and Schmitz 2016; Plikynas and Raudys 2016, among many others).

The idea of cooperation as a basis of cultural differentiation is resounding heavily in archaeology and anthropology. Madsen and Lipo (2015) have introduced an extension of the Axelrod's model of cultural differentiation in which traits have prerequisite relationships, and where social learning is dependent upon the ordering of those prerequisites. Their results point to ways in which archaeologists can build more comprehensive explanations of the archaeological record of the Paleolithic as well as other cases of technological change.

Phillips et al. (2014) test the hypothesis that the development of extra-somatic weapons could have influenced the evolution of human cooperative behavior. In their simulations, the authors found that cooperative strategies performed significantly better, and non-cooperative strategies significantly worse, under simulated weapons use. They conclude that the development of extra-somatic weapons throws new light on the evolution of human altruistic and cooperative behavior, and particularly 'strong reciprocity'. The notion that distinctively human altruism and cooperation could have been an adaptive trait in a past environment that is no longer evident in the modern world provides a novel addition to theory that seeks to account for this major evolutionary puzzle. With a stronger substantive goal, Shennan et al. (2015) have analyzed two distinct material cultures (pottery and personal ornaments) from Neolithic Europe, in order to determine whether archaeologically defined "cultures" exhibit marked discontinuities in space and time, supporting the existence of a population structure, or merely isolation-by-distance. They have investigated the extent to which cultures can be conceived as structuring "cores" or as multiple and historically independent "packages". More theoretical studies are those by Burtsev (2005), who has validated a model of cooperation based on the assumptions of heritable markers, constrained resource, and local interactions with the real data on aggression in archaic egalitarian societies, and Briz et al. (2014a, b), Santos et al. (2015) who suggest a model providing insight on how the spatial concentration of resources and agents' movements in the space can influence cooperation. Through carefully calibrating the model parameters with ethnoarchaeological data from ancient Patagonia fisher-foragers, the authors conclude that the emergence of informal and dynamic communities that operate as a vigilance network preserves cooperation and makes defection very costly. Also using ethnographical data on hunter-gatherers, Janssen and Hill (2014) have explored the implications of social living, cooperative hunting, variation in group size and mobility. Their simulations show that social living decreases daily risk of no food, but cooperative hunting has only a modest effect on mean harvest rates. This research is related with their results in Chap. 3 in this book.

Savarimuthu et al. (2011b) use an agent based model to simulate a hunter-gatherer society where the norms of the society are affected by changing environmental conditions. In particular, the authors are interested in exploring how norms might change in a society based on the changes to the type of resources available in the society. Also based on ethnoarchaeological data to calibrate empirically the model parameters, Barceló et al. (2013b, 2015) have simulated how small sized groups (less than 10 households) died by starving because the impossibility to build a high enough number of social ties. Given that the probabilities of interaction and labor exchange are conditioned on the existence of some shared belief elements, agents should be able to adapt their identity in response to the identity of agents with them they have arrived to cooperate successfully. Cultural consensus is built adaptively from the communalities among individual identities of agents connected at a precise time-step. The higher the interaction, the higher identity likelihood. It is also assumed that the higher the perceived similarity in reference cognitive models (social memory), the higher the probabilities of cooperating and creating social aggregates conditioning social reproduction and how individual identities are transmitted to new generations.

Consequently, the study of intentionality in the remote past is not a question of individual "intelligence" or "rationality". The examples here quoted contribute to sustain the view that prehistoric people did not die as often as imagined as a direct consequence of scarcity. Instead of the traditional image of prehistoric hunters fighting for survival in hard environments, modern research based on computer simulation suggests that social exchange networks were easy to build and negotiate, allowing hunting success even in the case of low availability of resources and the poor efficacy of working instruments (Younger 2003, 2004; Ladefoged et al. 2008; Helbing et al. 2011; Gurven et al. 2012; Neumann and Secchi 2016).

This explanation is based on the assumption that "cooperation" when survival is not individually attained implies an investment in labor that produces a common benefit. Such investment comes from agents whose survival has been effectively attained individually, and it is produced at no cost, because there is no surplus accumulation beyond the survival level. The benefit is not only individual (some agents survive thanks to the help of others), but also common: a social aggregation emerges allowing technological diffusion and increasing a cultural consensus which can be necessary in the future. In that sense, positive interaction is not only the result of bounded rational decision making, but it is filtered by the specific social (cultural) identity of agents, a parameter that changes constantly because it is probabilistically conditioned by a number of social factors. Among hunter-gatherers, positive interaction depended on the predictable benefits of working together and sharing the results of collective work. The higher the interaction, the higher the probability of hunting success. It is not the same as arguing that the higher the number of hunters, the higher the amount of meat. In some scenarios, the total amount of energy per person can be lesser, but hunting success is more frequent in the long run, that is, it is more probable. In the usual circumstances of small bands with hardly efficient instruments for hunting and transport, the absence of cooperation made uncertain the probability of survival, given the increasing risk for hunting failure, even in the case of high animal availability in the area.

In this line of research, making emphasis on "collective" decision making, rather than on optimal rationality we can mention current work on technological change and innovation. Prehistoric people were not rude savages without any idea or necessity for innovate (Mithen 1990, 1991), rather they experimented constantly new materials and new abilities to expand their technology and increase the success of hunter and gathering activities needed for survival. Innovation was not the result of the individual geniality of a very clever man, "inventing" for his community. It was a collective phenomenon of experimentation and the higher probability of adopting some new tools or behaviors and rejecting others.

In a recent simulation of prehistoric hunter and gatherer populations from Patagonia (the southernmost part of South America), Barceló and colleagues have created an artificial world in which subsistence was obtained by individual households by means of labor with the contribution of its own technology, whose efficiency was estimated according a parameter that range from 0.01 to 2. High efficiency indicates that all local resources can be managed independently of its difficulty of acquisition given the extreme performance of available technology. Low values are characteristic of human groups with hardly evolved instruments, in such a way that only a part of locally available resources are effectively managed. The efficiency of food preservation techniques is another technological factor, related with the overall level of development of means of production. Both factors —quantity of people to work and technological efficiency act upon the difficulty of acquiring and transforming resources into subsistence and hence on survival. But technological efficiency is not a fixed parameter; it changes because hunter-gatherers learn from others in the environment different ways of making tools. They compare the new tools when they cooperate and adapt some characteristics—but not all—from most successful hunters (Del Castillo et al. 2014; Barceló et al. 2015). The result is an *S*-shaped curve of technological innovation that exactly reproduce modern mechanisms of technological change. This characteristic model can be understood as the number of adopters of a new technique or tool rises slowly at first, when there are only few adopters in each time period. The curve then accelerates to a maximum until half of the individuals in the system have adopted. Then it increases at a gradually slower rate as fewer and fewer remaining individuals adopt the innovation. The *S*-shape of a typical development curve can be viewed as the result of the process of exhausting a 'solution space' of potential improvements: as the pool is explored and exploited there are fewer and fewer improvements remaining to be discovered, slowing the pace of improvement if the number of trials stays the same. Again, the *S*-curve is produced in a setting where there is a finite potential for improvement. This result call for the resemblance between the process of technological change and innovation in the most remote past and the immediate present. Innovations to hunting equipment and storing technology followed similar trajectories as hybrid corn among Iowa farmers, bottle-feeding practices among impoverished Third Worlders, new governance practices among Fortune 500 companies, chemical fertilizers among small-scale farmers, and the practice of not smoking among Americans. "Intelligence" of prehistoric people was like "intelligence" of our contemporaries (White 2008).

Creating a generative model of technological change is an interdisciplinary effort that should include researches in various fields, like demography, anthropology, paleo genetics, and human ecology. Important questions that should be addressed before we can quantify the parts of a population adopting an innovation or changing their cultural features include the establishment of methods for inferring past population structure, the timing of the adoption or change, the relative importance of demographic variations, and the possibilities of alternative hypotheses like demographic transitions, colonization events, and/or population extinctions. Among current computer simulations along this lines of research, we can mention Heinrich (2001), Ma and Nakamori (2005), Dawid (2006), O'Brien and Bentley (2011), Rush (2011), Zenobia and Weller (2011), Kiesling et al. (2012), Vespignani (2009, 2012), Boyd et al. (2013), Laciana et al. (2013), Papachristos et al. (2013), Nan et al. (2014), O'Brien et al. (2015), Porčić (2015), Spaiser and Sumpter (2016).

1.2.5 The Myth of the Good Prehistoric Savage: The Origins of Social Differentiation and Complexity

An obvious consequence of this way of considering social organization as an emergent property of the mechanisms of cooperation (or the lack of it) and cultural transmission, is that the origins of social diversity, hierarchy and complexity can also be considered as emergent properties of relatively basic social mechanisms. Caldas and Coelho (1999) have argued that what we call today "institutions" were in fact solutions to recurring problems of social interaction in small-scale societies, and should be understood as preconditions for social life, unintended outcomes, and human devised constraints.

If for 99 % of its history humanity lived forming small scale, "egalitarian" communities, why those early undifferentiated groups diversified and coercion, power, inequality and hierachization have marked social evolution? First of all, what is "social complexity"? We should approach this term in the sense of a conceptual framework and not as a particular kind of society. The idea of complexity refers to phenomena with many parts and many possible arrangements of the relationships between those parts. Herbert Simon was one of the seminal thinkers in the study of complexity and also on computer simulation and artificial intelligence. In 1962, he put forward several key ideas: "(…) roughly, by a complex system I mean one made up of a large number of parts that interact in a no simple way. In such systems, the whole is more than the sum of the parts, not in an ultimate, metaphysical sense, but in the important pragmatic sense that, given the properties of the parts and the laws of their interaction, it is not a trivial matter to infer the properties of the whole. In the face of complexity, an in-principle reductionist may be at the same time a pragmatic holist. (Simon 1962: 468). Therefore, when we are speaking about social complexity we are speaking on the internal differentiation of subgroups of people within a well-defined group, and the existence of differentiated patterns of relationships or arrangement among those subgroups.

An important corollary to the very definition of complexity in social groups is that the behavior of the complex social system is difficult to predict because of the no simple interactions among the constituting social sub-groups. In a complex system we cannot provide a simple aggregation model of the system that adds up the independent behaviors of the parts; rather, the parts are influenced in their behaviors by the behaviors of other components. The state of the social system is fixed by the interdependent dynamics of agents and groups of agents; which implies that collective behavior can oscillate wildly with apparently similar initial conditions.

Cultural evolutionists usually speak of human societies evolving toward greater complexity or higher degrees of organization. This is an important aspect of any historical investigation. Is social inequality an immutable result of the destiny of any agglomeration of people, or the emergent consequence of the interaction between individuals and groups of individuals (households, communities, tribes, territories, etc.)? The increase in complexity in the course of social evolution that can be observed in historical terms is, however, neither inevitable nor universal. There is no reason to regard the evolutionary process as one of inevitable progress, nor is an increase in complexity of human societies inevitable (Nowotny 2005; Dundes and Harlow 2005; Anderson et al. 2014; Vanhée et al. 2014; Neumann and Secchi 2016).

If we equate social inequality with the formal definition of disorder, we would implement a computer model of social evolution in terms of an evolution from order—hunter gatherer intrinsic egalitarianism—to disorder—economic inequality, exploitation, social and political hierarchy and class struggle-. In physics, the terms order and disorder designate the presence or absence of some symmetry or correlation in a many-particle system. The strictest form of physical order in a solid is lattice periodicity: a certain pattern (the arrangement of atoms in a unit cell) is repeated again and again to form a translationally invariant tiling of space. Lattice periodicity implies long-range order: if only one unit cell is known, then by virtue of the translational symmetry it is possible to accurately predict all individual (atomic) positions at arbitrary distances. A system is said to present disorder when some parameters defining its behavior are random variables, that is, when not all components have the same values, and the distribution of values does not follow a regular pattern. This is also characteristic of societies defined in terms of the unequal character of access to means of production, coherence and social and political hierarchy: some agents are more powerful than others are because they influence decisively in the economic and social reproduction decisions they are able to take. There is not a single type of complex societies, but different degrees of internal differentiation.

Nature tends from order to disorder in isolated systems. That means that "disorder" is a more probable state of any system than order. Its measure is often called entropy (Kubat and Zeman 1975). The mathematical basis with respect to the association entropy has with order and disorder began, essentially, with the famous Boltzmann formula, $S = k \ln W$, which relates entropy S to the number of possible states W in which a system can be found. In the case of social systems, the entropy of a collection of social agents within the system can be defined as a measure of their disorder or equivalently, how close a system is to equilibrium—that is, to perfect internal inequality. A more precise way to characterize social entropy is in terms of the different number of diverse arrangements along a given temporal trajectory. Thus, an increase in entropy means a greater number of microstates for the final state than for the initial state, and hence more possible arrangements of a system arrangement at any one instant. Here, a greater 'dispersal of the total energy of a system' means the existence of many possibilities (Lambert 2002).

Annila and Salthe (2009), among many others (see also Tesfatsion 2003; Deguchi 2011), have regarded economic activity as an evolutionary process governed by the 2nd law of thermodynamics. The universal law, when formulated locally as an equation of motion, reveals that a growing economy develops functional machinery and organizes hierarchically in such a way as to tend to equalize energy density differences within the economy and in respect to the surroundings it is open to. Diverse economic activities result in flows of energy that will preferentially channel along the most steeply descending paths, leveling a non-Euclidean free energy landscape. This principle of 'maximal energy dispersal', equivalent to the maximal rate of entropy production, gives rise to economic laws and regularities. The law of diminishing returns follows from the diminishing free energy while the relation between supply and demand displays a quest for a balance among interdependent energy densities. Economic evolution is dissipative motion where the driving forces and energy flows are inseparable from each other. When there are multiple degrees of freedom, economic growth and decline are inherently impossible to forecast in detail. Namely, trajectories of an evolving economy are non-integrable, i.e., unpredictable in detail because a decision by a player will affect also future decisions of other players. We propose that decision making is ultimately about choosing from various actions those that would reduce most effectively subjectively perceived energy gradients.

Social structure is a common phenomenon in nature, and it is not a necessary characteristic of human "intelligence" or rationality. Specifically, many species of the order of primates show different patterns of "complex" social structure. The limits of collective action and the emergence of patterns of social affiliation and differentiation in primate societies have been recently simulated (Bryson et al. 2007; Puga-Gonzalez et al. 2009, 2014; De Vries 2009; Evers et al. 2011, 2012; King and Sueur 2011; Sueur et al. 2011; Dolado et al. 2014; Smith et al. 2016; Will 2016). For instance, Witkowski and Ikegami (2016) have created a virtual world in which agents progressively evolve the ability to use the information exchanged between each other via signaling to establish temporary leader-follower relations. These relations allow agents to form swarming patterns, emerging as a transient behavior that improves the agents' ability to forage for the resource. Once they have acquired the ability to swarm, the individuals are able to outperform the non-swarmers at finding the resource.

The basis for many of those studies is a model for the origins of domination in animal populations proposed by Hemelrijk (1999, 2002, 2004), Hemelrijk et al. (2005). In this virtual world, artificial entities live in a homogeneous world and only aggregate, and upon meeting one another and may perform dominance interactions in which the effects of winning and losing are self–reinforcing. Whether an agent will initiate an attack depends on the chance it has to defeat its opponent. If the risk of losing is large the likelihood that the agent will start an attack is small ('risk-sensitive attack strategy'). When a dominance interaction actually takes place the outcome of the fight is decided probabilistically by the relative win chance. Defeating an opponent having a small probability to win increases the winner's dominance value less than defeating an opponent that has a large probability to win ('damped positive feedback'). The ordering of the agents according to this hypothetical value can be read as the emergence of a 'real hierarchy'. The agent's DOM value is intended to correspond with a real animal's capacity to win fights. By varying the intensity of aggression only, one may switch from egalitarian to despotic virtual communities. In addition, artificial despotic communities show a clearer spatial centrality of dominants and, counter–intuitively, more rank overlap between the sexes than the egalitarian ones. Because of the correspondence with patterns in real animals, the model makes it worthwhile comparing despotic and egalitarian species for socio–spatial structure and rank overlap too. Furthermore, it presents with parsimonious hypotheses which can be tested for patterns of aggression, spatial structure and the distribution of social positive and sexual behavior.

To sum up, violence and revenge may reduce the survival probability of the population. Flight from known aggressors enhanced the survival of the total population, at the expense of social cohesion. These examples show the possible role of violence and aggression on the evolution towards increasing social complexity (see also Ilachinski 2004; Taylor et al. 2004; Clements and Hughes 2004; Younger 2005, 2011; Lim et al. 2007; Philips et al. 2014).

Rather than an unconscious solution to instinctive violence, we may suggest that it was the rational and conscious emergence of social norms constraining free will what characterized social evolution and the development of more complex social systems (Savarimuthu et al. 2011a). It has been suggested that social norms help people self-organizing in many situations without relying on a centralized and omnipresent authority (Villatoro and Sabater-Mir 2009; De la Cruz et al. 2012; Vila et al. 2013. See also Makowsky and Smaldino 2015; Roos et al. 2015; Gelfand and Jackson 2016; Horiuchi 2015; Santos et al. 2016; Thürmel 2016). On the contrary to institutional rules, the responsibility to enforce social norms is not the task of a central authority but a task of each member of the society (Ghorbani and Bravo 2016).

Castelfranchi et al. (1998) suggested the need of a social norm prescribing: "attack an eater unless the food item being eaten is marked as 'owned' by that agent". The multi-agent system is composed out of two different sub-populations: agents either respect the finder-keeper precept (the Respectful) or not (the Cheaters). Either through experience or through communications the agents learn whether another agent is a Respectful or a Cheater. The 'normative' algorithm of the Respectful is modified so that they respect the norm only with agents known to be Respectful. This looks like a sanction towards the Cheaters, but as the finder-keeper precept does not hold for any Cheater—it is in fact not prescribed for them—they cannot violate it, and therefore they cannot be sanctioned. The Cheaters are defined as non-normative, i.e., self-interested agents. In this respect, in the Castelfranchi, Conte and Paolucci model, it is the Respectful who violate the finder-keeper norm if they do not respect the Cheaters. It is rational that the Respectful only respect themselves, but how do we know, that decisions about the respect or disrespect of norms are the result of a rational calculus? Is it rational that the Cheaters always disrespect the finder-keeper norm? Under the title of deviant behavior, there is a long research tradition in sociology that investigates the reasons for a lack of respect of norms, which could advance theory construction here. Working on the results of this model, Saam and Harrer (1999) have studied the hypothesis, which can be traced back to Marx, stating that the "finder-keeper" norm while controlling aggression efficaciously reduces social inequality holds only in quite egalitarian societies. Throughout a variety of non-egalitarian societies, it instead increases social inequality. The authors have remodeled the model's normative behavior from a sociological point of view by implementing Haferkamp's theory of action approach to deviant behavior, demonstrating that it is possible to integrate power into computational models of norms.

Gavrilets (2012) shows that the differences in fighting abilities lead to the emergence of hierarchies where stronger individuals take away resources from weaker individuals and, as a result, have higher reproductive success. He has shown that the logic of within-group competition implies under rather general conditions that each individual benefits if the transfer of the resource from a weaker group member to a stronger one is prevented. This effect is especially strong in small groups. This effect can result in the evolution of a particular, genetically controlled psychology causing individuals to interfere in a bully–victim conflict on the side of the victim. A necessary condition is a high efficiency of coalitions in conflicts against the bullies.

Ray and Liew (2003) adopt a different approach by assuming that leaders are the better performing individuals that help others in the society to improve through an intrasociety information exchange. "Better" may refer to different behaviors: more successful in hunting or sharing resources with others, more efficient in fighting against violence and aggression, etc. Such "leaders" would improve only through an intersociety information exchange that results in the migration of a leader from a society to another that is headed by better performing leaders. This process of leader migration would halve helped the "better" performing societies to expand and survive where others disaggregate and disappear.

Hazy (2008) defines leadership as those aspects of agent interactions which catalyze changes to the local rules defining other agents' interactions. According to this author, there are five distinct aspects of leadership to be observed. Leadership involves actions among agents that: (a) identify or espouse a cooperation strategy or program, (b) catalyze conditions where other agents choose to participate in the program, (c) organize choices and actions in other agents to navigate complexity and avoid interaction catastrophe (sometimes called "complexity catastrophe"), (d) form a distinct output layer that expresses the system as a unity in its environment, and (e) translate feedback into structural changes in the influence network among agents. Leadership in all of its aspects serves three functional demands in supporting the purposes of participating agents and groups of agents. Generative leadership identifies and generates variety in the programs of action, resources and capabilities available to the community. Convergent leadership increases the perceived benefit to cost ratio of participating in a program of action; this deepens and makes less rugged the attractor basin associated with agents choosing to adopt a particular program of action. Unifying leadership promotes collective identity, or "unity," and catalyzes actions and communications that pressure others to conform to a program; it clarifies boundaries and enables increased participation and cooperation at the margin within an attractor basin. See also Boal and Schultz (2007) about this view on "strategic" leadership.

Accepting dominance and creating institutionalized forms of leadership has been considered as an answer to conflict (Spisak et al. 2011). Particular attention has been given to the role of the "follower" and the specific pressures encouraging "followership investment" and the emergence of traits intended to signal potential leadership ability. This is a source of internal differentiation, and hence of "complexity" as leaders differentiate from the rest of the population. Eguiluz et al. (2005) have created a virtual world in which leaders are individuals getting a large payoff who are imitated by a considerable fraction of the population, conformists are unsatisfied cooperative agents that keep cooperating, and exploiters are defectors with a payoff larger than the average one obtained by cooperators. The dynamics generate a social network that can have the topology of a small world network. The network has a strong hierarchical structure in which the leaders play an essential role in sustaining a highly cooperative stable regime. But disruptions affecting leaders produce social crises described as dynamical cascades that propagate through the network. "Prestige" increases the different nature of leaders, coming into existence to signal the level of skill held by their owners, in order to gain deference benefits from learning individuals in exchange for access.

Clemson and Evans (2012) have simulated a virtual world in which agents can choose to follow the choices made by a neighbouring agent in a social network (the future "leader"). The authors investigated three different types of possible social network (the Erdős–Rényi random graph, the scale-free network, and the regular-ring network), chosen to represent various extremes in terms of their substrate degree distributions, and investigated each using a variety of network sizes. Results highlight the apparently universal aspects of social behaviour. This universal form shows that, irrespective of the type of underlying social network, the leadership structure which emerges has an initial power-law section. That is, there are always a few agents whose actions are copied by many others. However, the authors have also found that the nature of the social network linking agents does have a significant effect on the 'fatness' of the leadership distribution. The virtual abstract worlds investigated here are clearly not realistic in many senses, but they can capture some of the basic features of competition dynamics thorough history. It is clear that the copying of strategies from a local social neighbourhood does lead to the emergence of a leadership structure, regardless of the nature of the social network.

Among the agent-based models that explicitly take into account social inequality and conflict, we can mention Smith and Choi (2007), who have simulated the emergence of inequality in small-scale societies. The model is predicated on the assumption that a limited number of asymmetries, such as differential control over productive resources, can explain the emergence of institutionalized inequality. They also draw on contemporary evolutionary theory in order to avoid the pitfalls of naïve functionalism and teleology. Their approach is not to deny any possibility of collectively beneficial outcomes or directionality to sociopolitical evolution, but rather to show how it emerges from the interaction of individual agency, social structure, and environmental constraints. In their computer simulation, some agents (depicted as "Patrons") control limited areas with greater per capita resource endowments, and can trade access to these for services from less fortunate agents (depicted as "Clients"). There is also an additional set of isolated agents which simply defend richer patches for their exclusive use, while others (depicted as "Doves") share any resources on their patch with other non-territorial agents (Doves or Clients). In the initial simulation, all agents are Doves, randomly distributed over a heterogeneous environment, so each agent has different probabilities to become a Patron or a Client depending on its behavior and the productivity of the area it is placed. Under default parameter values, non-territorial strategies dominate, split equally between Dove and Client types, and isolated and Patron types are about equally represented in the remaining areas. However, a stable patron-client regime emerges in about one third of all runs, and takes over the population about 10 percent of the time. Obviously, environmental heterogeneity is critical, as Patrons capitalize on their relatively rich patch endowments to participate in exchanges with Clients, and hence variation in property endowment, provides the initial opportunity for the emergence of inequality. Yet this is not sufficient, nor can this be glossed as "environmental determinism", since alternative strategies, interacting with similar resource heterogeneity do not generate socioeconomic inequality. Demographic parameters have also a strong effect on the relative success of territorial and non-territorial strategies. When mortality is high or reproductive rate low, the initial (all-Dove) population expands slowly so that isolated and Patron agents are able to spread and control rich patches, effectively keeping Dove and Client numbers low at equilibrium. Conversely, low mortality or high reproductive rate allows Doves to proliferate rapidly, and territorial agents are locked out (with Clients arising in modest numbers through mutation and drift). Increased mutation rates are favorable to the spread of Client and Patron strategies, but only because this retards the initial proliferation of Doves.

Although this model may be considered as too restricted and limited, it allows exploring the hypothesis that a limited number of asymmetries can explain most cases of emergence of institutionalized inequality through history, specially in ancient times. These might include asymmetries in control over productive resources, control over external trade, differential military ability (and resultant booty and slaves), or control of socially significant information. As simulations suggest, these asymmetries need not be employed coercively, as long as they are economically defensible and can provide an advantage in bargaining power sufficient to allow the concentration of wealth and/or power in the hands of a segment of the social group or polity. The modeling indicates that such asymmetries can be self-reinforcing, and thus quite stable to moderate perturbations over time. Because most of the social transactions based on them are mutual rather than coercive, it can be suggested that such systems are likely to be more stable than the stratified social systems (e.g., nation states) that eventually succeed them.

Dwight Read (2002, 2003) has followed a very similar approach and shows how competition is shown to play a critical role in the way interaction—among decision-making, demographic parameters, and social units that organize resource ownership and procurement—either promotes or inhibits change in social organization.

Koykka and Wild (2015) have simulated how group dispersal may be initiated by leaders. The authors use a theory of inclusive fitness to examine the incentives for leading and following in this context. High relatedness, significant reductions in the cost of dispersal due to dispersing in groups, and reproductive skew in favor of followers facilitates the emergence of group dispersal. In contrast to some previous theoretical work, which has either concluded that leadership is uniformly altruistic or that it is uniformly selfish, this investigation suggests that at evolutionary equilibrium the incentives for leading can be either selfish or altruistic. The nature of result (selfish or altruistic) depends on ecological and social conditions such as the cost of dispersal and the relatedness between leaders and followers. The model demonstrates that kin selection is sufficient and that individual differences in condition and ability are not necessary to promote the emergence and maintenance of leader–follower relationships. It has been suggested (Layton et al. 2012) that band formation evolved in humans from the more transient fissioning behavior as a solution to the conflicting pressures of sustaining higher levels of cooperation required in hunting and the division of labor in a more dispersed community. If disputes break out, or if resources in the band territory are temporarily depleted, the existence of a wider community continues to be adaptive. Van der Post et al. (2015) have studied the evolutionary progression from "leader-follower" societies to "fission-fusion" societies, where cooperative vigilance in groups is maintained via a balance between within- and between-group selections. Group-level selection can be seen as generated from an assortment that arises spontaneously when vigilant and non-vigilant agents have different grouping tendencies. The evolutionary maintenance of small groups, and cooperative vigilance in those groups, is therefore achieved simultaneously. The evolutionary phases, and the transitions between them, depend strongly on behavioral mechanisms.

An obvious consequence of the emergence of leader-follower dominance relationships is the signaling of this difference, that is, the origins of prestige as a way to express hierarchical difference. Plourde (2008) argues that strategies towards signaling social difference can invade a non-signaling population and can be evolutionarily stable under a set of reasonable parameter values. Increasing competition levels can be likely the selective force driving the adoption of this novel strategy. Two changes in the social context in which prestige processes operate have been also tentatively identified as leading to increased levels of competition for prestige: (1) increasing group sizes and (2) increasing complexity or size of the existing cultural repertoire (see also Reyes-García et al. 2008; Heinrich 2009; Bentley et al. 2011; Halevy et al. 2012; Cheng et al. 2013). Similar approaches are being considered for analyzing social evolution from egalitarian human communities to "complex" and internally diversified human groups with complex interaction links between groups hierarchically organized (Pauketat 1996; Cohen 1998; Walby 2007; Heinrich and Boyd 2008; Helbing 2012; Hoffrage and Hertwig 2012; Edmonds and Meyer 2013; Hofstede 2013; Perch et al. 2013; Gavrilets and Fortunato 2014; von Rueden 2014; Skyrms 2014).

But conflict, violence and domination are not the only sources of social diversification and the increase of social entropy in small scale societies with scarce development of their means of production (hunter-gatherer societies). Empirical evidence suggests that division of labor in animal societies is positively related to group size. Frolova and Korobitzin (2002), Robinson-Cox et al. (2007) and Dyble et al. (2015) have simulated the emergence of gender stratification in artificial societies of hunter-gatherers. Jeanson et al. (2007) have simulated how group size influences division of labor using a fixed response-threshold model. They have investigated how expected by-products of increased population size, including demand (total work need relative to total work force available) and task number, affect this relationship. Their results indicate that both low demand and high task number positively influence division of labor. If social division of labor is an emergent property of group size and the need of increasing productivity, Bentley et al. (2005) have explored how an exchange network coevolves with the changing specializations of the agents within it. Through simulation, the authors keep track of who is connected to whom through a mapping of the network and the specializations of each agent, and they test the effects of simplified individual motivations for exchange, the make-up of the initial population of agents, and abstract representations of basic ideological dispositions such as the belief in private ownership. The aim was to test whether specialization and wealth inequalities are natural, self-organizing qualities of a small-scale economy. Internal differentiation can emerge, even in the absence of conflict, violence and the needs of protection (see also Crabtree 2015). Chiang (2015) argues that the way inequality evolves as a result of egalitarian sharing is determined by the structure of "who gives whom": social networks make a difference in how egalitarian sharing influences the evolution of inequality.

Social structure is an emergent property of a group of individuals; it cannot be the property of any single agent. Explanations for the evolution of complex societies assume that the organizational benefits of complexity are the reason it evolves (Edmonds et al. 2009). Among others, Rosenberg (2009) proposes that complexity is a product of group selection. He suggests that the organizational benefits are exaltations, built on authority only after it already exists, and which first develops to provide a more primitive benefit, conflict resolution. He further argues that in contexts where the maintenance of group unity confers a net top-down advantage to an egalitarian group's members, even after factoring in loss of personal autonomy, egalitarian ideology will be abandoned and replaced by hierarchical ones.

It is obvious that much more research is needed in this area, not only as developments of abstract social theory, but computer simulations calibrated with historical data in well-defined scenarios (see later, Sect. 1.2.6).

1.2.6 Simulating Economic, Social and Cultural Change in Prehistory. Why Humans Have Made Life so Complex and Difficult

Cultural diversity, social division of work and social hierarchization can be studied in terms of the complex (non-linear) accumulative consequence of relatively simple social mechanisms acting along time on non-isolated and dynamic aggregates of social agents. Therefore, we can explore computationally the study of cultural shift and change (Read 1987; Kondrashin 1997; Frantzeskaki et al. 2008; Xu et al. 2013; Sanders 2015). The span of this definition of cultural shift comprises from technical or technological changes, the development of means of production, the emergence of new social structures, the adoption of a different set of political tires, the transformation of religious beliefs, the adoption of a new language by a society, etc. (Weidlich 2002; Bentley et al. 2004; Bergman et al. 2008; Schilperoord et al. 2008; de Haan and Rothmans 2011; Holtz 2011; Safarzynska et al. 2012; Kandler and Shennan 2013; Zeppini et al. 2014; Carrignon et al. 2015; Nicholson and Sibani 2015; Marsh 2016).

Isern and Fort contribution to this volume (Chap. 7) focus on a specific kind of cultural shift: language shift. The birth of a new language is a slow process which usually includes several successive minor processes that spread throughout the population over the course of millennia, until eventually the language has diverged enough from the original language as for them to be mutually unintelligible. These are often considered random processes, analogous to genetic drift, which may include the invention of new words—e.g., for innovations—, acquisition of loan-words from other languages in contact, phonetic changes. The other process of language shift, the displacement of the local language by a foreign one that becomes the new prominent language in the region, once started, is usually a much faster process, which can take place in as short a time as a single generation. The authors present a language competition model devised to predict the evolution of the number of speakers when an external language is displacing the native one. In the model, the authors are interested especially in language displacement processes which do not imply large movements of people or even population substitution. Isern and Fort mathematically model the progress of a linguistic frontier over time and space, when the displacement mechanism is due to language acquisition rather than population substitution, with a reaction-diffusion model similar the wave of advance models (see Fort et al., Chap. 5, this volume), that is, a model where cultural shift is simplified to increase or decrease in the population number due factors such as population growth or conversion into another population group. For a review of historical linguistics simulation see: Cangelosi and Parisi (2002), Steels (2011), Steiner et al. (2011), Gong and Shuai (2013), Martins et al. (2014).

Beyond language evolution, the study of social transitions comprises global changes with crucial impact on the evolution of human history, which besides the technical changes directly related to the adoption of agriculture, entailed as well changes in using organization, social structures and belief systems that may be the initial seed of the present sociocultural organization. The adoption of agriculture, herding and stockbreeding is one of the traditional domains for understanding the complex dynamics in cultural shift. Archaeologically known as the Neolithic, in this period human populations began to produce their own food substituting predator and forager practices that were in use for the most part of human history. There are many hypotheses about why this could have happened in a precise place and time (Gremillion et al. 2014). The suggested explanations are a mix of natural (environmental) factors affecting evolutionary behavior and adaptation to new environments, or even the creative nature of human minds, able to learn from natural process of biological reproduction, interfere with them in an intentionally way and building as a result a new artificial environment.

This is the obvious domain for computer simulations. Can agriculture and related practices of animal control emerge "mechanically" in a group of agents originally defined as foragers and predators? The technological side of this transition is not the result of the "intelligence" of some individuals who "invented" something new. As computational simulations have proved (Cribb 1987; Grosman 2005; Ch'ng and Stone 2006; Conolly et al. 2007; Pearsall 2007; Allaby et al. 2010, 2015; Schreinemachers et al. 2011; Fuller et al. 2012; Gerbault et al. 2014; Larson and Burger 2013; Smith 2015a, b; Perrot et al. 2016; van Vliet et al. 2016), domestication of plants and animals is an evolutionary emergent result. Therefore it seems that there are some possibilities that one of the most relevant transitions in the history of humanity had also a mechanical basis.

The following case studies are a good example of the way early agriculture can be simulated computationally. Lancelotti et al. (2014) have created a simple Agent Based Model in which agents relied on a pure subsistence strategy based on domesticated plants and animals. The model explores the role of climate, agricultural production and surplus, and animal availability on the resilience of agro-pastoralists communities on a simplified version of a semi-arid environment. The world where the agents move is divided in three randomly distributed types (dune, interdune and water). The environment state is tracked by the entity World, which takes care of generating the rain, updating the biomass quantity of the cells (depending on their state and type). Interdune type cells can be in one of three states: wild, crop and fallow. The agents derive their caloric intake form crop cells. The relationship rain-biomass-crop-calories is derived by ethnographic and ecological sources and it is based on species of small-millets. The data considered regard rain-fed, manual agriculture, which is believed to be the closest to incipient cultivation system. The agent is modelled as a couple with possible offsprings and the demography tracked yearly, based on the number of days in the year when the agent does not meet her caloric needs (starvation rate). Agent behaviour is focused on resource management. For this reason the model is based on 3 types of actions: (1) searching a suitable place where to settle (which allows both sedentary and some forms of spatial-residential mobility; (2) managing farm activities: harvest the calories from the plots by transforming wild cells in crop once the agents select them as their potential plot; (3) managing animals: in those cases when the agents do not meet their caloric intake with the crops they can use the calories provided by the meat of the animals in their herd.

Barton (2014) has simulated prehistoric swidden cultivation. The model can be run in controlled and adaptive modes. In the controlled mode, the researcher controls all the parameters that govern land-use, and sets them prior to running the model. These land-use parameters include: (1) the initial number of households that start a simulation, (2) the minimum amount of accumulated resources for a household to fission and form a new household, (3) the maximum distance farmers travel to cultivate fields, and (4) the level of low resource returns at which a household will decide to abandon a farm and move to a new locale. All households begin with an arbitrary 100 energy units. These energy units serve as the currency for land use costs, returns, and decisions. The researcher also controls a number of environmental parameters, including: (1) harvest return, (2) costs to clear land, and (3) costs to farm—all expressed as percentages of the initial energy units—along with (4) the rate at which fertility is lost when a parcel of land is farmed, and (5) is regained by soil when a patch is left fallow (in energy percentage lost/gained per time unit). A percentage of bad years can be set during which harvests are only half the normal. Finally, there are settings for land ownership and an adaptive mode that will be discussed below. The landscape of the virtual world that farming households inhabit is initially covered completely by woodland. Households select land parcels that they clear of vegetation to farm. Each modeling cycle, each household selects a parcel to cultivate within the radius of the maximum distance it will travel to farm. Land is selected so as to maximize farming returns and minimize the labor costs of land clearance and walking from farmstead to field. Land farmed in a previous cycle needs less labor for clearing, but will produce lower returns because fertility declines the more it is cultivated. If a parcel is left fallow, it begins to regrow vegetation and can return to woodland after 50 modeling cycles. Fallowed land may also regain fertility if the researcher has set a non-zero rate for soil rejuvenation.

Aagesen and Dragićević (2014) have developed a model to examine the spatio-temporal land-use changes and population responses of early agricultural communities under a variety of environmental and cultural conditions. Complex systems theory and geographical information systems (GIS) are integrated into the design of the model. The resulting Early Agricultural Resources and Land-use Investigation (EARLI) model couples agent-based modeling (ABM) and cellular automata (CA) techniques within a GIS framework. The model examines how both cultural and environmental factors influence land use change under multiple scenarios.

A naturalistic explanation of the origins of plant domestication and agriculture, not making any reference to human motivations nor intentions has been presented by Lemmen and colleagues (Lemmen and Wirtz 2006; Lemmen et al. 2011a, b, 2015; Lemmen 2012, 2015a, b). GLUES, a computer program simulating human population density, technological change and agricultural activity directly, based on the concept of gradient adaptive dynamics, where adoption of a subsistence lifestyle, e.g., Neolithic agriculture, by any given group of people at any particular time depends on endogenous environmental and social factors, e.g., potential productivity, population density, and exogenous factors, including the presence of farming people in neighbouring regions. Simple rules in GLUES, including continent size and climate, allow the model to simulate the spontaneous transition to farming in certain regions of the world. Once farming is established, the model simulates the advection of peoples and diffusion of ideas and technology across environmental gradients. The model is driven by static maps of potential productivity and climate on regions of ca. 1000 km^2 that are defined as areas of relatively homogeneous climate and productivity. GLUES can further use information on climate variability prescribed as discrete events in space and time to influence human activities and populations. GLUES' prognostic outputs include population density, relative proportions of farming people in the region, and the level of technology used by the farming people. The major disadvantage of this computer simulation of the origins of agriculture is that it may produce histories of society-environment interactions that are at-odds with reality, e.g., the spontaneous development of agriculture in places where it is not known to have occurred. Saqalli and Baum (Chap. 8) offer a deep examination of GLUES and related explanatory models of agriculture origins.

If Lemmen's model does not take into account human rationality in the origin of agriculture, Tisdell and Svizzero (2016) and Sterelny (2015) have explore more behavioral approaches, such as satisficing types of behavior. Particular attention is given to social embedding as a constraint on economic change and to non-marginal limitations to economic evolution. The authors assume rational optimizing, and argue that satisficing theories provide a superior explanation of transition (and non-transition) by some hunter-gatherers. They conclude that many of the concepts associated with neoclassical economics are shown to be inadequate for analyzing the choice problems involved. Behavioral models take into account the relationship between human behavior and economic evolution paying attention to the way that decision-making is embedded in social structures.

There is a lot of interest modeling the transition towards agriculture as a wave of advance generated by the spatio-temporal spread of a new population (see Fort et al., Chap. 5). Based on the pioneering work by Cavalli-Sforza and Ammermann (1979), Cohen (1992), Ackland et al. (2007, 2014), Cohen and Ackland (2012a, b) has developed the original model based on fundamental concepts of food production, birth and death rates for various cultures. He and his collaborators showed how some cultures could expand at the expense of others. In the case of Neolithic farming, the form of the equation is similar to Fisher's, but since it was derived rather than postulated, it was also possible to deduce more subtle features. In particular, the equations only allow for a wave of advance of farming if the farmers have a birthrate higher than that of the Mesolithic hunters and gatherers they are displacing or absorbing. This may be due to their more sedentary lifestyle making childcare easier, a hypothesis which is borne out by observation in contemporary farming and nomadic societies. More unexpectedly, the model required that farmers should be less well-nourished and have shorter lifespans than the hunter gatherers they displaced, showing that the strategy more successful for advancing the culture may not be better for the individuals practicing it.

Parisi et al. (2003), Cecconi et al. (2006) follow a different approach within the same problem using cellular automata, which can be seen as a simplified version of an agent-based model. They have simulated the agricultural colonization of Europe from the VII to the IV millennium BC, and its possible similarity with the prehistoric differentiation of European languages. A similar simulation has been developed by Drechsler and Tiede (2007) in the case of the spread of Neolithic herders within the Near East, towards the Arabian Peninsula. In the model, environmental local features influence a global innovation diffusion pattern. Here, computational agents represent mobile populations. The spreading process itself is simulated by a repeated generation of random agents in space. The random component represents the archaeology incomprehensible decisions that lead to human displacements. Because it is more likely that "wandering groups" populate nearby places than faraway places, the possibility for the adoption on an innovation like agriculture is highest in the direct neighborhood of prior acceptance of innovation. Therefore, the random agents cluster spatially more frequently around the "parent" nodes. The spreading surface represents a combination of environmental parameters that are considered fundamental to the dispersal of Neolithic herders across the Arabian Peninsula. These parameters were evaluated for their influence on the movement of human groups, reclassified, and combined to obtain a spreading surface that represents local resistance to the process of spreading. As a result:

- Every place in each generation decreases the underlying raster value simulating the drain on resources and its exploitation value.
- The number of descendants at each place in each generation depends on the value of the underlying raster. The higher the value ("better conditions"), the greater will be the number of descendants in the next generation.
- The actual spreading distance ("how far a new generation will go") also depends on the underlying raster value. The lower the raster value at a specific point, the higher the spreading distance.

The origin of agriculture and production economies as a consequence of the combination of demic processes and cultural transmission mechanisms is now a relatively popular subject of research. Joaquim Fort and Neus Isern have published extensively on this point (Fort 2011, 2012, 2015; Fort and Méndez 1999; Isern and Fort 2008, 2010, 2012; Isern et al. 2012). Fort et al. (Chap. 5) suggest a combination of demic processes of population substitution and cultural transmission, that is, the spread of ideas (hunter-gatherers becoming farmers) instead of populations. They consider an abstract population of preindustrial farmers, initially located in some region, and assume they can disperse into other regions that are also suitable for farming but initially empty of farmers. The idea is that the next generations of farmers will disperse away from their parents and agriculture will propagate to neighbor areas as a wave of advance. The authors modify the classical Fisher's reactive model to predict the specific dynamics of such a wave of advance, taking also into consideration an integro-difference cohabitation model between newcomers (farmers) and indigenous populations (hunter-gatherers) in which cultural transmission from farmers to hunter-gatherers leads to a more complicated model.

Other relevant work exploring many alternative hypothesis on the causes of human movement and the spread of innovation with such historic contexts have been published by Barbujani et al. (1995), Di Piazza and Pearthree (1999), Excoffier et al. (2008), Cabana et al. (2008), Connolly et al. (2008), Boquet-Appel et al. (2009), Barton et al. (2010a, b), Baggaley et al. (2012), Hervella et al. (2012), Rasteiro et al. (2012), Currat and Silva (2013), Düring (2013), Gerbault et al. (2013), Ullah (2013), Guedes et al. (2014), Le Néchet et al. (2015), Silva and Steele (2015), Bernabeu et al. (2015), Gordó et al. (2015).

Sakahira and Terano (Chap. 10) also deal with a similar issue. These authors analyze the arrival of Chinese-Korean immigrants during the establishment of the agrarian culture of the Yayoi period (300 BC–250 AD) in Japan. The agrarian culture is reported to have been imported from China-Korea. Thus, the presence of Chinese-Korean immigrants was evidently of importance during the establishment of the Yayoi culture when agriculture became the social and economic foundation of society. However, several factors pertaining to these immigrants remain unclear within Japanese anthropology and archaeology. Specifically, these relate to the immigrants' place of origin, the initial immigrant population size, the sex ratio of the immigrants, and whether native hunter-gatherer people or farmer immigrants played a formative role in the establishment of agrarian culture during the Yayoi period. This contribution focus on two issues: (1) the sex ratio of the immigrants, and (2) the question of who played a formative role in the development of the agrarian culture during the Yayoi period. This simulation model demonstrates that in the event that most of the initial immigrants were male, and that an agrarian culture was widely adopted by native hunter-gatherers people during the early stage of its development, it is probable that after 300 years, the majority of people shared the same traits as the immigrants. The authors have simulated three possible scenarios. In the first, immigrants were polygamous and the agrarian culture was only inherited from a parent agent (not diffused from neighboring agents). In this case, the descendants of agriculturalists at an early stage were either immigrants or both immigrants and native hunter-gatherers people. Thus, immigrants played a formative role in the establishment of an agrarian culture. In the second case, immigrants were polygamous and the agrarian culture was inherited from a parent agent as well as diffused from neighboring agents. However, the diffusion of the agrarian culture occurred slowly. In this case, the descendants of the agriculturalists at an early stage were mostly immigrants with few native hunter-gatherer people. As in the first case, immigrants played a formative role in the establishment of an agrarian culture. In the last case, the diffusion of the agrarian culture was significantly more rapid. In this case, the majority of descendants of agriculturalists were immigrants at the earliest stage, but shortly thereafter, native hunter-gatherer descendants were evident during a subsequent early stage. Here, mostly Jomon people and a few immigrants played a formative role in the establishment of an agrarian culture. Of these three probable cases, the last is the most consistent with anthropological and archaeological evidence for the following reasons. In the first case, the diffusion rate of agriculture was too low.

Matsumoto and Sasakura (Chap. 11) develop the same case study as Sakahira and Terano (Chap. 10), that is, hunter-gatherer to farmer transitions in Japan as a consequence of the arrival of new populations with a new economy and the hybridizing with local populations. Drastic socio-cultural changes in subsistence, material culture and settlement structure occurred in the northern part of Kyushu Island around 10th–8th centuries BC., and they seem related with the arrival of new populations, and the consequent pattern of interaction between populations and cultural transmission between newcomers and local settlers, which ended with the acculturation of indigenous populations. The authors consider that decisions concerning cultural integration, transformation and adoption/rejection of cultural elements were important factors in this transition, but they only focus on cultural transmission aspects for the sake of simplicity. A simulation of 500 years of accumulated changes shows that cultural skill could have spread quickly without much loss in the case of biased transmission, even in case the migration rate was very low, and that the spread of cultural skill without significant genetic influence was possible even when cultural transmission was restricted to between relatives. The result gives an inspiration for possible explanatory models of hunter-gatherer/farming transition in Japan in which indigenous people play more significant roles in areas remote from the locus of Yayoi cultural origin. Among their main results, we can quote:

- The rate of population increase can considerably vary due to chance factors, while the spread of genetic value is almost constant as the same marriage rules and move rate were applied to all runs.
- Cultural skill can spread quickly without much loss in the case of biased transmission, even when migration rate is maintained very low.
- The spread of cultural skill without significant genetic influence is possible even when cultural transmission is restricted within relatives.
- Nonrandom migration based on family relationship may facilitate the spread of g-value.

These models of social transition built on the assumption of population spread rely on complex mechanisms of population growth. Important work has been done on this aspect, trying to model the mechanisms of social reproduction, fertility, marriage and mortality in small-scale early agricultural societies (Artzrouni and Komlos 1985; Komlos and Nefedov 2002; Low et al. 2002; Jager and Janssen 2003; Fletcher et al. 2011; Baggaley et al. 2012; Machálek et al. 2012; Rasteiro et al. 2012; Rogers et al. 2012; Geard et al. 2013; Séguy and Buchet 2013; Lemmen 2014; Puleston et al. 2014; Diachenko and Zubrow 2015; Shennan 2015; Sajjad et al. 2016; Winterhalder et al. 2015). As an example of these kind of investigations we can quote Iwamura et al. (2014), who have developed a holistic model framework with agent-based modeling to examine interactions between demographic growth, hunting, subsistence agriculture, land cover change, and animal population in a particular geographical area, investigating the conditions under which indigenous communities relying on hunting and subsistence agriculture alter their impacts on an ecological system through land use change. This is a spatially-explicit household simulation mode, and it is meant to analyze the feedback between human activities and natural resource systems. The authors use an extensive field dataset from social surveys, animal observation records and hunting kill locations along with satellite images. The model exhibits feedback loops between a growing human population and depletion of local natural resources. The model can reproduce the population size of two different villages along with landscape patterns without further calibration. This model has been used for understanding the conditions of sustainability for indigenous communities relying on subsistence agriculture and hunting, and for scenario analyses to examine the implications of external interventions.

In the same way as Chaps. 3 and 4 tried to reproduce in silico hunting and gathering ways of living in prehistory, we can reproduce computationally the social life of first farmers. Figueiredo and Velho (2001) have programmed a system based on three different kinds of agents: cattle, hunters, and farmers. These agents compete for natural resources (plants). The success of each type of agent is determined not only by the availability of the natural resource but also by the capability of other agents to gather those resources for themselves. Running the model consists of creating a landscape and introducing initial populations of animal and hunters. The initial group of hunters follows the cattle around killing them whenever possible. The killing rule relates the energy of the animal to the number of humans in cells around it. So the kills are determined by the patterns of movements of animals and hunters. As the animals follow the concentration of plants, and hunters the concentration of animals, the two groups move close together. Farming disturbs the natural availability of resources. Farmers are located in the same locations were animals eat. Cattle are competitors for farmers, hunters are competitors for hunters, farming increase the number of cattle. Vaart et al. (2006) used a similar approach to understand the consequences of the different social mechanisms related to the management of wild preys and domesticated cereals. Saqalli et al. (2014) describe another spatialized Agent-Based model, reconstructing the society system of the oldest central European farming communities (Linear Band Keramik, circa 5500–4500 BC) functioning at the village level. The idea was to reconstruct in the same model the functioning along a local grid level (1 ha/cell) of village societies. The goal of this combination of scale was that small variations at the farming/livestock keeping/hunting-gathering system do have exponential effects on a larger scale.

Saqalli and Baum (Chap. 8) discuss different "Terroir"-based environmentally constrained models based on information from local archaeological data regarding environmental characteristics (soil, vegetation, local climate, distance to village) and cropping and livestock-keeping practices, to evaluate the environmental impact of human settlements over several village territories, along several farming scenarios (shifting, intensive garden and non-intensive cultivation) and diet assumptions.

Tilman Baum (Chap. 9, see also Baum 2014) analyses some aspects of the economic and social life of first farmers in Europe. He presents WELASSIMO, an Agent-Based Model simulating land use of Neolithic wetland settlements in the Swiss and German pre-alpine forelands. Its aims are to test whether any of the existing hypotheses would justify a settlement relocation for systemic reasons. It is shown that for relatively small communities, the non-finite resources related to their land-use most likely have not been limiting and thus did not determine the observed settlement pattern. Instead, it is argued that the continuous duration of moderate land-use did increase the economic value of the evolving landscape. Thus, it is proposed, that relocations happened mostly inside of the relevant landscapes as a combined consequence of the poor durability of wooden houses in waterlogged environs and the spatiotemporal variability of suitable timber. This does not exclude the possibility, that also cultural/social reasons may have been involved. The aim of WELASSIMO to fill this gap and, more specifically, to answer the following questions:

- What implications and systemic feedbacks go alongside with the published hypotheses on land-use systems?
- What was the spatial and temporal availability of non-finite resources?
- Can excessive resource use have caused the observed dynamic settlement pattern?

Within the research domain of agricultural societies, the VIRTUAL ANASAZI project (Dean et al. 2000; Axtell et al. 2002) is another example of agent-based modeling designed to investigate where early agricultural prehistoric communities of the American Southwest would have situated their households based on both the natural and social environments in which they lived. The idea was to define nuclear families (households, the smallest social unit consistently definable in the archaeological record) as agents, and loosed them on landscapes, which have been archaeologically studied for different historical periods, and plenty of paleo-productivity data exist. The model has been used to predict individual household responses to changes in agricultural productivity in annual increments based on reconstructions of yearly climatic conditions, as well as long-term hydrologic trends, cycles of erosion and deposition, and demographic change. The performance of the model is evaluated against archaeological data of population, settlement, and organizational parameters. By manipulating numbers and attributes of households, climate patterns, and other environmental variables, it is possible to evaluate the roles of these factors in prehistoric culture change. Here the household is a theoretical construct, but it moves on a historically defined environment, which is the most precise available archaeological data allow. Simulated population levels closely follow the historical trajectory. In the first 200 years, the model understates the historical population, whereas the peak population just after A.D. 1100 is somewhat too high in the model. The historical clustering of settlements along the valley zonal boundaries is nicely reproduced. Although the ability of the model to predict the actual location of settlements varies from year to year, the progressive movement of the population northward over time, clear in the historical data, is also reproduced in the simulation. Long House Valley was abandoned after A.D. 1300. The agent model suggests that even the degraded environment between 1270 and 1450 could have supported a reduced but substantial population in small settlements dispersed across suitable farming habitats located primarily in areas of high potential crop production in the northern part of the valley. The fact that in the real world of Long House Valley, the supportable population chose not to stay behind but to participate in the exodus from the valley indicates the magnitude of socio-cultural "push" or "pull" factors that induced them to move. Thus, comparing the model results with the actual history helps differentiate external (environmental) from internal (social) determinants of cultural dynamics. It also provides a clue—in the form of the population that could have stayed but elected to go—to the relative magnitude of those determinants.

Ultimately, "to explain" the settlement and farming dynamics of Anasazi society in Long House Valley is to identify rules of agent behavior that account for those dynamics (Dean et al. 2000). To "explain" an observed spatiotemporal history is to specify agents that generate—or grow—this history. By this criterion, this strictly environmental account of the evolution of this society during this period goes a long way toward explaining this history (Axtell et al. 2002). The simulation imitates the target data by computing the individual agents' behavior in response to some input environmental data, by computing the effects of the individual behaviors on the environment, and by computing the repercussions these environmental effects have on individual agents. As shown, this 'best fit' still does not necessarily accurately replicate the historical findings. In particular, it simulates a higher population early on, and does not replicate the complete eclipse of the settlement in around 1300. The authors point out that better fits can be achieved by increasing the number of household attributes and their heterogeneity, possibly introducing non-uniform distributions.

The evolution of the Virtual Anasazi project can be seen in the similar but at a much higher scale "Village Ecodynamics" project by Kohler and his colleagues (Kohler 2003, 2013; Kohler and Carr 1997; Kohler and Yap 2003; Kohler et al. 2000, 2005, 2007; Kohler et al. 2012; Kohler and Varien 2012; Johnson et al. 2005; Crabtree 2015). Some interesting details of this model are also discussed in Saqalli and Baum contribution to this volume (Chap. 8), Kohler and associates began by entering paleo environmental data on a digitized map of the area, and then placed the agents—simulated households—randomly on the map. The primary area of research is the study of the effect of exchange relationships upon the formation of larger social groups. Since agricultural yields varied greatly from year to year, farmers needed to adapt mechanisms to reduce their uncertainty of future yields. One such mechanism thought to be important is reciprocity between households. After a reasonable model of agent planting was constructed, agents were endowed with balanced reciprocity behaviors and adaptive encodings of exchange, placing the households into a social and an economic network or other (related and unrelated) households. This network is flexible enough to evolve according to agent interactions and changes in the world environment. The authors are also trying to include the natural production and human degradation of what they consider Critical Natural Resources into the agent-based simulation modeling of household settlement patterns. By demonstrating the ease with which populations could have depleted fuels in this environment, for instance, the simulation builds a context in which changes in food preparation, craft production, architecture, frequency of axes, and so forth, which might be responsive to fuel scarcity, become more plausibly interpreted as having been intended to do so (Johnson et al. 2005).

In recent simulations, the authors have extend the previous model by adding the ability of agents to perform symmetrically initiated or asymmetrically initiated generalized reciprocal exchange (Reynolds et al. 2004a, b, 2005a, b; Kobti and Reynolds 2005). According to this model, the decision made by the group is a not consensus based upon the weights and opinions of the members, but the individual knowledge is pooled and used by a central decision maker to produce a decision (Reynolds and Peng 2005). Selected individuals contribute to the cultural knowledge, which is stored and manipulated based on individual experiences and their successes or failures.

A small world social network emerged and the resultant agent populations were shown to be more resilient to environmental perturbations. When allowing agents more opportunities to exchange resources, the simulation produced more complex network structures, larger populations, and more resilient systems. Furthermore, allowing the agents to buffer their requests by using a finite state model improved the relative resilience of these larger systems. Introducing reciprocity that can be triggered by both requestors and donors produced the largest number of successful donations. This represents the synergy produced by using the information from two complementary situations within the network. Thus, the network has more information with which it can work and tended to be more resilient than otherwise (Crabtree 2015).

Cockburn et al. (2013), Crabtree (2015) have developed the original model by introducing a new model for agent specialization in small-scale human societies that incorporates planning based on social influence and economic state. Agents allocate their time among available tasks based on exchange, demand, competition from other agents, family needs, and previous experiences. Agents exchange and request goods using barter, balanced reciprocal exchange, and generalized reciprocal exchange. The authors use a weight-based reinforcement model for the allocation of resources among tasks. In the base model, agents represent households seeking to minimize their caloric costs for obtaining enough calories, protein, fuel, and water from a landscape which is always changing due to both exogenous factors (climate) and human resource use. Compared to the baseline condition of no specialization, specialization in conjunction with barter increases population wealth, global population size, and degree of aggregation. Differences between scenarios for specialization in which agents use only a weight-based model for time allocation among tasks, and one in which they also consider social influence, are more subtle. The networks generated by barter in the latter scenario exhibit higher clustering coefficients, suggesting that social influence allows a few agents to assume particularly influential roles in the global exchange network.

The Virtual Anasazi and the Village Ecodynamics models are among the most influential computer simulations of prehistoric societies. This impact is easily observed in modern publications that model different aspects of social life in early agrarian societies (MacMillan and Huang 2008; Gabler 2012; Barton et al. 2014).

SimpopLocal is a stylized model describing an agrarian society in the Neolithic period, during the primary "urban transition" manifested by the appearance of the first cities (Schmitt et al. 2015). It is designed to study the emergence of a structured and hierarchical urban settlement system by simulating the growth dynamics of a system of settlements whose development remains hampered by strong environmental constraints. This exploratory model seeks to reproduce a particular structure of the Rank-Size distribution of settlements well defined in the literature as a generalized stylized-fact: for any given settlement system throughout the time and continents, the distribution of sizes is strongly differentiated, exhibiting a very large number of small settlements and a much smaller number of large settlements.

Ortega et al. (2014, 2016) examines an alternative approach to previously proposed models of prehistoric exchange to explain the distribution of obsidian across the Near East during the Neolithic period. Obsidian exchange is a complex system where multiple factors interact and evolve in time and space. Through Agent-Based Modelling simulations of an hypothetical exchange network where some agents (villages) are allowed to attain long-distance exchange partners through correlated random walks, the authors suggest that when additional variables (population density, degree of collaboration between villages…), a type of small-world exchange network could explain the breadth of obsidian distribution (up to 800 km from source) during the Near Eastern Neolithic.

In the same line, Cleuziou (2009) suggests modeling social evolution in conjunction with environmental changes by using non-linear multi-agent models is a much more fruitful way to understand the shift from coastal to inner environments by mid-3rd millennium BC and the apparent depopulation of the Oman Peninsula by 2000 BC. Rouse and Weeks (2011) have recently investigated the role of specialized production strategies in the development of socio-economic inequalities in Bronze Age south-eastern (SE) Arabia, and particularly, the ways in which a localized, internal exchange economy may have produced stress and instability in the SE Arabian socio-economic system. The agent-based model the authors have built with that perspective suggests the nature of the internal exchange economy in SE Arabia itself may have precipitated the social conditions necessary for change by allowing individuals to profit disproportionately.

In the Bronze/Iron Age, approximately 1500/500 years before our era, most human societies adopted production economies in the Old World, and some early forms of social complexity began to develop. Widgren (1979) was one of the very first researchers in modeling how those ancient economic systems worked. Kowarik et al. (2012, 2015) have modelled social life and ancient production techniques of the Bronze Age salt mining complex of Hallstatt/Austria (1458–1245 BC). The authors have addressed the complexity of production structures and especially their interaction with the natural and socioeconomic surroundings: what were the demands concerning workforce, means of production and subsistence? How many people had to be supplied with means of production and subsistence? Were the local resources sufficient? The authors have used Agent-Based Simulation to build a model of the working processes in one mining hall (breaking salt, collecting salt, transporting salt to the shaft), in order to gain insights into spatial organization, allocation of tasks and workload balance and to relate the time span of mining to the size of the workforce and the amount of mined salt. A System Dynamics Simulation was applied to correlate the size of the workforce (population dynamics) with food consumption and demand for mining tools. Through Process Simulation, the authors were able to display and analyze the workflow of an entire shaft system encompassing several mining halls.

Štekerová and Danielisová contribution to this book (Chap. 12) can also be regarded as an example of simulating farming economic systems before the full consolidation of social complexity. Authors approach computer modelling as a tool for understanding Celtic society and cultural changes at the end of the East European Iron Age. They focus on development of agent-based models of daily economic activities of inhabitants of Late Iron Age agglomerations (oppida), aiming to verify hypotheses about the probable self-subsistence of oppida by means of models of the population dynamics and socio-economic behavior of one particular site, the Staré Hradisko oppidum in Bohemia. The core concept is the idea of society pursuing agro-pastoral activities within the given temporal and spatial scale which is tested against subsistence, surplus production and carrying capacity factors. They aim to explore the dynamics of the food production and isolate possible crisis factors imposed either by environment or by unsustainability of the economic strategies pursued. Main questions throughout the chapter are:

- What is the maximum population that can be sustained in a given environment and when is this maximum reached?
- Using what cultivation strategies and labor input can the population most effectively exploit natural resources in order to be self-sufficient?
- What are the dynamics of production with constantly growing or declining population (subsistence–surplus–success rate–diminishing returns)?

In Štekerová and Danielisová's model, the whole Iron Age world despite its technological innovations, specialization and economic contacts, or its level of complexity, was still principally a world of the common farmer. It appears as part of a socio-economically advanced environment, together with a distinctive intensification of settlement patterns. Central places are programmed in historically reliable environments as "total consumers". That generally means that they were too specialized and hence engaged in other activities, so they were not capable of producing any foodstuffs. This fact should have eventually contributed decisively to the collapse of the Iron Age society in the 1st century BC. Some of these settlements surely had to overcome or accept some environmental constrains (imposed for example by higher altitude) or were forced to adapt their subsistence practices (e.g., develop an alternative approach to the exploitation of land). To answer these questions, they developed three models: the population dynamics model, subsequent food production and land use model and workforce allocation model. The model of population dynamics generates data on synthetic population for four alternative depopulation scenarios, the model of food production and land use is designed to enable experimenting with carrying capacity of the environment with respect to alternative exploitation scenarios, and finally, the work-force model is used for studying allocation of working capacities during the harvest season which is understood to be one of "bottlenecks" of the agricultural year. The aim is especially to ascertain the resilience of the food production system (i.e., carrying capacity) of the oppida under the dynamically changing (increasing/decreasing) population. The models are designed to enable experimenting with alternative scenarios and strategies with the aim to test various upper limits of self-subsistence of the oppidum and to verify general theoretical hypotheses related to the functioning of the oppida within particular landscape environment and the ecological and economic rules that were shaping them.

The same authors have also explored related subjects, like the effects of population growth (Olševičová-Štekerová et al. 2013), and the configuration of a settlement network (Olševičová-Štekerová et al. 2015; Danielisová et al. 2015).

The work by Kim (2015) on the simulation of Bronze Age Korea can also be related with the economic and political evolution of prehistoric agricultural societies. The author argues that sociopolitical development in the central and southern parts of the Korean Peninsula during the Early Bronze Age–Middle Bronze Age transition might have been closely related to economic intensification. This can be understood from a perspective that emphasizes elite control over basic economic resources as a significant factor in this development.

1.2.7 Why Humans Have Made Life Even More Complex and Difficult. The Making of the State and the Origins of Class Struggle

The economic change implied in the transition from predator and forager based survival to full productive economies based on agriculture, herding and stockbreeding subsistence settled the basis for a new social organization and new forms of political decision making. Computer modeling allows researchers to understand major transitions as involving several interacting processes: evolution of cooperation among lower-level units, selection which acts on higher-level "collectives," policing mechanisms which suppress "free riders" and competition among lower-level units, and increased functional integration of collectives which makes them increasingly organism-like (Turchin 2013). Eventually, higher-level collectives become so well integrated that they can be treated as "individuals" in their own right (and can serve as lower-level units for the next evolutionary transition).

Different authors have generated computer simulations to understand how hierarchical decision-making could have affected inter-group conflicts sometime through the historical evolution of human society (Mark 1998; Suleiman and Fischer 2000), the dynamics of status symbols in hierarchically ordered societies (Pedone and Conte 2001), the consequences of wealth distribution (Impullitti and Rebmann 2002), the coevolution of farming and private property (Bowles and Choi 2013; Bowles et al. 2010; Cockburn et al. 2013; Angourakis et al. 2015; Biscione et al. 2015; Gallagher et al. 2015), the deification of historical figures and the emergence of priesthoods (Dávid-Barrett and Carney 2015), the origins of war (Duering and Wahl 2014) and the Neolithic transition from egalitarianism to leadership and despotism (Levine and Modica 2013; Powers and Lehman 2015). Those models and simulations explain how, despite being an unlikely event, farming and a new system of property rights jointly emerged when they did, as an emergent property of the new possibilities of unambiguously demarcate and defend the new wealth produced and stored by farmers—crops, dwellings, and animals—. Farming and private property may have spread as a result of adoption by most individuals in a group occurring either as the result of changes within the group or from emulation by a group of foragers and their subsequent adoption of the new institutions and technology.

Computer simulations results thus challenge unicausal models of historical dynamics supposedly driven by advances in technology, population pressure, adaptation to climatic change or other exogenous influences (Pujol et al. 2005). Especially important to understand the development of means of production and the consequent emergence of new relations of production is the possibility to simulate computationally the emergence of specialization, in which different individual agents spontaneously assuming different roles in the execution of the task (Parisi and Nolfi 2005). The most effective strategy includes primitive forms of "situated" specialization in which identical individuals play different roles according to the circumstances such as leading or following the group. These forms of functional specialization seem to be due to the need to reduce interference between potentially conflicting sub-goals such as moving toward the rest of the group to maintain aggregation and moving toward the target. Imagine a group of agents that has to reach a target in the environment but to be rewarded they must approach the target by maintaining reciprocal proximity. If the agents are initially dispersed in the environment, they may be unable to perceive each other and therefore they may be unable to aggregate and then move together toward the target. The solution is to evolve some signaling behavior that allows the group to aggregate. On this question, Cokburn et al. (2013) add the effect of social influence to increase the level of specialization. Building on these assumption, these authors have created a model that incorporates both economic state and social influence. Agents are influenced by competition from other agents in their topographically based social network. It is expected that there should be more task specialization in this socially influenced system than in the models without social influence. Further, specialization and social influence may have effects on populations of agents, and as social influence interacts with exchange networks, it is expected that specialization may introduce changes in the structure of global populations.

To sum up, it is the mechanism of change itself which produces the emergence of new social configurations. This idea is basic to understand the evolution from prehistoric small-scale societies to historical complex polities. This has been a traditional topic for archaeologists, anthropologists, historians and social and political theorists (Lull and Micó 2011), and we can read more different theories than theoreticians have thought thereof. Fortunately for us, Henri Francfort has shown how 2000 years of historical narratives can be easily resumed in a few hundred lines of computer code (Francfort et al. 1989; Francfort 1997). In any case, politogenesis should be never reduced to the only one evolutionary pathway leading to the statehood (Grinin 2009). The early state formation was only one of many versions of development of complex late archaic social systems. The state is nothing more than one of many forms of the post-primitive socio-political organization; these forms are alternative to each other and are able in certain conditions to transform to one another without any loss in the general level of complexity.

Foundational work on the idea to simulate the historical processes towards the origin of state societies and complex polities was Epstein and Axtell's Sugarscape model. It simulates the behavior of artificial people (agents) located on a landscape of a generalized resource (sugar). Agents are born onto the Sugarscape with a vision, a metabolism, a speed, and other genetic attributes. Their movement is governed by a simple local rule: "look around as far as you can; find the spot with the most sugar; go there and eat the sugar." Every time an agent moves, it burns sugar at an amount equal to its metabolic rate. Agents die if and when they burn up all their sugar. A remarkable range of social phenomena emerge. For example, when seasons are introduced, migration and hibernation can be observed. Agents are accumulating sugar at all times, so there is always a distribution of wealth. Based on this simplified scenario, Epstein and Axtell attempted to grow a metaphoric "proto-history" of civilization. It starts with agents scattered about a twin-peaked landscape; over time, there is self-organization into spatially segregated and culturally distinct "tribes" centered on the peaks of the Sugarscape. Population growth forces each tribe to disperse into the sugar lowlands between the mountains. There, the two tribes interact, engaging in combat and competing for cultural dominance, to produce complex social histories with violent expansionist phases, peaceful periods, and so on. The proto-history combines a number of ingredients, each of which generates insights of its own. One of these ingredients is sexual reproduction. In some runs, the population becomes thin, birth rates fall, and the population can crash. Alternatively, the agents may over-populate their environment, driving it into ecological collapse. When Epstein and Axtell introduce a second resource (spice) to the Sugarscape and allow the agents to trade, an economic market emerges. The introduction of pollution resulting from resource-mining permits the study of economic markets in the presence of environmental factors (Epstein and Axtell 1996).

This computing example shows how complexity unconsciously emerges as a side effect of individual decisions (Mark 1998). Here complexity refers to diversified patterns of social organization and political institutions controlling, constraining and determining social behavior. The original Sugarscape model has been updated and modified many times (Costopoulos 2015). The Virtual Anasazi project, as reviewed in the preceding section, was a direct consequence of Epstein work, addressed to the empirical testing of the social principles behind the model (Swedlund et al. 2015). Flentge et al. (2001) have extended the sugarscape model giving the agents the possibility to claim possession of a "plot" of land. Memes regulate the behavior of the agents regarding the land claims of others. It turns out that the probability for the survival of the population is much higher when possession claims of others are respected. However, there exist short term disadvantages for agents respecting the possessions of others. Thus, the need for a possession norm arises. The introduction of sanctions provides a good possibility to enforce the norm as long as no costs arise for sanctioning agents. Rahman et al.

(2009), have added social classes (poor, mid, and rich) and have studied the consequences of wealth distribution among all agents. Bruno (2011) has explored the economic properties of trade networks emerging from agents' interaction. Pan (2011) has studied the emergence of solution of violence in a sugarscape-derived artificial society using Greed and Grievance Theory of Civil Conflicts. Elsenbroich and Gilbert (2014) consider the influence of environmental factors on social norms; using the sugarscape scenario of a scarce resource environment, the emergence of a possession norm is explored as is the function of such a norm for society.

Sugarscape derived models are not the only ones to understand the formation of heavily institutionalized groups of people. Some alternative models emphasizes the "benefits" of leadership and the long term consequences of social division of labor in the process towards increasing hierarchy in the political organization. Especially relevant for this purpose are mathematical models showing how wealth accumulation depends on the 'social relation' between two classes: owners or workers. As a result, a society may evolve towards an unequal outcome with few rich and many poor individuals (Roemer 1985; Walby 2007; Chadefaux and Helbing 2010; Russo 2014).

For instance, Powers and Lehman (2014) have modeled the historical coevolution of individual preferences for hierarchy alongside the degree of despotism of leaders, and the dispersal preferences of followers. They show that voluntary leadership without coercion can evolve in small groups, when leaders help to solve coordination problems related to resource production. An example is coordinating construction of an irrigation system. Their model predicts that the transition to larger despotic groups will then occur when: (1) surplus resources lead to demographic expansion of groups, removing the viability of an acephalous niche in the same area and so locking individuals into hierarchy; (2) high dispersal costs limit followers' ability to escape a despot. Jahanbazi et al. (2014) have formally modeled the transition from kinship tribes to nation states. Their agent-based simulation, based on existing observational and analytical studies of pre-contact Pacific Island hunter-gatherer societies, examine how different societies' structures were affected by various characteristics and strategies of their chiefs. The model represents the influence of societies' structure on how agents fulfil their basic needs and the consequences of an agent's action on both short term and long term society's survival. The evolving societal structures of the model have long-term effects on wealth inequality and whether the society grows or collapses. The results encourage the idea that significantly different outcomes in social welfare do not necessarily require massive changes to all the agents, but can be achieved by relatively moderate modifications in social structure and the governance of societies.

The most popular computational theories of the origin of state are those considering the nonlinear effects of violence and warfare on the emergence of complex polities. Most of these models are reexaminations of the classical hypothesis by Carneiro (1970). However, the particular characteristics of computational models have allowed to integrate both extremes of the same continuum: altruism—benefiting fellow group members at a cost to oneself—and conflict hostility toward individuals not of one's own ethnic, racial, or other group—. The idea is that neither violence nor altruism would have been viable singly, but by promoting group conflict, they could have evolved jointly (Bowles 2008, Choi and Bowles 2007).

Spencer (1998) proposed a mathematical model of political growth in chiefdoms (societies with centralized but not internally specialized authority) and states (societies with centralized and also internally specialized authority), based on differential equations. A major conclusion of the exercise is that the emergence of a primary state is likely to be accompanied by a considerable expansion in the political-economic (sustaining) territory of the polity. A related issue is how peoples who successfully resist incorporation can help shape the developmental trajectory of an expanding state. Spencer (2014) proposes a model of the dynamic between an expanding polity and its neighbors suggesting that the effectiveness of incorporation is positively related not simply to the size of the expanding polity, but rather to a positive rate of change in the expanding polity's growth relative to that of resisting polities. Variable relationships of incorporation and resistance will cause the shape of the expanding state's growth trajectory to be not regular and symmetric, but instead asymmetric and non-uniform.

Reynolds and Lazar (2002) added the effects of aggregation to a computer model of territorial expansion. With increased aggregation it was no longer possible for a single individual to monitor the entire aggregation. In order to control thousands of farmers, laborers, and warriors, it was required that many tasks be delegated to administrative, scribal, architectural, craft, and military specialists. This resulted in the formation of the state. In order to produce larger degrees of aggregation the span of leadership needed to be extended. This level of aggregation was achieved by changing the meaning of existing relations, implying that only the immediate offspring of current leaders had the right and duty to lead. This allowed leaders to aggregate wealth and resources over generations and extend alliances over larger numbers of surrounding villages. These changing relationships produced a system in which the actors were relentlessly competing, resulting in periodic outbursts of violence. In this system, the culturally defined goals of a leader were to have as many farmers, craftspeople, and warriors under his control as possible. The two main strategies for reaching those goals were: (1) alliance building-through feasting, gift-giving, and bride exchange; and (2) warfare, mostly at the level of raiding and burning rival villages. The escalating warfare lead to a major shift in emphasis on site location from access to high quality agricultural land to the need for defensible locations. This change supported the shift from a ranked society to a stratified one by restricting the ability of lower ranks to marry with those from upper ones. This over time resulted in two basic strata, the elites and the commoners. The pragmatics behind this shift in the meaning of social relationships was engendered by the need to incorporate other conquered, highly ranked elites into the fold via intermarriage valley wide (Jayyousi and Reynolds 2013).

Griffin and Stanish (2007, 2008), Griffin (2011) have modeled how complex early polities expand in size over time to accommodate population growth. Polities also expand due to fusion with other polities, when adjacent polities came into conflict when no empty land separating them remained for expansion. The net result is consolidation, which can be explained in terms of overt conquest or intimidation, forming alliances, religious legitimization, rewarding loyalty, marriage, etc. Internally there was competition between factions within each polity. It seems reasonable to expect that the larger a polity the greater the number of internal factions and hence the more likely resistance would occur. This relationship can be modeled by assuming that the probability of resistance for any one settlement was constant, so the likelihood of resistance somewhere in a polity increased as the number of its settlements grew. The same effect was achieved in the current model by spatially uniform random occurrences of resistance. Polities came into conflict when a settlement is added and bridges the gap between two or more polities. This corresponds to one or more of these neighboring polities attempting to expand into the buffer zone separating them. The center of the prevailing polity retained its current location and became the center of the newly constituted fused polity. The other competing centers became satellite settlements in the new larger polity. The competition's winner is determined by comparing the effective strengths of two, three or four competing centers with the strongest being the winner. The assumption was that the strength of agrarian polities would have been determined by a combination of center's population size and resources discounted by distance. The simulation of these mechanisms concludes that:

- Population rank-size distribution for an area surrounding a single dominant center will be primate immediately before fission and transition to convex thereafter.
- Strengthening each of four integrative processes by adjusting its associated parameter will decrease the time averaged rank-size convexity for the entire grid.
- Subordinate population centers articulated to a primate center or another subordinate center will be observed within polities.

Gavrilets et al. (2014) have developed a spatially explicit agent-based theoretical model of the emergence of early complex polities via warfare. In this model polities are represented as hierarchically structured networks of villages whose size, power, and complexity change as a result of conquest, secession, internal reorganization (via promotion and linearization), and resource dynamics. A general prediction of our model is continuous stochastic cycling in which the growth of individual polities in size, wealth/power, and complexity is interrupted by their quick collapse. The model dynamics are mostly controlled by two parameters, one of which scales the relative advantage of wealthier polities in between and within-polity conflicts, and the other is the chief's expected time in power. Our results demonstrate that the stability of large and complex polities is strongly promoted if the outcomes of the conflicts are mostly determined by the polities' wealth/power, if there exist well-defined and accepted means of succession, and if control mechanisms are internally specialized. The authors present a dynamic quantitative model exploring the origin and operation of early human complex society, focusing on both the size and complexity of emerging polities as well as their longevity and settlement patterns. They systematically examine the effect of parameters such as system size, the effect of polity power on the probability of winning a conflict, tribute level, variation in productivity between individual villages, span of control, and chief's average time in power. The polities in the model exhibit a strikingly fluid nature resembling so-called "chiefly cycles." Unexpectedly, the largest effect on results is due to just two parameters: the scaling of the polity power to the probability of winning a conflict, and the chief's average time in power.

Rowthorn et al. (2014) have developed the effects of behavioral and populational differences in an artificial society divided into 2 hereditary classes: a warrior elite and a productive class. The model entails that the extra cost warriors must incur to train and equip their children for war determines the relative sizes of both classes and the degree of economic inequality. Higher costs of warrior children imply a greater economic advantage for warriors and a smaller ratio of warriors to producers.

Nevertheless, what characterizes complex polities is not only conflict, authority and coercion, but ultrasociety, the ability of humans to cooperate in large groups of genetically unrelated individuals (Centola et al. 2005; Turchin 2015). Such cooperation can take many forms: volunteering for the army when the country is attacked, willingly paying taxes, voting, helping strangers, refusing to take bribes, etc. In each case, the result of cooperation is production of a public good, while the costs of cooperation are born privately. Sustained cooperation requires a solution to the collective action problem stemming from the tension between the public nature of benefits yielded by cooperation and private costs borne by cooperating agents. Social norms and institutions are among the most important ways of solving this problem. Ultrasocial institutions are institutions that enable cooperation at the level of larger-scale human groups. They are characterized by the tension between benefits they yield at the higher level of social organization and costs borne by lower-level units. Of particular interest are ultrasocial institutions, which play a role in the integration of largest-scale human groups; institutions that enabled the transition from middle-range societies (simple and complex chiefdoms) to archaic urban states and subsequently to large-scale empires and modern nation-states (Turchin 2015).

Strong macrohistorical regularities suggest that the rise of any particular mega-empire was not a random result of a concatenation of unique events; general social mechanisms must have been at work. Building on the ideas of the fourteenth century thinker Khaldun, Turchin (2003, 2009; Turchin and Gavrilets 2009; Turchin et al. 2013) has proposed a "mirror-empire" model as one common route to mega-empire. This model postulates that antagonistic interactions between nomadic pastoralists and settled agriculturalists result in an autocatalytic process, which pressures both nomadic and farming polities to scale up polity size, and thus military power. In many cases, as happened repeatedly in China and Ancient Egypt, the result of this process is the simultaneous rise of an agrarian empire and a nomadic imperial confederation on their respective sides of the steppe frontier. However, if the agrarian state does not have a deep hinterland to expand into, it may lose the scaling-up race to the nomadic polity, and is conquered by it. What is the balance of forces favoring cooperation of lower-level units and, therefore, their ability to combine into higher-level collectives? Here "units" and "collectives" are social groups at different levels of hierarchical complexity. For a society to grow in size, it has to make repeated transitions from the *i*th *to* ($i + 1$)th level. The success of each transition depends on the balance of forces favoring integration versus those favoring fission. Thus, evolution of traits promoting integration at the $i + 1$ level is favored by (1) increasing cultural variation among collectives and decreasing variation among lower-level units, and (2) increasing the effect of the trait on the fitness of collectives and reducing the effect at the lower level. Consequently, it is expected that large states should arise in regions where very different people are culturally in contact, and where interpolity competition (i.e., warfare) is particularly intense.

Instead of using computational theory to understand the evolution of complex political systems in history, Mezza-García et al. (2014) have refined computer theory in terms of what they known on hierarchical political systems. According to these authors, the similarity between a Turing machine and hierarchical political systems can be explained by how the transformation of 'inputs' into decisions in the latter is achieved, namely via sequential routes of rule-based activities that are assumed to take place in a closed manner amongst a selected group of individuals—the government. For those individuals who do not form part of the regime, and even for those who are members of a separate subsection of government, the computation of the decision takes place in a 'black box' until the moment of the 'halt' and the output of a political decision is made available. Decisions in such political systems are made with a type of information processing that works in a linear framework of reference, but which is limited when finding optimal solutions in spaces of high complexity. In the suggested model, heterarchical political organizations operate with decision-making dynamics whose computation is performed by an open system, i.e., that is in interaction with the world in various levels simultaneously in a distributed, parallel, diffuse, real time and decentralized manner. Inputs and conditions can be modified during the computation, and external agents can therefore also interact with this process. Ideally, 'outputs' or decisions are produced bottom-up from local interactions, rather than only implemented in a top-down manner at the expense of the complexity of human social systems and their environments.

As an example of computational models to understand the origins and formation of complex polities, Bogle and Cioffi-Revilla contribution to this volume (Chap. 13) implement a model about politogenesis in Sub-Saharan Africa. ZambeziLand demonstrates how a society of initially small and egalitarian groups could evolve into a complex society with a few large groups in response to changes in how individual members perceive their group and the state of extant leadership. The authors are interested in how ancient political centers originated and why they dissolved, analyzing sociopolitical phase transitions, whereby polities form and dissolve as people migrated to larger, more complex communities. The punctuated process of sociopolitical phase transitions, typical of polity cycling is explained by modeling the dynamic interplay among leaders and society members (individuals and groups) experiencing fluctuating conditions of leadership and loyalty during recurring times of stress affecting the local community. Larger and more complex polities were generated through a recursive, iterative process of collective action successes and failures by individuals and groups. The authors assume that the main structure of the fast process is universal and invariant, but the exact branching paths realized vary, depending on contingencies such as a situational change having endogenous or exogenous causes, a society perceiving or not the situational change, collective action occurring or not, success or failure in collective action being realized: hence, the term canonical. As situational changes recur in this particular society's model, a "fast process" punctuated by contingent events begins, including subsequent collective action choices made by society members (leaders and followers). Collective action may succeed or fail, depending on other contingent events. The outcome of each fast process results in the polity generating greater or lesser complexity when examined on a longer time scale or "slow process." Recursive fast processes occur relatively quickly as the society succeeds or fails in solving collective action problems that arise in the normal course of its history, with sociopolitical results and effects accumulating over time in the slow process. The most significant result of the Cioffi-Revilla and Bogle's model is the demonstration via computational simulation that an initially egalitarian, homogeneous society can quickly coalesce into a small number of much larger differentiated groups.

A similar approach applied to Inner Asia (Central Eurasia) in the past 5,000 years has been published by Cioffi-Revilla et al. (2007, 2013, 2015), Rogers (2013), Rogers et al. (2015). In all cases, the simulations are based on Cioffi-Revilla's computational theory for the emergence of social complexity accounts for the earliest formation of systems of government (pristine polities) in prehistory and early antiquity. The theory is based on a fast process of stressful crises and opportunistic decision-making through collective action. This core iterative process is canonical in the sense of undergoing variations on a main recurring theme of problem solving, adaptation and occasional failure. When a group is successful in managing or overcoming serious situational changes (endogenous or exogenous to the group, social or physical) a probabilistic phase transition may occur, under a well-specified set of conditions, yielding a long-term (slow) process of emergent political complexity and development. A reverse process may account for decay (Cioffi-Revilla 2005, 2009).

1.2.8 Simulating Social Life After Prehistory

As soon as we enter those historical periods in which written sources can be found, read and analyzed, the effort for a computational formalization of historical explanation is less evident in the current scientific literature. It seems as if the narrative basis of available data from the past constrains the causal explanation of this past imposing a similar narrative. As we have been suggesting all along this introduction, as in the rest of the book, the nature of available data from the past should not affect the logical form of the historical explanation in the present.

We can use agent-based models or any other algorithmic presentation of social mechanisms implied in the historical events whose causal relationships we intend to analyze. Obviously, the higher amount of data can force the researcher to change the scale of the analysis, moving for the quasi-abstract or theoretical social units considered in the case of hardly known prehistoric events, to more detailed social units, at better logical resolution, up to the level of the individual, if you have data about individual behaviors.

The exception to this apparent lack of interest in the computer simulation of ancient societies can be the study of the rise-and-demise of ancient empires, a historical subject that has been an important topic for computer simulation. Since the early days of authors like Hosler et al. (1977) and Dickson (1980), computer algorithms have been used to reproduce and to understand the collapse of ancient worlds (Lowe 1985; Renfrew 1987; Parisi 1998; Brunk 2002; Janssen and Scheffer 2004; Dalfes 1997; Hunt and Elliott 2005). Most of those methods used non-linear equations to model the way an economic system ceased to be efficient sometime in history. This is still an important area of research (Davidson 2010; Scarborough and Burnside 2010; Flores et al. 2011; Knappett et al. 2011; Reuveny 2012; Heckbert 2013; Heckbert et al. 2014; Faulseit 2015). Although of great interest, many of such studies seem to be too limited and are prone to be considered as overtly deterministic (Butzer and Endfield 2012). We need to go beyond the trivial relationship between ecology, natural resources and human society to really understand the highs and lows of historical trajectories.

There is a single contribution in this book related to the computer simulation non-prehistoric worlds for which we have appropriated written sources. Trescak et al. (Chap. 14) present a novel approach that can significantly decrease the cost and effort required for simulating everyday life of ancient inhabitants of virtual cities, while still capturing enough detail to be useful in historical simulations. The authors show how it is possible to design a small number of individual avatars and then automatically simulate a substantially large crowd of virtual agents, which will live their lives in the simulated city, perform choirs and rituals as well as other routine activities that are consistent with their social status. The key novelty of this approach that enables simulating such sophisticated crowds is the combination of physiological needs—for generating agent goals, emotions and personality—for choosing how to fulfil each goal and genetically informed propagation of appearance and personality traits—to propagate aspects of appearance and behavior from a small sample of manually designed individuals to large agent groups of a desired size. The usefulness of the approach is demonstrated by applying it to simulating everyday life in a reconstruction of the ancient city of Uruk, 3000 B.C. In the model, the authors have enriched computational agents with personalities and emotions, which affect their decisions when creating a plan for a current goal. This approach may even lead to emergent agent behavior that appears to be closer to human-like reasoning. As an example, the chapter details the case of a fisherman agent with no personality and emotions that catches fish when it's hungry. The agent will fish until it succeeds, or until it dies of hunger, unless the programmer manually specifies a possible change of plans when hunger level raises to a critical value. In contrast, the same can be computationally built by making the same fisherman having personality and emotions that may get frustrated when being hungry and unsuccessful. This agent may "decide" to stop fishing when frustration level overwhelms the rational decision for fishing and will search for alternatives to feed, such as begging or stealing food. The decision whether to beg or steal would depend on agent's personality.

In the previous example, fisherman represents a specific social group of the simulated population. Social groups combine certain classes of individuals that fulfill their goals in a similar way. Combining individuals into social groups allows the authors to define and program actions on a group level, rather than having to do this on individual level, reducing effort in defining crowd behavior. They consider again the case of an ancient Mesopotamian fisherman who has to trade fish with a spear maker in order to replace his broken fishing spear. The solution implies the explicitly formalization of social norms that, captures rules and protocols that drive agent interactions. As a result, agents can use these norms in reasoning to create plans for their current goal. This provides agents the ability to automatically perform their actions depending on their assigned social group. In order for agents to be able to select an action that is most relevant for their personality, such action has to be annotated by following personality facets: temptation, gregariousness, assertiveness, excitement, familiarity, straightforwardness, altruism, compliance, modesty and correctness. Using values of personality facets, the agent selects an action that provides the highest utility for its personality type. To define social groups, their actions and interactions, the authors specify virtual institutions that may have existed hypothetically in ancient Uruk in the form of an Organisation-Centred Multi-Agent System (OCMAS), establishing what agents are permitted and forbidden to do as well as the constraints and the consequences of their actions. In general, such virtual institution regulates multiple, distinct, concurrent, interrelated, dialogic activities, and each one involving different groups of agents playing different roles. In the presented case study, the authors defined all components of the Virtual Institution, with roles of fisherman, spear-maker, pot-maker, pries, king and wife.

Researchers at the University of Chicago and Argonne National Laboratory (Altaweel 2008; Altaweel et al. 2006; Altaweel and Christiansen 2004; Christiansen and Altaweel 2004, 2006; Wilkinson et al. 2007a, b, 2013) take a different approach for the historical understanding of ancient Mesopotamian societies. They have modeled the trajectories of development and demise of Bronze Age settlement systems for both the rain-fed and irrigated zones of Syria and Iraq. The reconstructed landscape near the ancient city of Assur is used as the example setting to test the effectiveness of simulated cultivation strategies. These methods include sole dependence on biennial fallow and rainfall, gravity flow irrigation, application of manure, and the integration of all these approaches. Results obtained within this computer model attempt to delineate agricultural constraints and potential benefits of the specific anthropogenic processes and strategies addressed. The investigation intends to prove that systems of ancient Near Eastern cities co-evolved in an intimate relationship with their environment, primarily by means of the aggregation through time of smaller fundamental units (e.g., households). The model allows for the scaling up of a settlement from a single household to a village, and ultimately to an urban center with its appropriate array of subsidiary and neighboring settlements. Agrarian production (specifically in light of environmental stresses) and social interaction is modeled at a mutually consistent, fairly detailed level that will support a realistic representation of feedback processes, nonlinear behavior mechanisms, and some degree of self-organization in Bronze Age settlement systems. Emphasis is on the development of the household model and its transformation into higher-order settlements. Everyday decisions in farming are also being incorporated into the model (e.g., when to plant, whether to fallow or crop annually, etc.), as well as social factors such as the pooling of resources. Moreover, the full model includes mechanisms that allow for the growth of social differentiation and that enable some households to grow and others to become subordinate.

The first empires in the Old World seem to be an ideal domain for computer simulation using historical information to calibrate the key model parameters. Palmissano and Altaweel (2015) have simulated explanatory models of settlement hierarchy in Central Anatolia during the Old Assyrian Colony period. Symons and Raine (2008) have investigated the spread of information and population aggregation in a somewhat ideal agrarian society based on an abstracted Egyptian landscape containing villages, flood plain, and river. The agents represent farming households which exchange information and migrate around the landscape motivated by the availability of surplus food (used as a proxy for quality of life). The model follows the aggregation of hamlets into larger villages that occurred during the pre-dynastic period. The results presented are intended to correspond to a one hundred to five hundred year time-span in the period roughly 3800–3300 BC. One of the drivers of Symons and Raine model is the variability of the Nile flood, since this determines the changing fertility of the land. The fertility is modelled as a function of perpendicular distance from the Nile. There are no records of land tenure in the pre-dynastic period. Therefore the authors have extrapolated back from later practice to implement a simplified form of land tenure. Thus, they have included in the model the 'buying' of fields whenever a village has more labor available than the fields it 'owns'. Once bought these fields remain under the ownership of the village even if the population declines. For simplicity, ownership is assigned to a village as a whole, rather than to individual households. The algorithm to decide which fields to buy is based on three factors. The first is the fertility of the field. The second factor is the distance to the fields, which makes a field less attractive the further away it is from the village. The final factor is the undesirability of owning fields adjacent to those already owned, as an insurance policy against fluctuations in yield. A key feature of all of the simulated scenarios is the aggregation of population. The movement of the population towards the Nile and the abandonment of the more distant villages are to be expected on the grounds of the distribution of fertility. Each household simply tries to optimize their quality of life. As a result it turns out that they aggregate into larger villages. The outcome is not even the most desirable from the point of view of overall average quality of life for an individual household over time in any of the models. The movement of the population consumes resources and therefore reduces the overall quality of life, and the agglomeration into larger villages does not exploit the full potential fertility of the landscape. The driving force that produces larger village units is the unpredictable variability of the flood that provides relative safety in numbers.

The regions bordering the Aegean Sea were also witnesses of important historical events some 4000 years ago. Knappett et al. (2008) have created a spatial network model to understand the scale of cultural (and economic) interaction between the Cyclades, Crete, the Greek mainland, the Dodecanese and coastal Asia Minor during the later periods of the Middle Bronze Age (c. 2000–1600 BC). In this period, there appear to be substantial changes in transport technology between the Early Bronze Age and the later Middle Bronze Age, with the advent of the sail. The main hypothesis is that the centrality and size of the historic site of Knossos (Crete) and the growth of Minoanisation, may be related. The authors propose a mathematical model of 'imperfect optimisation' to describe such historical maritime networks, encoding, metaphorically, the notion of gravitational attraction between objects in space. The 'gravitation' in this case is a balance of social forces, expressed by networks with settlements of particular sizes and links of particular strengths. The model can be tweaked by giving different relative importance to the cultivation of local resources or to trade, and to show what happens when a member of the network suddenly disappears. The model incorporates some sense of function: regional interaction networks must accrue some benefit, balanced against their costs. Hence the model works on the assumption of some basic optimisation. Secondly, the model takes account of geographical distances while not being strictly determined by them. The model is neither fully bottom up like agent-based modelling, which tends to aggregate scales very coarsely, nor entirely top down; it is set up in such a way that the interactions between the level of the site and that of the network as a whole can be explored.

Investigating further in the same historical domain, Chliaoutakis and Chalkiadakis (2015, 2016) have developed a functional ABM system prototype for simulating an artificial ancient society of autonomous agents residing at the Malia area of the island of Crete during the Early Bronze Age. At its current implementation, the ABM allows exploring the sustainability of specific agricultural technologies in use at the time, so we can examine their impact on population size and dispersion; and it allows for the incorporation of any other technology that needs to be modeled. In addition, it allows us to assess the influence of different social organization paradigms on land use patterns and population growth. Importantly, the model incorporates the social paradigm of agents self-organizing into a "stratified" social structure, and continuously re-adapting the emergent structure, if required. The investigation is based on a self-organization algorithm incorporating a set of agent relations influencing the various social interactions, and a decentralized structural adaptation mechanism, suitable for open and dynamic organizations. Simulation results demonstrate that self-organizing agent populations are the most successful, growing larger than populations employing different social organization paradigms. Specifically, self-organization is compared to egalitarian-like and static hierarchical organization models. The success of this social organization paradigm that gives rise to "stratification" that is, non-egalitarian societies, and provides support for so-called "managerial" archaeological theories which assume the existence of different social strata in very early period; and consider this early stratification a pre-requisite for the emergence of the Minoan Palaces, and the hierarchical social structure evident in later periods.

Insights into historical region-wide political consolidation have been suggested by simulation results from an agent-based model based on historical data of human societies circa 2500 BC to AD 1000 in the Lake Titicaca basin of Peru and Bolivia (Griffin and Stanish 2007). The agents' behavior was modeled as micro-level condition-action rules based on the hypothesized causal factors of: agriculture, migration, competition, and trade. The approach to modeling political dynamics was inspired by Lars-Erik Cederman's agent-based Emergent Polarity model of early nation-state geopolitics (1997, 2002), which the authors adapted for pre-Inka historical scenario. This model simulated the consolidation of small polities into large ones which may then fission back into small independent entities and subsequently consolidate again, reminiscent of the recycling pattern observed in pre-state chiefdoms. The spatial end state of each simulation run has been classified as one of several alternative political configurations, based on the number of sovereign states remaining: unipolar, bipolar, multipolar, or nonpolar. In the same way, each simulation run of the current model was classified as one of seven alternative Titicaca political prehistories, one of which corresponded to what the record indicates to us actually happened. The authors have insisted in the temporal dimension to the classification scheme to distinguish not only the end state but the trajectory through time to reach that configuration.

Some models emphasize the key role of the interactions between households, institutions or spatial entities to generate a processual explanation of the emergence of a hierarchical urban system (Batty, 2001; Schmitt and Pumain 2013). In terms of transition, the model should simulate the transition from a loose position (random or uniform seeding of the entities) to the emergence of a spatial hierarchical and organized structurement without such an objective contained in the rules of model. Among the relevant models, we can mention the SIMPOP model, in which the settlement entities are the agents, the assumption being that there are interaction processes at the meso-geographic level that cause the trajectory of the settlement system in one direction rather than another. Starting from an initial situation in which we only count for agricultural villages poorly differentiated in function and size of cities emerging crescent acquire new functions and the possibility to exchange with broader geographic ranges. The growth or decline of a city will depend on the success of its trade with other villages and cities with which it interacts (Sanders et al. 1997; Pumain et al., 2009). The interference zones of influence of other cities creates a context of long distance competition in which the city must develop its position.

An interesting domain for applying these models to the historical formation of ancient cities is Greece. Rivers and Evans (2014) have re-examined the onset of centralisation in mainland Greek city states of the 9th and 8th centuries BCE. The aim is to model the onset of 'urbanisation', by which is meant the emergence of dominant settlements within community territories as a result of a transference of 'sovereignty' from villages to create larger associations centred upon these dominant settlements. The authors have compared two cost-benefit model in which the benefits arise from exchange between sites, assuming that larger sites getting most benefit from exchanging with larger sites. These non-linear benefits are offset against the cost of sustaining the network, assumed linear in the total network activity.

Around the 10th century BC, the rural villages in South Etruria (now Tuscany and Latium, Italy) began to disappear and a number of cities started to arise. The accepted grounds of these events deal with defense and safety reasons. Bianchi and Marcialis (2013) attribute the birth of the proto-cities to a sustainability crisis in the mining villages and asserts that mining technicians imposed such transition on farmers in order to carry out a sustainable reorganization of the whole system of settlements and, as a corollary, to strengthen their ruling role. The authors illustrate the proposed hypothesis by means of a simulation model roughly reproducing the described event. The model is based on the idea that the city birth can be interpreted as a discontinuity in the social system behavior. An unsustainable growth may have caused a crisis in the Etruscan village system. The formation of a new form of social aggregation, the city, would have achieved an organizational change and restored sustainability.

Ceconni et al. (2015), address the same historical case. In this simulation, the Etrurian territory is divided into a grid of square cells, with each cell characterized by three properties—(a) soil quality and presence of natural resources, (b) existence of water courses, (c) morphology of the ground from the point of view of defensibility—and the model assumes that each settlement decides what to do on the basis of these properties. The simulation reproduces the process that led to the appearance towards the end of the second millennium of a few large centers in well-defended sites and numerous small settlements. During each cycle of the simulation, each settlement (a) takes into consideration its N (number of inhabitants), (b) defines its zone of control with respect to the surrounding area, and (c) calculates how many resources are available for its inhabitants, resulting in the relative value of resources per capita. The simulation can develop according to two different types of dynamics; a positive and a negative dynamics. A positive dynamics means that the number of inhabitants of a settlement increases together with an increase in the size of its zone of control. Therefore, the available resources also increase and the value of the resources per capita remains high. The settlement is a prosperous one. On the contrary, a negative dynamics implies an increase in the number of inhabitants but not of the settlement's zone of control because of the presence of the zones of control of other settlements or because the zone of control is made of soil with low productivity. In this case, the resources per capita become insufficient, and the settlement is in trouble. When the resources do not meet the needs of a settlement's inhabitants, the number of inhabitant decreases and, if is reduced to zero, the settlement disappears. The virtual Ancient Southern Etruria appears to be divided into five main zones of control and four of these five zones of control correspond to the historical proto-urban centers of Orvieto-Volsinii,

Tarquinia, Cerveteri and Veio. In the simulation, already during the virtual Early Bronze Age the system seems to undergo a collapse, going from 250 villages to about 60, while in the following centuries it remains roughly stable, with limited fluctuations. This diverges from what we know from the archaeological evidence which tells us that, after an increase between the beginning of the Early Bronze Age and Middle Bronze Age, the total number settlement remains pretty stable until, in the First Iron Age, the number of settlements is drastically reduced. This phenomenon is interpreted as due to a gradual but steady population growth but it is not captured by our simulation.

Crabtree (2016) has explored trade relationships between Etruscans and the native Gauls. She examines the first five centuries of wine consumption (from ~600 B.C. to ~100 B.C.), analyzing how preference of one type of luxury good over another created distinctive artifact patterns in the archaeological record. She has created a simple agent-based model to examine how the trade of comestibles for wine led to a growing economy and a distinctive patterning of artifacts in the archaeological record of southern France. This model helps shed light on the processes that led to centuries of peaceable relationships with colonial merchants, and interacts with scholarly debate on why Etruscan amphorae are replaced by Greek amphorae so swiftly and completely.

Heckbert (2013) has presented preliminary results from his MayaSim model, an integrated agent-based, cellular automata, and network model representing the ancient classical Maya social-ecological system (ca. 250–900 AD). The model represents the relationship between population growth, agricultural production, soil degradation, climate variability, primary productivity, hydrology, ecosystem services, forest succession, and the stability of trade networks. Agents representing settlements develop and expand within a spatial landscape that changes under climate variation and responds to anthropogenic impacts. The model is able to reproduce spatial patterns and timelines somewhat analogous to that of the ancient Maya. This investigation aims to identify candidate features of a resilient versus vulnerable social-ecological system, and employs computer simulation to explore this topic, using the ancient Maya as an example. Complex systems modelling identifies how interconnected variables behave, considering fast-moving variables such as land cover change and trade connections, meso-speed variables such as demographics and climate variability, as well as slow-moving variables such as soil degradation.

Watts (2013) has modeled some aspects of Hohokam economics. The Hohokam were an ancient Native American culture centered on the present-day US state of Arizona during the period AD 200–1450. The objective of this research has been to first identify a variety of economic models that may explain patterns of artifact distribution in the archaeological record. Those models were abstract representations of the real-world system reconstructed on the basis of microeconomic theory, and economic anthropology hypotheses. Those hypotheses have been implemented into an agent-based model, and run to assess whether any of the models were consistent with Hohokam ceramic datasets. The results su workshop procurement and shopkeeper merchandise, provided the means of distributing pottery from specialist producers to widely distributed consumers. Perhaps unsurprisingly, the results of this project are broadly consistent with earlier researchers' interpretations that the structure of the Hohokam economy evolved through time. Growing more complex throughout the Preclassic, and undergoing a major reorganization resulting in a less complicated system at the transition to the Classic Period.

Those investigations show the relevant paper of the advanced production economies in ancient times and how computer simulation allows reconstructing its functioning from incomplete and sometimes partial written sources from the past. Among the aspects we need to consider there is the practice of irrigation in ancient kingdoms to increase productivity. Irrigation systems, with their many entities, social and physical, their many interactions within a changing environment and emergent properties, are typical examples of systems for which agent-based modelling could yield fruitful analysis because of the highly detailed and complex relations between human actions and the social and material context. Ertsen (2011), Murphy (2012) and Altaweel (2013) show how interactions between humans, hydrology and hydraulics within irrigation systems have historically created patterns of water use. Both studies are based on a modelling-based approach generating flows in ancient irrigated environments, as it yields new insights in the way irrigation has succeeded in sustaining human civilization—or failed to do so, pointing out to the fact that we should not explain how irrigation-based societies collapse after centuries or even millennia, but why these societies did not collapse each and every day. It is the combination of modelling daily interactions by agents and water fluxes that will build better understanding of irrigation systems as anthropogenic landscapes resulting from activities of individuals, households, and groups, within hydraulic and hydrological boundaries setting the material context.

Kuznar and Sedlmeayer (2005) have developed a flexible agent-based computer simulation of pastoral nomad/sedentary peasant interaction that can be adapted to particular historical and social settings. The authors focus on how environmental and material factors may have conditioned individual agent response has allowed the modeling of how collective behaviors (mass raiding, genocide) can emerge from individual motives and needs. Many factors influence tribal conflict in the modern world (ethnicity, global politics). However, these simulations reinforce the analyses of some social scientists that argue such conflicts are the inevitable result of the breakdown of land use in the face of growing populations, marginal habitats, and an unprecedented ecological crisis. An alternative model has been offered by Cohen and Ackland (2012a b). Angourakis et al. (2014) have created an abstract agent-based model describing a mechanism of competition for land use between farming and herding addressed to understanding "oases" economic systems in historical central Asia. The aim is the exploration of how mobility, intensity, and interdependence of activities can influence land use pattern. After performing a set of experiments the authors compare the implications of each condition for the corroboration of specific land use patterns. In this way, the overall extension of farming in oases can be explained by the competition for land use between farming and herding, assuming that it develops with little or no interference of climatic, geographical, and historical contingencies.

A particular application of this way of studying the historical sources of inter-cultural conflict is Altaweel and Paulette (2013), who have investigated the long-term effects of economic interaction between nomadic and sedentary groups in the Bronze Age Near East. To keep things as simple as possible, they have modeled only a single, small sedentary community and a single nomadic group. The nomadic group visits the village for a portion of each year as a part of its annual migration pattern, and it is during these visits that economic exchanges take place. In a series of simulation runs, the authors varied the timing of the nomadic visit and the resources available to each group, and they tracked the impact of these changes on the economic life of the settlement and its inhabitants.

Cioffi-Revilla et al. (2007, 2010; see also Rogers 2013; Rogers et al. 2015) have simulated the rise and fall of polities in Inner Asia over a long time span, on the basis of nomadism effects on the economic, social and political structure. The time is defined as sufficiently long to include significant climate change. When climate changed, the biomass distribution on the landscape also changed, which in turn generated changes in the biological and social dynamics of animals and people, respectively. HouseholdsWorld is a spatial agent-based model of pastoral nomads living in a simple socio-natural system. The target system is a generic locality smaller than a region of Inner Asia shortly after ca. 500 BCE, the time period just prior to the rise of the Xiung-nu polity (ca. 200 BCE). The primary sources used for developing the HouseholdsWorld model were epigraphic, archaeological, ethnographic, and environmental, as detailed in the subsections below. Several of the patterns produced by simulation bear significant qualitative and quantitative resemblance to comparable patterns in the target system. For example, the distribution of wealth has the approximate form of a log-normal distribution, as a real-world distribution of household wealth usually should. Similarly, household movements show marked periodic fluctuations, as in the real world when nomads undergo seasonal travel following their herds. While the model does not attempt to produce a specific historical or empirically replicated replication, the overall qualitative and quantitative behavior of households, herds, and seasons are supported by known features of the target system.

Concerning the study of later periods in ancient times, there is a growing interest in modeling Roman economy in terms of micro-behaviors, feedback, and local interaction. Before anyone can ask questions about growth, or market integration, or the degree to which Rome was 'primitive' versus 'modern', some scholars are focusing on individual decision making and networks of individuals at all geographical scales and then using those networks as the substrate for computationally simulating individuals' economic activities (Brughmans 2012). The idea that network relationships (and the institutions that emerge to promote these) are the mechanism through which ancient economies deal with incomplete knowledge is a powerful one because we can find and outline the traces of these networks through archaeology. The simplest of these essays are those by Graham (2005, 2006) who has tried to understand the geography of the Empire from the point of view of a person traveling through ancient roads. The author takes the lists in the historical written Itineraries, and recast them as networks of interconnected cities. The purpose is to know whether there are any significant differences between provinces' connective network topography in terms of the transmission of information. One agent is given a piece of 'knowledge', which it may or may not share with those he encounters. The rate at which knowledge is transmitted therefore depends on the chance of transmission in any given encounter, and on the topology of the itinerary network. By controlling for the different variables, significant differences in how the different provinces' networks facilitate the transmission of information may be observed.

Graham and Weingart (2015) have developed an agent-based model of the Roman extractive economy which generates various kinds of networks under various assumptions about how that economy works. This simulation of an ancient economy is based on four key mechanisms: (a) the generation of small parcels of capital to combat risk; (b) little homogenization of products; (c) opportunism; and (d) social networks where there is high local clustering and a few long-distance links. These mechanisms correspond well with the archaeology of the Roman economy and the picture we know from legal and other historical textual sources. The authors have formalized in Netlogo code their ideas concerning how economic networks might be formed; they then sweep the parameter space, the entire landscape of possible outcomes; they compare that generated landscape of the model against known archaeological networks; and in the degree of conformity or disjuncture between the model and observed networks they reevaluate the stories that have been told about the past, creating new models in the process. They assume they will never be able to simulate perfectly the formation processes that give rise to a particular archaeological network. To do so would require making a map as large as the territory it is intended to describe. The computer translation of a hypothetical model of Roman economy, and the role of social networks within that model should be couched in all appropriate caveats and warnings. Networks can be discerned and drawn out from archaeology, prosopography, and historical sources. If we can align networks from the ancient evidence to those generated from the model's simulation of the ancient economy, we have a powerful tool for exploring antiquity, for playing with different ideas about how the ancient world worked.

Brughmans and Poblome (2016) take a very similar approach. They have presented an agent-based network model simulating the social networks which represent the flow of information and goods between roman traders. The concept of social networks is here used as an abstraction of the commercial opportunities of traders, acting as a medium for the flow of information and products. In the model 2000 traders are located at 100 sites and are connected in a social network. Four products are produced at four different 'production sites', and are subsequently distributed through commercial transactions between pairs of traders that are connected in the social network according to shortest-path-length links to reproduce the idea of "small world". Preliminary results suggest that the local-knowledge variable has a limited effect on the wideness of goods distribution, whilst the proportion of inter-site links variable has a strong effect. Limited commercial knowledge can still give rise to wide differences in distributions, but only in systems with highly integrated markets. This means that the local-knowledge variable is not instrumental in giving rise to the pattern of interest, whilst the proportion-inter-site-links variable is. Limited availability and high uncertainty of information, and a weak integration of different markets in an economy governed by supply and demand, is unlikely to give rise to large differences in the distribution patterns of commercial goods. Preliminary results of this model therefore reject the claim that limited market integration, availability and reliability of commercial information in ancient Rome gave rise to differences in the wideness of products' distributions.

It can be of interest to compare this new research on Roman economy with medieval and post-medieval economies. Ewer et al. (2001) have created a multiagent-based model to understand the role of deliberative Agents in Analyzing Crisis Management in Pre-modern Towns. The model distinguishes among merchants, craftsmen, laborers and local authorities. Agents interact as consumers and suppliers via several markets. Within the course of simulation local authorities are capable of intervening in market processes and implementing measures for crisis management. Hodgson and Knudsen (2008) have developed a behavioural explanation for the emergence of high levels of property rights enforcement in Europe in Medieval times (11th to 13th centuries). The merchant guilds have a central role in our explanation. The authors have developed an agent-based model that allows a number of important but previously unexplored issues to be considered (such as the joint importance of price variation, guild stability and the effect of uncoordinated embargo pressures among multiple guilds). The main result is that almost perfect levels of property rights enforcement can emerge solely as a result of multiple guilds' uncoordinated embargo pressures and medium to high levels of price variation. In fact, both conditions were fulfilled in the Middle Ages. In this model, no reputation mechanisms are required; our results solely depend on behavioural adjustment. High levels of property rights enforcement can emerge instead as a result of guilds' embargo.

Frantz et al. (2013, 2015) have studied the functioning of the Maghribi Traders Coalition—a historically significant trader collective that operated along the North African coast between the 10th and 13th centuries, which acted as a closed group whose interactions were governed by informal institutions. Bekar and Read have studied of eleventh and fourteenth centuries in England, when innovations in property rights over land induced peasants to respond by trading small parcels of land as part of their risk coping strategy (Bekar and Read 2009; see also Ewert and Sunder 2001 for a related experiment with trading networks in Medieval North Europe). Those times witnessed a dramatic increase in inequality in the distribution of peasant estimates of the quantitative impact of land trades (motivated by behavior toward risk) on the distribution of landholdings. The authors employ an agent based modeling strategy in which decisions regarding pooling, saving, labor supply, and land transactions are rule based. Agents are initially endowed with an exogenous landholding. Each period agent draws a harvest realization from a random normal distribution transformed by the requisite mean and variance. Harvests are independent across agents and through time. Agents pool and save out of current harvests. Smallholders work in the labor market; largeholders hire labor. Incomes are compared to a subsistence consumption bundle. An agent facing a subsistence crisis with a positive land position offers a parcel of land for sale. If, after depleting their land position, the agent is still below subsistence it experiences a subsistence crisis. An agent sufficiently above subsistence purchases parcels offered for sale. Agents sell land only when all other forms of insurance have been exhausted and they still face a serious subsistence crisis—treating land sales as an insurance mechanism of last resort. The authors test their explanation by simulating the dynamics of the land market, including differential reproductive success, partible inheritance, pooling and saving behavior, production parameters linking harvest realizations through time, crisis levels of income, wage rates, and land prices. Our simulations reveal that transactions in the land market coupled with population growth produce levels of inequality and skew consistent with those observed in the data. Population growth alone, coupled with partible inheritance, can only explain a small portion of the observed inequality.

Suárez and Sancho (2011) have investigated using computer simulations a theoretical model of cultural dynamics in which the individuals' behavior plays a strong role derives from the many cultural communities involved and the different scales used to study the spread of the baroque culture from Europe to America at the beginning of the Early Modern Period. The research explains the origins, evolution, transmission, and effectiveness of baroque artistic patterns, through the development of a model that rationalized the cultural and symbolic movements between Europe and Latin America, as well as the transformations and mutations that cultural objects undergo in their successive interactions with the variety of ecosystems and groups through which they pass on their journeys. The authors have created a Virtual Cultural Laboratory (VCL) using agent-based computational modeling that helps study how human culture has been historically transformed and transmitted through acts of learning, imitation, and the creation of cultural objects as they might be experienced by any human being from birth to death, independently of the specific community to which the cultural object or individual belongs. In general terms, the VCL addresses three different issues that are relevant for the historian and the cultural researcher. First, the VCL offers a platform to check on the effects of historical events and processes about which the researcher has comprehensive sets of data. Having the data lets the researcher to refine the model he is using to explain the given cultural and historic processes, as both data and model have to show a mutually coherent behavior. Second, when the researcher does not have good data about the phenomena he is studying, the VCL helps test the hypotheses and the assumptions used by the historian, and double-check the results of the simulation with the logic of those hypotheses. Third, the researcher can take advantage of the VCL by rehearsing different what-if scenarios that he knows did not happen, but whose results would be important to shed light into the context in which actual events took place.

But not only economic mechanisms should be taken into account for understanding social life in ancient times. The history of religion and the historical evolution of religiosity (Altran and Heinrich 2010; Whitehouse et al. 2012) can be an interesting domain for simulating historical non-economic dynamics. Czachesz (2007a, b) has advanced some algorithmic models of social behavior for understanding religiosity and look for ways of applying such models to the emergence of early Christian religion. The author puts forward the hypothesis that religious ideas emerge as a necessary consequence of the sophisticated "flocking" rules of human societies. Religion emerges from the interaction of a great number of participants with each other and their environment. Rituals are repetitive actions that emerge from these interactions. Texts (public representations) are environmental components that have been formed by the agents. Beliefs and experiences are generated by texts and rituals and describe the internal states of the agents. On a different level, however, also beliefs and experiences can be studied as distributed phenomena, inasmuch as they are emerging from the interaction of different parts within the human mind. His suggestion is that religious ideas emerge as a necessary side-effect of the sophisticated "flocking rules" of human societies. The large-scale dynamics of human societies emerge as agents make decisions based on interactions with our neighbors as well as on simulations of unknown, distant, and foreign human individuals. Some of the latter simulations are maintained in stabilized, stereotyped, and socially transmitted forms, such as national stereotypes. Ideas of religious agents are long-standing, stabilized, stereotyped, and socially transmitted simulations of distant or abstract persons. Religious agents, in fact, are often important family members, rulers, or distant, exotic people.

On a similar subject, Turchin (2003) has explored three alternative mechanisms of religious conversion and ethnic assimilation through history: the noninteractive, the autocatalytic, and the threshold models. Each model predicts a qualitatively different trajectory (the proportion converted/assimilated as a function of time). This means that using a model the historian can determine which theory better reflects the reality if he/she can find data on the temporal course of conversion. When fitting the model with historical data on conversion to Islam in Iran and Spain, results strongly supported the autocatalytic model and were nothing like trajectories predicted by the two alternatives. Turchin concludes from this result that all models are by definition wrong, because they oversimplify the complex reality, but the autocatalytic model is less wrong than the alternatives. It appears that the assumptions of the conversion process built into the autocatalytic model capture some important aspect of the historical reality of those territories at that time: once world religions got going, they generated a kind of momentum that allowed them to expand at approximately constant (per capita) rate. Dramatic events—world wars, imperial collapses, and nomadic invasions—did not derail these massive macrohistorical processes, at least in these particular cases (of course, certain kinds of events, such as the Christian Reconquista in Spain, are capable of reversing the tide of religious conversion).

Tomlinson (2009) has studied how ancestor veneration and other forms of commemoration may help to reduce social distance within groups, thereby encouraging reciprocity and providing a significant survival advantage. In his simulation, a prototypical form of ancestor commemoration arises spontaneously among computational agents programmed to have a small number of established human capabilities. Specifically, ancestor commemoration arises among agents that: (a) form relationships with each other, (b) communicate those relationships to each other, and (c) undergo cycles of life and death. By demonstrating that ancestor commemoration could have arisen from the interactions of a small number of simpler behavioural patterns, this simulation may provide insight into the workings of human cultural systems, and ideas about how to study ancestor commemoration among humans.

As examples of other non-economic models for understanding ancient worlds, we can mention a simulated Polynesian society that has been used to explain why, in Polynesia, growing stratification did not result in a devaluation of women's status, as most theorists had suggested (Small 1999). The computer model used to explore this problem—called TongaSim—attempts to emulate the basic social dynamics of Tonga, a Western Polynesian society. The program is capable of simulating the operation of a chiefdom with up to 100+ chiefly lines whose descendants marry and have children, create and maintain kinship relationships, exact and pay tribute, produce and redistribute agricultural wealth, expand in territory and go to war, and attempt to gain personal and group status. TongaSim was used to simulate the effect of warfare (a prime mover of stratification) on women's status, specifically the custom of "fahu" that asserts the spiritual superiority of sisters and sister's lines over brothers and their lines. Because of intermarriage patterns, this custom also serves to make higher status chiefly lines superior in kinship to lower status chiefly lines and, thus, supports traditional political power. The simulation showed that, despite the initial conflict between the interests of rising military chiefs and the fahu custom, the custom was appropriated by these rising chiefs, turning fahu's political effects "on its head." Ultimately in the simulation, the fahu custom provided a vehicle for military chiefs to gain status and power. This, it is argued, is consistent with the lack of any historical evidence that the fahu was challenged and toppled during periods of growing warfare and stratification.

In a related way, Froese et al. (2014) have simulated the political life in ancient Teotihuacan, México, from 100 AD to 500 AD. The authors have devised a mathematical model of the city's hypothetical network of representatives as a formal proof of concept that widespread cooperation was realizable in a fully distributed manner. In the model, decisions become self-organized into globally optimal configurations even though local representatives behave and modify their relations in a rational and selfish manner. This self-optimization crucially depends on occasional communal interruptions of normal activity, and it is impeded when sections of the network are too independent. The authors relate these insights to theories about community-wide rituals at Teotihuacan and the city's eventual disintegration.

Livni and Stone (2015) have simulated some aspects of pre-monarchic life in iron Age Israel, taking into account the potential cultural, civic, and social role of religious rituals and beliefs (i.e., the weekly Sabbath), in controlling deviation from social norms. The model begins with an analogy between spread of transgression (defined as lack of conformity with social norms) and of biological infection. Borrowing well-known mathematical methods, the authors have derived solution sets of social equilibrium and study their social stability. The work shows how a particular ritual in a complex polity could in theory enhance social resilience. The examination reveals that an institutionalized ritual had the potential to ensure a stable organization and suppress occasional appearances of transgression from cultural norms and boundaries. Subsequently, the model is used to explore an interesting question: how old is the Sabbath? The work is interdisciplinary, combining anthropological concepts with mathematical analysis and with archaeological parallels in regards to the findings.

War and violence have been regarded as relevant aspects for understanding historical evolution and social change (Younger 2012; Turchin et al. 2013). As a result of this interest in the formal study of conflict in ancient times, the computer replica of ancient battles has been one of the recurrent subjects of computer simulation (Cederman 2003; Stover 2007; Graham 2009; Findley 2008; Findley et al. 2010; Stilman et al. 2011; Craenen et al. 2012; Loper and Turnitsa 2012; Wittek and Rubio-Campillo 2012; Sabin 2012). War in the origins of humanity (Philips et al. 2014), during the Neolithic (Duering and Wahl 2014), the Trojan War (Flores and Bologna 2013), in roman times (Rubio-Campillo et al. 2015), in the medieval period (Murgatroyd et al. 2012) or later (Girardin and Cederman 2007; Rubio-Campillo et al. 2013) has been simulated. Models of ancient and modern armies can be then used as a virtual laboratory, where different hypotheses are tested under varying scenarios what allows the study behavioral action at any scale, involving tens of thousands of agents within the context of modelling logistical arrangements relating to the battle, or taking into account how the resilience of formations to combat stress may increase exponentially when they contain just a small percentage of homogeneously distributed individual agents (warriors) with higher psychological resistance. In this way, the computer model of a battle can show different possible courses of action, the influence of random movements, the influence of landscape, the consequences of the differences in weaponry or soldiers training, logistics and the "geniality" of generals and commanders. Distributed simulation is the only viable approach to deal with a problem of such scale and complexity.

The other side of violence is mortality. Computational simulation can be the most obvious way to explore the consequences of famines in historical perspective, be there the result of violence, structural problems of the economic mechanisms or climatic transformations (Watkins and Menken 1985; Wassermann 2007; Curran et al. 2015). Ewert et al. (2003, 2007) have explored using agent-based technology the relationship between hunger and early market dynamics in order to understand the consequences of mortality crises in Pre-Modern European towns explains how to implement a model in which historical famines may be simulated. Zhang et al. (2011) considers the role of climate-change.

Mortality can also be the result of epidemics. Black Death in the middle ages is one of the best known historical examples (Bossack and Welford 2015). Voigtländer and Voth (2013) have simulated how a major shock to population can trigger a transition to a new steady state with higher per-capita income. The Black Death was such a shock, raising wages substantially. The model shows that demand for urban products increased and urban centers grew in size. European cities were unhealthy, and rising urbanization pushed up aggregate death rates. This effect was reinforced by diseases spread through war, financed by higher tax revenues. In addition, rising trade also spread diseases. In this way higher wages reduced population pressure. The authors suggest in a calibration exercise that our model can account for the sustained rise in European urbanization as well as permanently higher per capita incomes in 1700, without technological change. Europe's precocious rise to economic riches can be explained as the result of complex interactions of the plague shock with the belligerent political environment and the nature of post-medieval cities. Other related approaches to the computational investigation of the social, political and economic effects of historical epidemics are Duncan et al. 1993; Lagerlöf 2003; Monecke et al. 2009; Gaudart et al. 2010; Kausrud et al. 2010.

1.2.9 Simulating the Recent Past

There are two key factors that can be used to fix the begining of "modernity": industrial revolution at the end of 18th century and the French revolution and the posterior historical trend towards parliamentary political regimes. The Industrial Revolution was the transition to new manufacturing processes in the period from about 1760 to sometime between 1820 and 1840. This transition included going from hand production methods to machines, new chemical manufacturing and iron production processes, improved efficiency of water power, the increasing use of steam power, and the development of machine tools. It marks a major turning point in history; almost every aspect of daily life was influenced in some way. In particular, average income and population began to exhibit unprecedented sustained growth, but also new forms of inequality emerged. Only some aspects of this series of historical events have been explored using computational methods (but see Atack 1979; Komlos 1989; Komlos and Artzrouni 1994; Foley 1998; Malerba et al. 1999 and Garavaglia 2010; Spaiser and Sumpter 2016). Harley and Crafts (2000) used a classical computational general equilibrium (CGE) trade model with diminishing returns in agriculture and realistic assumptions about consumer demand. Their results show that while technical change in cottons and iron were major spurs to exportation of those specific goods, the need for food imports also stimulated exports generally. In any case, why did England industrialize first? And why was Europe ahead of the rest of the world? To answer these questions, Voigtländer and Voth (2006) built a probabilistic two-sector model where the initial escape from Malthusian constraints depends on the demographic regime, capital deepening and the use of more differentiated capital equipment. Weather-induced shocks to agricultural productivity cause changes in prices and quantities, and affect wages. In a standard model with capital externalities, these fluctuations interact with the demographic regime and affect the speed of growth. Voigtländer and Voth model has been calibrated to match the main characteristics of the English economy in 1700 and the observed transition until 1850. The authors capture one of the key features of the British Industrial Revolution emphasized by economic historians—slow growth of output and productivity. Fertility limitation is responsible for higher per capita incomes, and these in turn increase industrialization probabilities. Simulations using parameter values for other countries show that Britain's early escape was only partly due to chance. France could have moved out of agriculture and into manufacturing faster than Britain, but the probability was less than 25 %. Contrary to recent claims in the literature, 18th century China had only a minimal chance to escape from Malthusian constraints (Zhou 2008). This line of enquire has also been further explored by Galor et al. (2009), Desmet and Parente (2012), Mejía Cubillos (2015). Social aspects of emerging inequality as a consequence of industrialization have been explored by Crayen and Baten (2010). The third industrial revolution that is the transition to the Information Age has been computationally explored by Veneris (1990).

The French Revolution of 1789 was much more than a mere uprising of the "people" against the State. Its historical relevance comes from the fact that the main guidelines for the future parliamentary forms of government were defined then (Sharp and Weisdorf 2012). Why some street fighting in Paris at that time could have had so enduring consequences? Although there is not any specific computer simulation of what happened in France at the end of eighteenth century, we may suggest a general model of a social revolution based on a conjunction of events that were, themselves, and each independently caused (Grossman 1991). These events would include state crises, popular uprisings and elite actions. As they unfolded, these events may have been shaped by international forces that would have impinged on the states in question. In response to these events, the state and other elite actors may have found themselves constrained by some crisis (typically financial, often deepened by the exigencies of war) and therefore increasingly susceptible to the revolutionary challenges. The role for quasi-independent social actors, and the historically unique forms and sequencing of events can make the model suppler, and better able to represent diverse scenarios than prior theories. As an example, we can consider the MASON RebeLand model (Cioffi-Revilla and Rouleau (2010), based on: (i) an explicit polity model with politically complete structure and processes; (ii) social and natural model components within integrated socio-natural systems; and (iii) generative dynamics where insurgency and the state of the polity (stable, unstable, failing, failed, and recovering) occur as emergent phenomena under a range of social and environmental conditions.

In other words, instead of "reproducing" the "storming of the Bastille" or the activities of Robespierre and his committee of Public Safety we can "calibrate" an abstract model of the causal factors of insurrection, civil conflict and political transformation with empirical data from historical sources. This approach was suggested by Sewell (1985), Skocpol (1985), Goldstone (1991), and computationally enriched by Squazzoni (2008a, b), Cederman et al. (2010), Sallach (2010), and Altaweel et al. (2012). In this way, we can investigate the outbreak of different historical situations (Hermann and Hermann 1967; Bremer 1977; Mintz 1981; Hanneman 1988; Schrodt 1988; Chadwick 2000; Fogu 2009). Beyond the emergence of social conflict, revolutions and uprisings, the historical process towards parliamentary political regimes can be formally explored using computational tools (Cederman 2001, 2005; Ulfelder and Lustik 2007). The historical origins and emergence of political democracy should be studied as a macro-historical process that expanded from a small number of democracies to about 50 % of all states. In order to account for this development, Cederman and Gleditsch (2004) introduced an agent-based model combining natural-selection logic with adaptive mechanisms of regime change. The latter is implemented as an empirically calibrated, contextual rule that prompts democratization as an *S*-shaped function of the democratic share of a state's immediate neighborhood. A similar transition rule governs regime change in the opposite direction. The computational results show that regime change and collective security are necessary to produce realistic trajectories of democratization at the systemic level.

Kroneberg and Wimmer (2012) have explored some historical aspects of France socio-political evolution from 1500 to 1900. They have analyzed in formal and computational terms the conditions under which political modernization lead to nation building, to the politicization of ethnic cleavages, or to populism by modeling these three outcomes as more or less encompassing exchange relationships between state elites, counterelites, and the population. The authors show how social actors seek coalitions that grant them the most advantageous exchange of taxation against public goods and of military support against political participation (see also Wimmer 2014).

Sandberg (2011) and Jansson et al. (2013) have experimented system dynamics for studies of the global diffusion of democracy from 1800 to 2000. The dynamic explanation proposed focuses on transitions to democracy, soft power, and communication rates on a global level. The analysis suggests that the transition from democratic experiences ('the soft power of democracy') can be estimated from the systems dynamics simulation of an extended adoption-of-innovations model. Soft power, fueled by the growth in communications worldwide, is today the major force behind the diffusion of democracy. The findings indicate the applicability of system dynamics simulation tools for the analysis of political change over time in the world system of polities.

These are not the only historical subjects that can be explored using computational simulation tools and techniques. The amount of information coming from sources as historical census has allowed an interest for simulating demographic trends from the recent past (Silverman et al. 2011, 2014). An early example of this trend is Whitmore's work on simulating Amerindian depopulation in colonial Mexico (Zubrow 1990; Whitmore 1992). Gonzalez-Bailón and Murphy (2013) have built an agent-based simulation, incorporating geographic and demographic data from nineteenth-century France, to study the role of social interactions in fertility decisions. The simulation made experimentation possible in a context where other empirical strategies were precluded by a lack of data. The authors evaluated how different decision rules, with and without interdependent decision-making, caused variations in population growth and fertility levels. The analyses show that incorporating social influence into the model allows empirically observed behavior to be mimicked, especially at a national level. These findings shed light on individual-level mechanisms through which the French demographic transition may have developed. Bar and Leukhina (2010) have worked on the demographic transition related with the industrial revolution (see also Skirbekk et al. 2015). Going beyond pure demographic models, Wu et al. (2011) have created an agent-based simulation of the spatial evolution of the historical population in China. (See also Zhao 2000).

Also related with the modeling of population trends in the recent past, there is an increasing interest in historical changes in land use as a subject of computer simulations to understand the evolution of modern cities and urbanization processes (Ruggles 1993; Zhao 1994; Parker et al. 2003; Manson 2005; Matthews et al. 2007; Entwisle et al. 2008; Rindfuss et al. 2008; Arce-Nazario 2007; Bretagnolle and Pumain 2010; Komlos and Kim 1990; Le et al. 2010; Fu et al. 2010; Long et al. 2014; Magliocca et al. 2015; Chang-Martínez et al. 2015; Heppenstall et al. 2016). In many cases, cellular automata and agent integrated models are developed based on the prior research of to simulate land use and cover change. In such integrated cases, every cell is used to store the land use change related information of the location where the cell posits, and sense the land use change information of the cells in the neighborhood. Agents, with different roles, calculate the information stored in the cells and do the logistic decision of whether the cells change their states. Therefore, the model has capability of complex computation and a global dynamics.

Gasmi et al. (2015) propose a methodology to build agent-based models of the management of floods in Hà Nội (Việt Nam) in 1926. The authors have collected, digitized and indexed numerous historical documents from various sources, built a historical geographic information system to represent the environment and flooding events and finally designed an agent-based model of human activities in this reconstructed environment. They then show how this model can be useful to understand the decisions made by the different actors during this event, testing multiple scenarios and answering several questions concerning the management of the flooding events.

A possible criticism about the idea of simulating the past and the analytical explanation of social dynamics that generated our social, economic, political and cultural present would be the impossibility of simulating the historical evolution of complex polities in modern times for reasons of scale: to be fully capable of understanding historical dynamics of ancient empires and modern nations we would need to create artificial societies of such complexity that any computer could run the simulation. Nevertheless, the current use of agent-base modeling and related techniques to understand modern economics and modern social and political organization clearly indicates the opposite. If we consider the number of actual publications, it would seem that simulating the present is easier than simulating the past, and that simulating the recent past should be easier than simulate the most ancient human societies (Tesfatsion 2002; Batty 2007; Squazzonni 2012; Cioffi-Revilla 2014).

The amount of qualitative and quantitative historical data about the recent present may allow the historian-computationalist to go beyond the generic and abstract scales we have detailed up to now (households, families, communities, institutions, etc.) and introduce the replica of real people that once existed and we know for certain what they really did. Saqalli and Baum (Chap. 8) suggest the idoneity of two general scales for the computer simulation of social dynamics:

- The level of the village/hamlet (defined here along the more adequate word "terroir") unit is often used because it is the functional unit of management of a landscape, the geographic expression of a combination of rationalities that have to interact altogether. Building a model of one simulated entity below this level is impossible regarding the importance of such interactions, both direct (marriages and other social interactions but also mutual manpower support for instance). Roughly, it is the level in which micro-economic rationality can be considered in order to analyze and explain differences in the use of natural resources;
- The level of the territory that corresponds to a culture or a group of cultures. Roughly, it is the level in which macro-economic rationality can be assessed, assuming a certain homogeneity regarding the use of natural resources within this culture comparing to others. A main aspect here is to analyze the impacts of a homogenous use of these resources;

Would it be possible going beyond those general scales? Some experiments have been published to consider the historical simulation at the level of the individual. Yang et al. (2010) propose the use of a pattern oriented inverse simulation (PIS) to analyze a particular family line with more successful candidates in the civil service examination in imperial China. Two relevant patterns observed in the real family system are employed to decode family strategies along such an elite family line. The authors implemented PIS through inverse simulation techniques, by fitting the simulated results to the real genealogical data arranged in time-series as patterns. In case all those techniques allow us to use the individual as a real unit of analysis in a history study, then can we simulate the past at the level of what historic people really did? For instance, can we create a model for European artistic development in the last centuries with virtual simulations of known artists and musicians? We have detailed life stories of those individuals and given the current technology of agent based systems, there is no doubt that we can recreate the world, understanding individual behavior (Düring et al. 2011; Novak et al. 2014). Some pioneering work on this line has been initiated by Schich et al. (2014), Medina (2014), Park et al. (2015). The same could be made for other historical events, like World War II, from the point of view of Churchill, Himmler, Guderian, Montgomery, Eisenhower or any private that we know fought on that war and whose actions affected other people (see Alexander and Danowski 1990; Wetherell 1998; Gould 2003; Lemercier 2005, 2012; Boyer 2008; Hamill and Gilbert 2009).

Simulating historical events in full detail can be enormously costly, however. Therefore most computer simulations today vary the detail at which they simulate various events. In general, the level of detail appropriate for any one place depends on how much more expensive it is to produce such detail, and on how influential larger errors are in producing errors in the final results of interest. Since it is harder to vary the simulation detail in role-playing simulations containing real people, these simulations tend to have some boundaries in space and time at which the simulation ends (Hanson 2001).

1.3 Predicting the Future

As it has been shown all along this introductory chapter, the use of simulations that integrate disparate quantitative time series data and other time-oriented information into a unified formal presentation can reveal patterns, causes, probabilities, and possibilities across complex social, technological, economic, and political systems. Cycles, waves, logistics curves, and other archetypal patterns, when laid over historical data, can provide a deeper understanding of the dynamics of change. Timelines and these archetypal change patterns can also be used in the study of human change in the long run. In fact, a big number of publications are addressed precisely to this goal (Korotayev 2005, 2006; Korotayev et al. 2014; Grinin 2012; Grinin and Korotayev 2009; Sulakshin 2010; Hazy and Ashley 2011; Broadberry 2012; Foreman-Peck 2014; el-Muwaqqar 2014). Beyond the obvious interest of this endeavor for understanding the logic of the present in which we live in terms of the dynamics on very long periods of time, we need to ask whether we can go beyond and make the biggest question: would it be possible to predict the future given that we have already simulated the historical period that brought us until the present? In the last few decades, the reality of global changes has led many areas of science to explore possible futures. Public awareness and demand are indeed now pressing for clear results and tools to facilitate decision making.

One of the most influential arguments against scientific history was formulated by the philosopher Karl Popper (1957). Popper's main point was that because the future course of human history is critically affected by the development of knowledge, and because future scientific and technological discoveries cannot be predicted, a predictive science of human history is in principle impossible. However, the notion of *prediction* in science is not limited to forecasting the future. The paradigmatic example is the weather, which cannot be forecast more than 7–10 days in the future, even though we perfectly well understand the laws of hydrodynamics underlying weather fluctuations. However, because the dynamical system governing weather is in a chaotic regime and our measurements of initial conditions are not infinitely accurate, long-term prediction of weather is impossible.

In fact, the future is in principle unpredictable. In social life rare events with huge consequences, occur with greater frequency than in purely physical applications (Taleb 2010). The difference, however, is quantitative, not qualitative. Bridges collapse, space shuttles explode, and hurricanes strike from seemingly blue skies. However, we do not decide, on the basis of such prediction failures, that there are no laws of physics. Prediction is an inherent part of science, but not in the narrow sense of forecasting the future. *Scientific prediction* (to distinguish it from the common usage, which is closer in meaning to "prophecy") is used in empirical tests of scientific theories. Scientific prediction inverses the logic of forecasting: whereas in making forecasts we assume the validity of the underlying theory and want to know what will happen to observables, in a scientific prediction exercise we want to use the degree of match between observables and predictions to infer the validity of the theory (Turchin 2008, 2011).

Thinking about the future can take numerous forms, varying from planning actions to foreseeing possible scenarios by means of knowledge and informed guesses, or speculations and intuitions, or imagination and creativity (Von Stackelberg 2009; de Vito and Della Sala 2011). We are limiting the possibilities here to what can be formally extrapolated from the knowledge of the past. If there some kind of linearity in the dependence relationships empirically determined between temporally ordered events, we can extrapolate new events using linear and non-linear multiple regression statistical methods (Kantz and Schreiber 2004). Obviously, nothing in historical dynamics is so easy, and here unpredictability seems to reign. According to Hunemann (2012), the idea of future predictability intuitively means that when the initial state of a system is changed, there is some polynomial function of the predicted result that would yield the correct prediction for the subsequent new final state. Imagine a system with a given initial state (i), i.e., an initial value of the descriptive state variables or initial position in the state space, and a small range (d) of values around those initial values. This system allows predictions if the final values it reaches, starting from all different initial values in $[i - d; i + d]$, are in a range $f(d)$ which is not too much larger than the range (d) of initial values. If not, it means that the margin of error (represented here by d) of measurements of those initial values will not ensure that the final result yielded by calculating the final state is in a same or analogous margin of error, so there will be no possible prediction. If the future is unpredictable, then tracking down the causal trajectory of one event in the present will quickly become computationally intractable and thus impossible.

To our surprise, many aspects of human life can be extrapolated to some comparatively near future using relatively simple statistical models. This approach has had certain success in economy, as a side effect of path analysis studies (Nelson and Winter 1982; David 2001; Garrouste and Ioannides 2001; Höjer and Mattsson 2000; Martin and Sunley 2006; Vergne and Durand 2010). Chen et al. 2003 have presented a novel methodology for predicting future outcomes that uses small numbers of individuals participating in an imperfect information market. By determining their risk attitudes and performing a nonlinear aggregation of their predictions, we are able to assess the probability of the future outcome of an uncertain event and compare it to both the objective probability of its occurrence and the performance of the market as a whole.

In the same way, the future of political issues can also be examined from the point of view of the directed temporal dependencies among a set of social or cultural events. Relevant here is the pioneering work by Douglass North (1994), who generalized path dependence analysis making it the basis of a theory of institutional change. North's translation of the path dependence thesis to institutional change associates historical continuity of all kinds with the path dependence conception. The path dependence thesis serves as an explanation for long-term stability of institutions with different degrees of success and for the predominance of technologies and products, the optimality of which is called into question. The arguments primarily turn against economic equilibrium models in which efficiency is achieved in a state of equilibrium. They are also directed against the notion that "perfect" markets ensure efficient institutions ("invisible hand"). The currently very intense discussion of the path dependence concept in the social sciences is particularly influenced by the work of political scientist Paul Pierson (Pierson 2000; Kay 2005; Howlett and Rayner 2006; Schrodt 2006; Attinà 2007; Brandt et al. 2011; Schreyögg et al. 2011). As an example, we can quote the research work by Bechtel and Leuffen (2010) forecasting European Union politics using time series analysis. Authors like Bennet (2008), Bhavnani et al. (2008), Rost et al. (2009), Ward et al. (2010), Braha (2012), Schrodt et al., (2013) have used agent-based computational framework for predicting the onset and duration of civil wars as a consequence of the particular dependence between natural resources, ethnicity and politics. These investigations attempt to provide the policy making community with systematic ex ante forecasts of political events and trends (Agami et al., 2008; Schneider et al. 2010).

Visualizing possible futures of humanity is no more a science fiction dream (Kelly and Kelly 2002; Bishop et al. 2007; Duinker and Greig 2007; Schubert 2015; Zackery et al. 2015). The Integrated History and future of People of Earth (IHOPE) initiative is a global network of researchers and research projects with the goal of projecting, with more confidence and skill, options for the future of humanity and Earth systems. These projections will be based on models that have been tested against the integrated history and with contributions from knowledge of the Earth's integrated record of biophysical and human system changes over past millennia and tested human-environment system models against the integrated history to better understand the socio-ecological dynamics of human history (Costanza et al. 2012; Braje 2015). And this is not the only project for developing possible future scenarios that can be considered the consequences of what we are doing now, and what our ancestors did before us (Hajkovitz et al. 2012).

Anticipating the future is both a social obligation and intellectual challenge that no scientific discipline can escape. In any case, we should ask whether the future of human events will resemble what we know about the past. The use of formal computational and mathematical approaches does not impose such conclusion, because the same causal mechanism can produce different consequences according to the local circumstances. After all, the extrapolated future is just a probabilistic prediction and not a real fact (Tetlock 1999): once a relevant path has been defined between successive events, when looking into the future, the degree of predictability gradually goes down the further we look and uncertainty goes up. In the very short-term, predictability may be high and forecasting is the working planning mode of choice. In the very long term, everything is uncertain and attempts to planning demonstrate diminishing returns. In the middle zone, there is a level of predictability nut, considerable uncertainty scenarios (Kaivo-oja et al. 2004). Whatever the specific definition, the common denominator of any kind of prediction is a reference to the future. This implies that all sources of uncertainty associated with describing present and past must also be associated with forecasting —and one more: the specification error inherent in the future dimension. In particular, this error should be associated with the distinction between causality and correlation, i.e., the understanding of behavior, the necessary prerequisite for prediction. Thus, the key representational problem, the gap between model and reality, and the conditions for controlling that gap, becomes particularly evident in forecasting (Strand 1999).

1.4 Conclusions. Rethinking the Way the Past Can Be Made Understandable

As suggested by Saqalli and Baum in their contribution to this volume (Chap. 8), three goals may be assigned to modelling past social dynamics: describing, understanding and predicting. As it is the fate of history and archaeology to draw conclusions on a sometimes very narrow database, because we hardly know everything having happened years, centuries or millennia ago, it is necessary to continuously develop and adapt hypotheses to conceptualize the most probable historical scenario proposals and to eliminate the less plausible ones, the overly too simplistic, such as the one "single cause" cliché (climate, volcano, flood). This is possible, because a wide range of historical scenarios may be reconstructed by varying certain input parameters. In the computer, we would explore (by altering the variables) the entire possible range of outcomes for different past behaviors. The idea is then simulating inside a computer what we know about actions having been performed in the past and experimenting with the effects they may produce in such a virtual world. History runs only once. However, in the computer, it can run over and over again.

By conceptualizing a dynamical and extensible simulation platform, researchers and domain experts are provided with a tool for specifying and formulating own hypotheses, assumptions and discoveries (Timm et al., Chap. 2). Crucially, the simulation itself is claimed to carry the central explanatory role: it is the fit of the generated data, or the identification of generating agents and their rules of behavior, that purportedly does the explaining. The simulation either may provide a test of the models and its underlying theory, if any, or may simply allow the experimenter to observe and record the behavior of the target system. As the emphasis shifts from describing the behavior of a target system to the proper understanding of social systems through time, so the objective of historical research changes to the experimental manipulation of a possible scenario. With the possibility of constructing artificial systems reproducing in silico what the scientist believes people did in the past, a new methodology of scientific inquiry becomes possible. In this model of research, the target is no more a natural society but an artificial one, existing only as lines of computer code, and giving the idea of social activity. The value of creating artificial societies is not to create new entities for their own sake, but observing theoretical models performing on a testbed.

A common place of development of the historical simulations should be this focus on the understanding of the processes underlying social change, the evolution of the simulation with the representation of stability and change of social simulated process. May be this is what really matters to us, understanding the process and not only making emphasis on the results and the possible predictions of the models. The way an economist or a sociologist mainly seek to understand analytical results to understand the models is a clear example. To simulate is to understand how a model behaves, a social historical model is a formalization of an historical explanation and it is also the explicitation of all the assumptions implicit in the proposed model. The main value of creating artificial societies is not to create new entities for their own sake, but observing theoretical models performing on a testbed.

Computer simulation imitates the past through a computer reproduction of individual actions of agents, in response to a historically justified calibration of the virtual world in which they moved (Caughey 1972). Thus computed results are obtained as the effects of individual actions in a virtual environment and the impact that these environment has over the agents. The fact that the results "fit" with the empirical description of change it does not mean that the causes of changes are isomorphic to the actions implemented in the simulation. A computational model that is able to generate results similar to the available empirical evidence of a historical situation is necessary but not sufficient for explanation (Güner-Yanoff 2009). The level of abstraction of a model will depend on previous decisions about the scale use in the model, about what intends to explain and about the data available to compare the model predictions with what we can observe in the real world. The result is never a plurality of possible explanations, but a potentially very high number of degrees of freedom in any explanatory implicit decision. The decisions we make when accepting an explanation could be multiple and diverse.

It is important to recognize that, as a series of languages, rather than as a single technique, computer simulation can be used for different purposes and in a variety of theoretical frameworks. The use of artificial intelligence theories and techniques offers different advantages to scholars with a "post-modern" or hermeneutic idea of humanities. On the one hand it is important to mention the current trend on cognitive modeling and belief-desire-intention architectures for designing more "human-like" computer agents. It may help researchers in exploring non rational ways of decision making. On the other hand, the fact that a virtual past resides in a computer and it can be modified according to the needs of the human agent interacting with it contributes to change the traditional idea of the immutability of scientific theories. A computer program can be modified and altered at any time, and the consequences of modifications are immediately available to the user. Explanations appear to be as a result as flexible tools in the hands of people, used for anything the user need.

Is this a radically new way of understanding the past? In 2001, R. Hanson wrote: "We expect our descendants to run historical simulations for several different kinds of reasons. First, some historical simulations will be run for academic or intellectual interest, in order to learn more about what actually happened in the past, or about how history would have changed if conditions had changed. Other historical simulations, however, perhaps the vast majority, will be created for their story-telling and entertainment value" (Hanson 2001). Some interesting advances have already been made in this second aspect, in the use of virtual reality methods and simulated historical scenarios as a teaching tool in e-learning environments (Luch and Tamura 1999; Squire and Barab 2004; Allison 2008; Greengrass and Hughes 2008; Bogdanovych et al. 2012; Winnerling 2014; Smart et al. 2015; Telles and Alves 2015). Nevertheless, if we look at the actual impact of formal theories and computational tools and techniques in the domain of academic research, the results are slightly disappointing. They are not disappointing because "computing" has failed to do what it intended to do, which was to provide "history" with computerized tools and methods historians could use to expand the possibilities and to improve the quality of their research, but because most "historians" have failed to acknowledge many of the tools "computing" had come up with (Munro 2000; Boonstra et al. 2004). Within the humanities, computational modeling is infrequent at best, given the reticence of a significant portion of the humanistic community to technology, and the doubts [of many] as to whether the complex behavior of humans is even open to modelling through the reduction of our behavior to a few fundamental elements, that is to say, those that define us as human (Suarez and Sancho 2011).

Turchin (2008, 2011) considers there are two major reasons explaining this failure. First, computational simulation has been inspired directly by successes in physical sciences. Yet physicists traditionally chose to deal with systems and phenomena that are very different from those in history. Physicists tend to choose very simple systems with few interacting components (such as the solar system, the hydrogen atom, etc.) or with systems consisting of a huge number of identical components (as in the modynamics). As a result, very precise quantitative predictions can be made and empirically tested. But even in physical applications, such systems are rare, and in social sciences only very trivial questions can be reduced to such simplicity. Real societies always consist of many qualitatively and quantitatively different agents interacting in very complex ways. Furthermore, societies are not closed systems: they are strongly affected by exogenous forces, such as other human societies and by the physical world. Thus, it is not surprising that traditional physical approaches based on simple models should fail in historical applications. The second reason considered by Peter Turchin is that quantitative approaches typically employed by physicists require huge amounts of precisely measured data. For example, a physicist studying nonlinear laser dynamics would without further ado construct a highly controlled lab apparatus and proceed collecting hundreds of thousands of extremely accurate measurements. Then she or he will analyze these data with sophisticated methods on a high-powered computer. Nothing could be further from the reality encountered by a historical sociologist, who typically lacks data about many aspects of the historical system he is studying, while possessing fragmentary and approximate information about others. For example, one of the most important aspects of any society is just how many members it has. But even this kind of information usually must be reconstructed by historians on the basis of much guesswork.

If these two problems are the real reason why previous attempts failed, then some recent developments in natural sciences provide a basis for hope. First, during the last 20–30 years physicists and biologists have mounted a concerted attack on complex systems. A number of approaches can be cited here: nonlinear dynamics, synergetics, complexity, and so on. The use of powerful computers has been a key element in making these approaches work. Second, biologists, and ecologists in particular, have learned how to deal with short and noisy datasets. Again, plentiful computing power was a key enabler, allowing such computer-intensive approaches as nonlinear model fitting, bootstrapping, and cross-validation.

The main challenges for historical disciplines in operationalizing computational concepts in a science of long-term social dynamics is how can we systematically track and explain non-linear chains of causality that cascade from multi-scale inter-actions among individuals, groups, and the biophysical world up to the emergent level of social organization. This is especially difficult when traditional analyses and narratives are inherently linear and our knowledge of the past is static. Some equation-based models of human behavioral ecology and related approaches can account for non-linear dynamics (Levin et al. 2013; Anderies 2015). However, even these models have difficulty in adequately dealing with the kinds of multi-scale interactions of many spatially and culturally heterogeneous, independent actors. Furthermore, even with a firm understanding of the dynamics of human societies, how can we recognize and account for historical complex dynamics when key features are not preserved in the historical record? Meeting these challenges will require the development and application of robust theory about drivers and nature of long-term social change. Of course, it is impossible to carry out real-world experiments with past human systems—or even with modern ones at the scales of interest to most historians and archaeologists. Computational simulation modeling offers a valuable protocol for combining social theory and historical knowledge to create experimental environments in which to explore non-linear causality in complex systems and generate results that can be evaluated against the empirical historical data.

Therefore, we want to close this introduction to simulating the past theories, techniques and technologies remembering that the starting point of the explanation of prehistoric and ancient times by means of computer methods is not the creation of a particular artificial society that may reproduce what really happened in a remote past but the investigation of the mathematically possible development of specific classes of model systems (pure systems). As these pure systems usually generate a lot more different paths of development than are known from real human history, we should limit these possibilities by introducing constraints from well documented historical and ethnographical narratives or from archaeological data. The historically interesting question is then why these constraints appeared in reality. This approach can be traced back to Gibson's formulation of affordance theory (Gibson 1977, 1979). The relationship between successive historical events afforded by a potential causal factor can be termed an affordance. On this view, an event's historical function reflects the actions that may have been performed there and then by social agents, given both the particular situation (context) and the apparent directionality of the trajectory configured by previous events. In other words, the future state of a society is not predefined as a form of destiny, but there is a sense of directionality in the historical sequence of social actions with a dynamic, sometimes even adaptive, nature. Therefore, understanding those elements of the past that have been seen in the present assumes that the perceived strength of causes can be analyzed under the form of particular connections between the potential cause and the observed effect (Van Overwalle and Van Rooy 1998). In this way, we can understand that affordances are not properties, or at least not always properties (Chemero 2003). Affordances are relations between the abilities of people, their intentions, and what the concrete situation allow to be performed.

For this sort of "affordance-based" explanation be operative, the historian should discover what precipitating conditions generate an increase in the probability of the historical occurrence of an action at some place and moment and constrained by the social and environmental context. Beyond a simple addition of individual random decisions, what happened in the past should be defined in terms of social dispositions or capacities within a system of subjects, intentions, activities, actions and operations, some of them rational, others clearly indeterminate, impulsive or unconscious. The fact that the performance of some social action *A*, in circumstances *T*, had a probability *P* of having caused a change *Y* in some entity *N* (social agent, community of social agents or the nature itself), is a property of the social action *A*. It is a measurement of the intensity of the propensity, tendency, or inclination of certain events to appear in determined causal circumstances. In general, if the potentiality (occurring in a state *S*) to have state property *X* has led to a state *S*′ where indeed *X* holds, then this state property *X* of state *S*′ is called the fulfillment or actualization of the potentiality for *X* occurring in state *S*. A social action or sequence of social actions will be causally related with a state change if and only if the probability for the new state is higher in presence of that action that in its absence. Causal significance of a factor *C* for a factor *E* corresponds to the difference that the presence of *C* makes on *E*. That is, observed changes in the historical record of that particular event are not necessary determined univocally by the agent's will alone, but there is some probability that in some productive, distributive or use contexts, some values are more probable than others are. We are not suggesting that the cause is a probabilistic relationship, but it should be expressed probabilistically given the implicit uncertainty and the lack of any direct reference to what really happened there and then. In these circumstances, a historical situation should be defined as a relatively constant background condition consisting of possible stimuli afforded by the situation itself (the social agents and their environment). Thus, the primary explanandum of historical theory is social capacities: the capacity to work, to produce, to exchange, to interact, to obey, to impose something or someone. Social action appears as transformational processes to which social scientists attribute the achievement of some new state of the world: an end, goal, or result.

In any case, the purpose should be not to replicate the actual processes of historical change, but to obtain useful insights in terms of potentialities, dispositions or causal powers to construct a model to explain the long term social dynamics. Therefore, the starting point of the explanation of social systems by means of computer simulation is not the simulation of one particular system but the investigation of the mathematically possible development of specific classes of model systems (pure systems). As these pure systems usually generate a lot more different paths of development than are known from real human history, the automated archaeologist has to limit these possibilities by introducing known social constraints from social reality. The socially interesting question is then why these constraints appeared in reality. This particular procedure is aptly described by Bateson with the concept of "cybernetic explanation" (Bateson 1957).

We hope that a future society will very likely have the technological ability and the motivation to create large numbers of completely realistic social simulations. Simulated worlds created by such a future society to solve policy, strategic and research issues would most likely be retrospectives, i.e., historical simulations in which artificial intelligence would genuinely address human matters, rather than merely playing the role of a surrogate. These simulations will provide a rich source of information to a future society about how it arrived at its current stage of development as well as how it could avoid repeating the mistakes of the past. Someone has proposed that this future is very near, ca. 2050 (Jenkins 2006). We will rewrite this introduction in 35 years!

Acknowledgments As a direct consequence of an international conference, this chapter (and even the book) could not have been possible without the contribution of many people. We thank all the students and colleagues that contributed to the organization. Special thanks are due to Enrico Crema, Marco Madella, Laura Mameli, Francesc Xavier Miguel Quesada, Flaminio Squazzoni, Xavier Rubio-Campillo and Xavier Vilà. The conference and the book arrived to a safe harbor thanks to founding by the Universitat Autònoma de Barcelona, The Catalan Government-Generalitat de Catalunya (2014 SGR 1169), The Spanish Ministry of Science and Innovation, through Grant No.HAR2012-31036 awarded to J.A. Barceló and Project CSD2010-00034 «Social and environmental transitions: Simulating the past to understand human behavior (CONSOLIDER-INGENIO 2010 program by Spanish Ministry of Science and Innovation, see: http://www.simulpast.es).

We also acknowledge all people at Springer Verlag for their efforts and enthusiasm with this book, and obviously to all authors and contributors to this volume.

References

Aagesen S, Dragićević S (2014) EARLI: a complex systems approach for modeling land-use change and settlement growth in early agricultural societies. In: Computational models of complex systems. Springer International Publishing, pp 119–139

Abbott A (1983) Sequences of social events: concepts and methods for the analysis of order in social processes. Hist Methods: J Quant Interdiscip Hist 16(4):129–147

Acerbi A, Ghirlanda S, Enquist M (2014) Regulatory traits: cultural influences on cultural evolution. In: Evolution, complexity and artificial life. Springer, Berlin, Heidelberg, pp 135–147

Acevedo-Rocha CG, Hoebenreich S, Reetz MT (2014) Iterative saturation mutagenesis: a powerful approach to engineer proteins by systematically simulating Darwinian evolution. In: Directed evolution library creation. Springer, New York, pp 103–128

Ackland GJ, Henry AY, Williams A, Cohen MH (2014) Cultural collapse and system survival due to environmental modification. Computation 2(3):83–101

Ackland GJ, Signitzer M, Stratford K, Cohen MH (2007) Cultural hitchhiking on the wave of advance of beneficial technologies. Proc Natl Acad Sci 104:8714–8719

Agami NME, Omran AMA, Saleh MM, El-Shishiny HEED (2008) An enhanced approach for trend impact analysis. Technol Forecast Soc Change 75(9):1439–1450

Agustí J, Rubio-Campillo X (2016) Were Neanderthals responsible for their own extinction? Quatern Int. doi:10.1016/j.quaint.2016.02.017

Alexander MC, Danowski JA (1990) Analysis of an ancient network: personal communication and the study of social structure in a past society. Soc Netw 12:313–335

Allaby RG, Gutaker R, Clarke AC, Pearson N, Ware R, Palmer SA, Smith O (2015) Using archaeogenomic and computational approaches to unravel the history of local adaptation in crops. Philos Trans R Soc Lond B: Biol Sci 370(1660):20130377

Allaby RG, Brown TA, Fuller DQ (2010) A simulation of the effect of inbreeding on crop domestication genetics with comments on the integration of archaeobotany and genetics: a reply to Honne and Heun. Veg Hist Archaeobotany 19(2):151–158

Allison J (2008) History educators and the challenge of immersive pasts: a critical review of virtual reality 'tools' and history pedagogy. Learn Media Technol 33(4):343–352

Altaweel MR (2008) Investigating agricultural sustainability and strategies in northern Mesopotamia: results produced using a socio-ecological modeling approach. J Archaeol Sci 35(4):821–835

Altaweel MR (2013) Simulating the effects of salinization on irrigation agriculture in southern Mesopotamia. In: Wilkinson TJ, Gibson M, Widell M (eds) Models of Mesopotamian landscapes: how small-scale processes contribute to the growth of early civilizations. Archaeopress, pp 219–239

Altaweel MR, Christiansen J (2004) Simulating a Bronze Age city state under stress. Modeling long-term culture change. Workshop at the Santa Fe Institute, Oct 2004. http://oi.uchicago.edu/OI/PROJ/MASS/papers/SFI2004_MASS_2.pdf. Accessed Apr 2010

Altaweel M, Paulette T (2013) Modeling nomad-sedentary interactions. In: Wilkinson TJ, Gibson M, Widell M (eds) Models of Mesopotamian landscapes: how small-scale processes contribute to the growth of early civilizations. Archaeopress, pp 204–218

Altaweel MR, Alessa LN, Kliskey AD (2009) Forecasting resilience in Arctic societies: creating tools for assessing social-hydrological systems. J Am Water Resour Assoc 45(6):1379–1389

Altaweel M, Sallach D, Macal C (2012) Mobilizing for change: simulating political movements in armed conflicts. Soc Sci Comput Rev 0894439312451106

Altaweel M, Paulette T, Christiansen J (2006) Modeling dynamic human ecologies: examples from Northern Mesopotamia. In: BANEA conference, Edinburgh. http://oi.uchicago.edu/OI/PROJ/MASS/papers/PresentationBanea.pdf. Accessed Apr 2010

Altaweel MR, Alessa LN, Kliskey A, Bone C (2010) A framework to structure agent-based modeling data for social-ecological systems. Struct Dyn 4(1). http://escholarship.org/uc/item/7kw1h48n

Ammerman AJ, Cavalli-Sforza L (1979) The wave of advance model for the spread of agriculture in Europe. In: Transformations: mathematical approaches to culture change, pp 275–294

An L (2012) Modeling human decisions in coupled human and natural systems: review of agent-based models. Ecol Model 229:25–36

Anastassakis G, Panayiotopoulos T (2014) A transparent and decentralized model of perception and action for intelligent virtual agents. Int J Artif Intell Tools 23(04):1460020

Anderies JM (2015) Understanding the dynamics of sustainable social-ecological systems: human behavior, institutions, and regulatory feedback networks. Bull Math Biol 77(2):259–280
Andersson C, Törnberg A, Törnberg P (2014) Societal systems–complex or worse? Futures 63:145–157
Angourakis A, Rondelli B, Stride S, Rubio-Campillo X, Balbo A, Torrano A, Gurt JM (2014) Land use patterns in Central Asia. Step 1: the musical chairs model. J Archaeol Method Theory 21(2):405–425
Angourakis A, Santos JI, Galán JM, Balbo AL (2015) Food for all: an agent-based model to explore the emergence and implications of cooperation for food storage. Environ Archaeol 20(4):349–363
Annila A, Salthe S (2009) Economies evolve by energy dispersal. Entropy 11(4):606–633. doi:10.3390/e11040606
Arce-Nazario JA (2007) Human landscapes have complex trajectories: reconstructing Peruvian Amazon landscape history from 1948 to 2005. Landscape Ecol 22(1):89–101
Arenas M (2012) Simulation of molecular data under diverse evolutionary scenarios. PLoS Comput Biol 8(5):e1002495
Artzrouni M, Komlos J (1985) Population growth through history and the escape from the Malthusian trap: a homeostatic simulation model. Genus 21–39
Atack J (1979) Fact in fiction? The relative costs of steam and water power: a simulation approach. Explor Econ Hist 16(4):409–437
Atran S, Henrich J (2010) The evolution of religion: How cognitive by-products, adaptive learning heuristics, ritual displays, and group competition generate deep commitments to prosocial religions. Biol Theory 5(1):18–30
Attinà F (2007) Theories of long-term change and the future of world political institutions. In: Globalization as evolutionary process: modeling global change, vol 108
Aubin D, Dalmedico AD (2002) Writing the history of dynamical systems and chaos: longue durée and revolution, disciplines and cultures. Historia Mathematica 29(3):273–339
Axelrod R (1997a) Advancing the art of simulation in the social sciences. In: Hegselmann Rainer, Terna Pietro (eds) *Simulating social* phenomena In Rosario Conte. Springer, Berlin, pp 21–40
Axelrod R (1997b) The dissemination of culture: a model with local convergence and global polarization. J Conflict Resolut 41:203–226
Axtell RL (2000) Why agents? On the varied motivations for agent computing in the social sciences. Center on Social and Economic Dynamics Working Paper, 17
Axtell RL, Epstein JM, Dean JS, Gumerman GJ, Swedlund AC, Harburger J, Chakravarty S, Hammond R, Parker J, Parker M (2002) Population growth and collapse in a multiagent model of the Kayenta Anasazi in Long House Valley, vol 99. National Academy of Sciences
Baggaley AW, Boys RJ, Golightly A, Sarson GR, Shukurov A (2012) Inference for population dynamics in the Neolithic period. Ann Appl Stat 6(4):1352–1376
Bak P (2013) How nature works: the science of self-organized criticality. Springer Science & Business Media
Balbo AL, Rubio-Campillo X, Rondelli B, Ramírez M, Lancelotti C, Torrano A, Salpeteur M, Lipovetzky N, Reyes-García V, Montañola C, Madella M (2014) Agent-based simulation of Holocene monsoon precipitation patterns and hunter-gatherer population dynamics in semi-arid environments. J Archaeol Method Theory 21:426–446
Balke T, Gilbert N (2014) How do agents make decisions? A survey. J Artif Soc Soc Simul 17:4
Ball P (2003) The physical modelling of human social systems. Complexus 1(4):190–206
Ball P (2004) Critical mass: how one thing leads to another. Macmillan
Ball P (2007) Social science goes virtual. Nature 448
Balzer W (2015) Scientific simulation as experiment in social science. Philos Inquiry 39(1):26–37
Bankes SC, Lempert R, Popper S (2002) Making computational social science effective: epistemology, methodology, and technology. Soc Sci Comput Rev 20:377–388
Bar M, Leukhina O (2010) Demographic transition and industrial revolution: a macroeconomic investigation. Rev Econ Dyn 13(2):424–451

Barbosa LA, Fontanari JF (2009) Culture–area relation in Axelrod's model for culture dissemination. Theory Biosci 128(4):205–210
Barbujani G, Sokal RR, Oden NL (1995) Indo-European origins: a computer-simulation test of five hypotheses. Am J Phys Anthropol 96(2):109–132
Barceló JA, Bogdanovic I, Del Castillo F (2012) Etnicidad en la prehistoria neolítica. Un estudio computacional. Rubricatum: revista del Museu de Gavà 5:531–538
Barceló JA, Del Castillo MF (2012) Why hunter and gatherers did not die more often? Simulating prehistoric decision making. Archaeology in the digital era. In: Earl G, Sly T, Chrysanthi A, Murrieta-Flores P, Papadopoulos C, Romanowska I, Wheatley D (eds) Papers from the 40th conference on computer applications and quantitative methods in archaeology (CAA), Southampthon, UK. Amsterdam University Press
Barceló JA, Del Castillo MF, Mameli L (2015) The probabilities of prehistoric events: a Bayesian network approach. In: Barceló JA, Bogdanovic I (eds) Mathematics and archaeology. CRC Press, pp 464–483
Barceló JA, Del Castillo MF, Del Olmo R, Mameli L, Miguel FJ, Poza D, Vila X (2013) Social interaction in hunter-gatherer societies. Simulating the consequences of cooperation and social aggregation. Social science computer review. SAGE Publications y Social Science Computing Association
Barceló JA, Del Castillo MF, Del Olmo R, Mameli L, Miguel Quesada FJ, Poza D, Vila X (2013) Simulating Patagonian territoriality in prehistory: space, frontiers and networks among hunter-gatherers. In: Wurzer G, Kowarik K, Reschreiter H (eds) Agent-based modeling and simulation in archaeology. Advances in geographic information science series. Springer, Berlin, p 200
Barton CM (2013) Stories of the past or science of the future? Archaeology and computational social science. In: Bevan A, Lake MW (eds) Computational approaches to archaeological spaces. Left Coast Press, Walnut Creek, pp 151–178
Barton CM (2014) Complexity, social complexity, and modeling. J Archaeol Method Theory 21(2):306–324
Barton CM, Riel-Salvatore J (2012) Agents of change: modeling biocultural evolution in Upper Pleistocene western Eurasia. Adv Complex Syst 15(01–02):1150003
Barton CM, Ullah I, Mitasova H (2010) Computational modeling and Neolithic socioecological dynamics: a case study from southwest Asia. Am Antiq 364–386
Barton CM, Ullah II, Bergin S (2010b) Land use, water and Mediterranean landscapes: modelling long-term dynamics of complex socio-ecological systems. Philos Trans R Soc Lond A: Math Phys and Eng Sci 368(1931):5275–5297
Barton CM, Riel-Salvatore J, Anderies JM, Popescu G (2011) Modeling human ecodynamics and biocultural interactions in the late Pleistocene of western Eurasia. Hum Ecol 39(6):705–725
Barton CM, Ullah IIT, Bergin SM (2012) Looking for the future in the past: long-term change in socioecological systems. Ecol Model 241:42–53. doi:10.1016/j.ecolmodel.2012.02.010
Batty M (2001) Polynucleated urban landscapes. Urban Stud 38(4):635–655
Batty M (2007) Cities and complexity: understanding cities with cellular automata, agent-based models, and fractals. The MIT Press
Bauch CT, McElreath R (2016) Disease dynamics and costly punishment can foster socially imposed monogamy. Nat Commun 7
Baum TG (2014) Models of wetland settlement and associated land use in South-West Germany during the fourth millennium BC. Veg Hist Archaeobotany 23(1):67–80
Baumer E, Tomlinson B (2006) The interconnected roles of abstraction and emergence in artificial societies. In: AAAI fall symposium. Interaction and emergent phenomena in societies of agents. Arlington, VA
Bearman P (2012) On analytical sociology. Sociologica 6(1):0–0
Bechtel W, Richardson RC (1993) Discovering complexity. Decomposition and localization as strategies in scientific research. Princeton University Press, Princeton
Bechtel MM, Leuffen D (2010) Forecasting European Union politics: Real-time forecasts in political time series analysis. Eur Union Polit 11(2):309–327

Bedau MA (2003) Artificial life: organization, adaptation and complexity from the bottom up. Trends Cogn Sci 7(11):505–512
Bedny GZ, Karwowski W (2004) Activity theory as a basis for the study of work. Ergonomics 47(2):134–153
Bekar CT, Reed C (2009) Risk, asset markets and inequality: evidence from Medieval England, vol 79
Belew RK (1990) Evolution, learning, and culture: Computational metaphors for adaptive algorithms. Complex Syst 4(1):11–49
Bell JA (1987) Simulation modelling in archaeology: Reflections and trends. Eur J Oper Res 30(3):243–245
Bennett DS (2008) Governments, civilians, and the evolution of insurgency: modeling the early dynamics of insurgencies. J Artif Soc Soc Simul 11(4):7
Bentley A, Ormerod P (2012) Agents, intelligence, and social atoms. In: Creating consilience: integrating the sciences and the humanities, vol 205
Bentley RA, Brock WA, Caiado CC, O'Brien MJ (2016) Evaluating reproductive decisions as discrete choices under social influence. Philos Trans R Soc B 371(1692):20150154
Bentley RA, Ormerod P, Batty M (2011) Evolving social influence in large populations. Behav Ecol Sociobiol 65(3):537–546
Bentley RA, O'Brien MJ (2015) Collective behaviour, uncertainty and environmental change. Philos Trans R Soc A 373(2055):20140461
Bentley RA, Hahn MW, Shennan SJ (2004) Random drift and culture change. Proc R Soc B 271:1443–1450
Bentley RA, Lake MW, Shennan SJ (2005) Specialisation and wealth inequality in a model of a clustered economic network. J Archaeol Sci 32(9):1346–1356
Bergman N, Haxeltine A, Whitmarsh L, Köhler J, Schilperoord M, Rotmans J (2008) Modelling socio-technical transition patterns and pathways. J Artif Soc Soc Simul 11(3):7
Berman M, Nicolson C, Kofinas G, Tetlichi J, Martin S (2004) Adaptation and sustainability in a small arctic community: results of an agent-based simulation model. Arctic 57(4):401–414
Bernabeu J, Barton CM, Gordó SP, Bergin SM (2015) Modeling initial Neolithic dispersal. The first agricultural groups in West Mediterranean. Ecol Model 307:22–31
Bevan A (2011) Computational models for understanding movement and territory. In Mayoral Herrera V, Celestino Pérez S (eds) Tecnologías de Información Geográfica y análisis Arqueológico del Territorio. Anejos de Archivo Español de Arqueología, Mérida, pp 383–394
Beyer J (2010) The same or not the same-on the variety of mechanisms of path dependence. Int J Soc Sci 5(1):1–11
Beyin A (2011) Upper Pleistocene human dispersals out of Africa: a review of the current state of the debate. Int J Evol Biol 2011, Article ID 615094, 17 pp. (2011). doi:10.4061/2011/615094
Bhavnani R, Miodownik D, Nart J (2008) REsCape: an agent-based framework for modeling resources, ethnicity, and conflict. J Artif Soc Soc Simul 11(27)
Bianchi NP, Marcialis R (2013) The endogenous genesis of Etruscan proto-cities. In: The 31st international conference of the system dynamics society, 21–25 July. Cambridge, MA. http://www.systemdynamics.org/conferences/2013/proceed/papers/P1093.pdf. Accessed 6 Aug 2015
Billari FC, Prskawetz A (eds) (2012) Agent-based computational demography: using simulation to improve our understanding of demographic behaviour. Springer Science & Business Media
Biscione V, Petrosino G, Parisi D (2015) External stores: simulating the evolution of storing goods and its effects on human behaviour. Interact Stud 16(1):118–140
Bishop P, Hines AA, Collins T (2007) The current state of scenario development: an overview of techniques. Foresight 9(1):5–25
Bleed P, Scott DD (2011) Contexts for conflict: conceptual tools for interpreting archaeological reflections of warfare. J Conflict Archaeol 6(1):42–64
Blount J, Gelfond M, Balduccini M (2014) Towards a theory of intentional agents. In: Knowledge representation and reasoning in robotics. AAAI spring symposium series, pp 10–17
Boal KB, Schultz PL (2007) Storytelling, time, and evolution: the role of strategic leadership in complex adaptive systems. Leadersh Q 18(4):411–428

Bocinsky RK (2014) Landscape-based null models for archaeological inference. Ph.D. Disserstation. Washington State University

Bocquet-Appel J-P (2011) The agricultural demographic transition during and after the agriculture inventions. Curr Anthropol 52(S4):S497–S510

Bocquet-Appel JP, Moussa R, Dubouloz J (2014) Multi-agent modelling of the Neolithic LBK. In: Computers applications and quantitative methods in archaeology, Paris, pp 22–25

Bogdanovych A, Ijaz K, Simoff S (2012) The city of uruk: teaching ancient history in a virtual world. In: Intelligent virtual agents. Springer, Berlin, Heidelberg, pp 28–35

Bölöni L (2014) Autobiography based prediction in a situated AGI agent. In: Artificial general intelligence, pp 11–20. Springer International Publishing

Bongard JC (2013) Evolutionary robotics. Commun ACM 56(8):74–83

Boone RB, Galvin KA (2014) Simulation as an approach to social-ecological integration, with an emphasis on agent-based modeling. In: Understanding society and natural resources. Springer, Netherlands, pp 179–202

Boonstra O, Breure L, Doorn P (2004) Past, present and future of historical information science. Hist Soc Res/Historische Sozialforschung 4–132

Bortolini M (2007) Analytical sociology and its discontents. Eur J Soc Theory 10(1):153–172

Bossak BH, Welford MR (2015) Spatio-temporal characteristics of the medieval Black Death. In: Spatial analysis in health geography, Part II infectious disease. Ashgate's geographies of health series

Bosse T, Memon ZA, Treur J (2011) A recursive BDI agent model for theory of mind and its applications. Appl Artif Intell 25(1):1–44

Bostrom N (2012) The superintelligent will: motivation and instrumental rationality in advanced artificial agents. Mind Mach 22(2):71–85

Boudon R (2003) Beyond rational choice theory. Annu Rev Sociol 29(1):1–21

Bouissac P (2015) The grounding of archaeological representation: from imagination to simulation In: How do we imagine the past? In: Gheorghiu D, Bouissac P (eds) On metaphorical thought, experientiality and imagination in archaeology. Cambridge Scholarly Publishers

Boumans IJMM, Hofstede GJ, De Boer IJM, Bokkers EAM (2014) Modeling feeding behavior and associated welfare and productivity of pigs: an agent-based approach. In: Proceedings of measuring behavior 2014

Boumans R, Roman J, Altman I, Kaufman L (2015) The Multiscale Integrated Model of Ecosystem Services (MIMES): simulating the interactions of coupled human and natural systems. Ecosyst Serv 12:30–41

Bowles S (2008) Being human: conflict: Altruism's midwife. Nature 456(7220):326–327

Bowles S (2011) Cultivation of cereals by the first farmers was not more productive than foraging. Proc Natl Acad Sci 108(12):4760–4765

Bowles S, Gintis H (2004) The evolution of strong reciprocity: cooperation in heterogeneous populations. Theor Popul Biol 65(1):17–28

Bowles S, Choi J-K (2013) Coevolution of farming and private property during the early Holocene. Proc Natl Acad Sci 110(22):8830–8835

Bowles S, Smith EA, Mulder MB (2010) The emergence and persistence of inequality in premodern societies. Curr Anthropol 51(1):7–17

Boyd R, Richerson PJ (1987) Evolution of ethnic markers. Cult Anthropol 2:65–79

Boyd R, Richerson PJ, Henrich J (2013) The cultural evolution of technology: facts and theories. In: Cultural evolution: society, technology, language, and religion, pp 119–142

Boyer C (2008) Netzwerke und Geschichte: Netzwerktheorien und Geschichtswissenschaften. In Unfried B (ed) Transnationale Netzwerke im 20. Jahrhundert: Historische Erkundungen zu Ideen und Praktiken, Individuen und Organisationen. (ITH-Tagungsberichte, n° 42). AVA Akad. Verl.-Anst, Leipzig, pp 47–58

Braha D (2012) Global civil unrest: contagion, self-organization, and prediction. PLoS ONE 7(10): e48596. doi:10.1371/journal.pone.0048596

Braje TJ (2015) Earth systems, human agency, and the anthropocene: Planet Earth in the human age. J Archaeol Res 1–28

Brandenburg J-T, Austerlitz F, Toupance B (2012) Impact of fertility transmission and other sociodemographic factors on reproductive success and coalescent trees. Genet Res 94(03): 121–131

Brandt PT, Freeman JR, Schrodt PA (2011) Real time, time series forecasting of inter-and intra-state political conflict. Conflict Manage Peace Sci 28(1):41–64

Brantingham PJ (2003) A neutral model of stone row material procurement. Am Antiq 68: 487–509

Brantingham PJ (2007) A unified evolutionary model of archaeological style and function based on the Price equation. Am Antiq 72(3), 395e416

Bratman ME (1999) [1987] Intention, plans, and practical reason. CSLI Publications. ISBN: 1-57586-192-5

Bremer SA (1977) Simulated worlds: a computer model of national decision-making. Princeton University Press

Bretagnolle A, Pumain D (2010) Simulating urban networks through multiscalar space-time dynamics (Europe and the United States, 17th-20th Centuries). Urban Stud 47(13):2819–2839

Brilhante MF, Gomes MI, Pestana D (2012) Extensions of Verhulst Model in population dynamics and extremes. Chaotic Modell Simul 2(4):575–591

Briz i Godino I, Izquierdo LR, Álvarez M, Caro J, Galán JM, Santos JI, Zurro D (2014a) Ethnoarchaeology of hunter-fishergatherers societies in the Beagle Channel (Tierra del Fuego): ethnographical sources and social simulation. Revista de Arqueología Americana 32:75–98

Briz i Godino I, Santos JI, Galán JM, Caro J, Álvarez M, Zurro D (2014b) Social cooperation and resource management dynamics among late hunter-fisher-gatherer societies in Tierra del Fuego (South America). J Archaeol Method Theory 21(2):343–363

Broadberry, S. (2012) Recent developments in the theory of very long run growth: a historical appraisal. Jahrbuch für Wirtschaftsgeschichte/Econ Hist Yearbook 53(1):277–306

Brookfield JFY (2001) Predicting the future. Nature 411(6841):999–999

Brughmans T (2012) Thinking through networks: a review of formal network methods in archaeology. J Archaeol Method Theory 19:2

Brughmans T, Poblome J (2016) MERCURY: an agent-based model of tableware trade in the Roman East. J Artif Soc Soc Simul 19(1)

Brunk GG (2002) Why do societies collapse? A theory based on self-organized criticality. J Theor Polit 14(2):195–230

Bruno F (2011) Trade networks and economic properties of sugarscape. In: Student papers complex adaptive systems Fall 2011, vol 18

Bryson JJ (2015) Artificial intelligence and pro-social behaviour. In: Collective agency and cooperation in natural and artificial systems. Springer International Publishing, pp 281–306

Bryson JJ, Ando Y, Lehmann H (2007) Agent-based modelling as scientific method: a case study analysing primate social behaviour. Philos Trans R Soc B: Biol Sci 362(1485):1685–1699

Buehner, M. J. (2012) Understanding the past, predicting the future causation, not intentional action, is the root of temporal binding. *Psychological science*, 0956797612444612

Bulbulia J (2011) The hypnotic stag hunt. J Cogn Cult 11(3–4):353–365

Bunge M (1972) Teoría y Realidad. Editorial Ariel, Barcelona

Bunge M (1985) Racionalidad y Realismo. Alianza Editorial, Madrid

Burch S, Shaw A, Dale A, Robinson J (2014) Triggering transformative change: a development path approach to climate change response in communities. Clim Policy 14(4):467–487

Burtsev MS (2005) Artificial life meets anthropology: a case of aggression in primitive societies. Advances in artificial life. Springer, Berlin, Heidelberg, pp 655–664

Butzer KW, Endfield GH (2012) Critical perspectives on historical collapse. Proc Natl Acad Sci 109(10):3628–3631

Caballero A, Botía J, Gómez-Skarmeta A (2011) Using cognitive agents in social simulations. Eng Appl Artif Intell 24(7):1098–1109

Cabana GS, Hunley K, Kaestle FA (2008) Population continuity or replacement? A novel computer simulation approach and its application to the Numic expansion (western Great Basin, USA). Am J Phys Anthropol 135(4):438–447

Cai D (2012) An economic growth model with endogenous carrying capacity and demographic transition. Math Comput Model 55(3):432–441

Caiado CC, Brock WA, Bentley RA, O'Brien MJ (2016) Fitness landscapes among many options under social influence. J Theor Biol

Caldas JC, Coelho H (1999) Te origin of Institutions: socioeconomicsprocesses, choice, norms and conventions. J Artif Soc Soc Simul 2(2). http://jasss.soc.surrey.ac.uk/2/2/1.html

Calisto H, Chandía KJ, Bologna M (2014) Effects of a fluctuating carrying capacity on the generalized Malthus-Verhulst model. Adv Math Phys

Callaghan RT (2003) Prehistoric trade between Ecuador and West Mexico: a computer simulation of coastal voyages. Antiquity 77(298):796–804

Callegari S, Weissmann JD, Tkachenko N, Petersen WP, Lake G, Ponce de León M, Zollikofer CPE (2013) An agent-based model of human dispersals at a global scale. Adv Complex Syst (ACS) 16(04)

Campennì M (2016) Cognitively rich architectures for agent-based models of social behaviors and dynamics: a multi-scale perspective. In: New frontiers in the study of social phenomena, pp 11–40. Springer International Publishing

Cangelosi A, Parisi D (eds) (2002) Simulating the evolution of language. Springer Science & Business Media

Carneiro RL (1970) A theory of the origin of the state. Science 169:733–738

Carrignon S, Montanier JM, Rubio-Campillo X (2015) Modelling the co-evolution of trade and culture in past societies. In: 2015 Winter simulation conference (WSC). IEEE, pp 3949–3960

Cartwright N (1989) Nature's capacities and their measurement. Clarendon Press, Oxford

Castelfranchi C, Conte R, Paolucci M (1998) Normative reputation and the costs of compliance J Artif Soc Soc Simul 1(3). http://jasss.soc.surrey.ac.uk/1/3/3.html

Caughey JL (1972) Simulating the past: a method for using ethnosemantics in historical research. Am Q 626–642

Cecconi F, Parisi D, Antinucci F, Natale F (2006) Simulating the expansion of farming and the differentiation of European languages. In: Laks B (ed) Origin and evolution of languages: approaches, models, paradigms. Oxford University Press

Cecconi F, di Gennaro F, Parisim D (2015) Simulating the emergence of proto-urban centres in ancient Southern Etruria. In: Barceló JA, Bogdanovic I (eds) Mathematics and archaeology. CRC Press, pp 449ff

Cederman LE (2001) Modeling the democratic peace as a Kantian selection process. J Conflict Resolut 45(4):470–502

Cederman LE (2003) Modeling the size of wars: from billiard balls to sandpiles. Am Polit Sci Rev 97(01):135–150

Cederman LE, Gleditsch KS (2004) Conquest and regime change: an evolutionary model of the spread of democracy and peace. Int Stud Q 48(3):603–629

Cederman LE, Wimmer A, Min B (2010) Why do ethnic groups rebel? New data and analysis. World Polit 62(01):87–119

Cederman LE (2005) Computational models of social forms: advancing generative process theory. Am J Sociol 110(4):864–893

Cegielski WH, Rogers JD (2016) Rethinking the role of agent-based modeling in archaeology. J Anthropol Archaeol 41:283–298

Centola D, Gonzalez-Avella JC, Eguiluz VM, San Miguel M (2007) Homophily, cultural drift, and the co-evolution of cultural groups. J Conflict Resolut 51(6):905–929

Centola D, Willer R, Macy M (2005) The emperor's dilemma: a computational model of self-enforcing norms. Am J Sociol 110(4):1009–1040

Ch'ng E, Gaffney VL (2013) Simulation and visualisation of agent survival and settlement behaviours in the hunter-gatherer colonisation of Mesolithic landscapes. In: Visual heritage in the digital age. Springer, London, pp 235–258

Chadefaux T, Helbing D (2010) How wealth accumulation can promote cooperation. PLoS ONE 5(10):e13471

Chadwick RW (2000) Global modeling: origins, assessment, and alternative futures. Simul Gaming 31(1):50–73
Chan MH, Hawkes K, Kim PS (2016) Evolution of longevity, age at last birth and sexual conflict with grandmothering. J Theor Biol
Chandrasekaran B (ed) (2013) Intelligence as adaptive behavior: an experiment in computational neuroethology, vol 6. Academic Press
Chang-Martínez LA, Mas JF, Valle NT, Torres PSU, Folan WJ (2015) Modeling historical land cover and land use: a review from contemporary modeling. ISPRS Int J Geo-Inf 4(4): 1791–1812
Chapman M (1980) Infanticide and fertility among Eskimos: a computer simulation. Am J Phys Anthropol 53(2):317–327
Chella A, Manzotti R (2013) Artificial consciousness. Andrews UK Limited
Chemero Anthony (2003) An outline of a theory of affordances. Ecol Psychol 15(2):181–195
Chen KY, Fine LR, Huberman BA (2003) Predicting the future. Inf Syst Front 5(1):47–61
Cheng JT, Tracy JL, Foulsham T, Kingstone A, Henrich J (2013) Two ways to the top: evidence that dominance and prestige are distinct yet viable avenues to social rank and influence. J Pers Soc Psychol 104(1):103
Chiang Y-S (2015) Good samaritans in networks: an experiment on how networks influence egalitarian sharing and the evolution of inequality. PLoS ONE 10(6):e0128777
Chliaoutakis A, Chalkiadakis G (2015) Utilizing agent-based modeling to gain new insights into the ancient Minoan civilization. In: Proceedings of AAMAS'14, 5–9 May 2014, pp 1371–1372. http://www.intelligence.tuc.gr/~angelos/WorkingPaper.pdf. Accessed16 June 2015
Chliaoutakis A, Chalkiadakis G (2016) Agent-based modeling of ancient societies and their organization structure. Auton Agents Multi-Agent Syst 1–45
Ch'ng E, Stone RJ (2006) Enhancing virtual reality with artificial life: reconstructing a flooded European mesolithic landscape. Presence: Teleoper Virtual Environ 15(3):341–352
Ch'ng E, Gaffney V, Hakvoort G (2014) Stigmergy in comparative settlement choice and palaeoenvironment simulation. Complexity
Choi J-K, Bowles S (2007) The coevolution of parochial altruism and war. Science 318 (5850):636–640
Christiansen, J. and M. Altaweel (2004) Agent-based holistic simulations of Bronze Age Mesopotamian settlement systems. In: Figueiredo A, Velho G (eds) The world is in your eyes. Computer applications in archaeology 2005 Proceedings, CAA. Tomar, Portugal
Christiansen J, Altaweel M (2005) Understanding ancient societies: a new approach using agent-based holistic modeling. Struct Dyn: J Anthropol Rel Sci 1 (2):Article 7
Christiansen J, Altaweel M (2006) Simulation of natural and social process interactions: an example from Bronze Age Mesopotamia. Soc Sci Comput Rev 24(2):209–226
Churchland PM (1989) A neurocomputational perspective: the nature of mind and the structure of science. MIT Press
Cioffi-Revilla C (2005) A canonical theory of origins and development of social complexity. J Math Sociol 29(2):133–153
Cioffi-Revilla C (2009) Simplicity and reality in computational modeling of politics. Comput Math Organ Theory 15(1):26–46
Cioffi-Revilla C (2014) Introduction to computational social science. Principles and applications. Texts in computer science. Springer, Berlin and New York
Cioffi-Revilla C, Rouleau M (2010) MASON RebeLand: an agent-based model of politics, environment, and insurgency. Int Stud Rev 12(1):31–52
Cioffi-Revilla C, Honeychurch W, Rogers JD (2015) MASON hierarchies: a long-range agent model of power, conflict, and environment in inner Asia. In: The complexity of interaction along the Eurasian steppe zone in the first millennium AD: empires, cities, nomads and farmers, Bonn contributions to Asian archaeology. Bonn University Press, Bonn, pp 39–63
Cioffi-Revilla C, Rogers JD, Latek M (2010) The MASON HouseholdsWorld model of pastoral nomad societies. In: Simulating interacting agents and social phenomena. Springer, Japan, pp 193–204

Cioffi-Revilla C, Luke S, Parker DC, Rogers JD, Fitzhugh WW, Honeychurch W, Frohlich B, DePriest P, Amartuvshin C (2007) Agent-based modeling simulation of social adaptation and long-term change in inner Asia. In: Takahashi S, Sallach D, Rouchier J (eds) Advancing social simulation: the first world congress in social simulation. Springer, Tokyo, pp 189–200

Cioffi-Revilla C, Paus S, Luke S, Olds JL, Thomas J (2004) Mnemonic structure and sociality: a computational agent-based simulation model. In: Sallach D, Macal C (eds) Proceedings of the agent 2004 conference on social dynamics: interaction, reflexivity and emergence. Argonne National Laboratory and University of Chicago, Chicago, IL

Cioffi-Revilla Claudio, Honeychurch William, Rogers J Daniel (2013) MASON hierarchies: a long-range agent model of power, conflict, and environment in inner Asia. In: Bemmann J, Brosseder U (eds) The complexity of interaction along the Eurasian Steppe Zone in the first millennium AD: empires, cities, nomads and farmers. Bonn University Press, Bonn

Clancey WJ (1997) Situated cognition: on human knowledge and computer representations. Cambridge University Press, Cambridge

Clark JK, Crabtree SA (2015) Examining social adaptations in a volatile landscape in Northern Mongolia via the agent-based model Ger Grouper. Land 4(1):157–181

Clarkson C, Haslam M, Harris C (2015) When to retouch, haft, or discard? Modeling optimal use/maintenance schedules in lithic tool use. Lithic Technol Syst Evol Theory 117

Clements RR, Hughes RL (2004) Mathematical modelling of a Mediaeval battle: the battle of agincourt, 1415. Math Comput Simul 64(2):259–269

Clemson T, Evans TS (2012) The emergence of leadership in social networks. Physica A 391(4): 1434–1444

Cleuziou S (2009) Extracting wealth from a land of starvation by creating social complexity: a dialogue between archaeology and climate? C R Geosci 341:726–738

Cockburn D, Crabtree SA, Kohler TA, Bocinsky RK (2013) Simulating social and economic specialization in small-scale agricultural societies. J Artif Soc Soc Simul 16(4):4

Codding BF, Bird DW (2015) Behavioral ecology and the future of archaeological science. J Archaeol Sci 56:9–20

Cohen MN (1998) The emergence of health and social inequalities in the archaeological record. Hum Biol Soc Inequality 39:249

Cohen MH (1992) Nonlinearity, disorder, and the spread of neolithic farming and the origin of the Indo-European Languages. In: Abdullaev F, Bishop AR, Pnevmatikos S (eds) Nonlinearity with disorder. Springer, Berlin, Heidelberg, Germany, pp 161–170

Cohen MH, Ackland GJ (2012a) Boundaries between ancient cultures: origins and persistence. Adv Complex Syst 15(01–02):1150004

Cohen MH, Ackland GJ (2012b) Boundaries between ancient cultures: origins and persistence. Adv Complex Syst 15. doi:10.1142/S0219525911003220

Collard M, Buchanan B, Ruttle A, O'Brien MJ (2011) Niche construction and the toolkits of hunter–gatherers and food producers. Biol Theory 6(3):251–259

Collins HM, Kusch M (1998) The shape of actions: what humans and machines can do. MIT Press Cambridge, Massachuset

Conolly J, Colledge S, Shennan S (2008) Founder effect, drift, and adaptive change in domestic crop use in early Neolithic Europe. J Archaeol Sci 35(10):2797–2804

Conte R (2009) From simulation to theory (and backward). In: Squazzoni F (ed) EPOS 2006, LNAI 5466. Springer, Berlin, Heidelberg, pp 29–47

Coreau A, Treyer S, Cheptou PO, Thompson JD, Mermet L (2010) Exploring the difficulties of studying futures in ecology: what do ecological scientists think? Oikos 119(8):1364–1376

Costanza R, Graumlich L, Steffen W, Crumley C, Dearing J, Hibbard K, Leemans R, Redman C, Schimel D (2007) Sustainability or collapse: what can we learn from integrating the history of humans and the rest of nature? AMBIO: J Hum Environ 36(7):522–527

Costanza R, van der Leeuw S, Hibbard K, Aulenbach S, Brewer S, Burek M, Steffen W (2012) Developing an integrated history and future of people on earth (IHOPE). Curr Opin Environ Sustain 4(1):106–114

Costopoulos A (2001) Evaluating the impact of increasing memory on agent behaviour: adaptive patterns in an agent based simulation of subsistence. J Artif Soc Soc Simul 4(4). http://www.soc.surrey.ac.uk/JASSS/4/4/7.html
Costopoulos A (2002) Playful agents, inexorable process: elements of a coherent theory of iteration in anthropological simulation. Archeologia e Calcolatori 13
Costopoulos A (2015) How did sugarscape become a whole society model? In: Wurzer G, Kowarik K, Reschreiter H (eds) Agent-based modeling and simulation in archaeology. Advances in geographic information science. Springer, Berlin, pp 259–269
Costopoulos A, Lake MW (eds) (2010) Simulating change: archaeology into the twenty-first century. University of Utah Press
Cowley SJ (2016) Cognition beyond the body: using ABM to explore cultural ecosystems. In: Agent-based simulation of organizational behavior. Springer International Publishing, pp 43–60
Crabtree SA (2012) Why can't we be friends? Exchange, alliances and aggregation on the Colorado Plateau. Doctoral dissertation, Washington State University
Crabtree SA (2015) Inferring ancestral Pueblo social networks from simulation in the central Mesa Verde. J Archaeol Method Theory 22(1):144–181
Crabtree SA (2016) Simulating littoral trade: modeling the trade of wine in the Bronze to Iron age transition in Southern France. Land 5(1):5
Crabtree SA, Kohler TA (2012) Modelling across millennia: Interdisciplinary paths to ancient socio-ecological systems. Ecol Model 241:2–4
Craenen B, Theodoropoulos G, Suryanarayanan V, Gaffney V, Murgatroyd P, Haldon J (2010) Medieval military logistics: a case for distributed agent-based simulation. In: Proceedings of the 3rd International ICST conference on simulation tools and techniques. ICST (Institute for Computer Sciences, Social-Informatics and Telecommunications Engineering), p 6
Craenen B, Murgatroyd P, Theodoropoulos G, Gaffney V, Suryanarayanan V (2012) MWGrid: a system for distributed agent-based simulation in the digital humanities. In: Proceedings of the 2012 IEEE/ACM 16th international symposium on distributed simulation and real time applications. IEEE Computer Society, pp 124–131
Craver C (2001) Role functions, mechanisms, and hierarchy. Philos Sci 68:53–74
Crayen D, Baten J (2010) New evidence and new methods to measure human capital inequality before and during the industrial revolution: France and the US in the seventeenth to nineteenth centuries. Econ Hist Rev 63(2):452–478
Creary L (1981) Causal explanation and the reality of natural component forces. Pac Philos Q 62 (2):148–157
Crema ER (2014) A simulation model of fission–fusion dynamics and long-term settlement change. J Archaeol Method Theory 21(2):385–404
Crema ER, Edinborough K, Kerig T, Shennan SJ (2014a) An approximate Bayesian computation approach for inferring patterns of cultural evolutionary change. J Archaeol Sci 50:160–170
Crema ER, Kerig T, Shennan S (2014b) Culture, space, and metapopulation: a simulation-based study for evaluating signals of blending and branching. J Archaeol Sci 43:289–298
Cribb R (1987) The logic of the herd: a computer simulation of archaeological herd structure. J Anthropol Archaeol 6(4):376–415
Cristiano C (2000) Through the agents' minds: cognitive mediators of social action. In: Rosselli F (ed) Mind and society: cognitive studies in economics and social sciences, vol 1, no 1, pp 109–140
Curran D, Luciuk L, Newby AG (eds) (2015) Famines in European economic history: the last great European Famines reconsidered. Routledge
Currat M, Silva NM (2013) Investigating European genetic history through computer simulations. Hum Hered 76(3-4):142–153
Czachesz I (2007a) The emergence of early Christian religion toward a naturalistic approach. In: Luomannen P, Pyysiäinen I, Uro R (eds) Explaining early Judaism and Christianity: contributions from cognitive and social science. Brill Biblical Interpretation Series, Leiden, p 89

Czachesz I (2007b) The transmission of early Christian thought: toward a cognitive psychological model. Stud Relig/Sci Religieuses 36(1):65–83
Czaczkes TJ, Czaczkes B, Iglhaut C, Heinze J (2015) Composite collective decision-making. Proc R Soc B 282(1809):20142723
Dalfes HN (1997) Environmental vulnerability of early societies: some reflections on modeling issues. Third millennium BC climate change and old world collapse. Springer, Berlin Heidelberg, pp 691–697
Danielisová A, Olševičová-Štekerová K, Cimler R, Machálek T (2015) Understanding the Iron Age economy: sustainability of agricultural practices under stable population growth. In: Agent-based modeling and simulation in archaeology. Springer International Publishing, pp 183–216
Darden L (2002) Strategies for discovering mechanisms: schema instantiation, modular subassembly, forward/backward chaining. Philos Sci 69:354–365
Dautenhan K (1998) The art of designing socially intelligent agents: science, fiction, and the human in the loop. Appl Artif Intell 12(7–8):573–617
Dautenhan K, Ogdenand B, Quick T (2002) From embodied to socially embedded agents—Implications for interaction-aware robots. Cogn Syst Res 3(3):397–428
David PA (2001) Path dependence, its critics and the quest for 'historical economics'. Evolution and path dependence in economic ideas: Past and present 15:40
David PA (2007) Path dependence: a foundational concept for historical social science. Cliometrica 1(2):91–114
Dávid-Barrett T, Carney J (2015) The deification of historical figures and the emergence of priesthoods as a solution to a network coordination problem. Relig Brain Behav 1–11
Davidson DJ (2010) The applicability of the concept of resilience to social systems: some sources of optimism and nagging doubts. Society and Natural Resources 23(12):1135–1149
Davidsson, P. (2000) Multi Agent Based Simulation: Beyond Social Simulation. In *Multi-Agent-Based Simulation*. S. Moss, P. Davidsson (Ed.). Berlin: Springer-Verlag (Lecture Notes in Computer Science, 1979)
Davidsson, P. (2001) Categories of artificial Societies. In *Engineering Societies in the Agents World II*. A. Omicini, P. Petta, R. Tolksdorf (Ed.). Berlin: Springer (Lecture Notes in Computer Science, 2203)
Davies B, Holdaway SJ, Fanning PC (2015) Modelling the palimpsest: an exploratory agent-based model of surface archaeological deposit formation in a fluvial arid Australian landscape. The Holocene 0959683615609754
Davydov, V. (1999) The content and unsolved problems of activity theory. En perspectives on Activity Theory. Editado por Y. Engeström, R. Miettinen, R.L. Punamäki. Cambridge University Press
Dawid H (2006) Agent-based models of innovation and technological change. Handbook of computational economics 2:1235–1272
De Boer J (2013) A stag hunt with signalling and mutual beliefs. Biol Philos 28(4):559–576
Florio De, Vincenzo et al (2013) Models and concepts for socio-technical complex systems: towards fractal social organizations. Syst Res Behav Sci 30(6):750–772
De la Cruz D, Estévez J, Noriega P, Pérez M, Piqué R, Sabater-Mir J, Villatoro D (2012) Normas en Sociedades Cazadoras-Pescadoras-Recolectoras. Argumentos para el uso de la simulación social basada en agentes. Cuadernos de Prehistoria y Arqueología de la Universidad de Granada 20:149–161
De Oliveira PMC, Stauffer D, Wichmann S, De Oliveira SM (2008) A computer simulation of language families. J Linguist 44(03):659–675
De Vito S, Della Sala S (2011) Predicting the future. Cortex 47(8):1018–1022
Dean JS, Gumerman GJ, Epstein JM, Axtell RL, Swedlund AC, Parker MT, McCarroll S (2000) Understanding Anasazi culture change through agent-based modeling. In: Dynamics in human and primate societies: agent-based modeling of social and spatial processes. Oxford University Press, pp 179–205

Dearing JA, Bullock S, Costanza R, Dawson TP, Edwards ME, Poppy GM, Smith GM (2012) Navigating the perfect storm: research strategies for socialecological systems in a rapidly evolving world. Environ Manage 49(4):767–775

Deguchi H (2011) Economics as an agent-based complex system: toward agent-based social systems sciences. Springer Science & Business Media

Del Castillo MF, Barceló JA, Mameli L, Moreno E (2010) Etnicidad en cazadores-recolectores patagónicos: enfoques desde la simulación computacional. Revista Atlántica-Mediterránea de Prehistoria y Arqueología Social 12(1):35–58

Del Castillo MF, Barceló JA, Mameli L (2013) Formalización y dinámica social: la simulación computacional en arqueología. Atek Na [En la tierra] 3:35–73

Del Castillo MF, Barceló JA, Mameli L, Miguel F, Vila X (2014) Modeling mechanisms of cultural diversity and ethnicity in hunter-gatherers. J Archaeol Method Theory 21(2):364–384. Skibo J, Cameron C (eds) Springer, US

Del Castillo MF, Barceló JA (2013) Why hunter and gatherers did not die more often? Simulating prehistoric decision making. In: Earl G, Sly T, Chrysanthi A, Murrieta-Flores P, Papadopoulos C, Romanowska I, Wheatley D (eds) Archaeology in the digital era. Amsterdam University Press. ISBN: 978 90 8964 663 7

Dendrinos DS, Sonis M (2012) Chaos and socio-spatial dynamics, vol 86. Springer Science & Business Media

Desmet K, Parente SL (2012) The evolution of markets and the revolution of industry: a unified theory of growth. J Econ Growth 17(3):205–234

Di Piazza A, Pearthree E (1999) The spread of the 'Lapita people': a demographic simulation. J Artif Soc Soc Simul 2(3)

Diachenko A, Zubrow EB (2015) Stabilization points in carrying capacity: population growth and migrations. J Neolithic Archaeol 17:1–15

Diamond J, Robinson JA (2010) Natural experiments of history. Harvard University Press

Dickson DB (1980) Ancient agriculture and population at Tikal, Guatemala: an application of linear programming to the simulation of an archaeological problem. Am Antiq 697–712

Dietrich E (ed) (2014) Thinking computers and virtual persons: essays on the intentionality of machines. Academic Press

Dolado R, Beltran FS, Quera V (2014) Modeling the emergence of social structure from a phylogenetic point of view. J Artif Soc Soc Simul 17(1):8

Doran JE, Palmer M (1995b) The EOS project: modelling prehistoric sociocultural trajectories. In: Aplicaciones informaticas en Arqueologia: Teoria y Sistemas, vol I (Proceedings of first international symposium on computing and archaeology, Paris 1991), Nov 1995. Gastiburo S. L., Bilbao, pp 183–198

Doran JE, Palmer M (1995a) The EOS Project: integrating two models of Palaeolithic social change In: Gilbert N, Conte R (eds) Artificial societies: the computer simulation of social life. UCL Press, London, pp 103–125

Doran JE (2000) Trajectories to complexity in artificial societies: rationality, belief and emotions. In: Dynamics in human and primate societies—agent-based modeling of social and spatial processes, pp 89–105

Doran JE, Palmer M, Gilbert GN, Mellars- P (1994) The EOS project: modelling upper paleolithic social change. In: Gilbert GN, Doran J (eds) Simulating societies: the computer simulation of social phenomena. UCL Press, London

Dorward AR (2014) Livelisystems: a conceptual framework integrating social, ecosystem, development, and evolutionary theory. Ecol Soc 19(2):44. doi:10.5751/ES-06494-190244

dos Anjos PL, Aylett R, Cawsey A (2007) Affective adaptation of synthetic social behaviour. In: Affective computing and intelligent interaction. Springer, Berlin, Heidelberg, pp 434–439

Dow SM, Lea SE (2013) Foraging in a changing environment: simulations in the operant laboratory. Quant Anal Behav 6:89–113

Drechsler P, Tiede D (2007) The spread of neolithic herders –a computer aided modeling approach. In: Figueiredo A, Velho G (eds) The world is in your eyes. Computer applications in archaeology. Tomar (Portugal). CAAPortugal, pp 231–236

Drogoul A, Ferber J, Corbara B, Fresneau D (1992) A behavioral simulation model for the study of emergent social structures. In: Toward a practice of autonomous systems, pp 161–170
Düring A, Wahl J (2014) A massacred village community? Agent-based modelling sheds new light on the demography of the Neolithic mass grave of Talheim. Anthropol Anz 71(4): 447–468
Düring BS (2013) Breaking the bond: investigating the Neolithic expansion in Asia Minor in the seventh millennium BC. J World Prehist 26(2):75–100
Düring M (2014) The potential of agent-based modelling for historical research. In: Complexity and the human experience: modeling complexity in the humanities and social sciences, vol 121
Düring M, Kronenwett M, Bixler M, Stark M (2011) VennMaker for Historians: sources, social networks and software. In: Redes: revista hispana para el análisis de redes sociales, vol 21, pp 0421–0452
Duinker PN, Greig LA (2007) Scenario analysis in environmental impact assessment: Improving explorations of the future. Environ Impact Assess Rev 27(3):206–219
Duncan SR, Scott S, Duncan CJ (1993) The dynamics of smallpox epidemics in Britain, 1550–1800. Demography 30(3):405–423
Dutton JE, Roberts LM, Bednar J (2010) Pathways for positive identity construction at work: Four types of positive identity and the building of social resources. Acad Manag Rev 35(2):265–293
Dyble M, Salali GD, Chaudhary N, Page A, Smith D, Thompson J, Migliano AB et al (2015) Sex equality can explain the unique social structure of hunter-gatherer bands. Science 348 (6236):796–798
Dyke B, MacCluer JW (eds) (2014) Computer simulation in human population studies. Academic Press
Edling C (2012) Analytical sociology is a research strategy. Sociologica 6(1):0–0
Edmonds B, Norling E, Hales D (2009) Towards the evolution of social structure. Comput Math Organ Theory 15:78–94
Edmonds B, Meyer R (2013) Simulating social complexity. Springer, Berlin
Edmonds B, Moss S (2011) The importance of representing cognitive processes in multi-agent models. In: Dorffner G, Bischof H, Hornik K (eds) Artificial neural networks—ICANN 2001, Lecture notes in computer science, vol 2130, pp 759–766
Edwards A (2000) Looking at action research through the lenses of sociocultural psychology and activity theory. Educ Action Res 8(1):195–204
Eells E (1991) Probabilistic causality. Cambridge University Press, Cambridge
Eerkens JW, Bettinger RL, Richerson PJ (2013) Cultural transmission theory and hunter-gatherer archaeology. In: Cummings V, Jordan P, Zvelebil M (eds) The Oxford handbook of the archaeology and anthropology of hunter-gatherers, pp 1127–1142
Eguíluz VM, Zimmermann MG, Cela-Conde CJ, San Miguel M (2005) Cooperation and the emergence of role differentiation in the dynamics of social networks. Am J Sociol 110(4): 977–1008
Eiben AE (2014) Grand challenges for evolutionary robotics. Front Robot AI 1:4
el-Muwaqqar Q (2014) Long-term landscape, environment and climate change studies, from the past through to predictive models for future developments. Bull Counc Br Res Levant 9(1)
El-Nasr MS, Yen JJ, Ioerger TR (2000) Flame—fuzzy logic adaptive model of emotions. Auton Agent Multi-Agent Syst 3(3):219–257
Elsenbroich C, Gilbert N (2014) The environment and social norms. In: Modelling norms. Springer, Netherlands, pp 85–93
Elster J (1989) Nuts and bolts for the social sciences. Cambridge University Press
Engels F [1883] (1968) Dialéctica de la naturaleza. Editorial Grijalbo, México
Engeström Y (1987) Learning by expanding. Orienta-Konsultit Oy, Helsinki
Enquist M, Ghirlanda S, Eriksson K (2011) Modelling the evolution and diversity of cumulative culture. Philos Trans R Soc B: Biol Sci 366(1563):412–423
Entwisle B, Malanson G, Rindfuss RR, Walsh SJ (2008) An agent-based model of household dynamics and land use change. J Land Use Sci 3(1):73–93

Epstein JM, Axtell R (1996) Growing artificial societies—social science from the bottom up. MIT Press, Cambridge MA
Epstein JM (2006) Generative social science. studies in agent-based computational modeling. Princeton University Press, Princeton
Eriksson A, Manica A (2012) Effect of ancient population structure on the degree of polymorphism shared between modern human populations and ancient hominins. Proc Natl Acad Sci 109(35):13956–13960
Eriksson A, Betti L, Friend A, Lycett S, Singarayer JS, von Cramon-Taubadel N, Valdes PJ, Balloux F, Manica A (2012b) Proc Natl Acad Sci USA 109(40):16089–16094
Ertsen MW (2011) Modelling human agency in ancient irrigation. In: Variabilités Environnementales, Mutations Sociales: Nature, intensités, échelles et temporalités des changements: Proceedings of the XXXIIe rencontres internationales d'archéologie et d'histoire d'Antibes. APDCA
Evers E, de Vries H, Spruijt BM, Sterck EH (2012) Look before you leap-individual variation in social vigilance shapes socio-spatial group properties in an agent-based model. Behav Ecol Sociobiol 66(6):931–945
Evers E, de Vries H, Spruijt B, Sterck EH (2011) Better safe than sorry-socio-spatial group structure emerges from individual variation in fleeing, avoidance or velocity in an agent-based model. PLoS ONE 6(11)
Ewert UC, Sunder M (2011) Trading networks, monopoly, and economic development in Medieval Northern Europe: an agent-based simulation of early hanseatic trade. In: 9th European historical economics society conference, Dublin
Ewert UC, Roehl M, Uhrmacher AM (2001) The role of deliberative agents in analyzing crisis management in pre-modern towns. Sozionik aktuell 3:43–57
Ewert UC, Roehl M, Uhrmacher AM (2003) Consequences of mortality crises in pre-modern European towns: a multiagent-based simulation approach. Physica A 175–196
Ewert UC, Roehl M, Uhrmacher AM (2007) Hunger and market dynamics in pre-modern communities: insights into the effects of market intervention from a multi-agent model. Hist Soc Res/Historische Sozialforschung 122–150
Excoffier L, Ray N (2008) Surfing during population expansions promotes genetic revolutions and structuration. Trends Ecol Evol 23(7):347–351
Faulseit RK (2015) 1. Collapse, resilience, and transformation in complex societies: modeling trends and understanding diversity. In: Beyond collapse: archaeological perspectives on resilience, revitalization, and transformation in complex societies, vol 3, no 34
Faur C, Clavel C, Pesty S, Martin JC (2013) PERSEED: a self-based model of personality for virtual agents inspired by socio-cognitive theories. In: 2013 Humaine association conference on affective computing and intelligent interaction (ACII). IEEE, pp 467–472
Feldman MS, Orlikowski WJ (2011) Theorizing practice and practicing theory. Organ Sci 22(5):1240–1253
Feola G (2014). Societal transformation in response to global environmental change: a review of emerging concepts. Ambio 1–15
Fernández-Márquez CN, Vázquez FJ (2014) A simple emulation-based computational model. J Artif Soc Soc Simul 17(2):8
Figueiredo A, Velho GLC (2001) Complexity in action: the emergence of agro-pastoral societies. In: Stancic Z, Veljanovski T (eds) Computing archaeology for understanding the past (BAR International Series, vol 931). Oxford, ArchaeoPress
Findley M (2008) Agents and conflict: adaptation and the dynamics of war. Complexity 14:22–35
Findley M, Young JK, Shellman SM (2010) Modeling dynamic violence: integrating events, data analysis and agent-based modeling. In: APSA 2010 annual meeting paper
Fishwick PA (1995) Simulation model design and execution: building digital worlds. Prentice Hall
Fitzpatrick SM, Callaghan R (2008) Seafaring simulations and the origin of prehistoric settlers to Madagascar. In: Islands of inquiry: Colonisation, seafaring and the archaeology of maritime landscapes, pp 47–58

Flentge F, Polani D, Uthmann T (2001) Modelling the emergence of possession norms using memes. J Artif Soc Soc Simul 4(4)
Fletcher JB, Apkarian J, Hanneman RA, Inoue H, Lawrence K, Chase-Dunn C (2011) Demographic regulators in small-scale world-systems. Struct Dyn 5(1). http://escholarship.org/uc/item/6kb1k3zk
Flores JC, Bologna M (2013) Troy: A simple nonlinear mathematical perspective. Physica A 392 (19):4683–4687
Flores JC, Bologna M, Urzagasti D (2011) A mathematical model for the Andean Tiwanaku civilization collapse: climate variations. J Theor Biol 291:29–32
Fogu C (2009) Digitalizing historical consciousness. Hist Theory 48(2):103–121
Foley D (1998) Simulating long-run technical change. Department of Economics, Barnard College, Columbia University, New York
Foreman-Peck J (2014) Economic-demographic interactions in long-run growth. Handbook of cliometrics. Springer, Berlin Heidelberg, pp 1–21
Fort J (2011) Vertical cultural transmission effects on demic front propagation: theory and application to the Neolithic transition in Europe. Phys Rev E 83(5):056124
Fort J (2012) Synthesis between demic and cultural diffusion in the Neolithic transition in Europe. PNAS 109:18669–18673
Fort J (2015) Demic and cultural diffusion propagated the Neolithic transition across different regions of Europe. J R Soc Interface 12(20150166):1–8
Fort J, Méndez V (1999) Time-delayed theory of the Neolithic transition in Europe. Phys Rev Lett 82(4):867
Fort J, Crema ER, Madella M (2016) Modelling demic and cultural diffusion—an introduction. Hum Biol 87(3):2
Francfort HP (1997) Archaeological interpretation and non linear dynamic modelling: between metaphor asndf simulation. In: van der Leeuw SE, McGlade J (eds) Time, process and structured transformation in archaeology. Londfon, Routledger
Francfort HP, Lagrange MS, Renaud M (1989) Application des systèmes experts à l'Archéologie de civilisations protohistoriques. CNRS-UPR 315. Technical report. Paris
Frantz C, Purvis MK, Nowostawski M, Savarimuthu BTR (2015) Analysing the apprenticeship system in the maghribi traders coalition. In: Multi-agent-based simulation XV. Springer International Publishing, pp 180–196
Frantz C, Purvis MK, Nowostawski M (2013) Agent-based modeling of information transmission in early historic trading. Soc Sci Comput Rev 0894439313511931
Frantzeskaki N, van Daalen E, Slinger JH (2008) Detecting and directing socioecological transitions—a transitions management approach. In: International society of ecological economics, 8th International conference ISEE 2008 Nairobi: applying ecological economics for social and environmental sustainability, pp 7–11
Friedenberg J (2011) Artificial psychology: the quest for what it means to be human. Psychology Press
Froese T, Gershenson C, Manzanilla LR (2014) Can government be self-organized? A mathematical model of the collective social organization of ancient Teotihuacan, Central Mexico. PLoS ONE 9(10):e109966
Frolova J, Korobitsin V (2002) Simulation of gender artificial society: multi-agent models of subject-object interactions. In: Computational science—ICCS 2002. Springer, Berlin, Heidelberg, pp 226–235
Fu Q, Song J, Mao F, Zhou W (2010) Simulation of city development using cellular automata and agent based integrated model—a case study of Qingdao city. In: 2010 18th International conference on geoinformatics. IEEE, pp 1–4
Fuller DQ, Asouti E, Purugganan M (2012) Cultivation as slow evolutionary entanglement: comparative data on rate and sequence of domestication. Veg Hist Archaeobotany 21(2): 131–145
Gabler BM (2006) Ethnic boundary maintenance and historical archaeology from an agent-based modeling perspective. In: Clark JT, Hagemeister EM (eds) Proceedings CAA conference

digital discovery. Exploring New Frontiers in Human Heritage. CAA2006-computer applications and quantitative methods in archaeology. Proceedings of the 34th conference, Fargo, USA
Gabler BM (2012) Modeling livestock's contribution to the duration of the village farming lifeway in pre-state societies. J Ecol Anthropol 15(1):5–21
Gabora L, Russon A (2011) The evolution of intelligence. In: The Cambridge handbook of intelligence, pp 328–350
Gabora L, Saberi M (2011) An agent-based model of the cognitive mechanisms underlying the origins of creative cultural evolution. In: Proceedings of the 8th ACM conference on Creativity and cognition. ACM
Gabora L, DiPaola S (2012) How did humans become so creative? A computational approach. In: Third international conference on computational creativity
Gabora L, Chia WW, Firouzi H (2013) A computational model of two cognitive transitions underlying cultural evolution. arXiv:1310.4086
Gallagher EM, Shennan SJ, Thomas MG (2015) Transition to farming more likely for small, conservative groups with property rights, but increased productivity is not essential. Proc Natl Acad Sci 112(46):14218–14223
Galor O, Moav O, Vollrath D (2009) Inequality in landownership, the emergence of human-capital promoting institutions, and the great divergence. Rev Econ Stud 76(1):143–179
Garavaglia C (2010) Modelling industrial dynamics with "History-friendly" simulations. Struct Change Econ Dyn 21(4):258–275
Gardner A (2012) Agency uncovered: archaeological perspectives on social agency power and being human. Taylor & Francis
Garfinkel AP, Young DA, Yohe RM (2010) Bighorn hunting, resource depression, and rock art in the Coso Range, eastern California: a computer simulation model. J Archaeol Sci 37(1):42–51
Garrouste P, Ioannides S (eds) (2001) Evolution and path dependence in economic ideas: past and present. Edward Elgar Publishing
Garson GD (2009) Computerized simulation in the social sciences a survey and evaluation. Simul Gaming 40(2):267–279
Gasmi N, Grignard A, Drogoul A, Gaudou B, Taillandier P, Tessier O, An VD (2015) Reproducing and exploring past events using agent-based geo-historical models. In: Multi-agent-based simulation, vol XV. Springer International Publishing, pp 151–163
Gaudart J, Ghassani M, Mintsa J, Waku J, Rachdi M, Doumbo OK, Demongeot J (2010) Demographic and spatial factors as causes of an epidemic spread, the copule approach: application to the retro-prediction of the black death epidemy of 1346. In: 2010 IEEE 24th International conference on advanced information networking and applications workshops (WAINA). IEEE, pp 751–758
Gavin M (2014) Agent-based modeling and historical simulation. Digit Humanit Q 8(4). http://www.digitalhumanities.org/dhq/
Gavrilets S (2012) On the evolutionary origins of the egalitarian syndrome. Proc Natl Acad Sci 109(35):14069–14074
Gavrilets S, Fortunato L (2014) A solution to the collective action problem in between-group conflict with within-group inequality. Nat Commun 5 (2014)
Gavrilets S, Anderson DG, Turchin P (2014) Cycling in the complexity of early societies. Hist Math: Trends Cycles 136
Geard N, McCaw JM, Dorin A, Korb KB, McVernon J (2013) Synthetic population dynamics: a model of household demography. J Artif Soc Soc Simul 16(1):8
Geary DC (2015) Social competition and the evolution of fluid intelligence. In: Handbook of intelligence. Springer, New York, pp 105–119
Gelfand MJ, Jackson JC (2016) From one mind to many: the emerging science of cultural norms. Curr Opin Psychol 8:175–181
Gelfond M, Kahl Y (2014) Knowledge representation, reasoning, and the design of intelligent agents: the answer-set programming approach. Cambridge University Press

Gerbault PASCALE et al (2013) Inferring processes of Neolithic gene-culture co-evolution using genetic and archaeological data: the case of lactase persistence and dairying. In: The origins and spread of domestic animals in Southwest Asia and Europe

Gerbault PI, Grimaldi M, Allaby RG, Rudzinski A, Boivin N, Pires JC, Vigueira C, Dobney K, Gremillion KJ, Barton L, Arroyo Kalin M, Purugganan MD, Rubio de Casas R, Bollongino R, Burger J, Fuller DQ, Bradley DG, Balding DJ, Richerson PJ, Gilbert PTM, Larson G, Thomas MG (2014) Story telling and story testing in domestication: can modeling help? Proc Natl Acad Sci 111:6159–6164

Gerbault P, Roffet-Salque M, Evershed RP, Thomas MG (2013) How long have adult humans been consuming milk? IUBMB Life 65(12):983–990

Gerring J (2008) The mechanismic worldview: thinking inside the box. Br J Polit Sci 38(01): 161–179

Ghorbani A, Bravo G (2016) Managing the commons: a simple model of the emergence of institutions through collective action. Int J Commons 10(1)

Gibson JJ (1977) The theory of affordances. Hilldale, USA

Gibson JJ (1979) The ecological approach to visual perception. Mifflin, Boston

Girardin L, Cederman LE (2007) A roadmap to realistic computational models of Civil Wars. In: Advancing social simulation: the first world congress. Springer, Japan, pp 59–69

Glennan SS (1996) Mechanisms and the nature of causation. Erkenntnis 44(1):49–71

Glennan SS (2002) Rethinking mechanistic explanation. Philos Sci 69(S3):S342–S353

Goertzel B, Pennachin C, Geisweiller N (2014) A generic architecture of human-like cognition. In: Engineering general intelligence, Part 1. Atlantis Press, pp 143–154

Goldstone JA (1991) Revolution and rebellion in the early modern world. University of California Press, Berkeley, CA

Goldstone RL, Ashpole BC (2004) Human foraging behavior in a virtual environment. Psychon Bull Rev 11(3):508–514

Goldstone RL, Roberts ME (2006) Self-organized trail systems in groups of humans. Complexity 11(6):43–50

Goldstone RL, Ashpole BC, Roberts ME (2005) Knowledge of resources and competitors in human foraging. Psychon Bull Rev 12(1):81–87

Goldstone RL, Janssen MA (2005) Computational models of collective behavior. Trends Cogn Sci 9(9):424–430

Gong T, Shuai L (2013) Computer simulation as a scientific approach in evolutionary linguistics. Lang Sci 40:12–23

Gong T, Shuai L (2016) Simulating the effects of cross-generational cultural transmission on language change. In: Towards a theoretical framework for analyzing complex linguistic networks. Springer, Berlin, Heidelberg, pp 237–256

González-Bailón S, Murphy TE (2013) The effects of social interactions on fertility decline in nineteenth-century France: an agent-based simulation experiment. Popul Stud: J Demogr 67(2):135–155. doi:10.1080/00324728.2013.774435

Goodhall SJ (2002) Multi-agent simulation of hunter-gatherer behavior, M.A. Dissertation, Wayne State University

Gordó SP, Bernabeu J, Puchol OG, Barton CM, Bergin SM (2015) The origins of agriculture in Iberia. Documenta Praehistorica 42:117–131

Gould RV (2003) Uses of network tools in comparative historical research. In: Mahoney James, Rueschemeyer Dietrich (eds) Comparative historical analysis in the social sciences. Cambridge University Press, Cambridge, pp 241–269

Gowdy J, Krall L (2014) Agriculture as a major evolutionary transition to human ultrasociality. J Bioecon 16(2):179–202

Gowdy J, Krall L (2015) The economic origins of ultrasociality. Behav Brain Sci 1–63

Gracia-Lázaro G, Lafuerza LF, Floria LM, Moreno Y (2009) Residential segregation and cultural dissemination: an Axelrod-Schelling model. Phys Rev Evol 80(2, 4),046123.1–046123.5

Graham S (2006) Networks, agent-based modeling, and the antonine itineraries. J Mediterranean Archaeol 19(1):45–64

Graham S (2009) Behaviour space: simulating Roman social life and civil violence. Digit Stud/Le champ numérique 1(2)
Graham S (2012) Towards the computational study of the Roman economy: draft. http://electricarchaeology.ca/2012/05/29/towards-the-computational-study-of-the-roman-economy-draft/. Accessed 27 Aug 2015
Graham S, Weingart S (2015) The Equifinality of archaeological networks: an agent-based exploratory lab approach. J Archaeol Method Theory 22(1):248–274
Grand S (2012) Playing god: the historical motivations of artificial life. In: Origin(s) of design in nature. Springer Netherlands, pp 733–748
Gratch J, Hartholt A, Dehghani M, Marsella SS (2013) Virtual humans: a new toolkit for cognitive science research. Appl Artif Intell 19:215–233
Greengrass M, Hughes LM (eds) (2008) The virtual representation of the past, vol 1. Ashgate Publishing, Ltd
Gremillion KJ, Barton L, Piperno DR (2014) Particularism and the retreat from theory in the archaeology of agricultural origins. Proc Natl Acad Sci 111(17):6171–6177
Griffin AF (2011) Emergence of fusion/fission cycling and self-organized criticality from a simulation model of early complex polities. J Archaeol Sci 38(4):873–883
Griffin AF, Stanish C (2007) An agent-based model of prehistoric settlement patterns and political consolidation in the Lake Titicaca Basin of Peru and Bolivia. Struct Dyn 2(2)
Griffin AF, Stanish C (2008) Emergent patterns of political consolidation in ABM simulations of pre-Inca Andean cultures. In: Society for American Archaeology 73rd annual meeting, Vancouver BC, Canada, 28 Mar 2008
Griffith CS, Long BL, Sept JM (2010) HOMINIDS: An agent-based spatial simulation model to evaluate behavioral patterns of early Pleistocene hominids. Ecol Model 221(5):738–760
Grinin LE (2009) The pathways of politogenesis and models of the early state formation. Soc Evol Hist 8(1):92–132
Grinin L (2012) State and socio-political crises in the process of modernization. Cliodyn: J Theor Math Hist 3(1)
Grinin L, Korotayev A (2009) Social macroevolution: growth of the World system integrity and a system of phase transitions. World Futures 65(7):477–506
Grosman L (2005) Computer simulation of variables in models of the origins of agriculture in the Levant. Ph.D. thesis. The Hebrew University, Jerusalem
Gross M (1998) Molecular computation. In: Gramss T et al (eds) Non standard computation. Wiley-VCH, Weinheim
Grossman HI (1991) A general equilibrium model of insurrections. Am Econ Rev 912–921
Grüne-Yanoff T (2015) A cooperative species: human reciprocity and its evolution. J Econ Methodol 22(1):128–134
Grüne-Yanoff T (2009) The explanatory potential of artificial societies. Synthese 169:539–555
Guastello SJ (2013) Chaos, catastrophe, and human affairs: applications of nonlinear dynamics to work, organizations, and social evolution. Psychology Press
Guddemi P (2014) How minds are made, or made up. Cybern Hum Knowing 21(3):81–87
Guedes JD'A, Butler EE (2014) Modeling constraints on the spread of agriculture to Southwest China with thermal niche models. Quat Int 349:29–41
Guillot EG, Hazelton ML, Karafet TM, Lansing JS, Sudoyo H, Cox MP (2015) Relaxed observance of traditional marriage rules allows social connectivity without loss of genetic diversity. Mol Biol Evol msv102
Gumerman GJ, Swedlund AC, Dean JS, Epstein JS (2003) The evolution of social behavior in the prehistoric American Southwest. Artif Life 9(4):435–444
Gummerman GJ (ed) (2003) Dynamics in human and primate societies: agent-based modelling of social and spatial processes. Oxford University Press, New York, pp 107–143
Gurven M, Stieglitz J, Hooper PL, Gomes C, Kaplan H (2012) From the womb to the tomb: the role of transfers in shaping the evolved human life history. Exp Gerontol 47(10):807–813
de Haan JH, Rotmans J (2011) Patterns in transitions: understanding complex chains of change. Technol Forecast Soc Chang 78(1):90–102

Hajkowicz SA, Cook H, Littleboy A (2012) Our future world: global megatrends that will change the way we live. The 2012 revision. CSIRO, Australia
Halevy N, Chou EY, Cohen TR, Livingston RW (2012) Status conferral in intergroup social dilemmas: behavioral antecedents and consequences of prestige and dominance. J Pers Soc Psychol 102(2):351
Hamill L, Gilbert N (2009) Social circles: a simple structure for agent-based social network models. J Artif Soc Soc Simul 12(2):3
Hammond RA, Axelrod R (2006) The evolution of ethnocentrism. J Conflict Resolut 50(6): 926–936
Hanneman RA (1988) Computer-assisted theory building: Modeling dynamic social systems. Sage Publications, Inc.
Hanson R (2001) How to live in a simulation. J Evol Technol 7(1)
Harley CK, Crafts NF (2000) Simulating the two views of the British Industrial Revolution. J Econ Hist 60(03):819–841
Harton HC, Bullock M (2007) Dynamic social impact: a theory of the origins and evolution of culture. Soc Pers Psychol Compass 1(1):521–540
Hatala KG, Wunderlich RE, Dingwall HL, Richmond BG (2016) Interpreting locomotor biomechanics from the morphology of human footprints. J Hum Evol 90:38–48
Haubrich T, Seele S, Herpers R, Bauckhage C, Becker P (2015) Modeling sensation for an intelligent virtual agent's perception process. In: Intelligent virtual agents. Springer International Publishing, pp 87–97
Hawick KA (2013). Dimensional and neighbourhood dependencies of phase transitions in the Axelrod culture dissemination model. In: Proceedings of the IASTED international conference, vol 201, no 3, pp 1–1
Hazelwood L, Steele J (2004) Spatial dynamics of human dispersals: constraints on modelling and archaeological validation. J Archaeol Sci 31(6):669–679
Hazy JK (2008) Toward a theory of leadership in complex systems: computational modeling explorations. Nonlinear Dyn Psychol Life Sci 12(3):281
Hazy JK, Ashley AS (2011) Unfolding the future: bifurcation in organizing form and emergence in social systems. Emergence: Complex Organ 13(3):57
Heckbert S (2013) MayaSim: an agent-based model of the ancient maya social-ecological system. J Artif Soc Soc Simul 16(4):11
Heckbert S, Costanza R, Parrott L (2014) Achieving sustainable societies: lessons from modelling the Ancient Maya. Solution J. http://www.thesolutionsjournal.com/node/237204
Hedström P (2005) Dissecting the social: on the principles of analytical sociology. Cambridge University Press, Cambridge
Hedström P, Bearman P (2009b) What is analytical sociology all about? An introductory essay. In: The Oxford handbook of analytical sociology, pp 3–24
Hedström P, Bearman P (eds) (2009a) The Oxford handbook of analytical sociology. Oxford University Press
Hedström P, Swedberg R (eds) (1998) Social mechanisms. an analytical approach to social theory. Cambridge University Press
Helbing D (ed) (2012) Social self-organization: agent-based simulations and experiments to study emergent social behavior. Springer
Helbing D, Balietti S (2013) How to do agent-based simulations in the future: from modeling social mechanisms to emergent phenomena and interactive systems design. Agent-based modeling. In: Helbing D (ed) Social self-organization. Springer, Berlin, pp 25–70
Helbing D, Yu W, Rauhut H (2011) Self-organization and emergence in social systems: modeling the coevolution of social environments and cooperative behavior. J Math Sociol 35(1–3): 177–208
Hemelrijk CK (1999) An individual–orientated model of the emergence of despotic and egalitarian societies. Proc R Soc Lond B: Biol Sci 266(1417):361–369
Hemelrijk CK (2002) Despotic societies, sexual attraction and the emergence of male 'tolerance': an agent-based model. Behaviour 139(6):729–747

Hemelrijk CK (2004) The use of artificial-life models for the study of social organization. In: Thierry B, Singh M, Kaumanns W (eds) Macaque societies: a model for the study of social organization, vol 41. Cambridge University Press

Hemelrijk CK, Wantia J, Gygax L (2005) The construction of dominance order: comparing performance of five methods using an individual-based model. Behaviour 142:1043–1064

Hendriks-Jansen H (1996) Catching ourselves in the act. situated activity, interactive emergence, evolution, and human thought. The MIT Press, Cambridge (MA)

Henrich J (2001) Cultural transmission and the diffusion of innovations: adoption dynamics indicate that biased cultural transmission is the predominate force in behavioral change. Am Anthropol 103(4):992–1013

Henrich J (2004) Demography and cultural evolution: how adaptive cultural processes can produce maladaptive losses: the Tasmanian case. Am Antiq 69:197–214

Henrich J (2009) The evolution of costly displays, cooperation and religion: credibility enhancing displays and their implications for cultural evolution. Evol Hum Behav 30(4):244–260

Henrich J, Henrich N (2007) Why humans cooperate: a cultural and evolutionary explanation. Oxford University Press, New York

Henrich J, Boyd R (2008) Division of labor, economic specialization, and the evolution of social stratification. Curr Anthropol 49(4):715–724

Henrich J, Gil-White FJ (2001) The evolution of prestige: freely conferred deference as a mechanism for enhancing the benefits of cultural transmission. Evol Hum Behav 22(561):196

Heppenstall A, Malleson N, Crooks A (2016) "Space, the Final Frontier": how good are agent-based models at simulating individuals and space in cities? Systems 4(1):9

Hermann CF, Hermann MG (1967) An attempt to simulate the outbreak of World War I. Am Polit Sci Rev 61(02):400–416

Hervella M et al (2012) Ancient DNA from hunter-gatherer and farmer groups from Northern Spain supports a random dispersion model for the Neolithic expansion into Europe. PLoS ONE 7(4):e34417

Hmeljak, DM, Goldstone RL (2016) Avatars and behavioral experiments: methods for controlled quantitative social behavioral research in virtual worlds. In: Handbook on 3D3C platforms. Springer International Publishing, pp 179–213

Ho WC, Dautenhahn K, Nehaniv CL (2006) A study of episodic memory-based learning and narrative structure for autobiographic agents. In: Proceedings of adaptation in artificial and biological systems, AISB 2006 conference, vol 3, pp 26–29

Hoban S, Bertorelle G, Gaggiotti OE (2012) Computer simulations: tools for population and evolutionary genetics. Nat Rev Genet 13(2):110–122

Hodgson GM, Knudsen T (2008) The medieval emergence of property rights enforcement: a behavioural model without reputational effects. J Econ Behav Organ 68(1):48–62

Hoffrage U, Hertwig R (2012) Simple heuristics in a complex social world. Soc Judgment Decis Making 135–150

Hofstede GJ (2013) Theory in social simulation: status-power theory, national culture and emergence of the glass ceiling. In: Social coordination: principles, artefacts, and theories, pp 21–28

Höjer M, Mattsson LG (2000) Determinism and backcasting in future studies. Futures 32(7): 613–634

Holtz G (2011) Modelling transitions: an appraisal of experiences and suggestions for research. Environ Innov Soc Transitions 1(2):167–186

Hölzchen E, Hertler C, Timm I, Lorig F (2015) Evaluation of Out of Africa hypotheses by means of agent-based modeling. Quat Int

Horiuchi S (2015) Emergence and collapse of the norm of resource sharing around locally abundant resources. J Artif Soc Soc Simul 18(4):7

Hosler D, Sabloff JA, Runge D (1977) Simulation model development: a case study of the Classic Maya collapse. Soc Process Maya Prehist 553–590

Howlett M, Rayner J (2006) Understanding the historical turn in the policy sciences: a critique of stochastic, narrative, path dependency and process-sequencing models of policy-making over time. Policy Sci 39(1):1–18

Hritonenko N, Yatsenko Y (2013) Mathematical models of biological populations. Mathematical modeling in economics, ecology and the environment. Springer, US, pp 133–156

Hughes HP, Clegg CW, Robinson MA, Crowder RM (2012) Agent-based modelling and simulation: the potential contribution to organizational psychology. J Occup Organ Psychol 85(3):487–502

Huneman P (2012) Determinism, predictability and open-ended evolution: lessons from computational emergence. Synthese 185(2):195–214

Huneman P (2014) Mapping an expanding territory: computer simulations in evolutionary biology. Hist Philos Life Sci 36(1):60–89

Hunt BG, Elliott TI (2005) A simulation of the climatic conditions associated with the collapse of the Maya civilization. Clim Change 69(2–3):393–407

Hurley RA (2012) The science of stories: human history and the narrative philosophy of science. Ph.D. thesis, Victoria University of Wellington (Australia). http://researcharchive.vuw.ac.nz/xmlui/bitstream/handle/10063/2227/thesis.pdf?sequence=2. Accessed 24 Aug 2015

Huttegger SM, Skyrms B (2013) Strategic interaction in humans and other animals. Biol Theory 8(2):125–126

Ilachinski A (2004) Artificial war: multiagent-based simulation of combat. World Scientific Publishing, Singapore

Impullitti G, Rebmann CM (2002) An agent-based model of wealth distribution. CEPA Working Paper 2002-15. http://www.newschool.edu/cepa/papers/archive/cepa200215.pdf. Accessed July 2008

In: Thierry B, Singh M, Kaumanns W (eds) Macaque societies: a model for the study of social organization. Cambridge University Press, Cambridge, pp 295–313

Inverno MD, Luck M (2003) Understanding Agent Systems. Springer, Berlin

Isern N, Fort J (2012) Modelling the effect of Mesolithic populations on the slowdown of the Neolithic transition. J Archaeol Sci 39(12):3671–3676

Isern N, Fort J (2008) Cohabitation effect on the slowdown of the Neolithic expansion. © EPL (Europhys Lett) 96, 58002, 2011

Isern N, Fort J (2010) Anisotropic dispersion, space competition and the slowdown of the Neolithic transition. New J Phys 12(12):123002

Isern N, Fort J, Vander Linden M (2012) Space competition and time delays in human range expansions. Application to the neolithic transition. PLoS ONE 7(12)

Iwamura T, Lambin EF, Silvius KM, Luzar JB, Fragoso JM (2014) Agent-based modeling of hunting and subsistence agriculture on indigenous lands: understanding interactions between social and ecological systems. Environ Model Softw 58:109–127

Iwamura T, Lambin EF, Silvius KM, Luzar JB, Fragoso J (2016) Socio–environmental sustainability of indigenous lands: simulating coupled human–natural systems in the Amazon. Front Ecol Environ 14(2):77–83

Iwanaga S, Namatame A (2002) The complexity of collective decision. Nonlinear Dyn Psychol Life Sci 6(2):137–158

Jager W, Janssen MA (2003) Diffusion processes in demographic transitions: a prospect on using multi agent simulation to explore the role of cognitive strategies and social interactions. Physica-Verlag HD

Jahanbazi M, Frantz C, Purvis M, Nowostawski M (2014) Agent-based modelling of primitive human communities. In: 2014 IEEE/WIC/ACM International Joint Conferences on Web Intelligence (WI) and Intelligent Agent Technologies (IAT), vol 3. IEEE, pp 64–71

Janssen MA (2010) Population aggregation in ancient arid environments. Ecol Soc 15(2)

Janssen MA, Ostrom E (2006) Governing social-ecological systems. Handb Comput Econ 2: 1465–1509

Janssen MA, Scheffer M (2004) Overexploitation of renewable resources by ancient societies and the role of sunk-cost effects. Ecol Soc 9(1):6

Janssen MA, Hill K (2014) Benefits of grouping and cooperative hunting among ache hunter–gatherers: insights from an agent-based foraging model. Hum Ecol 42(6):823–835

Janssen MA, Sept JM, Griffith CS (2005) Foraging of *Homo ergaster* and *Australopithecus boisei* in East African environments. In:, Annual Conference of the North American Association for computational social and organizational science NAACSOS Conference 2005, 26–28 June 2005, Notre Dame, Indiana, USA

Jansson F, Lindenfors PP, Sandberg M (2013) Democratic revolutions as institutional innovation diffusion: Rapid adoption and survival of democracy. Technol Forecast Soc Chang 80(8): 1546–1556

Jayyousi TW, Reynolds RG (2013) Using Cultural Algorithms to generate models for archaic urban centers: the Monte Alban example. In: 2013 IEEE Congress on evolutionary computation (CEC). IEEE, pp 300–308

Jeanson R, Fewell JH, Gorelick R, Bertram SM (2007) Emergence of increased division of labor as a function of group size. Behav Ecol Sociobiol 62:289–298

Jenkins P (2006) Historical simulations-motivational, ethical and legal issues. J Futures Stud 11(1):23–42

Johnson CD, Kohler TA, Cowan JA (2005) Modeling historical ecology, thinking about contemporary systems. Am Anthropol 107:96–108

Jones M, Richter T (2014) Long-term landscape, environment and climate change studies, from the past through to predictive models for future developments. In: Environments for multi-agent systems. Lecture notes in computer science, vol 3374, pp 127–149

Kaivo-oja JY, Katko TS, Seppälä OT (2004) Seeking convergence between history and futures research. Futures 36(5):527–547

Kalff, C., T. T. Hills and J. M. Wiener (2010) Human foraging behavior: A virtual reality investigation on area restricted search in humans. *Proceedings of the 32nd Annual Conference of the Cognitive Science Society*

Kalter F, Kroneberg C (2014) Between mechanism talk and mechanism cult: new emphases in explanatory sociology and empirical research. KZfSS Kölner Zeitschrift für Soziologie und Sozialpsychologie 66(1):91–115

Kandler A, Shennan S (2013) A non-equilibrium neutral model for analyzing cultural change. J Theor Biol 330:18e25

Kang JH, Ha SY, Kang K, Jeong E (2014) How do cultural classes emerge from assimilation and distinction? An extension of the Cucker-Smale flocking model. J Math Sociol 38(1):47–71

Kang Y, Tan AH (2013) Self-organizing cognitive models for virtual agents. Intelligent virtual agents. Springer, Berlin, Heidelberg, pp 29–43

Kantz H, Schreiber T (2004) Nonlinear time series analysis, vol 7. Cambridge University Press

Kaur H, Kaur A (2015) Population dynamics in artificial agent societies: a review. Population 4:3

Kausrud KL, Begon M, Ari TB, Viljugrein H, Esper J, Büntgen U, Stenseth NC (2010) Modeling the epidemiological history of plague in Central Asia: palaeoclimatic forcing on a disease system over the past millennium. BMC Biol 8(1):112

Kawecki TJ et al (2012) Experimental evolution. Trends Ecol Evol 27(10):547–560

Kay A (2005) A critique of the use of path dependency in policy studies. Public Adm 83(3): 553–571

Kealy S, Louys J, O'Connor S (2015) Islands under the Sea: a review of early modern human dispersal routes and migration hypotheses through Wallacea. J Island Coastal Archaeol

Keane RE, Parsons RA, Hessburg PF (2002) Estimating historical range and variation of landscape patch dynamics: limitations of the simulation approach. Ecol Modell 151(1):29–49

Kelly SJ, Kelly S (2002) Simulating future trends in wealth inequality. University of Canberra. National Centre for Social and Economic Modelling

Kempe M, Lycett SJ, Mesoudi A (2014) From cultural traditions to cumulative culture: parameterizing the differences between human and nonhuman culture. J Theor Biol 359:29–36

Kempe M, Lycett SJ, Mesoudi A (2012) An experimental test of the accumulated copying error model of cultural mutation for Achedulean handaxe size. PLoS ONE 7(11):e48333

Kennedy WG (2012) Modelling human behaviour in agent-based models. In: Agent-based models of geographical systems. Springer, Netherlands, pp 167–179
Kiesling E, Günther M, Stummer C, Wakolbinger LM (2012) Agent-based simulation of innovation diffusion: a review. Central Eur J Oper
Kim B (2015) Socioeconomic development in the Bronze Age: archaeological understanding of the transition from the early to Middle Bronze Age, South Korea. Asian Perspect 54(1): 144–184
Kim DW, Kim JH, Park SL, Kim KC, Park CS (2013) Traditional vs. cognitive agent simulation. In: 13th International conference of the international building performance simulation association
Kim J-W (2010) Evolution of cultural groups and persistent parochialism. Struct Dyn: eJ Anthropol Rel Sci 4(2). http://escholarship.org/uc/item/2cr2681m
King AJ, Sueur C (2011) Where next? Group coordination and collective decision making by primates. Int J Primatol 32(6):1245–1267
Klemm K, Eguıluz VM, Toral R, San Miguel M (2003) Role of dimensionality in Axelrod's model for the dissemination of cultura. Phys A 327(2003):1–5
Klemm K, Eguíluz VM, Toral R, San Miguel M (2005) Globalization, polarization and cultural drift. J Econ Dyn Control 29:321–334
Kline MA, Boyd R (2010) Population size predicts technological complexity in Oceania. Proc R Soc Lond B: Biol Sci 277(1693):2559–2564
Klügl F, Fehler M, Herrler R (2005) About the role of the environment in multi-agent simulations. In: Environments for multi-agent systems. Springer, Berlin, Heidelberg, pp 127–149
Klüver J (2000) The dynamics and evolution of social systems: new foundations of a mathematical sociology, vol 29. Springer Science & Business Media
Klüver J, Stoica C, Schmidt J (2003) Formal models, social theory and computer simulations: some methodical reflections. J Artif Soc Soc Simul 6(2)
Knappett C, Rivers R, Evans T (2011) The Theran eruption and Minoan palatial collapse: new interpretations gained from modelling the maritime network. Antiquity 85(329):1008–1023
Knappett C, Evans T, Rivers R (2008) Modelling maritime interaction in the Aegean Bronze Age. Antiquity 82(318):1009–1024
Kobti Z, Reynolds RG (2005) Modeling protein exchange across the social network in the village multi-agent simulation. IEEE Int Conf Syst Man Cybern 4(10–12):3197–3203
Koenig A, Scarry CJ, Wheeler BC, Borries C (2013) Variation in grouping patterns, mating systems and social structure: what socio-ecological models attempt to explain. Philos Trans R Soc B: Biol Sci 368(1618):20120348
Kohler TA (2013) How the Pueblos got their sprachbund. J Archaeol Method Theory 20(2): 212–234
Kohler TA, Varien MD (eds) (2012) Emergence and collapse of early villages: models of Central Mesa Verde archaeology. University of California Press
Kohler TA, van der Leeuw SE (eds) (2007) The model-based archaeology of socionatural systems. School for Advanced Research Press
Kohler TA, Crabtree SA, Bocinsky RK, Hooper PL (2015) Sociopolitical evolution in midrange societies: the prehispanic Pueblo Case. In: Principles of complexity: an introduction to complex adaptive systems and human society. http://www.santafe.edu/media/workingpapers/15–04-011.pdf. Accessed 2 June 2016
Kohler TA, Bocinsky RK, Cockburn D, Crabtree SA, Varien MD, Kolm KE, Kobti Z (2012) Modelling prehispanic Pueblo societies in their ecosystems. Ecol Modell 241:30–41
Kohler TA, Carr E (1997) Swarm-based modeling of prehistoric settlement systems in Southwestern North America. In: Johnson I, North M (eds) Proceedings of colloquium II, UISPP, XIIIth Congress, Forli, Italy, Sept 1996. Sydney University Archaeological Methods Series 5. Sydney University, Sydney, Australia
Kohler TA, Gummerman G (eds) (2000) Dynamics in human and primate societies. Santa Fe Institute Studies in the Sciences of Complexity. Oxford University Press

Kohler TA, Yap L (2003) Modeling reciprocal exchange in southwestern societies. Paper presented at the 68th annual meeting of the Society for American Archaeology, Milwaukee, WI. http://www.wsu.edu/%7Evillage/Kohler%20&%20Yap%20SAA%202003.pdf. Accessed July 2007

Kohler TA, Johnson CD, Varien M, Ortman S, Reynolds R, Kobti Z, Cowan J, Kolm K, Smith S, Yap L (2007) Settlement ecodynamics in the prehispanic central Mesa Verde Region. In: Kohler T, van der Leeuw SE (eds) Model-based archaeology of socionatural systems. SAR Press

Kohler TA, Gumerman GJ, Reynolds RG (2005) Simulating ancient societies. Sci Am 293(1): 76–83

Kohler TA, Kresl J, Van West CR, Carr E, Wilshusen R (2000) Be there then: a modeling approach to settlement determinants and spatial efficiency among late ancestral pueblo populations of the Mesa Verde Region, U.S. Southwest. In: Kohler TA, Gumerman GJ (eds) Dynamics in human and primate societies: agent-based modeling of social and spatial processes. Santa Fe Institute and Oxford University Press, pp 145–178

Kohler TA (2003) Agent-based modeling of mesa verde region settlement systems: introduction. Paper presented in symposium "Building Models for Settlement Systems in the Late Prehispanic Mesa Verde Region: An Interdisciplinary Approach" 68th annual meeting of the Society for American Archaeology, Milwaukee, April. http://www.wsu.edu/%7Evillage/Kohler%20SAA%20%2703.pdf. Accessed Mar 2007

Komlos J (1989) Nutrition and economic development in the eighteenth-century Habsburg monarchy: an anthropometric history. Princeton University Press

Komlos J, Kim JH (1990) Estimating trends in historical heights. Hist Methods: J Quant Interdiscip Hist 23(3):116–120

Komlos J, Artzrouni M (1994) Ein Simulationsmodell der Industriellen Revolution. VSWG: Vierteljahrschrift für Sozial-und Wirtschaftsgeschichte, pp 324–338

Komlos J, Nefedov S (2002) A compact macromodel of pre-industrial population growth. Hist Methods: J Quant Interdiscip Hist 35(2):92–94

Kondrashin I (1997) Dialectics of matter. The Pentland Press Ltd, Durham

Koopmans R, Rebers S (2009) Collective action in culturally similar and dissimilar groups: an experiment on parochialism, conditional cooperation, and their linkages. Evol Hum Behav 30(3):201–211

Korotayev A (2005) A compact macromodel of world system evolution. J World-Syst Res 11(1):79–93

Korotayev AV (2006) The world system history periodization and mathematical models of socio historical processes. In: History and mathematics: the problems of periodization of historical macroprocesses, pp 116–167

Korotayev AV, Markov AV, Grinin LE (2014) Mathematical modeling of biological and social phases of big history. In: Teaching and researching big history: exploring a new scholarly field, p 188

Kovacevic M, Shennan S, Vanhaeren M, d'Errico F, Thomas MG (2015) Simulating geographical variation in material culture: were early modern humans in Europe ethnically structured? In: Learning strategies and cultural evolution during the palaeolithic. Springer, Japan, pp 103–120

Kowarik K, Reschreiter H, Wurzer G (2012) Modelling prehistoric mining. Math Model 7(1): 17–29

Kowarik K, Reschreiter H, Wurzer G (2015) Mining with agents: modelling prehistoric mining and prehistoric economy. In: Agent-based modeling and simulation in archaeology. Springer International Publishing, pp 141–159

Koykka C, Wild G (2015) The evolution of group dispersal with leaders and followers. J Theor Biol 371:117–126

Kramer KL, Otárola-Castillo E (2015) When mothers need others: the impact of hominin life history evolution on cooperative breeding. J Hum Evol

Kroneberg C, Wimmer A (2012) Struggling over the boundaries of belonging: a formal model of nation building, ethnic closure, and populism. Am J Sociol 118(1):176–230

Kubat L, Zeman J (1975) Entropy and information in science and philosophy. Elsevier
Kuhn SL (2012) Emergent patterns of creativity and innovation in early technologies. In: Origins of human innovation and creativity. Elsevier, Amsterdam, pp 69–88
Kurzweil R (2012) How to create a mind: the secret of human thought revealed. Penguin
Kutsukake Nobuyuki, Innan Hideki (2013) Simulation-Based likelihood approach for evolutionary models of phenotypic traits on phylogeny. Evolution 67(2):355–367
Kuznar LA (2006) High-fidelity computational social science in anthropology prospects for developing a comparative framework. Soc Sci Comput Rev 24(1):15–29
Kuznar LA, Sedlmeyer R (2005) Collective violence in Darfur: an agent-based model of pastoral nomad/sedentary peasant interaction. Math Anthropol Cult Theory: Int J 1 (4)
Laciana CE, Rovere SL, Podestá GP (2013) Exploring associations between micro-level models of innovation diffusion and emerging macro-level adoption patterns. Phys A: Stat Mech Appl 392(8):1873–1884
Ladefoged TN, Lee CT, Graves MW (2008) Modeling life expectancy and surplus production of dynamic pre-contact territories in leeward Kohala, Hawai 'i. J Anthropol Archaeol 27(1): 93–110
Lagerlöf NP (2003) Mortality and early growth in England, France and Sweden. Scand J Econ 105(3):419–440
Lake MW (2000) MAGICAL computer simulation of Mesolithic foraging. In: Kohler T, Gummermann G (eds) Dynamics in human and primate societies: agent-based modelling of social and spatial processes. Santa Fe Institute, pp 107–143
Lake MW (2014) Trends in archaeological simulation. J Archaeol Method Theory 21(2):258–287
Lake MW (2015) Explaining the past with ABM: on modeling philosophy. In: Wurzer G, Kowarik K, Reschreiter H (eds) Agent-based modeling and simulation in archaeology. Advances in geographic information science. Springer, pp 3–36
Lambert FL (2002) Disorder-a cracked crutch for supporting entropy discussions. J Chem Educ 79:187
Lancelotti C, Madella M, Rubio-Campillo X, Balbo AL, Salpeteur M (2014) Testing the resilience of agro-pastoralists communities in arid margins through ABM. In: Miguel, Amblard, Barceló, Madella (eds) Advances in computational social science and social simulation. Autònoma University of Barcelona, Barcelona. DDD repository: http://ddd.uab.cat/record/128053/
Lanchier N (2012) The Axelrod model for the dissemination of culture revisited. Ann Appl Probab 22(2):860–880
Lane M (2010) The carrying capacity imperative: assessing regional carrying capacity methodologies for sustainable land-use planning. Land Use Policy 27(4):1038–1045
Lanen RJ, Kosian MC, Groenewoudt BJ, Jansma E (2015) Finding a way: modeling landscape prerequisites for Roman and Early-Medieval routes in the Netherlands. Geoarchaeology 30(3):200–222
Larson G, Burger J (2013) A population genetics view of animal domestication. Trends Genet 29(4):197–205
Layton R, O'Hara S, Bilsborough A (2012) Antiquity and social functions of multilevel social organization among human hunter-gatherers. Int J Primatol 33(5):1215–1245
Le Néchet F, Mathian H, Sanders L, Coupé C, Hombert JM (2015) Simulating the effects of local interactions on the Neolithic Bantu migrations. Plurimondi. An international forum for research and debate on human settlements, vol 7, no 15
Le QB, Park SJ, Vlek PL (2010) Land Use Dynamic Simulator (LUDAS): a multi-agent system model for simulating spatio-temporal dynamics of coupled human–landscape system: 2. Scenario-based application for impact assessment of land-use policies. Ecol Inf 5(3):203–221
Leaf M (2008) Indigenous algorithms, organizations, and rationality. Struct Dyn 3(2)
Lee MH, Lacey NJ (2003) The influence of epistemology on the design of artificial agents. Minds Mach 13(3):367–395
Lehman J, Stanley KO (2014) Investigating biological assumptions through radical reimplementation. Artif Life 21(1)

Lei PL, Lin SS, Wang DY, Sun CT (2013) The design of social agents that introduce self-reflection in a simulation environment. J Educ Technol Soc 16(3):152–166
Lemercier C (2005) Analyse de réseaux et histoire. Revue d'histoire moderne et contemporaine 52(2) (Avril-Juin)
Lemercier C (2012) Formal network methods in history: why and how?. Osterreichische Zeitschrift für Geschichtswussenschaften, vol 1. http://halshs.archives-ouvertes.fr/halshs-00521527/fr/
Lemmen C (2012) Changing human-environment interactions in regional transitions to agriculture. Quat Int 279:276
Lemmen C (2015a) Malthusian assumptions, Boserupian response in transition to agriculture models. In: Ester Boserup's legacy on sustainability. Springer Netherlands, pp 87–97
Lemmen C (2015b) Gradient adaptive dynamics describes innovation and resilience at the society scale. In: Barceló JA, Bogdanovic I (eds) Mathematics and archaeology. CRC Press, Boca Raton (FL), pp 405–415
Lemmen C, Wirtz K (2006) Socio-technological revolutions and migration waves re-examining early world history with a mathematical model. The Spread of the Neolithic to Central Europe, Mainz
Lemmen C, Khan A (2011) A simulation of the Neolithic transition in the Indus valley. arXiv: 1110.1091
Lemmen C, Gronenborn D, Wirtz KW (2011) A simulation of the Neolithic transition in Western Eurasia. J Archaeol Sci 38(12):3459–3470
Lemmen C, Haberkorn K, Blender R, Fraedrich K, Wirtz KW (2015) Global land use and technological evolution simulations to quantify interactions between climate and pre-industrial cultures. In: Integrated analysis of interglacial climate dynamics (INTERDYNAMIC). Springer International Publishing, pp 103–108
Leont'ev AN (1974) The problem of activity in psychology. Sov Psychol 13(2):4–33
Lercari N (2016) Simulating history in virtual worlds. In: Handbook on 3D3C platforms. Springer International Publishing, pp 337–352
Letendre K (2012) Variation and organization in social behavior: infectious disease and human intergroup conflict and warfare; and the organization of foraging behavior in harvester ants. The University of New Mexico, Diss
Levin S, Xepapadeas T, Crépin AS, Norberg J, De Zeeuw A, Folke C, Walker B (2013). Social-ecological systems as complex adaptive systems: modeling and policy implications. Environ Dev Econ 18(02):111–132
Levine DK, Modica S (2013) Anti-Malthus: conflict and the evolution of societies. Res Econ 67(4):289–306
Lewontin RC (1996) Evolution as engineering. In: Collado-Vides J, Magasanik B, Smith TF (eds) Integrative approaches to molecular biology. The MIT Press, Cambridge (MA), pp 1–10
Lieberman P (2016) The evolution of language and thought. J Anthropol Sci 94:1–20
Liebowitz SJ, Margolis S (1995) Path dependence, lock-in and history. J Law Econ Organ 11: 205–226. http://wwwpub.utdallas.edu/~liebowit/paths.html
Lim M, Metzler R, Bar-Yam Y (2007) Global pattern formation and ethnic/cultural violence. Science 317(5844):1540–1544
Livni J, Stone L (2015) The stabilizing role of the Sabbath in pre-monarchic Israel: a mathematical model. J Biol Phys 41(2):203–221
Lombardo C (2015) More than a set of principles: analytical sociology at work. Revue européenne des sciences sociales 53(1):293–301
Long Y, Jin X, Yang X, Zhou Y (2014) Reconstruction of historical arable land use patterns using constrained cellular automata: a case study of Jiangsu, China. Appl Geogr 52:67–77
Loper ML, Turnitsa CD (2012) History of combat modeling and distributed simulation. In: Engineering principles of combat modeling and distributed simulation, pp 331–355
Lotka AJ (1910) Contribution to the theory of periodic reaction. J Phys Chem 14(3):271–274
Low BS, Simon CP, Anderson KG, Kermyt G (2002) An evolutionary ecological perspective on demographic transitions: modeling multiple currencies. Am J Hum Biol 14(2):149–167

Lowe JW (1985) The dynamics of apocalypse: a systems simulation of the classic Maya collapse. University of New Mexico Press
Luck M, McBurney P, Preist C (2004) A manifesto for agent technology: towards next generation computing. Auton Agents Multi-Agent Syst 9(3):203–252
Lull V, Micó Pérez R (2011) Archaeology of the origin of the state: the theories. Oxford University Press
Lush NW, Tamura EH (1999) Teaching history through simulation: the Guomindang-communist struggle in rural China. Hist Teacher 355–380
Ma J, Fan M, Ma Y (2012) Programmed interpretation of the life evolution and computer simulation. In: International conference on biomedical engineering and biotechnology (iCBEB), 2012. IEEE
Ma T, Nakamori Y (2005) Agent-based modeling on technological innovation as an evolutionary process. Eur J Oper Res 166(3)
Ma ZS (2015) Towards computational models of animal cognition, an introduction for computer scientists. Cogn Syst Res 33:42–69
Machálek T, Olševičová-Štekerová K, Cimler R (2012) Modelling population dynamics for archaeological simulations. Math Methods Econ 536–539
Machamer P (2002) Activities and causation: the metaphysics and epistemology of mechanisms. Int Stud Philos Sci 18(1)
Machamer P, Darden L, Craver CF (2000) Thinking about mechanisms. Philos Sci 1–25
Macmillan W, Huang HQ (2008) An agent-based simulation model of a primitive agricultural society. Geoforum 39(2):643–658
Makowsky MD, Smaldino PE (2015) The evolution of power and the divergence of cooperative norms. J Econ Behav Organ
Macy MW, Willer R (2002) From factors to actors: computational sociology and agent-based modeling. Annu Rev Sociol 28(1):143–166
Madella M, Rondelli B (eds) (2014) Simulating the past: exploring change through computer simulation in archaeology. Monographic number of J Archaeol Method Theory 21(2)
Madsen ME, Lipo CP (2015) Behavioral modernity and the cultural transmission of structured information: the semantic axelrod model. In Learning strategies and cultural evolution during the palaeolithic. Springer, Japan, pp 67–83
Magliocca NR, Rudel TK, Verburg PH, McConnell WJ, Mertz O, Gerstner K, Ellis EC (2015) Synthesis in land change science: methodological patterns, challenges, and guidelines. Reg Environ Change 15(2):211–226
Mahoney J (2015) Process tracing and historical explanation. Secur Stud 24(2):200–218
Mainzer K (2004) Thinking in complexity. The computational dynamics of matter, mind, and mankind. Springer, Berlin
Malerba F, Nelson R, Orsenigo L, Winter S (1999) History-friendly' models of industry evolution: the computer industry. Ind Corp Change 8(1):3–40
Malleson N (2012) Using agent-based models to simulate crime. Agent-based models of geographical systems. Springer, Netherlands, pp 411–434
Manson SM (2005) Agent-based modeling and genetic programming for modeling land change in the Southern Yucatan Peninsular Region of Mexico. Agricult Ecosyst Environ 111(1):47–62
Manzo G (2010) Analytical sociology and its critics. Eur J Sociol 51(01):129–170
Manzo G (2014) Data, generative models and mechanisms: more on the principles of analytical sociology. In: Analytical sociology. Actions and networks. Wiley, London, pp 4–53
Marean CW et al (2015) A new research strategy for integrating studies of paleoclimate, paleoenvironment, and paleoanthropology. Evol Anthropol: Issues News Rev 24(2):62–72
Mark N (1998) Beyond individual differences: social differentiation from first principles. Am Sociol Rev 309–330
Marsh EJ (2016) The disappearing desert and the emergence of agropastoralism: An adaptive cycle of rapid change in the mid-Holocene Lake Titicaca Basin (Peru, Bolivia). Quat Int. http://dx.doi.org/10.1016/j.quaint.2015.12.081

Martin AE, Fahrig L (2016) Reconciling contradictory relationships between mobility and extinction risk in human-altered landscapes. Funct Ecol
Martin R, Sunley P (2006) Path dependence and regional economic evolution. J Econ Geogr 6(4):395–437
Martins M, Raju A, Ravignani A (2014) Evaluating the role of quantitative modelling in language evolution. In: The past, present and future of language evolution research, pp 84–93
Marwick B (2016) Computational reproducibility in archaeological research: basic principles and a case study of their implementation. J Archaeol Method Theory 1–27
Matthews J (2008) The longevity of distinct cultures in an agent-based model of memetic drift. Artif Life XI:398–403
Matthews RB, Gilbert NG, Roach A, Polhill JG, Gotts NM (2007) Agent-based land-use models: a review of applications. Landscape Ecol 22(10):1447–1459
Maurer A (2016) Social mechanisms as special cases of explanatory sociology: Notes toward systemizing and expanding mechanism-based explanation within sociology. Anal Kritik 38(1):31–52
Mayfield JE (2007) Minimal history, a theory of plausible explanation. Complexity 12(4):48–53
McElreath R, Boyd R, Richerson PJ (2003) Shared norms and the evolution of ethnic markers. Curr Anthropol 44(1):122–129
McHugh KA, Yammarino FJ, Dionne SD, Serban A, Sayama H, Chatterjee S (2016) Collective decision making, leadership, and collective intelligence: tests with agent-based simulations and a Field study. Leadersh Q 27(2):218–241
McRorie M, Sneddon I, McKeown G, Bevacqua E, De Sevin E, Pelachaud C (2012) Evaluation of four designed virtual agent personalities. IEEE Trans Affect Comput 3(3):311–322
Medina MA (2014) Network theory and its applications in arts practice and history of arts. Rupkatha J Interdiscip Stud Humanit 6(3)
Mejía Cubillos J (2015) The evolution of economic history since 1950: from cliometrics to cliodynamics. Tiempo Economia 2(2):79–103
Mella P (2008) Observing collectivities. The combinatory systems approach in social sciences. Int J Interdiscip Soc Sci 3:213–223
Mesoudi A (2007) Using the methods of experimental social psychology to study cultural evolution. J Soc Evol Cult Psychol 1(2):35
Mesoudi A (2011) Cultural evolution: how Darwinian theory can explain human culture and synthesize the social sciences. University of Chicago Press
Mesoudi A (2014) Experimental studies of modern human social and individual learning in an archaeological context: people behave adaptively, but within limits. In: Dynamics of learning in Neanderthals and modern humans, vol 2. Springer, Japan, pp 65–76
Mesoudi A, O'Brien MJ (2008) The cultural transmission of Great Basin projectile-point technology II: an agent-based computer simulation. Am Antiq 627–644
Messer PW (2013) SLiM: simulating evolution with selection and linkage. Genetics 194(4): 1037–1039
Mezza-García N, Froese T, Fernández N (2014) Reflections on the complexity of ancient social heterarchies: toward new models of social self-organization in pre-hispanic Colombia. J Sociocybern 12:3–24
Miller DL (2013) Introduction to collective behavior and collective action. Waveland Press
Millington JD, O'Sullivan D, Perry GL (2012) Model histories: narrative explanation in generative simulation modelling. Geoforum 43(6):1025–1034
Millington JD, Wainwright J, Mulligan M (2013) Representing human decision-making in environmental modelling. In: Environmental modelling: finding simplicity in complexity, 2nd edn, pp 291–307
Mintz A (1981) A validation study of computer simulations of the European "Major Power" system: 1870-1914. Conflict Manage Peace Sci 6(1):19–38
Mithen S (1990) Thoughtful foragers: a study of prehistoric decision making. Cambridge University Press, New York

Mithen SJ (1991) A cybernetic wasteland? Rationality, emotion and mesolithic foraging. In: Proceedings of the prehistoric society, vol 57, no 02. Cambridge University Press, pp 9–14
Mithen SJ, Reed M (2002) Stepping out: a computer simulation of hominid dispersal from Africa. J Hum Evol 43:433–462
Mitri S, Wischmann S, Floreano D, Keller L (2013) Using robots to understand social behaviour. Biological Reviews 88(1):31–39
Mode CJ, Sleeman CK, Raj T (2013) Simulating the emergence of mutations and their subsequent evolution in an age-structured stochastic self-regulating process with two sexes. Int J Stochast Anal
Monecke S, Monecke H, Monecke J (2009) Modelling the black death. A historical case study and implications for the epidemiology of bubonic plague. Int J Med Microbiol 299(8):582–593
Moreira JA, Pinheiro FL, Nunes A, Pacheco JM (2012) Evolutionary dynamics of collective action when individual fitness derives from group decisions taken in the past. J Theor Biol 298:8–15
Moschovakis YN (2001) What is an algorithm. In: Mathematics unlimited–2001 and beyond, pp 919–936
Moschovakis YN, Paschalis V (2008) Elementary algorithms and their implementations. In: New computational paradigms. Springer, New York, pp 87–118
Moya C, Snopkowski K, Sear R (2016) What do men want? Re-examining whether men benefit from higher fertility than is optimal for women. Philos Trans R Soc B 371(1692):20150149
Munro R (2000) Exploring and explaining the past: ICT and history. Educ Media Int 37(4): 251–256
Murgatroyd P, Gaffney V (2014) Calm before the storm? In: Miguel, Amblard, Barceló, Madella (eds) Advances in computational social science and social simulation. Autònoma University of Barcelona, Barcelona. DDD repository: http://ddd.uab.cat/record/126346
Murgatroyd P, Craenen B, Theodoropoulos G, Gaffney V, Haldon J (2012) Modelling medieval military logistics: an agent-based simulation of a Byzantine army on the march. Comput Math Organ Theory 18(4):488–506
Murphy JT (2012) Exploring complexity with the Hohokam water management simulation: a middle way for archaeological modeling. Ecol Modell 241:15–29
Muscolo GG, Recchiuto CT, Sellers W, Molfino R (2014) Towards a novel embodied robot bio-inspired by non-human primates. In: Proceedings of ISR/Robotik 2014; 41st International Symposium on Robotics. VDE
Nakoinz O, Knitter D (2016) Modelling human behaviour in landscapes. Springer International Publishing
Nan N, Zmud R, Yetgin E (2014) A complex adaptive systems perspective of innovation diffusion: an integrated theory and validated virtual laboratory. Comput Math Organ Theory 20(1):52–88
Nardi BA (1996) Studying context: a comparison of activity theory, situated action models, and distributed cognition. In: Context and consciousness: Activity theory and human-computer interaction, pp 69–102
Nelson R, Winter S (1982) An evolutionary theory of economic change. Harvard University Press
Neumann M (2009) Emergence as an explanatory principle in artificial societies. Reflection on the bottom-up approach to social theory. In: Epistemological aspects of computer simulation in the social sciences. Springer, Berlin, Heidelberg, pp 69–88
Neumann M, Cowley SJ (2016) Modeling social agency using diachronic cognition: learning from the Mafia. In: Agent-based simulation of organizational behavior. Springer International Publishing, pp 289–310
Neumann M, Secchi D (2016) Exploring the New Frontier: computational studies of organizational behavior. In: Agent-based simulation of organizational behavior. Springer International Publishing, pp 1–16
Nicholson AE, Sibani P (2015) Cultural evolution as a nonstationary stochastic process. Complexity
North DC (1994) Economic performance through time. Am Econ Rev 359–368
Novak J, Micheel I, Wieneke L, Düring M, Melenhorst M, Garcia Moron J, Fraternali P (2014) HistoGraph–a visualization tool for collaborative analysis of networks from historical social

multimedia collections. In: 2014 18th International conference on information visualisation (IV). IEEE, pp 241–250
Nowotny H (2005) The increase of complexity and its reduction emergent interfaces between the natural sciences, humanities and social sciences. Theory Cult Soc 22(5):15–31
O'Brien MJ, Bentley RA (2011) Stimulated variation and cascades: two processes in the evolution of complex technological systems. J Archaeol Method Theory 18(4):309–335
O'Brien MJ, Boulanger MT, Buchanan B, Bentley RA, Lyman RL, Lipo CP, Eren MI (2015) Design space and cultural transmission: case studies from Paleoindian Eastern North America. J Archaeol Method Theory 1–49
Oliver PE (1993) Formal models of collective action. Annu Rev Sociol 271–300
Oliver PE, Marwell G, Teixeira R (1985) A theory of the critical mass. I. Interdependence, group heterogeneity, and the production of collective action. Am J Sociol 522–556
Olševičová-Štekerová K, Cimler R, Machálek T (2013) Agent-based model of Celtic population growth: NetLogo and Python. Adv Methods Comput Collect Intell. Springer, Berlin, Heidelberg, pp 135–143
Olševičová-Štekerová K, Procházka J, Danielisová (2015) Reconstruction of prehistoric settlement network using agent-based model in NetLogo. In: Highlights of practical applications of agents, multi-agent systems, and sustainability-the PAAMS collection. Springer International Publishing, pp 165–175
Opp KD (2013) What is Analytical Sociology? Strengths and weaknesses of a new sociological research program. Soc Sci Inf 52(3):329–360
O'Reilly RC, Munakata Y (2002) Psychological function in computational models of neural networks. In: Gallagher M, Nelson R (eds) Handbook of psychology, vol 3, Biological psychology. Wiley, New York
Ortega D, Ibañez JJ, Khalidi L, Méndez V, Campos D, Teira L (2014) Towards a multi-agent-based modelling of obsidian exchange in the Neolithic Near East. J Archaeol Method Theory 21(2):461–485
Ortega D, Ibáñez JJ, Campos D, Khalidi L, Méndez V, Teira L (2016) Systems of interaction between the first sedentary villages in the near east exposed using agent-based modelling of Obsidian exchange. Systems 4(2):18
Ossowski S (1999) Co-ordination in artificial agent societies. social structures and its implications for autonomous problem-solving agents. Lecture notes in computer science, vol 1535. Springer, Berlin
Pacheco JM, Santos FC, Souza MO, Skyrms B (2011) Evolutionary dynamics of collective action. In: The mathematics of Darwin's legacy. Springer, Basel, pp 119–138
Palmissano A, Altaweel M (2015) Simulating past human landscapes: models of settlement hierarchy in Central Anatolia during the Old Assyrian Colony period. In: Proceedings of the 1st Kültepe International Meeting. Kültepe, 19–23 Sept 2013. Studies Dedicated to Kutlu Emre. Brepols, pp 131–146
Pan R (2011) Rebellion on sugarscape: case studies for greed and grievance theory of civil conflicts using agent-based models. In: Social computing, behavioral-cultural modeling and prediction. Springer, Berlin, Heidelberg, pp 333–340
Pantelis PC, Gerstner T, Sanik K, Weinstein A, Cholewiak SA, Kharkwal G, Feldman J (2016) Agency and rationality: adopting the intentional stance toward evolved virtual agents. Decision 3(1):40
Papachristos G, Sofianos A, Adamides E (2013) System interactions in socio-technical transitions: extending the multi-level perspective. Environ Innov Soc Transitions 7:53–69
Parisi D (1998) A cellular automata model of the expansion of the Assyrian empire. In: Cellular automata: research towards industry. Springer, London
Parisi D, Cangelosi A (2002) A unified simulation scenario for language development, evolution and historical change. In: Simulating the evolution of language. Springer, London, pp 255–275
Parisi D, Nolfi S (2005) Sociality in Embodied Neural Agents. In: Sun R (ed) Cognition and Multi-Agent Interaction. University Press, Cambridge

Parisi D, Cecconi FF, Natale F (2003) Cultural change in spatial environments: the role of cultural assimilation and of internal changes in cultures. J Conflict Resolut 47:163–179

Park D, Bae A, Schich M, Park J (2015) Topology and evolution of the network of western classical music composers. EPJ Data Sci 4(1):1–15

Parker DC, Manson SM, Janssen MA, Hoffmann MJ, Deadman P (2003) Multi-agent systems for the simulation of land-use and land-cover change: a review. Ann Assoc Am Geogr 93(2): 314–337

Pastor JM, Garcıa-Algarra J, Galeano J, Iriondo JM, Ramasco JJ (2015) A simple and bounded model of population dynamics for mutualistic networks. Netw Heterogen Media 10(1)

Pauketat TR (1996) The foundations of inequality within a simulated Shan community. J Anthropol Archaeol 15(3):219–236

Pearsall DM (2007) Modeling prehistoric agriculture through the palaeoenvironmental record: theoretical and methodological issues. In: Rethinking agriculture: archaeological and ethnoarchaeological perspectives, pp 210–230

Peart DC (2015) Continuous or pulse? Simulating speciation and extinction from East and South African fauna at Plio-Pleistocene fossil sites. Dissertation, The Ohio State University

Pedone R, Conte R (2001) Dynamics of status symbols and social complexity. Soc Sci Comput Rev 19(3):249–262

Peeters H, Romeijn J-W (2016) Epistemic considerations about uncertainty and model selection in computational archaeology: a case study on exploratory modeling. In: Uncertainty and sensitivity analysis in archaeological computational modeling. Springer International Publishing, pp 37–58

Perc M, Gómez-Gardeñes J, Szolnoki A, Floría LM, Moreno Y (2013) Evolutionary dynamics of group interactions on structured populations: a review. J R Soc Interface 10(80):20120997

Perrot N, De Vries H, Lutton E, van Mil HG, Donner M, Tonda A, Axelos MA (2016) Some remarks on computational approaches towards sustainable complex agri-food systems. Trends Food Sci Technol 48:88–101

Petersen AC (2012) Simulating nature: a philosophical study of computer-simulation uncertainties and their role in climate science and policy advice. CRC Press

Petters D (2014) Bringing together different pieces to better understand whole minds. In: From animals to robots and back: reflections on hard problems in the study of cognition. Springer International Publishing, pp 1–7

Pfau J, Kirley M, Kashima Y (2013) The co-evolution of cultures, social network communities, and agent locations in an extension of Axelrod's model of cultural dissemination. Phys A: Stat Mech Appl 392(2):381–391

Phillips T, Li J, Kendall G (2014) The effects of extra-somatic weapons on the evolution of human cooperation towards non-kin. PLoS ONE 9(5):e95742

Pierson P (2000) Increasing returns, path dependence, and the study of politics. Am Polit Sci Rev 94(02):251–267

Plikynas D, Raudys S (2016) Towards nonlocal field-like social interactions: oscillating agent based conceptual and simulation framework. In: Agent-based simulation of organizational behavior. Springer International Publishing, pp 237–263

Plourde AM (2008) The origins of prestige goods as honest signals of skill and knowledge. Hum Nat 19(4):374–388

Pointeau G, Petit M, Dominey PF (2013) Embodied simulation based on autobiographical memory. Biomimetic and biohybrid systems. Springer, Berlin, Heidelberg, pp 240–250

Polechová J, Barton NH (2015) Limits to adaptation along environmental gradients. Proc Natl Acad Sci 112(20):6401–6406

Polhill JG, Filatova T, Schlüter M, Voinov A (2016) Modelling systemic change in coupled socio-environmental systems. Environ Modell Softw 75:318–332

Pollock JL (1995) Cognitive carpentry: a blueprint for how to build a person. The MIT Press, Cambridge (MA)

Polly PD, Stayton CT, Dumont ER, Pierce SE, Rayfield EJ, Angielczyk KD (2016) Combining geometric morphometrics and finite element analysis with evolutionary modeling: towards a synthesis. J Vertebr Paleontol e1111225
Pomeranz KL (2011) Labeling and analyzing historical phenomena: some preliminary challenges. Cliodynamics 2(1)
Ponse A (1996) Computable processes and bisimulation equivalence. Formal Aspects Comput 8(648):678
Pop CM (2015) Simulating lithic raw material variability in archaeological contexts: a re-evaluation and revision of Brantingham's neutral model. J Archaeol Method Theory 1–35
Popper K (1957) The poverty of historicism. Routledge, London
Porčić M (2015) Exploring the effects of assemblage accumulation on diversity and innovation rate estimates in neutral, conformist, and anti-conformist models of cultural transmission. J Archaeol Method Theory 22(4):1071–1092
Portugali J (1999) Population, society, and environment on the verge of the 21st century: an overview. Discrete Dyn Nat Soc 3(2–3):77–79
Powers ST, Lehmann L (2014) An evolutionary model explaining the Neolithic transition from egalitarianism to leadership and despotism. Proc R Soc Lond B: Biol Sci 281(1791):20141349
Pradhan GR, Tennie C, van Schaik CP (2012) Social organization and the evolution of cumulative technology in apes and hominins. J Hum Evol 63(1):180–190
Premo LS (2005) Patchiness and prosociality: an agent-based model of plio/pleistocene hominid food sharing. In: Davidsson P, Takadama K, Logan B (eds) Multi-agent and multi-agent-based simulation. Lecture notes in artificial intelligence, vol 3415. Springer, Berlin, pp 210–224
Premo LS (2012) Local extinctions, connectedness, and cultural evolution in structured populations. Adv Complex Syst 15(1e18) 1150002
Premo LS (2015) Mobility and cultural diversity in central-place foragers: implications for the emergence of modern human behavior. In: Learning strategies and cultural evolution during the palaeolithic. Springer, Japan, pp 45–65
Premo LS, Kuhn SL (2010) Modeling effects of local extinctions on culture change and diversity in the Paleolithic. PLoS ONE 5(12):e15582
Pringle H (2013) The origins of creativity. Sci Am 308(3):36–43
Puga-Gonzalez I, Hildenbrandt H, Hemelrijk CK (2009) Emergent patterns of social affiliation in primates, a model. PLoS Comput Biol 5(12):e1000630. doi:10.1371/journal.pcbi.1000630
Puga-Gonzalez I, Butovskaya M, Thierry B, Hemelrijk CK (2014) Empathy versus parsimony in understanding post-conflict affiliation in monkeys: model and empirical data. PLoS ONE 9(3): e91262
Pujol JM, Flache A, Delgado J, Sangüesa R (2005) How can social networks ever become complex? Modelling the emergence of complex networks from local social exchanges. J Artif Soc Soc Simul 8(4)
Puleston C, Tuljapurkar S, Winterhalder B (2014) The invisible cliff: abrupt imposition of Malthusian equilibrium in a natural-fertility, Agrarian society. PLoS ONE 9(1)
Pumain D, Sanders L, Bretagnolle A, Glisse B, Mathian H (2009) The future of urban systems: exploratory models. In: Lane D, Pumain D, van der Leeuw S, West G (eds) Complexity perspectives on innovation and social change, Methods series. Springer, pp 331–359
Racko G (2011) The whole is greater than the sum of its parts: some remarks on the Oxford handbook of analytical sociology. Eur Sociol Rev 27(6):772–789
Rahman A, Setayeshi S, Zafarghandi MS (2009) Wealth adjustment using a synergy between communication, cooperation, and one-fifth of wealth variables in an artificial society. AI Soc 24(2):151–164
Rammer W, Seidl R (2015) Coupling human and natural systems: simulating adaptive management agents in dynamically changing forest landscapes. Global Environ Change 35:475–485
Rao AS, Georgeff MP (1998) Decision procedures for BDI logics. J Logic Comput 8(3):293–343
Rashevsky N (1968) Looking at history through mathematics. MIT Press, Cambridge, MA

Rasteiro R, Bouttier PA, Sousa VC, Chikhi L (2012) Investigating sex-biased migration during the Neolithic transition in Europe, using an explicit spatial simulation framework. Proc R Soc Lond B: Biol Sci rspb20112323
Raub W, Buskens V, Van Assen MA (2011) Micro-macro links and microfoundations in sociology. J Math Soc 35(1–3):1–25
Ray T, Liew KM (2003) Society and civilization: an optimization algorithm based on the simulation of social behavior. Trans Evol Comp 7(4):386–396. http://dx.doi.org/10.1109/TEVC.2003.814902
Read DW (1987) Foraging society organization: a simple model of a complex transition. Eur J Oper Res 30(3):230–236
Read DW (1998) Kinship based demographic simulation of societal processes. J Artif Soc Soc Simul 1(1). http://www.soc.surrey.ac.uk/JASSS/1/1/1.html
Read DW (2003) Emergent properties in small-scale societies. Artif Life 9(4):419–434
Read DW (2008) An interaction model for resource implement complexity based on risk and number of annual moves. Am Antiq 599–625
Read DW (2010) Agent-based and multi-agent simulations: coming of age or in search of an identity? Comput Math Organ Theory 16(4):329–347
Read DW, LeBlanc S (2003) Population growth, carrying capacity, and conflict. Curr Anthropol 44(1):59–85
Reisenzein R, Hudlicka E, Dastani M, Gratch J, Hindriks K, Lorini E, Meyer JJC (2013) Computational modeling of emotion: toward improving the inter-and intradisciplinary exchange. IEEE Trans Affect Comput 4(3):246–266
Renfrew AC (1987) Problems in the modelling of socio-cultural systems. Eur J Oper Res 30(2):179–192
Reuveny R (2012) Taking stock of Malthus: modeling the collapse of historical civilizations. Annu Rev Resour Econ 4(1):303–329
Reyes-Garcia V, Molina JL, Broesch J, Calvet L, Huanca T, Saus J, TAPS Bolivian Study Team (2008) Do the aged and knowledgeable men enjoy more prestige? A test of predictions from the prestige-bias model of cultural transmission. Evol Hum Behav 29(4):275–281
Reynolds RG (1986) An adaptive computer model for the evolution of plant collecting and early agriculture in the Eastern Valley of Oaxaca. In: Guila Naquitz: Archaic foraging and early agriculture in Oaxaca, Mexico, pp 439–507
Reynolds RG, Lazar A (2002) Simulating the evolution of Archaic states. In: Proceedings of the 2002 congress on evolutionary computation, 2002. CEC'02, vol 1. IEEE
Reynolds RG, Peng B (2005) Cultural algorithms: computational modeling of how cultures learn to solve problems: an engineering example. Cybern Syst: Int J 36(8):753–771
Reynolds RG, Peng B, Mostafa ZA (2008) The role of culture in the emergence of decision-making roles: an example using cultural algorithms. Complexity 13(3):27–42
Reynolds RG, Ali M, Alomari RS (2006) Optimization problem solving using predator/prey games and cultural algorithms. In: 2006 IEEE symposium on computational intelligence and games. IEEE, pp 119–125
Reynolds RG, Vitale K, Che X, O'Shea J, Salaymeh A (2013) Using virtual worlds to facilitate the exploration of ancient landscapes. Int J Swarm Intell Res (IJSIR) 4(2):49–83
Reynolds RG, Whallon R, Ali MZ, Zadegan BM (2006) Agent-based modeling of early cultural evolution. In: IEEE Congress on evolutionary computation, 2006. CEC 2006. IEEE, pp 1135–1142
Reynolds RG, Kobti Z, Kohler TA (2004a) The effect of culture on the resilience of social systems in the village multi-agent simulation. In: IEEE International congress on evolutionary computation, Portland (OR), 19, 24, June 2004, pp 1743–1750
Reynolds RG, Kobti Z, Kohler TA (2004b). The effects of generalized reciprocal exchange on the resilience of social networks: an example from the prehistoric Mesa Verde region. J Comput Math Organ Theory 229–254
Reynolds RG, Kobti Z, Kohler TA (2006a) Learning in dynamic multi-layered social networks: a Mesa Verde example. In: Proceedings of geo-computation 2005

Reynolds R, Kobti Z, Kohler T, Yap L (2006b) Unraveling ancient mysteries: re-imagining the past using evolutionary computation in a complex gaming environment. IEEE Trans Evol Comput 9(6):707–720
Reynolds R, Kobti Z, Kohler T (2006c) The emergence of social network hierarchy using cultural algorithms. Int J Artif Intell Tools 15:963–978
Reynolds RG, Whallon R, Goodhall S (2001) Transmission of cultural traits by emulation: an agent-based model of group foraging behavior. J Memetics—Evol Models Inf Transm 4. http://jom-emit.cfpm.org/2001/vol4/reynolds_r&al.html
Ribeiro FL (2015) A Non-phenomenological model of competition and cooperation to explain population growth behaviors. Bull Math Biol 77(3):409–433
Richardson K (2003) On the limits of bottom-up computer simulation: towards a nonlinear modeling culture. In: Proceedings of the 36th annual Hawaii international conference on system sciences, 2003. IEEE, pp 9–pp
Riebling JR, Schmitz A (2016) ZombieApocalypse: Modeling the social dynamics of infection and rejection. Methodol Innov 9:2059799115622767
Rindfuss RR, Entwisle B, Walsh SJ, An L, Badenoch N, Brown DG, Verburg PH et al (2008) Land use change: complexity and comparisons. J Land Use Sci 3(1):1–10
Rivers R, Evans TS (2014) New approaches to Archaic Greek settlement structure. Nouvelles de l'archéologie 135:21–28
Roberts BW, Vander Linden M (2011) Investigating archaeological cultures: material culture, variability, and transmission. Springer, New York, pp 1–21
Robinson-Cox JF, Martell RF, Emrich CG (2007) Simulating gender stratification. J Artif Soc Soc Simul 10 (3)
Rodgers J, Kohler HP (eds) (2012) The biodemography of human reproduction and fertility. Springer Science & Business Media
Rodríguez J, Mateos A, Hertler C, Palombo MR (2015) Modelling human presence and environmental dynamics during the Mid-Pleistocene revolution: new approaches and tools. Quat Int
Roemer J (1985) A general theory of exploitation and class. Harvard University Press
Rogers JD (2013) Pastoralist mobility and social controls in Inner Asia: experiments using agent-based modeling. Struct Dyn 6(2)
Rogers JD, Cioffi-Revilla C, Linford SJ (2015) The Sustainability of wealth among nomads: an agent-based approach. In: Barceló JA, Bogdanovic I (eds) Mathematics and archaeology. CRC Press, pp 431ff
Rogers JD, Nichols T, Emmerich T, Latek M, Cioffi-Revilla C (2012) Modeling scale and variability in human–environmental interactions in Inner Asia. Ecol Modell 241:5–14
Rohde DL, Olson S, Chang JT (2004) Modelling the recent common ancestry of all living humans. Nature 431(7008):562–566
Rohlf FJ, Davenport D (1969) Simulation of simple models of animal behavior with a digital computer. J Theor Biol 23(3):400–424
Romanowska I, Gamble C, Bullock S, Sturt F (2016) Dispersal and the Movius Line: testing the effect of dispersal on population density through simulation. Quat Int. doi:10.1016/j.quaint.2016.01.016
Roos P, Gelfand M, Nau D, Lun J (2015) Societal threat and cultural variation in the strength of social norms: An evolutionary basis. Organ Behav Hum Decis Process 129:14–23
Rorabaugh AN (2014) Impacts of drift and population bottlenecks on the cultural transmission of a neutral continuous trait: an agent based model. J Archaeol Sci 49:255–264
Rorabaugh AN (2015) Modeling pre-European contact coast salish seasonal social networks and their impacts on unbiased cultural transmission. J Artif Soc Soc Simul 18(4):8. doi:10.18564/jasss.2911
Roseman CC, Auerbach BM (2015) Ecogeography, genetics, and the evolution of human body form. J Hum Evol 78:80–90

Rosenberg M (2009) Proximate causation, group selection, and the evolution of hierarchical human societies: system, process, and pattern. In: Macroevolution in human prehistory. Springer, New York, pp 23–49

Ross CT, Richerson PJ (2014) New frontiers in the study of human cultural and genetic evolution. Curr Opin Genet Dev 29:103–109

Rost N, Schneider G, Kleibl J (2009) A global risk assessment model for civil wars. Soc Sci Res 38(4):921–933

Roth SF (1998) Past into present: effective techniques for first-person historical interpretation. Univ of North Carolina Press

Rounsevell MDA, Robinson DT, Murray-Rust D (2012) From actors to agents in socio-ecological systems models. Philos Trans R Soc B: Biol Sci 367(1586):259–269

Rouse LM, Weeks L (2011) Specialization and social inequality in Bronze Age SE Arabia: analyzing the development of production strategies and economic networks using agent-based modeling. J Archaeol Sci 38(7):1583–1590

Rowthorn R, Guzmán RA, Rodríguez-Sickert C (2014) The economics of social stratification in premodern societies. J Math Soc 38(3):175–202

Rubio-Campillo X (2016) Model selection in historical research using approximate Bayesian computation. PLoS ONE 11(1):e0146491

Rubio-Campillo X, Cela JM, Cardona FXH (2013) The development of new infantry tactics during the early eighteenth century: a computer simulation approach to modern military history. J Simul 7(3):170–182

Rubio-Campillo X, Valdés Matías P, Ble E (2015) Centurions in the Roman legion: computer simulation and complex systems. J Interdiscipl Hist 46(2):245–263

Ruggles S (1993) Confessions of a microsimulator: problems in modeling the demography of kinship. Hist Methods: J Quant Interdiscip Hist 26(4):161–169

Rush DE (2011) A simulation of evolving sustainable technology through social pressure. In: 2011 AAAI fall symposium series

Russo A (2014) A stochastic model of wealth accumulation with class division. Metroeconomica 65(1):1–35

Saam NJ, Harrer A (1999) Simulating norms, social inequality, and functional change in artificial societies. J Artif Soc Soc Simul 2(1):2

Sabin P (2012) Simulating war: Studying conflict through simulation games. A&C Black

Safarzyńska K, Frenken K, Van Den Bergh J (2012) Evolutionary theorizing and modeling of sustainability transitions. Res Policy 41(6):1011–1024

Sajjad M, Singh K, Paik E, Ahn CW (2016) A data-driven approach for agent-based modeling: simulating the dynamics of family formation. J Artif Soc Soc Simul 19(1)

Salali GD, Whitehouse H, Hochberg ME (2015) A life-cycle model of human social groups produces a U-shaped distribution in group size. PLoS ONE 10(9):e0138496

Salgado M, Noguera JA, Miguel FJ (2014) Modelling cooperation mechanisms: some conceptual issues. J Archaeol Method Theory 21(2):325–342

Sallach DL (2010) Social science model validation: domain-specific challenges. In: McNamara LA, Trucano TG, Geisler C, Perry JL (eds) Challenges in computational social modeling and simulation for national security decision-making. Defense Threat Reduction Agency, Fort Belvoir, VA

Salmon W (1984) Scientific explanation and the causal structure of the world. Princeton University Press, Princeton

Samuels ML (1982) POPREG I: a simulation of population regulation among the Maring of New Guinea. Hum Ecol 10(1):1–45

San Miguel M, Eguiluz VM, Toral R, Klemm K (2005) Binary and multivariate Stochastic models of consensus formation. Comput Sci Eng 6–7:67–73

Sandberg M (2011) Soft power, world system dynamics, and democratization: a bass model of democracy diffusion 1800-2000. J Artif Soc Soc Simul 14(1):4

Sanders L (2012) Regards croisés de géographes, économistes et archéologues sur la hiérarchie des systèmes de peuplement: de l'empirie aux systèmes complexes. Région et Développement 36:127–146
Sanders L (2015) Un cadre conceptuel pour modéliser les grandes transitions des systèmes de peuplements de 70 000 BP à aujourd'hui. Bulletin - Société géographique de Liège 63:5–19
Sanders L, Pumain D, Mathian H, Guérin-Pace F, Bura S (1997) SIMPOP: a multi-agents system for the study of urbanism. Environ Plann B 24:287–305
Sansores Pérez C (2007) Metodología para el estudio de Sociedades Artificales. Universidad Complutense de Madrid, Tesis Doctoral
Santos FC, Santos MD, Pacheco JM (2008) Social diversity promotes the emergence of cooperation in public goods games. Nature 454(7201):213–216
Santos Fernando P, Santos Francisco C, Pacheco Jorge M (2016) Social norms of cooperation in small-scale societies. PLoS Comput Biol 12(1):e1004709
Santos JI, Pereda M, Zurro D, Álvarez M, Caro J, Galán JM, Briz I, Godino I (2015) Effect of resource spatial correlation and hunter-fisher-gatherer mobility on social cooperation in tierra del fuego. PLoS ONE 10(4):e0121888
Santow G (2012) A simulation approach to the study of human fertility, vol 5. Springer Science & Business Media
Saqalli M, Salavert A, Bréhard S, Bendrey R, Vigne JD, Tresset A (2014) Revisiting and modelling the woodland farming system of the early Neolithic Linear Pottery Culture (LBK), 5600–4900 BC. Veg Hist Archaeobot 23(1):37–50
Saqalli M, Bielders CL, Gerard B, Defourny P (2010) Simulating rural environmentally and socio-economically constrained multi-activity and multi-decision societies in a low-data context: a challenge through empirical agent-based modeling. J Artif Soc Soc Simul 13(2):1
Sarjoughian HS, Mayer GR, Ullah II, Barton CM (2015). Managing hybrid model composition complexity: human–environment simulation models. In: Concepts and methodologies for modeling and simulation. Springer International Publishing, pp 107–134
Savarimuthu BTR, Cranefield S (2011) Norm creation, spreading and emergence: a survey of simulation models of norms in multi-agent systems. Multiagent Grid Syst–Int J 7(1):21–54
Savarimuthu BTR, Arulanandam R, Savarimuthu S (2011b) Emergence of a sharing norm in a simulated hunter-gatherer society. In: Proceedings of the 2011 IEEE/WIC/ACM international conferences on web intelligence and intelligent agent technology, vol 02. IEEE Computer Society, pp 34–37
Sawyer RK (2005) Social emergence: Societies as complex systems. Cambridge University Press
Scarborough VL, Burnside WR (2010) Complexity and sustainability: perspectives from the ancient Maya and the modern Balinese. Am Antiq 327–363
Scheffer M, Carpenter S, Lenton T, Bascompte J, Brock W, Dakos V, van de Koppel J, van de Leemput IA, Levin SA, van Nes EH, Pascual M, Vandermeer J (2012) Anticipating critical transitions. Science 338
Schelling T (1978) Micromotives and macrobehavior. Norton, New York
Schich M, Song C, Ahn Y, Mirsky A, Martino M, Barabási AL, Helbing D (2014) A network framework of cultural history. Science 345(6196):558–562
Schieve WC, Allen PM (eds) (2014) Self-organization and dissipative structures: Applications in the physical and social sciences. University of Texas Press
Schilperoord M, Rotmans J, Bergman N (2008) Modelling societal transitions with agent transformation. Computational and Mathematical Organization Theory 14(4):283–301
Schlötterer C., R. Kofler, E. Versace, R. Tobler, Franssen, S.U. (2014). Combining experimental evolution with next-generation sequencing: a powerful tool to study adaptation from standing genetic variation. *Heredity*. 2014. doi:10.1038/hdy.2014.86
Schlueter M, McAllister RR, Arlinghaus R, Bunnefeld N, Eisenack K, Hoelker FF, Stöven M (2012) New Horizons for Managing the Environment: A Review of Coupled Social-Ecological Systems Modeling. Natural Resource Modeling 25(1):219–272
Schmidt, B. (2000). *The modelling of human behaviour*. Society for Computer Simulation International

Schmitt C, Rey-Coyrehourcq S, Reuillon R, Pumain DD (2015) Half a billion simulations: evolutionary algorithms and distributed computing for calibrating the SimpopLocal geographical model. Environ Plann B: Plann Des 42(2):300–315
Schmitt C, Pumain D (2013) Modélographie multi-agents de la simulation des interactions sociétés-environnement et de l'émergence des villes. Cybergeo 643
Schneider G, Gleditsch NP, Carey SC (2010) Exploring the past, anticipating the future: a symposium. Int Stud Rev 12(1):1–7
Schönbrodt FD, Asendorpf JB (2011) The challenge of constructing psychologically believable agents. J Media Psychol: Theories Methods Appl 23(2):100–107
Schreinemachers P, Berger T (2011) An agent-based simulation model of human–environment interactions in agricultural systems. Environ Modell Softw 26(7):845–859
Schreyögg G, Sydow J, Holtmann P (2011) How history matters in organisations: the case of path dependence. Manage Organ Hist 6(1):81–100
Schrodt PA (1988) PWORLD: a precedent-based global simulation. Soc Sci Comput Rev 6(1): 27–42
Schrodt PA (2006) Forecasting conflict in the Balkans using hidden Markov models. Programming for Peace. Springer, Netherlands, pp 161–184
Schrodt PA, Yonamine J, Bagozzi BE (2013) Data-based computational approaches to forecasting political violence. In: Handbook of computational approaches to counterterrorism. Springer, New York, pp 129–162
Schubert C (2015) Situating technological and societal futures. Pragmatist engagements with computer simulations and social dynamics. Technol Soc 40:4–13
Séguy I, Buchet L (2013) Current demographic models. In: Handbook of palaeodemography. Springer International Publishing, pp 99–112
Sept J (2007) Modeling the significance of paleoenvironmental context for early hominin diets. In: Evolution of the human diet: the known, the unknown, and the unknowable, pp 289–307
Seth AK (2007) The ecology of action selection: Insights from artificial life. Philos Trans R Soc B: Biol Sci 362(1485):1545–1558
Sewell WH (1985) Ideologies and social revolutions: reflections on the French case. J Modern Hist 57:57–85
Shamrani M, Waldispühl J, Major F (2015) Evolution by computational selection. arXiv:1505. 02348
Sharp PR, Weisdorf JL (2012) French revolution or industrial revolution? A note on the contrasting experiences of England and France up to 1800. Cliometrica 6(1):79–88
Shaw L (2015) Mechanics and dynamics of social construction: modeling the emergence of culture from individual mental representation. Poetics 52:75–90
Shennan S (2015) Demography and cultural evolution. In: Scott RA, Kosslyn SM (eds) Emerging trends in the social and behavioral sciences: an interdisciplinary, searchable, and linkable resource, pp 1–14
Shennan SJ, Crema ER, Kerig T (2015) Isolation-by-distance, homophily, and "core" vs. "package" cultural evolution models in Neolithic Europe. Evol Hum Behav 36(2):103–109
Shoham Y, Tennenholtz M (1997) On the emergence of social conventions: modeling, analysis, and simulations. Artif Intelli 94(1):139–166
Silva F, Steele J (2015) Two-dimensional models of human dispersals: tracking reaction-diffusion fronts on heterogeneous surfaces. In: Barceló JA, Bogdanovic I (ed) Mathematics and archaeology. CRC Press, Boca Raton (FL), pp 416–430
Silverman E, Bijak J, Noble J (2011) Feeding the beast: can computational demographic models free us from the tyranny of data? In: Lenaerts T, Giacobini M, Bersini H, Bourgine P, Dorigo M, Doursat R (eds) Advances in a Artificial life, ECAL 2011. MIT Press, Cambridge, MA, pp 747–754
Silverman E, Bijak J, Noble J, Cao V, Hilton J (2014) Semi-artificial models of populations: connecting demography with agent-based modelling. In: Advances in computational social science. Springer, Japan, pp 177–189
Simon H (1962) The architecture of complexity. Proc Am Philos Soc 106:467–482

Skirbekk V, Stonawski M, Alfani G (2015) Consequences of a universal European demographic transition on regional and global population distributions. Technol Forecast Soc Change (Article in press). Accessed 21 May 2015

Skocpol T (1985) Cultural idioms and political ideologies in the revolutionary reconstruction of state power. A rejoinder to Sewell. J Modern Hist 57:86–96

Skyrms B (2001) The stag hunt. In: Proceedings and addresses of the American Philosophical Association. American Philosophical Association, pp 31–41

Skyrms B (2004) The stag hunt and the evolution of social structure. Cambridge University Press

Skyrms B (2010) Signals: evolution, learning, and information. Oxford University Press

Skyrms B (2013) Natural social contracts. Biol Theory 8(2):179–184

Skyrms B (2014) Evolution of the social contract. Cambridge University Press

Slator BM, Borchert O, Hokanson G (2015) Learning by doing history with smart historical gaming. In: Smart education and smart e-Learning. Springer International Publishing, pp 207–217

Sloman A (20140 How can we reduce the gulf between artificial and natural intelligence? In: Proceedings of the 2nd international workshop on artificial intelligence and cognition (AIC 2014), 2014, pp 1–13

Sloman A, Chrisley R (2003) Virtual machines and consciousness. J Conscious Stud 10(4–5): 133–172

Smaldino PE, Newson L, Schan JC, Richerson PJ (2013) Simulating the evolution of the human family: cooperative breeding increases in harsh environments. PLoS ONE 8(11):e80753. doi:10.1371/journal.pone.0080753

Small C (1999) Finding an invisible history: a computer simulation experiment (in virtual Polynesia). J Artif Soc Soc Simul 2(3):6

Smith AL, Benazzi S, Ledogar JA, Tamvada K, Pryor Smith LC, Weber GW, Spencer MA, Lucas PW, Michael S, Shekeban SA, Al-Fadhalah K, Almusallam AS, Dechow PC, Grosse IR, Ross CF, Madden RH, Richmond BG, Wright BW, Wang Q, Byron C (2015). The feeding biomechanics and dietary ecology of Paranthropus boisei. *The Anatomical Record* 298.1: 145–167

Smith BD (2015) A comparison of niche construction theory and diet breadth models as explanatory frameworks for the initial domestication of plants and animals. J Archaeol Res 1–48

Smith EA, Choi J-K (2007) The emergence of inequality in small-scale societies: simple scenarios and agent-based simulations. In: Kohler TA, Van der Leeuw SE (eds) Model-based archaeology of socionatural systems. SAR Press, Sante Fe, pp 105–120

Smith JE, Gavrilets S, Mulder MB, Hooper PL, El Mouden C, Nettle D, van Vugt M et al (2016) Leadership in mammalian societies: emergence, distribution, power, and payoff. Trends Ecol Evol 31(1):54–66

Sokolowski J, Banks C (2009) Modeling and simulation for analyzing global events. Wiley, New Jersey

Song Z, Feldman MW (2013) The coevolution of long-term pair bonds and cooperation. J Evol Biol 26(5):963–970

Song Z, Vaughan RT (2013) Sustainable robot foraging: adaptive fine-grained multi-robot task allocation for maximum sustainable yield of biological resources. In: 2013 IEEE/RSJ international conference on intelligent robots and systems (IROS). IEEE, pp 3309–3316

Spaiser V, Sumpter DJTS (2016) Revising the human development sequence theory using an agent-based approach and data. J Artif Soc Soc Simul

Spencer CS (1998) A mathematical model of primary state formation. Cult Dyn 10(1):5–20

Spencer CS (2014) Modeling the evolution of bureaucracy: political-economic reach and administrative complexity. Soc Evol Hist 13(1):42–66

Spisak BR, Nicholson N, Van Vugt M (2011) Leadership in organizations: an evolutionary perspective. Evolutionary psychology in the business sciences. Springer, Berlin, Heidelberg, pp 165–190

Squazzoni F (2008a) A (computational) social science perspective on societal transitions. Comput Math Organ Theory 14(4):266–282
Squazzoni F (2008b) The micro-macro link in social simulation. Sociologica 2(1). http://www.sociologica.mulino.it/journal/article/…/Journal:ARTICLE:179. Accessed Jan 2011
Squazzoni F (2012) Agent-based computational sociology. Wiley
Squire K, Barab S (2004) Replaying history: engaging urban underserved students in learning world history through computer simulation games. In: Proceedings of the 6th international conference on Learning sciences. International Society of the Learning Sciences, pp 505–512
Stajich JE, Hahn MW (2005) Disentangling the effects of demography and selection in human history. Mol Biol Evol 22(1):63–73
Stanley SD, Salaymeh AJ, Palazzolo TJ, Warnke DM (2014) Analyzing prehistoric hunter behavior with cultural algorithms. In: 2014 IEEE Congress on Evolutionary Computation (CEC). IEEE
Starnini M, Sánchez A, Poncela J, Moreno Y (2011) Coordination and growth: the Stag Hunt game on evolutionary networks. J Stat Mech: Theory Exp 5:P05008
Steels L (2011) Modeling the cultural evolution of language. Phys Life Rev 8(4):339–356
Steiner L, Stadler PF, Cysouw M (2011) A pipeline for computational historical linguistics. Lang Dyn Change 1(1):89–127
Sterelny K (2015) Optimizing engines: rational choice in the neolithic? Philos Sci 82(3):402–423
Sterman JD (1984) Appropriate summary statistics for evaluating the historical fit of system dynamics models. Dynamica 10(2):51–66
Stettiner O (2016) From silico to vitro: computational models of complex biological systems reveal real-world emergent phenomena. In: Computing and philosophy. Springer International Publishing, pp 133–147
Stilman B, Yakhnis V, Umanskiy O (2011) The primary language of ancient battles. Int J Mach Learn Cybern 2(3):157–176
Stinchcombe AL (1991) The conditions of fruitfulness of theorizing about mechanisms in social science. Philos Soc Sci 21(3):367–388
Stoica C, Klüver J (2006) Social constrains as cybernetic explanations. In: Unifying themes in complex systems. Springer, Berlin, Heidelberg, pp 367–376
Stover WJ (2007) Simulating the cuban missile crisis: crossing time and space in virtual reality. Int Stud Perspect 8(1):111–120
Strand S (1999) Forecasting the future: pitfalls in controlling for uncertainty. Futures 31(3): 333–350
Strogatz S (2003) SYNC—the emerging science of spontaneous order. Hyperion, New York
Stutz AJ (2012) Culture and politics, behavior and biology: seeking synthesis among fragmentary anthropological perspectives on hunter-gatherers. Rev Anthropol 41(1):23–69
Suárez JL, Sancho F (2011) A virtual laboratory for the study of history and cultural dynamics. J Artif Soc Soc Simul 14(4):19
Sueur C, Deneubourg JL, Petit O, Couzin ID (2011) Group size, grooming and fission in primates: a modeling approach based on group structure. J Theoret Biol 273(1):156–166
Sulakshin S (2010) A quantitative political spectrum and forecasting of social evolution. Int J Interdiscip Soc Sci 5(4):55–66
Sun R (2006) Cognition and multi-agent interaction: from cognitive modeling to social simulation. Cambridge University Press
Swedlund AC, Sattenspiel L, Warren AL, Gumerman G (2015) Modeling archaeology: origins of the artificial Anasazi project and beyond. In: Wurzer G, Kowarik K, Reschreiter H (eds) Agent-based modeling and simulation in archaeology. Advances in geographic information science. Springer, Berlin, pp 37–50
Symons S, Raine D (2008) Agent-based models of ancient Egypt. In: Proceedings of Informatique et Égyptologie. Piscataway, NJ. http://www.physics.le.ac.uk/ComplexSystems/papers/AgentBasedModelsEgypt2008.pdf. Accessed 28 May 12

Taillandier P, Therond O, Gaudou B (2012) A new BDI agent architecture based on the belief theory. Application to the modelling of cropping plan decision-making. In: International environmental modelling and software society (iEMSs)

Tang T, Ye H (2016) The blessing of sexuality: evolution of altruism with mating preference. J Artif Soc Soc Simul 19(2)

Taylor G, Frederiksen R, Vane RR, Waltz E (2004) Agent-based simulation of geo-political conflict. In: Innovative applications of artificial intelligence (IAAI). http://www.soartech.com/pubs/IAAI04-GTaylor-AGILE.pdf. Accessed July 2009

Telles HV, Alves L (2015) Narrative, history, and fiction: history games as boundary works. Comunicação e Sociedade 27:319–333

Tenenbaum JB, Kemp C, Griffiths TL, Goodman ND (2011) How to grow a mind: statistics, structure, and abstraction. Science 331(6022):1279–1285

Tesfatsion L (2002) Agent-based computational economics: growing economies from the bottom up. Artif life 8(1):55–82

Tesfatsion L (2003) Agent-based computational economics: modeling economies as complex adaptive systems. Inf Sci 149(4):262–268

Tetlock PE (1999) Theory-driven reasoning about plausible pasts and probable futures in world politics: are we prisoners of our preconceptions? Am J Polit Sci 335–366

Thompson NE, Demes B, O'Neill MC, Holowka NB, Larson SG (2015) Surprising trunk rotational capabilities in chimpanzees and implications for bipedal walking proficiency in early hominins. Nat Commun 6

Thornton PH, Ocasio W, Lounsbury M (2012) The institutional logics perspective: a new approach to culture, structure, and process. Oxford University Press

Thürmel S (2016) Exploring social and asocial agency in agent-based systems. In: Agent-based simulation of organizational behavior. Springer International Publishing, pp 221–236

Tisdell C, Svizzero S (2016) Different behavioral explanations of the Neolithic transition from foraging to agriculture: a review. Economic theory, applications and issues working paper series 75, School of Economics, The University of Queensland

Toffoli T (2005) Nothing makes sense in computing except in the light of evolution. Int J Unconvent Comput 1:1–29

Tomasello M, Melis AP, Tennie C, Wyman E, Herrmann E (2012) Two key steps in the evolution of human cooperation. Curr Anthropol 53(6):673–692

Tomlinson B (2009) A proximate mechanism for communities of agents to commemorate long dead ancestors. J Artif Soc Soc Simul 12(1):7

Topa P, Komosinski M, Bassara M, Tyszka J (2016) eVolutus: a configurable platform designed for ecological and evolutionary experiments tested on Foraminifera. In: Man–machine interactions, vol 4. Springer International Publishing, pp 269–278

Turchin P (2003) Why states rise and fall. Studies in complexity. Princeton University Press, Princeton (NJ)

Turchin P (2008) Arise 'cliodynamics'. Nature 454(7200):34–35

Turchin P (2009) A theory for formation of large empires. J Glob Hist 4:191–207

Turchin P (2011) Toward cliodynamics. Cliodynamics 2(1):175

Turchin P (2013) The puzzle of human ultrasociality how did large-scale complex societies evolve? In: Richerson PJ, Christiansen MH (ed) Cultural evolution: society, technology, language, and religion. Strüngmann Forum Reports, vol 12. MIT Press, Cambridge, MA

Turchin P (2015) Ultrasociety: how 10,000 years of war made humans the greatest cooperators on Earth. Beresta Books

Turchin P, Gavrilets S (2009) Evolution of complex hierarchical societies. Soc Evol Hist 8: 167–198

Turchin P, Currie TE, Turner EA, Gavrilets S (2013) War, space, and the evolution of old world complex societies. Proc Natl Acad Sci 110(41):16384–16389

Ulfelder J, Lustik M (2007) Modelling transitions to and from democracy. Democratisation 14(3):351–387

Ullah I (2013) The consequences of human land-use strategies during the PPNB-LN transition a simulation modeling approach. Ph.D. dissertation, Arizona State University

Upal MA (2015) A framework for agent-based social simulations of social identity dynamics. In: Conflict and complexity. Springer, New York, pp 89–109

Urban C, Schmidt B (2001) PECS–agent-based modelling of human behaviour. In: Emotional and intelligent–the tangled knot of social cognition, AAAI fall symposium series, North Falmouth, MA. http://www.or.unipassau.de/5/publik/urban/CUrban01.pdf

Vaart E, Whittington R (2012) Strategy-as-practice: taking social practices seriously. Acad Manage Ann 6(1):285–336

Van Der Vaart E, Hankel A, De Boer B, Verheij B (2006) Agents adopting agriculture: modeling the agricultural transition. In: Proceedings of From animals to animats 9, 9th international conference on simulation of adaptive behavior, SAB 2006, Rome, Italy, 25–29 Sept 2006. Lecture notes in computer science, vol 4095. Springer, Berlin, pp. 750–761

Vahia MN, Ladiwala U, Mahathe P, Mathur D (2016) Population dynamics of early human migration in Britain. PLoS ONE 11(5):e0154641

Valori L, Picciolo F, Allansdottir A, Garlaschelli D (2012) Reconciling long-term cultural diversity and short-term collective social behavior. Proc Natl Acad Sci 109(4):1068–1073

Van Den Bergh J, Truffer B, Kallis G (2011) Environmental innovation and societal transitions: introduction and overview. Environ Innov Soc Transitions 1(1):1–23

Van der Post DJ, Verbrugge R, Hemelrijk CK (2015) The evolution of different forms of sociality: behavioral mechanisms and eco-evolutionary feedback. PLoS ONE 10(1):e0117027

Van Overwalle F, Van Rooy D (1998) A connectionist approach to causal attribution. In: Read SJ, Miller LC (eds) Connectionist models of social reasoning and social behavior. Erlbaum, New York, pp 143–171

van Vliet N, Cornelis D, Beck H, Lindsey P, Nasi R, LeBel S, Jori F et al (2016). Meat from the wild: extractive uses of wildlife and alternatives for sustainability. In: Current trends in wildlife research. Springer International Publishing, pp 225–265

Vanhée L, Ferber J, Dignum F (2014) Agent-based evolving societies. Adv Soc Simul. Springer, Berlin, Heidelberg, pp 283–294

Vegvari C, Foley RA (2014) High selection pressure promotes increase in cumulative adaptive culture. PLoS ONE 9(1):e86406

Veneris Y (1990) Modeling the transition from the industrial to the informational revolution. Environ Plann A 22(3):399–416

Vergne JP, Durand R (2010) The missing link between the theory and empirics of path dependence: conceptual clarification, testability issue, and methodological implications. J Manage Stud 47(4):736–759

Vespignani A (2009) Predicting the behavior of techno-social systems. Science 325(5939):425

Vespignani A (2012) Modelling dynamical processes in complex socio-technical systems. Nat Phys 8(1):32–39

Vila A, Perez M, Estevez J, Sabater-Mir J, de la Cruz D, Villatoro D, Vila A (2013) Ethnoarchaeology meets artificial intelligence. an ongoing experience. In: Social coordination: principles, artifacts and theories. AISB annual convention 2013. http://social.path.sintelnet.eu/papers/paper%20vila.pdf. Accessed Aug 2015

Villmoare B (2013) Morphological integration, evolutionary constraints, and extinction: a computer simulation-based study. Evol Biol 40(1):76–83

Voigtländer N, Voth HJ (2006) Why England? Demographic factors, structural change and physical capital accumulation during the industrial revolution. J Econ Growth 11(4):319–361

Voigtländer N, Voth HJ (2013) The three horsemen of riches: plague, war, and urbanization in early modern Europe. Rev Econ Stud 80(2):774–811

Volterra V (1926) Variazioni e fluttuazioni del numero d'individui in specie animali conviventi. Mem Acad Lincei Roma 2:31–113

Von Rueden C (2014) The roots and fruits of social status in small-scale human societies. In: The psychology of social status. Springer, New York, pp 179–200

Von Stackelberg P (2009) Footprints of the future: timelines and exploratory forecasts in futures research. J Futures Stud 13(4):13–34

de Vries H (2009) On using the DomWorld model to evaluate dominance ranking methods. Behaviour 146(6):843–869

Wagner EO (2012) Evolving to divide the fruits of cooperation. Philos Sci 79(1):81–94

Wainwright J (2008) Can modelling enable us to understand the role of humans in landscape evolution? Geoforum 39(2):659–674

Walby S (2007) Complexity theory, systems theory, and multiple intersecting social inequalities. Philos Soc Sci 37(4):449–470

Wan PY (2012) Analytical sociology: a Bungean appreciation. Sci Educ 21(10):1545–1565

Ward MD, Greenhill BD, Bakke KM (2010) The perils of policy by p-value: predicting civil conflicts. J Peace Res 47(4):363–375

Wassermann S (2007) Let's have a famine! connecting means and ends in teaching to big ideas. Phi Delta Kappan 290–297

Watkins SC, Menken J (1985) Famines in historical perspective. Popul Dev Rev 647–675

Watts J (2013) The organization and evolution of the hohokam economy: agent-based modeling of exchange in the Phoenix Basin, Arizona, AD 200–1450. Ph.D., Arizona State University (ASU), School of Human Evolution and Social Change. The Digital Archaeological Record. http://core.tdar.org/document/391253. doi:10.6067/XCV8V125PD

Weber K (2007) Erklärung historischer Abläufe mit Computersimulationen. Historical Social Research/Historische Sozialforschung 94–121

Weidlich W (2002) Sociodynamics-a systematic approach to mathematical modelling in the social sciences. Nonlinear Phenom Complex Syst-Minsk 5(4):479–487

Wertsch JV (1995) The need for action in sociocultural research. Sociocul Stud Mind 56–74

West GB (2011) Can there be a quantitative theory for the history of life and society? Cliodynamics 2

Wetherell C (1998) Historical social network analysis. Int Rev Soc Hist 43(S6):125–144

White AA (2008) A developmental perspective on technological change. World Archaeol 40(4):597–608. doi:10.1080/00438240802453351

White AA (2013) Subsistence economics, family size, and the emergence of social complexity in hunter–gatherer systems in eastern North America. J Anthropol Archaeol 32(1):122–163

White AA (2014) Mortality, fertility, and the OY ratio in a model hunter–gatherer system. Am J Phys Anthropol 154(2):222–231

White AA (2016) The sensitivity of demographic characteristics to the strength of the population stabilizing mechanism in a model hunter-gatherer system. In: Uncertainty and sensitivity analysis in archaeological computational modeling. Springer International Publishing, pp 113–130

Whitehouse H, Kahn K, Hochberg ME, Bryson JJ (2012) The role for simulations in theory construction for the social sciences: case studies concerning divergent modes of religiosity. Relig Brain Behav 2(3):182–201

Whitley TG (2016) Archaeological simulation and the testing paradigm. In: Uncertainty and sensitivity analysis in archaeological computational modeling. Springer International Publishing, pp 131–156

Whitmore TM (1992) Disease and death in early colonial Mexico: simulating Amerindian depopulation, Dellplain Latin American geography series 28. Westview Press, Boulder

Widgren M (1979) A simulation model of farming systems and land use in Sweden during the early Iron Age, c. 500 b.c.–a.d. 550. J Hist Geogr 5:21–32

Widlok T, Aufgebauer A, Bradtmöller M, Dikau R, Hoffmann Th, Kretschmer I, Panagiotopoulus K, Pastoors A, Peters R, Schäbitz F, Schlummer M, Solich M, Wagner B, Weniger G-Ch, Zimmermann AA (2012) Towards a theoretical framework for analyzing integrated socio-environmental systems. Quat Int 274:259–272

Wilkinson TJ, Gibson M, Christiansen J, Widell M, Schloen D, Kouchoukos N, Woods C, Sanders JC, Simunich K, Altaweel M, Ur JA, Hritz C, Lauinger J, Paulette T, Tenney J (2007b) Modeling settlement systems in a dynamic environment: case studies from Mesopotamia. In:

Kohler TA, van der Leeuw S (eds) The model-based archaeology of socionatural systems. School of American Research, Santa Fe, pp 175–208
Wilkinson TJ, Christiansen J, Ur JA, Widell M, Altaweel M (2007a) Urbanization within a dynamic environment: modelling bronze age communities in upper Mesopotamia. Am Anthropol 109:52–68
Wilkinson TJ, Christensen J, Altaweel M, Widell M (2013) Output from the agent-based modeling program. In Wilkinson TJ, Gibson M, Widell M (eds) Models of Mesopotamian landscapes: how small-scale processes contribute to the growth of early civilizations. Archaeopress, pp 177–204
Will TE (2016) Flock leadership: understanding and influencing emergent collective behavior. Leadersh Q 27(2):261–279
Wimmer A (2014) Nation building. a long-term perspective and global analysis. Eur Sociol Rev jcu078
Winnerling T (2014) The eternal recurrence of all bits: how historicizing video game series transform factual history into affective historicity. Eludamos. J Comput Game Cul 8(1): 151–170
Winterhalder B, Puleston C, Ross C (2015) Production risk, inter-annual food storage by households and population-level consequences in seasonal prehistoric agrarian societies. Environ Archaeol 20(4):337–348
Wischmann S, Floreano D, Keller L (2012) Historical contingency affects signaling strategies and competitive abilities in evolving populations of simulated robots. Proc Natl Acad Sci 109(3):864–868
Witkowski O, Ikegami T (2016) Emergence of swarming behavior: foraging agents evolve collective motion based on signaling. PLoS ONE 11(4):e0152756
Witt U, Schwesinger G (2013) Phylogenetic footprints in organizational behavior. J Econ Behav Organ 90:S33–S44
Wittek P, Rubio-Campillo X (2012) Military reconstructive simulation in the cloud to aid battlefield excavations. In: 2012 IEEE 4th International conference on cloud computing technology and science (CloudCom). IEEE, pp 869–874
Wobcke WR (1998) Agency and the Logic of Ability. In: Wobcke WR, Pagnucco M, Zhang C (eds) Agents and multi-agent systems. Springer, Berlin
Woo KL, Rieucau G (2011) From dummies to animations: a review of computer-animated stimuli used in animal behavior studies. Behav Ecol Sociobiol 65(9):1671–1685
Wood KA, Stillman RA, Goss-Custard JD (2015) Co-creation of individual-based models by practitioners and modellers to inform environmental decision-making. J Appl Ecol 52(4): 810–815
Wooldridge M (2000) Reasoning about rational agents. The MIT Press. ISBN: 0-262-23213-8
Wren CD, Xue JZ, Costopolous A, Burke A (2014) The role of spatial foresight in models of hominin dispersal. J Hum Evol 69:70–78
Wren CD (2014) The effect of spatial environmental heterogeneity on hominin dispersal events and the evolution of complex cognition. Ph.D. dissertation, McGill University
Wright-Maley C (2015) Beyond the "Babel problem": defining simulations for the social studies. J Soc Stud Res 39(2):63–77
Wu J, Rayman Mohamed M, Wang Z (2011) Agent-based simulation of the spatial evolution of the historical population in China. J Hist Geogr 37(1):12–21
Wurzer G, Kowarik K, Reschreiter H (eds) (2015) Agent-based modeling and simulation in archaeology. Advances in Geographic Information Science. Springer
Xu G, Yang J, Li G (2013) Simulating society transitions: standstill, collapse and growth in an evolving network model. PLoS ONE 8(9):e75433
Xu J, Yao L, Lu Y (2014) Ecological capacity evaluation. Innovative approaches towards low carbon economics. Springer, Berlin, Heidelberg, pp 155–175
Yang C, Kurahashi S, Ono I, Terano T (2010) Pattern-oriented inverse simulation for agent-based modeling: an analysis of family strategies. In: Proceedings of the 12th annual conference companion on Genetic and evolutionary computation. ACM, pp 1801–1808

Ylikoski P (2011) Social mechanisms and explanatory relevance. In: Demeulenaere P (ed.) Analytical sociology and social mechanisms. Cambridge University Press
Ylikoski P (2012) Micro, macro, and mechanisms. In: The Oxford handbook of philosophy of the social sciences, pp 21–45
Young DA (2002) A new space-time computer simulation method for human migration. Am Anthropol 104(1):138–158
Younger SM (2005) Violence and revenge in Egalitarian societies. J Artif Soc Soc Simul 8(4)
Younger SM (2011) Leadership, violence, and warfare in small societies. J Artif Soc Soc Simul 14(3):8
Younger SM (2003) Discrete agent simulations of the effect of simple social structures on the benefits of resource sharing. J Artif Soc Soc Simul 6(3)
Younger SM (2012) Calculating chiefs: simulating leadership, violence, and warfare in Oceania. LAP LAMBERT Academic Pub
Youngman PA, Hadzikadic M (eds) (2014) Complexity and the human experience: modeling complexity in the humanities and social sciences. CRC Press
Zacharias GL, Macmillan J, Van Hernel SB (eds) (2008) Behavioural modeling and simulation: from individuals to societies. The National Academies Press, Washington, DC
Zackery A, Shariatpanahi P, Zolfagharzadeh MM, Pourezzat AA (2015) Toward a simulated replica of futures: classification and possible trajectories of simulation in futures studies. Futures
Zanini F, Neher RA (2012) FFPopSim: an efficient forward simulation package for the evolution of large populations. Bioinformatics 28(24):3332–3333
Zenobia BA, Weber CM (2011) Opening the black box of technology adoption: the motive-technology-belief framework. Int J Innov Technol Manage 8(04):535–555
Zeppini P, Frenken K, Kupers R (2014) Thresholds models of technological transitions. Environ Innov Soc Transitions 11:54–70
Zhang DD, Lee HF, Wang C, Li B, Pei Q, Zhang J, An Y (2011) The causality analysis of climate change and large-scale human crisis. Proc Natl Acad Sci 108(42):17296–17301
Zhao Z (1994) Demographic conditions and multi-generation households in Chinese history. Results from genealogical research and microsimulation. Popul Stud 48(3):413–425
Zhao Z (2000) Corresidential patterns in historical China: a simulation study. Popul Dev Rev 26(2):263–293
Zhou X (2008) The great escape: modelling the industrial revolution. Ph.D. dissertation. University of California, Davis
Zubrow EB (1990) The depopulation of native America. Antiquity 64(245):754–765
Zubrow EB (1971) Carrying capacity and dynamic equilibrium in the prehistoric Southwest. Am Antiq 127–138

Chapter 2
Multi-scale Agent-Based Simulation of Long-Term Dispersal Processes: Towards a Sophisticated Simulation Model of Hominin Dispersal

Ingo J. Timm, Fabian Lorig, Ericson Hölzchen and Christine Hertler

Abstract According to the Out-of-Africa-Hypothesis, the geographic origin of hominins known to be ancestors of anatomically modern humans, such as homo sapiens, is located in Africa. Due to the discovery of numerous fossils there is archaeological evidence on the existence of waves of early dispersal from Africa to Eurasia. Yet, the reason as well as the actual route of migration are being discussed controversially among experts. However, there is a scientific consensus that a conjunction of several local factors, such as climatic changes or carnivore competition, caused the global effect of hominids migrating to Eurasia to occur. In order to understand these emergent phenomena and to validate different scientific hypotheses, the dispersal processes need to be reproduced. In this article we propose the use of agent-based modeling for developing a simulation platform which enables researchers to evaluate assumptions and hypotheses using artificial and customizable scenarios. Furthermore, potential fields are proposed as a first step approach for modeling and simulating environmental factors influencing migration processes.

I.J. Timm (✉) · F. Lorig
University of Trier, Business Informatics I, 54286 Trier, Germany
e-mail: ingo.timm@uni-trier.de

F. Lorig
e-mail: fabian.lorig@uni-trier.de

E. Hölzchen · C. Hertler
Senckenberg Research Institute, ROCEEH, 60325 Frankfurt am Main, Germany
e-mail: ericson.hoelzchen@senckenberg.de

C. Hertler
e-mail: christine.hertler@senckenberg.de

J.A. Barceló and F. Del Castillo (eds.), *Simulating Prehistoric and Ancient Worlds*,
Computational Social Sciences, DOI 10.1007/978-3-319-31481-5_2

2.1 Introduction

The question of where mankind originated from has been of peculiar interest for generations. In 1871, Charles Darwin argued that the origin of anatomically modern humans, such as homo sapiens, is located in Africa. As great apes, e.g., chimpanzees and gorillas, are known to be human relatives and live in Africa, this assumption seems obvious. However, Darwin could not provide any evidence for this assumption. Therefore, numerous researchers refused Africa as an origin of mankind and proposed Asia instead. This theory received further support as Dubois found fossils of the so called *Java Man*. In the following decades, further archaeological excavations provided even more evidence for Asia being the origin of mankind (Antón and Swisher III 2004).

A change of thinking was achieved in 1924, when fossils—found in Southafrica—were accepted as human ancestors by leading researchers in paleoanthropology. From that point of time the *Out-Of-Africa-Hypothesis* obtained acceptance (Stringer 2000).

Nowadays, the discovery of numerous fossils supports the existence of waves of early dispersal from Africa to Eurasia, too. According to this, *homo erectus* initiated the migration process towards Eurasia 1.8 million years ago. Yet, the reason as well as the concrete route of migration are still controversially discussed by experts.

Modern geochronological methods enable researchers to date fossils by measuring end products of radioactive decay occurring in findings. As a result of this, evidence concerning the stay of hominins at certain points of time was provided. However, a detailed and complete reconstruction of the path taken cannot be achieved using current methods. Likewise, further archaeological excavations are not promising as well due to the huge size of the area. Thus, four competing hypotheses (Abbate and Sagri 2012; Armitage et al. 2011; Bar-Yosef and Belfer-Cohen 2001; Derricourt 2005) concerning possible routes of human dispersal out of Africa have been established:

- Along the Bad-el-Mandeb Strait, which connects the Red Sea to the Gulf of Aden,
- the Levantive Corridor located between the Mediterranean Sea and the deserts connecting Africa to Eurasia,
- the Strait of Sicily, nowadays separating Tunisia and Sicily,
- and the Strait of Gibraltar, separating the Atlantic and the Mediterranean Sea.

When comparing the scenarios mentioned above it becomes obvious that a combination of several different factors was responsible for the dispersal processes. Each scenario provides conditions making it suitable for migrating from Africa to Eurasia. Among other things ecological variations and demographic pressure likely influenced the dispersal of hominins (Abbate and Sagri 2012).

The increasing number of members may have required tribes to split up in to smaller tribes in order to keep group sizes manageable. Furthermore, changes in climatic, geographical or sea-level conditions may have been responsible for hominins to move towards Eurasia, too. They either made habitable tracts of land uninhabitable or vice versa. Especially when considering potential routes of dispersal, changes of the sea-level may have supported migration or even provided new possibilities (Abbate and Sagri 2012; Blain et al. 2010; Leroy et al. 2011; Van der Made 2011).

But also changes of physical abilities increasing the hominin's stamina as well as the absence or occurrence of diseases outside their former habitat may have caused migration. Finally, other carnivores hunting the same prey might have caused hominins to move to other areas providing a sufficient amount of food (Turner 1992). There is a scientific consensus that a conjunction of the local circumstances and interactions mentioned above caused the global effect of hominins migrating to Eurasia. In order to understand these emergent phenomena and to validate different hypotheses concerning reasons and motivations causing hominins to move to Eurasia, the dispersal processes need to be reproduced.

During the last decades, computer simulation has been established as standard means for reproducing and analyzing the behavior of complex systems. Based on abstract models describing relevant environmental conditions and characteristics of the object to be examined simulation experiments can be conducted. Considering the influencing factors mentioned above, a variety of differentiated yet independent domain models is available. Therefore, this article aims at proposing a method for integrating a set of models representing different factors influencing hominin dispersal processes into a holistic simulation platform. By enabling paleoanthropological researches to formulate hypothesis and assumptions concerning routes hominins may have chosen on their way to Eurasia, the simulation platform proposed in this article provides a tool for validating these theories by simulating the dispersal processes with regards to scenarios created by the researchers.

2.2 Understanding Hominin Dispersal

Hominin fossils discovered by archaeologists do not provide sufficient evidence regarding the concrete route our manlike ancestors have taken on their way from Africa to Eurasia. Therefore, a number of opposing hypotheses and assumptions are suggested by researchers. However, further excavations will likely neither provide certainty concerning the actual route taken nor give indication of the reason hominins migrated. By modeling these dispersal processes, which occurred 1.5–0.5 million years BC, we aim at providing a simulation platform for validating the hypotheses and assumptions by creating individual artificial dispersal processes.

As the access to real pieces of evidence is limited, paleoanthropological researchers are restricted to the use of established technologies and methods. The possibilities of validating hypotheses and analyzing how certain assumptions regarding the environment or the behavior of hominins and other creatures influenced migration processes have been exhausted. Yet, feedback whether or not the hypotheses apply and how assumptions influence the entire system's behavior are essential for researchers in order to gain further insights.

The scope of research questions is wide and evaluating which of the potential routes hominins have chosen to get from location A to location B is only a first step

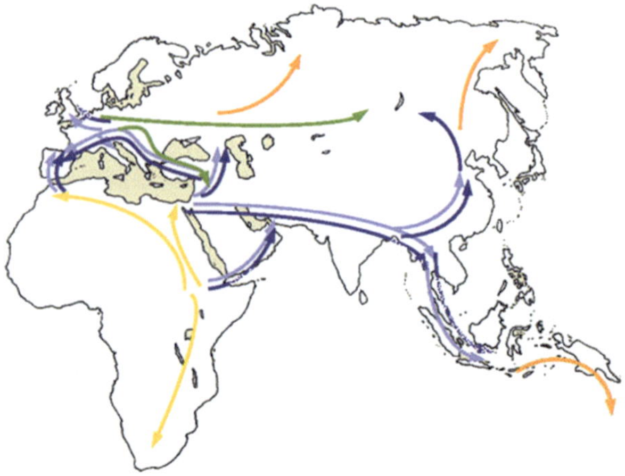

Fig. 2.1 Potential expansion routes between 2 million and 20.000 years before present (ROCEEH 2014)

(see Fig. 2.1). Even estimating probabilities for different routes may help archaeologists on their search for further fossils or other relics. Additionally, insights regarding the time hominin populations needed to complete a route or a segment of a route as well as the preconditions (ecological, physiological/anatomical, technological or cultural) required for the resettlement are of peculiar interest, too. Concerning this, factors determining the dispersal processes most significantly need to be identified first.

The simulation platform (see Fig. 2.2) proposed in this article aims at enhancing the research process at this point. In this regard, by considering a computer science view, it is an important challenge to enable domain experts, i.e. researchers in the field of hominin dispersal processes, to specify hypotheses and to support the interpretation of results by providing the possibility to navigate through them in an adequate way. By conceptualizing a dynamical and extensible simulation platform, researchers and domain experts are provided a tool for specifying and formulating own hypotheses, assumptions and discoveries. Based on this, multiple simulation runs can be performed and artificial scenarios are being created. Thus, the platform provides simulation-based evaluation of hypotheses. As a visionary approach, we are working on assistance functionalities for performing and varying simulation runs in an automated way to avoid the demand of simulation engineers supervising and controlling the execution of simulation experiments (Lattner 2013).

In case of researchers requiring an exact reproduction of simulation runs it is possible to repeat the same scenario but also to vary certain parameters for the purpose of comparability. The output generated by different simulation runs can then be integrated, visualized on a map, and analyzed individually. As a result, researchers can learn from these simulation runs and formulate further hypotheses and assumptions. An iterative process emerges supporting the generation of knowledge with respect to hominin dispersal processes from Africa to Eurasia.

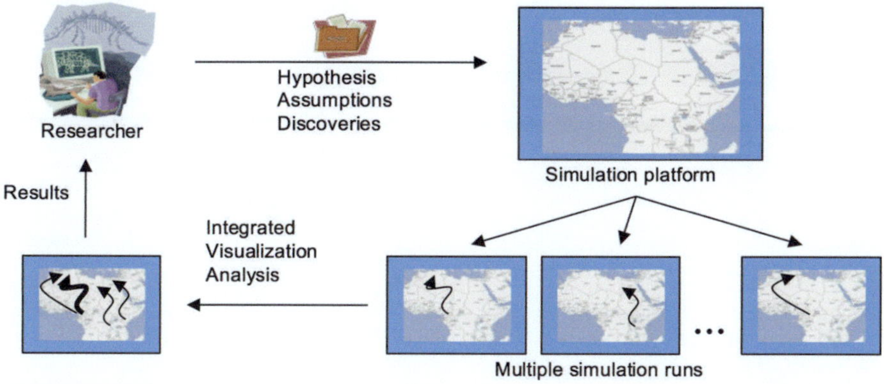

Fig. 2.2 How the simulation platform can be integrated into the process of validation hypotheses

The dispersal processes themselves originated from group dynamics and hominins interacting and reacting with regard to the environment. In the research field of systems theory these effects are referred to as *emergence effects*. They are characterized by the fact that global features, structures, or behaviors of a system arise from local interactions of its components. Yet, these global observations can only partially be reduced to features of the system's components. Out of this, the necessity of applying a modeling technique taking these effects into account is derived.

2.3 Agent-Based Computer Simulation

When reconstructing emergent phenomena in complex environments, like the conditions given by the Out-Of-Africa-Hypothesis, a consideration of each individual actor being involved in the scenario is required. In contrast to describing a system using sets of differential equations or stochastic modeling, a more individualized modeling technique needs to be used. In computer science the concept of *software agents* has been established for modeling interacting individuals.

2.3.1 Software Agents

Wooldridge describes computer systems as software agents, in case they comply with the following two requirements:

- The computer system is *situated in some environment* and
- it is capable of *autonomous action in this environment* in order to meet its designers objectives.

These so called autonomous actions are not meant to be compared to the basic exchange of data. Interactions performed by software agents are rather inspired by human social behavior such as cooperation, coordination or negotiation between individuals (Woolridge and Wooldridge 2001).

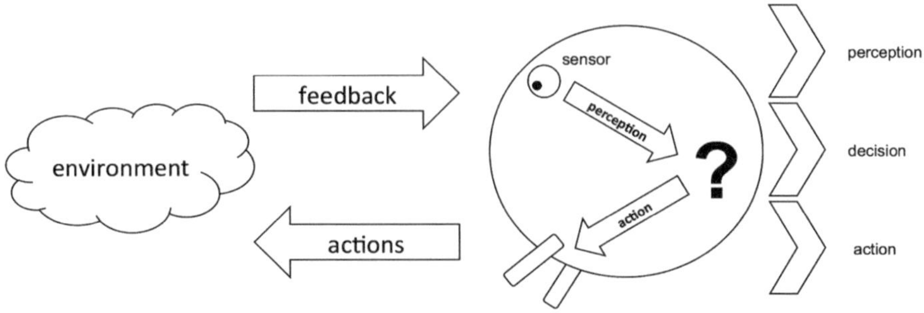

Fig. 2.3 A software agent located in its environment (Woolridge and Wooldridge 2001; Russell and Norvig 2003)

Awareness of the current state of the world (the agent's environment) and changes occurring in the world are necessary for making autonomous behavior possible. By using sensors for observing the environment agents can perceive different states of the world and react according to its objectives to be achieved, as shown in Fig. 2.3. As agents have to choose the most suitable action from a set of possible actions, a differentiated decision function (also called *agent function*) is required. Agent functions can either be simple mathematical functions mapping certain perceptions to predefined actions or more sophisticated mechanisms enabling agents to behave "*intelligent*".

Intelligent agents, as a special type of software agents, are characterized by applying proactive behavior for accomplishing goals given. For this purpose, the use of techniques from the area of *artificial intelligence* is required, as agents need to learn from recent behavior or observations and use practical reasoning in order to achieve more sophisticated goals. Furthermore, a social ability is required, as intelligent agents are meant to interact with other agents.

Based on the environment agents are located in and the goals agents are given to achieve, the design needs to be individual. The degree of *intelligence* required for accomplishing tasks influences the amount of considerations which are necessary before making a decision. Figure 2.4 shows structures of different agent types.

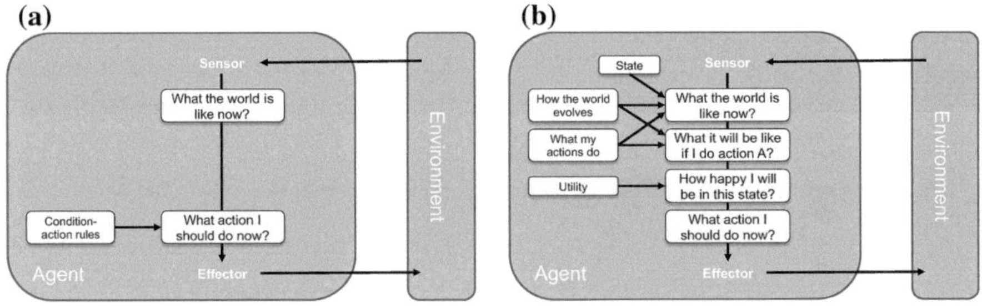

Fig. 2.4 Schematic structure diagrams of different agent types (Russell and Norvig 2003). **a** Simple reflex agent. **b** Utility-based agent

Fig. 2.5 Agent function of a simple reflex agent in charge of a heating control

$$Agent(condition) = \begin{cases} \text{heater off} & \text{if condition = temperature OK} \\ \text{heater on} & \text{otherwise} \end{cases}$$

Simple relfex agents are the most elementary type of software agents. Actions are chosen by ignoring the history of events which occurred in the agent's environment. Instead, only current observations are considered for selecting the next action. These predefined connections leading from sensor-aided perceptions to agent behavior are called *condition-action-rules*. For example in case of an agent being in charge of a heating control linked to the heather of a house, the condition-action-rules might be defined as shown in Fig. 2.5.

Considering more complex scenarios where agents are meant to control more sophisticated entities, simple differentiations by cases likely lack of specialization. When choosing an agent's next action a detailed consideration of the action's consequences might be necessary. The hypothetical condition of the world, after the agent has performed its action, may influence the decision of the agent. Even though an action might appear to be useful or appropriate regarding the current state of the agent's world, changing the environment by performing the action might cause a disadvantage to the agent. For example, when thinking of an agent located in a natural environment, harvesting and eating the remaining wheat results in the satisfaction of hunger, however, using it to grow more wheat would have provided a food supply in the long term.

By comparing different states of the world resulting from an action, agents can select the most beneficial action. To provide a consistent way of measuring the performance of each possible state, agents' are provided *utility functions*. These *utility-based agents* then choose their actions by trying to maximize the utility expected when applying a certain action.

Simple reflex agents and utility-based agents are only two examples for possible structures of software agents. However, comparing these two structures shows that software agents can be applied in diverse scenarios and for solving problems at different levels of difficulty. Either as a reactive unit for unambiguous decisions-making or as a highly specialized autonomous entity planing its actions ahead.

2.3.2 Agent-Based Modeling and Simulation

When trying to understand, analyze or optimize a real world system, the transformation of processes and entities into a model has been established as a first step. By modeling systems based on its components, a profound basis for the representation of emergent phenomena is provided. So called *agent-based models* (ABM), consisting of individual actors having opportunities for decisions and actions, are used for gaining further insights into the behavior of actors when certain rules are given. Due to diverse areas of application for intelligent software agents, they are particularly even seen as a way of thinking rather than a technology for implementing autonomous entities (Bonabeau 2002).

When using ABM to create systems of agents trying to solve problems, *multi-agent systems* (MAS) are formed (Ferber 1999). In order to simplify the creation of MAS, a number of software toolkits like NetLogo[1] or RePast[2] were developed since the beginning of the nineties. As a result of this even non-informatical sciences, such as social sciences or economics, adopted ABM as inherent part of their set of research methods.

MAS can be used to generate or reconstruct emergent behavior by executing agent-based models and simulating interactions between the agents. The process of executing models is called *computer simulation* and provides a series of benefits. In case real world experiments would influence or even damage the real system, using computer simulation prevents risk to the real system. Furthermore, experiments might be too sophisticated in order to be executed in real systems or real systems are not accessible to researchers. Finally, and this is the most relevant aspect when analyzing long-term dispersal processes, even systems that are not or no longer existent can be examined by using computer simulation.

Fujimoto defines computer simulation as follows:

> A computer simulation is a computation that models the behavior of some real or imagined system over time (Fujimoto 2000).

This definition names three relevant components of computer simulation: the system, the model and the simulation itself (see Fig. 2.6).

A *system*, also referred to as *original system* or *real world system*, is the object of study. It contains a holistic view on relationships between entities and processes. The original system is then being mapped to a *model* or *model system*, a formal description of certain effects or phenomena being part of the original system. This is accomplished by the use of domain specific methods for describing the behavior of the system. However, the process of mapping real systems to models is associated with a loss of precision. Models, by definition, are never equivalent to the original system, as the only adequate model of a real system is the system itself. Nevertheless, it meets certain appropriate features or relationships of the original system's object of study. Simulation can therefore be used for performing experiments with the model. By this means either the real system's model or artificial scenarios generated by altering the model can be analyzed (Klügl 2001).

In order to use simulation results for predicting the original system, two requirements need to be met: *verification* and *validation*. Verification describes the process

[1]https://ccl.northwestern.edu/netlogo/.

[2]http://repast.sourceforge.net/.

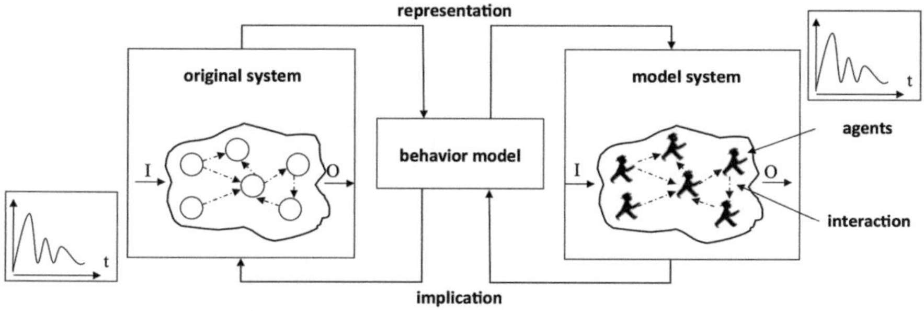

Fig. 2.6 Relation between original system and model system (Timm and Hillebrandt 2006)

of evaluating whether the software itself is designed and programmed in a correct manner, whereas determining the model's appropriateness for representing the original system is called validation. However, a detailed consideration of how to verify and validate a computer simulation will not be part of this article as a variety of methods is sufficiently described in literature (Kleijnen 1995).

When providing a valid and verified model of a real world scenario, which depends on the research of domain experts, computer simulation can be used for gaining knowledge from experiments. By applying assumptions to the simulation model, artificial scenarios can be created and analyzed. Furthermore, hypotheses concerning the behavior of the system under certain circumstances can be evaluated. Therefore, and due to the condition given in the context of the Out-of-Africa-Hypothesis, we propose the application of agent-based modeling as an innovative methodology for modeling, simulating and analyzing artificial societies for understanding the dynamics of hominin dispersal processes.

2.4 Modeling Dispersal Processes

In order to use agent-based simulation for understanding the reason why hominins migrated from Africa to Eurasia and to reconstruct the actual route taken by them, a sophisticated agent model needs to be created. As emergent phenomena were a reason for dispersal processes to occur, decisions and actions of each individual need to be modeled. Based on the agent models introduced in the previous section, intelligent utility-based agent seems to be most suitable for this task.

Assuming that hominins had a concrete reason to leave their original habitat, a detailed consideration of potential influencing factors seems necessary. Utility-based agents, in contrast to simpler agent structures, consider changes of their environment and evaluate the consequences of their actions in advance. Furthermore, the happiness regarding new states created by performing an action will be considered as well. Transfered to the challenges hominins faced when crossing Africa towards Eurasia, this happiness might be equated with the sufficient availability of food and other

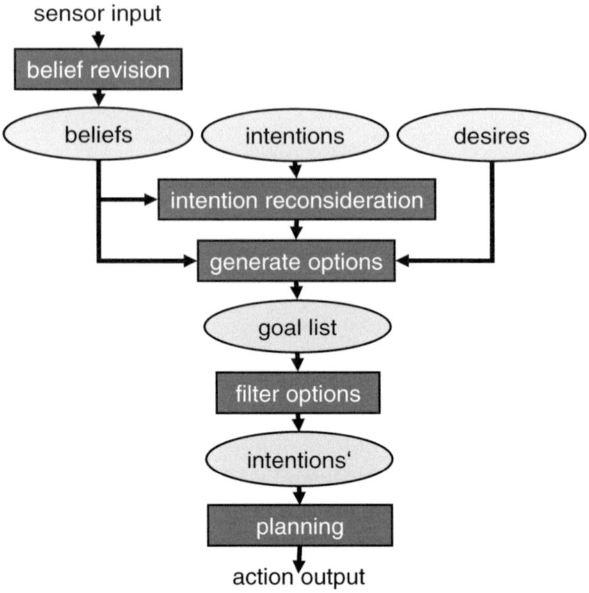

Fig. 2.7 Sequence of a BDI agent's reasoning process (Timm 2004)

resources of vital importance. Alternatively, the level of happiness was likely being influenced by the absence of predators or other hostile creatures. With other words, we can assume that the path of hominins was influenced by the pursuit of multiple goals.

When transferring a multi-goal scenario into agent-based modeling the so called *BDI* architecture for software agents has proven to be suitable. In the *belief-desire-intention software model*, as shown in Fig. 2.7, a distinction is made between the selection and the execution of the agent's plan. According to the model of human practical reasoning developed by Bratman, the BDI architecture consists of three components: (Rao et al. 1995; Bratman 1987)

- **Beliefs**: The agent's beliefs represent its perception. All information collected about the environment and other agents located inside this environment as well as information about the agent itself are stored in a *beliefset*.
- **Desires**: The motivational state of an agent is stored as its desires. Desires may be perceived as the objectives agents want to accomplish. However, the term *goal* is not equivalent to the term *desires* when talking about BDI agents. A goal is a specific desire which is actively pursued by an agent. Hence, the desires of an agent may be contradictory whereas the goals of an agent must not be.
- **Intentions**: The deliberative component of a BDI agent is represented by its intentions. In order to attain its goal, agents are provided a set of plans. The plans purposefully chosen by the agent are referred to as the agent's intentions. A plan consists of a sequence of actions which can be performed by the agent, yet, plans may be composed of other plans.

Transfered to the modulation and simulation of dispersal processes, hominins may be modeled using a BDI architecture. As hominins were able to perceive their environment and had to choose certain actions according to their needs, this way of modeling seems suitable. Hence, the recurrent reasoning process of BDI agents (see Fig. 2.7) needs to be fit to the behavior of hominins.

Initially, the beliefs already known to the agent need to be revised using recent sensor input. New perceptions need to be added or changes in the environment need to be considered for further planning. Based on the updated beliefset, agents need to consider whether the execution of the current plan is still expedient or even possible. Changes in the environment or new observations may cause the current goal to become unattainable pursuing the current plan or the selection of another goal might have become more reasonable. For instance the observation of a group of carnivores close to a nearby river crossing might require a tribe of hominins to discard their current goal of crossing a river course at a certain place. Instead another crossing located further away may need to be chosen instead.

Generating the agents' new options by considering the updated beliefset, desires and feasible plans, a new list of goals is being created as well. Based on this goal list a new plan is chosen and the actions which are necessary to accomplish this plan are executed. Executing BDI agents requires this process to be performed over and over again in order to consider changes of the world.

However, hominins are not the only actors which are part of the Out-of-Africa-Hypothesis that deliberate their behavior in regard to their actions. The behavior of carnivores might for example be modeled by using a BDI architecture as well. Choosing appropriate prey as well as selecting, defending and marking their territory are processes which can be modeled using intelligent software agents. Yet, specialized domain models is a need to be provided by domain experts.

2.5 Environmental Abstraction

But not all aspects of the Out-of-Africa-Hypothesis can and should be modeled as intelligent software agents. There are also other factors affecting the dispersal processes such as outside influences (weather or climatic changes) or the condition of the landscape (vegetation or geological formation). These factors cannot be implemented by using software agents. Instead, they are meant to be modeled as part of the environment the agents are located in. Hence, another modeling technique is needed for abstracting these aspects.

On closer consideration, all factors mentioned in Sect. 2.1 have in common that they influence the suitableness of land for hominin dispersal. The influence can either be positive, as for example an abundant vegetation providing a sufficient food supply, or negative, as geographical conditions can make a trace of land impassable to hominins. However, the impassableness can be caused due to physical reasons, for example a mountain which is too sheer, or a lack of appropriate tools, for instance

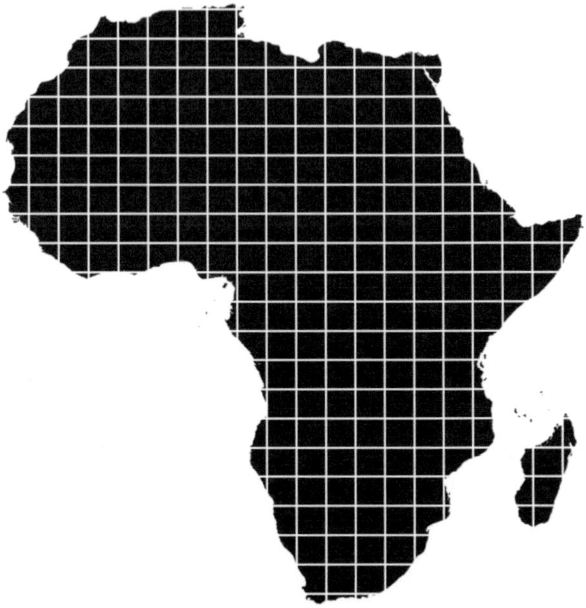

Fig. 2.8 Segmentation of a map of the African continent into equal cells as used for the modulation and implementation of potential fields

for building a raft for crossing a broad river. To put it another way, all of these factors influence the land's potential for hominin dispersal. Yet, the potential is not a constant value but it may change over time.

As part of earlier work an approach for simulating migration processes on potential field based landscapes has been proposed (Dallmeyer et al. 2010). Dividing a landscape into subsegments of equal size provides the possibility of calculating an individual potential for hominins to migrate to each cell (Fig. 2.8). By combining different domain models evaluating specific aspects of the overall potential of a certain cell, a detailed estimation can be given.

A geographer might provide a domain model for estimating the potential of landscapes. In this case a desert might be assessed with a low score and the borderlines of freshwater areas with a high score. A biologist might then complete this model with statements about how the landscape's potential mentioned above influences the settlement of prey or the vegetation which can be expected due to the potential of the landscape. But also weather models need to be taken into account as they can change the potential of a cell as well, for example due to the absence of rain. Finally, a holistic model arises for evaluating the potential of individual cells.

In computer science the use of *cellular automata* has been established for implementing spatially discrete dynamical systems. A regular grid of cells is the basis of each cellular automaton. Each of these cells can have a state, yet, the state is calculated using a mathematical function whose variables are defined as the states of cells located in a cell's neighborhood. However, the definition of which cell is considered as a certain cell's neighbor may vary. Two prominent definitions of neighborhoods are shown in Fig. 2.9 (Toffoli and Margolus 1987).

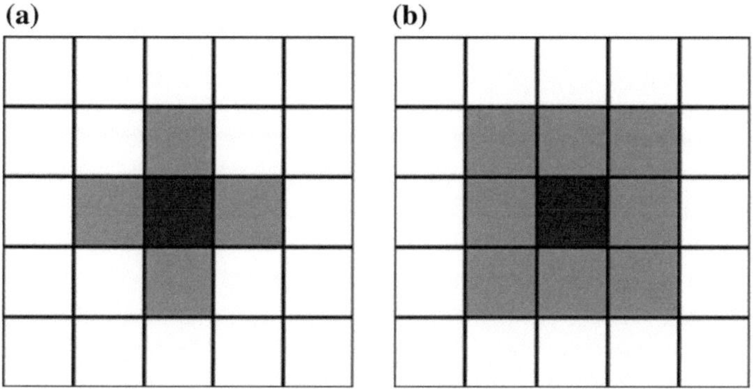

Fig. 2.9 Visualization of different neighborhoods in cellular automata. **a** von Neumann neighborhood. **b** Moore neighborhood

Starting from the dark cell shown in the center of each grid in Fig. 2.9 the *von Neumann neighborhood* contains the direct neighbors on each side of the cell. The *Moore neighborhood* instead contains the cells located diagonally from the starting cell as well. Depending on the environmental definition given by the model neighborhoods can be implemented individually in cellular automata.

When modeling and simulating hominin dispersal processes the potential of each cell may be implemented as the cell's current state. Depending on the influencing factors being regarded for the calculation of a cell's potential, the neighborhood needs to be defined according to the domain models. In case of weather models this might even imply the definition of a three-dimensional cellular automaton, as weather phenomena like rainfall or wind occur from multiple directions. Certainly when modeling rain a distinction between the vertical rainfall and the horizontal drain of rain water needs to be considered.

When modeling rainfall and its impact to the potential of a certain cell in a cellular automaton, the amount of water falling on each cell needs to be defined. Depending on the capacity of the soil, defined by geological domain models, and the liquid requirements of the plants, being part of a biological domain model, a certain amount of the rainfall will not be retained by the cell's components. This surplus of water will then drain off to the neighbor cells, as defined by a geographical domain model and become another factor of the calculation of the cell's potential.

Analogous to this description the dependencies and interferences of each domain model as well as effects towards cells in its neighborhood need to be defined. Based on this an overall potential for hominin dispersal may be calculated in order to simplify decision making of hominin agents.

2.6 Challenges for Scaling Agent-Based Modeling

As described in the previous sections, agent-based modeling may significantly improve the understanding of hominin dispersal processes. However, a number of challenges is existing as well which scientists may face during the modeling and simulation of the platform described. Contrary to usual fields of simulation application, the special feature of this scenario is its enormous size. Either linked to the domain model's level of detail, the long lapse of time, the spatial extent or the amount of individual actors, simulation of hominin dispersal processes will most likely cause challenges in scaling agent-based simulation the models being used. Therefore, we identify five major challenges as part of this article:

Scale 1: *Expertise*. A variety of highly complex domain models, e.g., weather, climate, or botany, needs to be integrated.

As described in Sect. 2.5 a large number of highly specialized domain models needs to be integrated into the simulation platform for modeling the environment and the actors being part of it. The development of each of these models is the responsibility of domain experts as they possess knowledge about the mechanisms controlling the behavior of a particular factor or entity. These mechanisms and further features need to be transfered into a formal model, which then can be interpreted and integrated by the simulation platform. As mentioned in the previous chapters the integration can either be accomplished by the use of agent-based modeling or as part of a complex mathematical formula determining the potential of a piece of land as cell of a cellular automaton.

Furthermore, besides design and implementation issues, the specification of a multi-disciplinary modeling language is required. In order to achieve a common understanding of the subject among all groups of participants adequate techniques for formalizing and visualizing domain specific insights and to provide an optimal human-computer interaction need to be created.

Scale 2: *Space*. The model's granularity concerning the spatial and temporal resolution of the simulation needs to be determined.

Nowadays, due to the availability of cloud-computing and networked systems, computer disk space becomes less important to private users. However, the amount of data being generated when simulating hominin dispersal processes on a detailed level is inconceivable. The area of Africa is currently stated as 30 million km^2. When modeling the African environment using potential fields, each cell having the size of one square kilometer and each potential requiring 4 bytes[3] of disk space, a total amount of 115 MB of space is required for each update of the potential field.

As users of the simulation platform are going to simulate a long lapse of time and as stepwise analysis of the simulation progress is required, intermediate data need to be stored as well. Considering an interval of 1.5M years and steps of 100 years,

[3]4 bytes of disk space is the amount of space required for an *integer* value, a whole number, to be stored in *Java* programming language.

almost 1.7 TB[4] of disk space will be occupied. When considering smaller time steps and a significantly higher amount of disk space required for the simulation of software agents, which have not been regarded in the calculation shown above, the challenge of defining a manageable yet informative modeling and simulation granularity becomes apparent.

Scale 3: *Time*. Particularly influenced by the granularity, scaling challenges emerging from the extraordinary long lapse of time being simulation need to be solved.

Certainly due to the use of agent-based modeling and intelligent software agents the time lapse of simulation needs to be kept in mind. As described in Sect. 2.4 intelligent software agents can memorize the world they are located in and changes that occurred during their execution. In case the time steps are not chosen wisely when performing simulation experiments, a considerable amount of data can be collected in no time. As a result of this a new area of agent research needs to be faced: *intentional forgetting*. In order to keep the mental state of an agent manageable mechanisms for discarding information on purpose need to be developed and implemented.

Scale 4: *Actor*. A consideration of the actor's level of details needs to be made. Is it sufficient to model each tribe or is the presence of each of the tribes' members relevant?

Depending on the hypotheses defined by researchers, the level of detail regarding individual tribes might vary. In case an ant inspired behavior for discovering new sources of food or fresh water supplies by randomly spreading into all directions, the simulation of each member of a tribe as a single software agent is required. However, in case assumptions defining a continuous movement of a tribe are made the consideration of each member of a tribe might no longer be relevant. Instead, one software agent representing the entire tribe might be sufficient.

Scale 5: *Validity*. As a consequence of the previous four scales the question of how to validate models of this enormous complexity arises.

Verification and validation is a key aspect of modeling and simulation. The model should correspond to the real world in such a way that effects identified in the simulation are related to the real world behavior of a system. Ensuring verification and validity is a challenge for simulation by itself. Each dimension introduced so far increases the validation complexity significantly. Another challenge arises from the non-existence of hominin dispersal processes in our days such that empirical evidence is not provided.

2.7 Conclusions

According to the Out-of-Africa-Hypothesis, the geographic origin of anatomically modern humans is located in Africa. But, hominin fossils discovered by archaeologists do not provide sufficient evidence regarding the actual route hominins have

---

[4] 1.7 TB $\approx$ 1.700.000 MB.

taken on their way from Africa to Eurasia. Therefore, a number of opposing hypotheses and assumptions are suggested by researchers. Furthermore, a number of influencing factors has been identified which may have caused the migration to happen. However, further excavations will likely neither provide certainty concerning the actual route taken not give some indication for the reason hominins migrated. By modeling these dispersal processes, which occurred 1.5-0.5M years BC, we aim at providing a simulation platform for validating hypotheses and assumptions by creating individual artificial dispersal processes. In contrast to other approaches we propose to develop a sophisticated simulation model consisting of cognitive decision making as well as discretized models for integrating environmental influence factors rather then applying stochastic process simulation.

When modeling actors being part of the Out-of-Africa-Hypothesis as intelligent software agents, processes of deliberation regarding different environmental factors can be recreated and analyzed by researchers. Furthermore, different artificial scenarios can be set up and dispersal processes can be simulated individually.

The approach proposed within this article is meant to be understood as a first conception of how to simulate hominin dispersal processes in order to provide a simulation platform for researchers from multiple disciplines. For this purpose five challenges in terms of scaling issues has been identified. However, we are aware that further research is required considering the formalization of hypotheses and assumptions as well as the integration of diverse domain models into a holistic simulation system in order to implement an operative simulation platform. Nevertheless, our workgroup aims at contributing significant aspects.

Acknowledgments Parts of the concepts presented here, i.e., applying potential fields to dispersal simulation, have been developed together with Tjorben Bogon and Jörg Dallmeyer.

References

Abbate E, Sagri M (2012) Early to Middle Pleistocene Homo dispersals from Africa to Eurasia: geological, climatic and environmental constraints. Quat Int 267:3–19

Antón SC, Swisher III CC (2004) Early dispersals of homo from Africa. Annu Rev Anthropol 271–296

Armitage SJ, Jasim SA, Marks AE, Parker AG, Usik VI, Uerpmann H-P (2011) The southern route out of Africa: evidence for an early expansion of modern humans into Arabia. Science 331(6016):453–456

Bar-Yosef O, Belfer-Cohen A (2001) From Africa to Eurasia early dispersals. Quat Int 75(1):19–28

Blain H-A, Bailon S, Cuenca-Bescós G, Bennàsar M, Rofes J, López-García JM, Huguet R, Arsuaga JL, de Castro JMB, Carbonell E (2010) Climate and environment of the earliest West European hominins inferred from amphibian and squamate reptile assemblages: Sima del Elefante Lower Red Unit, Atapuerca, Spain. Quat Sci Rev 29(23):3034–3044

Bonabeau E (2002) Agent-based modeling: methods and techniques for simulating human systems. Proc Natl Acad Sci 99(suppl 3):7280–7287

Bratman M (1987) Intention, plans, and practical reason

Dallmeyer J, Bogon T, Lorion Y, Timm IJ (2010) Migration simulation on potential field based landscapes. In: Proceedings of the 3rd International ICST conference on simulation tools and techniques. ICST (Institute for Computer Sciences, Social-Informatics and Telecommunications Engineering), p 73

Derricourt R (2005) Getting out of Africa: sea crossings, land crossings and culture in the hominin migrations. J World Prehist 19(2):119–132

Ferber J (1999) Multi-agent systems: an introduction to distributed artificial intelligence, vol 1. Addison-Wesley Reading

Fujimoto RM (2000) Parallel and distributed simulation systems, vol 300. Wiley, New York

Kleijnen JP (1995) Verification and validation of simulation models. Eur J Oper Res 82(1):145–162

Klügl F (2001) Multiagentensimulation, vol 1. Addison-Wesley

Lattner AD (2013) Towards automation of simulation studies. KI-Künstliche Intelligenz 27(3):287–290

Leroy S, Arpe K, Mikolajewicz U (2011) Vegetation context and climatic limits of the Early Pleistocene Hominin dispersal in Europe. Quat Sci Rev 30(11):1448–1463

Rao AS, Georgeff MP et al (1995) BDI agents: from theory to practice. ICMAS 95:312–319

ROCEEH (2014) Potential expansion routes between 2 million and 20.000 years before present. http://www.roceeh.net/home

Russell SJ, Norvig P (2003) Artificial intelligence: a modern approach, 2 edn. Pearson Education

Stringer C (2000) Palaeoanthropology: coasting out of Africa. Nature 405(6782):24–27

Timm IJ (2004) Dynamisches Konfliktmanagement als Verhaltenssteuerung Intelligenter Agenten, vol 1. infix AKA Verlagsgruppe

Timm IJ, Hillebrandt F (2006) Reflexion als sozialer mechanismus zum strategischen management autonomer softwaresysteme. In: Reflexive soziale Mechanismen. Springer, pp 255–288

Toffoli T, Margolus N (1987) Cellular automata machines: a new environment for modeling. MIT press

Turner A (1992) Large carnivores and earliest European hominids: changing determinants of resource availability during the Lower and Middle Pleistocene. J Hum Evol 22(2):109–126

Van der Made J (2011) Biogeography and climatic change as a context to human dispersal out of Africa and within Eurasia. Quat Sci Rev 30(11):1353–1367

Woolridge M, Wooldridge MJ (2001) Introduction to multiagent systems. Wiley, New York, NY, USA

Chapter 3
An Agent-Based Model of Resource Distribution on Hunter-Gatherer Foraging Strategies: Clumped Habitats Favor Lower Mobility, but Result in Higher Foraging Returns

Marco A. Janssen and Kim Hill

3.1 Introduction

Animal behavioral ecologists have long proposed that greater environmental patchiness changes the optimal strategy for a variety of social behaviors (e.g. MacArthur and Pianka 1966). Following this lead, primatologists and human behavioral ecologists generally propose a relationship between group size and movement and whether resources are dispersed or clumped in space (e.g. Crook 1970; Jarman 1974; Wrangham 1980; Winterhalder and Smith 1981; Slobodchikoff 1984; Terborgh and Jansen 1986; Kelly 1995). While some ecological models focus on the effects of group size on predation risk, or inter-group competitive ability to monopolize resources, other have focused on cooperation and feeding competition (e.g. MacDonald 1983; White and Wrangham 1988; Chapman et al. 1995; Janson and Goldsmith 1995; Creel 1997). When patches are large feeding competition should be lower, and optimal group size will increase if there are advantages to grouping (Clark and Mangel 1986). Applications of this logic to human foraging societies are tempting. For example, Kelly (1995: 215) following Horn (1968) predicts that hunter-gatherer group size should increase with increased environmental patchiness.

In a similar manner, animal ecologists have proposed (and provided some evidence) that levels of resource patchiness affect movement patterns of foraging species

M.A. Janssen (✉)
School of Sustainability, Arizona State University, Tempe, USA
e-mail: Marco.Janssen@asu.edu

K. Hill
School of Human Evolution and Social Change, Arizona State University, Tempe, USA
e-mail: kim.hill@asu.edu

J.A. Barceló and F. Del Castillo (eds.), *Simulating Prehistoric and Ancient Worlds*, Computational Social Sciences, DOI 10.1007/978-3-319-31481-5_3

(e.g. Hart 1981). The general prediction is that movement should be less frequent in patchy environments because foragers should stay within a patch until foraging gain rates drop below some critical value before moving on (Charnov 1976). While most hunter-gatherer mobility models predict that mobility decreases with more abundant resources (an intuitive outcome if movement is costly), Kelly also predicted that more patchy environments should result in less frequent mobility for hunter-gatherer societies (1995: 120) even when resource density is held constant.

In this paper we explore these predictions using agent-based modeling, and examine how optimal group size, movement frequency, are affected by more dispersed or more clumped resource distributions, when the absolute number of resources in the environment is held constant. We also examine the effect of targeted camp movement (vs. random) on the return rate that can be obtained in more patchy environment. The model uses real measured parameters from a modern foraging society to create an agent-based model, which subsequently allows us to simulate a more patchy or less patchy environment in order to determine how those changes affect optimal group size and mobility.

3.2 Model Description

We developed an agent-based model (ABM) of foraging behavior of the Ache hunters by assuming hunting behavior consistent with Optimal Foraging Theory and based on ecological parameters of the environment and prey characteristics measured in the Mbaracayu Reserve, Paraguay (Janssen and Hill 2014). Model documentation and code used for this publication can be found at: https://www.openabm.org/model/4538/version/1/view. The Mbaracayu Reserve is part of the traditional foraging territory of the native Ache population whose foraging patterns have been extensively studied from an optimal foraging perspective (e.g. Hawkes et al. 1982; Hill et al. 1987; Kaplan and Hill 1992).

The model landscape consists of 58,408 one-hectare cells representing the Mbaracayu Reserve. Each 100 × 100 m cell in the model was assigned a vegetation type based on ground truth transects and subsequent supervised GIS classification with remote sensing using the Landsat 7 TM image with 6 optical bands and one thermal band (Naidoo and Hill 2006). Seven major vegetation habitat types were distinguished: (1) meadow/grassland; (2) large bamboo forest; (3) riparian forest; (4) high forest; (5) low forest; (6) small bamboo understory; and (7) liana forest (Hill et al. 1997). For each hectare cell with an assigned vegetation type, an expected encounter rate for 26 prey types was assigned based on 9 million meters of random diurnal transect monitoring of game encounter rates (Hill et al. 2003; Janssen and Hill 2014).

Our model consists of two types of agents; hunters, and camps, that move on the model landscape. Based on GPS measurements hunters move at a speed of 100 m per 5 min while searching for prey in any of the seven vegetation types. Given the empirically measured mean hunt-day length of 355 min for Ache men (Hill et al.

1985; Hill and Kintigh 2009), hunters can potentially cover on average 7.1 km each day, searching for prey on the simulated landscape.

For each of the 26 prey types in our ABM the following empirically measured characteristics apply: mean live weight of a harvested prey item, mean pursuit time if the prey is hunted upon encounter, and mean probability of a kill (success rate) for all pursuits attempted (see Hill and Kintigh 2009; Janssen and Hill 2014). After the initial assignment of prey densities based on corresponding vegetation types, there are four ways by which prey encounter rates can change through time:

1. *Encounter Rate Suppression* (*ERS*). The probability of encountering a prey is reduced for the rest of the day when hunters pass through a cell since they frighten the animals in the cell to hide or move for some time period.
2. *Prey Capture* (*PC*). The probability of encountering a prey is adjusted to zero for a cell and some number of surrounding cells whenever a hunt is successful an animal is harvested. The number of cells emptied depends on the density of the species (see Janssen and Hill 2014).
3. *Migration* (*M*). Every 3 months there is an update of the prey encounter values by assuming that some animals in nearby cells move into "empty" cells after a conspecific has been harvested. This is an oversimplification adopted for computational reasons, but sensitivity analysis show that more frequent updating does not significantly change the results.
4. *Reproduction* (*R*). Once a year we include a reproduction event which follows logistic growth assumptions and increases the probability of encountering prey in cells that were previously emptied after prey harvest.

Each of the 26 prey encounter rates is updated every 5 min in every cell in the model landscape based on ERS and PC. Prey encounter rates are also updated in every cell each three months based on M and once a year due to R.

All hunters live in camps with other hunters, and the location of the next campsite (an agent in the model) often moves each morning (see below). During each 5 min time step through the day, hunters either move/search or hunt/pursue prey without moving. Hunters are constrained to initially travel in the approximate direction of the campsite for the end of the day (Janssen and Hill 2014).

Each time step that a hunter is not in pursuit of a specific prey item, the hunter moves to an adjacent cell and then checks the list of potential prey species in that habitat type in random order to determine whether an encounter takes place in that cell (Fig. 3.1). Prey encounters are assigned probabilistically to match actual measured encounter rates from diurnal transect monitoring. If a prey is encountered, the hunter decides whether to pursue that prey type, and if pursuit is elected, the hunter terminates the probability of encountering any remaining potential prey in that cell. The decision to pursue is based on the expected profitability (kg/h) of the encountered prey type and the mean experienced return rate (kg/h) in the previous 20 days of foraging.

If a hunter is in pursuit during any time step, he remains in pursuit until the assigned prey type pursuit time expires (a defined number of time steps required for each prey

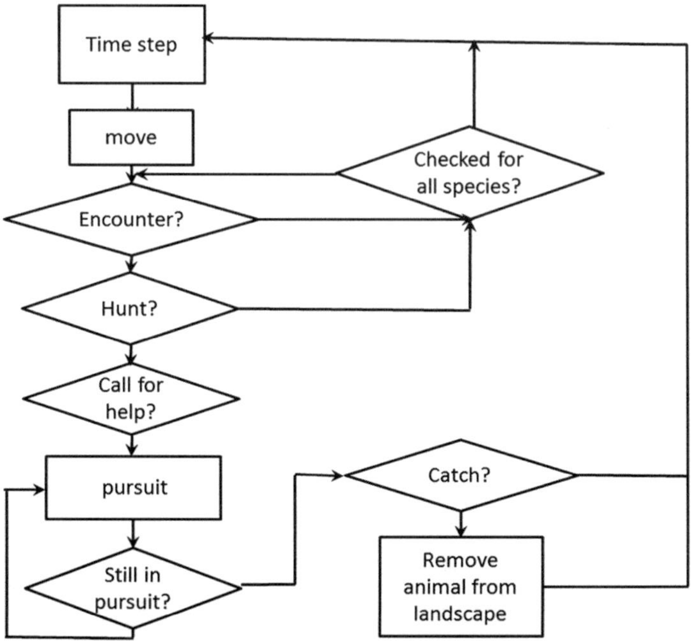

Fig. 3.1 Decision tree for hunters and their related decisions in the agent-based model of foraging

type). If the hunter is not in a pursuit, he checks whether there is still time left in the day to search for prey. If so, the hunter can either turn and move one cell (to repeat the above sequence), or continue moving forward in his previous direction. There is a probability p_S that the hunter continues walking straight, and thus a (1-p_S) probability that the hunter reorients. As the remaining time left in the day decreases, the hunter becomes more likely to reorient directly towards the next campsite in order to make it to the assigned campsite by the end of the allowed foraging period. Ongoing pursuits continue to termination near the end of the day even if this requires more time than the average assigned foraging day. In the case of an extra-long foraging day due to pursuit, a new time budget is calculated for the following day that will result in the average hunting time per day of 355 min over the long run.

When other hunters are searching nearby, Ache hunters engage in cooperative pursuits for the following species: capuchin monkey, coati, paca, armadillos, and peccaries. Hunters that encounter these prey, often call for others to join a pursuit. Cooperative pursuits increase the total harvest for a band (Hill and Hawkes 1983), but in order for hunters to join in cooperative pursuits, they must move though the landscape in a semi coordinated fashion. In this paper we only include coordinated search with cooperative pursuits for some species. Janssen and Hill (2014) presented analysis of other types of hunter behavior.

The previously published version of the Mbaracayu foraging model allowed us to examine the implications of social living (congregating in camps at the end of each day), cooperative hunting, variation in group size and mobility, under Ache-like ecological conditions. Simulations showed that group living (with presumed sharing) greatly decreased daily risk of no food, but group-based cooperative hunting had only a modest effect of increasing harvest rates. Analysis also showed that bands containing 7–8 hunters that move nearly every day will achieve the best combination of high harvest rates and low probability of no meat in camp (Janssen and Hill 2014). The model predictions of group size, camp mobility, composition of prey harvest, time spent in pursuit, and overall harvest rates corresponded very closely to actual empirically observed patterns by the Ache hunters who live in the study area (Ibid.).

In this paper we extend the prior analysis by exploring the implication how changes in spatial distribution patterns of prey affect optimal camp mobility, camp location and corresponding search patterns by foragers. In the natural Mbaracayu landscape, measured prey encounter rates in each of the seven vegetation habitat types are approximately equal. This probably explains why random walk as a search pattern is such a good null model (Janssen and Hill 2014). However, most other hunter-gatherer landscapes are likely to be more clumped and patchy, with prey densities that probably vary more between habitat types. How sensitive are the payoffs from Ache-like camp mobility, location and hunting strategies, to landscapes that are more patchy and with higher prey variability across space? To answer this question, we vary the original Ache-like model landscape by modifying the clumpiness of vegetation patterns and the distribution of prey species among vegetation types, while keeping the total prey availability the same. We have chosen to model camp mobility patterns under six alternative habitat conditions: three levels of increasingly clumped habitat types, and two levels of increased variation in prey densities between habitat types (see Table 3.1, Column 1 and Row 1 headings). The model derived from the actual measured Mbaracayu environment we refer to as the "original" environment. It consists of medium clumpiness of vegetation, and low variation in prey biomass between vegetation habitats.

3.2.1 Strategies of Camp Movement

In addition to hunters, our models also include mobile agents that represent campsites. The default model behavior that determines the position of a campsite at the end of each day is to randomly relocate the future camp to a spot 2 km from the

Table 3.1 Types of landscapes

Clumpiness	Original variation in prey biomass	High variation in prey biomass
Low	Low	Low
Medium	**Original**	**Medium**
High	High	High

current camp location each morning. Agents move towards the new camp during the day. This allows us to explore alternative decisions about camp location.

In the ***targeted*** campsite version of the model, agents move their camp location into a preferred (high prey density) vegetation type each day. Agents also keep track where each camp has been and do not reuse old campsites for some time period. The targeted condition constrains the new camp location to cells at least 1 km from a recent campsite. When a camp moves, the nearest vegetation type with the highest return rate which has not been visited during the last 30 days, is the top priority relocation site. This allows foraging agents to spend more time in the highest return vegetation type in an area that has not been recently depleted. If there are no campsites available meeting these criteria, camp will be located in the next highest return vegetation type, and so on, as future campsites are prioritized in descending order of expected foraging return rate in the vegetation habitat where they will be located.

When the direction is defined, we will check whether the targeted camp location is between 1 and 3 km. If so, the new camp location will be the target. Otherwise, the camp will move 2 km in the direction earlier defined towards the highest return vegetation type.

The original Ache model specified that camp location always moved after a specified number of days (e.g. one day). In the new ***adaptive*** mobility version of the model, the agents residing in a camp together determine whether the average weight of meat hunted over the last few days is above a certain threshold. If so, the camp remains in its location for another day, if not, the campsite is moved to a new location at the beginning of the day.

These two decision criteria define four broad strategies for a camp: whether it is ***adaptive*** or not, and whether new locations are ***targeted*** or not. This leads to a decision tree on how camps are moved through the landscape (Fig. 3.2).

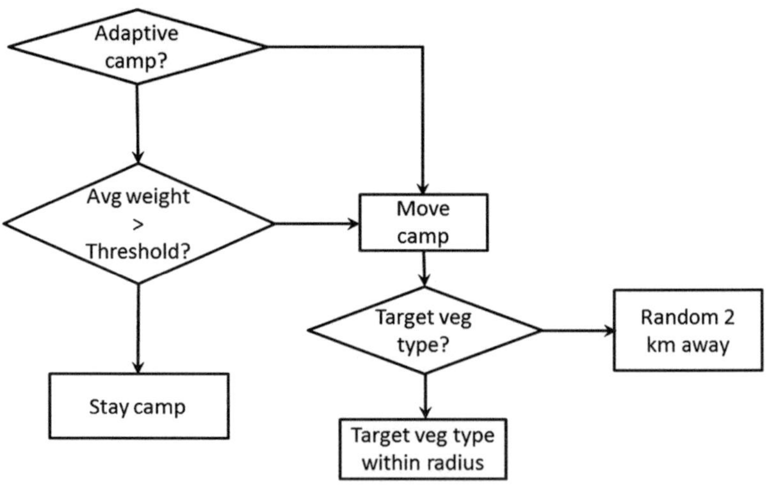

Fig. 3.2 Decision tree for movement of camps including adaptive and targeted movement

Nested within the four camp mobility strategies that we allowed, we can examine several variants. For this paper we varied the threshold for the daily harvest weight that determines whether an adaptive camp stays or moves each day. We explored the threshold values 2, 2.5, 3, 3.5 and 4 kg per hunter per day. We also allowed a range of different group sizes for each camp (1, 2, 3, 4, 5, 6, 7, 8, and 15 hunters) and vary the number of groups to keep the hunting pressure similar. This leads to 108 configurations of camp size and mobility strategies that are imposed on the six different landscape configurations (648 different combinations of camp mobility rules and vegetation habitat configurations).

3.2.2 *Alternative Landscapes*

In our first publication we examined Ache foraging and camp movement patterns that could maximize foraging gain rates in the actual Mbaracayu environment in which they live. Here we explore optimal strategies when the environment is more clumped and more variable across space. To that end we created alternative resource distributions on the landscape and varied the degree to which vegetation types were more or less productive and the extent to which the cells of different vegetation types were clustered.

The return rates characterizing each of the seven vegetation types are rather equal in the original landscape. Here we amplify the small prey density differences by increasing the encounter rates in the most productive habitat types, and decreasing prey encounter rates in the least productive habitats. Specifically, for the high variation environment we multiplied the prey encounter rates in riparian habitat by 3 and multiplied prey encounter rates in high forest by 2. The remaining 5 vegetation types are multiplied by factors less than one with final prey encounter rates balanced so that the total population of available prey and biomass remains the same over the entire model landscape. Here we assume encounter rate directly relates to the population density of species. This is derived by adjusting the multipliers $M_{v,s}$ such that

$$\sum_{v} enc_{v,s} \cdot M_{v,s} \cdot ha_v = \sum_{v} enc_{v,s} \cdot ha_v,$$

for each species s and where v denotes vegetation type. Encounter rate is defined for each species and vegetation type, $enc_{v,s}$ and the number of hectares of vegetation type is denoted as ha_v. Hence if $M_{v,s}$ is increased for two vegetation types, the others will have to be lower than 1 to meet the condition listed above. The multipliers lead to a more unequal distribution of expected return rates for the different vegetation types (Fig. 3.3), with riparian habitat more than ten times as productive as the meadow habitat.

In addition to amplifying the variation or prey densities in habitat types we also modified the landscape by changing the spatial configuration of vegetation types but without changing the total area covered by each habitat type in the model. The natural landscape of the Mbaracayu reserve is composed of multiple habitat types that are distributed in very small patches (often less than 500 m across). To increase the mean size of habitat patches we take the original landscape and perturb this by applying an algorithm which checks if randomly swapping the land cover of two cells leads to a higher degree of similarity between directly neighboring cells. We also applied the inverse algorithm make the landscape more fined grained, with extremely small patches of similar habitat. In the original landscape a one hectare cell has on average 60 % of the cells with the same vegetation type from the 8 neighboring cells that touch it. In our simulations we created artificial landscapes with 30 and 90 % of the neighboring cells containing the same vegetation type (Fig. 3.4).

3.3 Analysis

We ran 64,800 simulations with the Ache model, 100 runs for each of the about 108 configurations on each of the 6 landscapes. Note that we always assume cooperative hunting and coordination between the hunters. The landscape variants are "original" (O) and "high" (H) variance in prey density across habitats, and "low" (30), "medium" (60), and "high" (90) degrees of clumped habitat.

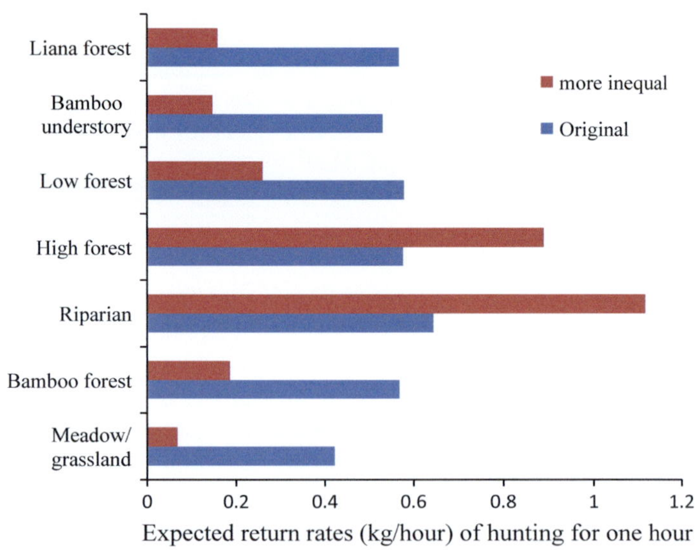

Fig. 3.3 Expected mean return rates on the 7 vegetation types based on prey densities with the original measured values and with the modified encounter rate distribution of higher vegetation variability

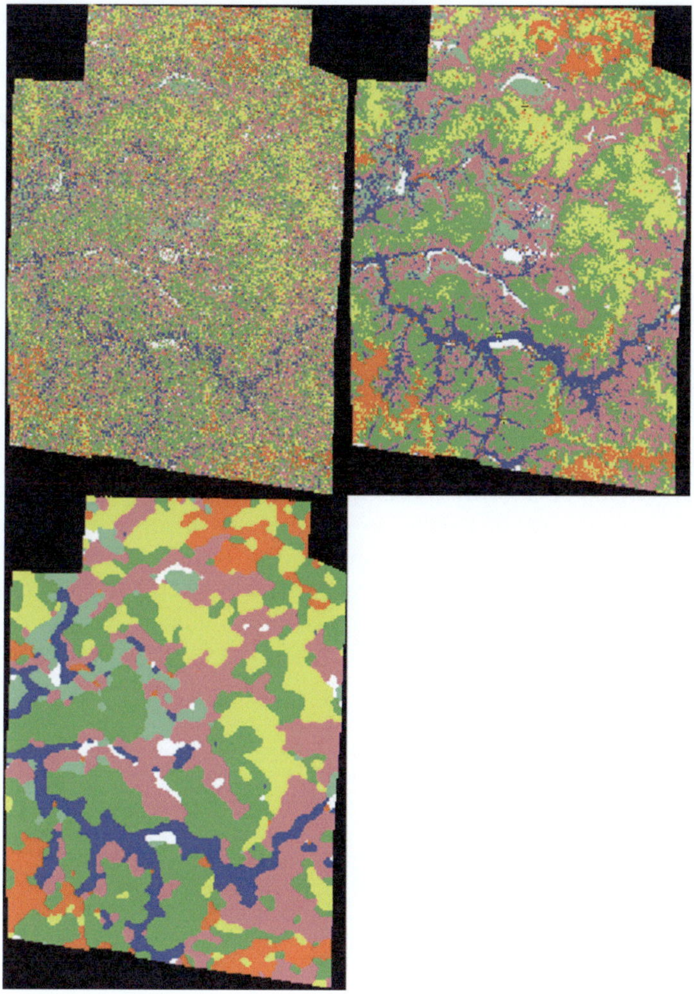

Fig. 3.4 Vegetation maps for less clumped habitat (30), original landscape (60), and more clumped habitat (90) conditions

Figure 3.5 zooms into the results of the targeted movement of the camps. The outcomes of 9 different group sizes are connected to illustrate the effect of group size. Janssen and Hill (2014) used isoclines to find the optimal group size as the combination that leads to high return rates with a low fraction of days without meat. Figure 3.5 shows that for adaptive strategies, the return rates are reduces but the shape is similar.

In Fig. 3.6 we depict for each landscape the results of the 108 camp movement configurations by plotting the average amount of meat per hunter day as well as the fraction of days that camp residents would consume no meat (because no hunter makes a kill).

Results show that for landscapes with the original measured habitat return rates (O), the best strategy is for groups move each day regardless of clumpedness, and not use an adaptive threshold to determine camp mobility. When the landscape is modified to produce increased variation in return rates among habitat types, the adaptive camp strategy produces increasingly better results than high mobility as the patchiness of the environment increases.

Targeted camp movement is actually worse than random movement when habitats differ little and resources are highly dispersed (O30). When habitats differ little or when habitat types are not clumped, there is no real difference between targeted versus random camp moves. However, when habitat types differ greatly in productivity and when habitats are more clumped in space (H60, H90) substantially greater hunting returns can be obtained by targeting camp moves to prioritize the highest return habitat types.

Without developing a formal model, we presume that foragers prefer both more meat and lower chances of having no game to consume on any given day. In Fig. 3.6 hypothetical isoclines of assumed equal biological utility can be constructed for combinations of return rates and risk of no meat that may be equivalent value to foragers. These isoclines indicate increasing utility to foragers as we move from the lower left to upper right corner in the figure. In all landscapes we find that 7 hunters will maximize the desired combination of higher hunting returns and

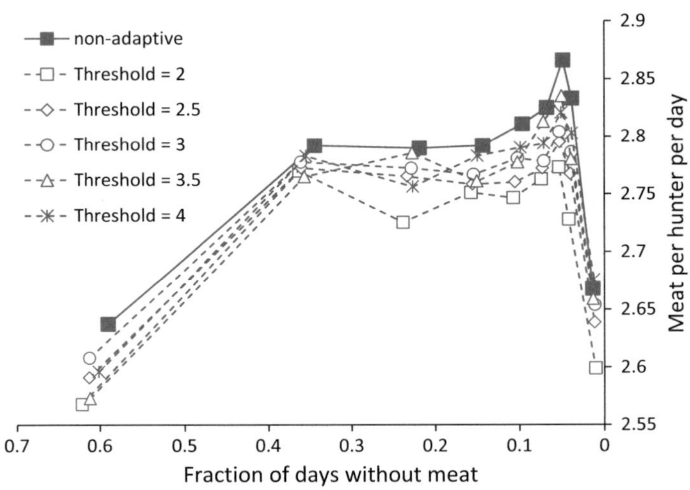

Fig. 3.5 Return rate and days with no meat for 54 permutations of targeted camp movement rules in the original Ache model landscape (O60). Combinations are assumed to have higher biological value moving from *lower left* to *upper right* (increasing utility isoclines indicate higher daily return and lower probability of no meat). Camp sizes increase from 1 hunter (*far left points*) to 15 hunters (*far right points*) for each condition. The optimal combination of high returns and low probability of no-meat is for 7 hunters to move every day (non-adaptive camp mobility)

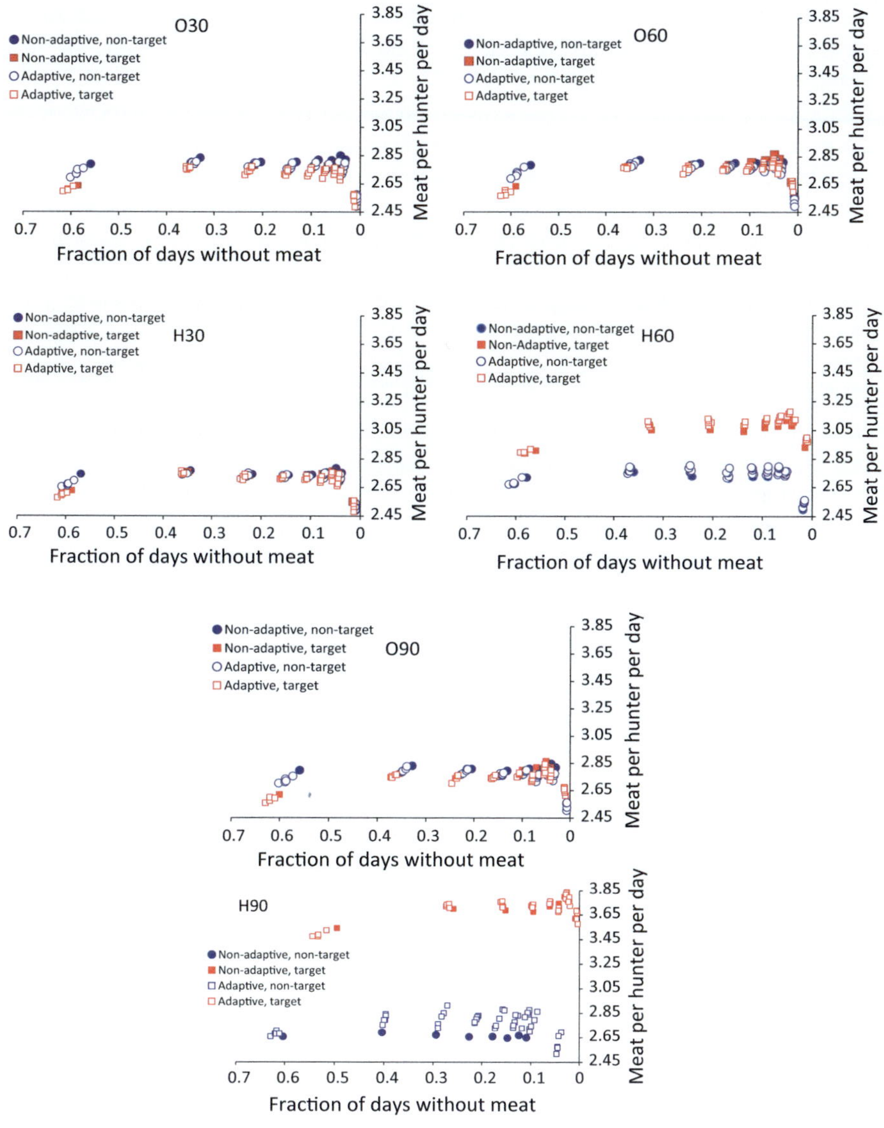

Fig. 3.6 Return rate and days with no meat for 108 permutations of the camp movement rules and in the six different model landscapes described. Combinations are assumed to have higher biological value moving from *lower left* to *upper right* (increasing utility isoclines indicate higher daily return and lower probability of no meat) The six figures correspond to the six landscape types defined above (e.g. O90 = original variation between habitats and highly clumped habitat types). Camp sizes increase from 1 hunter (*far left points*) to 15 hunters (*far right points*) for each condition. Adaptive threshold generally decreases in each cluster of unfilled symbols as the y values increase (lower adaptive staying thresholds usually result in higher return rates)

lower probability of no meat obtained on single days (see Janssen and Hill 2014). Based on our previous analysis (Ibid.) the optimal group size is found to be a consequence of the advantages of risk reduction with more hunters and the disadvantages of encounter suppression as group size grows. In our simulations, if we reduce the parameter of encounter suppression larger groups are favored, while increasing the impact of encounter suppression reduces the optimal group size. Since we have no empirical measures of this parameter we will stick with our original estimate and for the remainder of this paper we assume a group size of 7 hunters.

We see that for most landscapes the best mobility strategy is for groups to move each day (Table 3.2). Only under high variance in prey density and relatively clumped landscapes does it pay to stay in one camp until daily returns drop below some threshold value. On the other hand, the targeted mobility strategy is more robust, producing higher returns in all environments except those in which habitat types are highly dispersed with little clumping in space. This is because targeted movement allows hunters to spend more time in the best habitat types as long as the camp is located in a reasonable large patch of that habitat type.

In Table 3.3 we present the meat per hunter per day under different conditions and for different mobility strategies. For the adaptive camps we depict the results of the threshold that leads to the best results. We see that the actual Ache mobility pattern (non targeted and non adaptive camp) results in the same food acquisition

Table 3.2 Optimal strategies for different landscapes

Clumpiness	Original vegetation variability	High vegetation variability
Low (30)	Non-targeted camp, non-adaptive camp	Non-targeted camp, non-adaptive camp
Original (60)	**Targeted** camp, non adaptive camp	**Targeted** camp, **adaptive** camp. Threshold = 2 kg
High (90)	**Targeted** camp, non-adaptive camp	**Targeted** camp, **adaptive** camp. Threshold = 2.5 kg

Table 3.3 The results for different strategies. For each of the 6 landscapes and each of the four strategies, we provide two numbers: the mean amount of meat per hunter per day (kg/day), and the fraction of days hunters of the camp have not obtained meat from hunting

	Non targeted, non adaptive camp	Non targeted, adaptive camp	Targeted, non-adaptive camp	Targeted, adaptive camp
O30	2.850; 0.041	2.807; 0.040	2.795; 0.050	2.764; 0.052
O60	**2.835; 0.041**	2.827; 0.047	2.866; 0.049	2.835; 0.050
O90	2.845; 0.041	2.803; 0.046	2.865; 0.052	2.842; 0.054
H30	2.785; 0.049	2.759; 0.053	2.761; 0.055	2.757; 0.058
H60	2.746; 0.069	2.797; 0.067	3.115; 0.051	3.178; 0.045
H90	2.667; 0.125	2.876; 0.103	3.789; 0.032	3.836; 0.026

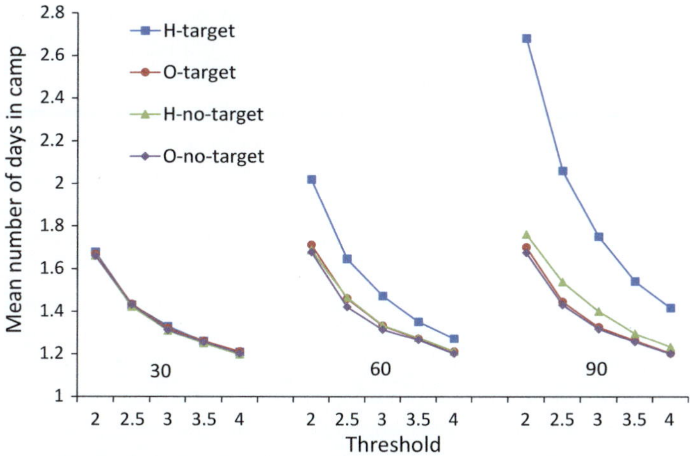

Fig. 3.7 The relationship between the mean number of days *adaptive* camps remain in the same location on different landscapes, and adopting different mobility thresholds. Camps are expected to remain longer in one place when resources are more clumped and habitats are more variable (H90)

rates on most landscapes, with a slight drop in efficiency on landscapes with more heterogeneity in prey density between habitats. Likewise, on the landscape in which the Ache currently reside (row O60) different mobility strategies lead to very similar results. The strategy Ache hunters use may be the simplest to implement.

Figure 3.7 shows that when the landscape is more patchy and clumpy, hunters will achieve higher return rates by camping multiple days in the same camp spot. When the resources on the landscape are more evenly dispersed there is little reason to stay longer in the same location more than one day, and mobility is very high, just as we observe ethnographically among the Ache.

Adopting an adaptive movement strategy or a set mobility interval does not seem to make much difference in our model. This is partially because we have incorporated not cost of camp movement into the model (in both cases men simply hunt along the way to the new campsite). Instead, the key decision in our simulation is when to target specific vegetation types. When two of the vegetation types have much higher return rates and the vegetation types are clustered (H60 and H90) we see major improvement in the overall return rate of hunters when they target certain vegetation types for the location of their camps.

3.4 Conclusions

The distribution of resources on the landscape have a modest effect on determining which camp mobility strategies are most effective. This empirically based model analysis shows that the ethnographically observed Ache pattern of extremely high mobility and randomly placed campsites would not be effective if relevant prey species were concentrated in a few habitat patches within the landscape. But in moderately heterogeneous landscapes, like their current Mbaracayu home range, the Ache mobility strategy performs very well relative to alternatives. But the most surprising result is that much greater heterogeneity in resource distributions in the environment does not favor larger camp size in our model, nor does it change camp mobility very much (2.8 mean days in camp in a highly variable clumped environment vs. 1 day in camp for the natural and relatively homogeneous environment). We did discover, however that hunters would increase their mean return rates by about a 30 % in clumped heterogeneous environments by targeting the most productive habitats in camp moves. This is an important insight. Human foragers more efficient at exploiting patchy rather than homogenous environments because they can recognize and exploit the patchiness in a manner that reduces their search time in unproductive environments. While this might seem intuitively obvious, we were surprised at the magnitude of the increase in efficiency on patchy landscapes even when the biomass of prey on the landscape was the same.

Ecological hypothesis about how resource distributions through time and space affect hunter-gatherer group size and mobility are generally accepted as fact due to their logical coherence and their origins in animal behavioral ecology where they are qualitatively supported. Nevertheless here we found minimal changes in optimal group size or mobility patterns as environments contained more dispersed or more clumped prey distributions. The environmental differences we simulated were quite substantial, from very minor differences in prey abundance across 7 vegetation types to more than 10 fold differences in prey abundance across vegetation types. We also examined a wide range of patchiness, from many small habitat patches of only a few hectares to a landscape where 52 % the habitat was found in patches of greater than 1000 ha. Despite this variation the optimal group size under all conditions was 7 hunters per camp. This group size not only maximizes the mean expected hunting return rate, but it is far superior for both maximizing return rate and simultaneously minimizing the probability of no hunted game in camp on any particular day. The best return rates in the model come from group sizes in which the benefits of cooperative hunting are maximal relative to the costs encounter rate depression from frightening game in the same search area (i.e. feeding competition).

The impact of increased patchiness on mobility is also very moderate. Under natural conditions return rates are maximized by moving every day of the year (congruent with ethnographic observation), but in our simulated highly variable and patchy environment, the best performing strategy is found to have a mean camp staying time of 2.1 days. It is important to note however that our model includes no costs of movement outside that of localized depletion if the hunters remain in an already hunted area.

Finally, when habitats are more heterogeneous and clumped, targeted movement, in which camps are located in the best habitats whenever possible, increases the hunting return rate by about 30 % over a pattern in which camps are simply moved in a random direction each day. Thus *targeted* moves in addition to *adaptive* camp movement, remaining at a camp spot until prey are depleted below some threshold, would allow simulated Ache hunters to increase their mean daily hunting return rate by 35 % in a more patchy and variable environment even when it contains exactly the same number of prey animals as their natural environment containing more dispersed prey. This is quite a substantial and biologically meaningful increase in food intake simply by exploiting patterned distribution of prey even when absolute densities do not change. Human foragers, by knowing the landscape and the spatial location of better habitats, and moving to facilitate hunting in those areas, gain a substantial advantage from that knowledge.

Acknowledgments Portions of this research were funded by NSF-IPG grant BCS-1138073.

References

Chapman CA, Chapman LJ, Wrangham RW (1995) Ecological constraints on group size: an analysis of spider monkey and chimpanzee subgroups. Behav Ecol Sociobiol 36(1):59–70

Charnov EL (1976) Optimal foraging, the marginal value theorem. Theor Popul Biol 9(2):129–136

Clark CW, Mangel M (1986) The evolutionary advantages of group foraging. Theor Popul Biol 30 (1):45–75

Creel S (1997) Cooperative hunting and group size: assumptions and currencies. Anim Behav 54 (5):1319–1324

Crook JH (1970) Social organization and the environment: aspects of contemporary social ethology. Anim Behav 18:197–209

Hart DD (1981) Foraging and resource patchiness: field experiments with a grazing stream insect. Oikos 46–52

Hawkes K, Hill K, O'Connell J (1982) Why hunters gather: optimal foraging and the Ache of eastern Paraguay. Am Ethnologist 9(2):379–398

Hill K, Hawkes K (1983) Neotropical hunting among the Ache of eastern Paraguay. In: Hames R, Vickers W (eds) Adaptive responses of native Amazonians. Academic Press, New York, pp 139–188

Hill K, Kintigh K (2009) Can anthropologists distinguish good from poor hunters: implications for hunting hypotheses, sharing conventions, and cultural transmission. Curr Anthropol 50 (3):369–377

Hill K, Kaplan H, Hawkes K, Hurtado A (1985) Men's time allocation to subsistence work among the Ache of eastern Paraguay. Human Ecol 13:29–47

Hill K, Hawkes K, Kaplan H, Hurtado A (1987) Foraging decisions among Ache hunter-gatherers: new data and implications for optimal foraging models. Ethol Sociobiol 8:1–36

Hill K, Padwe J, Bejyvagi C, Bepurangi A, Jakugi F, Tykuarangi R, Tykuarangi T (1997) Impact of hunting on large vertebrates in the Mbaracayu Reserve, Paraguay. Conserv Biol 11 (6):1339–1353

Hill K, McMillan G, Fariña R (2003) Hunting-related changes in game encounter rates from 1994 to 2001 in the Mbaracayu Reserve, Paraguay. Conserv Biol 17(5):1312–1323

Horn HS (1968) The adaptive significance of colonial nesting in the Brewer's blackbird (*Euphagus cyanocephalus*). Ecology 49:682–694

Janson CH, Goldsmith ML (1995) Predicting group size in primates: foraging costs and predation risks. Behav Ecol 6(3):326–336

Janssen MA, Hill K (2014) Benefits from grouping and cooperative hunting among Ache hunter-gatherers: insights from an agent-based foraging model. Human Ecol 42(6):823–835

Jarman P (1974) The social organisation of antelope in relation to their ecology. Behaviour 48 (1):215–267

Kaplan H, Hill K (1992) Evolutionary ecology of food acquisition. In: Smith EA, Winterhalder B (eds) Evolution, ecology, and human behavior. Chicago, Aldine, pp 167–202

Kelly RL (1995) The foraging spectrum: diversity in hunter-gatherer lifeways. Smithsonian Institution Press, Washington, DC

MacArthur RH, Pianka ER (1966) On optimal use of a patchy environment. Am Nat 100:603–609

Macdonald DW (1983) The ecology of carnivore social behaviour. Nature 301(5899):379–384

Naidoo R, Hill K (2006) Emergence of indigenous vegetation classifications through integration of traditional ecological knowledge and remote sensing analyses. Environ Manage 38(3):377–387

Slobodchikoff CN (1984) Resources and the evolution of social behavior. In: Price PW, Slobodchikoff CN, Gaud WS (eds) A new ecology: novel approaches to interactive systems. Wiley, New York, pp 227–251

Terborgh J, Janson CH (1986) The socioecology of primate groups. Annu Rev Ecol Syst 17:111–136

White FJ, Wrangham RW (1988) Feeding competition and patch size in the chimpanzee species *Pan paniscus* and *Pan troglodytes*. Behaviour 105(1):148–164

Winterhalder B, Smith EA (eds) (1981) Hunter-gatherer foraging strategies: ethnographic and archeological analyses. University of Chicago Press, Chicago

Wrangham RW (1980) An ecological model of female-bonded primate groups. Behaviour 75 (3):262–300

Chapter 4
Testing Brantingham's Neutral Model: The Effect of Spatial Clustering on Stone Raw Material Procurement

Simen Oestmo, Marco A. Janssen and Curtis W. Marean

4.1 Introduction

The archaeological record shows that foragers varied their stone tool raw material preferences, even when several types of stone material were available. The changing use, and co-use of different stone tool raw materials is well known from a wide range of environmental and climatic contexts, time-periods, and 'cultures' (Andrefsky 1994; Bamforth 1990; Bar-Yosef 1991; Clark 1980; Jelinek 1991; Kuhn 2004, 1991). What explains this changing raw material preference is a question of great interest, and it is debated whether changes in stone tool raw material frequencies in an archaeological assemblage could be considered a reliable proxy for human forager adaptive variability (Brantingham 2003; Féblot-Augustins 1993; Kuhn 1995; Mellars 1996). Explanations for change in raw material usage

S. Oestmo (✉) · C.W. Marean
School of Human Evolution and Social Change, Institute of Human Origins, Arizona State University, 900 S. Cady Mall, Rm. 233, Tempe, AZ 85281, USA
e-mail: soestmo@asu.edu

C.W. Marean
e-mail: Curtis.Marean@asu.edu

M.A. Janssen
School of Sustainability, Center for Behavior, Institutions, and the Environment, Arizona State University, Tempe, USA
e-mail: Marco.Janssen@asu.edu

C.W. Marean
Faculty of Science, Nelson Mandela Metropolitan University, Port Elizabeth, Eastern Cape 6031, South Africa

J.A. Barceló and F. Del Castillo (eds.), *Simulating Prehistoric and Ancient Worlds*, Computational Social Sciences, DOI 10.1007/978-3-319-31481-5_4

frequency include climate/environmental change and its co-variability with mobility and procurement strategies (Ambrose and Lorenz 1990; Binford and Stone 1985; Kuhn 2004), selection of certain raw materials for their physical properties (Braun et al. 2009; Gould and Saggers 1985; Minichillo 2006), changes in demography (Clark 1980), the preference for appearance or color (Akerman et al. 2002; Clendon 1999; Stout 2002), symbolic value (Wurz 1999), and style (Close 2002).

Brantingham (2003) challenges these explanations and provides a neutral model that was argued to explain some of the observed patterns in the record of raw material abundance. Brantingham argues that in order to demonstrate the deliberate selection of raw materials, patterning must be shown to be different from the results of the neutral model, which provides a baseline for comparison where archaeologists can be certain that observed raw material patterns is not the result of strategic selection.

We agree with Brantingham's sentiment. However, Brantingham (2003: 505) points out that a "…appropriate criticism of the present model would suggest that a forager "could" never engage in a random-walk foraging strategy and "could" never ignore the differences between stone raw material types." Here we explore if such a criticism is valid. In addition, we follow Brantingham's suggestion that quantitative development of the observations presented in his study requires calibration of the agent-based model to run in simulated "worlds" built around the known geographic distributions of actual raw material sources. Here we partly address that suggestion by first exploring two major limitations of the neutral model as currently described. First, the raw material sources are distributed randomly without any clustering across the model landscape, which is not the case on most real landscapes where potential raw material source locations are controlled by the underlying geological structure and geophysical processes. An example of such structures and processes, drawn from our research region, are coastal cliffs and embayed beaches that can produce cobble beaches along a stretch of coastline (Thompson and Marean 2008). Source locations thus appear clustered due to the geological structure and geophysical processes of the landscape.

The second limitation addressed here is the unrealistic assumption that each raw material location in the model represents a unique raw material. Five thousand raw material sources are possible over an extended landscape but not 5000 unique raw materials. It is more likely that a smaller amount of different raw materials, say 1–25, are represented by the 5000 source locations. In addition, the 1–25 unique raw materials are not randomly distributed in isolation away from same type raw materials. As discussed above, not only are source locations clustered due to the underlying geological structure and geophysical processes, several sources of the same material can be available in a cluster, depending on the geological formation.

4.2 Test Case and Model Description

4.2.1 Mossel Bay Region

The test case is the landscape around the town of Mossel Bay, Western Cape, South Africa. The Mossel Bay region has several archaeological sites that offers a long sequence of change in raw material selection (Brown et al. 2012; Thompson and Marean 2008; Thompson et al. 2010). The local geology is well understood (Malan and Viljoen 2008; Viljoen and Malan 1993; Roberts et al. 2012; Thamm and Johnson 2006), and thorough surveys for potential raw material sources have been undertaken (Oestmo et al. 2014). In total, 38 potential stone tool raw material sources have been discovered, which is likely an underestimate. These sources range greatly in size (Fig. 4.1), are clustered according to geological structures and geophysical processes, and only 6–7 raw materials are represented among the 38 sources.

4.2.2 Model Description

Original Neutral Model Brantingham (2003) created a simple model of one forager with a mobile toolkit of fixed capacity that is randomly placed on the environment. At each time step, the forager moves to one of the nearest eight neighboring cells or stays in the present cell, with equal probability (=1/9). At each

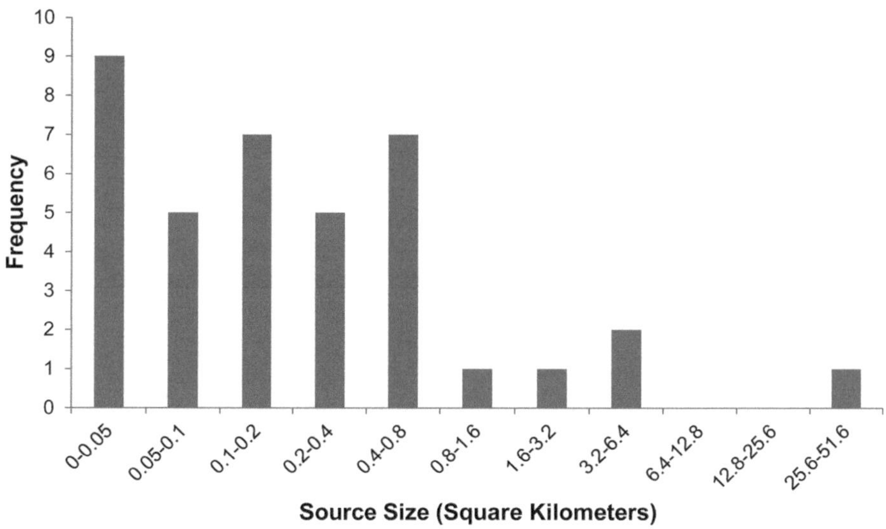

Fig. 4.1 Frequency of stone tool raw material sources by size bin in the Mossel Bay region

time step a fixed amount of raw material is consumed dependent only upon its frequency in the mobile toolkit. If a raw material source is encountered, the toolkit is re-provisioned up to its maximum capacity before moving again at random. If no raw material source is encountered, the forager moves immediately at random. Simulations are run until 200 unique raw material sources are encountered, or the edge of the simulation world is reached. The model is replicated in Netlogo by Janssen and Oestmo (2013).

New Analysis For the initial configuration and analysis in this paper, a maximum capacity of the tool kit equal to 100 was used, the environment was set to 500 × 500 cells and consisted of 5000 unique raw material sources. To include clustering of sources, the probability p_r was included. When the 5000 material sources were placed on the landscape there was a probability p_r determining where the new material source was placed on a randomly chosen empty cell. Five different values of p_r were used (Fig. 4.2) with probability $1 - p_r$, a new material source was placed on a randomly chosen empty cell that had at least one neighbor (one of 8 neighboring cells) that already contained a material source (see Fig. 4.3 for landscape examples for each p_r value used in this paper). Every simulation-run lasted 35,000 time steps, and each type of simulation with different walk behaviors was run 100 times.

Three different model outcomes are addressed here: raw material richness (the number of different raw material types), distance materials move before being discarded, and steps taken without raw material in the toolkit. The two first outcomes are the same as Brantingham (2003) used in his original study to evaluate his neutral model. Here they will be used to evaluate the effect of spatial clustering on the neutral model outcomes. The last model outcome, steps taken without raw

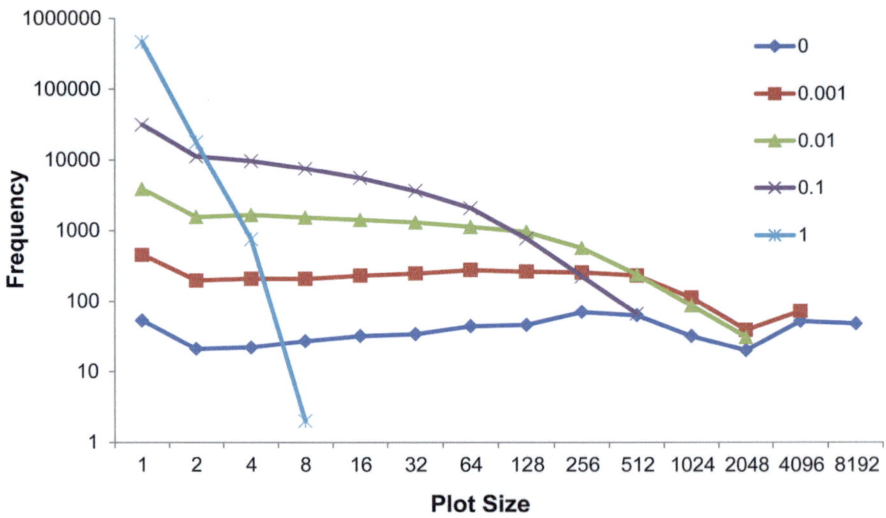

Fig. 4.2 Distribution of source sizes in generated landscapes with different p_r values

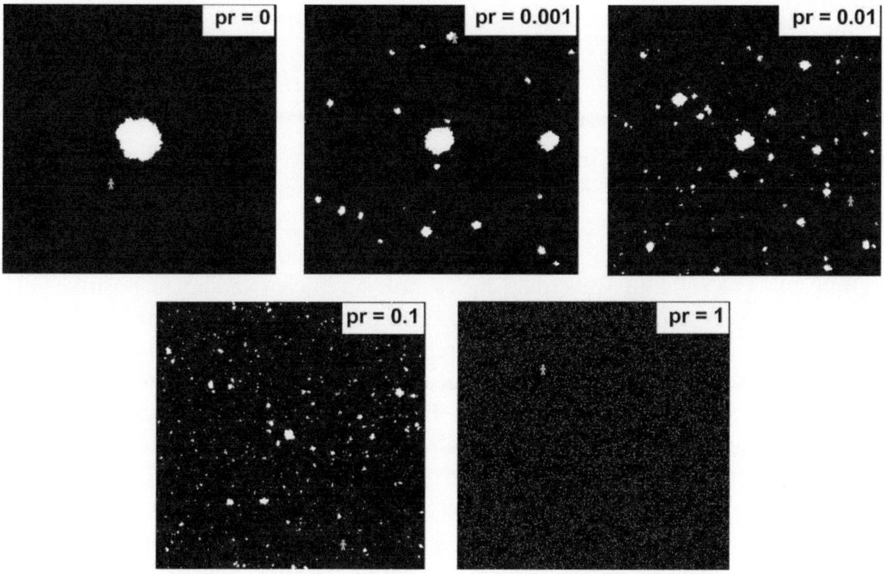

Fig. 4.3 Spatial view of distribution of material sources in generated landscapes with different p_r values

material in the toolkit, is used to evaluate whether the criticism that a forager can never engage in random walk in an environment is a valid criticism.

To address the second limitation that 5000 unique raw materials on an extended landscape is unrealistic, a second model configuration is run where 20 unique raw materials are distributed among the 5000 raw material positions. This can lead to, by chance, a cluster with a majority of one unique raw material distributed next to each other.

In addition to the original random walk behavior, two other walk behaviors will be simulated for both the original configuration with 5000 unique raw materials and with the configuration with 20 unique raw materials. The first one is here called "seeking walk". The seeking walk behavior could be seen as an analogy for returning to a stone cache at a central location. During seeking walk simulations, the forager will move towards the nearest material source if the level of the materials in the toolkit is lower than a certain number. Here the number will be 0. This means that at any moment when a foragers' toolkit is empty it will seek to acquire new material.

The second alternative walk model is termed the "wiggle walk" where it is assumed that a forager has a direction and moves forward one cell each time step. At each time step, the forager changes the direction by taking a left turn with a degree drawn from a uniform distribution between 0 and 90°, and then a right turn with a degree drawn from a uniform distribution between 0 and 90°.

4.3 Model Analysis Results and Discussion

4.3.1 Assuming 5000 Unique Raw Materials

Raw Material Richness in Tool Kit Two different patterns are visible when investigating raw material richness. First, when a forager engages in random or wiggle walk, a more clustered environment leads to lower average raw material richness in the toolkit (Fig. 4.4). However, these relationships are not statistically significant. The random walk data has a non-significant moderate positive relationship with the p_r values (Spearman's $rs = 0.6$; $p = 0.23$), while the wiggle walk data has a non-significant weak positive relationship with the p_r values (Spearman's $rs = 0.3$; $p = 0.52$). Because the forager will consume a unit of raw material at every time step if material is available in the tool kit and will refill the toolkit to the maximum when encountering a source, a high encounter frequency in combination with encountering new sources evenly distributed across the map will increase the richness. This is because no single raw material has a chance to dominate the frequency make-up of the tool kit. As clustering increases, the forager will on average move longer periods without encountering a source. Due to this and the fact that the forager use a material at every step, the forager will then when encountering a source fill up the tool kit to the maximum capacity resulting in one raw material dominating the make-up of the tool kit in terms of frequency. However, as noted above, this relationship is not statistically significant.

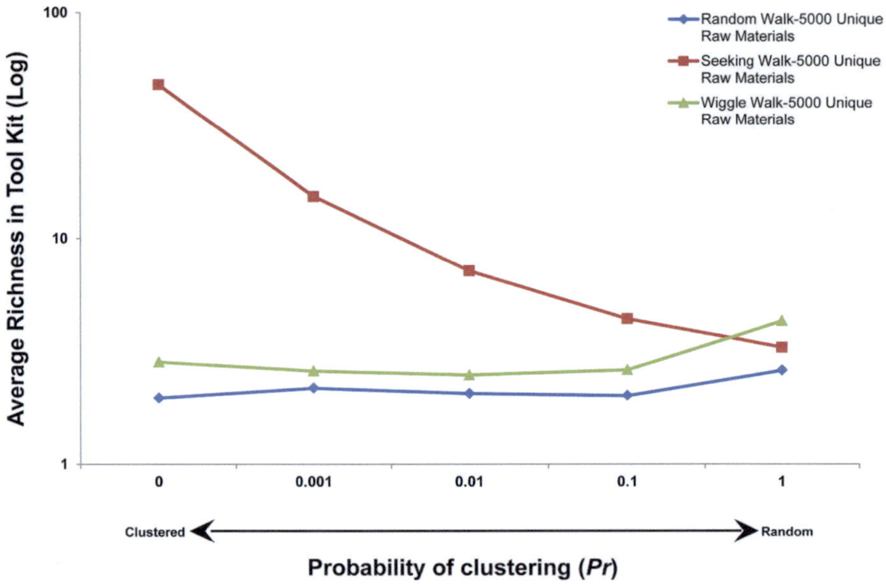

Fig. 4.4 Average richness of toolkit. Y values are shown as log values. Each *curve* is based on the average of 100 simulation runs

In the other pattern, the forager engages in a seeking walk and seeks the closest raw material sources when the tool kit is empty. In this case, the increased clustering of raw material sources leads to increased raw material richness (Fig. 4.4). The seeking walk data has a significant negative strong relationship with the p_r values (Spearman's $rs = -1$; $p = 0.02$). The richness increases because when the forager seeks the nearest raw material source, and this nearest raw material source is clustered with other sources, it increases the chance of encountering other sources in close proximity that in turn could lead to increased richness.

Distance Materials Travel Until Discarded In terms of the distances that raw materials travel until discarded, two patterns can be observed (Fig. 4.5). In the first pattern, when a forager engages in random or wiggle walk, increased clustering leads to decreased travel distance (Fig. 4.5). However, not both of these relationships are statistically significant. The random walk data has a strong but non-significant relationship with the p_r values (Spearman's $rs = 0.7$; $p = 0.2$), while the wiggle walk data has very strong and significant relationship with the p_r values (Spearman's $rs = 1$; $p = 0.02$). Because raw material richness increases with increased random distribution of sources as shown above, the probability that any one raw material is consumed decreases. This decreased probability means that there is increased chance that any one raw material will stay in the tool kit for a longer time, which results in raw materials being carried for longer distances before being consumed.

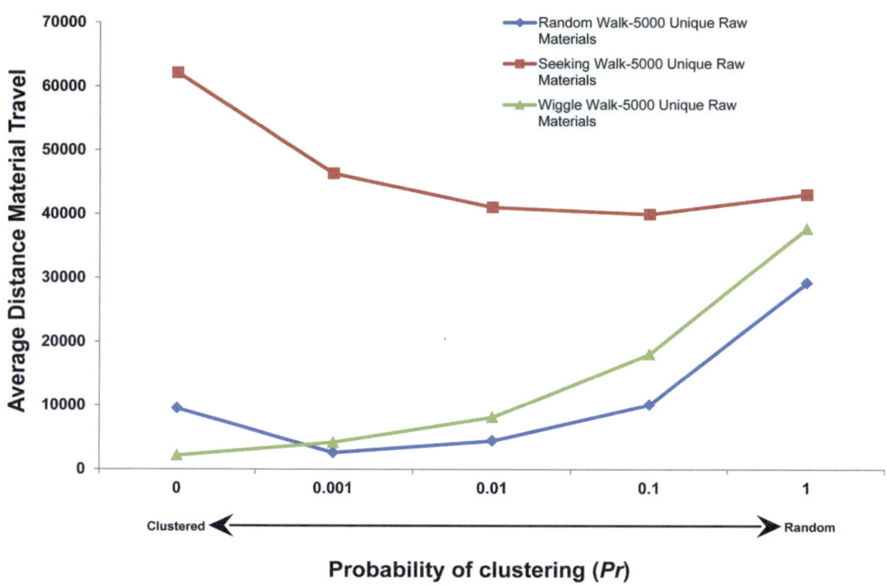

Fig. 4.5 Average distance materials are travelling from the source. Each *curve* is based on the average of 100 simulation runs

On the other hand, when the forager engages in a seeking walk, increased clustering leads to increased travel distance (Fig. 4.5). However, this relationship is not significant although there is a strong negative correlation (Spearman's $rs = -0.7$; $p = 0.2$). As noted above, tool kit richness controls how long a raw material travels before being consumed. Increased richness results in increased distances that any one raw material travels before being consumed because the probability that any one raw material is consumed at each time step is decreased.

Time Steps Without Material in Tool Kit When investigating how much time the forager spends without material in the tool kit one clear pattern can be observed: clustering leads to increased time without materials in the tool kit. Across all three simulated walk behaviors, the analysis shows that when resources are more clustered than simulated in the original neural model, we can expect that foragers run out of materials for longer periods of time (Fig. 4.6). All three walk behaviors have significant and strongly negative relationships with the p_r values (Table 4.1). Table 4.2 shows the estimated time steps without raw materials. If engaging in random or wiggle walk, the forager will on average spend about 55 time steps without materials when the raw materials are randomly placed as simulated in the neutral model. However, as the clustering of the raw material sources increases to mimic a realistic landscape, one can observe that time spent without materials increases 10–30 times. This is because increased clustering leads to more spaces between sources leading to an increased probability that a forager will use up all the raw materials in the tool kit before encountering a new source. Hence, the original neutral model might not be an appropriate model for landscapes with raw material sources clustered like is often typical of most environments. It is unrealistic to expect that foragers go extended periods of time without raw materials in their tool kit to create and repair tools.

Although ethnoarchaeological work and ethnographic description offer some evidence that stone procurement was a daily exercise for some groups (Hayden and Nelson 1981; MacCalman and Grobelaar 1965; Miller 1979; Sillitoe and Hardy 2003; Stout 2002) it has to be noted that this behavior cannot be considered a universal behavior, and that caches of stone to provision daily use can also be maintained at a central location where the foragers operate (Parry and Kelly 1987). An important distinction needs to be made here. If the forager returns to such a central location where a cache is situated, then the forager could go extended periods of time without procuring materials as long as the forager returns to such a central cache and refills the tool kit. However, if random walk takes the forager away from the central location and never or very seldom returns then it is unrealistic to assume that random walk is a realistic behavior because the probability that the foragers runs out of materials is high.

Not surprisingly, when the forager is engaging in seeking walk behavior, the time spent without materials is decreased drastically compared to random and wiggle walk simulations (Fig. 4.6). However, even in seeking walk simulations an

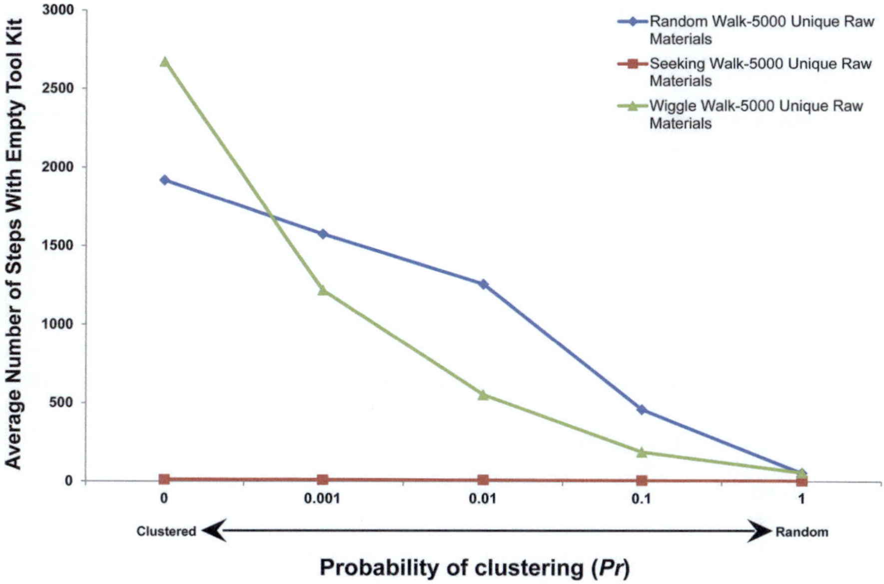

Fig. 4.6 Average number of time steps a tool kit is empty. Each *curve* is based on the average of 100 simulation runs

Table 4.1 Spearman's *rs* test results

	Random walk	Wiggle walk	Seeking walk
p value	0.02	0.02	0.02
rs coefficient	−1	−1	−1

Table 4.2 Time steps spent without material in tool kit

p_r	Random walk	Wiggle walk	Seeking walk
0	1919	2673	12
0.001	1575	1217	11
0.01	1257	552	10
0.1	458	189	8
1	54	57	4

increased clustering of the raw material sources leads to more time without any raw materials in the toolkit. This is because there is an increased probability that a forager can find itself further from a cluster or any single source because of the increased space between any sources. This means that the forager has to travel further to find the nearest material, which leads to increased time without material in the tool kit.

4.3.2 Assuming 20 Unique Raw Materials

Raw Material Richness in Tool Kit When a forager engages in random walk, a more clustered environment leads to lower average raw material richness in the toolkit (Fig. 4.7). The random walk data has a significant strong positive relationship with the p_r values (Spearman's $rs = 0.99$; $p = 0.0002$). Compared to the result of the three different walk modes when assuming 5000 unique raw materials, the random walk while assuming 20 unique raw materials produces, not surprisingly, on average a much lower richness in the tool kit. However, as seen above, when clustering increases, the forager will on average move longer periods without encountering a source. Coupled with the fact that the forager uses a material at every step, the forager will then when encountering a source fill up the tool kit to the maximum capacity, which results in one raw material dominating the make-up of the tool kit in terms of frequency.

Distance Materials Move Until Discarded In terms of the distances that raw materials are moved until discarded, when the forager engages in random walk, greater clustering leads to increased travel distance (Fig. 4.8). However, this relationship is not statistically significant. The random walk data has a non-significant and moderate negative relationship with the p_r values (Spearman's $rs = -0.6$; $p = 0.2$). Similar to random walk simulations with the assumption of 5000 unique raw materials, the raw material richness increases with increased random

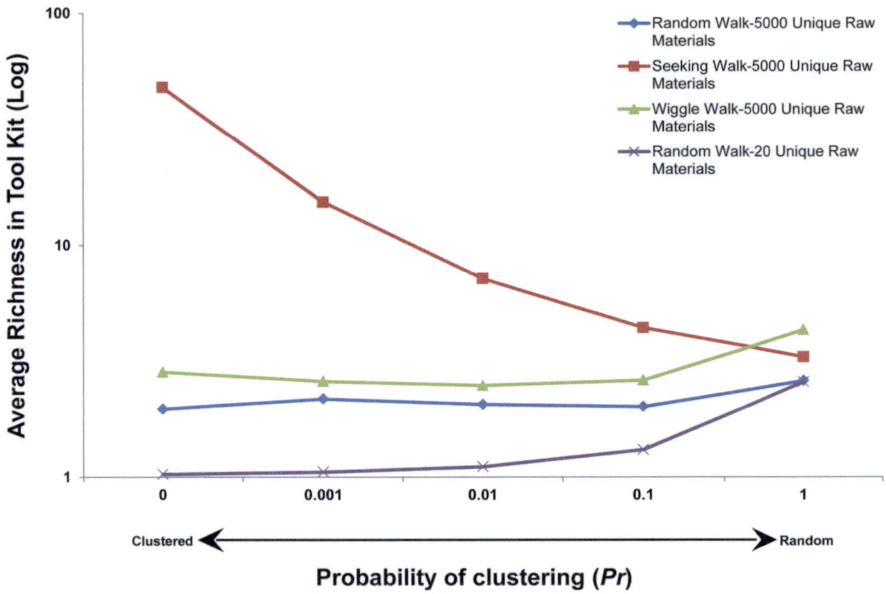

Fig. 4.7 Average richness of toolkit. Y values are shown as log values. Each *curve* is based on the average of 100 simulation runs

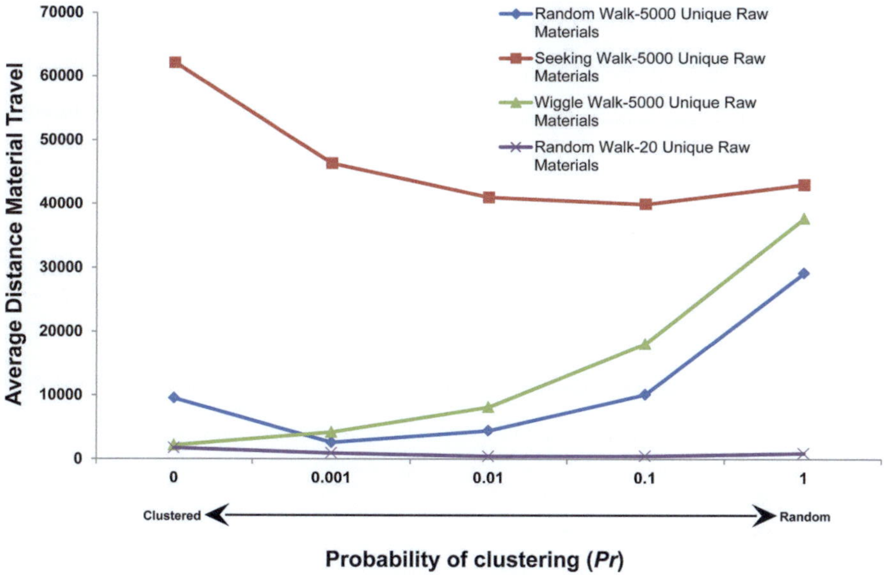

Fig. 4.8 Average distance materials are travelling from the source. Each *curve* is based on the average of 100 simulation runs

distribution of sources in turn leading to a decreased probability that any one raw material is consumed. This decreased probability means that there is increased chance that any one raw material will stay in the tool kit for a longer time. However, compared to the 5000 unique raw materials assumption, here a maximum of 20 raw materials could be available out of the 100 possible in the tool kit. This means that compared to a situation where there are 100 unique raw materials available for consumption, this overall low richness increases the probability that any one raw material is consumed, which results in similar types of raw materials being carried for shorter distances before being consumed.

Time Steps Without Material in Tool Kit The result shows that when resources are more clustered than simulated in the original neutral model, we can expect that foragers run out of materials for longer periods of time (Fig. 4.9). The random walk data has a significant and strong negative relationship with the p_r values (Spearman's $rs = -0.9$; $p = 0.02$). Compared to the analysis with 5000 unique raw materials, the 20 unique materials analysis numbers are very similar. If engaging in random walk, the forager will on average spend about 104 time steps without materials when the raw materials are randomly placed on the landscape as in the original neutral model (Table 4.3). As clustering increases, the time steps without raw materials in the tool kit increases 10–15 times. Decreasing the number of unique raw materials does not affect the finding that increased clustering leads to increased time without raw materials in the tool kit.

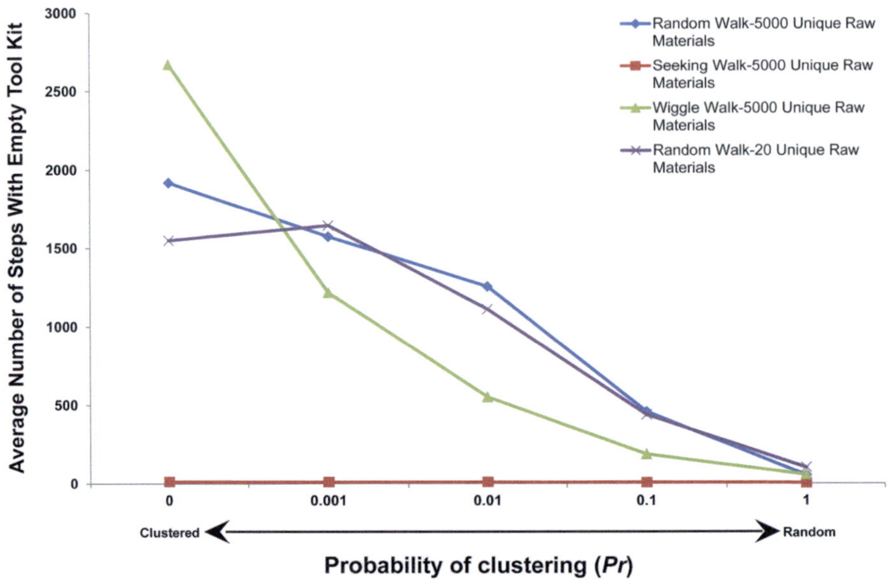

Fig. 4.9 Average number of time steps a tool kit is empty. Each *curve* is based on the average of 100 simulation runs

Table 4.3 Time steps spent without material in tool kit

p_r	Random walk
0	1550
0.001	1646
0.01	1112
0.1	440
1	104

4.4 Archaeological Implications and Predictions

Both the seeking walk, which is a simplified analogy for a forager that returns to a stone cache, and the random walk behavior both show that increased clustering of the raw material sources leads to increased time without raw materials in the tool kit. However, time between procurement instances and time without materials in the tool kit have different implications. If a forager can stockpile a cache at a central location and can return to such a place then the forager can go extended periods without procuring because it could return to the cache to fill up on raw materials. On the other hand, these results suggest that if random walk takes the forager away from the central location and never or very seldom returns directly to a stone cache then random walk is an unrealistic or at least risky strategy because the probability that the foragers runs out of materials is high.

A next step will be to project a map in an ABM of the Mossel Bay region that shows the location of archaeological sites in question, and that has potential raw materials sources and their real extent plotted on it. The forager will then be started at any one archaeological site and will move in a random walk to procure raw materials. Based on the results in this study one can predict several things: first, raw material richness should be low comparatively to the default neutral model as the actual number of unique raw materials on the landscape will be low. Second, as the agent is moving about the landscape the time spent without any raw materials in the tool kit will be high, in the order of days and weeks. This suggests that alternative procurement strategies need to be evaluated that meets the demands of the stone tool economy.

Acknowledgments The majority of this research was funded by the National Science Foundation (USA; grants # BCS-1138073, BCS-9912465, BCS-0130713, and BCS-0524087 to Curtis Marean), the Hyde Family Foundation, the Institute of Human Origins, Arizona State University, NORAM, and the Andrew E. and G. Norman Wigeland Fund.

References

Akerman K, Fullagar R, van Gijn A (2002) Weapons and wunan: production, function and exchange of Kimberley points. Aust Aboriginal Stud 2002(1):13–42

Ambrose SH, Lorenz KG (1990) Social and ecological models for the middle stone age in southern Africa. In: Mellars P (ed) The emergence of modern humans: an archaeological perspective. Edinburgh University Press, Edinburgh, pp 3–33

Andrefsky W Jr (1994) Raw-material availability and the organization of technology. Am Antiq 59 (1):21–34. doi:10.2307/3085499

Bamforth DB (1990) Settlement, raw material, and lithic procurement in the central Mojave Desert. J Anthropol Archaeol 9(1):70–104. doi:10.1016/0278-4165(90)90006-Y

Bar-Yosef O (1991) Raw material exploitation in the Levantine Epi-Paleolithic. In: Montet-White A, Holen S (eds) Raw material economies among prehistoric hunter-gatherers. University of Kansas, Lawrence

Binford LR, Stone NM (1985) "Righteous Rocks" and Richard Gould: some observations on misguided "Debate". Am Antiq 50(1):151–153. doi:10.2307/280641

Brantingham PJ (2003) A neutral model of stone raw material procurement. Am Antiq 68 (3):487–509. doi:10.2307/3557105

Braun DR, Plummer T, Ferraro JV, Ditchfield P, Bishop LC (2009) Raw material quality and Oldowan hominin toolstone preferences: evidence from Kanjera South, Kenya. J Archaeol Sci 36(7):1605–1614. doi:10.1016/j.jas.2009.03.025

Brown KS, Marean CW, Jacobs Z, Schoville BJ, Oestmo S, Fisher EC, Bernatchez J, Karkanas P, Matthews T (2012) An early and enduring advanced technology originating 71,000 years ago in South Africa. Nature 491(7425):590–593. doi:10.1038/nature11660

Clark JD (1980) Raw material and African lithic technology. Man Environ 4:44–55

Clendon M (1999) Worora gender metaphors and Australian prehistory. Anthropol Linguist 41 (3):308–355

Close AE (2002) Backed bladelets are a foreign country. In: Elston RG, Kuhn SL (eds) Thinking small: global perspectives on microlithization, pp 31–44

Féblot-Augustins J (1993) Mobility strategies in the late Middle Palaeolithic of central Europe and western Europe: elements of stability and variability. J Anthropol Archaeol 12(3):211–265. doi:10.1006/jaar.1993.1007
Gould RA, Saggers S (1985) Lithic procurement in Central Australia: a closer look at Binford's idea of embeddedness in archaeology. Am Antiq 50(1):117–136. doi:10.2307/280637
Hayden B, Nelson MC (1981) The use of chipped lithic material in the contemporary Maya highlands. Am Antiq 46:885–898
Janssen MA, Oestmo S (2013) A neutral model of stone raw material procurement (version 1). CoMSES Computational Model Library. Retrieved from: http://www.openabm.org/model/3957/version/1
Jelinek AJ (1991) Observations on reduction patterns and raw materials in some Middle Paleolithic industries in the Perigord. In: Montet-White A, Holen S (eds) Raw material economies among prehistoric hunter-gatherers. University of Kansas Publications in Anthropology 19, Lawrence, pp 7–32
Kuhn SL (1991) "Unpacking" reduction: lithic raw material economy in the Mousterian of west-central Italy. J Anthropol Archaeol 10(1):76–106. doi:10.1016/0278-4165(91)90022-P
Kuhn SL (1995) Mousterian lithic technology: an ecological perspective. Princeton University Press, Princeton
Kuhn SL (2004) Upper Paleolithic raw material economies at Üçağızlı cave, Turkey. J Anthropol Archaeol 23(4):431–448. doi:10.1016/j.jaa.2004.09.001
MacCalman NR, Grobelaar BJ (1965) Preliminary report of two stone-working Ova Tjimba groups in northern Kaokoveld of South West Africa. Cimbebasia 13:1–39
Malan J, Viljoen J (2008) Southern Cape geology: evolution of a Rifted Margin. Field excursion FT07 guidebook. Prepared for the American Association of Petroleum Geologists international conference and exhibition, Cape Town, South Africa, 26–29 Oct 2008
Mellars PA (1996) The Neandertal legacy: an archaeological perspective from Western Europe. Princeton University Press, Princeton
Miller TO (1979) Stonework of the xeta Indians of Brazil. In: Hayden B (ed) Lithic use-wear analysis. Academic Press, New York, pp 401–408
Minichillo T (2006) Raw material use and behavioral modernity: Howiesons Poort lithic foraging strategies. J Hum Evol 50(3):359–364. doi:10.1016/j.jhevol.2005.08.013
Oestmo S, Schoville BJ, Wilkins J, Marean CW (2014) A middle stone age paleoscape near the pinnacle point caves, Vleesbaai, South Africa. Quatern Int 350:147–168
Parry WJ, Kelly RL (1987) Expedient core technology and sedentism. In: Johnson J, Morrow C (eds) The organization of core technology. Westview Press, Boulder, pp 285–304
Roberts DL, Karkanas P, Jacobs Z, Marean CW, Roberts RG (2012) Melting ice sheets 400,000 yr ago raised sealevel by 13 m: past analogue for future trends. Earth Planet Sci Lett 357–358:226–237
Sillitoe P, Hardy K (2003) Living lithics: ethnoarchaeology in highland New Guinea. Antiquity 77:555–566
Stout D (2002) Skill and cognition in stone tool production: an ethnographic case study from Irian Jaya. Curr Anthropol 43(5):693–722. doi:10.1086/342638
Thamm AG, Johnson MR (2006) The cape supergroup. In: Johnson MR, Anhauesser CR, Thomas RJ (eds) The geology of South Africa. Geological Society of South Africa, Johannesburg/Council for Geoscience, Pretoria, pp 443–460
Thompson E, Marean CW (2008) The Mossel Bay lithic variant: 120 years of Middle Stone Age research from Cape St Blaize Cave to Pinnacle Point. Goodwin Series 10:90–104
Thompson E, Williams HM, Minichillo T (2010) Middle and late Pleistocene Middle Stone Age lithic technology from Pinnacle Point 13B (Mossel Bay, Western Cape Province, South Africa). J Human Evol 59(3–4):358–377. doi:10.1016/j.jhevol.2010.07.009
Viljoen JHA, Malan JA (1993) Die Geologie van die Gebiede 3421 BB Mosselbaai en 3422 AA Herbertsdale. Department of Mineral and Energy Affairs, Pretoria
Wurz S (1999) The Howiesons Poort backed artefacts from Klasies River: an argument for symbolic behaviour. S Afr Archaeol Bull 54(169):38–50

Chapter 5
Population Spread and Cultural Transmission in Neolithic Transitions

Joaquim Fort, Neus Isern, Antonieta Jerardino and Bernardo Rondelli

5.1 Introduction

The Neolithic transition in Europe has been analyzed quantitatively since the seminal work by Ammerman and Cavalli-Sforza (1971). Because the oldest Neolithic sites are located in the Near East, Ammerman and Cavalli-Sforza (1971) fitted a straight line to the dates of European sites versus their distances to a Near Eastern site (Jericho). In this way they estimated a speed of about 1 km/y. Later Ammerman and Cavalli-Sforza (1973, 1984) applied a model due to Fisher (1937) to the spread of preindustrial famers. They found that this model predicts a speed of about 1 km/y, i.e. similar to the observed one. This indicates that a process based mainly on demic diffusion (spread of populations) agrees with the archaeological data in Europe. Here we report on models with a more refined description of population spread than Fisher's model (Fort et al. 2007, 2008). We also recall a recent model that incorporates the effect of cultural diffusion, i.e. the spread of ideas (hunter-gatherers becoming farmers) instead of populations (Fort 2012). This demic-cultural model is then compared to the archaeological data on the Neolithic spread in Europe and southern Africa.

J. Fort (✉) · N. Isern
ICREA/Complex Systems Lab and Physics Department,
Universitat de Girona, C/. Mª Aurèlia Capmany 61, 17071 Girona, Catalonia, Spain
e-mail: joaquim.fort@udg.edu

A. Jerardino
CaSEs Research Group, ICREA/Department of Experimental & Health Sciences,
Universitat Pompeu Fabra, Ramon Trias Fargas 25-27, 08005 Barcelona, Spain
e-mail: amsjerardino@gmail.com

B. Rondelli
ICREA/CaSEs Research Group, Department of Archaeology and Anthropology,
Institució Milà i Fontanals, CSIC, C/. Egipcíaques, 15, 08001 Barcelona, Spain
e-mail: bernardorondelli@yahoo.it

J.A. Barceló and F. Del Castillo (eds.), *Simulating Prehistoric and Ancient Worlds*,
Computational Social Sciences, DOI 10.1007/978-3-319-31481-5_5

5.2 Limitations of Fisher's Model

Consider a population of preindustrial farmers, initially located in some region. Assume they can disperse into other regions that are also suitable for farming but initially empty of farmers. The next generations of farmers will, in general, disperse away from their parents. Then Fisher's model predicts that a wave of advance (also called a front) of farmers will form and propagate with the following speed (Fisher 1937)

$$s_F = 2\sqrt{a_N D_N}, \tag{5.1}$$

where a_N is the initial reproduction rate of Neolithic farmers (which is easily related to their net fecundity and generation time) and D_N is the diffusion coefficient of Neolithic farmers (which is easily related to the probability that farmers disperse away from their parents as a function of distance). Equation (5.1) is very useful. Ammerman and Cavalli-Sforza (Ammerman and Cavalli-Sforza 1973, 1984) used observed values for a_N and D_N into Eq. (5.1) and found that Fisher's model predicts a speed of about 1 km/y, i.e. similar to the observed one for the Neolithic transition in Europe. In recent years, Fisher's model has been refined (Fort et al. 2007). Note that Eq. (5.1) predicts that, for a given value of D_N, the speed increases without bound ($s_F \to \infty$) for increasing values of the initial reproduction rate ($a_N \to \infty$). This is counterintuitive because, for a given value of D_N, the dispersal behavior of the population is fixed. Thus individuals can disperse up to some maximum distance, $\Delta_{\max}$. Then we should expect that (no matter how large is a_N) the speed s_F should not be faster than $s_{\max} = \Delta_{\max}/T$, where T is the time interval between two subsequent migrations (mean age difference between parents and their children). An integro-difference cohabitation model solves this problem (Fort et al. 2007, 2008, 2012). Then Eq. (5.1) is replaced by a more complicated and accurate equation that takes into account a set of dispersal distances per generation and their respective probabilities. However Fisher's speed, Eq. (5.1), is very useful as a first approximation. It is even quite accurate for some pre-industrial farming populations. For example, for the Yanomano (Isern et al. 2008) Fisher's speed (1.22 km/y) yields an error of only 6 % relative to the integro-difference cohabitation model (1.30 km/y). In other cases, Fisher's speed is not so accurate. For example, for the Issocongos (Isern et al. 2008) Fisher's speed (0.56 km/y) yields an error of 30 % relative to the integro-difference cohabitation model (0.80 km/y).

5.3 Possible Forms of the Cultural Transmission Term

The demic models above can be extended by including cultural transmission. Then Fisher's speed, Eq. (5.1) is generalized into (Fort 2012)

$$s = 2\sqrt{\left(a_N + \frac{C}{T}\right)D_N}, \tag{5.2}$$

where C is the intensity of cultural transmission (defined as the number of hunter-gatherers converted into farmers per farmer during his/her lifetime, in the leading edge of the front, i.e. a region where the population density of farmers is very low) (Fort 2012). In the absence of cultural transmission ($C = 0$), Eq. (5.2) reduces to Fisher's speed, Eq. (5.1), as it should.

Equation (5.2) and other models with cultural transmission take into account that hunter-gatherers can learn agriculture not only from incoming farmers, but also from converted hunter-gatherers, i.e. former hunter-gatherers that have (partially) become farmers (as well as their descendants).

An integro-difference cohabitation model with cultural transmission leads to a more complicated equation than Eq. (5.2), and generalizes the integro-difference model summarized in the previous section (Fort 2012).

Both demic-cultural models (i.e., Eq. (5.2) and the integro-difference cohabitation model) are based on cultural transmission theory (Cavalli-Sforza and Feldman 1981), which shows that the number of hunter-gatherers converted into farmers per farmer during his/her lifetime is (Fort 2012)

$$\frac{\Delta P_N}{P_N} = \frac{f\,P_P}{P_N + \gamma\,P_P}, \tag{5.3}$$

where P_N and P_P are the population densities of Neolithic farmers and Mesolithic hunter-gatherers, respectively, and f and γ are cultural transmission parameters. In the leading edge of the front ($P_N \approx 0$), Eq. (5.3) becomes

$$\frac{\Delta P_N}{P_N} = C, \tag{5.4}$$

with $C = f/\gamma$.

A comparison to other approaches is of interest here. In Ecology a widely used model is based on Lotka-Volterra equations, which assume that the interaction between two populations (ΔP_N) is proportional to their population densities (Murray 2003),

$$\frac{\Delta P_N}{P_N} = k\,P_P, \tag{5.5}$$

where k is a constant. This model has the problem that $\Delta P_N/P_N \to \infty$ if $P_P \to \infty$, which seems inappropriate in cultural transmission, for the following reason. Assume that a farmer converts, e.g., 5 hunter-gatherers during his lifetime ($\Delta P_N/P_N = 5$) if there are $P_P = 10$ hunter-gatherers per unit area. Then Eq. (5.5) predicts that he/she will convert $\Delta P_N/P_N = 50$ hunter-gatherers if there are

$P_P =$ 100 hunter-gatherers per unit area, $\Delta P_N/P_N =$ 500 hunter-gatherers if there are $P_P =$ 1000 hunter-gatherers per unit area, etc. Contrary to this, intuitively we expect that there should be a maximum in the number of hunter-gatherers that a famer can convert during his/her lifetime, i.e. that $\Delta P_N/P_N$ should have a finite limit if $P_P \rightarrow \infty$. This saturation effect is indeed predicted by Eq. (5.3), as shown by Eq. (5.4). Thus we think that Eq. (5.3) is more reasonable than the Lotka-Volterra interaction, Eq. (5.5).

This point has important consequences because for Eq. (5.3) the wave-of-advance speed is independent of the carrying capacity of hunter-gatherers, $P_{P\,\max}$ (see, e.g., Eq. 5.2). In contrast, for the Lotka-Volterra interaction the wave-of-advance speed does depend on $P_{P\,\max}$. For example, if Fisher's model is generalized by including the Lotka-Volterra interaction, the front speed is (Minedez et al. 1999) (see also Murray 2003 for a similar model)

$$s = 2\sqrt{\left(a_N + \frac{k\,P_{P\max}}{T}\right) D_N}. \tag{5.6}$$

The point is that, in contrast to Eq. (5.2), Eq. (5.6) depends on $P_{P\max}$. The same happens if the integro-difference cohabitation model (which is more precise than Fisher's model) is generalized by including the Lotka-Volterra interaction (Fort et al. 2008). These results are not surprising because in the front leading edge ($P_N \approx 0$, $P_P \approx P_{P\,\max}$) Eq. (5.5) becomes $\Delta P_N/P_N = k\,P_{P\max}$, which depends on $P_{P\,\max}$ (whereas Eq. 5.4 does not).

Finally, some language competition models use population fractions (rather than population densities) and interaction terms with non-linear powers of P_N and P_P (Abrams and Strogatz 2003). We first consider the linear case. In one such model, Eq. (5.5) above is replaced by (Isern and Fort 2014)

$$\frac{\Delta P_N}{P_N} = \frac{\eta\, P_P}{P_N + P_P}, \tag{5.7}$$

with η a constant. Equation (5.7) is a special case of Eq. (5.3), thus the wave-of-advance speed is independent of $P_{P\,\max}$ also in this model (Isern et al. 2014). It can be argued that the complete model in Isern et al. (2014) is useful for modern populations but not for the Neolithic transition, because it assumes the same carrying capacity for both populations. But a model that allows for different carrying capacities (Fort and Pérez-Losada 2012) also leads, in the linear case, to an equation with the form of Eq. (5.7). In conclusion, some models originally devised to describe language competition also lead to the conclusion we have stressed above, namely that the wave-of-advance speed is independent of $P_{P\,\max}$.

For completeness, in the non-linear case the following two limitations of the language-competition models discussed in the previous paragraph (Abrams and Strogatz 2003; Isern et al. 2014; Fort and Pérez-Losada 2012) should be noted in the context of the Neolithic transition.

(i) In the non-linear case, Eq. (5.7) above is generalized into (Isern et al. 2014)

$$\Delta P_N = \frac{\eta P_N^{\alpha} P_P^{\beta}}{(P_N + P_P)^{\alpha+\beta-1}} \tag{5.8}$$

with $\alpha \geq 1$ and $\beta \geq 1$ (Abrams and Strogatz 2003). Thus $\Delta P_N \to 0$ if $P_P \to \infty$, i.e. $\Delta P_N / P_N$ does not have a finite, non-vanishing limit (except in the linear case $\alpha = \beta = 1$, see Eq. (5.6). Alternatively, for the Abrams-Strogatz model in Ref. (Fort and Pérez-Losada 2012), namely

$$\Delta P_N = \kappa \left[\sigma P_P \left(\frac{P_N}{P_N + P_P} \right)^a - (1-\sigma) P_N \left(\frac{P_P}{P_N + P_P} \right)^a \right], \tag{5.9}$$

where $\sigma < 1$ is called the status of language N and $a \geq 1$ is the resistance to language change, we obtain a negative limit for $\Delta P_N / P_N$ if $P_P \to \infty$, which is counterintuitive (Isern et al. 2014) (except again in the linear case, $a = 1$). The main point here is that neither of both non-linear models displays the saturation effect discussed above.

(ii) Whereas Eq. (5.3) was derived from cultural transmission theory, the non-linear models introduced to describe language competition (Abrams and Strogatz 2003; Isern et al. 2014; Fort and Pérez-Losada 2012) (Eqs. 5.8 and 5.9) were not.

The non-linear models given by Eqs. (5.8) and (5.9) compare favorably to observed data in non-spatial linguistic systems (Abrams and Strogatz 2003; Isern et al. 2014), and may be applicable to other modern instances of cultural transmission. Perhaps the effects of mass-media, schools, etc. in modern societies avoid the saturation effect discussed above. Such effects are not included in the cultural transmission theory leading to Eq. (5.3) (Fort 2012).

In any case, due to reasons (i) and (ii) above, for the Neolithic transition we prefer not to apply language-competition non-linear models, Eqs. (5.8) and (5.9), neither the Lotka-Volterra interaction, Eq. (5.5). Instead, we apply cultural transmission theory, Eq. (5.3) (or its frequency-dependent generalizations, which take into account the conformist effect but lead to the same conclusions (Fort 2012)).

We stress that the conclusion that the wave-of-advance speed is independent of the hunter-gatherer population density $P_{P\,\max}$ follows from cultural transmission theory, and is ultimately due to the fact that there should be a maximum number of hunter-gatherers converted to agriculture per farmer (or converted hunter-gatherer) during his/her lifetime (this is the saturation effect discussed above).

5.4 Europe

The integro-difference cohabitation model that refines Eq. (5.2) by taking into account a set of dispersal distances per generation and their respective probabilities (see Sect. 5.2) has been applied to the Neolithic transition in Europe (Fort 2012). The results are reproduced in Fig. 5.1, where the horizontal hatched rectangle is the observed speed range from the archaeological dates, namely 0.9–1.3 km/y (Pinhasi et al. 2005). The vertical hatched rectangle is the observed range for the intensity of cultural transmission C from hunting-gathering into farming, according to ethnographic data (Fort 2012). The upper curve is the maximum predicted speed, i.e. that obtained from the model for the fastest observed reproduction rate of human populations that settled in empty space ($a_N = 0.033$ yr^{-1}) and the lowest observed value for the generation time ($T = 29$ yr). Similarly, the lower curve is the minimum predicted speed, i.e. that obtained from the model for the slowest observed reproduction rate of human populations that settled in empty space ($a_N = 0.023$ yr^{-1}) and the highest observed value for the generation time ($T = 35$ yr). Note that without taking into account the effect of cultural transmission ($C = 0$), the predicted speed is about 0.8 km/y (0.7–0.9 km/y), whereas for consistent values of C the speed increases up to 1.3 km/y. Thus the cultural effect is about 40 % (more precisely, 40 ± 8 % (Fort 2012)).

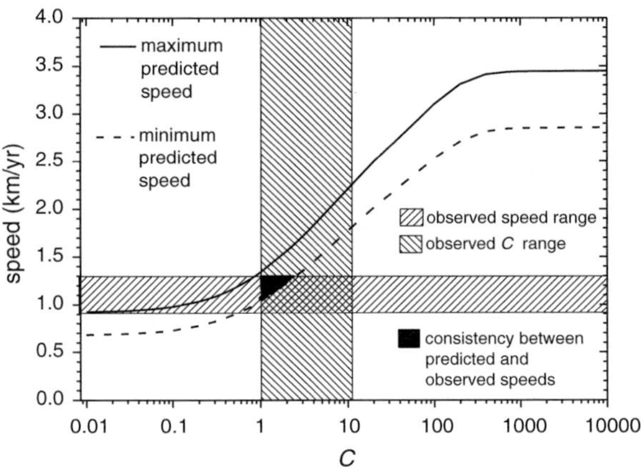

Fig. 5.1 The speed of the Neolithic transition in Europe, as a function of the intensity of cultural transmission C. The horizontal hatched rectangle is the observed speed range of the Neolithic transition in Europe (Pinhasi et al. 2005), and the vertical hatched rectangle is the observed range for the intensity of cultural transmission from hunting-gathering into farming (Pinhasi et al. 2005). Adapted from Ref. (Fort 2012)

5.5 Southern Africa

In southern Africa, the Neolithic transition was a shift from hunting-gathering into herding, not into farming and stockbreeding as in Europe. Another difference is that the speed was 1.4–3.3 km/y (Jerardino et al. 2014), therefore substantially faster than in the European case (previous section). From Fig. 5.1 we thus expect that the value of C (and, therefore, the cultural effect) will be higher in southern Africa than in Europe. This is indeed the case, as we shall now see. Figure 5.2 is the equivalent for southern Africa to Fig. 5.1 for Europe. Thus Fig. 5.2 follows exactly from the same model as Fig. 5.1. The curves are not the same in Figs. 5.1 and 5.2 only because the dispersal kernel (set of dispersal distances and probabilities) used was measured for populations of herders (Fig. 5.2) rather than farmers (Fig. 5.1). The kernel of herders (used in Fig. 5.2) was determined from 4,483 parent-offspring birthplace distances of herders collected by Mehrai (1984). But comparing Figs. 5.1 and 5.2, we note that the waves of advance of farmers and herders are in fact similar. Indeed, the speed obtained without cultural transmission ($C=0$) is about 1 km/y in both figures, and the fastest possible speed ($C \rightarrow \infty$) is again similar (about 3 km/y). Therefore, as expected, the fastest speed for the southern African Neolithic (1.4–3.3 km/y, horizontal rectangle in Fig. 5.2) as compared to Europe (0.7–0.9 km/y, horizontal rectangle in Fig. 5.1) implies higher values for C in Fig. 5.2 (e.g. $C=10$) compared to Fig. 5.1 ($C \leq 2.5$, black area in Fig. 5.1). This is why we find that the cultural effect was stronger in the southern African Neolithic. For example, without taking into account the effect of cultural transmission ($C=0$) the predicted speed is about 1.0 km/y (0.9–1.2 km/y), whereas for ethnographically realistic values of C ($6 \leq C \leq 15$, see Ref. (Jerardino et al. 2014)) the speed

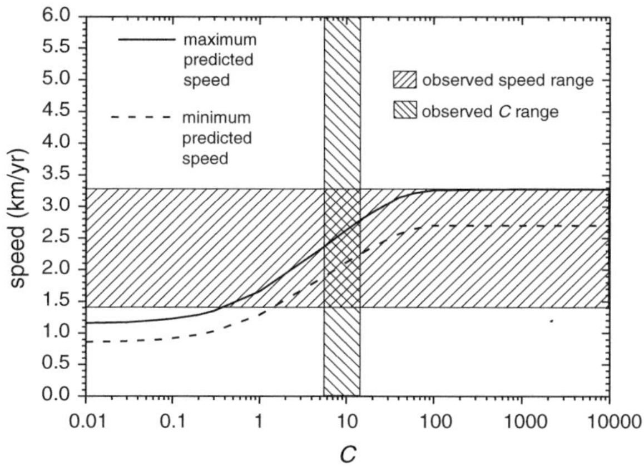

Fig. 5.2 The speed of the Neolithic transition in southern Africa, as a function of the intensity of cultural transmission C. The horizontal hatched rectangle is the observed speed range of the Neolithic transition in southern Africa, and the vertical hatched rectangle is the observed range for the intensity of cultural transmission from hunting-gathering into herding. Adapted from Ref. (Jerardino et al. 2014)

increases up to 2.8 km/y. Thus the cultural effect is about 60 % (more precisely, 57 ± 6 % (Fort 2012)) in southern Africa.

We conclude that the Neolithic transition was mainly demic in Europe (cultural effect about 40 %, i.e. <50 %, see the previous section) but mainly cultural in southern Africa (cultural effect 60 %, i.e. >50 %, as explained in this section). Because the reproductive and dispersal behavior of both populations (farmers in Europe, herders in southern Africa) is likely similar (Jerardino et al. 2014), this difference could be due to a higher ease for hunter-gatherers to learn herding in comparison with farming.

5.6 Conclusion

The European and southern African Neolithic spread are the two first examples in which the percentages of demic and cultural diffusion have been determined. Another interesting example could be the Bantu expansion of farming in Africa (Russell et al. 2014). Many other examples could be studied, provided of course that there were enough data were available to perform statistically sound estimations of the observed speed range. Potential applications include not only Neolithic transitions but also many other spread phenomena of cultural traits, such as the spread of horses in North America (Haines 1938), crop dispersals (Dickau et al. 2007), etc.

Acknowledgment This work was funded in part by ICREA (JF and AJ) and the MINECO grants SimulPast-CSD2010-00034 (all authors) and FIS-2012-31307 (JF and NI). The authors are very thankful to John Kinahan, Jayson Orton, Thembi Russell, Karim Sadr, and Lita Webley for providing useful bibliography.

References

Abrams DM, Strogatz SH (2003) Modelling the dynamics of language death. Nature 424:900

Ammerman AJ, Cavalli-Sforza LL (1971) Measuring the rate of spread of early farming in Europe. Man 6:674–688

Ammerman AJ, Cavalli-Sforza LL (1984) The Neolithic transition and the genetics of populations in Europe. Princeton Univ. Press, Princeton (NJ)

Ammerman AJ, Cavalli-Sforza, LL (1973) A population model for the diffusion of early farming in Europe. In: Renfrew C (ed) The explanation of culture change: models in prehistory. Duckworth, London, pp 343–357

Cavalli-Sforza LL, Feldman M (1981) Cultural transmission and evolution: a quantitative approach. Princeton University Press, Princenton

Dickau R, Ranere AJ, Cooke RG (2007) Starch grain evidence for the preceramic dispersals of maize and root crops into tropical dry and humid forests of Panama. Proc Natl Acad Sci USA 104:3651–3656

Fisher RA (1937) The wave of advance of advantageous genes. Ann. Eugenics 7:355–369

Fort J (2012) Synthesis between demic and cultural diffusion in the Neolithic transition in Europe. Proc Natl Acad Sci USA 109:18669–18673
Fort J, Pérez-Losada J (2012) Front speed of language replacement. Hum Biol 84:755–772
Fort J, Pérez-Losada J, Isern N (2007) Fronts from integrodifference equations and persistence effects on the Neolithic transition. Phys Rev E, 76, paper 031913
Fort J, Pérez-Losada J, Suñol JJ, Escoda L, Massaneda JM (2008) Integro-difference equations for interacting species and the Neolithic transition. New J Phys 24, paper 043045
Haines F (1938) The northward spread of horses among the plains Indians. Amer Anthropol 40:429–437
Isern N, Fort J (2014) Language extinction and linguistic fronts. J Roy Soc Interface, 11, paper 20140028. Eq. (2.6). Equation (7) here corresponds to the linear case, namely $\alpha = \beta = 1$
Isern N, Fort J, Pérez-Losada J (2008) Realistic dispersion kernels applied to cohabitation reaction-dispersion equations. J Stat Mec, 10, paper P10012
Jerardino A, Fort J, Isern N, Rondelli B (2014) Cultural diffusion was the main driving mechanism of the Neolithic transition in southern Africa. PLoS ONE 9:e113672
Mehrai H (2014) A demographic study of some populations in Shahrestan Nowshahr, Mazandaran, Iran, with reference to the genetic structure, 1984, p. 208. Ph.D. Thesis, Durham University. http://etheses.dur.ac.uk/7169/. Accessed 15 Mar 2014
Méndez V, Fort J, Farjas J (1999) Speed of wave-front solutions to hyperbolic reaction-diffusion equations. Phys Rev E 60:5231–5243. Eq. (50)
Murray JD (2003) Mathematical Biology, vol. 2. Springer, Berlin. Eqs. (1.2) and (1.10)
Pinhasi R, Fort J, Ammerman AJ (2005) Tracing the origin and spread of agriculture in Europe. PLoS Biol 3:e410
Russell T, Silva F, Steele J (2014) Modelling the spread of farming in the Bantu-speaking regions of Africa: an archaeology-based phylogeography. PLoS ONE 9:e87854

Chapter 6
Modelling Routeways in a Landscape of Esker and Bog

Yolande O'Brien and Stefan Bergh

6.1 Introduction

This paper is part of a wider research project which aims to understand how people in the past exploited natural routeways and manoeuvred around obstacles in the landscape. The archaeological evidence from North Offaly in the Irish midlands is the principle case study used to explore this question (Fig. 6.1). Segments of a known, but poorly defined, ancient routeway within the study area are discussed in this paper, with the objective of identifying a likely routeway using computer applications, supported by fieldwork and documentary sources. Routeways can wax and wane in importance depending on factors such as settlement, expressions of control or technology, but this paper aims to describe how people interact with the natural features of the landscape in a cumulative fashion to form routeways. This concept can be applied to any landscape or period, with the caveat that certain ritual practices, taboos or cultural rivalries also have an effect on how movement is performed. The case study in question, however, incorporates evidence ranging from the Neolithic period to as late as the 16th century, when the Tudors drastically altered the landscape through widespread clearance of woodland.

Two digital approaches are used, namely Least Cost Paths to *calculate* a routeway, and Agent-Based Modelling to *grow* (Epstein and Axtell 1996) one. ArcGIS 9.3 is used in what is considered a routine method to identify potential routes through the application of Least Cost Paths. NetLogo 5.1.0. (Wilensky 1999) is used to emulate individual actions of heterogeneous agents which cumulatively contribute to the evolution of routeways. Least Cost Path procedures have gained

Y. O'Brien (✉) · S. Bergh
National University of Ireland, Galway, Ireland
e-mail: y.obrien2@nuigalway.ie

S. Bergh
e-mail: stefan.bergh@nuigalway.ie

J.A. Barceló and F. Del Castillo (eds.), *Simulating Prehistoric and Ancient Worlds*, Computational Social Sciences, DOI 10.1007/978-3-319-31481-5_6

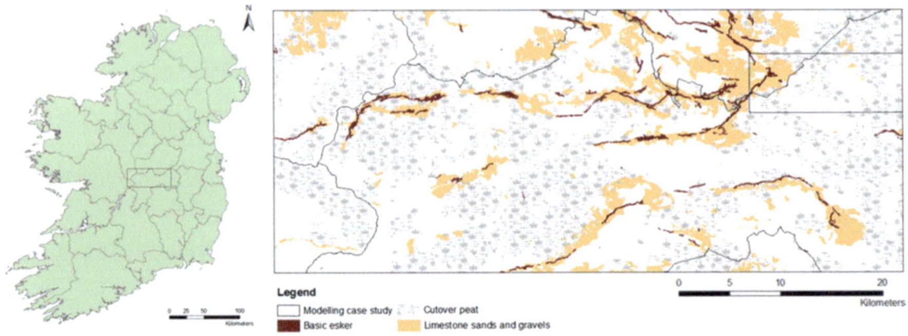

Fig. 6.1 Location of study area and modelling case study area

popularity in archaeological landscape studies since the 1990s, and particular attention has been paid to how it might be performed without reducing the role of people in the landscape to passive individuals with no autonomy or agency. In fact, it is quite possible to create a Least Cost Path based on genuine human decision, as the values assigned to these models are derived from legitimate factors which influence movement, such as distaste for steep slopes, the relative difficulties of traversing different soil types, and absolute obstacles. As Llobera (2000) observes, 'Topography is basic for it is always present and its influence is continuous in every landscape. Hence it constitutes the background on which other factors operate.' Social factors need not be ignored either, and taboos, traditions, exclusivity etc. can also be easily incorporated into such models by increasing or decreasing values as appropriate. Agent-Based Modelling makes this decision-making process explicit, as each action performed by the agents involves a decision based on the environment, informed by any number of physical, social or cultural factors.

While Least Cost Path procedures are ideal for identifying the optimal path through a landscape, agents on the ground are not exposed to the level of global information which is used to calculate the path in this way. Modelling allows us to investigate the overall evolution of a routeway as individual agents have access only to local information, allowing them to approach the optimal path over time through a process of iterative attempts to traverse a landscape.

The outputs from Least Cost Paths and Agent-Based Modelling may be used to point to parts of the landscape that merit further research in the field and through documentary sources. Existing archaeological and documentary evidence such as extant monuments, lines of sight and records of roads can support the potential of the modelled routeways. By comparing the hypothetical and the physical in this way, the parameters of both models can be improved in the hope of finding a useful methodology for areas without such rich records.

6.2 The Study Area

The landscape of North Offaly is dominated with esker, bog and, in the past, extensive natural woodland (Fig. 6.1). An esker is a long, sinuous ridge of sand and gravel, which are the remains of deposits left by rivers of melt-water beneath the surface of glaciers 15,000 years ago. In Ireland, a series of these ridges stretches from the east coast to the west coast and are known by the collective name of the *Eiscir Riada*. Some of the finest examples of high-sided and single-crested eskers are found in the study area (Tubridy and Meehan 2006). The bogs, which are slightly younger, began to form about 10,000 years ago as glacial retreat filled dips and valleys with nutrient-rich meltwater. Poor drainage caused these shallow lakes to build up with partially decomposed plant material and eventually, as they changed from being fed by ground water to rain water, they grew into the typical dome shape of raised peat bogs. The Irish midlands are renowned for their raised bogs, often referred to in the singular as the Bog of Allen, and a number of archaeological surveys and excavations have demonstrated their importance since early prehistoric times (Moloney et al. 1995; Irish Archaeological Wetland Unit 2002a, b, c,d, e; Irish Archaeological Wetland Unit 2003a, b, c; Whitaker and O'Carroll 2009). A stretch of dry land, known as the Midland Corridor (Smyth 1982), bisects this landscape in a northeast by southwest orientation, acting as a major inter-regional routeway and valuable agricultural land. When Ireland was populated by Mesolithic hunter-gatherers around 8000 BC, the eskers were already in place, but many bogs were still in the early stages of development as lakes or reed swamps. Nevertheless, they were an important feature in the landscape which impacted on the execution of movement, and both of these landscape features have influenced human activities since the arrival of the first settlers in Ireland.

6.2.1 Eskers

The eskers, being well-drained, elevated, relatively straight, and flanked by wetlands, are quite suitable for movement, as is clear from the number of trails and roads currently located on these ridges (Fig. 6.2). The Early Medieval routeway known as the *Slighe Mór*, which is associated with the birth of King Conn Céadcathach and therefore usually dated to the early 2nd century AD, is defined for much of its course by the *Eiscir Riada*. From the Early Medieval period onwards, there was a considerable increase in the amount of ecclesiastical settlement in particular along the course of the eskers. It appears that the Midland Corridor would have been a more important inter-regional routeway in prehistory, while the esker probably functioned as a local routeway. The bogs would have been wetter early in their developments, and the eskers would have been attractive features in the attempt to negotiate them. This attraction is demonstrated by the presence of standing stones and burials in proximity to the eskers, suggesting a prehistoric importance to these features.

Fig. 6.2 Roads often follow esker ridges

6.2.2 *Bogs*

While bogs are obstacles, they are not necessarily impenetrable if one is prepared to invest time and energy in the construction of a trackway. Archaeological investigations have revealed numerous timber trackway constructions in these wetland locations ranging in date across prehistory and the medieval periods (Moloney et al. 1995; Irish Archaeological Wetland Unit 2002a, b, c, d, e; Irish Archaeological Wetland Unit 2003a, b, c; Whitaker and O'Carroll 2009). This suggests that there were incentives to traversing the bog, rather than diverting around it on to dry land. The principle incentive would most likely have been the saving of time and energy by substantially shortening a journey. The initial effort of constructing the trackway would be very quickly offset by the ease with which subsequent crossings could be taken. The trackway may have been periodically maintained or replaced as the bog would continue to grow, and this often results in a succession of trackways over a prolonged period. Edercloon, Co. Longford, for example, revealed 48 structures in an area which measured only 170 m by 30 m, demonstrating a consistency of movement in this area from the Neolithic to the Medieval period (Moore 2008). This persistency of construction and consistency in crossing the bog at the same location makes the crossing point a place of relevance and an active node in the landscape. Typically, trackways traverse the bog at narrow points, although exceptions exist, such as Ballybeg Bog within the study area, or Mountdillon Bog, Co. Longford. Examples such as these are sometimes speculated to be for ritual purposes, or perhaps local access to resources within the bog. This indicates the trackways can be divided into two categories, those crossing the bog which treat it as an obstacle, and those accessing the bog which treat it as an objective.

6.2.3 Hills and Landmarks

The terrain throughout the North Offaly is relatively flat, ranging from 40 m OD around the River Shannon basin in the West, to 90 m in the East. Apart from Croghan Hill, with a height of 234 m, most rises are quite low, but nevertheless highly visible. The practice of navigating through a landscape is most often done by moving in reference to landmarks in a process known as piloting. Hills and other highly visual features tend to act as landmarks to pilot by, and facilitate the development of cognitive maps (see Golledge 2003 for full discussion). While individuals are typically only exposed to local information, hills are a means of introducing more global information, by offering distant landmarks to pilot by, and by offering a vantage point to assess more distant terrain. Such locations are frequently mythologised and ritualised, demonstrating the importance of these places to sense of place. In the landscape of North Offaly in particular, rises are often found either side of narrow points in the bogs, meaning they are found at the most appropriate crossing points. As such, they are attractive features to travelers who seek to cross a bog, observe the landscape, and plan a journey.

6.2.4 The Slighe Mór

The *Slighe Mór* routeway is often described as following the course of the *Eiscir Riada*, but the "esker" is in fact a series of multiple, discontinuous and sometimes parallel ridges, which make it quite difficult to define the exact course of the routeway. A number of suggested courses have been described (O'Lochlainn 1940; Fitzpatrick and O'Brien 1998; O'Keeffe 2001; Geissel 2006), and each suggestion almost certainly represents places where movement took place. However, it is not the intention of this research to identify the exact path of the *Slighe Mór*. In fact, it is perhaps more appropriate to think of the *Slighe Mór* as a concept, rather than a fixed path, and the name may have been applied to several paths at different, or even simultaneous, times. Rather, the itinerary produced by Colm O'Lochlainn (1940) for the *Slighe Mór* is used as a list of nodes between which movement demonstrably happened. O'Lochlainn produced this itinerary through a study of documentary sources and mythologies which record the travels of historical and mythological characters. While exact paths were not recorded, settlements along the way were named. Models are run between these locations in order to understand how movement may have taken place between them. Within the study area, O'Lochlainn describes the *Slighe Mór* as passing through Rhode, Croghan, Kiltober, Durrow, Ballycumber, Togher, Ballaghurt and Clonmacnoise. The records usually refer to ecclesiastical settlements, so ecclesiastical sites were chosen, where possible, as the sources and destination points. For locations without a suitable ecclesiastical site, castles were chosen as nodes as they were often placed in reference to routeways.

6.3 Methodology

As discussed above (Sect. 6.2.4), the methodology for this study began with identifying nodes between which we know movement took place. The computer applications described below (Sects. 6.3.1 and 6.3.2) were then used to respectfully *calculate* and *grow* potential routeways between these nodes. The proposed routes were then walked and compared against the archaeological and documentary evidence, as well as the existing road network (Sect. 6.3.3). The study therefore combines a range of conventional fieldwork and desk-based research with the possibilities of computer modelling.

6.3.1 Least Cost Paths

The natural features which create potential routeways or obstacles in this landscape are characterised by subsoil type more so than slope, so soil was weighted at 75 % and slope was allocated 25 % to produce a Cost Surface. A scale value of one to ten was applied to each soil type, ten being the most difficult to traverse and one the easiest. These values were admittedly subjective, and were arrived at through fieldwork and personal experience (Table 6.1).

Wetland areas are difficult to traverse and were therefore assigned high values, while the glacial sediments represented by eskers, sands and gravels, and till are suitably drained to facilitate ease of movement, and were therefore assigned low values.

ArcGIS Least Cost Paths are anisotropic, or direction dependent. As such, each segment was run in both directions in order to determine the extent of differences associated with direction. It is not unusual to take a different path, depending on direction of travel, as one would attempt to avoid steep slopes, or to maintain a straight course for as long as possible before changing direction. Even in the case of established roads and paths, for instance, where an agent's decisions are based on a limited number of potential paths, it is common for pedestrians to return via a different path from the initial journey.

Table 6.1 Weight applied to subsoils

Cutover peat—10	Fen peat—10
Water—10	Lake sediment—10
Alluvium—8	Rock—6
Marl—6	Karstified limestone—6
Made ground—4	Limestone till—2
Limestone sands and gravels—2	Sandstone till— 2
Basic esker—1	

6.3.2 Agent-Based Modelling

The NetLogo world was constructed using the NetLogo GIS extension to import the relevant shapefiles to the model, including soil types and elevation data (Fig. 6.3). This model was similarly run in both directions in order to consider the effect of direction on the evolution of a routeway. The variables explored included the number of agents, or *turtles* in NetLogo terminology, as well as their release interval and the dimensions of the cones of vision. The turtles are created at one settlement and include a single *leader* breed while the rest are *followers*. They leave the settlement at the rate of release controlled by the slider and their task is to reach the target at the opposite settlement. The distance and angle of the cones of vision are controlled by an *in-cone* reporter, and this limits access to landscape information until they are within visual range of the turtles.

The *leader* turns its heading to the target and proceeds to navigate through the landscape. Anthropological studies have shown cognitive mapping to be powerful enough to allow for dead reckoning, particularly when there are highly visual landscape features to act as landmarks (Golledge 2003). In the case of the examples in this paper, the targets are next to obvious landmarks in the form of hills and eskers, which act as visual cues to pilot by in the real landscape. The aim of navigating to a known settlement presupposes a minimum pre-existing cognitive map, which may be constructed from personal experience, third-party knowledge and *topographical gossip* (Widlock 1997) so it was deemed sufficiently realistic to set the heading from the beginning of the journey in this way. The *leader* is then instructed to negotiate the landscape using a series of simple commands.

Rather than assigning values as is performed in Least Cost Path models, Booleans were used to differentiate between *obstacle* and *not obstacle*, with bogs acting

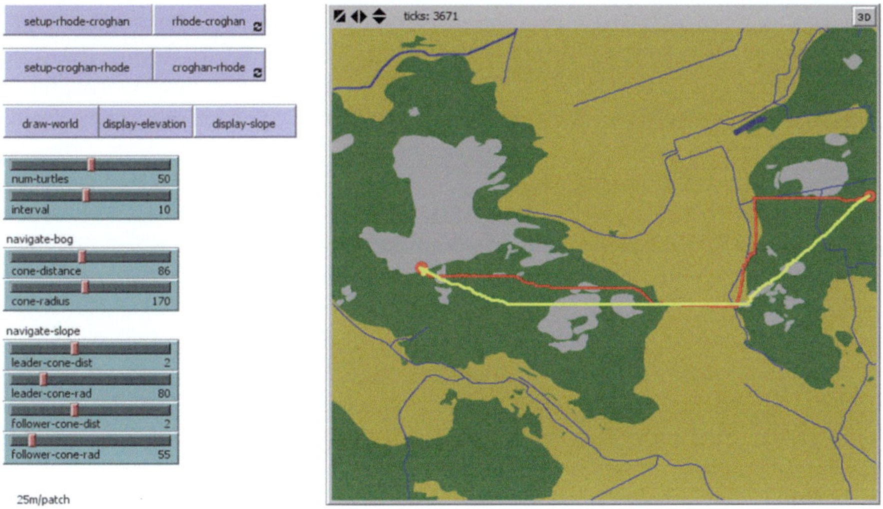

Fig. 6.3 Paths created by NetLogo model of Rhode to Croghan

as obstacles. When a bog is encountered, the turtle is obliged to find a suitable crossing point within the user-defined cone of vision to find dry land within a set distance and radius. A range of variables were tested for each of the parameters. It is possible to see c. 4.8 km over land if unobstructed, but this would be substantially less in a landscape with vegetation, uneven contours etc. It is also an unrealistically long crossing for bogs of the dimensions found in landscape. Within the overall study area, the longest bog crossing suggested by surviving trackways is c. 2.15 km, so an approximation of this distance was used, as it represents the upper limits of an ideal bog crossing and falls well within the potential distance of human vision. The angle of vision has been set at 170°. Values below this were not effective in finding the narrowest point in the bog, while higher values cause the turtles to move in circular motions. With this code and these values, the leading turtle can find the most efficient crossing point within a reasonable distance without having to circle the entire bog.

The *leader* turtle was also instructed to favour the least slope values within a distance and radius defined by sliders. It was found that the most effective values were to aim for the patch of least slope within two patches (c. 50 m) and 80°. While the process of crossing bogs requires a deviation of path, it is preferable to maintain a straighter course on dry land, calling for a narrower cone of vision. Each time step, or *tick*, calls the turtle to return their heading to the target before managing slope. This minimises the deviation when making corrections for slope, while representing the attention which a traveler would pay to a landmark while piloting a landscape.

All subsequent turtles, known by the *follower* breed, are released at regular intervals. Iterations with short intervals of release required a higher number of turtles to reach the most efficient solution, while longer release times necessitated less turtles. This is not reflective of reality, but a product of the *follow* procedure outlined below. *Followers* have the same capabilities as the *leader* to solve any obstacles encountered. They have the advantage, however, of having already had the problem solved by the *leader*, albeit in an inefficient way. Using the same method as the Ant Lines model (Wilensky 1997), each follower turns its heading to its immediate predecessor. The *followers* retain the ability to manage obstacles on their own and to factor slope into the path selection. This has the effect of smoothing the path over time. Rather than moving directly towards the target and negotiating an obstacle only when it presents itself, turtles later in the sequence aim straight towards the first solution to an obstacle, because they are defining their orientation based on their predecessors' movements. This cumulative process approaches an efficient path, with the path of the final turtle producing a path which is very similar to the path produced with Least Cost Path analysis.

As is usual with Agent-Based Modelling, different iterations of the model may produce slightly different results when using the same parameters. In order to compare the model to the Least Cost Path results, the path from a single, but representative, iteration each was used per segment and direction. The crucial points for problem solving are the bog crossings, which are always performed almost identically, while variations in other parts of the landscape are minor.

6.3.3 Evaluating the Models

These methods were applied to two segments described in O' Lochlainn's (1940) itinerary of the *Slighe Mór*. Potential paths are suggested in both directions from Rhode to Croghan (Figs. 6.3 and 6.4), and Croghan to Kiltober (Figs. 6.6 and 6.7). The paths are then assessed against the archaeological and documentary evidence. Where the digital models correlate with the record, it is good evidence for the existence of a routeway in this location. It also supports the values and parameters which have been used in the Least Cost Paths and Agent-Based Modelling, which demonstrates that the factors considered are important in the decision-making process of individuals negotiating the landscape.

6.4 Rhode to Croghan

The settlements of Rhode and Croghan in the northeast of Offaly occupy slight elevations which are surrounded by a series of hills of volcanic origin and are separated by Ballybeg Bog (Fig. 6.4). O'Lochlainn (1940) tells us that the *Slighe Mór* linked these two settlements in the Early Medieval period, so a routeway must have existed between them despite the obstacle of the bog. Clonin Hill, which overlooks Rhode, is topped with a large Bronze Age ring barrow, while Croghan Hill is the location of an extremely prominent burial mound. The dating of this monument is uncertain, but the lack of an external ditch may suggest that it is a Neolithic cairn, rather than a Bronze Age barrow. Within the bog itself, the remains of Late Neolithic and Early Bronze Age occupation have been found. Minor secondary and tertiary trackways are present which do not appear to have crossed the bog, and they seem to have been intended to access a particular part of the bog, probably the ancient Lough Nashade (Irish Archaeological Wetland Unit 2002e). As discussed (Sect. 6.2.2), trackways leading into the bog are characteristically different to those which are intended to cross it. The presence of a contemporary bow stave (Murray 2004) suggests these trackways were probably associated with hunting within the wetlands, and so they do not provide an answer for how the bog may have been crossed. However, the site of the existing road which crosses the bog may conceal earlier trackways. Indeed, it is known as the Togher of Croghan and documentary evidence from the Annals of the Four Masters suggest it is at least 600 years old (Lucas 1985). The presence of prehistoric archaeology in this area demonstrates a prolonged use of this landscape, and the two areas of occupation on either side of the bog, represented by the burials and highly visible hills at Rhode and Croghan, would have to have been linked by a routeway to facilitate this. The presence of Late Neolithic and Early Bronze Age archaeology in particular suggests a routeway may have existed here at that time.

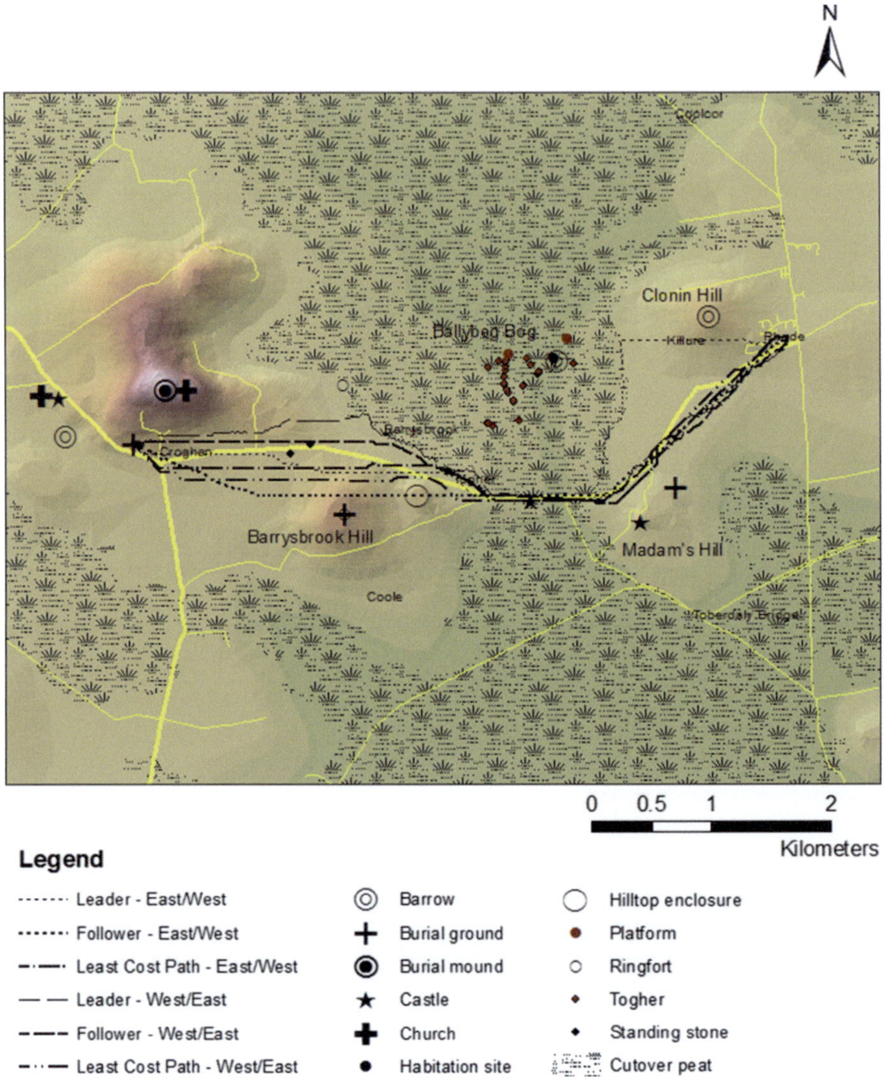

Fig. 6.4 Rhode to Croghan

6.4.1 Least Cost Path Results

The Least Cost Paths predictably traverse the bog at the narrowest point (Fig. 6.4). This point is flanked by Madam's Hill in Toberdaly, on the east side of the bog, and Barrysbrook Hill to the west. The paths skirt the lower slopes of these hills, using their elevation and drainage to emerge onto suitably dry land from the bog. It is not necessary to climb more than a few metres to access dry ground, and the steep slope and higher values for the exposed rock are thus avoided.

6.4.2 Agent-Based Modelling Results

A direct path from Rhode to Croghan and vice versa would traverse Ballybeg Bog at an unsuitable crossing point, so the *leader* is obliged to search for a narrower point, which it finds between Toberdaly and Barrysbrook, in the same location as the Least Cost Path (Figs. 6.3 and 6.4). Each *follower* is able to shorten the path to the crossing point, leading to an eventual path which makes straight for the crossing, with minor corrections made for slope. With the bog crossing complete, the remainder of the trip is unimpeded and a relatively straight route can be taken to the target.

6.4.3 Archaeological Evidence

The path taken by both programs through Ballybeg Bog coincides with the existing roadway which crosses this obstacle. A map dating to c. 1563 illustrates this crossing point as a causeway between Cnocarderin and a series of hills east of Croghan (Fig. 6.5). The feature is labelled as a togher and depicted as being defended by a castle, demonstrating the strategic importance of this crossing (see

Fig. 6.5 Togher of Croghan. With permission © The British Library Board. Cotton Augustus MS I ii 40. *North to right* of image

Irish Archaeological Wetland Unit 2002a for discussion of the location of this castle). The Togher of Croghan, or *Tóchar Cruachain Brí Éile*, is mentioned in the Annals of the Four Masters at least as early as 1385 (Lucas 1985), so the current roadway, and the path suggested by the modelling, mark a crossing of some antiquity. Given the prehistoric archaeology in the area, it would be likely that this crossing would have been exploited at an earlier date also.

The road separating Croghan Hill and Barrysbrook Hill appears to be closely related to the paths suggested by the modelling (Fig. 6.4), and was once flanked by two standing stones, of which one still survives. Standing stones are sometimes associated with routeways, but this road dates back only as far as the 19th century. An older road circles south of Barrysbrook Hill, before meeting a crossroads by which one can move north towards Croghan. When crossing Ballybeg Bog, it is clear that the series of hills which make up this landscape (Clonin Hill, Madams Hill, Barrysbrook Hill and Croghan Hill) create visual cues to pilot by when navigating the terrain. In particular, the targets on either side of the map are towards a low point on the slope, offering a suitably dry area for comfortable walking without an unnecessarily high climb, and providing an ideal vantage point to view the ground ahead. With this in mind, it would make no sense in terms of navigation and energy consumption to move south of Barrysbrook Hill to reach Croghan, obscuring Croghan Hill and adding needless distance to the journey.

There are a number of reasons why this circuitous route may exist. The road south of Barrysbrook is a better option for travelers bypassing Croghan in favour of Kilclonfert, 5.5 km to the west. This is another Early Christian site which was reputedly on the *Slighe Mór* and which was prestigious enough to be decorated with Romanesque features in the 12th century (Fitzpatrick and O'Brien 1998). In addition to this, the current road bisects the lands of Croghan Demesne, while the older road clearly adheres to its southern boundary. Movement through these lands would have been discouraged in the lifetime of the demesne, necessitating a different route which respected the boundary. Prior to this, Croghan was a royal site through which rights of movement would similarly have been carefully controlled.

Despite the later date for this section of the existing road, the compelling trajectory which the landscape impresses on the traveler through visual cues and landmarks suggests that there ought to have been a routeway here if movement between Rhode and Croghan took place. The standing stones are the best evidence for the existence of this route and, along with the modelled paths which move between the hills and associated monuments; they demonstrate that a path is likely to have existed in this location. Indeed, this path and the ritual landscape created by the burial mound on Croghan Hill and the standing stones below it may have been the impetus for the development of this landscape as a royal site.

The Togher of Croghan is a crucial point in the landscape because of its role in crossing Ballybeg Bog which would lead to its emergence as a place in its own right. This is demonstrated, not just from its depiction in the historical map of Leix and Offaly, but by its association with a castle. The Agent-Based Model shows turtles later in the sequence move directly towards this crossing point. It is clear that the Togher of Croghan becomes more than simply an interim point in the journey between Rhode and Croghan, but emerges as a place of note in the landscape which would appear in the cognitive maps of those who made use of it. By viewing the landscape in this movement-centric way, it may be possible to reconstruct how the people occupying it in the past constructed their cognitive maps.

6.5 Croghan to Kiltober

The landscape between Croghan and Kiltober is dominated by limestone till and cutover bog, with rock on the hills and occasional alluvium in the lowlands, but the western side is made up of limestone sands and gravels with a very substantial esker (Fig. 6.6). The Rahugh Esker is an excellent example of a steep-sided, single-crested esker, and it was evidently an important landscape feature as it creates the townland boundary between Kiltober and Monasset, and the other townlands which flank it. This is an important part of the esker, as it marks the point where the eskers become well defined and lengthy. Eskers north and east of this point are of short and more dispersed character, and as such are less useful for paths or boundaries. It also marks where the *Slighe Mór* intersects with the Midland Corridor, making it a crossroads of two major routeways. The importance of this intersection is demonstrated by the distribution of barrows in prehistory and

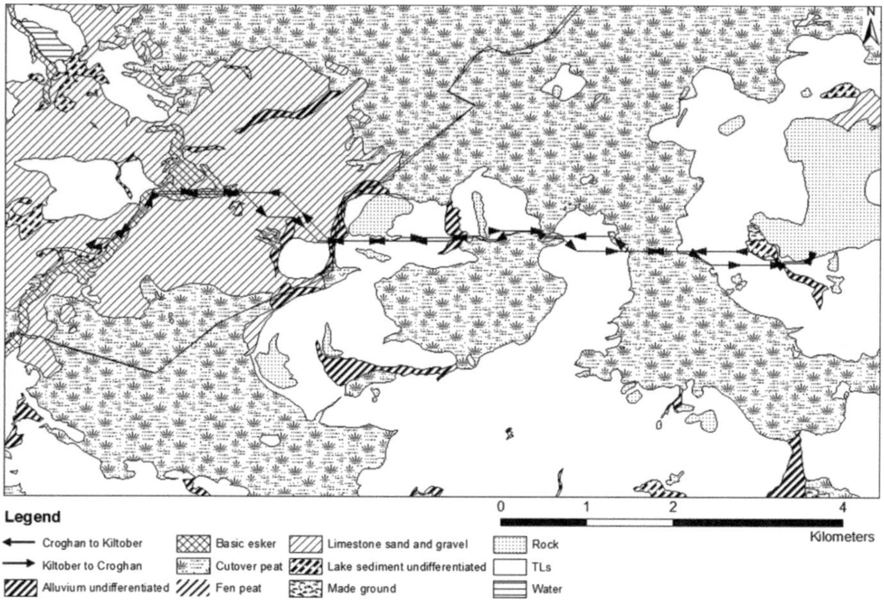

Fig. 6.6 Croghan to Kiltober Least Cost Path and soils

ringforts in the Medieval period, particularly in areas with limestone sand and gravel subsoil, west of the esker.

Clonearl Bog and Raheenmore Bog are located between Croghan and Kiltober, and these must be negotiated to move between the settlements. A series of low hills lie between Croghan and Kiltober, at Oldcroghan, Kilduff, Clonagh and Mullagharush Hill, which flank the narrowest points of the bogs.

6.5.1 Least Cost Path Results

The Least Cost Paths for this segment similarly traverse the bogs at the narrowest points available without deviating course more than a few degrees (Figs. 6.6 and 6.7). Clonearl Bog is crossed at the narrowest point, which is defined on the east side by a rise in Oldcroghan, and on the west by Kilduff Hill. The paths skirt the southern base of Clonagh Hill and Mullagharush Hill, and cross Raheenmore Bog where it narrows to only 10 m, which probably marks a patch of ground which was dry land until recent centuries. The hills mark the most convenient crossing points, but they are only climbed as much as is necessary to gain dry land. The esker is climbed at a suitably gentle point on its northeastern extent, after which this level, single-crested esker leads directly to Kiltober.

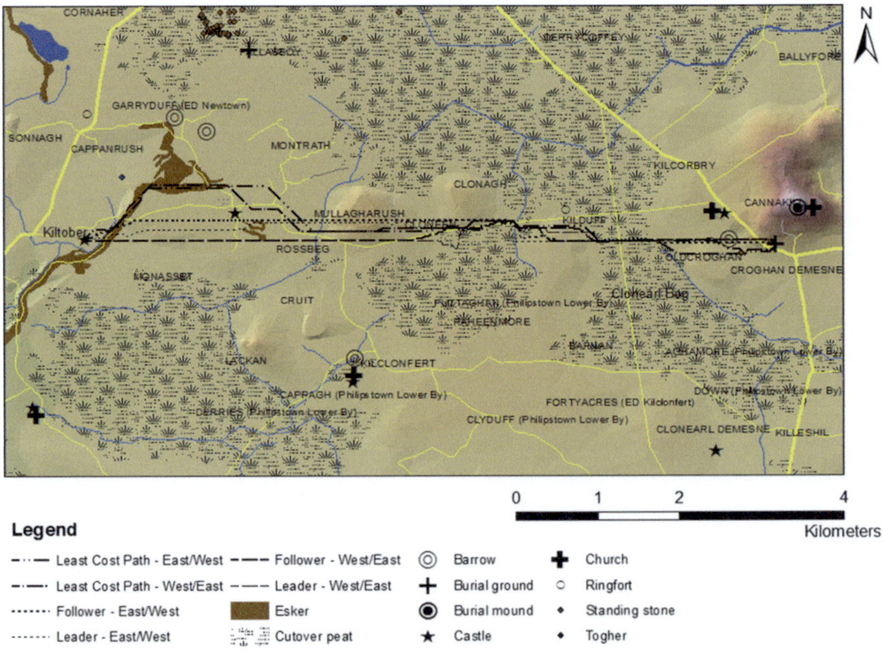

Fig. 6.7 Croghan to Kiltober

6.5.2 Agent-Based Modelling Results

The journey from Croghan to Kiltober requires the crossing of Clonearl Bog and Raheenmore bog. The *leader* finds the narrowest points in these bogs, which is the same as the crossing points suggested by Least Cost Paths (Fig. 6.7). The model deviates from the ArcGIS version on the western extent where the esker is accessed. The model does not include in-built preference to the esker subsoil type, but is controlled in this context by slope. The *leader*, when moving from east to west, does not move northwest to climb the esker, as the Least Cost Path model shows, but crosses the esker much closer to the target. The final *follower* crosses the esker 132 m from where an existing road transects the esker. This coincides with a slight drop in the contours east of the esker, which naturally direct movement to this point.

6.5.3 Archaeological Evidence

Clonearl Bog is most recognised for the Iron Age bog body found there in 2003. Oldcroghan Man, as he is known, was found 1.3 km southeast of the proposed crossing, where the bog is at its widest (Plunkett et al. 2009). As discussed above (Sect. 6.2.2), activities in the bog can be separated between those which treat the bog as an obstacle and those which treat it as an objective. The deposition of Oldcroghan Man was a ritual activity and it is no surprise that it should take place in a different location to simple negotiation of an obstacle. However, it is indicative of activity in the area, from which we can assume movement took place in the Iron Age.

The archaeological evidence in this segment is minimal. The paths pass a ring barrow in Oldcroghan and do not encounter any further known archaeology until in view of the esker. The most compelling evidence supporting the potential paths is their similarity to the existing road network. The predicted paths closely correlate with existing roads at the Raheenmore Bog crossing and along the southern slopes of Clonagh and Mullagharush Hill. The paths from both models are very similar in this segment. Except for the more obvious deviation on the western extent, they follow the same general corridor of movement with paths separated by a maximum distance of only 250 m. It is clear that major obstacles, such as the bogs, produce the most uniformity between the models and the existing road network.

The Rahugh esker is associated with a flanking road on the east side, and the presence of two castles along its course suggests the esker itself was used as a path in the Medieval period, with the earlier of the castles dating to the late 12th or early 13th century. A standing stone sits 220 m from the esker, which implies a significance to this landscape feature in prehistory also. The linear nature of the esker makes it an ideal feature by which to maintain orientation and to pilot by. Travelers can rely on such a feature to plan movement from a distance in this fashion, but it also acts as a suitable surface to walk over. The height which it offers provides a means of seeing some distance and planning a journey accordingly, while also being well-drained and linear.

6.6 Discussion

Those natural features which are conducive to movement must be exploited and established in the mental map of individuals before they can truly be called routeways. While ArcGIS can effectively show us the end product and a potential routeway, NetLogo can be used to explain how routeways are established through a series of discrete actions around those natural features, acted out by individual agents over time. The ability of agents to effectively learn from their predecessors, demonstrated through the use of the Ant Lines model, allows for quicker problem-solving on the part of the individual and more efficient routeways than initial attempts would produce.

In real world problem-solving, this would appear as a series of trails which impress upon any subsequent traveler. If an opportunity arises to smooth the course of a trail through cutting corners it is usually done. This can be seen in managed parklands or city green areas, where the paths laid down by the authorities are routinely ignored by walkers as they cut corners and create their own network of *desire lines*. The most effective path becomes the most established one both mentally, through repeated experiences, and physically, through repeated use. This can be further promoted through construction, providing a visually obvious option and usually requiring less energy expenditure. Thus, if a togher has been constructed across a bog, travelers are unlikely to deviate from that crossing point by walking over more unpredictable bog surfaces. In this way, a stable macrostructure emerges from the interaction of local agents and feedback from microstructures (Epstein and Axtell 1996).

The process of testing each model in both directions did not yield any major differences in path. The low gradient of the landscape made novel paths unnecessary, but where they do exist, they tend to be along slopes. The differences between these paths are minor—up to 260 m between Least Cost Paths and 460 m in some areas between Agent-Based Models—but the most intriguing areas are where the models agree at bog crossings and while winding between hills.

By combining Least Cost Paths with Agent-Based Modelling and conventional documentary research, it can be shown that Least Cost Paths have the capacity to emulate real human decisions as long as all the factors are considered by the program-user when producing the model. If the Least Cost Paths in these examples had been produced with only slope in mind, for example, the low slope values of the bogs would have been used to create wholly unrealistic paths which traversed the bogs in inefficient and dangerous ways. The consideration of the soil factor creates a model which is more realistic and closer to the real-world decisions which agents in the landscape are obliged to make, and while the values assigned were through subjective fieldwork, it is through the consideration of personal experience that modelling becomes its most effective, imitating real human behaviour rather that the ideal path. The Agent-Based Model is explicitly concerned with the decisions made by individuals and it produces very similar paths to those predicted by Least Cost Paths. Moreover, the documentary evidence for the Togher of Croghan, distribution of archaeological sites along both models and the close relationship between the model paths and the existing road network is persuasive evidence for the potential of both methods in predicting paths.

The models used in this research have demonstrated how attention to movement is essential in understanding the landscape of the past. The relationship between the suggested routeways and the archaeological evidence allow an enriched interpretation of those sites as part of an inter-connected landscape, as opposed to isolated areas of activity. Meanwhile, the difference in location between the Togher of Croghan and the trackways associated with Lough Nashade, for instance, demonstrate the different characteristics we should expect from routeways which are intended for different purposes. Where trackways deviate from the characteristics discussed in this paper, such as where the path bisects Croghan Demesne, we have an opportunity to ask questions relating to potential ritual, economic or social reasons for this deviation. In short, a movement-centric framework allows us to contextualise archaeological remains and understand landscape.

6.7 Conclusion

The use of these methodologies allows us to not only hypothesise the position of paths in the landscape, but to understand the processes which lead to their creation. The examples in this paper correlate very well with the archaeological and documentary evidence, as well as with current road networks. As Epstein (2006) wrote, ‘If you didn’t grow it, you didn’t explain its emergence.’ This consistency between method and data suggests that the appropriate factors were considered in each model to produce realistic paths, and the process of the emergence of those paths is explained. This demonstrates that the approach may be suitable in other landscapes, which do not have sufficient surviving evidence to suggest how movement may have taken place.

Acknowledgments This research has been funded by the Government of Ireland Postgraduate Scholarship and the Galway Doctoral Research Scholarship. The authors are grateful to Conor McDermott, University College Dublin, for providing survey data from the Irish Archaeological Wetland Unit, and to Alan Cunningham for comments on original drafts. Road data is © Open Street Map and Contributors CC-BY-SA.

References

Epstein JM (2006) Generative social science: Studies in agent-based computational modeling. Princeton University Press

Epstein JM, Axtell R (1996) Growing artificial societies: social Science from the bottom up. Brookings Institution Press

FitzPatrick E, O'Brien C (1998) The medieval churches of County Offaly. Wordwell, Ireland

Geissel H (2006) A Road on the Long Ridge: in search of the ancient highway on the Esker Riada. CRS Publications, Kildare

Golledge RG (2003) Human wayfinding and cognitive maps. In: Rockman M, Steele J (eds) Colonization of unfamiliar landscapes: the archaeology of adaptation. Routledge, London, pp 25–43

Irish Archaeological Wetland Unit (2002a) Peatland survey 2001. Archaeological survey report: Ballybeg Bog, Co. Offaly. Unpublished report, University College Dublin

Irish Archaeological Wetland Unit (2002b) Peatland survey 2001. Archaeological survey report: cavemount, Esker and Derryhinch Bogs, Cos. Meath, Westmeath and Offaly. Unpublished report, University College Dublin

Irish Archaeological Wetland Unit (2002c) Peatland Survey 2001. Archaeological Survey Report: Daingean Bog, Co. Offaly. Unpublished report, University College Dublin

Irish Archaeological Wetland Unit (2002d) Peatland survey 2001. Archaeological survey report of Clonad Bog, Co. Offaly. Unpublished report, University College Dublin

Irish Archaeological Wetland Unit (2002e) Peatland survey 2001: supplementary archaeological survey report. Unpublished report, University College Dublin

Irish Archaeological Wetland Unit (2003a) Peatland survey 2002. Archaeological survey report: Ballycon, Derrycricket & Mountlucas Bogs, Co. Offaly. Unpublished report, University College Dublin

Irish Archaeological Wetland Unit (2003b) Peatland survey 2002. Archaeological survey report: Derryarkin and Drumman Bogs, Cos Offaly & Westmeath. Unpublished report, University College Dublin

Irish Archaeological Wetland Unit (2003c) Peatland Survey 2003. Archaeological Survey Report: Ballykean Bog, Co. Offaly. Unpublished report, University College Dublin

Llobera M (2000) Understanding movement: a pilot model towards the sociology of movement. In: Lock G (ed) Beyond the map: archaeology and spatial technologies. NATO science series, vol 321. IOS Press, The Netherlands, pp 65–84

Lucas AT (1985) Toghers or causeways: some evidence from archæological, literary, historical and place-name sources. Proc Roy Irish Acad Sect C Archaeol Celt Stud Hist Linguist Lit 85C:37–60

Moloney A et al (1995) Blackwater survey & excavations. Artefact deterioration in peatlands loughmore, Co. Mayo. Irish archaeological Wetland unit transactions, vol 4. Crannóg Publication, Dublin

Moore C (2008) Old routes to new research: the Edercloon wetland excavations in County Longford. In: O' Sullivan J, Stanley M (eds) Roads, rediscovery and research: archaeology and the national roads authority monograph series 5. Wordwell, Dublin, pp 1–12

Murray C (2004) The barrysbrook bowstave. Past (46). http://www.ucl.ac.uk/prehistoric/past/past46.html#Bowstave. Accessed 29 Jun 2015

O'Keeffe PJ (2001) Ireland's principal roads: 123 AD-1608. National Roads Authority, Ireland

O'Lochlainn C (1940) Roadways in ancient Ireland. In: Ryan J (ed) Féil Sgríbinn Éoin Mhic Néill. Four Courts Press, Ireland, pp 465–474

Plunkett G et al (2009) A multi-proxy palaeoenvironmental investigation of the findspot of an Iron Age bog body from Oldcroghan, Co., Offaly, Ireland. J Archaeol Sci 36(2):265–277

Smyth AP (1982) Celtic leinster: towards an historical geography of early Irish civilization, A.D. 500–1600. Irish Academic Press, Ireland

Tubridy M, Meehan R. (2006) County Offaly esker survey 2006. Unpublished report, Offaly County Council

Whitaker J, O'Carroll E (2009) Peatland Excavations 1999–2000: Lemanaghan Group of Bogs, Co. Offaly. Archeological Development Services Limited, Dublin

Widlok T (1997) Orientation in the wild: the shared cognition of Hai||om Bushpeople. J Roy Anthropol Inst 3(2):317–332

Wilensky U (1997) Ant lines model. Evanston, IL: Center for Connected Learning and Computer-Based Modelling, Northwestern University. http://ccl.northwestern.edu/netlogo/models/AntLines. Accessed 29 Jun 2015

Wilensky U (1999) Evanston, IL: Center for Connected Learning and Computer-Based Modelling, Northwestern University. http://ccl.northwestern.edu/netlogo/. Accessed 29 Jun 2015

Chapter 7
Modelling Cultural Shift: Application to Processes of Language Displacement

Neus Isern and Joaquim Fort

7.1 Cultural Shift and Language Shift

Cultural shift, understood as the change in one or several cultural or social traits undergone by a human population, is present throughout human history. Indeed, we can find examples of cultural shift from the development and spread of tool construction techniques in prehistoric times, to the present time adoption of smartphones in our everyday lives.

The span of this definition of cultural shift comprises from technical changes (such as the examples above), to changes in religious beliefs or the adoption of a new language by a society. It comprises global changes with crucial impact on the evolution of human history—such as the Neolithic transition, which besides the technical changes directly related to the adoption of agriculture, entailed as well changes in housing organization, social structures and belief systems that may be the initial seed of the present sociocultural organization (Smith 1995). But cultural shift can happen at any level, always playing a role in shaping today's and the future cultural characteristics and diversity of our societies.

Here we will focus on a specific kind of cultural shift: language shift. And in particular, below we present a model devised to be applied to processes of language shift where the dominant language in an area is replaced by a foreigner language (usually from a neighbouring area), that for some reason is seen by the locals as being more advantageous to the population (Isern and Fort 2014).

As with the broader concept of cultural shift, there have been ongoing processes of language shift since the emergence of the first spoken languages. This is clearly evidenced by the amount of dead languages from which we have written testimony (Ancient Greek, Goth, Hittite, Tocharian, etc.), and the probably much larger

N. Isern (✉) · J. Fort
ICREA/Complex Systems Lab and Physics Department, University of Girona, C/Mª Aurèlia Capmany 61, 17071 Girona, Catalonia, Spain
e-mail: neus.isern@udg.edu

J.A. Barceló and F. Del Castillo (eds.), *Simulating Prehistoric and Ancient Worlds*, Computational Social Sciences, DOI 10.1007/978-3-319-31481-5_7

number of extinct non-literate languages from which we have little to none information; as well as by the historic testament of how dominant regional languages have changed during the last few millennia. However, processes of language change are not assimilated as easily or as often as, for example, the adoption of a new pottery style. As opposed to most technological innovations, language is frequently an important component of ethnic identity in a group (Barth 1998; Crystal 2000). Therefore, even though a new language can sometimes be related to the adoption of a new culture complex, this is not always the case and, in general, linguistic substitution (and probably other changes related to ethnicity) is not as readily integrated.

However, linguistic change does happen, and in the following section we will detail the most important processes that yield the replacement of the dominant language in an area, before discussing several models and presenting a language shift model that can be applied to predict the temporal and spatial evolution in processes of language displacement (Isern and Fort 2014).

7.2 Processes of Language Shift

The predominant language spoken in a certain region in the world will most probably have changed several times since the settlement of the first humans using verbal communication. But what are the underlying processes that lead to language change? In broad outline we can identify two basic processes: the local birth of a new language and the displacement of the local language by an extraneous language.

The birth of a new language is a slow process that usually includes several successive minor processes that spread throughout the population over the course of millennia (Renfrew 1987), until eventually the language has diverged enough from the original language as for them to be mutually unintelligible. These are often considered random processes, analogous to genetic drift, which may include the invention of new words—e.g., for innovations—, acquisition of loanwords from other languages in contact, phonetic changes—e.g., the use of occlusive sounds (*p*, *t*, *k*) in Latin, Greek and Sanskrit, as opposed to the fricative sounds (*f*, *th*, *h*) used in the Germanic languages, all of which share the same Indo-European origin (Lightfood 1999)—and ultimately the apparition of new grammatical forms (Renfrew 1987). A millennium would seem to be the minimum time span for this linguistic divergence to yield the birth of a new language (Cavalli-Sforza et al. 1994). Historical well known examples of language birth are the Romance languages from Latin, or the Indo-European languages from a probable common origin.

The other process of language shift, the displacement of the local language by a foreign one that becomes the new prominent language in the region, once started is usually a much faster process (McMahon 1994), and it can take place in as short a time as a single generation (Krauss 1992). However, as mentioned above, language is often strongly related with ethnicity and not so readily assimilated as other changes. So what are the mechanisms that may trigger a language displacement process? Renfrew (1987) described three main mechanisms that would yield to language displacement: *demography/subsistence*, *élite dominance* and *system collapse*.

The first mechanism, denoted *demography/subsistence,* would entail the arrival of new population into the territory, bearing some new exploitative technology that would allow them to subsist at significantly higher densities, thus outnumbering the local population and prompting their language to be the new dominant one. The spread of farming in Europe is known to have mostly taken place in such a way, and it may have well introduced their language into Europe alongside the farming technologies. Renfrew (1987) theorized that this language might be the Proto-Indo-European language from which most European and several Asian languages aroused. This theory has recently been supported by the results from a study that applied computational methods derived from evolutionary biology to infer an Indo-European language tree, as well as a chronology of the divergence times for every linguistic branch (Gray and Atkinson 2003). Their analysis estimated the initial Indo-European divergence to have taken place about 7800–9800 years BP, consistent with the initial spread of agriculture from Anatolia around 8000–9500 years BP (Gray and Atkinson 2003). Therefore, the spread of the Proto-Indo-European language into Europe would be an example of the *demography/subsistence* mechanism, and so would be some modern processes such as the spread of English (and its speakers) into Australia or North America—this last one including the use of the force of arms (Renfrew 1987).

The second mechanism, *élite dominance*, implies as well the arrival of foreign population but in this case, rather than introducing a new technology, the newcomers would be a reduced group with military superiority who would undertake the ruling of the region. This would lead to a period of bilingualism and the language of the élite may eventually become the dominant language. This is the case, for example, of the spread of the Latin language during the Roman empire; the Latin language was never imposed by the new Roman rulers, however, the language of the new rulers ended up being the dominant one at most of their empire (Rochette 2011). Nonetheless, *élite dominance* does not necessarily imply the displacement of the indigenous language, but it may be the new élite who end up being assimilated and their language forgotten (Renfrew 1987). This would be the case, for example, of the Norman invasion of Britain during the 11th century, where after a period of French dominance, English became again the dominant language at all social levels (especially reinforced by the posterior animosity between England and France), although with a clear French influence (Crystal 2003; Clairborne 1990).

Finally, the third main mechanism leading to language displacement described by Renfrew (1987) was as a consequence of *system collapse*. In this case the language displacement would be the consequence of the collapse of a rapidly growing, highly specialized society whose central authority would not be able to maintain control in case of environmental adversities. The collapse could entail the exodus of local people as well as the loss of the control over the frontiers, thus losing terrain (politically and linguistically) to neighbouring better structured societies. And precisely for this reason, Cavalli-Sforza et al. (1994) englobed this mechanism and the *élite dominance* under a single denomination: *conquest by a minority*. The collapse of a previous system may have been the mechanism that yielded the Nahuatl language to become dominant with the Aztecs in Mexico (Renfrew 1987).

Besides these mechanisms, Cavalli-Sforza et al. (1994) additionally noted that language displacement processes may also be observed without the need of population movements introducing a new language. In this case, the new language would be acquired as a result of continuous contact between neighbouring languages, with one of them becoming the new main language near the border—we may call it *neighbouring acquisition*. As a consequence of this process the linguistic border would retreat, although without the need of political or military intervention, nor of population replacement. Over time, the new languages may completely displace the indigenous one and become the prevalent language in the region. Cavalli-Sforza et al. (1994) observed this mechanism of language acquisition from a neighbour population with African pygmy people, and similar processes are observed nowadays in Europe with the shrinkage of the area of prevalence of several minority languages (Isern and Fort 2014).

Below we present a language competition model devised to predict the evolution of the number of speakers when an external language is displacing the native one. In the model, we are interested especially in language displacement processes which do not imply large movements of people. Therefore, this would mostly correspond to cases of language displacement due to the mechanisms of *élite dominance* or *neighbouring acquisition*, or a combination of both. In the next section we consider non-spatial models of such processes. In Sect. 7.4 we generalize them into spatial models (i.e., models of moving linguistic borders) to describe the case of neighbouring acquisition of a language. They can be also useful to describe élite dominance, but in this case we note that (i) there is usually a military conquest first, after which the language substitution process takes place; (ii) the new language spreads possibly from one or several geographic centres of political power, rather than from an outside adjacent area.

7.3 Modelling Language Shift

The study of language evolution and language shift has become a field of interest for many disciplines in the recent times, including the application of computational and mathematical methods to model these processes.

A fruitful area for the application of computational methods to linguistics has been the study of the emergence of internal linguistic changes leading to language birth—lexical emergence and diffusion, phonetic change, appearance of grammar structures—through the application of approaches such as game theory or probabilistic inference (Wang et al. 2004; Baronchelli et al. 2008; Nowak et al. 2002; Bouchard-Côté et al. 2013). In general, many of these applications can be of interest both for the study of current language evolution as well as to the historical events of linguistic divergence and language birth, although several studies are particularly focused on historical linguistics. The work by Bouchard-Côté et al. (2013) is precisely devoted to the reconstruction of protolanguages by means of probabilistic inference of sound change over time, producing results very close to those obtained through manual reconstruction by linguists. Another important line of computational research, related to historical linguistics and process of language birth, has been the inference of language trees through the application of phylogenetic methods. Such methods have been applied to infer linguistic relationships and to estimate chronologies of language divergences for the Celtic languages (Forster and Toth 2003), the Indo-European languages (Gray and Atkinson 2003), and even to the Eurasiatic macrofamily (Pagel et al. 2013).

Language displacement has also been an important topic of research both for computational and mathematical modelling, although the substantial difference between the mechanisms leading to the shift in language described above affects significantly the applied models. In the *demography/subsistence* mechanism, the means to the language shift is mostly related to population displacement. Therefore, an appropriate modelling approach here would be the application of wave-of-advance models (Ammerman and Cavalli-Sforza 1973). Indeed, such models have been widely applied to the spread of the Neolithic in Europe (Ammerman and Cavalli-Sforza 1973; Fort and Méndez 1999; Fort 2012)—which seems to have been related to the expansion of the Proto-Indo-European language (Renfrew 1987; Gray and Atkinson 2003). However, the Neolithic expansion in Europe was not a purely demic process in the whole continent, but in some regions agriculture was also transmitted by an acculturation process (Fort 2012). In those regions language may have or may have not been transmitted alongside agriculture —Refrew (1987) suggests that the assumed pre-Indo-European languages such as Basque or the now extinct Etruscan, may have survived in those processes of cultural transmission. But if in some areas language was indeed transmitted as well, it must have been part of the whole "Neolithic package," rather than a simple linguistic shift, and thus the process may be well described by demic-cultural models devised to describe the Neolithic transition as a whole (Fort 2012). The colonization of North America—with the subsequent spread of the English language—has also been successfully described with a wave-of-advance model modified to include the colonizing intent (Fort and Pujol 2007).

Language displacement may also take place in situations where there is little or no population movement. These would be the cases for the mechanisms of *élite dominance* and *neighbouring acquisition*. Although the reasons behind the language shift differ, after the new élite is established in the first mechanisms, both cases can be assumed mostly equivalent for modelling purposes. Both mechanisms lead to a competition for dominance between two languages, one of which having a higher status—either because it is the language of the élite, or because the neighbouring language is seen as more advantageous for some reason—within a population that is mostly unchanged. Of course, a linguistic imposition in the case of *élite dominance* may accelerate the displacement process, or on the contrary, it may cause a resistance effect giving a higher status to the indigenous language; such effects can be easily included into a language competition model by means of adapting the parameter values.

Therefore, language competition models are a good approach to model language displacement when there are no important changes in the population density due to immigration, or to an increase in the population density that is sustainable. In the recent years, several authors have developed mathematical and computational language competition models (for a review, see Kandler 2009). In 2003, Abrams and Strogatz (2003) developed a simple two-population model to describe the competition for speakers between two languages, A and B, coexisting in the same region, and which has been the basis for several other studies on linguistic shift (Patriarca and Heinsalu 2009; Fort and Pérez-Losada 2012). This model describes the evolution in time of the fraction of speakers of each language (p_A and p_B), with the fraction of speakers defined as the ratio between the number of speaker of a given language over the total population (e.g., $p_A = N_A/N = N_A/(N_A + N_B)$, and therefore $p_A + p_B = 1$). The evolution over time, represented by the time derivative, is expressed mathematically according to the following equations (Abrams and Strogatz 2003),

$$\begin{cases} \dfrac{dp_A}{dt} = \gamma\left(s p_A^{\alpha} p_B - (1-s)\, p_A p_B^{\alpha}\right), \\ \dfrac{dp_B}{dt} = -\gamma\left(s p_A^{\alpha} p_B - (1-s)\, p_A p_B^{\alpha}\right). \end{cases} \tag{7.1}$$

In broad lines, this equation shows that the evolution of the fraction of speakers of each language follows the same dynamics as the other one, though with an opposed sign; this means that the speakers lost by one language become speakers of the other one. In addition, the minus sign before $(1-s)$ indicates that a language may lose or gain speakers depending on the fraction of the population speaking each language, as well as the values of the of the parameters. In the model by Abrams and Strogratz (2003), γ is a parameter that scales time, so it accelerates or decelerates the process; s, with a value between 0 and 1, reflects the status of language A relative to B; and α determines the relative importance of the population fractions in attracting speakers to language A.

Although this model has been applied rather successfully to describe language evolution (Abrams and Strogatz 2003), it yields some problems when trying to extrapolate the model beyond the data over which they applied the model. From a mathematical point of view, these problems arise because of the existence of stable and unstable equilibrium points, depending on the parameter values (see a detailed mathematical discussion in Isern and Fort 2014). To put it in more general terms, we shall describe one of the possible problematic outcomes. Depending on the parameter values chosen, the language with a higher status displaces the other one until it is nearly extinct in the region, and then the process stops. This means that the model predicts that, without adding any extra particularity (such as part of the population living in a very secluded area), the language will remain alive as the main language for a reduced part of the population forever.

Such behaviour is historically unrealistic, and for this reason we opt for an approach conceptually simpler and which does not present the same extrapolating problems (Isern and Fort 2014). This alternative model also describes the dynamics of the transfer of speakers between two languages *A* and *B* in competition, one of which is seen by the population as being socially or economically more advantageous. This model is described as follows (Isern and Fort 2014)

$$\begin{cases} \dfrac{dp_A}{dt} = \gamma p_A^\alpha p_B^\beta, \\ \dfrac{dp_B}{dt} = -\gamma p_A^\alpha p_B^\beta. \end{cases} \tag{7.2}$$

As with the model by Abrams and Strogatz (2003), the temporal evolution of the population fraction (described mathematically as a derivative), depends on the population fraction speaking each language, p_A and p_B, and the values of three parameters. γ is a parameter that scales time, so it accelerates or decelerates the process. The parameters $\alpha, \beta \geq 1$ are related to the attraction or perceived value of each language. Since $p_A, p_B \leq 1$, α and β may be regarded as a measure of the difficulty of language *A* to attract speakers (α), and the resistance of language *B* to lose speakers (β).

Note that, again, the speakers lost by language *B* become speakers of language *A* (both equations have the same form but with a minus sign in the second equation). However, with this model, only one of the languages can gain speakers and the other loses them; in particular, *A* is the language seen as more advantageous and thus gaining speakers and displacing language *B*. In general, this is a reasonable simplification for processes where a foreign language is displacing the indigenous language in a given region. It is true that it cannot directly describe all historical situations, such as the case of the Norman invasion of Britain, where the French initially gained speakers, but the English language eventually recuperated its prevalence (Clairborne 1990); though neither can it be directly described by the model in Eq. 7.1. A reasonable alternative would be to divide the whole period into two subperiods, each with a different language defined as the high status one; after all, the status of the language is defined by the subjective perception of it by the population, rather than its political position.

Therefore, the new model in Eq. 7.2 is conceptually a reasonable approach to model processes of language displacement when a language is perceived by the population as being more advantageous socially or economically. Such cases could be related to processes of language shift due to *élite dominance* or *neighbouring acquisition* or combinations of both (for example, when the new élite come from an adjacent region, which may describe the situation of minority languages in current times when they are co-official in their territory, or even not officially recognized).

The process of language displacement after a situation of *system collapse* mentioned in the previous section may take place in many different ways, with or without population movement, with a change in the dominant élite, etc. and for this reason we may not propose specific models of application in such event.

7.4 Moving Linguistic Borders

From a geographical point of view, linguistic displacement can also take place in different ways. For example, when an incoming new élite takes the ruling power of the region, a possible pattern may be the apparition of several language shift sources —e.g., near government, education or religious emplacements. On the other hand, when the language shift mechanism implies population displacement (due to immigration and a subsequent rapid growth), there will be a moving linguistic border between the two languages that will understandably progress with the incoming population; usually such situation can be seen as an advancing front driven by the population growth and thus can be easily described through wave-of-advance models. However we can also have a moving linguistic frontier without the need of an immigrant population front. This is the case when the new language is introduced from a neighbouring region.

We can mathematically model the progress of a linguistic frontier over time and space, when the displacement mechanism is due to language acquisition rather than population substitution, with a reaction-diffusion model similar the wave-of-advance models; that is, a model where the population dynamics is simplified to short-range migration (e.g., due to marriage), and the increase or decrease in the population number is due to factors such as population growth or conversion into another population group. However, as opposed to the classic wave-of-advance model (Ammerman and Cavalli-Sforza 1973), now the main driver will be the language shift (conversion into another linguistic group) rather than the population growth.

A general reaction-diffusion model to describe the dynamics of two linguistic groups, where a language A is gaining speaker in detriment of language B, may be

$$\begin{cases} \dfrac{\partial n_A}{\partial t} = D\dfrac{\partial^2 n_A}{\partial r^2} + a n_A\left(1 - \dfrac{n_A + n_B}{K}\right) + C(n_A, n_B), \\ \dfrac{\partial n_B}{\partial t} = D\dfrac{\partial^2 n_B}{\partial r^2} + a n_B\left(1 - \dfrac{n_A + n_B}{K}\right) - C(n_A, n_B). \end{cases} \tag{7.3}$$

Note that the equations now do not deal with fractions of speakers (p_A and p_B) but with population densities (n_A and n_B). These equations estimate the evolution over time of the density of speakers of each language at every position and time instant in terms of three processes: diffusion, population growth and conversion. The first term on the right-hand side of the equations is the diffusion term, which is related to short-range migrations without colonizing intent. This diffusion is characterized by a diffusion coefficient D. The second term is related to the population growth. Population growth is often described by a logistic function where populations with low densities grow exponentially, with a growth rate a, but the process is self-limiting when the population density nears a saturating density defined as the carrying capacity K. In the equation above, Eq. 7.3, the growth is limited by the densities of both populations, since they all share the same land and resources (Isern and Fort 2010). In addition, since we assume that they all have, in principle, similar ways of live, the parameters D, a and K are the same for both linguistic groups. Finally, the last term corresponds to the conversion of speakers from language B to language A, with the shift rate depending on the densities of speakers of each language at every location. As in the previous Eqs. 7.1 and 7.2, the opposed sign in this last term of Eq. 7.3 means that the speakers lost by language B become speakers of language A.

However, since the introduction of the new language does not yield, in this case, the assimilation of new technologies leading to a rapid population growth, we may assume that the total population number will vary slowly over time, especially in comparison with the language shift rate. Therefore, as a first approximation, the growth term in Eq. 7.3 (second term on the right-hand side) can be dropped. Such approximation simplifies the described dynamics, since now we only have to deal with population diffusion and language shift, but it also allows us to rewrite Eq. 7.3 in terms of the population fraction, thus enabling us to replace the generic conversion term by the language displacement model introduced in the previous section, Eq. 7.2. The model is then expressed as follows (Isern and Fort 2014),

$$\begin{cases} \dfrac{\partial p_A}{\partial t} = D\dfrac{\partial^2 p_A}{\partial r^2} + \gamma p_A^{\alpha} p_B^{\beta}, \\ \dfrac{\partial p_B}{\partial t} = D\dfrac{\partial^2 p_B}{\partial r^2} - \gamma p_A^{\alpha} p_B^{\beta}. \end{cases} \tag{7.4}$$

This simplified system describes, for every point in the region, the evolution over time of the fraction of speakers of each language within a population that is not experimenting substantial changes in the total population number. This evolution depends on short-range migrations of the population and the language shift process, according to which the indigenous population acquires a new language that they see as more advantageous socially or economically.

Since we are assuming that the new language is introduced from an adjacent region, the language shift will happen initially near the border, and then the new language will be progressively introduced further into the territory. From the model above, described by Eq. 7.4, we can measure the speed of the linguistic frontier by resolving the equation numerically (that is, with a computational simulation). It is also possible to derive mathematical expressions from which we can obtain a range within which lies the real speed, without having to resort to computational simulations. This is possible by assuming that the moving frontier is mostly planar (which is realistic if the language shift "source" is a political border) and through variational analysis of Eq. 7.4 (Benguria and Depassier 1994, 1998), which leads to the following expression for the upper bound (Isern and Fort 2014)

$$c_U = 2\sqrt{\gamma D}\sqrt{\sup_{p_A \in (0,\,1)}\left[\alpha p_A^{\alpha-1}(1-p_A)^{\beta} - \beta p_A^{\alpha}(1-p_A)^{\beta-1}\right]}, \tag{7.5}$$

and the following one for the lower bound (Isern and Fort 2014)

$$c_L = \sqrt{\gamma D}\max_{\delta \in (0,\,1)} 2\delta\sqrt{1-\delta}\frac{\Gamma\left(1+\frac{\beta}{2}\right)\Gamma\left(\frac{\alpha}{2}+\delta-\frac{1}{2}\right)}{\Gamma\left(\frac{1}{2}+\frac{\alpha}{2}+\frac{\beta}{2}+\delta\right)}, \tag{7.6}$$

where the gamma function is defined by the following integral $\Gamma(x) = \int_0^{\infty} t^{x-1}e^{-t}dt$, for $x > 0$ (Murray and Liu 1999).

The values of the bounds are obtained from the previous Eqs. 7.5 and 7.6 by searching for the maximum result of the right-hand side expression for values of δ in the range $(0,\,1)$ for the lower bound, and for values of p_A in the range $(0,\,1)$ for the upper bound.

7.5 Application to a Modern Example of Language Shift

As evidenced in Sect. 7.2, there have been ongoing processes of language shift throughout history up to the present day. In fact, in recent times we have been experiencing a global process of linguistic convergence towards a few stronger languages—such as English, Spanish or Chinese—leading to the endangerment or extinction of many languages (Krauss 1992; Crystal 2000). Indeed, linguists estimate the about 96 % of the population speaks only about 4 % of the languages in the world (Crystal 2000), and that about 90 % of the current linguistic diversity may become extinct by the end of the century (Krauss 1992).

It is actually this concern over the future of minority languages that have prompted the development of several existing language competition models (e.g., Abrams and Strogatz 2003; Kandler et al. 2010; Isern and Fort 2014); studies that in turn provide a source of data to exemplify here the model presented above. We will focus on the evolution of the Welsh language during the twentieth century. Up to the 1970, when linguistic policies started to be applied, the number of Welsh speakers had been decreasing year after year (Kandler et al. 2010), and the linguistic border had been progressively retreating—at an approximate speed of 0.3–0.6 km/y, according to the estimates obtained from linguistic maps by Fort and Pérez-Losada (2012).

It corresponds therefore to a case of language acquisition from a neighbouring region with a moving linguistic border, and thus a good subject to test the models described above. Of course, since Wales is part of the United Kingdom, and with

English being the official language, there is a factor related to the *élite dominance* described above. However, Wales have been part of the UK for a long time and the most relevant language shift process has taken place in the recent time (Aitchison and Carter 2000); indeed, in the early 1900s, half of the population still spoke Welsh, while by 1980 less than 20 % of the population could speak the language (Abrams and Strogatz 2003).

Applying the language shift model described by Eq. 7.2 to the evolution of the Welsh and English languages during the twentieth century in the region of Monmouthshire yields a very good fit between model and data.[1] This is evidenced by the results in Fig. 7.1, where the line in the figure represents the best approximation to the historical demographic data (squares) obtained for Eq. (7.2). The parameter values yielding this best fit are $\alpha = 2.23$, $\beta = 1.76$ and $\gamma = 0.237$.

We now can apply the parameters found above into our spatial model, i.e. the model represented by Eq. 7.4, where we take into account the geographical evolution in addition to the temporal change, as well as into Eqs. 7.5 and 7.6, which provide an estimated range of speeds for the progress of the linguistic border. To do so we will consider two realistic values of the diffusion coefficient, $D = 5.08$ km^2/y and $D = 6.72$ km^2/y. Both are estimated from the expression $D = \langle \Delta^2 \rangle / 4T$ (Fort and Méndez 1999), where $\langle \Delta^2 \rangle$ is an estimation of the mobility of a population over a generation, and T the time span of a generation. In both cases we use a value of the generation time corresponding to modern human populations, $T = 25$y (Fort and Pérez-Losada 2012). Then, the first value for the diffusion coefficient is estimated from mobility data on modern populations in the Parma Valley, Italy, during the twentieth century and thus coetaneous with the data for the Welsh language; in this case $\langle \Delta^2 \rangle = 508\,\text{km}^2$ (Isern et al. 2008; Cavalli-Sforza and Bodmer 1999). The second value is estimated from mobility data in Catalonia, Spain, during the eighteenth and nineteenth centuries, with $\langle \Delta^2 \rangle = 672\,\text{km}^2$ (Heras de Puig 2000).

To compute the theoretical values for the front speed we have obtained the parameters from data corresponding only to the region of Monmouthshire rather than the data on all of Wales (also available in Abrams and Strogatz 2003). The reason behind this decision is that Monmouthshire is a rather rural area, representative for most of the extension of Wales, and thus of the region where the front speed was estimated by Fort and Pérez-Losada (2012). The data from all of Wales, by contrast, contains data from the large agglomerations near Cardiff (about 50 % of the population lives in 10 % of the area of Wales), where the language shift dynamics may well differ from that on the rest of Wales.

The predicted speeds of the linguistic frontier are shown in Table 7.1, for each of the two values of the diffusion coefficient. The second column corresponds to the results of the numerical simulation, and thus the exact speed of the linguistic front for a system whose dynamics may be described by Eq. 7.4; i.e. a population without substantial population growth and where the prevalent language from an

[1]As evidenced by Isern and Fort (2014), this model can also be satisfactorily applied to describe the evolution of the fraction of speakers for other current instances of language competition.

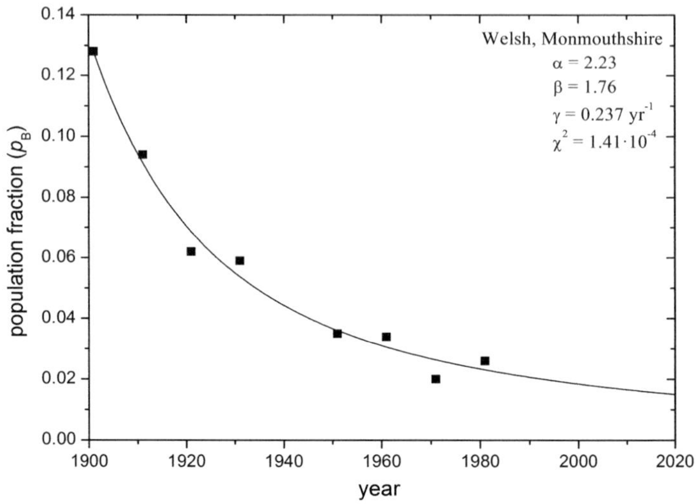

Fig. 7.1 Decline of the fraction of Welsh speakers over time (*squares*) and best fit (*line*) obtained with Eq. 7.2. (Adapted from Isern and Fort 2014)

Table 7.1 Numerical (c) and analytic (c_L, c_U) predictions of the English linguistic front replacing the Welsh language

D km²/y	c km/y	c_L km/y	c_U km/y
5.08	0.557	0.356	0.934
6.72	`0.641	0.409	1.750

adjacent regions is displacing the indigenous language. Comparing these theoretical values with the speed range estimated from data, 0.3–0.6 km/yr (Fort and Pérez-Losada 2012), we see that we obtain good agreement between model and observations. Therefore, the model can indeed predict with a fairly good accuracy the actual speed of the linguistic frontier.

In addition, the last two columns in Table 7.1 contain the values of the upper and lower analytic bounds calculated using Eqs. 7.5 and 7.6, respectively. We see that, as expected, the exact solution lies within those bounds. But, what is more important, we see that the ranges obtained are also fairly consistent with the observed data values, and thus, these equations can be used as a first approximation of the expected front of linguistic replacement without the need to apply numerical integration.

7.6 Conclusions

Processes of cultural shift, and in particular of language shift, are present throughout history and have had a great importance into shaping the current day society and diversity. Language is an inherent part of what people use to define their identity, and therefore, the study of the processes that yield a population to abandoning their own language in favour of an alien language is important to understand human evolution. Linguistic studies have described several mechanisms leading to language shift, such as language displacement due to a demographic substitution, due to being militarily conquered by speakers of another language, or as a result of language acquisition from a neighbouring region.

We are particularly interested in the last process, since it produces an advancing linguistic frontier whose speed can be predicted by a mathematical model. We have presented a model that has been developed to describe the dynamics of language shift in a region where the speakers of a native language are under the influence of a neighbour language regarded as being socially and economically more advantageous (Isern and Fort 2014). We have also applied our language shift model as an interaction term in a reaction-diffusion model in order to estimate the speed at which the more advantageous languages spreads geographically, increasing its range of prevalence and, in consequence, diminishing the area of influence of the minority language. Testing this model over modern data corresponding to the retreat of the Welsh-English border has yielded very accurate results, thus indicating that the model provides a good description of the process. In addition, on a wider context, the model presented here could be applied as well to the study of other cases of cultural shift for traits also related to national or ethnic identity, such as religious affiliations.

Acknowledgments This work was funded in part by FBBVA grant Neodigit-PIN2015, ICREA (JF) and the MINECO grants SimulPast-CSD2010-00034 and FIS-2012-31307 (all authors).

References

Abrams A, Strogatz SH (2003) Modelling the dynamics of language death. Nature 424:900

Aitchison J, Carter H (2000) Language, economy and society: the changing fortunes of the Welsh language in the twentieth century. University of Wales Press, Cardiff

Ammerman AJ, Cavalli-Sforza LL (1973) A population model for the diffusion of early farming in Europe. In: Renfrew C (ed) The explanation of culture change. Duckworth, London, pp 343–357

Baronchelli A, Loreto V, Steels L (2008) In-depth analysis of the naming game dynamics: the homogeneous mixing case. Int J Mod Phys C 19:785–801

Barth F (1998) Ethnic groups and boundaries: the social organization of culture difference. Waveland Press, Prospect Heights

Benguria RD, Depassier MC (1994) Validity of the linear speed selection mechanism for fronts of the nonlinear diffusion equation. Phys Rev Lett 73:2272–2274

Benguria RD, Depassier MC (1998) Speed of fronts of generalized reaction-diffusion equations. Phys Rev E 57:6493–6496
Bouchard-Côté A, Hall D, Griffiths TL, Klein D (2013) Automated reconstruction of ancient languages using probabilistic models of sound change. Proc Natl Acad Sci 110:4224–4229
Cavalli-Sforza LL, Bodmer WF (1999) The genetics of human populations. Dover, New York
Cavalli-Sforza LL, Menozzi P, Piazza A (1994) The history and geography of human genes. Princeton University Press, Princeton
Clairborne R (1990) The life and times of the English language: the history of our marvellous native tongue. Bloomsbury, London
Crystal D (2000) Language death. Cambridge University Press, Cambridge
Crystal D (2003) The Cambridge encyclopedia of the English language. Cambridge University Press, Cambridge
de Puig H (2000) Biografía, ó, explicació del arbre geneològich de la descendencia de casa Heras de Adri, 1350–1850. CCG Edicions, Girona
Forster P, Toth A (2003) Toward a phylogenetic chronology of ancient Gaulish, Celtic, and Indo-European. Proc Natl Acad Sci 100:9079–9084
Fort J (2012) Synthesis between demic and cultural diffusion in the Neolithic transition in Europe. Proc Natl Adak Sci 109:18669–18673
Fort J, Méndez V (1999) Time-delayed theory of the Neolithic transition in Europe. Phys Rev Lett 82:867–870
Fort J, Pérez-Losada J (2012) Front speed of language replacement. Hum Biol 84:755–772
Fort J, Pujol T, (2007) Time-delayed fronts from biased random walks. New J Phys 9, paper 234
Gray RD, Atkinson QD (2003) Language-tree divergence times support the Anatolian theory of Indo-European origin. Nature 426:435–439
Isern N, Fort J (2010) Anisotropic dispersion, space competition and the slowdown of the Neolithic 12, paper 123002
Isern N, Fort J (2014) Language extinction and linguistic fronts. J Roy Soc Interface 11, paper 20140028
Isern N, Fort J, Pérez-Losada J (2008) Realistic dispersion kernels applied to cohabitation reaction-dispersion equations. J Stat Mech Theor Exp, paper P10012
Kandler A (2009) Demography and language competition. Hum Biol 81:181–210
Kandler A, Unger R, Steele J (2010) Language shift, bilingualism and the future of Britain's Celtic languages. Phil Trans Roy Soc B 365:3855–3864
Krauss M (1992) The world's languages in crisis. Language 68:4–10
Lightfoot D (1999) The development of language: acquisition, change and evolution. Blackwell, Malden
McMahon AMS (1994) Understanding language change. Cambridge University Press, Cambridge
Murray RS, Liu J (1999) Mathematical handbook of formulas and tables, 2nd edn. McGraw-Hill, New York
Nowak MA, Komarova NL, Niyogi P (2002) Computational end evolutionary aspects of language. Nature 417:611–617
Pagel M, Atkinson QD, Calude AS, Meade A (2013) Ultraconserved words point to deep language ancestry across Eurasia. Proc Natl Adac Sci 110:8471–8476
Patriarca M, Heinsalu E (2009) Influence of geography on language competition. Phys A 388:174–186
Renfrew C (1987) Archaeology and Language: the puzzle of Indo-European origins. Johnatan Cape, London
Rochetter B (2011) Language policies in the Roman Republic and Empire. In: Clackson J (ed) Blackwell companion of the history of the Latin Language. Blackwell, New York, pp 549–563
Smith BD (1995) The emergence of agriculture. Scientific American Library, New York
Wang WS-Y, Ke J, Minett JW (2004) Computational studies of language evolution. In: Huang CR, Lenders W (eds) Computational linguistics and beyond: perspectives at the beginning of the 21st century. Institute of Linguistics, Academia Sinica, Taipei

Chapter 8
Pathways for Scale and Discipline Reconciliation: Current Socio-Ecological Modelling Methodologies to Explore and Reconstitute Human Prehistoric Dynamics

Mehdi Saqalli and Tilman Baum

8.1 Introduction

Reconstituting human past dynamics over a landscape or a territory is more than challenging:

- Modelling is a scientific methodology but also a de facto constructed agreement procedure among a group of scholars from different disciplines about the functioning of a society, an environment and their interactions. It is thereby subject to points of view, assumptions and considerations which, in such a comparatively low data modelling context, are difficult to counter-argue;
- It is nearly impossible to evaluate the importance of uncertainty and random events in the course of real history. One should acknowledge that any formalization of a historical reconstitution is actually the formalization of the *average and most probable* history within specific conditions, hypotheses and scenarios. Extraordinary environmental events, intra-society dynamics and breakouts are thereby impossible to reposition on their right time position. Nonetheless, a reconstruction of the complex system formed by man and his environment can help us to knit a web out of the loose ends of archaeological research.

This article describes several major modelling approaches with regard to past coupled human-environmental dynamics, with their specific strength, drawbacks

M. Saqalli (✉)
CNRS, University of Toulouse 2 Jean Jaurès, GEODE, 5 Allées a. Machado, 31058 Toulouse, France
e-mail: mehdi.saqalli@univ-tlse2.fr

T. Baum
University of Basel, IPNA, Vogelsangstrasse, 20, 72144 Dusslingen, Germany
e-mail: Tilman.baum@unibas.ch

J.A. Barceló and F. Del Castillo (eds.), *Simulating Prehistoric and Ancient Worlds*, Computational Social Sciences, DOI 10.1007/978-3-319-31481-5_8

and difficulties, thereby illustrating the scale gap we would like to illustrate. Thus we elaborate the methodological and epistemological orientation we plea for.

8.2 Modelling Past Rural Environment-Society Systems

8.2.1 Distinguishing Modelling Objectives, Subjects and Objects

Following Lieurain (1998); Garneau and Delisle (2002) or Bousquet and le Page (2004), three goals are assigned to modelling strategies: describe, understand and predict. As it is the fate of archaeology to draw conclusions on a sometimes very narrow database, it is necessary to continuously develop and adapt models to conceptualize most probable historical scenario proposals, i.e. eliminate least-probable ones. A second benefit of the modelling procedure is the identification of the driving forces and key elements of the simulated system. This is possible, because a wide range of historical scenarios may be reconstructed by varying certain input parameters. It can then for instance eliminate too simplistic or less plausible ones, such as the one "single cause Armageddon" cliché (climate, volcano, flood). As a third step it may be considered to validate theories and make predictions on the results of interacting system elements. Finally, following Edmonds and Moss (2005), this global « descriptive » methodology (considering that, without any previous analysis, one cannot determine which variable can be considered as negligible) can allow to display a simplified version of a reconstructed historically plausible scenario, i.e. to produce a series of theoretical models, each one corresponding to a "digested" research question, dedicated to the exploration of the possible variations of one or maximum two factors.

This trend of modelling the past is highly promising because it will help to solve large and theoretical questions, once parameterization and calibration have been established robustly to avoid the questioning over assumed postulates. One of the most famous simulations of the past, "Understanding Artificial Anasazi" can be categorized into such a scheme at a local "terroir"[1] level: from a study (Kohler and Carr 1996), several theorized modelling experiments were assessed (Dean et al. 1999; Axtell et al. 2002; Janssen et al. 2003; Janssen and Scheffer 2004; Kohler et al. 2005; Kohler 2008; Janssen 2009; Kohler et al. 2012; Crabtree and Kohler 2012).

Moreover, and following Landais and Deffontaines (1987), a model is a "theoretical and finalized representation of a reality formulated on the basis of situated

[1]The French word "terroir" is defined both geographically (the set of space managed and exploited by a village community: (Raison and Coniat 1997)) and socially (a socially defined territory containing a set of resources and associated rights to these resources: (Bassett et al. 2007)). It is therefore a geographically defined territory, but whose definition is social: it is the geographical framework of life of a rural society. It is important to specify for the land tenure issue that the "terroir' is defined on the basis of usufruct and not of property.

observations, of a predefined framework that will then be applied to study cases and permits to give representations quickly". A model serves to establish structural relationships and functions existing between the factors that one would like to analyse, and their respective importance (Parker et al. 2003). All models are designed for reaching a goal, an objective that can be problem solving, decision-support or simply experimentation (Roy 1992; Le Bars 2003). This definition adopts an operational standpoint, thereby insisting on the subjectivity and the need for an objective for every model. In our case, this should establish what research question is investigated with a model, i.e. what research subject and what research object is considered:

- If the *subject* is the history of the impact of the human expansion over an area, which can be either the Earth itself, a portion of it or a "terroir", the studied *object* is the area, including the related natural resources, from which humans are seen solely as a transforming force, whatever the refining of the behaviour of this force can be (inclusion of innovations, etc.). The main use of such models is in environmental disciplines.
- If the *subject* is the history of the population itself and the impact of the environment over its evolution (again regardless of its size), environment and related natural resources should be considered as an influencing force, even if humans themselves transform the capacity of this force, and the research *object* is the population itself. The main use of these models is in (pre-) historic disciplines.

8.2.2 Agent-Based Modelling Distributed Simulation: An Adequate Tool for Modelling Villagers and Fields

Humans form complex groups and societies that are bound to their environment in more or less intense interactions, the imprint of which are found in landscapes. One may note that this dependency on the environmental context and natural resources allows scientists to better feature and frame the field of potential evolutions of a rural society than of an urban society, because the evolution of the latter is less bound to direct environmental constraints, explaining thereby that most archaeologically related investigations using models focus on rural societies.

Thus, archaeological/palaeo-environmental models can either directly analyse the social interactions between agents, or use the landscape as a reference plane. The choice of the adequate modelling technique is strongly dependent on the research question, and in many cases also on the scientific background of the modeller. In any case, it is the mutual interdependence of humans and their environment that is in the focus: environment and natural resources are quickly and directly affected by human activities and at the same time, humans are directly and rapidly affected by the availability of natural resources. We see here the interest and the efficiency of agent-based modelling tools. In the Neolithic, power processes creating a public policy resulting in a large transformation of the access to and/or the nature of natural resources did not exist." Instead, such interactions are atomistic, i.e. they correspond to the repetition of small and direct transformations and uses of a territory at a lower spatial scale because of one or a small group of humans. De facto, they correspond well to the distributed way of conceiving large transformations of a landscape by repetitions of actions played by a multitude agents and actors that multi-agent modelling are the best to deal with. However, the large debate between descriptive and theoretical models initiated by Edmonds and Moss (2005) does have impact on the way multi-agent modelling is used for studying archaeological/palaeo-environmental issues.

8.2.3 Scales and Discipline Drivers: Categorizing Which Model You Are Working on

While a modellers' dream can be to construct global models that integrate data of all relevant research disciplines, more local reconstructions with a narrower focus are better suited to meet the needs of local to regional heritage management. The model census we have assessed non-exhaustively may lead to a classification of these models in four categories, different in their scale and drivers. They may roughly be presented following a matrix of *categories* combining scales on one hand and disciplines used as inputs and drivers in the other hand:

i. Scales:
   (a) The level of the village/hamlet (defined here along the more adequate word "terroir") unit is often used because it is the functional unit of management of a landscape, the geographic expression of a combination of rationalities that have to interact altogether. Building a model of one simulated entity below this level is impossible regarding the importance of such interactions, both direct (marriages & other social interactions but also mutual manpower support for instance). Roughly, it is the level in which micro-economic rationality can be considered in order to analyse and explain differences in the use of natural resources;
   (b) The level of the territory that corresponds to a culture or a group of cultures. Roughly, it is the level in which macro-economic rationality can be assessed, assuming a certain homogeneity regarding the use of natural resources within this culture comparing to others. A main aspect here is to analyse the impacts of a homogenous use of these resources;
ii. Involved disciplines and drivers:

(a) Archaeology and social science is used as the major input for the model and the expected results are focussing on palaeo-environmental issues;
(b) Paleo-environmental data are used as the main inputs for the model and the expected results are focussing on archaeological issues.

8.2.4 Genericness Criteria: Analysing the Validity Extension Methodology

Finally, we introduce a classification of different genericness *criteria* that models tend to achieve. In contrast to the binary categories of scale- and discipline-we describe above, (a model is either built on a rationality on a global scale, then tested on a lower scale - or the opposite; but cannot be both; a model uses disciplines as inputs and cannot therefore use the same inputs in a validation step), these genericness criteria are gradients on which one can position its model:

1. *The social and environmental spatial genericness:* The accuracy of fit possible when using local environment data and locally evidenced farming practices can hardly be generalized for a spatially broader model extent: one is then forced to establish adaptation "rules" of this modelled production system, thereby implying hidden or formalized rules regarding human rationality (securization, maximisation, constraints-based sequential rationality, etc.);
2. *the social-temporal genericness (innovations, adaptations, social evolutions):* The very same problem concerning space may be applied regarding time as well: one may have to introduce evolutions of techniques, practices and/or social relations that can adapt themselves along simple (reactive, elimination) or complex procedures (learning, cognitive adaptation, etc.) to get out from the "instantness" of these models;
3. *The Micro adequacies: local emergences and social differentiations.* Following Fraser (2003), Misselhorn (2005) or Olivier de Sardan et al. (2007), once a famine or any other plague occurs, they affect only portions of the population (families, groups), mainly the most fragile ones, and not the whole population. This means that only very specific and catastrophic "plagues" (for instance well-referenced and very harsh droughts), may constrain simulated populations because they affected the whole population (see Dean et al. 1999;Axtell et al. 2002; Janssen et al. 2003; Kohler (2008) on the Anasazi collapse). More generally, any social and economic dynamic may not be seen as affecting indifferently a whole population, but only portions of it, combining specific parameters (for instance at the level of a family, lack of manpower, low cropping surface per capita, bad gender repartition regarding inheritance access, etc.).

One can then position a model´s genericness extent and build its validity extension along these genericness criteria.

8.3 Modelling Environmentally-Constrained but Adaptable Society-Environment Systems

8.3.1 TEM ("Terroir"-Based Environmentally Constrained Models)

Following our classification, we describe here the "terroir" level models, where a society and its evolution is driven by their calorie and resource demand and constrained by environmental parameters. Important information used for the model originates in archaeology, such as tools and practices; knowledge on environmental factors is also important.

As an example of these models, Baum (2014) has formalized a GIS-based object model based on information from available and relevant literature and local archaeological data regarding environmental characteristics (soil, vegetation, local climate, distance to village) and cropping and livestock-keeping practices, to evaluate the environmental impact of human settlements over several village territories, along several farming scenarios (shifting, intensive garden and non-intensive cultivation) and diet assumptions (Fig. 8.1).

Further works with similar research interests include Coolen (2010), who has worked over different sites of the LBK (Linear Band Keramik) culture territory in Europe: thanks to a systematic geographical census of the archaeological sites of the LBK culture over a region, the agro-ecological characteristics of the implantation sites of this culture (pedology, climate, orientation, hydrology, relative distance to other sites) can be statistically determined. Combined with estimates on economic and agriculture-related parameters of this agropastoral system, this methodology aims at establish a spatial discrimination of a territory along site preferences and potentialities according to a specific culture agropastoral habits.

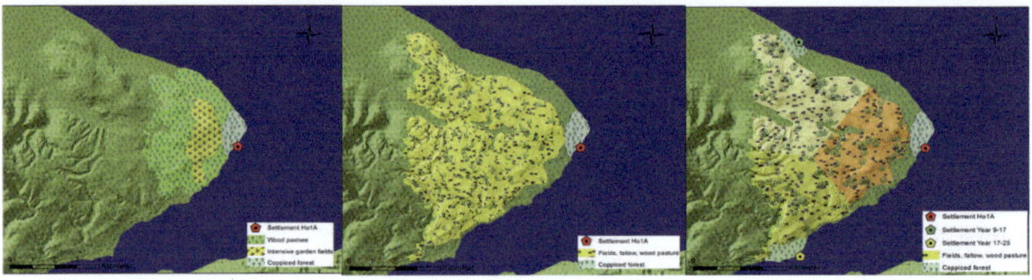

Fig. 8.1 Three "snapshot models" illustrating the model design in (Baum 2014). Economic areas are calculated using various hypotheses and their extent modeled in a GIS. *LEFT*: Intensive Garden Cultivation is applied, resulting in permanent, fields and "extra" wood pasture (*light green*); *CENTER*: Shifting Cultivation is applied, a large area is affected in 25 years. The resulting area exhibits elements of fallows, coppiced stands, and livestock browsing areas side by side. *RIGHT*: Two hypothetical settlements (*green* and *yellow*) have been added, and a relocation of the sites is assumed after 8 years. This might reduce maximum travel distances for agricultural activities

This methodology is equivalent in Burke et al. (2008); Tipping et al. (2009); Graves (2011); Carrer (2013). For instance, Yu et al. (2012) test on the Yiluo valley a combination of demographics and agriculture-based extrapolations and social assumptions based on what archaeology but also modern information provides.

Following their work on Swiss and German archaeological sites, Ebersbach and Schade (2004) have studied livestock-keeping needs and consequences on sustainability of environmental resources and livestock-based farming societies: through a GIS, they have estimated the impacts on an extended village territory of the necessary livestock to both feed the population and manure the fields that are necessary for crop production for feeding a population.

The research object of all these simulations is the area or the evolving landscape; the major tool is GIS input data comprise archaeological and paleo-environmental information. However, because the subject, i.e. the research question, differs, they are representative of the "discipline-as-input" factor differentiation: Coolen (2010) used environment as input and deduced site potentialities, with the hope that further archaeological excavations may provide confirmation. Baum (2014) and Ebersbach and Schade (2004) used archaeology as input and deduce the impact on the related territory and natural resources following various scenarios. These approaches are used to test the relevance and implication of certain model parameters, such as the crop husbandry or the size of the economic territory They set up spatial hypotheses which serve for explanatory purposes and as a reference plane for future works. The strength of such models is to estimate the constraints in which agro-socio-systems may evolve using local data and archaeological and/or agro-environmental assumptions on economic activities. Meanwhile, many of them establish the maximum potential level, i.e. a carrying capacity equivalent in those specific conditions and techniques such a society may reach, but not its fragility regarding social variables and temporal "coincidences" that are inherent to every society.

8.3.2 WEM: "World" Size Environmentally Constrained Models

Modelling prehistoric and pre-industrial society-environment systems is essential to understand the co-evolution of climate and humans over recent Millennia as well as the current state of the earth system. Such an analysis should be settled at the global scale, simply because it is the sole relevant scale for apprehending human-induced climate changes. Many of the ecosystems that are highly valued today for the services they provide to humanity are the result of long-term interactions between society and their environment. Because detailed observations of these interactions will always be limited in space and time, global human-environment models may be useful tools to bridge spatial and temporal gaps in data and to test hypotheses about the large-scale development of society and the environment.

Despite its promise, global modelling, however presents several additional challenges compared to the "terroir scale" described above. The foremost among these challenges concerns data both for driving the models and for evaluating their output. Outside of Europe and parts of East Asia, critical information on subsistence lifestyles, the timing of key transitions, and on paleo-demography needed to parameterize models is not available because of a lack of investigations in these regions or a poorly preserved archaeological record. Likewise, palaeo-environmental and ethnographic information, that is highly valuable for model evaluation, is largely absent from many continents where geographic conditions and local history led to poor preservation of archives, both natural and human.

Regarding the three points described in Sect. 8.2.4, WEM-type models obviously meet the spatial genericness criterion (1) but they methodologically do not completely fulfil the criterion (2) regarding time: rules of the model do apply all along simulations but the model lacks time-related adaptability. Finally, the criterion (3) is not answered as such models do belong to the ii. (b) palaeo-environmental "Disciplines used as inputs and drivers" scheme meaning that changes are environmentally driven.

Nevertheless, there are several promising methodologies that are currently being applied to understand society-environment systems at global scale. These models may be roughly divided into two categories:

- data-driven approach where demographic and subsistence data are inputs to the model;
- an "organic" approach, where the model simulates potential human population and subsistence lifestyle as prognostic variables. Both of these approaches have advantages and disadvantages and are currently under rapid further development.

The data driven approach is typified by the ALCC scenarios KK10 (Kaplan et al. 2009, 2011) and HYDE (Klein-Goldewijk et al. 2011). These scenarios are the result of empirical models that take geographically distributed estimates of population at any time in the past and combine them with information on climate and soils in order to estimate the magnitude and spatial distribution of land use. The models used to generate these scenarios assume subsistence lifestyle implicitly, i.e., everyone on earth at a given time is presumed to have the same type of subsistence strategy. While HYDE makes a simplistic distinction between land use for crop or pasture based upon present-day geographic patterns of land use, it does not consider changes in per capita land use over time (intensification). In contrast, KK10 models intensification as a non-linear function of population density itself, so that low population densities use relatively large amounts of land. This difference in the representation of per capita land use among the models leads to very large differences in the global pattern of land use in the past (Fig. 8.2).

As noted above, neither model takes directly into account the way in which different subsistence lifestyles may use the same landscape, e.g., foragers versus shifting cultivators versus permanent agriculturalists versus pastoralists. This distinction among land use types, in particular the shift from foraging to farming, may be critical

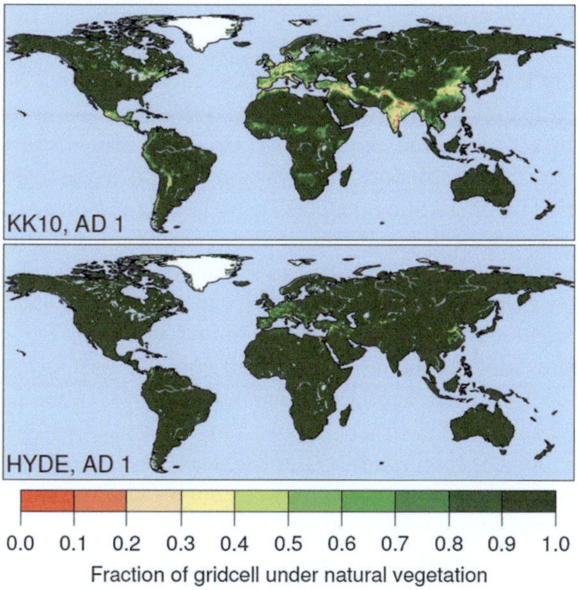

Fig. 8.2 Comparison between global anthropogenic land cover change scenarios KK10 and HYDE for the year AD 1. The large discrepancy between the scenarios in the maps is caused by differences in the treatment of per-capita land use. HYDE fixes the spatial pattern of per-capita land use observed in AD 1961 for all time periods in the past, whereas KK10 models per-capita land use as a function of population density, with intensification occurring at higher densities (courtesy of J. Kaplan)

for understanding the pattern of land cover change and human impact on the environment during pre-industrial time. While the agricultural transition could be prescribed in models based on archaeological records, lack of investigations or well-preserved sites implies that in many parts of the world prescription would be based on guesswork or assumptions. An alternative approach is to use a model that explicitly simulates subsistence lifestyle changes, as in the "organic" approach mentioned above.

Currently the best example of this approach that has been developed and applied at continental to global scale is the GLUES model (Global Land Use and technological Evolution Simulator (Lemmen et al. 2009). GLUES simulates human population density, technological change and agricultural activity directly, based on the concept of gradient adaptive dynamics, where adoption of a subsistence lifestyle, e.g., Neolithic agriculture, by any given group of people at any particular time depends on endogenous environmental and social factors, e.g., potential productivity, population density, and exogenous factors, including the presence of farming people in neighbouring regions. Simple rules in GLUES, including continent size and climate, allow the model to simulate the spontaneous transition to farming in certain regions of the world (Wirtz and Lemmen 2003). Once farming is established, the model simulates the advection of peoples and diffusion of ideas and technology across environmental gradients. The GLUES model is driven by static maps of potential productivity and climate on regions of ca. 1000 km2 that are defined as areas of relatively homogeneous climate and productivity. GLUES can further use information on climate variability prescribed as discrete events in space and time to influence human activities and populations. GLUES´ prognostic outputs include population density, relative proportions of farming people in the region, and the level of technology used by the farming people. The major disadvantage of GLUES is that it may produce histories of society-environment interactions that are at-odds with reality, e.g., the spontaneous development of agriculture in places where it is not known to have occurred. Additionally, GLUES in its current form cannot simulate major technological transitions beyond the initial adoption of agriculture, e.g., metallurgy, urbanization, or the development of complex societies, with focuses on specific sites such as Western Europe (Lemmen et al. 2011) or the Indus civilization (Lemmen and Khan 2012).

Such models answer the criteria (1) and (2) with a formal justification of the appearance of such technical innovations (Lemmen 2012). More globally, they cannot answer the criterion (3):

- Social innovations, such as socio-anthropological family evolutions and/or political structures, are less likely to be modelled, while such social innovations may have a determining impact on the "capacity" of a society for conquering new territories, following non-Malthusian hypotheses (Boserup 1965, 1976; Lemmen 2012). For instance, Todd (2011) has suggested large variations of the family structures in Eurasia, linked with the appearance of unequal families and the consequences on the cultures' differential "capacity" of expansion.
- The effects of "coincidences", i.e. emergences may disappear as such conjunctions are smoothed while going at a broader scale, both socially and spatially.

8.4 Modelling Innovative Societies in Its Environment

8.4.1 TSM: "Terroir"-Based Society-Driven Models

The focus on technical and/or social aspects of changes at the local level has been studied as well. Meanwhile, tending to answer the combination of criteria (1) and (3) (social-environmental genericness on one hand, and innovations and differentiations on the other hand), such studies are de facto related to a KISS approach (Edmonds and Moss 2005) for this specific question:

- The first possibility are theoretical KISS models, through which a question on innovations and conflicts is analysed (Bentley et al. 2005; Younger 2011)
- The second possibility, KIDS, is more focused on local situations on which many data and information are available and build some archaeological and/or socio-anthropological hypotheses to test, with the model as the test bed for

various social and/or technical scenarios (Allen et al. 2006; Altaweel, 2008; Murphy 2012; Rogers et al. 2012).

One of the major developments on modelling past local "terroirs" concerns the Anasazi people in the Southwestern United States. The innovation there was to include social factors along with environmental ones for modelling a "terroir" (Kohler et al. 2005; Kohler 2008). However, the advantage of describing an "island" territory, i.e. a closed system where no influence from outside may be considered, faced the default of this "island" situation: droughts did have such a huge impact that they overcame all social configurations. Such a modelling project may be more effective in study sites where environment is not a so blatant challenge.

Saqalli et al. (2014) describe another spatialized Agent-Based model, which aims was to reconstruct the LBK farming and society system functioning at the village level. The idea was to reconstruct in the same model the functioning along a very local grid level (1 ha/cell) of village societies, using assumptions from Bogaard (2002), Ebersbach (2003) and Schibler (2006). The goal of this combination of scale was that small variations at the farming/livestock keeping/hunting-gathering system do have exponential effects on a larger scale.

Because the purpose of this model was to raise hypotheses on socio-anthropological and economic organisations and was dedicated to analyse its impact on the environment, it takes for granted biophysical aspects and tends to integrate and combine environmental rules from literature and available data through inference: The use of databases from the European Commission provides the access to present-day soil characteristics (pedology and elevation), from which was deduced the pedology of the LBK period, following the soil retro-evolution methodology assessed by Schwartz et al. (2011). Within this simulated environment, family organisation and manpower availability are settled along with what archaeology and palaeo-analysis provides on the past farming system possibilities (for instance, family size can grow beyond mononuclear families, reconstituting thereby LBK houses and households, larger than Starçevo houses). Together with inferences from present-time agronomy and zootechny that both constrain the possible combinations of the farming system (for instance, the permanent fields), such a model may be used for testing hypotheses on the functioning of this past society. Similar models were built with the integration of demographic and social issues along environment, with environment and natural resources shortages and stresses as inputs and variable impacts on the population evolution and differentiation as outputs (Wilkinson et al. 2007; Verhagen and Whitley 2012).

The model is conditioned by food requirements and the demand in non-finite resources (firewood, timber, cultivable soils, livestock pasture or forests, hunting and gathering grounds) of individual households with household members varying from 1 to ∞ (mean: 5 to 7) but is driven along time according to family social organization & individually randomized dynamics. A first version of the model was settled using the CORMAS platform, written in Smalltalk and focusing on smaller territories of 20 * 20 km, i.e.. 40 000 1 ha pixels, of four typical LBK sites (Aisne valley in France, Aldenhoven and Hesse in Germany, Melk in Austria). The size of this small version of the model is big enough for allowing further household and village settlements after the first site building, depending on family splitting and departure rules (local ultimogeniture, patrilocality, choosing no side-effect inheritance) and then reconstructing the agglomerate-shaped expansion process.

This model should be considered as a scenario testing platform. 12 variables were considered (for instance, initial population, site choice procedure, colonization procedure, family organization, presence/absence of Mesolithic hunters-gatherers, integration of climatic variations according to the European Pollen Database), with 2 to 3 possible "alleles", inducing 108 864 combinations to explore. However, building such a model based on the inevitable assumption of a common complex of society rules faces the obvious critique from archaeologists that such an assumption cannot be applied on a so vast territory such as the LBK extent. More globally, one may question the genericness that formally comes from other sources and societies: Applying such hypotheses onto a past society implies considering them as generic and thereby applicable to broader spatial territories and cultures of the same period. Through this assumption, we raise the question whether the extension of any socio-ecosystem model from very local sites to global areas may be valid at all, i.e. is it possible to fulfil the criterion 1.

Another example of this model category with the name WELASSIMO is presented in chapter 9 of this book.

8.4.2 WSM: "World" Size Society- Driven Models

Several attempts were made to extend the previous category of models to a global scale, with the necessity to answer the criterion (1): social & environmental spatial genericness. A possible way can be seen in Meghan (2011, which assumes a specific theory (here: the circuit theory), and focuses on certain factors, movements of people in this case. Similar model attempts were built with the integration of demographic and social issues along environment, and natural resources and stresses as inputs and variable impacts on the population evolution and differentiation as outputs, such as one of the most achieved ones on ancient Maya (Heckbert 2013).

Another model was tried to be assessed for answering the three criteria we raised) for both the everyday life, including social, family and agro-ecological constraints, at the local scale and the population spatial and demographic dynamics at the global scale: The Obresoc project (Bocquet-Appel et al. 2009) tries to reconstitute the expansion of the LBK culture throughout non-Mediterranean Europe, even beyond the regions where LBK archaeological remnants were found, in order to not artificially constraint the settlement process. This was possible thanks to the assumption that what was collected from archaeology on spots related to the same culture is valid for all the sites of the same culture, thereby assuming the genericness criterion (1) without tending to prove it. The World Climate project (Hijmans et al. 2005) provide the access to present-day climate data (temperature and rainfall), from which was roughly reconstructed the climate and its variability at that time, as described in Saqalli (2015): The palynology-based climate reconstruction of Ortu et al. 2011 provides the average Europe temperature and rainfall time deviations with present-day figures, while the World Climate project provides the statistical deviations both in terms of time (seasonal variability based on 50 years of data) and space (with a precision of 10 km × 10 km cells, transposed and adapted to 1 ha-cell of the model). The work of Schwartz et al. (2011) was used for building the soil properties in the model, and Saqalli et al. (2014) supplied the background for the farming and society system and variability. Processes of reactive adaptation were formalized but no cognitive nor selective appearance of technical or social innovations may occur, i.e. it does not fulfill the criterion (2). Finally, the conjuncture adequacy or inadequacy between time, society and space and the related emergence was considered as the model agreed that the driving force, humans, act at the local scale, following the modelling scheme of Saqalli et al. (2014). This local driving force affects the dynamics at the global scale along the long era of the LBK culture thanks to the connection between access to natural resources and manpower availability, complying the criterion (3). Because the Europe-scale model encountered severe methodological and scale issues along its building process, mainly due to its computer requirements (320 millions of pixels treated sequentially four times a year (one time step = one season) along 800 years, with up to 4 millions of human household entities acting), this crucial connection between local and global scales was erased to simplify it but also for idealistic assumptions Renfrew (1987), thereby annihilating the emergence potential of this project.

More globally, hypotheses on the rationality that may have driven past societies should integrate the everyday constraints at the household level because it is at this very level that environmental, social and agro-ecological constraints are experienced differently from one household to another. Using present-time human socio-anthropology and especially theories of conflicting and limited rationality and planning, restricted information and interaction may be very useful for building a simple but acceptable cognition of the households. Acknowledging that all societies are not homeostatic may allow emergent properties in modelled rural societies, including "surprises", i.e. big expansion or total collapse without climate or other environmental constraints. For instance, the fact that family manpower should be actually seasonal and anthropologically restricted may have a huge impact on the productivity of such labour-constrained systems. Finally, the genericness point we raised may be partially reached through inference from "existing inferential frameworks (e.g., certain strands of evolutionary archaeology[2]) but that explicitly sociological simulation remains a challenge" (Lake 2014).

[2]We here include as well present-time originated anthropological theories.

8.5 Building a Grid of Analysis for Expanding the Genericness of a Past Society-Environment Model

8.5.1 *Objectives for Expanding Model Genericness*

One may point out that building a model that fulfils both scale & discipline categories (i. and ii. in Sect. 2) and temporal, spatial and emergence genericness criteria (1. 2 and 3. in Sect. 3.1) may be:

- Very difficult to build, both humanly and technically: it needs a lot of time to build a model with many disciplines, which means managing consortiums of thematic-oriented scholars for whom the value of a model depends on the spatial and temporal adequacy with their own data. Thereby, defining altogether within the consortium the model variables to consider but also to exclude, which is far more difficult, is a harsh task[3];
- Very challenging to validate: two validation steps are to be considered: confrontation with external data and sensitivity analysis (Amblard et al. 2006). As described by the latter and Bonaudo (2005), there is no absolute validation of a model. Following Popper (1985), a theory and therefore a model is temporarily accepted until it is rejected. Field data confrontation is challenging technically but not methodologically as far as a database was kept apart of the model building for confrontation purposes. On the other hand, sensitivity analysis complexity increases dramatically with the number of variables which are to be integrated in a model;
- Useful only under specific conditions: outputs of a very multidisciplinary model are harder to interpret for a monothematic scholar, meaning that the more a model is multidisciplinary; the more the use of it may be de facto restricted socially to modellers and the more publications are harsh to be published: journals are mainly thematic-oriented and model description increases with the number of disciplines, decreasing thereby their acceptance.

We can then deduce from these points that the ultimate goal of one modeller, at least for the present-time, is not to build the ultimate model that can answer and/or explore all the combinations of a past human-environment interaction.

Whatever the variable in a spatialized model, data are never fully and perfectly available, neither for present-time data and even less so for data concerning past periods. Such a perfect source cannot exist, once we acknowledge that spatial data can be completed only through reconstructions, at least partially, based on interpolations or inferences. Thereby, lacking data can be compensated by assumptions based on inference as well; The fact that data quality varies is not per se a criterion whether to use one type of data (and the corresponding variable and discipline) and to exclude another one. The sole criterion for deciding if a phenomenon should be included is the common agreement between scholars, even without data. Therefore and following Saqalli et al.

---

[3]Some co-modelling methodologies do exist such as ARDI (Etienne et al. 2011).

(2010), including a variable that is acknowledged as important,, is a smaller error than not considering it, even if this means to include it in a very simplistic way.

Finally, following An (2012) or Tzanopoulos et al. (2013), models where disciplines are combined but also interact may produce emergence of unexpected phenomena. More globally, one cannot always define ex ante the impact range of many variables. This applies especially for social variables, such as availability of manpower dedicated to rural activities, which may have multiplied impacts over the transformation power of humans over natural resources. We thus identify the following two desiderata:

- A methodology of model combination to answer the requirements we proposed above;
- A guideline of models according to objectives and available data.

8.5.2 Combining Four Objectives for Expanding Model Genericness

We then consider that analysing the validity of past society & environment models is performed as follows:

- Adequacy to scale and spatial genericness: simulation outputs correspond as much as possible to local data along time;
- environmental genericness: the model can be considered as reproducing correctly environmental dynamics of a broad territory;
- social genericness: the model is acceptable regarding social dynamics, including innovations' appearances, adaptations and social differentiations;
- Validity regarding emergence: It includes conjunctions, emergences, shocks, sudden events that may impact evolutions of a system.

The four types of models we described in the previous sections may be categorized along these four genericness paths, following Table 8.1:

Based on this classification, we propose a grid of pathways for expanding the genericness of the initial model one scholar may have built. Because each model is de facto a theory, i.e. a conceptualisation of a socio-ecological system (SES), it is also a methodology of test of this theory regarding scale, environment, society and emergence. Once a scholar has a model corresponding to one archetype we described in Table 8.1, different ways for expanding its genericness start from the initial model and may follow different procedures according to the genericness objective the scholar may have, itself defined by the pursued research question. The Fig. 8.3 illustrates the various patterns such pathways may follow.

These combinations of factors induces the definition of twelve pathways of genericness expansion, each one describing a methodology of model uses according to scales and drivers, each one allowing the exploration of one research question,

Table 8.1 Criteria of genericness for modelling past societies and their environments

Model types	Scale and spatial genericness	Environmental genericness	Social genericness	Validity regarding emergence
TEM	Yes: it is de facto an "instantané"	No, because of the scale	No	No
TSM	Yes, with variations along scenarios. ex.: 1 scenario = 1 innovation	No, because of the scale	Yes, with drivers ruling innovations' appearances or not, following theories	Yes, locally, thanks to social drivers. Environmental ones are less integrated because of scale
WEM	No, too broad	Yes, even with huge simplifications	Yes, with drivers ruling innovations' appearances or not, following theories[1]	No
WSM	No, too broad	Yes, through present time farming system inferences	No (not yet?)	Yes, socially and environmentally

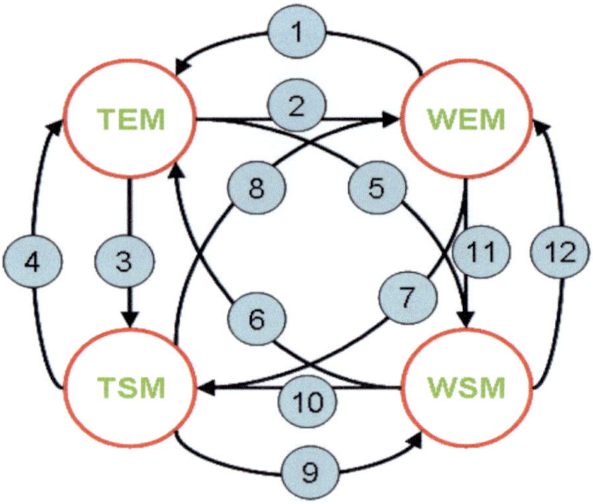

Fig. 8.3 Diagram of validity expansion paths, from one of the four model archetypes

that we described in Table 8.2. As a matter of fact, establishing a selection arborescence of procedures of combination and use of models according to different criteria (scale, disciplines as inputs and drivers, consistency principles, etc.) leads to so many combinations that a full arborescence is yet to be built.

Table 8.2 Paths of genericness for modelling past societies and their environments

Methodological procedure		Related research question
1	TEM → WEM procedure:	**Integrative world models improvement approach:** Step by step improving world models by including results from various local case study models
2	WEM → TEM procedure:	**World models testing approach:** Analysing world models results for specific locations, to compare with results from local archaeologically-constrained models; Building first trials of local models, to be compared with archaeological data
3	TEM → TSM procedure:	**Local impacts of innovations/adaptations evaluation approach:** Using a TEM model as a test-bed for analysing innovations & adaptations to shocks 'costs/benefits', not to compare with data
4	TSM → TEM procedure:	**Innovations appearance identification approach:** Several TSMs are tested to see if they fit better with archaeological data and TEM data: which innovations appearance and statistically-defined chaotic events explain farming system situation, sustainability AND diachronic evolution?
5	TEM → WSM procedure:	**Integrative world models improvement approach, including global shocks:** Step by step improving world models by including results from various local case study models AND integrating large scale variability (climate, for instance)
6	WSM → TEM procedure:	**World models testing approach:** Analysing world models results for specific locations, to compare with results from local archaeologically-constrained models and timely constrained "snapshot models"; Building first trials of local models, to be compared with archaeological data
7	TSM → WEM procedure:	**Integrative world models improvement approach, smoothing local shocks:** Step by step improving world models by including results from various local case study models, including local variability & innovations
8	WEM → TSM procedure:	**World models testing approach, including local shocks:** Analysing world models results for specific locations, to compare with results from local archaeologically-constrained models, including local variability to see if it is smoothed at large scale;
9	TSM → WSM procedure:	**Integrative world models improvement approach, including shocks:** Step by step improving world models by including results from various local case study models, transferring local variability & innovations at a global scale
10	WSM → TSM procedure:	**World models testing approach:** Analysing world models results for specific locations, to compare with results from local archaeologically-constrained but including innovations & shocks models; Building first trials of local models, to be compared with archaeological data

(continued)

Table 8.2 (continued)

Methodological procedure		Related research question
11	WEM → WSM procedure:	**Large scale shocks impact evaluation approach:** Analysing impacts of shocks at a global scale by using a WEM model as a test-bed for analysing innovations & adaptations to shocks 'costs/benefits', not to compare with data
12	WSM → WEM procedure:	**Large scale innovations appearance identification approach:** Several WSMs are tested to see if they fit better with archaeological data and WEM data (once one is settled): which innovations appearance and statistically-defined chaotic events explain farming system situations, sustainability AND diachronic evolutions?

Usually, choosing a model procedure depends practically on the availability of data: the more a model is global, the less such a system can be built along a systemic approach and the more it relies on paleo-environmental data, which are more or less the sole available at this scale. Thereby, the more the model is global, the more it tends to follow Malthusian environmentally-determined conceptions of human-environment interactions. We plea for avoiding this over-deterministic approach, chosen mainly for its practicability.

It means also to acknowledge that it is therefore important to start from the lower scale for avoiding this pro-environment prism but also to integrate archaeological information, which is the most conditioning information on SESs:

- The possible and plausible socio-anthropological societies, with no a priori consistency in its organization but solely in its functioning at the family level (whatever the organization of this last);
- The possible and plausible farming and environmental systems coming from inference from present-time non-mechanical farming systems, as well as the constraints and assets from its socio-anthropological organization as defined above and, its possible and plausible local "terroir"-level biophysical characteristics. Agronomy and zootechny may establish the agriculture consistency at the local level along a systemic "organic" approach (Rogers et al. 2012);
- The hazards, risks, and fluctuations at the same level (epidemics, plagues, family fluctuations) but also adaptation and resilience practices in present-time non-mechanical farming societies;

Transforming such a local model towards the global level implies trying to lose as less as possible the richness of the local scale, through:

- The simple iteration and juxtaposition of many "terroir" models with inclusions of exchange procedures (goods, information, humans, etc.) between models, reconstituting the global level. However, this procedure requires huge computer capacities;

- The "smart simplification" through the introduction of "terroir" agents, each agent being built based on parameters established from a sensitivity analysis of several "terroir"-like models, each one corresponding to a combined archetype of ecosystems and cultures. However, this procedure requires strong simplifications leading to an important loss of the emergence quality of the system.

The global level, once achieved, should acquire confidence, through:

- A confrontation with paleo-environmental data such as pollen databases;
- An independent territory reconstitution, through for instance GIS, purposely built for confronting its outputs with the ones from the model;

Finally and to conclude this formalization, we plea for acknowledging that a model is no more than a formalization of representations settled as a lab of experimentations:

- Its value is solely defined by a consensus among scholars;
- It has no value in itself apart from favouring the debate among scholars, formalizing scientific questions and exploring scenarios;
- It then can be used only as a test bed, through a plan of experiences, with series of scenarios, each one corresponding to a combination of alleles of several variables.

References

Allen E, Falconer S, Sarjoughian H, Barton MC and Fall P (2006) Modeling of agropastoral human activities using agent-based simulation. In: 70th Annual meeting of the society for American archaeology. Arizona State University, Santa Fe, Arizona, USA

Altaweel MR (2008) Investigating agricultural sustainability and strategies in northern Mesopotamia: results produced using a socio-ecological modeling approach. J Archaeol Sci 35(4):821–835

Amblard F, Rouchier J, Bommel P (2006) Evaluation et validation de modèles multi-agents. In: Amblard F, Phan D (eds) Modélisation et simulations multi-agents: application pour les sciences de l'Homme et de la Société. Hermes, Paris, France, pp 103–140

An L (2012) Modeling human decisions in coupled human and natural systems: review of agent-based models. Ecol Model 229:25–36

Axtell RL, Epstein JM, Dean JS, Gumerman GJ, Swedlund AC, Harburger J, Chakravarty S, Hammond R, Parker J, Parker MT (2002) Population growth and collapse in a multiagent model of the Kayenta Anasazi in Long House Valley. Proc Natl Acad Sci 99(3):7275–7279

Bassett TJ, Blanc-Pamard C, Boutrais J (2007) Constructing locality: the terroir approach in West Africa, Africa. J Int African Inst 77(1):104–112

Baum TG (2014) Models of wetland settlement and associated land use in South-West Germany during the fourth millennium B.C. Veg Hist Archaeobot 23(1):67–80

Bentley AR, Lake MW, Shennan SJ (2005) Specialisation and wealth inequality in a model of a clustered economic network. J Archaeol Sci 32(9):1346–1356

Bocquet-Appel JP, Berger JF, O'Connor M, Demoule JP, Sanchez-Goñi MF, Vigne JD (2009) OBRESOC: Un observatoire rétrospectif d'une société archéologique: La trajectoire du

néolithique Rubané. Document de Soumission. Agence Nationale de la Recherche, Programme changements Environnements planétaires, Paris, France
Bogaard A (2002) Questioning the relevance of shifting cultivation to Neolithic farming in the loess belt of Europe: evidence from the Hambach Forest Experiment. Veg Hist Archaeobot 11 (1–2):155–168
Bonaudo T (2005) La gestion environnementale sur un front pionnier amazonien. Ph.D. Agronomy, Institut National Agronomique Paris-Grignon, Paris, France
Boserup E (1965) The conditions of agricultural growth; the economics of agrarian change under population pressure. George Allen & Unwin Ltd, London, UK
Boserup E (1976) Environment, population, and technology in primitive societies. Popul Dev Rev 2(1):21–36
Bousquet F, Le Page C (2004) Multi-agent simulations and ecosystem management: a review. Ecol Model 176(3–4):313–332
Burke A, Ebert D, Cardille J, Dauth D (2008) Paleoethology as a tool for the development of archaeological models of land-use: the Crimean Middle Palaeolithic. J Archaeol Sci 35(4):894–904
Carrer F (2013) An ethnoarchaeological inductive model for predicting archaeological site location: a case-study of pastoral settlement patterns in the Val di Fiemme and Val di Sole (Trentino, Italian Alps). J Anthropol Archaeol 32(1):54–62
Coolen J (2010) Siedlungsgeografische Studien zum Frühneolithikum in der Umgebung von Melk, NÖ, Masterarbeit, Universität Wien. Historisch-Kulturwissenschaftliche Fakultät, Austrian Archaeological Institute, University of Vienna, Vienna, Austria
Crabtree SA, Kohler TA (2012) Modelling across millennia: interdisciplinary paths to ancient socio-ecological systems. Ecol Model 241(2–4):2–4
Dean JS, Gumerman GJ, Epstein JM, Axtell RL, Swedlund AC, Parker MT and McCarroll S (1999) Understanding Anasazi culture change through agent-based modelling in dynamics. In Kohler TA and Gumerman GJ (eds): Human and primate societies: agent-based modelling of social and spatial processes. Oxford University Press, Oxford, U.K, pp 179–205
Ebersbach R (2003) Paleoecological reconstructions and calculation of calorie requirement at Lake Zurich Paper presented at the The Archaeology of Landscape and Geographic Information SystemsArchäoprognose Brandenburg I Forschungen zur Archäologie im Land Brandenburg 8 (Wünsdorf 2003), Wünsdorf
Ebersbach R, Schade C (2004) Modeling the intensity of Linear Pottery land use: an example from the Mörlener Bucht in the Wetterau Basin, Hesse, Germany. In: Stadtarchäologie Wien (Ed), Enter the past: the E-way into the four dimensions of cultural heritage. CAA 2003. Computer applications and quantitative methods in archaeology, Proceedings of the 31st Conference, Vienna, Austria
Edmonds B, Moss S (2005) From KISS to KIDS: an 'anti-simplistic' modeling approach. In: Davidsson P et al (eds.) Multi agent based simulation 2004, Springer, Lect Notes Artif Intell 34 (15):130–144
Etienne M, Du Toit D, Pollard S (2011) ARDI: a co-construction method for participatory modelling in natural resources management. Ecol Soc 16(1):44
Fraser EDG (2003) Social vulnerability and ecological fragility: building bridges between social and natural sciences using the Irish Potato Famine as a case study. Conserv Ecol 7(2):9
Garneau T, Delisle S (2002) Programmation Orientée-Agent: Évaluation Comparative D'outils et Environnements". In: JFIADSMA'02 Journées Francophones pour l'Intelligence Artificielle Distribuée et les Systèmes Multi-Agents, Lille, France, Hermes, pp 111–123
Graves D (2011) The use of predictive modeling to target Neolithic settlement and occupation activity in mainland Scotland, J Archaeol Sci, 38(3), 633–656
Heckbert S (2013) MayaSim: an agent-based model of the ancient Maya social-ecological system. J Artif Soc Soc Simul 16(4):11
Hijmans R, Cameron S, Parra J, Jones P, Jarvis A (2005) Very high resolution interpolated climate surfaces for global land areas. Int J Climatol 25:1965–1978
Janssen MA (2009) Understanding artificial anasazi. J Artif Soc Soc Simul 12(4):13

Janssen MA, Scheffer M (2004) Overexploitation of renewable resources by ancient societies and the role of sunk cost effects. Ecol Soc 9(1):6
Janssen MA, Kohler TA, Scheffer M (2003) Sunk-cost effects and vulnerability to collapse in ancient societies. Curr Anthropol 44(5):722–728
Kaplan JO, Krumhardt KM, Zimmermann NE (2009) The prehistoric and preindustrial deforestation of Europe. Quatern Sci Rev 28(27–28):3016–3034
Kaplan JO, Krumhardt KM, Ellis EC, Ruddiman WF, Lemmen C, Klein-Goldewijk K (2011) Holocene carbon emissions as a result of anthropogenic land cover change. The Holocene 21 (5):775–791
Klein-Goldewijk K, Beusen A, van Drecht G, de Vos M (2011) The HYDE 31 spatially explicit database of human-induced global land-use change over the past 12,000 years. Glob Ecol Biogeogr 20(1):73–86
Kohler TA (2008) Evolutionary Archaeology. In: DM. Pearsall (ed.) Encyclopedia of archaeology. Academic Press, New York, pp 1332–1338
Kohler TA, Carr E (1996) Swarm-based modelling of prehistoric settlement systems in south-western North America. In: Johnson L, MacLaren I (eds) Archaeological applications of GIS: proceedings of Colloquium II. Forli, Italy
Kohler TA, Gumerman GJ, Reynolds RG (2005) Simulating ancient societies: computer modeling is helping unravel the archaeological mysteries of the American Southwest. Scientific American, pp 77–84
Kohler TA, Bocinsky KR, Cockburn D, Crabtree SA, Varien MD, Kolm KE, Smith S, Ortman SG, Kobti Z (2012) Modelling prehispanic Pueblo societies in their ecosystems. Ecol Model 241:30–41
Lake MW (2014) Trends in Archaeological Simulation. Journal of Archaeological Method Theory 21(2):258–287
Landais É, Deffontaines JP (1987) Les pratiques des agriculteurs. Etudes rurales, vol, Point de vue sur un courant nouveau de la recherche agronomique, p 109
Le Bars M (2003) Un Simulateur Multi-Agent pour l'Aide à la Décision d'un Collectif: Application à la gestion d'une ressource limitée agro-environnementale, Ph.D. Computer, Université Paris IX-Dauphine
Lemmen C (2012) Malthusian assumptions, Boserupian response in models of the transitions to agriculture. In: Society, nature and history: the legacy of ester Boserup, Springer, Vienna, Austria
Lemmen C, Khan A (2012) A Simulation of the Neolithic transition in the Indus Valley In: Giosan L., Fuller DQ, Nicoll K, Flad RK and Clift PD (eds.) Climates, landscapes and civilizations, chap. 6, American Geophysical Union, Washington, D. C. USA
Lemmen C, Wirtz KW, Gronenborn D (2009), Prehistoric land use and Neolithisation in Europe in the context of regional climate events in: EGU General Assembly, Vienna, Austria
Lemmen C, Gronenborn D, Wirtz KW (2011) A simulation of the Neolithic transition in Western Eurasia. J Archaeol Sci 38(12):3459–3470
Lieurain E (1998) Simulations Distribuées et Multi-Agents. Université Montpellier II Sciences et Techniques du Languedoc, Cirad Tera, M. Sc. Informatique. Montpellier, France
Meghan CL (2011) Multiple pathways across past landscapes: circuit theory as a complementary geospatial method to least cost path for modeling past movement. J Archaeol Sci 38(10):2523–2535
Misselhorn AA (2005) What drives food insecurity in southern Africa: A meta-analysis of household economy studies. Glob Environ Change 15(1):33–43
Murphy JT (2012) Exploring complexity with the Hohokam water management simulation: a middle way for archaeological modelling. Ecol Model 241:15–29
Olivier de Sardan JP, Ali Bako M, Guillermet E, Hamani O, Issa Y, Koné M and Moha M (2007) Analyse rétrospective de la crise alimentaire au Niger en 2005. Etudes & Travaux du LASDEL, vol. 59, Niamey, Niger
Ortu E, Sanchez-Goñi MF, Milzer G and Giraudeau J (2011) Dynamique du climat en région nord-atlantique et ses effets sur l'Europe centrale lors de l'expansion du Néolithique Rubané

(5750–4750 cal BC). 22ème Symposium de l'Association de Palynologues de Langue Francaise (APLF), Paris, France
Parker CD, Manson SM, Janssen MA, Hoffmann MJ, Deadman P (2003) Multi-agent systems for the simulation of land-use and land-cover change: a review. Ann Assoc Am Geogr 93(2):314–337
Popper KR (1985) Conjectures et réfutations la croissance du savoir scientifique. Payot, Paris, France
Raison JP, Coniat D (1997) Essai sur les montagnes de Tanzanie. Karthala, Paris, France
Renfrew CA (1987) Problems in the modelling of socio-cultural systems. Eur J Oper Res 30 (2):179–192
Rogers DJ, Nichols T, Emmerich T, Latek M, Cioffi-Revilla M (2012) Modeling scale and variability in human-environmental interactions in Inner Asia. Ecol Model 241:5–14
Roy B (1992) Science de la décision ou science de l'aide à la décision ?Revue Internationale de systémique, vol. 6, pp 497–529
Saqalli M (2015) Simple is beautiful? building a simple climate model for modelling archaeological issues. Journées Ateliers de Modélisation de l'Atmosphère, Toulouse, France
Saqalli M, Bielders CL, Defourny P, Gérard B (2010) Simulating rural environmentally and socio-economically constrained multi-activity and multi-decision societies in a low-data context: a challenge through empirical agent-based modelling. J Artif Soc Soc Simul, 13(2)
Saqalli M, Salavert A, Bréhard S, Bendrey R, Vigne JD, Tresset A (2014) Revisiting and modelling the woodland farming system of the early Neolithic Linear Pottery Culture (LBK), 5600-4900 BC. Veg Hist Archaeobot 23(1 Supplement):37–50
Schibler J (2006) The economy and environment of the 4th and 3rd millennia BC in the northern Alpine foreland based on studies of animal bones. Environ Archaeol 11(1):49–64
Schwartz D, Ertlen D, Berger JF, Davtian G, Bocquet-Appel JP (2011) Développement agricole et fertilité: comment évaluer la paléo-fertilité des sols aux échelles de temps millénaires? Quelques réflexions à partir d'une étude de cas: l'agriculture rubanée en Europe. In: Carpentier V, Marcigny C (eds) Des hommes aux champs II. Approche archéologique des économies agricoles, Caen, France
Tipping R, Bunting MJ, Davies AL, Murray H, Fraser S, McCulloch R (2009) Modelling land use around an early Neolithic timber hall in north east Scotland from high spatial resolution pollen analyses. J Archaeol Sci 36(1):140–149
Todd E (2011) L'origine des systèmes familiaux Tome 1: l'Eurasie. Gallimard, Paris, France
Tzanopoulos J, Mouttet R, Letourneau A, Vogiatzakis IN, Potts SG, Henle K, Mathevet R, Marty P (2013) Scale sensitivity of drivers of environmental change across Europe. Glob Environ Change 23(1):167–178
Verhagen P, Whitley TG (2012) Integrating archaeological theory and predictive modeling: a live report from the scene. J Archaeol Method Theory 19(1):49–100
Wilkinson TJ, Christiansen JH, Ur J, Widell M, Altaweel MR (2007) Urbanization within a dynamic environment: modeling bronze age communities in upper Mesopotamia. Am Anthropol 109(1):52–68
Wirtz KW, Lemmen C (2003) A global dynamic model for the Neolithic transition. Clim Change 59(3):333–367
Younger SM (2011) Leadership, violence, and warfare in small societies. J Artif Soc Soc Simul 14 (3):8
Yu Y, Guo Z, Wu H, Finke PA (2012) Reconstructing prehistoric land use change from archeological data: validation and application of a new model in Yiluo valley, Northern China. Agric Ecosyst Environ 156:99–107

Chapter 9 Simulating Land Use of Prehistoric Wetland Settlements: Did Excessive Resource Use Necessitate a Highly Dynamic Settlement System?

Tilman Baum

9.1 Introduction

From the archaeological investigation of findings in peat-bog and lake-shore sediments in the North-Western pre-alpine forelands, it is known that people built their wooden houses in these locations from the 5th to the first Millennium BC (Menotti 2004). In more than 150 years of interdisciplinary research, detailed knowledge has been gained from the excavations and analyses of the oxygen-depleted layers and the remains of wooden houses. However, a remarkable gap exists between highly resolved knowledge on certain issues, and some very fundamental, yet unsolved questions. Thus, it is known exactly which plant and animal species have been consumed (Jacomet 2009), but the husbandry and land use methods are contradictory discussed (Ehrmann et al. 2009; Bogaard 2002).

Evidence is for a highly dynamic settlement system and a short occupation time of many sites, yet the reasons are as unclear as the feedback mechanisms inside of the system (Ebersbach 2010). One reason for this disparity might be conditioned by the biased distribution of evidence that is concentrated in waterlogged locations. Inside of the sites, a lot of condensed information is stored, and in many cases, settlement structure, house architecture and consumption or production modes can directly be assessed from the excavations (e.g. de Capitani et al. 2002; Jacomet et al. 2004; Dieckmann et al. 2006; Schlichtherle et al. 2010). Yet the actions performed in the environment of the sites—and thus emergence of cultural landscapes—may only be inferred from the relevant findings in the sites, accompanied by sparse and punctual paleo-environmental information such as pollen profiles. Therefore, I present an approach to simulate landscape development around wetland sites as caused by the relevant anthropogenic and environmental processes.

T. Baum (✉)
IPAS - Integrated Prehistory and Archaeological Science, University of Basel,
Spalenring 145, Basel, Switzerland
e-mail: Tilman.baum@unibas.ch

J.A. Barceló and F. Del Castillo (eds.), *Simulating Prehistoric and Ancient Worlds*,
Computational Social Sciences, DOI 10.1007/978-3-319-31481-5_9

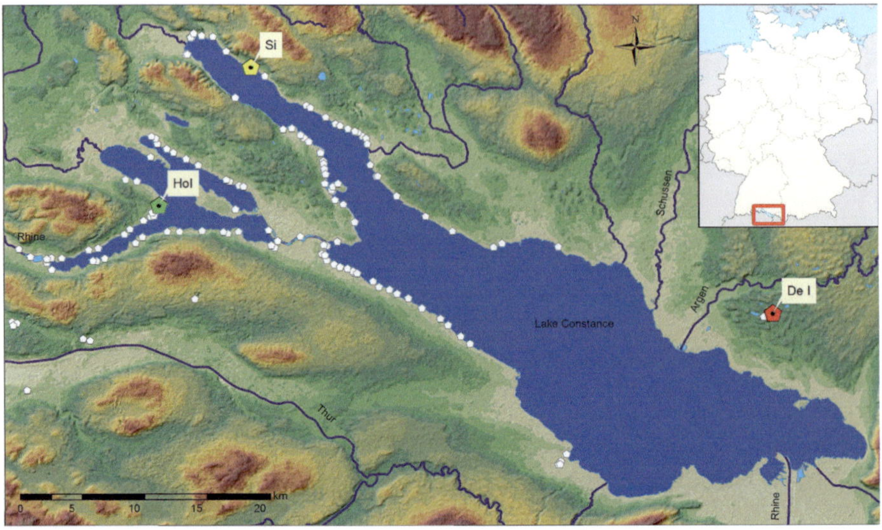

Fig. 9.1 Prehistoric pile dwellings around Lake Constance (not complete). The sites Ho I, Si and De I in *green*, *yellow* and *red* are discussed in the text (after Baum 2014, Fig. 1)

I mainly use GIS and ABM to integrate spatial, (paleo-) environmental and archaeological evidence with different competing models of land use in the wetland sites. The resulting scenarios are located in a hypothetical setting in order to underline the model character of WELASSIMO. To this aim, I chose a real landscape where no archaeological evidence is known, reconstructed a hypothetical natural environment integrating modern and paleo-environmental data, and simulated land-use activities in it as they have been reconstructed for the sites highlighted in Fig. 9.1, that were occupied in the early 4th Millennium BC. Thus it is possible to investigate the different pathways of landscape development and the systemic implications of certain hypotheses. The demand in non-finite resources such as livestock pasture, crop fields or suitable timber and their spatially and temporally varying availability can be assessed. In a second step, these hypothetical scenarios may be applied to specific archaeological sites integrating the local conditions, contributing to the understanding of the evolution of the earliest sedentary societies in this region.

9.2 Regional and Archaeological Setting

WELASSIMO is a tool to simulate the land-use of a hypothetical, idealized settlement, but I used data from several sites that have been excavated to a significant extent as a reference. Figure 9.1 shows the three main sites that were used to this aim. All sites are located in South-Western Germany in the vicinity of Lake

Constance. The larger Lake Constance area is shaped by the Würmian glaciation, as documented by numerous lakes of various sizes, kettle-hole peat-bogs, drumlin fields and wide areas of relatively fertile soils on glacial till. In the vicinity of Lake Constance, the sub-continental climatic conditions of the pre-alpine forelands are locally relatively favorable with moderate winters and mostly mild and humid summers. The site Ho1A (Hornstaad-Hörnle 1A, 3918—ca. 3905 BC) is located near the outlet of Lake Constance into the River Rhine. It was excavated to a large extent, and an impressive body of evidence is published on archaeological and ecological questions, e.g. Dieckmann et al. (2006), Matuschik (2011), Maier et al. (2001). Up to 45 houses were inhabited contemporaneously, each of which is interpreted by the authors as representing an individual economic unit. I use their interpretation for the sake of simplicity, despite new studies that demonstrate how the social system is likely to have been more complex than suggested by the equation house = household = nuclear family (Doppler et al. 2013). At the site Si (Sipplingen-Osthafen), up to 15 anthropogenic debris layers bear witness of frequent settlement activities from the 39th to the 24th century BC (Billamboz et al. 2010). Dendrotypological studies on the wooden house posts yield evidence of forest management systems, such as the use of primeval forest, the existence of coppiced forests, or intensive forest thinning (Billamboz and Köninger 2008; Billamboz 2014). For this project, I refer to the layers Si1 and Si2 (3919–3904 BC). The third settlement is De1A, which lies at the shores of Lake Degersee and was inhabited at the beginning of the 40th century BC for a few years only. It was partially excavated recently, and only preliminary results are published until now, e.g. (Maier et al. 2010).

9.3 The Economic System: Data and Hypotheses

The general properties of the socio-economic system of the wetland sites have been described by various authors in relative consistency, e.g. Menotti (2004), Jacomet (2009), Gross et al. (1990) and can thus be described as follows. The inhabitants of the wetland settlements lived on a mixed diet comprising of products from crop and livestock husbandry, hunting, gathering and fishing. The relative importance of these elements varied due to external and internal factors (e.g. Schibler and Jacomet 2010; Schibler 2006) but it is generally agreed on that cereals provided a large proportion of the calorie demand. Hypotheses on crop husbandry vary, but it is highly probable that the plough was not used during the 5th and the first half of the 4th millennium BC (Ebersbach 2002). People built elevated houses in close proximity to or directly in shallow lake areas or in peat bog. The average lifetime of the houses was only several years (Ebersbach 2010), and accordingly, the occupation time of many of the sites was short. Interpretation of published data by the individual authors with respect to the internal functioning of the subsystems, however, is not always consistent (e.g. Ehrmann et al. 2009; Bogaard 2002, 2004).

This is especially true for the crop husbandry system. The major hypotheses on crop husbandry systems are:

(1) Shifting Cultivation (SC). The main arguments for this hypothesis on crop husbandry and land-use is evidence for frequent large-scale fires and for an increase in scrubland vegetation dominated by hazel at the beginning of the 4th Millennium BC (Rösch et al. 2002; Rösch 2014), which is correlated with settlement activity (Lechterbeck et al. 2014). Several authors interpret these phenomena as a result of a land-use system that is based on ash fertilization of the crop fields, e.g. (Ehrmann et al. 2009; Schier 2009). In this system, high nutrient availability due to a burning procedure allows for high yields, while the high demand for wood for the burning and very intense weed growth in the second year after the fire necessitate an annual shifting of the fields. Based on experimental reconstruction of this system, I assume annually varying yields with a long-term average of 2700 kg/ha (100 % dry matter) for SC on soils of average quality (Ehrmann et al. 2009, p. 67). Annual variation of the yield due to weather conditions is accounted for in all simulated husbandry systems as described below. An important objection to this scenario is the evidence that backs the following hypothesis (IGC).
(2) Intensive Garden Cultivation (IGC). The weed content of well-preserved crop stores have been analyzed (e.g. Maier 1999; Bogaard 2004; Jacomet 2006) using, among others, the FIBS-approach (Charles et al. 1997). The ecological properties of the crop weed plants are interpreted as evidence for a crop husbandry regime, which is in contrast to SC—based on permanent fields that are cultivated for more than just a couple of years (Bogaard 2004, p. 41 ff.). The analysis of isotope relations of the cereal grains justify the assumption of the use of animal dung for manuring of the fields, so that a small-scale, permanent and highly intensive cultivation is reconstructed (Bogaard 2012; Bogaard et al. 2013). Based on data of the Rothamsted Research Station on long-term cultivation of wheat with manure application, I assume an average yield of 2000 kg/ha (100 % dry matter; Poulton 2006), also with annual variation due to weather events. IGC requires a large number of livestock for producing enough dung; however, archaeological reconstructions of the minimal number of animal individuals (MNI) in the lake-shore sites seldom meet these numbers (Ebersbach 2007; Ebersbach 2013). Furthermore, the hypothesis does not explain the peaks of charcoal and secondary forest found in the pollen stratigraphies.
(3) Non-Intensive Cultivation (NIC). This scenario is basically the same as IGC, but with the difference that no manure is applied and thus, yields are markedly lower and soil nutrient depletion may occur after some time. I assume an average yield of 800 kg/ha (100 % dry matter), also based on the Rothamsted dataset (Poulton 2006).
(4) Integrated Forest Horticulture (IFH). During the formulation of the model, it has become obvious that neither of the land-use models published so far (SC, NIC and IGC) is capable of integrating all data with confidence. Therefore, an

alternative scenario (IFH) has been formulated in the course of the modelling procedure, which combines elements of the other scenarios, but is in better agreement with the published archaeological and environmental evidence. In this scenario, a large amount of the calorie demand is covered by hazelnuts, the growth of which is promoted anthropogenically. Thus, the peaks of charcoal and secondary forest as documented by palynology (e.g. Rösch 2014) might result out of the targeted stimulation of hazel growth, not of cereal cultivation. Cereals, in contrast, could make up only a minor portion of the diet. Therefore, only small fields might be sufficient, and intensive cultivation and manuring as described for IGC can be performed with a lower livestock density. Both the observations that led to the formulation of the SC-Hypothesis and the evidence for manure application and small, permanent fields as in IGC are included in consistency.

Further models on economic subsystems include:

(5) Livestock husbandry regimes. The relative importance of livestock, especially cattle, is debated; while cattle bones with signs of butchery are found frequently, the reconstruction of an approximate number of cattle kept per person is difficult and varies spatially and chronologically (Ebersbach 2013). This is important not only with respect to the nutritional significance of livestock, but also in relation to the possible amount of manure available for IGC and IFH (see Bogaard 2012). As dense forests covered the land—at least at the beginning of the sequence—large areas were presumably needed for forest pasture and pollarding. As the fodder value (i.e. the amount of fodder per area) of secondary forest is much higher than that of old-growth primary forest, a further reason for the charcoal and hazel peaks may be found here.

(6) Forest management strategies. An ubiquitous and mostly well preserved element of the wetland sites are the remains of wooden construction piles. The analyses of their tree-ring patterns yields not only an absolute dating for the felling of the trees, but also information on the structural and compositional features of the forest stands they grew in (Billamboz and Köninger 2008; Bleicher 2009; Billamboz 2014). While coppiced forest or single tree selection dominated in some phases, in others only a few old trees seemed to be available. Likely for the ease of processing, quite young trees with a diameter of 5–20 cm were preferred in the beginning of the 4th Millennium. As these are not necessarily available in adequate numbers in a primeval forest, a suitable stand certainly constituted a valuable resource. Again, anthropogenically induced secondary forest growth might have been a valid strategy to improve resource availability.

(7) Foraging. Hunting, Gathering and Fishing are documented in most of the sites. The overall importance is difficult to assess for a number of reasons and may have varied largely (e.g. Schibler 2006; Jacomet 2006). Schlichtherle et al. (2010) stated a link between an increase in hunting and low crop harvests due to bad weather for the settlements at Lake Zürich. The importance of fish is not

well documented; however, Gross et al. (1990) stated that fish is low in calories and thus, a change in the quantity of fish cached would not necessarily make a large difference. Gathering of wild plants is documented regularly. Among the gathered plants are fruit, berries, herbs and especially nuts. Concerning the latter, it could be demonstrated that generally, they are extremely rich in calories and make an easy-to-store staple food (Holst 2010). While gathering activities are included in some detail within WELASSIMO, hunting and fishing are not treated as a single process but are instead merely represented in a schematic way.

9.4 The Model: Questions and Design

The proximate objective of WELASSIMO is an answer to the question, whether a need for a frequent settlement relocation (as documented by the archaeological record, e.g. Bleicher 2009; Dieckmann et al. 2006, p. 418; Ebersbach 2010) might have arisen out of the land use and the resource demand of the inhabitants of the wetland settlements at the beginning of the 4th Millennium BC. To this aim, I have programmed a simulation of the land use of a group of 1 to 20 households according to the relevant hypotheses integrating archaeological and (paleo-) environmental data. In contrast to the pattern observed by archaeology, households do not relocate after a number of years, but are permanently bound to one location. Thus, I want to observe whether resource scarcity arises after some time. Furthermore, an understanding of the systemic implications of different hypotheses on prehistoric land use as described above and of the resulting landscape is aimed at. I want to know, how large the economic area of the sites was, how the economic activities affected the environment—and vice versa, how the environmental conditions influenced the internal functioning of the sites. A more abstract objective is to analyze the human-environment-system and to define the fundamental parameters and factors. The research is facilitated by the large archaeobiological database published and the exact dating of settlement dynamics with annual resolution, as provided by dendrochronology. As a first step, I reconstructed the environment of a hypothetical settlement based on paleo-environmental and modern data. Therefore I chose an area of 5 × 5 km located in the Lake Constance area with similar geographic properties as in areas with well-known wetland settlements and a good availability of soil data and a high-resolution digital elevation model. This data (Table 9.1) was processed in Arc-GIS and transformed into grid cells with a

Table 9.1 Primary and derived data used to reconstruct the idealized environment of WELASSIMO. (DEM: © LGL Baden-Württemberg; Soil data: LGRB 2013)

Geodata	Derived grid cell data
Digital elevation model	Elevation; Slope; Aspect; Walking Chronozones
Modern soil map	Soil type; Vegetation cover

resolution of 25 × 25 m. These were used as the basis to generate a dynamic model environment with NETLOGO. Using the GIS-Extension of this agent-based programming software, a surface was created where every cell is characterized by a set of certain environmental parameters, some of which are static, such as elevation or soil type, others are dynamic and are updated in annual time steps, such as the state of the vegetation cover, the forest development phases or the quantity of relevant resources.

The modern soil map had to be adjusted to assumed Neolithic conditions, as certain modern soiltypes have only developed with intensified human impact since the Neolithic, and others have changed due to natural or anthropogenic processes (Gerlach 2006; Vogt 2014). Since the exact nature and amount of these changes is nearly impossible to assess, the reconstructions are necessarily tentative to a certain degree. Similarly, the allocation of a certain vegetation type to a grid cell is an idealized simplification. I defined standardized forest compositions, based on the naturally dominant tree species in the 4th Millennium as reconstructed by pollen analysis (Rösch 1990; Lechterbeck 2001) and on the modern natural vegetation in the region (Lang 1990), and assigned these communities to certain soil types. The age of the trees in primary lowland deciduous forests is not homogeneously distributed, but instead, these woods are characterized by a mosaic of stands of different development phases, as described by various authors (e.g. Härdtle et al. 2004, p. 85; Bernadzki et al. 1998; Bobiec 2012). Therefore also in WELASSIMO, the forest patches are grouped to "stands" randomly consisting of 1–20 cells sharing the same forest development phase. In the optimal and in the terminal phase, the characteristics and the resource availability are different from the regeneration and the juvenile phase. Especially, livestock fodder value, gathering value and timber availability vary. The stands mature with every model year and, by reaching a defined threshold, enter the next development phase. Thus, a simplified dynamic representation of vegetation succession and forest development phases is generated in a so-called cellular automaton.

The economic processes of interest are simulated as a second step inside of this environment. The basic unit (or "agent") of the model are the households = houses, which are idealized and represent a standardized group of assumed 6 persons comprising adults, children and elderly. The number of households is selectable in a range from 1 to 20, representing a population of 6–120 people. The main driver of the model is the annual demand in calories and non-finite resources of the households. The annual calorie demand of one household is defined as $365 * 6 * 2000 = 4{,}380{,}000$ kcal, which is the average demand of all potential inhabitants of the houses. In accordance with the objectives of this research, only non-finite resources that exhibit dynamic properties are considered: arable and fertile soil, livestock pasture, hunting/gathering/fishing areas, and suitable timber (see Table 9.2). Finite resources such as flint for tools or clay for pottery are not considered. The households have a set of subsistence strategies that they apply in order to meet their demand (see Fig. 9.2): crop husbandry, livestock husbandry, hunting/fishing and gathering, and timber extraction. While the basic properties, the timing and the functioning of these strategies is predefined and encoded inside of

Table 9.2 Quantitative data on resources per patch (1/16 ha = 25 × 25 m) as assumed in WELASSIMO. Numbers in brackets are the standard deviations of the specified mean. Values vary according to the forest development phase and environmental stochasticity (not for soil fertility). For livestock fodder, gather-value and soil fertility, the values are relative to 1 (the assumed maximum) and are further quantified in the model; values for suitable timber are absolute and give the range of numbers per patch

	Primary forest (beech) on luvisol	Primary forest (alder/ash) on gleysol	Primary forest (alder carr) on histosol	Young fallows	Secondary forest
Livestock fodder	0.2–0.3	0.3–0.4	0.2	1.0	0.5–0.6
Gather-value	0.005–0.01	0.005–0.01	0.005	0.05–0.6	0.6–1.0
Suitable timber	2–16	4–30	0	0	23–34 (7)
Soil fertility	1 (0.1)	0.7 (0.1)	0.2 (0.1)		

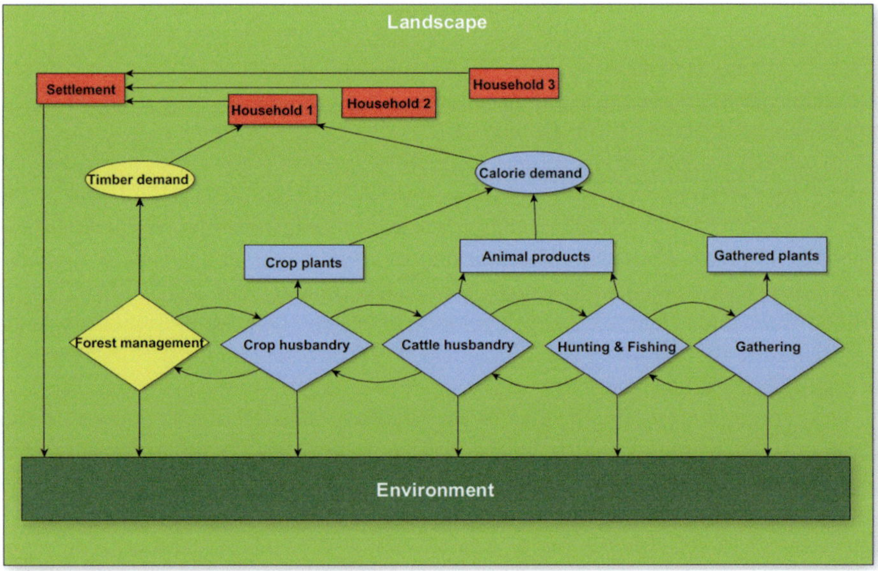

Fig. 9.2 Schema showing the interplay of the various elements of "Landscape" developing in the vicinity of a hypothetical wetland settlement in the 4th Millennium BC. Landscape is understood as the result of anthropogenic and natural processes shaping the human environment. Rectangles symbolize physical elements, diamonds denote processes, and ovals show system drivers. Arrows either denote influence on or affiliation to a certain element

the model, the exact configuration is defined by the observer, so that the outcome of various assumptions and hypotheses can be studied. The choice options for the observer are summarized in Table 9.3.

Table 9.3 Choice options for the observer

Cropping system	Importance of meat and fish	Source of plant calories (cultivated/gathered)	Source of meat calories (livestock/hunted and fished)
SC	Low (5 %)	100 % cultivated	100 % livestock
IGC	Medium (15 %)	80/20	75/25
NIC	High (25 %)	50/50	50/50
IFH	Not consumed	20/80	25/75
			100 % hunting and fishing

During a simulation run, the households cover their demand according to the chosen scenario. They always choose the patches with the desired properties which have the minimal traveling cost—a parameter that differs from the mere Euclidean distance in that realistic walking time is calculated by additionally taking into account the decreasing walking speed with increasing slope. For the crop fields, the soil type of the patches must be "Luvisol" and the slope must be below 25°, an arbitrary value. The other soiltypes that supposedly covered relevant areas in the Lake Constance area in the Neolithic are "Gleysol" and "Histosol", which are less well suited by far and therefore are excluded a priori. The size of the crop fields is calculated at the beginning of the simulation and remains fix for the subsequent years. The underlying assumption is that Neolithic people had acquired or inherited a knowledge about the most appropriate size of their fields, with respect to the available work force and the minimal proportion of crop calories aimed at. They definitely had experienced that crop yields fluctuate in wide ranges, and that the success and the fulfilling of the aims is dependent on external factors. To account for this context, the annual crop yield is calculated using the assumed average yield for the respective crop husbandry method as described above, modified by a factor for the soil fertility of the patch (which is dependent on the duration of crop production on this spot) and a factor which represents weather stochasticity. The rate of soil degradation is taken from a simulation performed with the crop simulation model "MONICA" (Nendel et al. 2011), while the influence of weather stochasticity is extracted from the same dataset and additionally from the yield series of the Rothamsted Experimental Station (Poulton 2006). An example of both the Rothamsted and the simulated yield series is shown in Fig. 9.3. This procedure means that if the observer chooses a diet comprising of 50 % cultivated plants to be produced with "IGC", the aim of one household would be to produce (4,380,000/2) = 2,190,000 kcal. As 1 kg of cereals equals 3000 kcal, and the average yield in IGC is assumed to be 2400 kg/ha, in this simulation run, one household cultivates an area of 0.3 ha equaling 5 patches. Yet due to stochasticity, yield success is likely to differ from the average yield. For reasons of simplicity, the only crop plant considered are cereals, although pulses, flax and poppy are also documented to a minor extent.

Average yields for the use in WELASSIMO are taken from the Rothamsted Dataset for IGC, IFH and NIC and from Ehrmann et al. (2009) for SC, while loss in

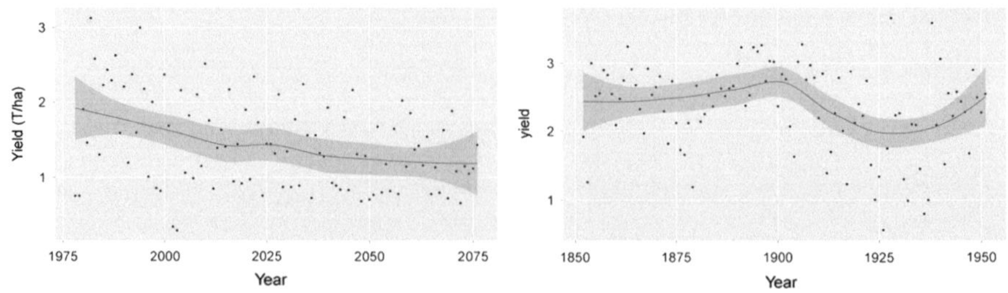

Fig. 9.3 *Left* Synthetic crop yield series (100 % dry matter) of 100 years simulated with the MONICA-model (Nendel et al. 2011). The scenario is IGC: annual application of manure (10 T/year/ha) and intensive weeding. The declining long-term trend is reflecting loss in soil fertility, while weather variability accounts for the annual variation. *Right* 100 years yield-series (100 % dry matter) as documented by Rothamsted Research. Yields increase slightly in the beginning due to a very high annual application of 35 T of manure per hectare. The decline in yields after 1900 AD is a consequence of reduced weeding, the rise of the curve is a consequence of renewed engagement and improved husbandry methods (Poulton 2006)

soil fertility is taken from the simulation. The annual demand in patches for livestock pasture and pollarding is dependent on the configuration set by the observer, and additionally on the vegetation cover of the patches. In the Neolithic wetland settlements, the minimum number of livestock individuals (MNI) per household lies between 0.1 and 4 (Ebersbach 2013). The livestock density in WELASSIMO uses these values as minimum and maximum values. Only cattle are considered, even if pigs, goat and sheep are also documented (e.g. Schibler 2006). If the importance of animal products and the proportion of domestics therein is set to high, or if IGC or IFH are selected and the need for animal dung is large, a higher MNI is used than if SC or NIC is chosen, and no livestock products are consumed at all. As shown by various authors, the area necessary to support one cow is highly dependent on the quality of the pasture or the area used for pollarding. While on grassland meadow (for which there is no proof in the Neolithic), 1.2 ha might be sufficient (Ebersbach 2002, p. 156), in a poor pine forest 20–30 ha are needed (Adams 1975, p. 148). In Welassimo, a minimum of 2 ha per cow on young fallowing areas and a maximum of 12 ha per cow in beech forest of the optimal and terminal phase are assumed. Livestock will choose patches with soil type not Histosol without crop fields with the least walking cost.

Also the area required for gathering is dependent on the model configuration as chosen by the observer and the vegetation cover of the respective patches. I assume that the maximal "gathering value" an area can have is reached when it is covered with secondary forest growth dominated by hazel, a vegetation type typical for the wetland sites as documented by palynology (e.g. Lechterbeck 2001; Rösch et al. 2014). Hazelnut kernels are extremely rich in calories (6000 kcal/kg). Using very conservative numbers given by Holst (2010), on one hectare of this vegetation type about 84 bushes may have grown in the Neolithic. 2000 nuts per bush may be harvested, adding up to an average of 900.000 kcal per year and hectare, divided by

16 for the patches (which have the size of 1/16 ha). These patches get the relative value of 1/16. The minimal gathering value a patch can have is arbitrarily set to 0.005/16. Thus, an area covered with mature hazelnut bushes yields 200 times more calories than the poorest areas (e.g. peat bog or optimal/terminal-phase beech forest). While the maximal value for nuts is backed by other studies, the lower number is speculative, and is open to discussion. The requirement in gathered calories of the households is the relative value of 1 * the proportion set by the observer, equaling a potential importance of minimum 0 and maximum 80 % of gathered calories. So, to meet this number, the households visit successively the patches beginning with the ones exhibiting the lowest travel costs, and add the respective gather value to their annual calories provision until the required amount is met.

The required area for hunting and fishing is not (yet) quantified, due to difficulties with finding reliable data. It is hypothetically assumed to have been sustainable; the simplifying assumption behind is that neither the populations of wild animals nor fish are severely limited in quantity as long as relatively small human populations exploit them. Furthermore, the degree of uncertainty with the decline in game or fish density due to human exploitation is dependent on too many factors to be simulated with confidence in this project. The only representation of these activities inside the model is the annual filling up of stocks according to the chosen parameters, with slight variations allowed for. The fluctuation of the success of calorie provision by livestock products, hunting, gathering and fishing in WELASSIMO is lower than the fluctuation of crop yields. If the observer chooses an importance of 5 % for one of these foodstuffs, than the actual value will be around 3–7 %. The reason for this is that field size is fix, and bad yields cannot be compensated by simply harvesting more patches. To the contrary, in hunting, fishing and gathering, endless resources are assumed, if the radius of action is extended. This is only possible because worktime limitations are not accounted for in WELASSIMO. The main reason is that they are used for validation; this is discussed below. As can be seen on the center panels of Figs. 9.4, 9.5, 9.6 and 9.7, in many cases the sum of all foodstuffs does not equal 100 % of the aim, but instead, over-and underachieving happens quite frequently. While in a real situation, people would try to mitigate this by increased investment in other calorie sources, this is not accounted for in WELASSIMO in order to highlight this effect.

The demand in timber is determined by the house age. A few logs are needed every year for reparations, while the probability of a complete reconstruction increases every year. In the year of the breakdown of the house, 120 logs of 5–20 cm are needed (combined after Luley 1992; Petrequin 1991). The area necessary to meet these numbers is dependent on the numbers of suitable timber per patch—again, patches with lowest travel cost are considered first, suitable timber extracted as needed and provided, and if needed, the next patch will be used as well. In the model, a beech forest in the optimal phase may have no suitable logs at all, while in the regeneration and in the juvenile phase of a mixed alder-ash forest, 400–600 such

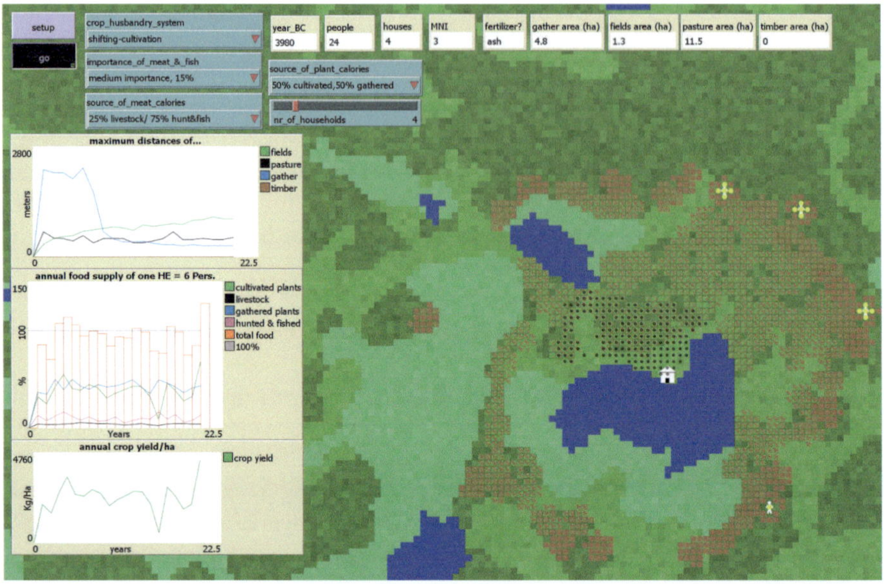

Fig. 9.4 Scenario 1 simulating land use, resource use and economic parameters of a hypothetical Neolithic wetland settlement relying on SC. *Grey* and *blue boxes* in the *upper left corner* are observer choice options, *white boxes* are monitors displaying current model conditions and results. (MNI = minimum number of individuals = livestock). *Blue areas* are lakes, different shades of *green* are forests of different species composition on specific soil, and brownish colors are fallowing patches. Only *dark green* colors (representing Luvisols) are soils suitable for agriculture. A *white house symbol* represents the settlement. *Black circles* mark patches affected by livestock browsing. One raster cell equals 25 * 25 m = 1/16 ha, the largest lake measures 750 m from east to west. Note that the maximum on the y-axis of the lowest panel is higher than in the other three scenarios

trees may be found (calculated after Korpel 1995, S. 127–137). On young secondary forest with ages of 20+ years, an assumed maximum of 700–800 suitable trees per hectare is simulated.

9.5 Four Scenarios

In order to exemplify the simulations, four scenarios with a configuration as described in Table 9.4 are presented in the Figs. 9.4, 9.5, 9.6 and 9.7, which show the simulations 20 years after the start (i.e. in the year 3980 BC). In order to highlight the implications of the cropping systems, the other parameters are unaltered or vary only to a minor extent. The model allows for any of the parameters in Table 9.4 to be changed, so the scenarios shown here represent only a few out of 320 possible configurations. The main window shows the landscape development due to the processes performed by the inhabitants of the households. In the upper

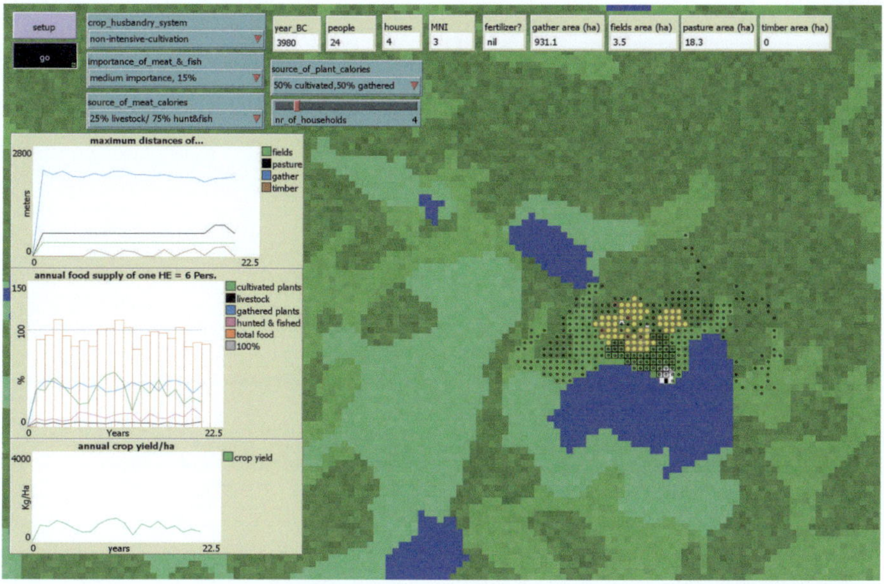

Fig. 9.5 Scenario 2 simulating land use, resource use and economic parameters of a hypothetical Neolithic wetland settlement relying on non-intensive cultivation. *Black boxes* are patches affected by timber extraction. The other symbols have been described in Fig. 9.4

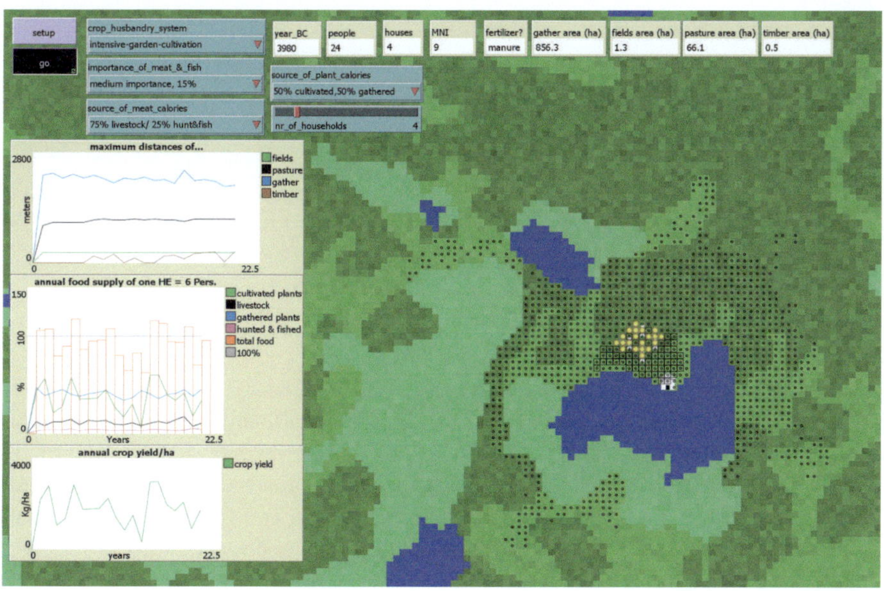

Fig. 9.6 Scenario 3 simulating land use, resource use and economic parameters of a hypothetical Neolithic wetland settlement relying on IGC. All symbols have been described in Figs. 9.4 and 9.5

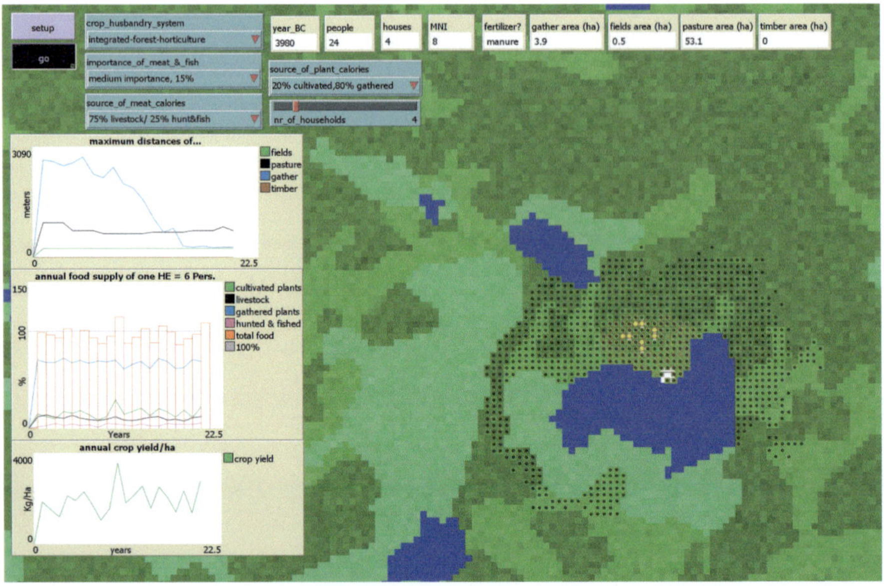

Fig. 9.7 Scenario 4 simulating land use, resource use and economic parameters of a hypothetical Neolithic wetland settlement performing IFH. All symbols have been described in Figs. 9.4 and 9.5

Table 9.4 Specifications of the Scenarios 1–4 as shown in Figs. 9.4, 9.5, 9.6 and 9.7 and discussed in the text. Abbreviations as above

	Cropping system	Importance of animal products	Source of plant calories	Source of meat calories
Scenario 1	SC	"Medium (15 %)"	"50 % cultivated, 50 % gathered"	"25 % livestock/75 % hunting and fishing"
Scenario 2	NIC	"Medium (15 %)"	"50 % cultivated, 50 % gathered"	"25 % livestock/25 % hunting and fishing"
Scenario 3	IGC	"Medium (15 %)"	"50 % cultivated, 50 % gathered"	"75 % livestock/25 % hunting and fishing"
Scenario 4	IFH	"Medium (15 %)"	"20 % cultivated, 80 % gathered"	":75 % livestock/25 % hunting and fishing"

left corner, model parameters can be specified. The small white boxes on the upper rim show details of the actual model status. On the lower left side of each of the panels, three monitors are located. The upper one shows the annual maximum distances for the economic activities of the settlers as conditioned by the model parameters. The panel in the center shows a graph where the annual food supply is plotted. Lines of different colors give the annual supply of the different categories adding to the calorie supply, while red bars show the total provisions in relation to the aim (=100 %), which may or may not be met due to stochastic factors of food production.

The lower panel displays the annual crop yield given in kg/ha, which is dependent on weather variability, soil fertility and the chosen cropping system. In each scenario, 24 persons in 4 households perform land and resource use in order to meet their requirements. The proportion of animal products is 15 % in all scenarios, while the cropping systems and the composition of the vegetal and the animal shares vary. Scenario one (Fig. 9.4) shows the application of SC. This practice allows for high yields per ha with a maximum of 4330 kg/ha in year 20 and thus, individual field size per year need not be large. Each household unit is burning and cultivating only 5 patches (yellow field symbol) equaling less than one third of a hectare. Altogether, the four households require an area of 1.3 ha to produce enough crop plants to cover (100 − 15)/2 = 42.5 % of their calorie demand (see Table 9.3). However, due to the additional forest area required to gain wood suitable for this specific burning procedure, large areas are affected in the course of twenty years. This is depicted by the brown patches symbolizing fallowing areas due to prior field use or forest cutting. As large forest areas are cleared annually, I assume that no additional areas for timber extraction are required. The fallowing areas provide possibly a very good livestock pasture, and only a small area is needed annually for this use category. Similarly, the growth of wild food plants such as berries, apples and especially hazelnuts is strongly stimulated on fallows of a certain age. Even when no direct anthropogenic promotion of these plants is assumed, the area necessary to cover a relevant proportion of the calorie demand by gathering is relatively low when the hazel bushes reach a certain age and start bearing nuts. Hazelnut—bushes need a few years to establish, and only from their 5th year on will they produce an annually increasing harvest of nuts in WELASSIMO. In year 15, they reach their maximum harvest potential and hold this for 35 years. In the upper panel of Fig. 9.4, the decreasing distances for gathering activities are observable. Pasture distances decrease less pronounced, as the difference in fodder—value between primary forest and fallowing land is not as large as in gathered human foodstuff. Additionally, the effect is masked by the low MNI and the large fallowing area from year two on. The farthest distance of economic activities is about 1000 m after twenty years, and the reason for this distance is the high land demand for SC. As can be seen in the center panel, food requirements are met in 9 years out of twenty. This is however not related to the cropping system, but is due to the built-in stochasticity of yields due to weather variability simulated by the model. A bad series of low crop yields occurs in years 1 and 2 and in the years 14 and 15 of the simulation. In WELASSIMO, this has no consequences for the settlers, as an assessment of the consequences of food shortages and demographic implications are not the aim of this research.

Scenario two shows the situation for NIC (Fig. 9.5). All model parameters except the cropping system are the same as in Scenario 1. As no fertilizing occurs, annual yields are quite low with a maximum of 1050 kg/ha in year 10, and nutrient depletion further affects the crops as cultivation duration increases. 14 patches are needed per household, equaling 3.5 ha for the four households. Successively, the households will relocate the fields when a certain threshold of soil fertility is reached and yields begin to decrease largely. Only a few fallowing patches are seen bordering the fields. As most other areas are primary forest, which is relatively low in animal fodder, a larger area than in scenario 1 is needed for the feeding of the livestock. The same holds true for wild edible plants, so in order to cover the same proportion of calorie demand from wild plants as in the SC scenario, a much larger area is needed (931 ha in comparison to 4.8 ha). Black boxes around patches in Figs. 9.5 and 9.6 symbolize areas affected by timber extraction. In the course of time, the distances for this activity increase, as nearest suitable trees to the settlement are felled first and more distant ones later. After 20 years, the distance to meet the demand in suitable construction timber has reached 200 m for the 4 households. The distance to the other economic activities does not change to a large extent in the course of time. The calorie requirements are met in 9 out of 20 years. In year 12, a bad crop yield occurs, and only 78 % of the food provisions are acquired.

Scenario three (Fig. 9.6) depicts the situation for IGC. All model parameters remain the same as before, except the source of meat calories as described below. Due to intensive weeding and manuring, permanent fields cultivated for several years may be assumed without relevant soil nutrient depletion. Field sizes are quite small due to relatively high yields per ha (avg. 2400 kg), and 5 patches equaling a third of a hectare are sufficient for one household. The fact that the number of patches for crop husbandry are the same as in scenario 1 is due to rounding of decimal places in the model; exact numbers differ, but this is not shown. The high manure application necessitates a quite large MNI (Minimal Number of Individuals, i.e. livestock). This is automatically accounted for inside the model script when IGC or IFH are selected; to highlight these relationships, I have raised the share of livestock for the supply with animal products (which remains medium = 15 %) deliberately to 75 %. The high MNI require a large area annually for forest-grazing and pollarding. As already discussed above, primary forest is lower in livestock fodder; thus in scenario three, very large areas are needed to feed the livestock. Yet similar as in scenario 2, the largest area is needed for gathering wild edible plants. While the distances of fields and pastures remain more or less stable, the need for suitable timber constantly leads to more distant timber areas as already shown in scenario two. The calorie requirements are met in 7 out of 20 years only, with a remarkable depression in calorie supply in the years 10–13—but again, this is not reflecting any other factor than the built-in stochasticity of yields due to weather variability.

Scenario four simulates the application of IFH. The source of calories of animal origin is 75 % livestock and 25 % hunted, as in scenario 3, but in contrast to the other scenarios, only 20 % of the vegetable calories are covered by crop plants, while 80 % are collected, the bulk of which is assumed to be hazelnuts. This represents the hypothesis that the well-documented hazel and charcoal peaks in the pollen profiles might rather reflect the use of fire for the opening and shaping of the vegetation cover, than being coincidental side-effects of SC. As the benefit of these measures would not only be the promotion of hazel growth, but as well good livestock browsing and presumably higher numbers of suitable timber than found in primary forest, the necessary zone of land-use activities may be smaller than in the

Table 9.5 An overview of the maximum distances for economic activities for a simulated settlement size of 4 households (=24 persons) as a result of WELASSIMO

Scenario	5 years, 4 households	20 years, 4 households
1	2.2 km, gathering	1.0 km, fields
2	2.0 km, gathering	2.0 km, gathering
3	2.1 km, gathering	2.1 km, gathering
4	2.8 km, gathering	0.7 km, pasture

previous scenarios. This effect will show after a few years of cultivation, as can be seen in the upper graph of Fig. 9.7. In the beginning of the simulation, when no nut-bearing hazel bushes exist, the high proportion of gathered calories causes a large radius for gathering activities (note the maximum value on the y-axis, which is different from the other three scenarios). After a couple of years, however, this distance is reduced drastically, and then the most distant activities are livestock browsing in 740 m distance—thus, IFH allows for the smallest economic area of all scenarios. The annual opening of new fields for the creation of new "forest gardens" is assumed to cover the need in timber, thus no extra area is needed similar as in scenario 1, and in contrast to scenarios 2 and 3. As intensive cultivation of the fields is assumed here similar to IGC, and due to the low proportion of cultivated plants, only two field patches per household are sufficient, which is equivalent to an eighth of a hectare per household or 0.5 ha for 4 households An MNI of 8 heads of livestock for the settlement results out of this configuration. The calorie requirements are met in 18 out of 20 years, with a set of bad harvest in collected plants paralleled by low crop yields in the years 5 and 6 of the simulation. Annual variation in the harvest of gathered plants is assumed to be less fluctuating than for crop yields, which is discussed below; the effect of this hypothesis is less variation and less pronounced extremes of food supply. This is especially evident in year 10 of the simulation, where a remarkable peak in crop yields of 3570 kg/ha results only in a minor over-achieving of the total provisions. Table 9.5 gives an overview of the maximum distances for economic activities resulting out of different configurations after 10 and 25 years of simulation for the scenarios described above.

9.6 Discussion

What can we learn from these scenarios? Are they plausible, and can the degree of credibility be estimated? Is it possible to validate such as model at all? WELASSIMO is a simulation of a complex system of human—environment interactions and processes, which took place 6000 years ago; it is impossible to validate such a model with the same degree of reliability as a model of recent processes, because of the lack of real, "living" analogies of the model. However, it is possible to check the general plausibility and perform some tests to build confidence. The basic properties are taken for granted and need not be validated, as they are evidenced unequivocally by archaeology and archaeobiology: people lived in wooden houses that were constructed in close vicinity of lakes and mires and lived on a diet comprising of cultivated and gathered plants and animal products of domestic and wild animals. Also, a general transferability of knowledge on recent ecosystem features to the reconstructed ecosystem of the 4th Millennium can be taken for granted. When it comes to the details in the data used, the difficulties arise; e.g. for the amount of calories that may be gathered on one hectare of primary deciduous forest (see Table 9.2), or for the rate of annual variation in the gathering success of the settlements. Such numbers are very difficult to verify, as modern analogies of hunter-gatherers especially in the biome of the mid-latitude deciduous forests are virtually non-existent and thus, ethnographic evidence is scarce. Thus, I regard these data as good estimations that are open to discussion. Here lies the first one of a number of advantages of the approach: the input data is transparent, and can be modified or supplemented quite easily, if necessary. If the validity of the database is generally agreed on, keeping the articulated uncertainties in mind, the next question concerns the plausibility of the different scenarios. With the presented approach, a broad variety of different assumptions and hypotheses can be displayed. This helps to reduce the danger of too narrow or fixed presumptions in the modeling process. But at the same time, the question arises how to evaluate the scenarios; is it possible to isolate the one "solution scenario", giving an answer to "how were things REALLY working back then"? The answer must be "no", because no validation method exists with the required degree of reliability. But can certain scenarios be ruled out for some reasons? Work load calculations are an important factor in this discussion. These are not included in WELASSIMO, because only independent data that is not used for the simulations can be used as a test for the scenarios. Furthermore, the temporal resolution of one year turned out to be unsuited to integrate work load in detail, which is relevant rather on a daily or even lower scale. To check whether the scenarios are in accordance with the available work force, I use data published by Kerig (2008). He could demonstrate that one person may prepare one ha of crop fields on already established plots in 29 days. Probably imposing a somewhat stronger limitation for field size was the labor associated with weeding and crop harvest; here, Kerig states that one worker with a silex-knife can process 0.9 ha during the harvesting season (Beginning of July—mid of September). If the available workforce of the households in WELASSIMO is assumed to be 2.5 full-working persons (two adults and one child), 2.5 ha can be seen as the potential maximum a household could handle. The largest fields in a permanent cultivation technique (for which Kerigs figures apply) are simulated to be 2 ha, if 100 % of the calories are provided by crop plants and NIC is assumed. IGC and IFH have higher yields per ha, which possibly decreases the associated work load—however, this might be neutralized due to the additional workload in these systems for manuring and intensive care. The work load associated with SC is described by Ehrmann et al. (2009) according to results obtained in a large-scale experiment in Forchtenberg, Germany. According to their research, 800 full working days are necessary for one hectare of fields in SC. With an assumed average yield of 3000 kg of cereal using SC, as found by Ehrmann et al. on soils of "average" quality, and 2.5 workers as above, 96 full working days per year are required in order to meet the calorie requirements discussed for scenario 1 (see above). Ehrmann et al. calculate with the value they found for "good" soils of 5000 kg/ha; thus, a total of 50 days would be needed with the other configurations unchanged. Even if a hypothetic proportion of 100 % crop plants is assumed, and parts of the work could be done outside of the time needed for field preparation and harvesting, the respective work load could be handled. To sum up, the work load associated with crop production would most probably not pose a severe limitation for any of the scenarios realized within WELASSIMO. To investigate on the combined work load of all subsistence practices together would require a simulation with daily resolution; this is aimed at in future projects. The work load associated with Hazelnuts is in detail discussed in Holst (2010). She states that the harvesting season for Hazelnuts lasts around 14 days in the end of September, so no conflict arises with crop harvest. In one hour, she could harvest 1.26 kg of Nutmeat (equivalent of 1400 Nuts with 0.9 g each). 2.5 workers could harvest at the very least 300 kg per season. With 6000 kcal per kg of nutmeat, this equals 1.800.000 kcal per group of 6 or 300,000 kcal per person. For the configuration as in Scenario 4 with 85 % vegetable foodstuff of which 80 % are gathered, the requirements are 496,000 kcal gathered. So these numbers do not seem realistic; but if the importance of gathered food is reduced to 50 %, the assumed 300 kg Hazelnuts per group of 6 are sufficient.

As stated above, it has become evident in the modelling process that neither of the previous land-use models (SC, NIC and IGC) is capable of integrating all data with confidence. This is better achieved with the alternative scenario of "Integrated Forest Horticulture (IFH)", which is formulated above. The fact that seemingly contradictory positive evidence on crop husbandry in the wetland settlements in the early 4th Millennium, which led to the formulation of the hypotheses SC, IGC or NIC, is included without being contradictory, is a hint that IFH might be the closest one to the Neolithic "reality" of all 4 land-use methods discussed. Until now, the charcoal and secondary forest peaks detected by pollen analyses were mainly seen as a by-product of SC (e.g. Rösch et al. 2014); if this was true, the evidence of manuring of the crop plants as documented for the site Ho1A (Bogaard et al. 2013) as well as the evidence for permanent fields with a distinct weed flora (e.g. Maier et al. 2001; Maier 1999; Jacomet et al. 2004, p. 136) would require explanation—which is very hard to give, then. Yet if it is assumed that the origin of the weed remains and the evidence for manuring is indeed a permanent and intensive form of crop husbandry, as interpreted by the researchers (e.g. Bogaard 2002; Bogaard et al. 2013), an explanation for the peaks documented by palynology is needed. As shown in scenario 4, a targeted promotion and facilitation of secondary forest growth by the use of fire and the parallel application of intensive cultivation methods for crop husbandry would be in good accordance with the existing data and at the same time provide systemic benefits, which could be demonstrated above. Here, the second advantage of an agent-based simulation approach becomes evident: the loose ends of the observed system, which are provided by the involved disciplines, may be woven into a stringent net of explanation, which considers the most of the available data. In the discussion of the increased value of patches with fallows or young secondary forest vegetation in contrast to their "wild" environment, the term "landscape" is so illustrative that I want to highlight its significance and sharpen its scope. One might as well use the term "cultural landscape", but this is actually a pleonasm; both denote a strip of land that has been anthropogenically shaped. In the case observed, the landscape offers a higher economic value than the "wild" environment (I set "wild" in quotation marks because most likely, even those areas were influenced by humans to a certain degree). This applies most drastically for the amount of calories from gathered plants, especially from hazelnuts. To a minor extent, also the quantity and quality of livestock fodder increases in these areas, and also the availability of suitable timber in the right dimensions for house construction is triggered by the initiation of secondary forest growth. It is likely, that even the density of certain wild animal species used for hunting is positively correlated with a certain degree of openness of the landscape. In spite of these advantages, I do not claim that IFH is depicting "true" Neolithic conditions without any doubt, and that the other hypotheses are wrong; to the contrary, it is highly probable that elements of SC, IGC and NIC have been realized as well, but not in an exclusive, but in an integrative manner. And even the IFH Scenario is simply a model that explains some data—many aspects are not included, others are generalized, rough assumptions are used: it has to be stressed that no model can ever display the full complexity of such a system.

9.6.1 Resource Use as a Need for Relocation?

The main question named initially is, whether a necessity for a settlement relocation arises due to the land and resource use of the people. Which subsistence strategy might contribute to this need, if any? For crop husbandry, the only scenario simulated in WELASSIMO, where a settlement shift after one or two house generations arguably makes sense, is SC. After this time, the distance to new fields might have grown large enough to motivate a settlement shift. If the parameters are set to force the maximum number of 120 people in WELASSIMO as far away as possible in a system that is still in accordance with the data—exhibiting the general properties as described above—then, a maximum distance of 2.5 km is necessary, which is reached after 30 years (SC, 5 % animal products, 80 % of plant calories are cultivated). In his investigation on current practices of SC in India, Pratap (2000, p.72) describes an example that daily walking distances to SC plots are normally 1–2 km. On the other hand, the same author states on p. 84 that "the axiom of settlement mobility, as a logical necessity in SC Systems, is itself an a priori assumption often overriding the complexity of real-world situations." Furthermore, Saradindu (1967) observes that fields are shifted annually in much larger radii of 6–7 miles. This means that daily travelling distances of 2.5 km are not necessarily forcing households to shift their location. Considering the alternative explanations of findings—

that were originally used to back the hypothesis of SC—as described in the IFH-scenario, I think, that the theoretical benefits of the SC-Hypothesis need not further be discussed, because there is positive bioarchaeological counterevidence against it as the dominant mode of husbandry. In the other scenarios 4, 3 and 2, no economic reason appears to be motivating a settlement shift (for 2 and 3, the same restrictions are valid as for scenario 1: they are rather theoretically relevant, because they do not explain all data). To the contrary: as described above, the economic value of a landscape would rather increase with ongoing duration of use through an increase in the amount of livestock fodder and especially the gathering value connected with hazelnuts. Furthermore, paths have formed and familiarity with the surroundings may be suspected. The only resource which causes slightly increasing distances for its extraction is timber; but distances are far less than for the other activities with a maximum of 200 m for 4 households after 20 years. From all this it seems plausible to assume a certain degree of spatial stability and commitment to the site—but nonetheless, in many cases, the contrary is evidenced: a highly dynamic settlement system with a frequent relocation of the sites (e.g. Ebersbach 2010). From the preceding considerations, it is highly implausible that the land use activity of a small community caused the observed relocation pattern. Even if the number of households is set to 20, this does not change the situation drastically. It is a different thing, however, when not a hypothetical determining necessity for a relocation, but the relative benefit of a settlement shift is considered. Even if the landscape around the settlement is something appraised that is to be maintained, low-distance relocations might nonetheless be assumed, as the appreciation of the economic area does not necessarily include the site itself. A similar situation is documented for the site of Ho1A: after the documented destruction of many of the houses in 3910, a number of new houses with the building year 3909 were constructed only a few hundred meters away in the site of Ho3 (Dieckmann et al. 2006, p.418; Billamboz 2006, p. 314). As the construction elements of the houses had a limited lifetime seldom exceeding the span of 10–20 years, a restoration or rebuilding was required quite frequently. Suitable timber in considerable numbers was thus needed in a temporal pattern of relatively high predictability. Additionally, the availability of fuel wood likely decreased in the proximity of the settlement in the course of several years. Furthermore, the specific site preferences might have caused a small-scale shift of the buildings, as lake levels of Lake Constance as well as of smaller lakes in the vicinity did fluctuate markedly and frequently. So if a house needed to be rebuilt for whatever reason, and a stand of suitable timber was growing adjacent to a suitable settlement location—maybe people rather carried their few belongings to a newly constructed house, than carrying (the timber of) their new house to their belongings, if all the economic benefits of the cultural landscape could be maintained. Drivers and benefits of the abandonment of a specific site and its relocation inside the cultural landscape may have been acts of convenience, of hygiene or of environmental forcing other than resource availability—or a combination of those. The above discussions are valid especially for smaller settlements with a relatively low population density of the landscape; a different situation might arise, if more and larger settlements in a defined landscape need more resources and affect their environment more intensely; a simulation to deal with this situation is currently prepared for the sites located near the effluence of Lake Zürich into the river Limmat.

9.7 Conclusions

In this chapter, I have presented an agent–based simulation of landscape development due to anthropogenic processes in the context of the Neolithic wetland settlements in the north-western pre-alpine forelands. WELASSIMO integrates (paleo-) environmental and archaeological data and is capable of dynamically displaying the implications of various hypotheses on land use. The requirements of the non-finite resources soil fertility, suitable timber, livestock fodder and gathered plants is dynamically quantified, while finite resources such as flint are not considered. The major motivation for this research is the question, why the inhabitants of the settlements shifted their houses and thus abandoned the settlements with the high frequency observed. The hypothesis was put forth, that this might be related to the land–use activities of the people and decreasing or degrading resources or ecosystem services. To test this hypothesis, 4 scenarios were simulated, which display 4 different models on crop husbandry: Shifting Cultivation (SC), Intensive Garden Cultivation (IGC), Non-intensive Cultivation (NIC) and Integrated Forest Horticulture (IFH), the latter of which has been described here for the first time. Most other specifications of the observed system such as livestock herding, foraging and timber extraction and the settlement size have been unchanged, while nutritional habits were changed to a minor extent to underline assumptions made in the formulation of the scenarios. The results of the simulations are indicating that for a relatively small settlement, the non-finite resources probably have not been limiting and thus did most likely not determine the observed settlement pattern, which is characterized by a high mobility. To the contrary, the landscapes around the settlements did most likely provide a higher economic value than their environments, and were thus probably regarded as a valuable resource in themselves. IFH is regarded as the most proximate scenario to the conditions in the early 4th Millennium BC, as it comprises all positive evidence that support the other hypothesis IGC, SC and NIC, without the necessity to ignore data. This implies the possibility that hazelnuts play a more important role than assumed before. Long-established proof for large areas covered with hazel scrubland in the environment of the settlements, the very high nutritional value of hazelnuts and the ease of processing and the high suitability for storage justify these assumptions.

Acknowledgments I thank the Lawes Agricultural Trust and Rothamsted Research for data from the e-RA database. The Rothamsted Long-term Experiments National Capability (LTE-NCG) is supported by the UK Biotechnology and Biological Sciences Research Council and the Lawes Agricultural Trust.

References

Adams S (1975) Sheep and cattle grazing in forests: a review. J Appl Ecol:143–152

Baum TG (2014) Models of wetland settlement and associated land use in South-West Germany during the fourth millennium BC. Veg Hist Archaeobotany 23(1):67–80

Bernadzki E, Bolibok L, Brzeziecki B, Zajączkowski J, Żybura H (1998) Compositional dynamics of natural forests in the Bialowieza National Park, northeastern Poland. J Veg Sci 9(2):229–238

Billamboz A (2006) Dendroarchäologische Untersuchungen in den neolithischen Ufersiedlungen von Hornstaad-Hörnle. In: Hornstaad-Hörnle 1A. Die Befunde einer jungneolithischen Pfahlbausiedlung am westlichen Bodensee, vol IX. Siedlungsarchäologie im Alpenvorland. Theiss, Stuttgart, pp 23–232

Billamboz A (2014) Regional patterns of settlement and woodland developments: Dendroarchaeology in the Neolithic pile-dwellings on Lake Constance (Germany). The Holocene 24 (10):1278–1287

Billamboz A, Köninger J (2008) Dendroarchäologische Untersuchungen zur Besiedlungs- und Landschaftsentwicklung des westlichen Bodenseegebietes. In: Dörfler W, Müller J (eds) Umwelt-Wirtschaft-Siedlungen im dritten vorchristlichen Jahrtausend Mitteleuropas und Südskandinaviens, vol 84. Offa—Bücher. Wachholtz, Neumünster

Billamboz A, Maier U, Matuschik I, Müller A, Vogt R, Out W, Steppan K (2010) Die Jung- und endneolithischen Seeufersiedlungen von Sipplingen-Osthafen am Bodensee: Besiedlungs- und Wirtschaftsdynamik im eng begrenzten Raum des Sipplinger Dreiecks. In: Matuschik I, Strahm C (eds) Vernetzungen. Festschrift für Helmut Schlichtherle. Lavori, Freiburg 2010

Bleicher N (2009) Altes Holz in neuem Licht. Hochschulschrift, Theiss, Stuttgart

Bobiec A (2012) Białowieża Primeval Forest as a remnant of culturally modified ancient forest. Eur J Forest Res 131(5):1269–1285

Bogaard A (2002) Questioning the relevance of shifting cultivation to Neolithic farming in the loess belt of Europe: evidence from the Hambach Forest experiment. Veg Hist Archaeobotany 11(1–2):155–168

Bogaard A (2004) Neolithic farming in central Europe. An archaeobotanical study of crop husbandry practices, 1st edn. Routledge, London

Bogaard A (2012) Middening and manuring in Neolithic Europe: issues of plausibility, intensity and archaeological method. In: Manure: historical, archaeological and ethnographic perspectives. Ashgate, Farnham, pp 25–40

Bogaard A, Fraser R, Heaton TH, Wallace M, Vaiglova P, Charles M, Jones G, Evershed RP, Styring AK, Andersen NH (2013) Crop manuring and intensive land management by Europe's first farmers. Proc Natl Acad Sci 110(31):12589–12594

Charles M, Jones G, Hodgson J (1997) FIBS in archaeobotany: functional interpretation of weed floras in relation to husbandry practices. J Archaeol Sci 24(12):1151–1161

DeCapitani A, Deschler-Erb S, Leuzinger U, Marti-Grädel E, Schibler J (2002) Die jungsteinzeitliche Seeufersiedlung Arbon/Bleiche 3: Funde. Archäologie im Thurgau Bd 11

Dieckmann B, Harwarth A, Hoffstadt J, Billamboz A (2006) Hornstaad-Hörnle 1A. Die Befunde einer jungneolithischen Pfahlbausiedlung am westlichen Bodensee, vol IX. Siedlungsarchäologie im Alpenvorland. Theiss, Stuttgart

Doppler T, Pichler S, Röder B, Schibler J (2013) Coping with Crises I: Subsistence variety and resilience in the neolithic lake shore settlement Arbon-Bleiche 3 (Switzerland). In: Kerig T, Zimmermann A (eds) Economic Archaeology. From structure to performance in european archaeology, vol 37. Universitätsforschungen zur prähistorischen Archäologie. Habelt, Bonn, pp 163–174

Ebersbach R (2002) Von Bauern und Rindern: eine Ökosystemanalyse zur Bedeutung der Rinderhaltung in bäuerlichen Gesellschaften als Grundlage zu Modellbildung im Neolithikum. Schwabe, Basel

Ebersbach R (2007) Glückliche Milch von glücklichen Kühen? Zur Bedeutung der Rinderhaltung in (neolithischen) Wirtschaftssystemen. In: Beiträge zum Göttinger Umwelthistorischen Kolloquium 2004–2006. Universitätsverlag Göttingen, p 41

Ebersbach R (2010) Vom Entstehen und Vergehen. Überlegungen zur Dynamik von Feuchtbodenhäusern und—siedlungen. In: Matuschik I, Strahm C (eds) Vernetzungen. Festschrift für Helmut Schlichtherle. Lavori, Freiburg

Ebersbach R (2013) Quantitative approaches to reconstructing prehistoric stock breeding. In: Kerig T, Zimmermann A (eds) Economic Archaeology. From structure to performance in European archaeology, vol 37. Universitätsforschungen zur prähistorischen Archäologie. Habelt, Bonn, pp 143–162

Ehrmann O, Rösch M, Schier W (2009) Experimentelle Rekonstruktion eines jungneolithischen Wald-Feldbaus mit Feuereinsatz, ein multidisziplinäres Forschungsprojekt zur Wirtschaftsarchäologie und Landschaftsökologie. Praehistorische Zeitschrift 84(1):44–72. doi:10.1515/pz.2009.003

Gerlach R (2006) Die Umgestaltung der Landschaft durch den Menschen seit dem Neolithikum. In: Kunow JWH (ed) Urgeschichte im Rheinland. Verlag des Rheinischen Vereins für Denkmalpflege und Landschaftsschutz, Köln, pp 87–98

Gross E, Jacomet S, Schibler J (1990) Stand und Ziele der wirtschaftsarchäologischen Forschung an neolithischen Ufer- und Inselsiedlungen im unteren Zürichseeraum (Kt. Zürich, Schweiz). In: Schibler J, Sedlmaier J, Spycher H (eds) Festschrift Hans R. Stampfli. Verlag Helbig &Lichtenhahn, Basel, pp 77–100

Härdtle W, Ewald J, Hölzel N (2004) Wälder des Tieflandes und der Mittelgebirge. Eugen Ulmer

Holst D (2010) Hazelnut economy of early Holocene hunter–gatherers: a case study from Mesolithic Duvensee, northern Germany. J Archaeol Sci 37(11):2871–2880

Jacomet S (2006) Plant economy of the northern Alpine lake dwellings—3500–2400 cal. BC. Environ Archaeol 11(1):65–85

Jacomet S (2009) Plant economy and village life in Neolithic lake dwellings at the time of the Alpine Iceman. Veg Hist Archaeobotany 18(1):47–59

Jacomet S, Leuzinger U, Bouchet F, De Capitani A (2004) Die jungsteinzeitliche Seeufersiedlung Arbon, Bleiche 3: Veröffentlichungen des Amtes für Archäologie des Kantons Thurgau. Umwelt und Wirtschaft. vol Bd. 3. Amt für Archäologie, Frauenfeld

Jacomet S, Schibler J (2010) Short climatic fluctuations and their impact on human economies and societies: the potential of the Neolithic lake shore settlements in the Alpine Foreland. Environmental archaeology 15(2):173–182

Kerig T (2008) Als Adam grub…. Vergleichende Anmerkungen zu landwirtschaftlichen Betriebsgrößen In prähistorischer Zeit. Ethnographisch-archaologische Zeitschrift 48(3): 375–402

Korpel S (1995) Die Urwälder der Westkarpaten. Gustav Fischer Verlag, Stuttgart

Lang G (1990) Die Vegetation des westlichen Bodenseegebietes: mit … 33 Tabellen im Text, sowie 86 Tabellen … im Anhang. 2., erg. Aufl. edn. G. Fischer, Stuttgart

Lechterbeck J (2001) "Human impact" oder "climatic change"? zur Vegetationsgeschichte des Spätglazials und Holozäns in hochauflösenden Pollenanalysen laminierter Sedimente des Steißlinger Sees (Südwestdeutschland). Tübingen

Lechterbeck J, Edinborough K, Kerig T, Fyfe R, Roberts N, Shennan S (2014) Is Neolithic land use correlated with demography? An evaluation of pollen-derived land cover and radiocarbon-inferred demographic change from Central Europe. The Holocene 24(10): 1297–1307

LGRB (2013) Bodenkarte 1: 50 000 (GeoLa. Regierungspräsidium Freiburg, Landesamt für Geologie, Rohstoffe und Bergbau: Geodaten der Integrierten geowissenschaftlichen Landesaufnahme (GeoLa). Freiburg

Luley H (1992) Urgeschichtlicher Hausbau in Mitteleuropa. Hochschulschrift, Habelt, Bonn

Maier U (1999) Agricultural activities and land use in a neolithic village around 3900 B.C.: Hornstaad Hörnle 1A, Lake Constance. Ger Veg Hist Archaeobotany 8(1–2):87–94

Maier U, Mainberger M, Merkt J, Kleinmann A, Vogt R, Späth S, Baum T (2010) Das DFG-Projekt "Degersee": Fortgang der Arbeiten und neue Entdeckungen. In: LfDiR Stuttgart (ed) Archäologische Ausgrabungen in Baden-Württemberg 2009. Konrad Theiss Verlag, Stuttgart

Maier U, Vogt R, Ahrens M (2001) Botanische und pedologische Untersuchungen zur Ufersiedlung Hornstaad-Hörnle IA, vol 74. Siedlungsarchäologie im Alpenvorland 6. Forsch.Ber.Ur-u. Frühgesch. Baden-Württemberg. Theiss, Stuttgart

Matuschik IM (2011) Die Keramikfunde von Hornstaad-Hörnle I-VI: Besiedlungsgeschichte der Fundstelle und Keramikentwicklung im beginnenden 4. Jahrtausend v. Chr. im Bodenseeraum. Siedlungsarchäologie im Alpenvorland, vol 12. Theiss, Stuttgart

Menotti F (ed) (2004) Living on the lake in prehistoric Europe. 150 years of lake dwelling research. Routledge, London/New York

Nendel C, Berg M, Kersebaum K, Mirschel W, Specka X, Wegehenkel M, Wenkel K, Wieland R (2011) The MONICA model: testing predictability for crop growth, soil moisture and nitrogen dynamics. Ecol Model 222(9):1614–1625

Pétrequin P (1991) Construire une maison 3000 ans avant J.-C. le lac de Chalain au néolithique [1] [1]. Ed. Errance, Paris

Poulton P (2006) Rothamsted research: guide to the classical and other long-term experiments, datasets and sample archive. Lawes Agric Trust Co, Harpenden, UK

Pratap A (2000) The hoe and the axe. Oxford University Press, New Delhi

Rösch M (1990) Vegetationsgeschichtliche Untersuchungen im Durchenbergried. In: Siedlungsarchäologie im Alpenvorland 2. Forsch. u. Ber. z. Vor- u. Frühgeschichte Bad.-Württ. 37. Stuttgart 1990, pp 9–56

Rösch M, Ehrmann O, Herrmann L, Schulz E, Bogenrieder A, Goldammer JP, Hall M, Page H, Schier W (2002) An experimental approach to Neolithic shifting cultivation. Veg Hist Archaeobotany 11(1–2):143–154

Rösch M, Kleinmann A, Lechterbeck J, Wick L (2014) Botanical off-site and on-site data as indicators of different land use systems: a discussion with examples from Southwest Germany. Veg Hist Archaeobotany 23(1):121–133

Saradindu B (1967) Carrying capacity of land under shifting cultivation. The Asiatic Society monograph series, vol 12. Asiatic Society, Calcutta

Schibler J (2006) The economy and environment of the 4th and 3rd millennia BC in the northern Alpine foreland based on studies of animal bones. Environ Archaeol 11(1):49–64

Schier W (2009) Extensiver Brandfeldbau und die Ausbreitung der neolithischen Wirtschaftsweise in Mitteleuropa und Südskandinavien am Ende des 5. Jahrtausends v. Chr. Praehistorische Zeitschrift 84(1):15–43

Schlichtherle H, Bleicher N, Dufraisse A, Kieselbach P, Maier U, Schmidt E, Stephan E, Vogt R (2010) Bad Buchau–Torwiesen II: Baustrukturen und Siedlungsabfälle als Indizien der Sozialstruktur und Wirtschaftsweise einer endneolithischen Siedlung am Federsee. In: Familie–Verwandtschaft–Sozialstrukturen: Sozialarchäologische Forschungen zu neolithischen Befunden., vol 1. Fokus Jungsteinzeit. Berichte der AG-Neolithikum. pp 157–178

Vogt R (2014) Kolluvien als Archive für anthropogen ausgelöste Landschaftsveränderungen an Beispielen aus der westlichen Bodenseeregion. Darmstadt

Chapter 10
Revisiting the Dynamics Between Two Ancient Japanese Descent Groups:

What Happened from the Jomon to the Yayoi Periods in Japan

Fumihiro Sakahira and Takao Terano

10.1 Introduction

The Yayoi period (300 BC–250 AD) was an era that marked the onset of rice-based agriculture in Japan. The Yayoi culture was established consequent to the integration of the Jomon hunter–gatherer culture, an antecedent of Yayoi culture, in the region. The agrarian culture is reported to have been imported from China-Korea. Additionally, investigations in anthropological morphology have revealed differences in human bones from the Yayoi period and the Jomon period (14,000 BC–300 BC). Therefore, it is believed that Chinese and Korean genetic influences on the Yayoi people were significant.

Thus, the presence of Chinese-Korean immigrants (*Trai-zin* in Japanese) was evidently of importance during the establishment of the Yayoi culture when agriculture became the social and economic foundation of society. However, several factors pertaining to these immigrants remain unclear within Japanese anthropology and archaeology. Specifically, these relate to the immigrants' place of origin, the initial immigrant population size, the sex ratio of the immigrants, and whether native Jomon people or immigrants played a formative role in the establishment of agrarian culture during the Yayoi period.

Anthropological and archaeological research indicates that the Korean Peninsula was the immigrants' place of origin. However, there are two competing hypotheses

F. Sakahira (✉) · T. Terano
Interdisciplinary Graduate School of Science and Engineering,
Tokyo Institute of Technology, 4259 Nagatsuda-cho, Midori-ku,
Yokohama, Kanagawa, Japan
e-mail: f-sakahira@hotmail.co.jp

T. Terano
e-mail: terano@dis.titech.ac.jp

F. Sakahira
Kozo Keikaku Engineering Inc., 4-5-3 Chuo, Nakano-ku, Tokyo, Japan

J.A. Barceló and F. Del Castillo (eds.), *Simulating Prehistoric and Ancient Worlds*,
Computational Social Sciences, DOI 10.1007/978-3-319-31481-5_10

proposing that the immigrant population was either large or small in size. The difference between human bones of the Yayoi and Jomon periods provides the rationale for the hypothesis positing a larger immigrant population size. Hanihara (1987) has estimated that the total size of the immigrant population over a period of 1,000 years ranged from about 310 million people based on a back calculation of the estimated population during the subsequent period. In contrast, the hypothesis of a smaller immigrant population size at the beginning of the Yayoi period is based on the characteristics of pottery and stone tools which retained the characteristic style of the Jomon period. Consequently, the size of the immigrant population was not considered sufficiently large to change the characteristics of the pottery and stone tools at the beginning of the Yayoi period. Moreover, pottery and tools in the immigrant style predominated during the subsequent middle Yayoi period (200 BC–0 AD).

Regarding the sex ratio of the immigrants, a leading hypothesis postulates that the immigrants were primarily male (Kaneseki 1976). One reason for this hypothesis is that, as mentioned, the characteristics of pottery and stone tools retained the Jomon style at the onset of the Yayoi period. Tsude (1982) has stated that pottery was made by females during the Yayoi period. This contention was based on the emergence of an extensive body of ethnographic literature reiterating that pottery was made by females (Murdok and Provost 1973). Therefore, Japanese archeologists have generally accepted that pottery was made by females during ancient times. Based on these studies, they have argued that the female ratio of the immigrants was not sufficiently high to change the characteristics of pottery from the Jomon to the Yayoi style. Further, this hypothesis postulates that even if the population was large, given that immigrants were primarily male, the characteristics of pottery and stone tools did not evidence rapid change at the onset of the Yayoi period.

The most pertinent question of whether native Jomon people or Chinese-Korean immigrants played a formative role in the establishment of agrarian culture during the Yayoi period has long been a source of controversy. This is an important research problem within Japanese anthropology and archaeology (Fujio 1999). Some archaeologists have suggested that the native Jomon people assimilated the new agrarian culture, thus assuming a key role in Yayoi agrarian culture. However, as previously discussed, this assertion is based on the characteristics of pottery and stone tools which retained the Jomon style at the inception of the Yayoi period. Consequently, it has been assumed that the immigrant population was small in size and that native Jomon people, comprising the majority of the population, played a major role in establishing the Yayoi agrarian culture. Conversely, some anthropologists have insisted that during ancient times, Chinese-Korean immigrants to Japan brought with them a systematic agrarian culture. As the population grew, their descendants became the key players in establishing the Yayoi agrarian culture (Kataoka and Iizuka 2006). This insistence can once again be attributed to differences found in human bones of the Yayoi and Jomon periods, revealed through investigations in anthropological morphology. Based on this finding, the immigrant population size was assumed to be sufficiently large to have had a significant genetic impact. Thus, according to this view, immigrants played a predominant role in the evolution of Yayoi agrarian culture. However, this dualistic conception has recently been revised. It is now thought that the evolution of the agrarian society was a collaborative process that was initiated by both Jomon people and immigrants (Fujio 1999).

To resolve these problems, an examination of population trends and of the food production systems of the Jomon people and of the descendants of the immigrants since the inception of agriculture is required. However, in the Northern Kyushu region where the agrarian culture took root, human bone material from the late Jomon period (1000 BC–300 BC) up to the early Yayoi period (300 BC–200 AD) is missing, despite the onset of the agrarian culture during this time.

10.2 Related Work

Nakahashi and Iizuka (1998, 2008) have provided insights into the initial size of the immigrant population and which group played a formative role in establishing Yayoi agrarian culture, based on their discriminant analysis of human bone material. They have indicated that people bearing similar traits to those of the immigrants accounted for approximately 80 % of the total population during the middle Yayoi period. Furthermore, they applied a mathematical equation model to propose features of ancient population dynamics up to the middle of the Yayoi period. Considering the differences in the population growth rates of the native Jomon people (0.1 % per annum) and immigrants (1.3 % per annum), they suggested that even a small number of immigrants could account for the large majority that prevailed a few hundred years later. That is, in contrast to conventional studies, these studies have demonstrated the possibility that even a small initial immigrant population could explain why anthropological investigations of the morphology of human bones have revealed differences during the Yayoi and Jomon periods. Kataoka and Iizuka (2006) have also estimated the population growth rate based on the inhabitants of excavated houses, determined by house plans, site locations, and settlement composition. They have suggested that only immigrants could account for the large majority that prevailed a few hundred years later. Therefore, only the immigrants could have played a key role in establishing the Yayoi agrarian culture.

These studies (Nakahashi and Iizuka 1998, 2008; Kataoka and Iizuka 2006) are remarkable in that they have adopted a quantitative approach, using mathematical models, to present objective results. However, a few unresolved issues remain. First, these studies are premised on a model that partially segregates native Jomon people and immigrants. Even assuming the composition of a mixed group of Jomon people and immigrants, a small sized mixed group population has been estimated with a low ratio of native Jomon people within the group. This assumption would be unreasonable if there was no barrier prohibiting marriage and inter-group contact, and if mating was possible between Jomon people and immigrants. That is, the effects of random mating between these groups have been ignored. Second, these studies have assumed that genetic traits and the food production system were not separated. Therefore, they did not consider the diffusion of the food production system. The fertility rate of a population depends on its food production system (Bentley et al. 1993). Thus, it is possible that the population growth rate also depended on a subsistence culture. These studies are, therefore, unable to address the fundamental question of who played a formative role in the establishment of the agrarian culture.

Additionally, the immigrant sex ratio remains an important unresolved factor. As previously mentioned, one leading hypothesis postulates that the immigrants were primarily male (Kaneseki 1976), based on the assumption that pottery and stone tools were primarily produced by females (Tsude 1982), and on the evident characteristics of pottery and stone tools that retained the Jomon style at the onset of the Yayoi period. This implies that, if native Jomon females produced pottery, then male immigrants mated with native Jomon females. Nakahashi and Iizuka (1998, 2008) have calculated that the majority of females in the mixed group population comprising native Jomon people and immigrants were Jomon females. However, these studies originally assumed the existence of a small mixed group. Thus, they were unable to estimate the sex ratio of the totality of immigrants. Furthermore, this hypothesis is inconsistent with studies that show that the haplotype frequency of the maternal mitochondrial DNA (mtDNA) of Jomon people differs significantly from that of people of the Yayoi period because of the genetic influence of Chinese-Koreans (Shinoda 2006). We, therefore, posit that the low ratio of immigrant females made it difficult to change the frequency of mtDNA between Jomon people and people of the Yayoi period. That is, at the beginning of the Yayoi period, the argument that pottery and stone tools retained the characteristics of Jomon style is inconsistent with the significant changes that occurred in the haplotype frequency of mtDNA between populations of the Jomon and Yayoi periods. Therefore, the problem of the immigrant sex ratio cannot be resolved through the application of a conventional static model.

In this study, we propose an alternative view of Japanese history using agent-based modeling techniques instead of using the mathematical model developed by Nakahashi and Iizuka (1998, 2008). In formulating this model, based on the reviewed literature, we assumed the following four points: (1) A large number of native Jomon people and a small number of Chinese-Korean immigrants coexisted in the Northern Kyushu region. (2) During the 300 years that followed immigration, people bearing immigrant traits accounted for 80 % of the total population. (3) The model incorporates both random mating and random diffusion of the agrarian culture. (4) We further examined the immigrant sex ratio by adding the pottery style and mtDNA inheritance. We used these assumptions and agent-based simulation (ABS) to examine the issue of who played a formative role in establishing Yayoi agrarian culture.

10.3 The Simulation Model

Our simulation model follows the Overview, Design concepts, and Details (ODD) protocol (Grimm et al. 2010). This protocol is intended to address the criticism that agent-based models lack reproducibility. Furthermore, it aims to improve the integrity and standardization of the model description.

10.3.1 Agent and State Variables

The agent in our model was defined as an ancient person with the following variables.

10.3.1.1 Identity (ID) Number and Spatial Placement

The following information was assigned to an agent: an *ID number* and a *coordinate position* (X: 50 cells, Y: 50 cells) within a two-dimensional space. This space represented only the Northern Kyushu region (a small portion of Japan) and not the entire chain of Japanese islands. The Northern Kyushu region is situated close to the Korean Peninsula and is the location where agriculture was first introduced and from where it rapidly diffused outward. In our simulation model, the simulation space is so abstract that the model space is not directly related to the real geographical one. Our study intends to provide an alternative perspective regarding the conclusions offered by Nakahashi and Iizuka (1998, 2008). Thus, we mainly focus on discussing the relative diffusion between agrarian culture and trait genes. Further, as described below, the diffusion speed of agriculture in our simulation model is determined by the probability of agricultural introduction and the range of diffusion. Therefore, considering the gene flow relative to the speed of agricultural diffusion, this abstract space is sufficient to discuss the issues at hand. The size of the space within our simulation is determined by the speed of diffusion of agrarian culture as described below.

10.3.1.2 Sex

The agent was *Male* or *Female*.

10.3.1.3 Life Expectancy and Age

Upon creation (birth), an agent was given a *life expectancy* based on the mortality table. If the *age* of the agent exceeded the *life expectancy*, the agent was removed (died). We created the mortality table by reflecting an infant mortality rate of 20 % up to recent years on that of the Jomon people (Nagaoka et al. 2008). We also presumed in our simulation model that the mortality table was the same for both the Yayoi and Jomon people.

10.3.1.4 Food Production System

The food production system variables were *hunting and gathering* or *agriculture*. This system changed from *hunting* and *gathering* to *agriculture* through the diffusion of agriculture based on the assumption that the cold climate from the late Jomon to the early Yayoi period introduced an opportunity for this conversion process (Miyamoto 2009). However, we assumed that the opposite condition did not hold, because there is no evidence of the diffusion of hunting and gathering during this period in the literature.

10.3.1.5 Marriage Institution

The marriage institution variable for the male agent was *monogamous* or *polygamous* for the Yayoi period. Polygamous marriage was assumed to occur based on descriptions of this type of marriage contained in "Gishi-Wazin-Den," an ancient Chinese text on Yayoi period customs. According to this text, some men of high status had four or five wives, and there were even some men of normal status who had two or three wives. To date, the type of marriage institution that prevailed during the Jomon period has not been ascertained. While both polygamy and polyandry may have existed during this period, the mathematical model formulated by Nakahashi and Iizuka (1998, 2008) assumed that monogamy prevailed among the Jomon people. Therefore, to present a clear alternate perspective in our study, we also assumed that monogamy was the marriage institution of the Jomon people. Additionally, we postulated that sustaining more than one wife—polygamous marriage—requires a surplus of food. Therefore, in our simulation model, if the male agent included both of the following variables: *polygamous* and a high yielding food production system, namely *agriculture*, then the agent was assumed to be married to three female agents. A new agent (child) inherited the father agent's marriage institution.

10.3.1.6 Pottery Style

The pottery style variable was either the *Jomon style* or the *immigrant style*. In our simulation model, for the sake of convenience, we restricted the pottery style to either the Jomon or immigrant styles. We assumed a continuous change in the characteristics of the pottery style and focused on the issue of which style was dominant. This did not mean that the distinction between these two styles was a discontinuous one.

The argument made by Tsude (1982) that females produced pottery during the Yayoi period is supported by an extensive ethnographic literature (Murdok and Provost 1973). Therefore, within the field of Japanese archaeology, it has generally been held that females produced pottery during ancient times. Additionally, Tanaka and Ozawa (2001) have discussed how cultural diffusion occurred through a vertical transmission process within society during the Yayoi period. Based on these descriptions in the literature, we assumed in our simulation model that the new agent (child) borne by a female inherited the mother agent's pottery style.

10.3.1.7 Trait Genes

Trait genes determine trait characteristics. Originally, it was thought that trait characteristics are determined through the involvement of many genes in a complex manner. However, to simplify this for the simulation, in our simulation model, following Nakahashi and Iizuka (1998, 2008), it is assumed to be composed of a major pair of alleles: the Jomon-type gene (*J*) and immigrant-type gene (*T*). When a new agent (child) is created (born), the agent inherits either of the father agent's and either of the mother agent's alleles. That is, the combination of alleles of an agent is JJ, TT, or JT. In accordance with these combinations, each agent is classified as one with Jomon or immigrant traits. Specifically, a JJ agent comprises traits of the Jomon people, a TT agent comprises immigrant traits, and a JT agent displays mixed traits (mixed people). Mixed people are also determined as those comprising a given ratio of immigrant traits.

10.3.1.8 mtDNA Macrohaplogroup

The mtDNA macrohaplogroup variable for an agent was *macrohaplogroup N* or *macrohaplogroup M*. The mtDNA, which is the cell organelle DNA of mitochondria, is inherited maternally and is relatively easy to extract from human bone remains. Therefore, mtDNA analysis is a useful way of investigating the origin of the maternal line of ancient peoples. The mtDNA of East Asian populations has been broadly classified into two groups: macrohaplogroup N and macrohaplogroup M (Kivisild et al. 2002; Kong et al. 2003). Results of mtDNA analyses of human bone remains have recently been compiled in Japan. The frequency of mtDNA macrohaplogroups N and M indicates major differences between people of the Jomon and Yayoi periods (Shinoda 2006). Specifically, for populations during the Jomon period, the frequency of mtDNA macrohaplogroups N and M were each about 50 %. In contrast, for populations during the Yayoi period, the frequency of mtDNA macrohaplogroups N and M were about 20 % and 80 %, respectively. In our simulation model, when a new agent (child) was created (born), the agent inherited the mother agent's mtDNA macrohaplogroup as described below.

10.3.2 Process Overview and Scheduling

Our simulation model proceeded according to annual time steps. Thus, the annual time step was a year. Each year, the three submodels of each agent were executed in turn as follows: diffusion of the agrarian culture rule, the marriage rule, and the moving rule. Additionally, agents were processed in a random order during each year.

10.3.3 Design Concepts

Our simulation model corresponded to seven out of the eleven design concepts contained in the ODD protocol (Table 10.1). The model was simple, and we considered that the description of the model and design concepts were sufficient to indicate reproducibility.

10.3.4 Submodels

10.3.4.1 Diffusion of the Agrarian Culture Rule

The diffusion of agrarian culture occurred through neighboring agents and inheritance from a parent agent. In our simulation model, we assumed that these very simple patterns of cultural transmission followed the conventional susceptible-infectious (SI) model of infectious diseases.

In the case of diffusion from a neighboring agent, if the agent's food production system was *hunting and gathering,* while that of all the other neighboring agents was *agriculture* within a given cell radius (the extent of diffusion occurring within a cell range was: one cell [narrow], three cells [moderate], and five cells [wide]), the agent's food production system would then be transformed into *agriculture*. This transformation was based on a given probability (introduction rate: impossible [0 %], difficult [0.1 %], middle [0.5 %], and easy [1.0 %]). Conversely, in the case of inheritance from a parent agent, and according to the marriage rule described below, when a new agent (child) was created (born), the agent inherited the food production system from either the father or mother agent. In this study, inheritance from the father or mother agent was simulated.

10.3.4.2 Marriage Rule

A new agent (child) was created (born) as a result of the marriage of a male and a female agent. The male agent was married to a female agent randomly selected

Table 10.1 Design concepts

No.	Design concepts	Elements
1	Basic principles	Trait gene, mitochondrial DNA (mtDNA) haplogroup, and pottery style was diffused under the increased population based on the food production system by the diffusion of agriculture
		• For the diffusion of agrarian culture, we apply the infection model (SI model)
		• For the increase of people, we apply Malthus' theory
		• For the inheritance of the trait gene, we apply Mendel's laws
2	Emergence	Diffusion of agrarian culture changes the composition ratio of each trait gene type of agrarian culture holders, the diffusion ratio of Jomon-style pottery and the frequency of mitochondrial DNA macrohaplogroup M
3	Adaptation	If an agent is near the other agent with agrarian culture, it introduces an agrarian culture in a given rate
4	Sensing	• Recognizing whether a male agent is near the other agent with agrarian culture
		• Recognizing whether an agent is near the female agent
5	Stochasticity	• Life expectancy
		• Spatial placement at the start of the simulation
		• Allocation of mtDNA macrohaplogroup at the start of the simulation
		• Introduction of agriculture
		• Selection of female agent for marriage
		• Sex of child agent
		• Combination of trait gene
		• Move in random direction
6	Collectives	Number of agents created is determined by the number of agents with "hunting and gathering" and "agriculture"
7	Observation	• Ratio of people with immigrant trait
		• Diffusion ratio of agrarian culture
		• Composition ratio of each descendant of agrarian culture holders
		• Diffusion ratio of Jomon-style pottery
		• Frequency of mitochondrial DNA macrohaplogroup M

from all of the female agents within three surrounding cells. Furthermore, a new agent was created according to the population growth rate of the mother agent's food production system and at the same spatial placement as that of the mother agent. The sex of the new agent was allocated according to a 50 % probability of being male or female, along with a life expectancy and age of 0. For the trait gene, as previously explained, the new agent inherited either of the father agent's alleles and either of the mother agent's alleles. Additionally, the new agent inherited the food production system from either the father or mother agent, the marriage institution from the father agent, and the pottery style and mtDNA macrohaplogroup from the mother agent. Moreover, as mentioned earlier, the male agent could be simultaneously married to three female agents only when associated with both the *polygamous* and *agriculture* variables.

10.3.4.3 Moving Rule

Within each step, an agent moved one cell in random directions within the simulated space.

10.3.5 Initialization

10.3.5.1 Time Span of the Simulation

The time span of our simulation was 300 years (300 steps), extending from the early to the middle Yayoi period. This value was the same as that of the calculated representative example in Nakahashi and Iizuka (1998, 2008). While a new hypothesis, based on Accelerator Mass Spectrometry radiocarbon dating, postulates the start of the Yayoi period to be 500 years earlier than the date suggested by conventional hypotheses, no clear conclusions have been reached. Therefore, in this study, the time span was 300 years which is a more stringent condition for a demographic transition in which the small size of the immigrant population could account for the large majority a few hundred years later.

10.3.5.2 Population Growth Rate Based on the Food Production System

The population growth rate of agriculturalists was higher than that of hunters and gatherers. We simulated two cases relating to the growth rate of each of the above populations as follows. The growth rate of each population for the first (high rate) case had the same value as that of the example of a representative calculation provided by Nakahashi and Iizuka (1998). The growth rate for each population in the second (low rate) case exhibited the lowest value shown in Nakahashi and Iizuka (1998).

- First (high rate) case: the growth rate of the hunting and gathering population was 0.1 % per year, while that of the agriculturalist population was 1.3 % per year.
- Second (low rate) case: the growth rate of the hunting and gathering population was 0.1 % per year, while that of the agriculturalist population was 0.5 % per year.

10.3.5.3 Speed of the Diffusion of Agrarian Culture

The speed of diffusion of agrarian culture in our simulation model comprised the range of cells associated with the diffusion and introduction rate. The range of diffusion cells corresponded to the distance within which cultural exchange would occur while they were in contact with each other. We assumed three degrees: narrow (one cell), moderate (three cells), and wide (five cells). The introduction rate corresponded to the difficulty associated with the introduction of an agrarian culture. Here, we assumed four degrees: impossible (0 %), difficult (0.1 %), medium (0.5 %), and easy (1 %). The level of difficulty did not relate to agricultural techniques, but rather to the adequacy of the environment and culture required for the acceptance of the new agrarian culture. These values were set assuming that even when the range of cells was narrow and the introduction rate was difficult, approximately 300 years were required for the majority of agents to have agriculture.

10.3.5.4 Inheritance of the Food Production System from a Parent

The inheritance of a food production system from a parent was unknown. Therefore, to investigate the extent to which the simulation result was impacted by inheritance from either the father or the mother, we simulated two cases as follows.

- First case (father): a new agent (child) inherited the food production system from the father agent.
- Second case (mother): a new agent inherited the food production system from the mother agent.

10.3.5.5 State Variables of the Initial Jomon People and Immigrants

The simulation run commenced with the initial Jomon people and immigrants whose state variables are described below.

Initial Jomon People

- Trait gene: *JJ*
- Food production system: *hunting and gathering*
- Marriage Institution: *monogamous*
- Pottery style: *Jomon style*
- MtDNA macrohaplogroup: with reference to Shinoda (2006), 50 % had *macrohaplogroup N* and 50 % had *macrohaplogroup M*.

Initial Immigrants

- Trait gene: *TT*
- Food production system: *agriculture*
- Marriage institution: *monogamous* or *polygamous* in each simulation case
- Pottery style: *immigrant style*
- MtDNA macrohaplogroup: In total, 62.5 % had *macrohaplogroup M* and 37.5 % had *macrohaplogroup N*. The haplogroup frequency of the immigrants' mtDNA is unknown. However, because immigrants are believed to have arrived via the Korean Peninsula, in this study, the frequency of macrohaplogroups within the current population of the Korean Peninsula (Shinoda 2006) was considered to be the same as that of the immigrants.

10.3.5.6 Spatial Placement of the Initial Jomon People and Immigrants

It is assumed that the immigrants initially arrived from northern coastal areas at the earliest stage. Therefore, in this study, the first immigrants were densely positioned in one area at the start of the simulation run. To investigate the extent to which the simulation result was influenced by this assumption, we simulated two cases pertaining to the spatial placement of the initial Jomon people and immigrants as follows.

- First (dense distribution) case: the initial Jomon people were uniformly randomly placed, while the initial immigrants were placed in the center of the upper side of the simulated space (X: 25, Y: 50), assuming that they came from the northern coastal area.
- Second (dispersed distribution) case: Both the initial Jomon people and immigrants were uniformly randomly placed.

10.3.5.7 Initial Numbers of Jomon People and Immigrants

The initial number of Jomon people was 200 agents and that of immigrants was 1,800 agents referring to the ratio of 9:1 of initial Jomon people and immigrants shown by Nakahashi and Iizuka (1998) in their example of a representative calculation. We set these absolute numbers of agents as the minimum numbers that were sufficient for matching the results of the numerical calculation provided by Nakahashi and Iizuka (1998) with those of our simulation runs. We used the same population growth rates but did not include the gene flow and agricultural diffusion between the two populations.

10.3.5.8 Sex Ratio of Initial Jomon People and Immigrants

A leading hypothesis states that the immigrants were primarily male (Kenasaki 1976). Therefore, to examine the sex ratio of the initial immigrants, we simulated three cases for the initial immigrants' sex ratio as follows. By contrast, the ratio of Jomon males and females was equal.

- First case (same): the number of males among the initial immigrants was 100 agents and the number of females was also 100 agents.
- Second case (more): 150 male agents and 50 female agents among the initial immigrants.
- Third case (majority): 175 male agents and 25 female agents among the initial immigrants.

10.3.5.9 Ratio Determining Mixed *JT* Individuals as Those with Immigrant Traits

If agents were genetically mixed, possessing the JT trait gene, then they displayed immigrant traits according to the given ratio. We simulated two cases for this ratio as follows.

- First case (100 %): individuals with immigrant traits at 100 %.
- Second case (50 %): individuals with immigration traits at 50 %.

In the first case, the individuals were determined to be immigrants based on the assumption that a person with even a small amount of immigrant traits is an immigrant.

10.3.6 The Number of Simulation Cases and the Evaluation Index

The total number of simulation cases was 441. This figure refers to cases combining each of the above parameters (Table 10.2) added to the representative example of a simple increase of calculation shown in Nakahashi and Iizuka (1998). The simple increase of calculation is a model based on the assumption that numbers of Jomon people and immigrants increased separately without random mating and cultural exchange occurring between them.

For the number of simulation runs, cases that combined a 1.3 % agriculturalist population growth rate with a dispersed spatial distribution of the initial Jomon people and immigrants were run once, considering computational costs. The other cases were run ten times. The random seed value of these ten runs was the same across cases.

Table 10.2 Values of parameters

Initialization parameters	Values
Time span of simulation	[300 years (steps)]
Population growth rate of hunting and gathering people	[0.1 %]
Population growth rate of agricultural people	[1.3 %], [0.5 %]
Range of cells of the diffusion	[Narrow: 1 cell], [Moderate: 3 cells], [Wide: 5 cells]
Introductory rate of agrarian culture	[Impossible: 0 %], [Difficult: 0.1 %], [Middle: 0.5 %], [Easy: 1.0 %]
Inheritance of food production system from a parent	[Father], [Mother]
Institution of marriage of the initial Jomon people	[Monogamous]
Institution of marriage of the initial immigrants	[Monogamous], [Polygamous]
Spatial placement of the initial Jomon people	[Dispersed distribution]
Spatial placement of the initial immigrants	[Dispersed distribution], [Dense distribution]
Sex ratio of the initial immigrants (Male, Female)	[Same: 100, 100], [More: 150, 50], [Majority: 175, 25]
Sex ratio of the initial Jomon people (Male, Female)	[900, 900]
Ratio determines the mixed people as those with immigrant traits	[100 %], [50 %]

The main evaluation index in our simulation results was the ratio of people with immigrant traits across all agents. Regarding the demographic transition that occurred during the middle Yayoi period, Nakahashi and Iizuka (1998) reported that 80 % or more people had immigrant traits. Therefore, determining whether this figure was close to 80 % or more after 300 years (steps) provided a measure of demographic transition in our simulation. In this study, we referred to the ratio of people with immigrant traits for each run of each case. Additionally, in simulation cases entailing demographic transition, to assess which group played a formative role in Yayoi agrarian culture, we depicted a time series of the diffusion ratio of agrarian culture and the composition ratio of each descendant of the agrarian culture holders.

The diffusion ratio of immigrant-style pottery and the frequency of the mtDNA macrohaplogroup M among the cases were also compared. We assumed that at the onset of the Yayoi period most pottery retained the characteristics of the Jomon style, with the immigrant-style pottery achieving predominance during the middle Yayoi period. Thus, starting with a situation in which immigrant-style pottery was less prevalent compared with Jomon-style pottery, we investigated whether the diffusion ratio of the immigrant-style pottery was higher 300 years later. Furthermore, considering that the frequency of macrohaplogroup M within the population during the Yayoi period was about 80 %, we determine whether the frequency of mtDNA macrohaplogroup M was higher 300 years later.

10.4 Results and Discussion

Of the 441 simulated cases, 111 demonstrated that more than 80 % of people exhibited immigrant traits after 300 years (steps). In the case of the representative example of a simple increase of calculation provided by Nakahashi and Iizuka (1998), based on the assumption that numbers of Jomon people and immigrants increased separately without random mating and cultural exchange occurring between them, 78.9 % of people had immigrant traits. This case did not include random mating and cultural exchange between native Jomon people and immigrants. The simulation result was very similar to the numerical calculations of Nakahashi and Iizuka (1998) based on the same population growth rate. Therefore, the result showed that the calculation of our simulation model was consistent with that of the mathematical model and that the initial absolute number of agents was appropriate.

In the following sections, we refer to differing results for cases relating to the spatial placement of the initial immigrants, the marriage institution, speed of the diffusion of agriculture, and sex ratio. Consequently, we only describe the results of cases combining inheritance of the food production system from the mother and 100 % determination of *JT* mixed individuals as those with immigrant traits.

10.4.1 Spatial Placement of the First Immigrants

In cases where both the initial Jomon people and immigrants were uniformly randomly placed, less than 80 % of people had immigrant traits. This could be used as a measure of demographic transition (Figs. 10.1 and 10.2). A summary of the results for cases combining a 1.3 % agricultural population growth rate and a dispersed distribution of the spatial placement of the initial Jomon people and immigrants is presented in Fig. 10.1. Considering other simulation results, even if these were each run 10 times, the stochasticity would not significantly change the ratio of people with immigrant traits after 300 years and we would observe less than 80 %.

In general, cases in which the speed of the diffusion of agrarian culture was slow (e.g., a narrow [one cell] range of diffusion cells and a difficult introduction rate

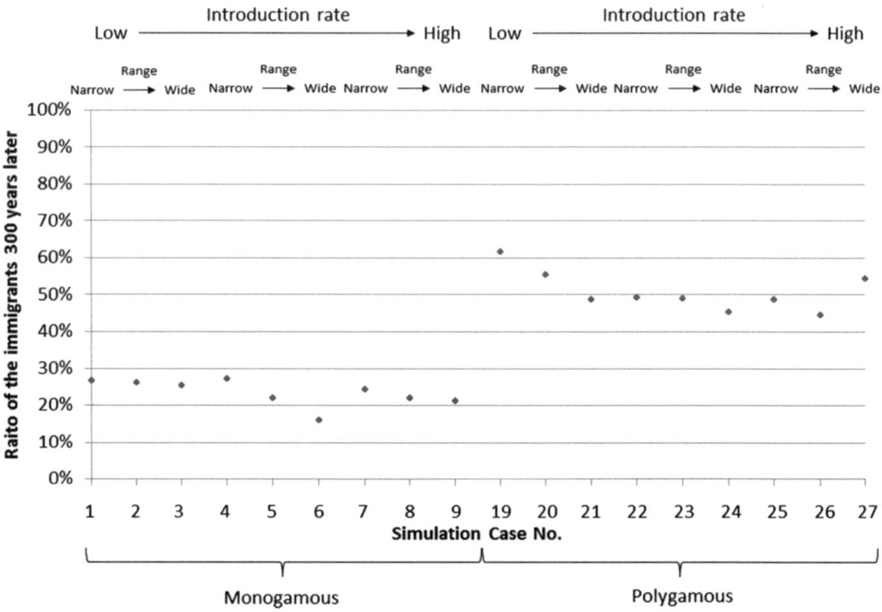

Fig. 10.1 Percentages of people with immigrant traits after 300 years in cases combining dispersed distribution, a 1.3 % agricultural population growth rate, and equal numbers of males and females

[0.1 %]) indicated a higher ratio of people with immigrant traits. Conversely, cases in which the speed of the diffusion of agrarian culture was rapid (e.g., a wide [five cells] range of diffusion cells and an easy introduction rate [1 %]) indicated a lower ratio of people with immigrant traits.

Some cases indicated the dense distribution of immigrants, with 80 % of people exhibiting immigrant traits 300 years later. This served as a measure of the demographic transition (Figs. 10.3 and 10.4). The immigrants in these cases were all *polygamous*. We elaborate on these cases in the following sections.

Demographic transition did not occur in cases where both the initial Jomon people and immigrants were uniformly randomly placed because there were many points of diffusion of agrarian culture. During an early stage, agrarian culture diffused among the native Jomon people and there was a high rate of increase of agriculturalists within the Jomon population. Therefore, even when the population growth rate of agriculturalists differed, the same result was obtained (Figs. 10.3 and 10.4). To generate demographic transition in which people with immigrant traits reached 80 % 300 years later, our results show that population densities of immigrants were probably high and that only a section of the neighboring native Jomon population made contact with them.

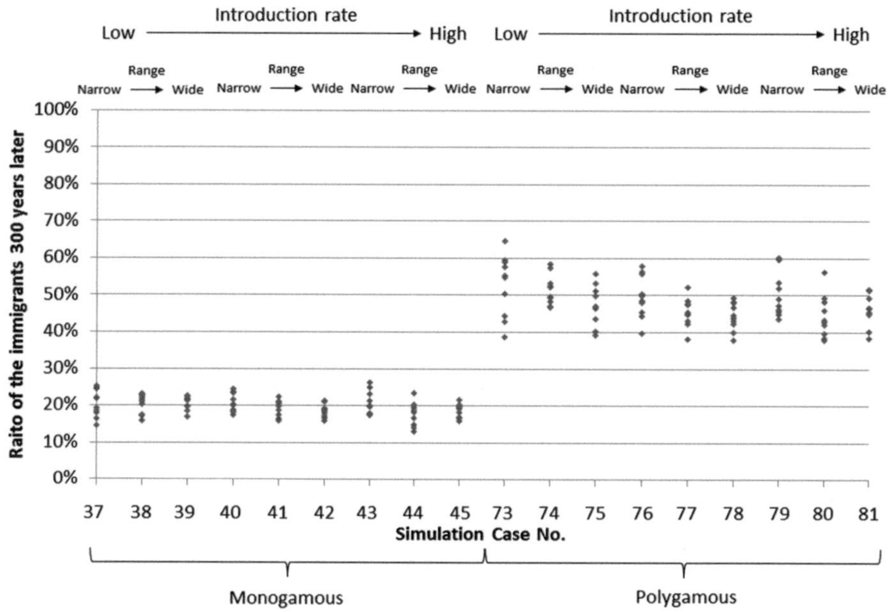

Fig. 10.2 Percentages of people with immigrant traits after 300 years in cases combining dispersed distribution, a 0.5 % agricultural population growth rate, and equal numbers of males and females

10.4.2 Marriage Institution and Speed of Agricultural Diffusion

10.4.2.1 Cases of Monogamous Marriage and Diffusion from Neighboring Agents

For cases combining dense distribution of immigrants, monogamous marriage, and the diffusion of agriculture from neighboring agents, the percentage of people with immigrant traits, 300 years later, was below the 80 % figure that indicated demographic transition (Figs. 10.3 and 10.4). The reason is the same as that described earlier. Once an agrarian culture had diffused among native Jomon people at an early stage, their population increased at the high rate of agricultural population growth. Therefore, cases entailing the slow diffusion of agrarian culture also indicated a high ratio of people with immigrant traits, while cases entailing the rapid diffusion of agrarian culture evidenced a low ratio of people with immigrant traits. Considering these results, even if we assume that preferential marriage occurred within the population, because the agrarian culture was diffused among native Jomon people, when the trait gene was diffused only within the population, demographic transition would not have occurred.

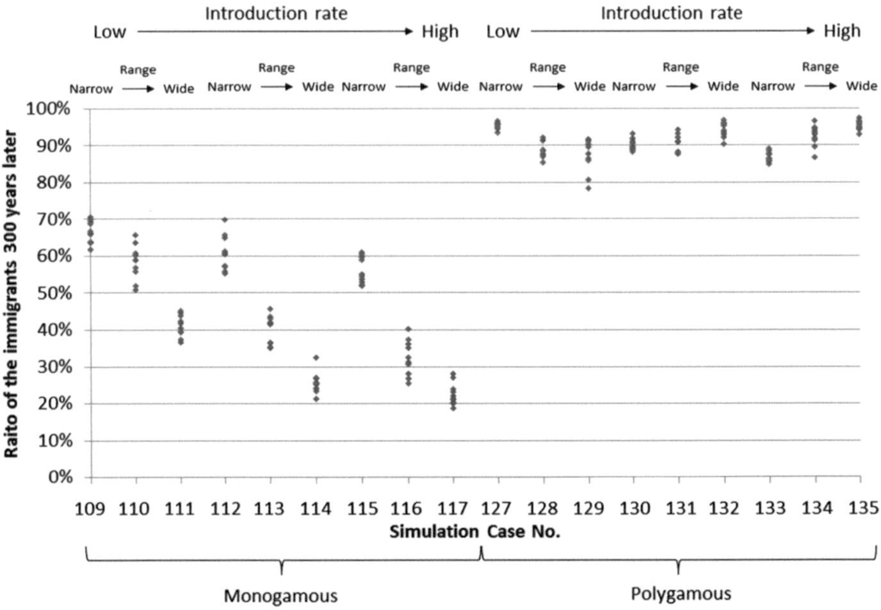

Fig. 10.3 Percentages of people with the immigrant traits after 300 years in cases combining dense distribution, a 1.3 % agricultural population growth rate, and equal numbers of males and females

10.4.2.2 Polygamous Marriage and Exclusive Inheritance from a Parent Agent

There were cases entailing polygamous immigrants and inheritance of the agrarian culture from only a parent agent (not diffused from a neighboring agent). Even with a lower growth rate (0.5 %) of the agriculturalist population, in some cases of immigrants reached the 80 % 300 years later (Fig. 10.4, No. 194). If the initial immigrants were polygamous, demographic transition would be probable. Additionally, considering these results, even if the population growth rate of agriculturalists was low (0.5 %), it would be sufficient to infer that demographic transition had occurred. That is, demographic transition in which people with immigrant traits came to constitute the majority a few hundred years later could occur through the diffusion of the trait gene within polygamous marriage, assuming the low population growth rate of agriculturalists. Given that agricultural technology had not attained maturity at this time, a 1.3 % agriculturalist population growth rate may be considered too high. Therefore, these results indicate high consistency for demographic transition even with a low growth rate of the agricultural population. Additionally, as described above, if we accept the hypothesis that the inception of the Yayoi period was 500 years earlier than commonly thought, even the lower rate of population growth could generate demographic transition.

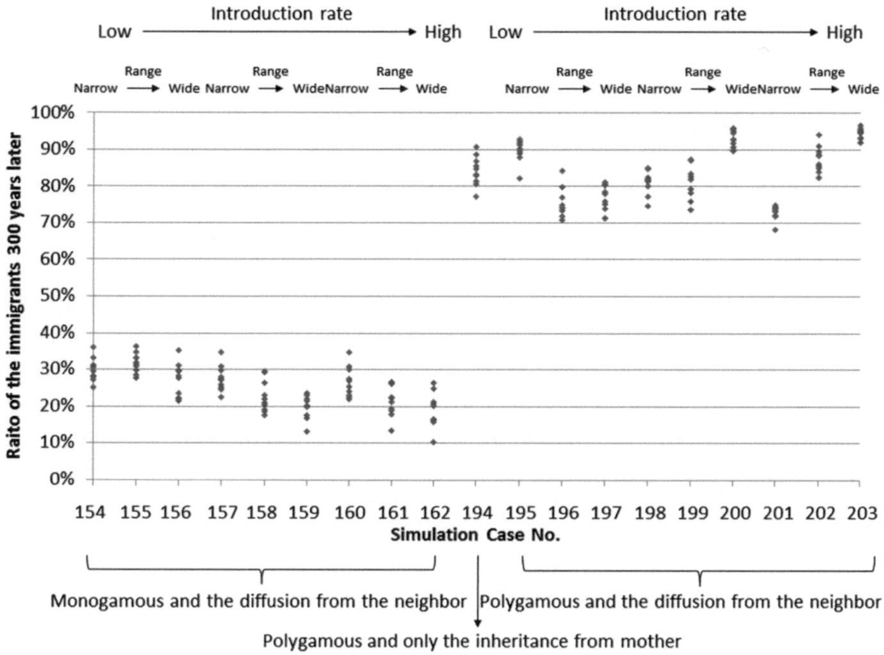

Fig. 10.4 Percentages of people with immigrant traits after 300 years in cases combining dense distribution, a 0.5 % agricultural population growth rate, and equal numbers of males and females

However, in these cases, the diffusion rate of the agrarian culture was very low (about 25 %) after 300 years, because the agrarian culture was only inherited from either the father or mother. Moreover, the composition ratio of descendants of these agriculturalists consisted of immigrants or both immigrants and Jomon people. These cases suggest, as our first hypothesis, that *immigrants played a formative role in the establishment of agrarian culture.*

10.4.2.3 Polygamous Marriage and Diffusion from Neighboring Agents

We now turn to cases entailing polygamous immigrants and agriculture that was not only inherited from a parent agent, but also diffused from neighboring agents. In such cases, the percentage of people with immigrant traits after 300 years varied depending on the speed of the diffusion of agrarian culture. When the population growth rate of agriculturalists was 0.5 % (the lower rate), some cases of slow-speed diffusion of agrarian culture did not attain the 80 % figure for people with immigrant traits after 300 years (Fig. 10.4). By contrast, cases demonstrating a significant speed of agrarian culture diffusion evidenced 80 % of the population with immigrant traits after 300 years. When the population growth rate of the agriculturalists was 1.3 % (the higher rate), regardless of the speed of the agrarian culture diffusion, 80 % of individuals in all cases evidenced immigrant traits after 300 years (Fig. 10.3). Nevertheless, the rapid speed of the diffusion of agrarian culture exceeded the percentage of people with immigrant traits 300 years later.

These results demonstrate that in cases in which polygamous marriage was combined with the diffusion of agriculture, demographic transition was facilitated by the wider diffusion of agrarian culture. This could be attributed to a time lag between the diffusion of agrarian culture and polygamous marriage, which influenced the increasing populations of Jomon people and immigrants. Specifically, the density distribution of immigrants meant that the number of immigrants increased during the earliest stage, and that in this process, the agrarian culture diffused among the Jomon people. However, polygamous marriage remained an immigrant trait because it was inherited from fathers. Consequently, the neighboring Jomon people came to possess an agrarian culture. Furthermore, in a situation in which immigrant neighbors, engaged in an agrarian culture, displayed a higher population growth rate, the immigrant trait gene type was diffused through polygamous marriage. That is, for wider diffusion of the immigrant trait gene type to occur, it was necessary for immigrant neighbors to demonstrate an agrarian culture and a higher population growth rate.

The composition ratio of descendants of those practicing an agrarian culture showed a slight degree of mixing of Jomon people and immigrants in cases that entailed slow diffusion of the agrarian culture at the early stage. Both groups of descendants thus came to account for most of those engaged in an agrarian culture by marriage (Fig. 10.5). These results suggest, as our second hypothesis, that *immigrants played a formative role in the establishment of agrarian culture.*

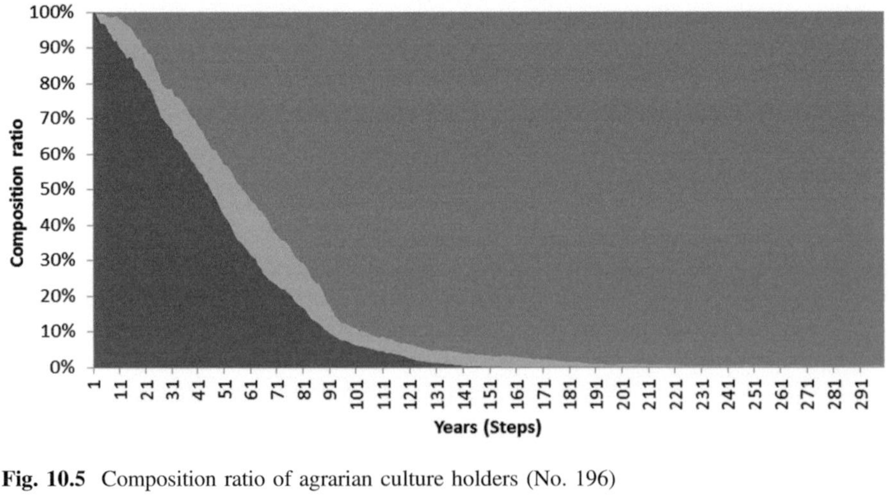

Fig. 10.5 Composition ratio of agrarian culture holders (No. 196)

In contrast, for cases demonstrating significant and rapid diffusion of the agrarian culture, and demographic transition, at the earliest stage, only the descendants of immigrants were the holders of the agrarian culture. However, shortly thereafter, Jomon descendants constituted the majority (Fig. 10.6). Consequently, both immigrant and Jomon descendants became the majority group through marriage. These results indicate that it is probable that even if the agrarian culture was widely diffused among the Jomon people, demographic transition could occur. These results suggest, as our third hypothesis, that *Jomon people played a formative role in the establishment of agrarian culture.*

10.4.3 Sex Ratio of Initial Immigrants

In general, cases involving primarily male immigrants demonstrated a slightly higher ratio of individuals with immigrant traits after 300 years than cases with equal numbers of males and females (Fig. 10.3 Nos. 127–135, Fig. 10.4 Nos. 195–203, Figs. 10.7 and 10.8). This was irrespective of the population growth rate of agriculturalists and the inheritance of agriculture either from the father or mother. However, regarding immigrant-style pottery, cases in which immigrants were primarily male after 300 years showed a lower ratio (Figs. 10.9, 10.10, and 10.11). Conversely, these results showed that even if the number of female immigrants was small, immigrant-style pottery predominated after 300 years. In our simulation study, we only considered the vertical transmission of a pottery style. Had we also considered horizontal transmission, the diffusion of the immigrant-style pottery

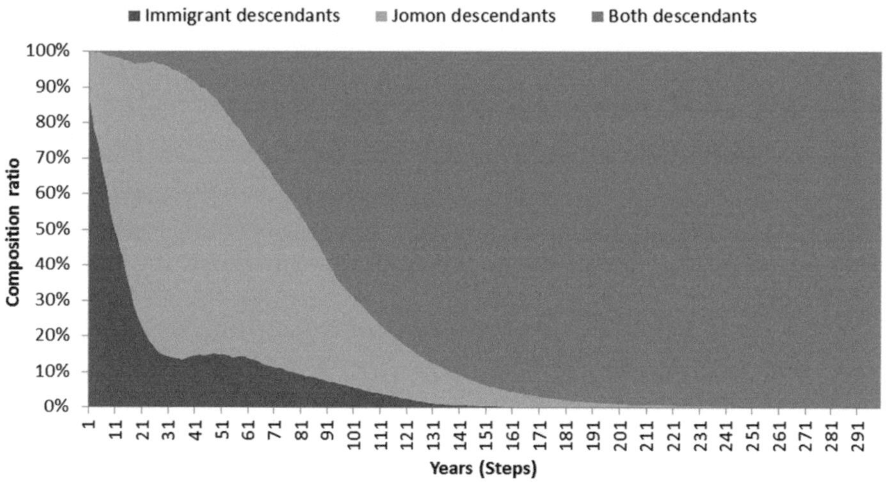

Fig. 10.6 Composition ratio of agrarian culture holders (No. 203)

would, in this case, have evidenced wider distribution than was indicated in our study. This would have more closely approximated the actual situation.

Moreover, regarding the frequency of the mtDNA macrohaplogroup, we found no clear difference between cases in which immigrants were primarily male and cases entailing equal numbers of males and females (Figs. 10.12, 10.13, and 10.14). The reason for this result was that the frequency of the mtDNA macrohaplogroup was largely influenced by random genetic drift. Conversely, these results show that when the immigrants were primarily male, the haplogroup frequency of the maternal mtDNA could significantly change. Our results indicate that even when the number of female immigrants was one-tenth that of female Jomon people, the frequency of the mtDNA macrohaplogroup changed significantly when the number of immigrants increased.

Based on these findings, it is evident that our simulation did not provide clear results regarding the sex ratio of the initial immigrants. On the one hand, when we examine the simulation results for the percentage of people with immigrant traits after 300 years, our results support the hypothesis that the immigrants were primarily male. On the other hand, when we examine the simulation results regarding the prevalence of immigrant-style pottery after 300 years, our results do not support the hypothesis that the immigrants were primarily male.

However, we only considered the vertical spread of the pottery style through inheritance from the mother. We did not consider the horizontal spread of a pottery

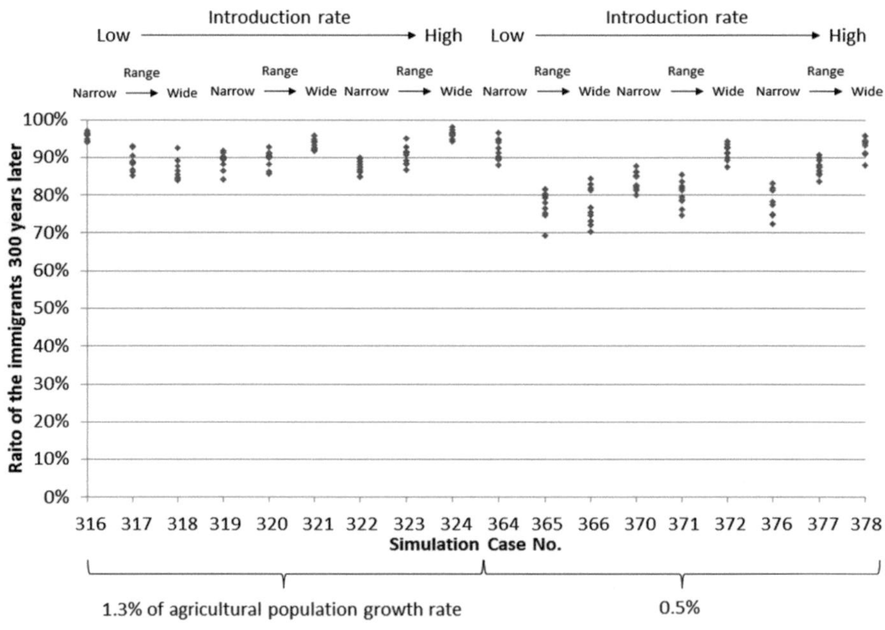

Fig. 10.7 Percentages of people with immigrant traits after 300 years in cases with more males than females

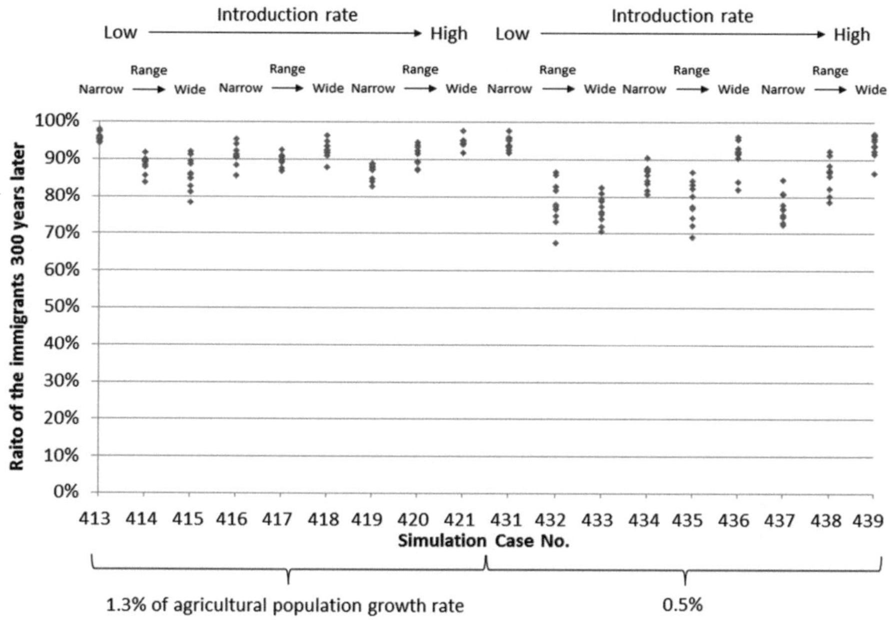

Fig. 10.8 Percentages of people with immigrant traits after 300 years in cases with a majority of males

style through diffusion from neighbors. Therefore, considering only the vertical spread of a pottery style in our simulation model led to a clear finding of a higher ratio of immigrant-style pottery 300 years later compared with the model described in our study. Much remains unknown regarding the manner of diffusion of a pottery style. Thus, our simulation model was inadequate in this regard, leaving room for improvement.

Therefore, considering the other more conclusive findings, our simulation results support the hypothesis that the immigrants were primarily male.

10.4.4 Who Played a Formative Role in the Establishment of Agrarian Cultures?

We now return to the problem of who played a formative role in the establishment of agrarian cultures during the Yayoi period. We simulated a situation initially entailing the coexistence of a large number of native Jomon people and a small number of immigrants, and the subsequent predominance of people with immigrant traits who accounted for 80 % of the total population a few hundred years later. The results of our simulation indicated the three probable cases described above. In the first, immigrants were polygamous and the agrarian culture was only inherited from

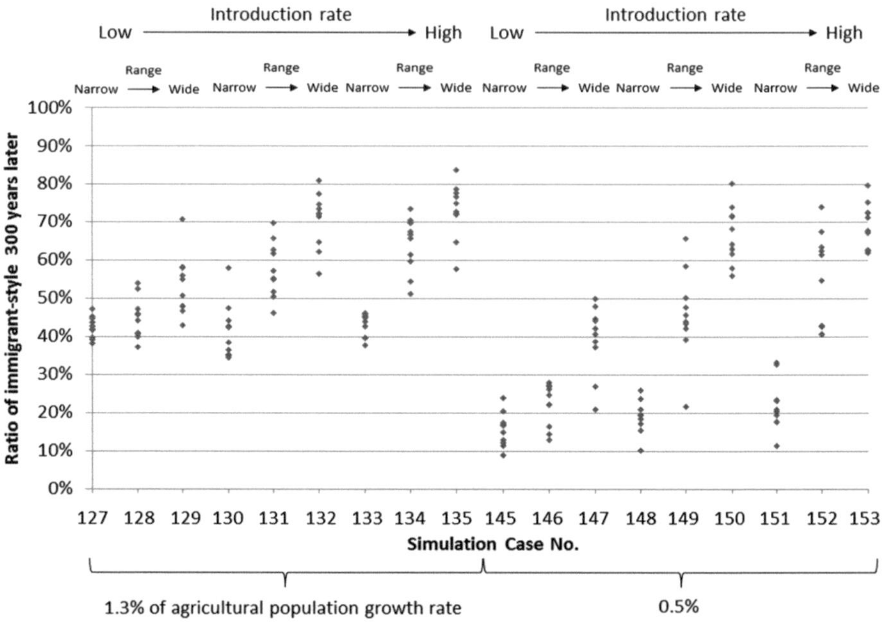

Fig. 10.9 Percentages of immigrant-style pottery after 300 years in cases with equal numbers of males and females

a parent agent (not diffused from neighboring agents). In this case, the descendants of agriculturalists at an early stage were either immigrants or both immigrants and Jomon people. Thus, immigrants played a formative role in the establishment of an agrarian culture. In the second case, immigrants were polygamous and the agrarian culture was inherited from a parent agent as well as diffused from neighboring agents. However, the diffusion of the agrarian culture occurred slowly. In this case, the descendants of the agriculturalists at an early stage were mostly immigrants with few Jomon people. As in the first case, immigrants played a formative role in the establishment of an agrarian culture. In the last case, the diffusion of the agrarian culture was significantly more rapid. In this case, the majority of descendants of agriculturalists were immigrants at the earliest stage, but shortly thereafter, Jomon descendants were evident during a subsequent early stage. Here, mostly Jomon people and a few immigrants played a formative role in the establishment of an agrarian culture.

Of these three probable cases, the last is the most consistent with anthropological and archaeological evidence for the following reasons. In the first case, the diffusion rate of agriculture was too low. Considering that the diffusion of agrarian culture began in the North Kyushu region, it is implausible to assume that the diffusion ratio at the place of origin of agriculture in Japan was low. Comparing the second and third cases, even when the population growth rate of agriculturalists was high, the rapid speed of diffusion of the agrarian culture was higher in the percentage of

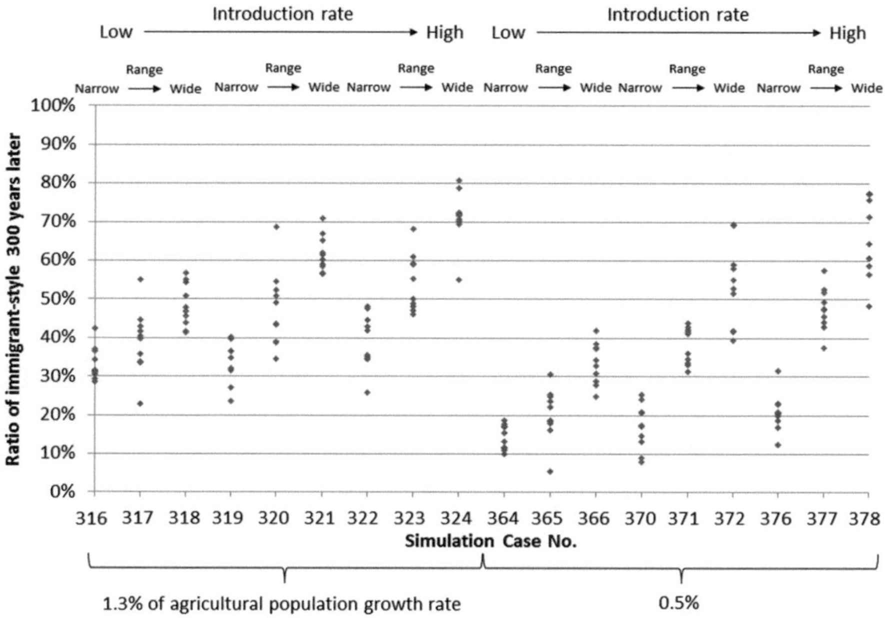

Fig. 10.10 Percentages of immigrant-style pottery after 300 years in cases with more males than females

people with immigrant traits after 300 years. When the population growth rate of agriculturalists was low, some of the cases demonstrating slow diffusion of the agrarian culture did not attain the 80 % figure in relation to immigrants after 300 years. As previously mentioned, considering that agricultural technology had not reached maturity at that time, the 1.3 % population growth rate of agriculturalists may have been too high. Therefore, the highest consistency occurred regarding cases in which even a lower population growth rate could generate demographic transition through rapid diffusion of the agrarian culture. Additionally, our investigation of immigrant-style pottery after 300 years revealed that the number of cases of rapid diffusion of agrarian culture exceeded that of cases demonstrating slow diffusion (Figs. 10.9, 10.10, and 10.11). However, in relation to immigrant-style pottery after 300 years, there were slightly fewer cases in which immigrants were primarily male (Fig. 10.3 No. 127–135, Fig. 10.4 No. 195–203, Fig. 10.7, and Fig. 10.8). However, of note is the finding that even when only inheritance of pottery style from the mother was considered, and the number of female immigrants was small, our simulation results indicated the predominance of immigrant-style pottery after 300 years.

Thus, our simulation results are consistent with anthropological and archaeological evidence that people with immigrant traits became the majority. In cases of rapid diffusion of agrarian culture, even if immigrant males constituted a majority and females were a minority, the immigrant-style pottery prevailed.

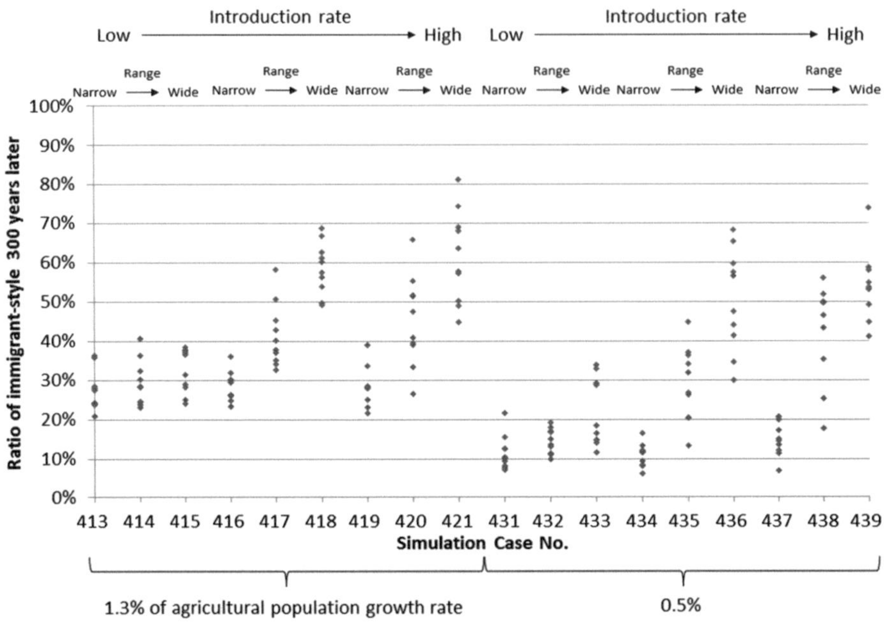

Fig. 10.11 Percentages of immigrant-style pottery after 300 years in cases with a majority of males

10.5 Concluding Remarks and Future Research

In this paper, we have described ABS and discussed its application in relation to historical and archaeological literature. We presented a simple model and extreme settings aimed at enhancing understanding of the factors affecting the behavior of the simulation results. Our results showed that in the case of initial coexistence of a large number of native Jomon people and a small number of immigrants, people with immigrant traits became the majority group a few hundred years later. Based on the simulation results, we offered three conjectures, or new falsifiable hypotheses for further discussion. The first relates to the following hypotheses: the population density of immigrants was high, and only a section of the neighboring native Jomon people made contact with them. Immigrants were polygamous and primarily male. Another conjecture related to the hypothesis that when an agrarian culture diffused among the native Jomon people, it was mostly Jomon people and only a few immigrants who played a formative role in the establishment of an agrarian culture.

Regarding the hypothesis that the population density of immigrants was high and that only a section of the neighboring native Jomon people made contact with them, there is no archaeological evidence that indicates the existence of an immigrant-only colony (Fujio 1999; Nakahashi and Iizuka 1998). However, our results relating to this hypothesis could be explained by an extremely low population density of Jomon people at the time that resulted in immigrant settlements

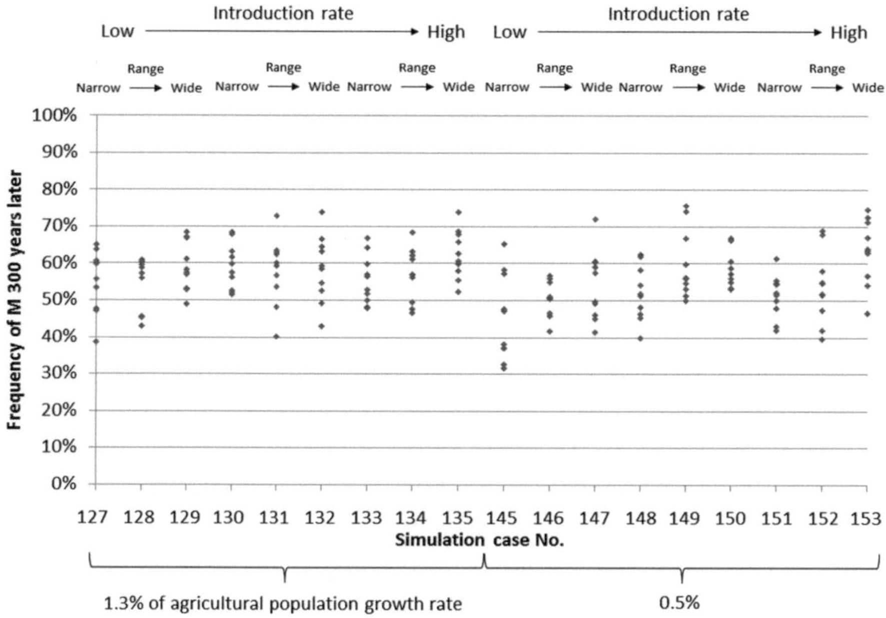

Fig. 10.12 Frequencies of macrohaplogroup M after 300 years in cases with equal numbers of males and females

(Kataoka and Iizuka 2006). There is also the possibility that the Jomon population significantly decreased, as evidenced by the small number of remains of the late Jomon period (Koyama 1984).

The discovery of bone remains of people with Jomon traits, along with artifacts verifying the existence of an agrarian culture, could support the hypothesis that when agriculture diffused among native Jomon people, it was mostly Jomon people and a few immigrants who played a formative role in the establishment of an agrarian culture. In fact, although agricultural artifacts have not been found, human bone remains characteristic of Jomon people were discovered in a Korean-style tomb at the Otomo site in Northern Kyushu.

Our simulation results indicate that mostly Jomon people and a few immigrants played a formative role in the establishment of an agrarian culture during the Yayoi period. This finding shows that within a context in which even a small number of immigrants generated demographic transition (Nakahashi and Iizuka 1998, 2008), the idea that agricultural society was a collaborative process initiated by both Jomon people and immigrants making up a living population (Fujio 1999) is highly plausible.

The hypotheses examined in this study have only offered some probabilities. The results of our simulation were generated through the application of a model based on several assumptions, with some of the simulation parameters based on those of Nakahashi and Iizuka (1998, 2008). These include the following: pottery was

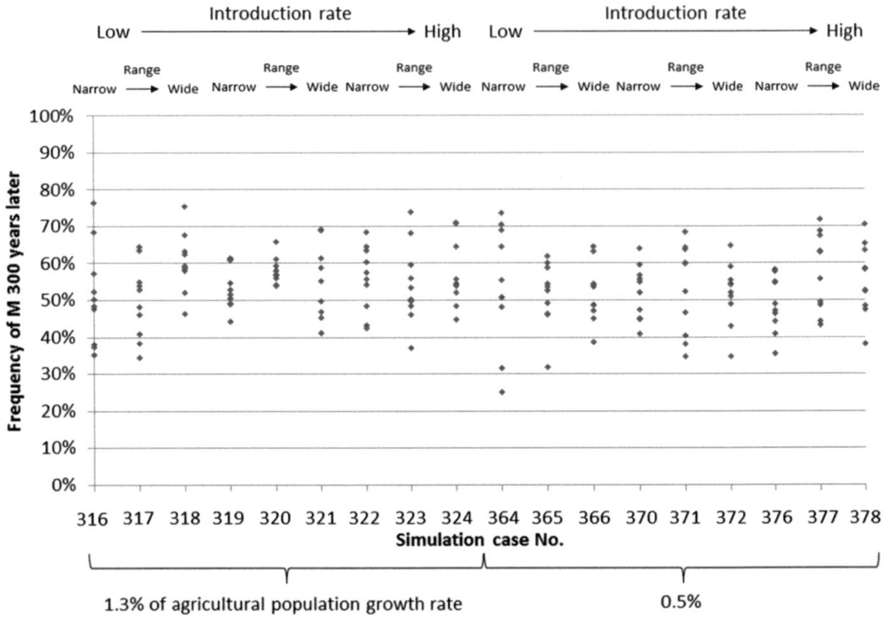

Fig. 10.13 Frequencies of macrohaplogroup M after 300 years in cases with more males than females

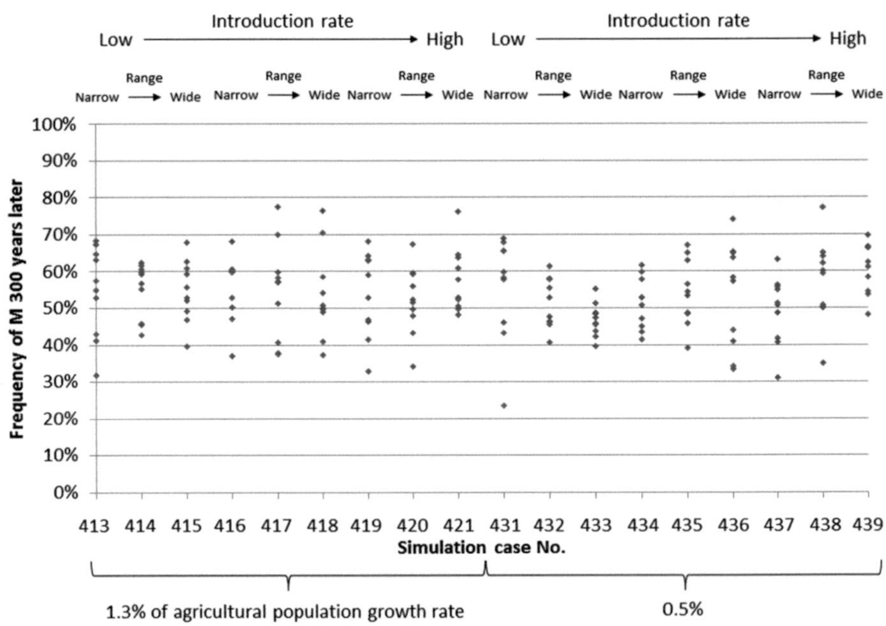

Fig. 10.14 Frequencies of macrohaplogroup M after 300 years in cases with a majority of males

inherited matrilineally, monogamy was the marriage institution within Jomon society, polygamy necessitated highly productive agriculture, and cultural transmission was based on a very simple pattern vis-à-vis the SI model of infectious diseases. These results could change if we employed different assumptions. These assumptions require further discussion as future issues. In the near future, some assumptions will be clarified through the analysis of ancient DNA. Specifically, an analysis of the diversity of Y chromosomes (paternally inherited) and mitochondrial DNA (maternally inherited) from human remains within a settlement will answer the question of whether the marriage institution within Jomon society was monogamy, polygamy, or polyandry. Additionally, the percentage of immigrants after 300 years, a prerequisite of our simulation, relied on the results of Nakahashi and Iizuka (1998). Therefore, any variation of the discriminant used in their study would require a different interpretation of the results of our study. It should be noted that demographic transition may also be caused by plague and war in addition to differing population growth rates. However, because there is no archaeological evidence to support these events (Nakahashi and Iizuka 1998), they were not considered in our simulation model.

The first objective of this study was to explore new simulation cases that matched the archeological evidence, and to investigate their underlying processes. Therefore, this paper does not include a detailed discussion of the validation work related to the exploration of the parameters. However, to investigate which conditions accord with archaeological evidence, further parameter tuning should be performed. These include developing regression trees with a random forests algorithm that could uncover which variables are more or less important, as well as Bayesian approximation methods that could isolate relevant parameter combinations. We have also proposed the pattern-oriented inverse simulation method in another history simulation study of ancient Chinese empires, which uses advanced evolutionary algorithms and high performance computation techniques (Yang et al. 2012). These methods are promising in terms of strengthening the application of our ABM approach to historical studies. The application of these advanced techniques offers considerable challenges to be addressed in our future work.

In conclusion, we believe that the ABS model and results of this study are widely applicable beyond the time frame and region of our investigation. The present study engages with the universal theme of population dynamics that unfolded after the introduction of agrarian culture. Furthermore, this study is the first to apply ABS to this anthropological and archeological issue in Japan. Within Japanese anthropology and archaeology, it is difficult to apply the ABS developed in famous pioneering studies on factors relating to the residential transition of the Anasazi tribe (Dean et al. 2000). For most anthropological and archaeological studies in Japan, the required data, especially paleo-environmental records, are not widely available as for these studies. However, even if there are less data available, as for the current study, ABS is able to compensate for this paucity of data. Therefore, it has the potential to become a powerful tool within Japanese anthropology and archaeology.

References

Bently GR, Jasinenska G, Goldberg T (1993) Is the fertility of agriculturalists higher than that of nonagriculturalists? Curr Anthropol 34:778–785

Dean JS, Gumerman GJ, Epstein JM, Axtell RL, Swedlund AC, Parker MT, McCarroll S (2000) Understanding Anasazi culture change through agent-based modeling. In: Kohler TA, Gumerman GJ (eds) Dynamics in human and primate societies. Oxford University Press, New York, pp 179–205

Fujio S (1999) The formation of Yayoi culture in Fukuoka Plain: The interaction between hunter-gatherers and agrarian. Bull Natl Mus Japan Hist 77:51–84 (in Japanese with English abstract)

Grimm V, Berger U, DeAngelis D, Polhill JC, Giske J, Railsback SF (2010) The ODD protocol: a review and first update. Ecol Model 221:2760–2768

Hanihara K (1987) Estimation of the number of early migrants to Japan: A simulative study. Anthropol Sci 95:391–403

Kaneseki T (1976) Nihonminzoku no kigen. Hosei University Press, Tokyo (in Japanese)

Kataoka K, Iizuka M (2006) A mathematical study of the increase of the "Yayoi migrant population". Kyushu Koukogaku 81:1–20 (in Japanese with English abstract)

Kivisild T, Tolk HV, Parik J, Wang Y, Papiha SS, Papiha HJ, Villems R (2002) The emerging limbs and twigs of the East Asia mtDNA tree. Mol Biol Evol 19:1737–1751

Kong QP, Yao YG, Sun C, Bandelt HJ, Zhun CL, Zhang YP (2003) Phylogeny of East Asian mitochondrial DNA lineages inferred from complete sequence. Am J Hum Genet 73:671–676

Koyama S (1984) Jomon zidai. Korin Sha, Tokyo (in Japanese)

Miyamoto, K (2009) Noukou no kigen wo saguru ine no kita michi. Yoshikawa koubunkan, Tokyo (in Japanese)

Murdok GP, Provost C (1973) Factors in the division of labor by sex: a cross-cultural analysis. Ethnology 12(2):203–225

Nagaoka T, Sawada J, Hirata K (2008) Did the Jomon people have a short lifespan? Evidence from adult age-at-death estimation based on the auricular surface of the ilium. Anthropol Sci 116:161–169

Nakahashi T, Iizuka M (1998) Anthropological study of the transition from the Jomon to the Yayoi periods in the Northern Kyushu using morphological and paleodemographical features. Anthropol Sci Japan Ser 106:31–53 (in Japanese with English abstract)

Nakahashi T, Iizuka M (2008) Anthropological study of the transition from the Jomon to the Yayoi periods in the Northern Kyushu using morphological and paleodemographical features (2). Anthropol Sci Japan Ser 116:131–143 (in Japanese with English abstract)

Shinoda K (2006) Idenshi de saguru Nihonjin no naritachi. In: National Science Museum (Ed.), Nihonrettutou no shizenshi. Tokyo, pp 296–307 (in Japanese)

Tanaka Y, Ozawa, Y (2001). Toraizin wo meguru syomondai. Yayoizidai niokeru Kyushu-Kanhanto kouryushi no kenkyu, 3–27 (in Japanese)

Tsude, H. (1982). Genshi zyosei to doki. In: Zyoseishi sougou kenkyukai (Ed.), Nihon zyosei shi 1.Tokyo University Press, Tokyo, pp 1–42 (in Japanese)

Yang C, Kurahashi S, Ono I, Terano T. (2012). Pattern-oriented inverse simulation for analyzing social problems: family strategies in civil service examination in Imperial China. Adv Complex Syst 15(7). doi:10.1142/S0219525912500385

Chapter 11
Cultural and Genetic Transmission in the Jomon–Yayoi Transition Examined in an Agent-Based Demographic Simulation

Naoko Matsumoto and Mariko Sasakura

11.1 Introduction

The transition from the Jomon to the Yayoi period of the Japanese archipelago is an East Asian case of a hunter-gatherer to farmer transition. Drastic socio-cultural changes in subsistence, material culture and settlement structure occurred in the northern part of Kyushu around the 10th–8th centuries BC. The major driver of this transition has been inferred as either immigration from the Korean peninsula or intentional adoption by native Jomon people (Harunari 1990; Kanaseki 1995). In reality, the Jomon–Yayoi transition is a complex process in which both human migration and cultural transmission played a major role (Imamura 1996; Matsumoto 2000; Fujio 2003).

Simulation studies can be very useful for understanding the nature of this transition as we can examine various hypotheses with different parameters to see how separate combinations would lead to alternative socio-cultural situations over a long period of time, and examine the resulting insights using real archaeological data. Interpretation of what happened in this period differs among researchers due to different assumptions concerning migration, cultural transmission, and the relationship between the two. As it is extremely difficult to calculate the long-term consequences of particular assumptions on genetic and cultural transmission, simulation can be a useful means for experimenting with particular sets of assumptions. However, simulation research remains undeveloped for this prehistoric event, except for a series of publications concerning demographic change in

N. Matsumoto (✉)
Graduate School of Humanities and Social Sciences, Okayamaa University, Okayama, Japan
e-mail: naoko_m@cc.okayama-u.ac.jp

M. Sasakura
Department of Computer Science, Okayamaa University, Okayama, Japan

J.A. Barceló and F. Del Castillo (eds.), *Simulating Prehistoric and Ancient Worlds*, Computational Social Sciences, DOI 10.1007/978-3-319-31481-5_11

terms of phenotypes (e.g., Hanihara 1987). An outline of these studies will be considered later.

The purpose of our research is not to replicate the actual processes of the Jomon–Yayoi transition, but to obtain useful insights regarding genetic and cultural transmission in order to construct a model explaining the prehistoric demographic and cultural dynamics involved. Such an effort is important, as our understanding of the socio-cultural process would remain intuitive without knowing about limits, patterns, and tendencies in dynamic relationships between population and culture.

How neolithic transitions spread has been the theme of active discussion in many parts of the world, among which the European case has been the target of the most intensive research. Whether neolithic expansions are driven mainly by demic or cultural diffusion is a major question to be answered in order to understand the transition process. Calibrated radiocarbon dates of the earliest Neolithic sites across Europe have made it possible to calculate the speed of that particular neolithic expansion. It has been demonstrated that the European Neolithic transition spread at a speed of about 1 km per year, and it has been recognized as indicating demic diffusion (Ammerman and Cavalli-Sforza 1971). On the other hand, the importance of cultural diffusion has also been pointed out (Ammerman and Cavalli-Sforza 1973, 1984; Fort 2012; Jerardino et al. 2004). Actually, archaeological evidence suggests that there can be various kinds of interactions between hunter-gatherers and farmers, and that the process of transition differs depending on the indigenous hunter-gatherers' population density and/or social complexity (Zvelebil 1986; Zvelebil and Lillie 2000).

The process of cultural transmission has recently been analyzed in an evolutionary framework, using such concepts as mutation, selection, and random drift. Cavalli-Sforza and Feldman (1981) examined how cultural evolution and diversity are produced by various modes of transmission: parent–child, peer–peer, and teacher–student. What we try to examine in this paper is a kinship-based transmission in a realistic demographic situation, hoping it can expand our understanding of the relationship between genetic and cultural transmission, and also contribute to the study of the spread of agriculture.

11.2 What We Do and Do not Know About the Jomon–Yayoi Transition

Before we move on to the simulation program and its outcome, we would like to summarize what we know about the Jomon–Yayoi transition from the archaeological evidence. The Jomon–Yayoi transition can be considered as a long-term process which started in the Late Jomon period with sporadic interactions between the southern part of the Korean peninsula and some areas in western Japan (Matsumoto 2002a), but the Jomon tradition of a basically hunter-gatherer lifestyle and material culture was maintained until the 10th–8th centuries BC when many aspects of Korean Bronze Age culture were adopted in northern Kyushu. The time frame of the Jomon–Yayoi transition has been hotly debated for more than a decade since the National Museum of History released new radiocarbon dates that pushed the date of the beginning of the Yayoi period 500 years earlier than previously thought (National Museum of Japanese History 2003). While the radiocarbon dates presented by the National Museum team distribute around the 10th century BC, a number of archaeologists insist that the start of the Yayoi period cannot be earlier than the 8th century BC based on comparative analysis of archaeological evidence between the continent and the Japanese archipelago (Nakamura 2012). It is difficult to determine the exact date of the beginning of the Yayoi, but most archaeologists agree that it should be much earlier than 500 BC as had been previously proposed.

This recent reexamination of the dating has made archaeologists reconsider the speed of the socio-cultural transformation from the Jomon to the Yayoi. Under the traditional framework, in which the Incipient and Early Yayoi periods are squeezed into less than 300 years, the spread of agriculture and the continental phenotype must have been quick. But with the same time periods extending more than 500 years in the new timeframe, the process can be slower. Although migration of significant numbers of people seemed likely under the former assumption, it may be unnecessary with the latter.

11.2.1 Archaeological Evidence and Questions

We have considerably rich archaeological data thanks to the huge number of excavations in Japan, most of which have been conducted by governmental institutions as a form of rescue archaeology. This wealth of archaeological information tells us that the actual process of the transition, i.e., the nature and extent of migration, adoption, or rejection of cultural information, etc., varied from region to region even in western Japan, where it had once been suggested that the spread of Yayoi culture was quick and uniform.

We will briefly introduce the following critical points of the Jomon–Yayoi transition. Although there are considerable differences regarding the details, most archaeologists agree that Yayoi culture first developed in northern Kyushu under strong influence from Korean Bronze Age culture, then spread eastward to the rest of the Japanese archipelago (Fig. 11.1). Except for some leap-frog diffusion to the Tohoku region during the Early Yayoi period, the spread of Yayoi culture halted in the middle of the archipelago for several hundreds of years. The Jomon tradition remained much stronger in eastern Japan.

Critical points of the Jomon–Yayoi transition which have been reconstructed based on archaeological data can be summarized as follows.

(1) There was a certain amount of migration from the Korean peninsula to northern Kyushu at the beginning of the Yayoi period (Nakahashi and Iizuka 1998).
(2) Yayoi culture was formed by integrating traditional Jomon culture and Korean Early Bronze Age culture in northern Kyushu (Matsumoto 2002b).

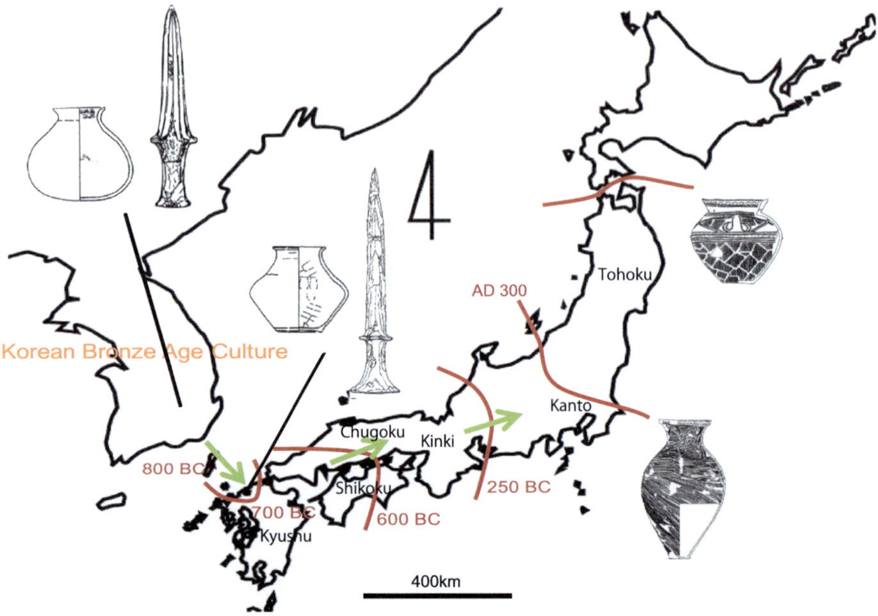

Fig. 11.1 The formation and spread of Yayoi culture. Yayoi culture was formed in northern Kyushu under strong influence from Korean Bronze Age culture, and spread to western Japan (Kyushu, Chugoku, Shikoku, and Kinki) while maintaining a certain level of uniformity. The dates beside the *red lines* indicate when each border was crossed. Adapted from Kobayashi (2013)

(3) Major components of Yayoi culture in northern Kyushu consist of wet rice agriculture, Itazuke type (Ongagawa-style) pottery, polished stone tools similar to those of Korean Bronze Age culture, and new burial customs also similar to those of the Korean Bronze Age.
(4) Immigrants from the Korean peninsula and indigenous Jomon groups lived in the same settlements in northern Kyushu.
(5) The spread of Yayoi culture to other parts of western Japan was achieved probably by both migration and acculturation, but actual conditions remain unclear.
(6) Several cases of the discovery of skeletal remains with a Jomon phenotype accompanied by Yayoi cultural traits indicate that indigenous adoption of new cultural elements was not rare.
(7) Some of the cultural elements such as placing stone weapons as burial goods were dropped in the process of diffusion from northern Kyushu to the Chugoku and Kinki regions (Nakamura 2011).
(8) Wet rice agriculture and Ongagawa-style pottery spread from northern Kyushu to the Chugoku and Kinki regions, a span of about 500 km, with considerable uniformity.

We can assume a certain amount of migration from the Korean peninsula to northern Kyushu at the beginning of the Yayoi period, based on systematic similarities in artifact style, technology, house structure, and burial customs. Yayoi culture was formed by integrating traditional Jomon culture and Korean Early Bronze Age culture in northern Kyushu. The earliest Yayoi pottery inherited stylistic and technological traditions from Mumun pottery of Korean Bronze Age culture, but was not the same as Mumun pottery. It represents the creation of a new tradition.

While wet rice agriculture and Ongagawa-style pottery spread uniformly from northern Kyushu to the Chugoku and Kinki regions, it is not a simple task to calculate the speed of the neolithic transition for the case of the Japanese archipelago as a whole. In addition to the difficulty in estimating distances due to the complicated geography of the islands, defining the earliest dates for each region can be problematic as the adoption of agriculture predates that of Yayoi material culture in a number of cases in Kyushu, Shikoku, and the Chugoku region. However, even when direct evidence of agriculture, such as paddy remains and agricultural implements, is not available, the first appearance of Ongagawa-style pottery in an area can be used as an indicator of the arrival of agriculture.

However, the absence of some burial customs beyond Kyushu indicates that parts of Yayoi culture were not transmitted, or intentionally rejected. Partial transformation and/or rejection of new culture are evident in eastern Japan as well, where the contents of Yayoi culture turned out quite different from western Japan.

Cultural continuity from the Jomon is evident in many aspects of finds at northern Kyushu settlements occupied by both Korean immigrants and indigenous Jomon groups, such as chipped stone tools, pottery style, and the custom of tooth ablation. Accordingly it is reasonable to assume that immigrants from the Korean peninsula did not exceed the indigenous population in number at these Incipient Yayoi settlements.

As the sociocultural processes were significantly different in western and eastern Japan, we made the heuristic decision to conduct our simulation taking the processes in western Japan as target. Also, while recognizing that decisions concerning cultural integration, and transformation and adoption/rejection of cultural elements, are certainly important factors in the Jomon–Yayoi transition, for the sake of simplicity we chose to focus only on the matter of transmission in this paper.

11.2.2 Physical Anthropological Evidence and Questions

As noted above, discoveries of skeletal remains with a Jomon phenotype accompanied by Yayoi cultural traits suggest that indigenous adoption of new cultural elements was commonplace. In the Incipient and Early Yayoi periods, skeletal remains with a so-called continental phenotype have only been found in a restricted area of northern Kyushu, while a number of individuals with a Jomon phenotype have been found in the context of Yayoi culture. At the Shinmachi site in Fukuoka prefecture, a middle-aged woman with a Jomon phenotype and Jomon-style tooth ablation was found buried in a grave covered with a dolmen, a custom newly adopted from the Korean peninsula. At the Shinpo site in Hyogo prefecture, three burials from the Early Yayoi period were excavated, each containing male skeletal remains with a Jomon phenotype along with Jomon-style tooth ablation. One of the graves yielded 18 stone arrowheads, indicating that the man might have been shot to death (Katayama 2000). The burials were accompanied by Yayoi pottery and stone tools.

It should be noted that skeletal evidence for this transitional period is rare, and it is very difficult to estimate the size and timing of the migration from the peninsula. But we do know that continental phenotypes are dominant in the Middle Yayoi period in northern Kyushu, as we have many skeletal remains from that period thanks to the practice of jar burial, which protected the bones from decay.

11.2.3 Prior Simulation Studies on the Jomon–Yayoi Transition

Prior applications of simulation to the study of the Jomon–Yayoi transition have mostly been restricted to demographic calculations. Hanihara (1987) proposed that more than a million people must have migrated from the continent to the Japanese archipelago during the Yayoi and Kofun periods based on his simulation of population increase, assuming that the population increase from the Final Jomon to the early historical period is inexplicable without a massive influx of population. Hanihara assumed that the annual population increase rate of the indigenous Japanese population did not exceed 0.2 %. The massive migration theory of Haninara has been criticized on two points: it does not fit very well with the archaeological data, and his assumption of the population increase rate may be too modest (Imamura 1996).

In order to clarify the mysterious gap between the modest estimation of the scale of immigration at the beginning of the Yayoi period and the dominance of continental physical features in the Middle Yayoi, Nakahashi and Iizuka carried out palaeodemographic simulations in which a higher population growth rate was assumed for immigrants (Nakahashi and Iizuka 1998, 2002, 2008). Nakahashi and Iizuka's study demonstrates that even a small number of immigrants from the Korean peninsula can lead to the dominance of continental physical features in the Middle Yayoi population in northern Kyushu that is evidenced in excavated skeletal remains. Thus they conclude that the immigrants were mainly responsible for the drastic cultural change.

While Nakahashi and Iizuka's model may provide a possible scenario concerning population dynamics in northern Kyushu, its assumptions on demographic processes may be too simple to understand the real dynamics of intermarriage and resulting genetic spread, as their simulation takes immigrants and the indigenous population separately. They do consider intermarriage of the two, but the mixed population is treated as a third category of population to which a separate rate of increase is applied. As pointed out above, however, archaeological evidence shows that immigrants and indigenous people basically cohabited the same villages and shared many cultural assets. Therefore, it seems unlikely that social categories of "immigrants" and "indigenous people" were maintained for hundreds of years and thus different population increase rates should be applied to each. In order to achieve a better understanding of the transition, we need to examine both the transmission of genetic traits and cultural skill to see how they are different but interrelated. An agent-based simulation would be one suitable method for this type of investigation.

Sakahira and Terano's approach (Sakahira and Terano 2014, Chapter 10 in this volume) is the first application of agent-based simulation to obtain new theoretical insights into the complex relationships between immigrants and indigenous people in the Jomon–Yayoi transition. Their main concern is the same as that of Nakahashi and Iizuka (1998, 2008), but they succeeded in providing a new possible scenario in which the dominance by the continental phenotype can be achieved. Their scenario posits that immigrants lived closely together in the first stage, that agriculture spread quickly, and that immigrants and their descendants were polygamous. The latter two points are highly speculative, and the first is not supported by archaeological evidence, as Sakahira and Terano have noted.

11.3 Agent-Based Simulation for Investigating Genetic and Cultural Transmission

11.3.1 Motivation

Our aim in using agent-based simulation is to experiment with a new set of parameters to broaden our horizons for reconstructing past phenomena. Our model is related to dual inheritance theory, as we want to observe how genetic and cultural traits spread, but the situation assumed in our model differs from the major models that have been established in other studies of neolithic expansion, being more focused on the relationship between kin-relations and the transmission of cultural skills in the context of realistic demographic dynamics.

Kinship is at the core of social structure for many segmented societies. Marriage is important as it creates and/or strengthens social relationships between groups. For hunter-gatherers, social networks based on kinship are important as a safety net in case of economic crisis, and also serve as the basic system for the transmission of information. In previous studies on the neolithic diffusion process, relocation of the next generation to obtain new land for cultivation has been considered the main mode of demic diffusion, and cultural diffusion mainly assumes adoption of cultivation by hunter-gatherers irrespective of kin relations to farmers. While such a clear distinction may be useful for examining differences between the two modes of diffusion, it may obscure the real process of transmission where kinship plays an important role.

As pointed out above, the nature and extent of migration from northern Kyushu eastward, and how different patterns of migration and acculturation may distribute both genes and cultural traits, are not well understood. Our simulation project intends to gain basic understandings of the relationships between the migration rate and the spread of genetic traits, and how social learning conditions affect the spread of cultural skills under realistic demographic dynamics.

There are no concrete arguments about the size and/or frequency of migrations within the Japanese archipelago in the Incipient and Early Yayoi periods; it is often assumed that the earliest settlement with Yayoi culture in each area was established partly or entirely by new Yayoi settlers. This image is similar to that of the wave-of-advance model proposed for agricultural expansion in Europe. The change from Jomon to Yayoi material culture looks drastic, but indigenous, local cultural traditions can also be recognized in the transitional period in each area. This means that people possessing Yayoi material culture and practicing agriculture did not just split and establish new villages, but always moved into areas or settlements where indigenous people lived, and intermingled with them.

The appearance of Yayoi cultural traits such as Ongagawa-style pottery and rice production as a set indicates that demic diffusion was involved to some extent, but settlement sites with the earliest Yayoi traits are almost always found close to Final Jomon sites in the same area. Some archaeologists regard this situation as evidence of the coexistence of hunter-gatherers who retained Jomon cultural traditions and newly arriving farmers with Yayoi culture. Although this may be the case in some instances, it is reasonable to consider that Yayoi culture may also have spread through other sequences of events. For example, at first a small number of inhabitants of a "Jomon" settlement may have started to adopt Yayoi cultural traits, then the number of such inhabitants increased, and when they finally became the majority they relocated their settlement to land more suitable for wet rice agriculture (Mikasa and Wakabayashi 2011).

In the Jomon period and probably also in the Incipient and Early Yayoi periods, population density in western Japan was low. Settlement size remained generally small and duration tended to be short, suggesting that life was rather mobile. In such small-scale societies, the movement of individuals from group to group should be easier compared to more sedentary societies with a strong sense of territoriality. Such sporadic movement of people would be beneficial for the reproduction of a small-scale population and for intergroup communication. Recent study shows that a number of pieces of Obora-style pottery, which is produced in the Tohoku region, have been found in Incipient and Early Yayoi sites in western Japan (Kobayashi 2013). While this may indicate that long-distance interactions played an important role in the transitional period, it also suggests there was some westward movement of people. Therefore, we should not restrict the direction of movement to eastward.

Neither a typical demic diffusion model nor a cultural diffusion model seems to fit the archaeological observations stated above. Therefore, before assuming a one-way, one-time event of a large-scale eastward migration, we should explore how cultural skills and genetic traits spread under ordinary, ad hoc movements of people. Moreover, it is readily imagined that the remarkably steady spread of cultural traits exhibited in the Yayoi case would be impossible without some form of transmission bias, should we adopt a low-level, random migration model.

Some cultural traits such as pottery decoration may be regarded as neutral and can be understood with models of drift and random transmission (Shennan and Wilkinson 2001; Shennan 2011). But the spread of Yayoi culture, whose central feature is the adoption of agriculture, is a case of the diffusion of innovation where biased transmission should play a major role. It is known that the spread of innovation usually takes an S-shaped increase when the adoption starts with a relatively small number of adopters at the first stage, followed by a rapid increase in adoption before a final phase of slowing down. It has been pointed out that some form of biased transmission is necessary for this pattern to emerge (Henrich 2001; Henrich and McElreath 2003). While there are various reasons for bias in cultural transmission, when it is grounded in the ways that individuals select their mentors for learning cultural skills, the bias could stem from direct assessments of the cultural skills, the social prestige of the person with the skill, or whether the majority of people possess the skill (Henrich 2001). Some form of model-based bias, probably a skill-bias or success-bias, is assumed in our model. New knowledge and skill in food production would likely be appreciated by hunter-gatherers who are already familiar with the cultivation of beans (Obata et al. 2007). It is also well known from ethnographies that hunter-gatherers often reject the adoption of agriculture even when they are in close contact with farmers, but such cultural barriers would be lowered if the bearer of new culture is not a stranger but a relative.

We should be careful in estimating the productivity of the earliest phase of rice agriculture, as population increase does not seem to have resulted soon after its adoption but becomes evident only after several hundred years. The adoption of agriculture definitely increased the productivity of the group, which eventually resulted in a significant population increase, so it is a more adaptive cultural trait. On the other hand, the transition from hunting and gathering to farming accompanies some risk. It is reported that skeletal remains from the Early Neolithic show more stresses compared to their hunter-gatherer predecessors (Cohen and Armelagos 1994), although an increase in stress at the beginning of agriculture is not evident in the case of the Jomon–Yayoi transition.

11.3.2 Simulation System

The simulation system we developed is a multi-agent system. In this system, an individual is implemented as an agent. The purpose of the simulation is to observe how genetic traits and cultural skills are transmitted through kin-relationships

Table 11.1 Simulation parameters

Parameter	Values/Descriptions
Number of years	500
Number of areas	5
Initial population per area	300
Destination of migration	Area(s) directly adjacent
Pattern of migration	M1: Individual migration with a probability of 0.001 per year M2: Individual migration with a probability of 0.01 per year M3: Family migration with a probability of 0.001 per year (agent plus her or his relatives within two degrees of relationship)
Marriage rule	Start looking for a spouse at the age of 15
	Age difference of a couple no greater than 10 years
	Monogamous
	No divorce
	Remarry after death of a spouse
Reproduction	Married females reproduce according to the birth rate (Table 11.2)
Genetic trait	One-locus two-allele model Yayoi type = YY, Jomon type = JJ, Hybrid type = YJ
Initial genetic distribution	Agents in the area A = YY, agents in areas B, C, D, E = JJ
Cultural skill	1 or 0
Initial skill distribution	Agents in the area A = 1, agents in areas B, C, D, E = 0
Age of skill acquirement	7
Transmission of skill	From an agent in the same area L1: Random L2: From a relative with a positive skill value if there is one within two degrees of relationship L3: Random from among relatives within two degree of relationship

without significant one-way migration as supposed in the wave-of-advance model. Parameters used in the simulation are shown in Table 11.1.

The system has areas that represent geographical divisions, or regional boundaries of populations. Areas are connected, and the connections of these areas can be logically represented as a graph in which an area is a node and a connection between areas is an edge. Individuals are born in one of the areas and can move through the connections to others, if she or he decides to move. The system determines if the migration occurs for each individual according to the migration rate.

In our simulation we set five areas connected in series, as areas A–E. Three hundred individuals are generated in each area at the start of the simulation, and data are taken for 30 years until the population structure stabilizes. The size of the initial population may be too modest if it is supposed to represent actual regional populations at the beginning of the Yayoi period, although the latter are difficult to estimate. In order to check if the number of agents affects qualitative features of the output, we experimented with an initial population of 3,000 per area. As the results showed no significant difference due to the increased number of agents, we decided to use the smaller number for efficiency.

Birth and death rates of an individual agent were based on ethnographic and obstetrical data and set to adjust as the population gradually increases (Tables 11.2 and 11.3). The birth rate is a combination of the pregnancy and successful delivery rates. The latter is defined according to age group. The maternal mortality rate is set at 0.01. We are aware that the birth rate setting, configured with a more micro-scale demographic analysis in mind, is too complicated for the current purpose of the simulation, but we kept it in that form because it would not affect the result. The death rate is defined according to age group, with higher death rates for babies and seniors. Population increase or decrease can be controlled to some extent by adjusting the birth and death rates, although the results can vary because of the stochastic nature of the simulation. An individual is born as a female or a male with a 50 % probability and has knowledge of her or his blood relationship, so that we can set an incest taboo.

Each agent has two parameters: a genetic trait and level of cultural skill. The genetic trait is intended to represent a set of genes responsible for the morphological difference between Jomon and Yayoi phenotypes and is defined by a simplified one-locus two-allele model. At the start of each run, all agents in the area A have

Table 11.2 Probability of pregnancy for each age category of married female agents. The probability of successful delivery is 0.8

Age category	Probability of pregnancy
0–14	0.0
15–19	0.25
20–29	0.35
30–35	0.3
36–42	0.2
≥ 43	0.0

Table 11.3 Probability of death for each age category

Age category	Probability of death
0	0.25
1–5	0.08
6–10	0.04
11–35	0.02
36–50	0.035
51–70	0.06
71–75	0.1
76–80	0.5
≥ 80	1.0

the Yayoi type genetic trait YY and those in the other areas have the Jomon type genetic trait JJ. A child inherits randomly one of the two alleles of each parent.

A simplified binary model is used for cultural skill which may represent knowledge and technology related to wet rice agriculture. An agent's cultural skill level is 0 at birth. If she or he reaches the age of seven, the individual chooses a master and copies that person's level of cultural skill. Copying errors are not considered in the model for simplification. The system has the following three conditions for choosing a master, to simulate the effect of social learning in a simplified manner.

L1. Choose one randomly from all individuals in the same area who are older than the individual.
L2. Choose one who has cultural skill among relatives within two degrees of relationship who live in the same area if available.
L3. Choose one randomly among older relatives within two degrees of relationship who live in the same area.

At the start of each run, all agents in area A have a cultural skill level of 1 and those in all other areas have a cultural skill level of 0.

As for migration, we experimented with the following three conditions to see the effect of the migration rate and whether kinship-based migration has any effect on the speed of genetic or cultural transmission.

M1. An individual moves alone with a probability of 0.001 per year.
M2. An individual moves alone with a probability of 0.01 per year.
M3. An individual moves with her or his relatives within two degrees of relationship with a probability of 0.001 per year.

Each individual can move to an adjacent area, meaning that individuals living in area A can move only to area B, while those in area B can move to either area A or C, at the specified rate of probability for each year.

We set the marriage rules as follows. An agent starts to look for her or his spouse at the age of 15. If an individual finds an unmarried agent of the opposite gender living in the same area, whose age is at least 15 and within ±10 years of the individual's own, they marry. For the sake of simplicity, monogamous marriage is the rule, although we are aware of the possibility that polygamy might have played an important role in the spread of genetic and cultural traits at the beginning of Yayoi culture, and have started examining its effect on genetic and cultural transmission (Matsumoto and Sasakura 2015). Agents can get married while they are alive, and remarry after the death of a spouse. Remarriage especially for younger females is considered vital due to the risk of the population dying out given the rather high mortality.

We ran 20 simulations for 500 years for each combination of the three conditions each for social learning (L1, L2, L3) and migration (M1, M2, M3), and examined the results of population increase, spread of genetic value, and spread of skill value.

11.3.3 Results

Means of the 20 runs are shown in the Fig. 11.2, 11.3, 11.4, 11.5, 11.6, 11.7 and 11.8. As the population increase and the spread of the Yayoi genetic trait were not affected by the social learning condition, only the results of the L1 condition are shown. The rate of population increase shows considerable fluctuation due to the stochastic nature of the simulation. The smallest population at the end of the simulation for 500 years in all runs was 749 (area A under the M3 condition) while

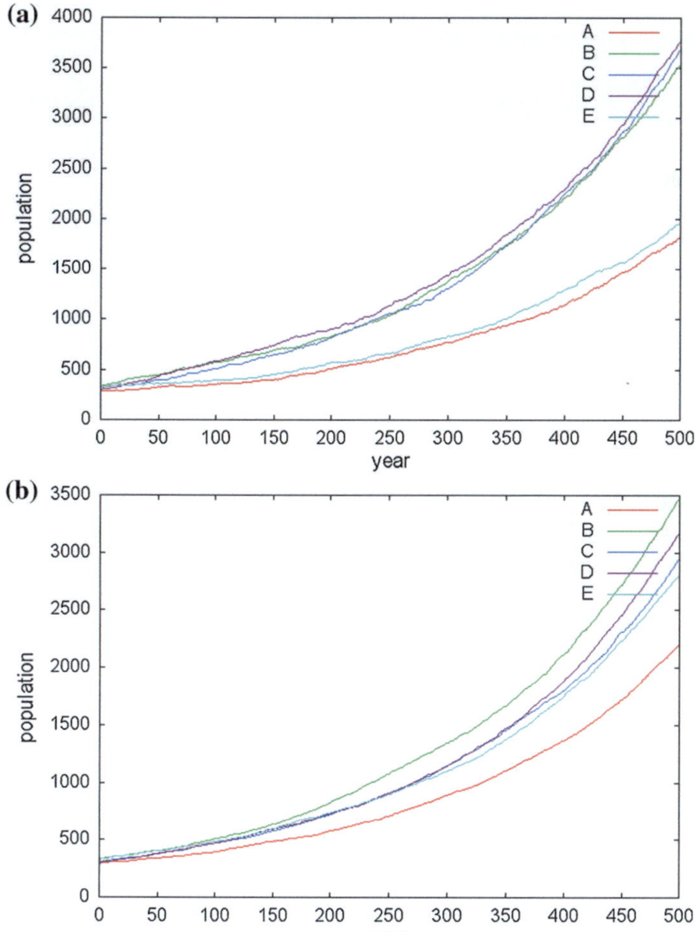

Fig. 11.2 **a** Population increase under conditions M3 (family migration with a probability of 0.001 per year) and L1 (random transmission of skill from an agent in the same area) **b** Population increase under conditions M1 (individual migration with a probability of 0.001 per year) and L3 (random transmission of skill from among relatives within two degree of relationship)

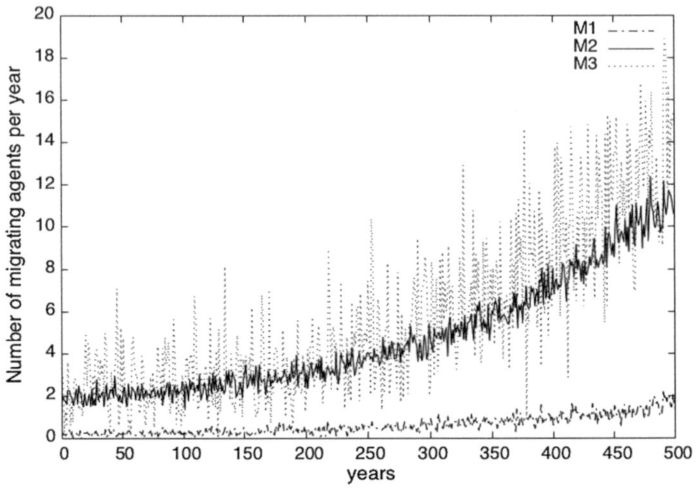

Fig. 11.3 Number of agents migrating per year for conditions M1 (individual migration with a probability of 0.001 per year), M2 (individual migration with a probability of 0.01 per year), and M3 (family migration with a probability of 0.001 per year)

the largest was 5,862 (area D under the M2 condition). In the case of conditions M2 and M3, the population increase rate in areas A and E tended to be slower than in other areas, probably due to a smaller incoming migration as those areas have only one place each supplying and receiving migrants, while the other three areas have two apiece (Fig. 11.2b). This effect is not significant in the M1 condition as the number of migrating agents is small (Fig. 11.2a).

The actual number of agents who move per year under the M1 condition is very small (Fig. 11.3). In the M2 condition, about two agents move every year from the start and the number of migrating agents increases to more than 10 agents near the end of the run. The number of migrating agents does not significantly differ between the M2 and M3 conditions, although the number of people moving per year shows much more fluctuation for M3, because it depends on the number of relatives of the person who decides to migrate.

Although our simulation is not intended to replicate the actual processes of the Jomon–Yayoi transition, the population increase rate in the simulation is consistent with the estimated population increase from the Final Jomon to the Yayoi period based on the number of archaeological sites. Population density in western Japan was quite low in the Jomon period but significantly increases in the Yayoi. Estimated population in the Early Yayoi period can be more than ten times that of the Final Jomon in many areas (Koyama 1978).

However, patterns of the spread of genetic value and skill value seem unaffected by such differences in population increase. The spread of genetic value was almost constant as different migration rates were applied. In the case of M1 where the migration rate is very low, the spread of the Yayoi genetic trait is also very slow

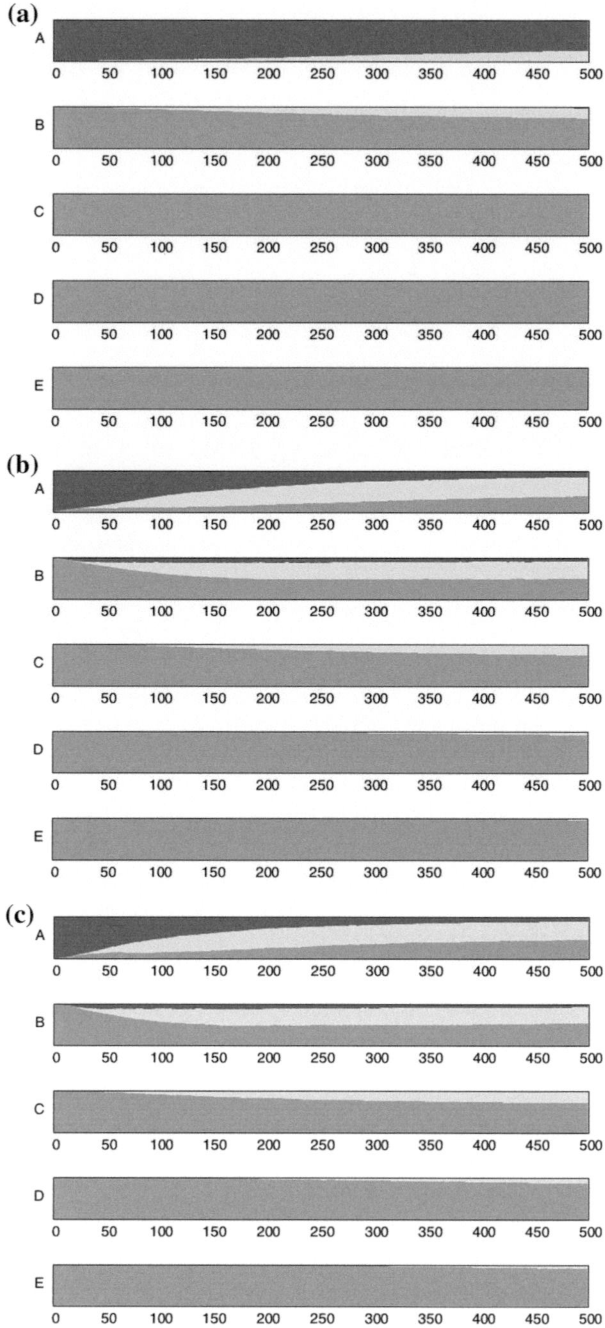

Fig. 11.4 Spread of the Yayoi genetic trait under conditions **a** M1 (individual migration with a probability of 0.001 per year) **b** M2 (individual migration with a probability of 0.01 per year) **c** M3 (family migration with a probability of 0.001 per year) *Dark gray* = Yayoi type; *light gray* = hybrid type; *gray* = Jomon type

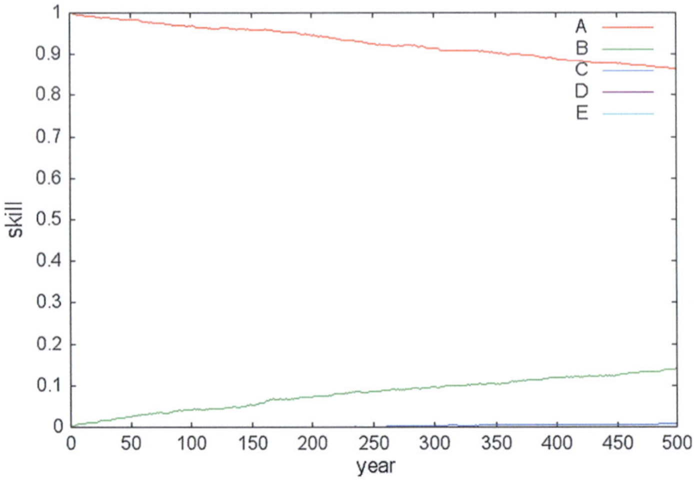

Fig. 11.5 Spread of cultural skill under conditions L1 (random transmission of skill from an agent in the same area) and M1 (individual migration with a probability of 0.001 per year)

(Fig. 11.4). There appear to be some heterozygous individuals slowly increasing in area B over 500 years, but the homozygous Yayoi population is almost entirely restricted to area A. In the case of M2, the number of migrating people is 10 times greater than that in the case of M1. In this condition, the Yayoi genetic trait spreads quicker and the ratio of homozygous Yayoi population decreases. The genetic composition in area B becomes similar to that of area A and about one fourth of the population in area C is heterozygous, but the Yayoi genetic trait barely enters areas D and E (Fig. 11.4a). This situation may fit the physical anthropological evidence in some respects. In the M3 condition, genetic traits spreads slightly quicker than in M2, although the difference is not significant (Fig. 11.4b, c).

On the other hand, the spread of cultural skill showed distinctly different patterns according to the way to choose a master. If individuals select masters at random in the same area, skill spreads very slowly. In the M1 condition, individuals who acquire cultural skill appear in area B soon but barely appear in area C around 250 years after the start (Fig. 11.5). The mean skill value learned at age 7 slightly increases in areas B and C, while that in area A gradually decreases.

If social learning is random, cultural skill spreads rather quickly when the number of migrating people increases in the M2 condition (Fig. 11.6a). Individuals with cultural skill appear in area E in about 200 years. By contrast, the ratio of agents with cultural skill in area A decreases to less than half of the population in 500 years. The result of the M3 condition is similar to that of M2, but the mean cultural skill of area A decreases slightly more (Fig. 11.6b). We have not been able to determine whether this difference is caused by the migration pattern or just by the difference in the number of migrating agents.

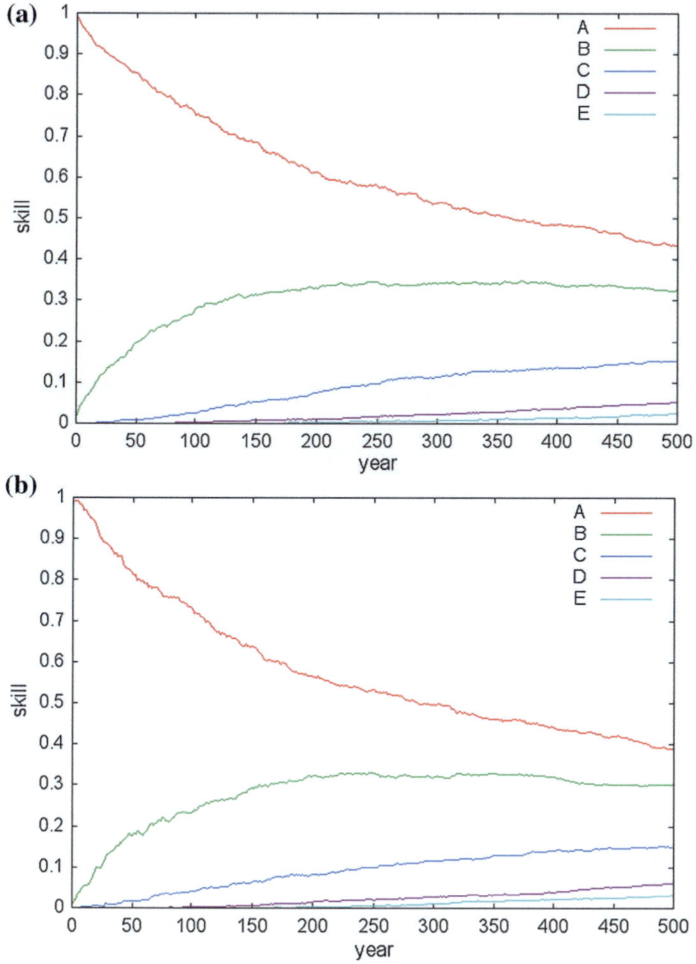

Fig. 11.6 Spread of cultural skill under conditions L1 (random transmission of skill from an agent in the same area) and **a** M2 (individual migration with a probability of 0.01 per year), **b** M3 (family migration with a probability of 0.001 per year)

In the L2 condition of biased transmission, a totally different pattern emerges. If one can learn from a skilled relative, about one third of the population in area B acquires cultural skill in 100 years even when the migration rate is very low (Fig. 11.7a). The level of skill does not drop during the diffusion process. Individuals with cultural skill appear in the most distant area E by around 300 years even in the M1 condition, although it takes a long time for the cultural skill to be shared by most of the population in the area. In the M2 condition, culture diffuses quickly (Fig. 11.7b). In about 300 years, cultural skill is held by everyone in all the areas. In the M3 condition, the spread of cultural skill is higher than in M2

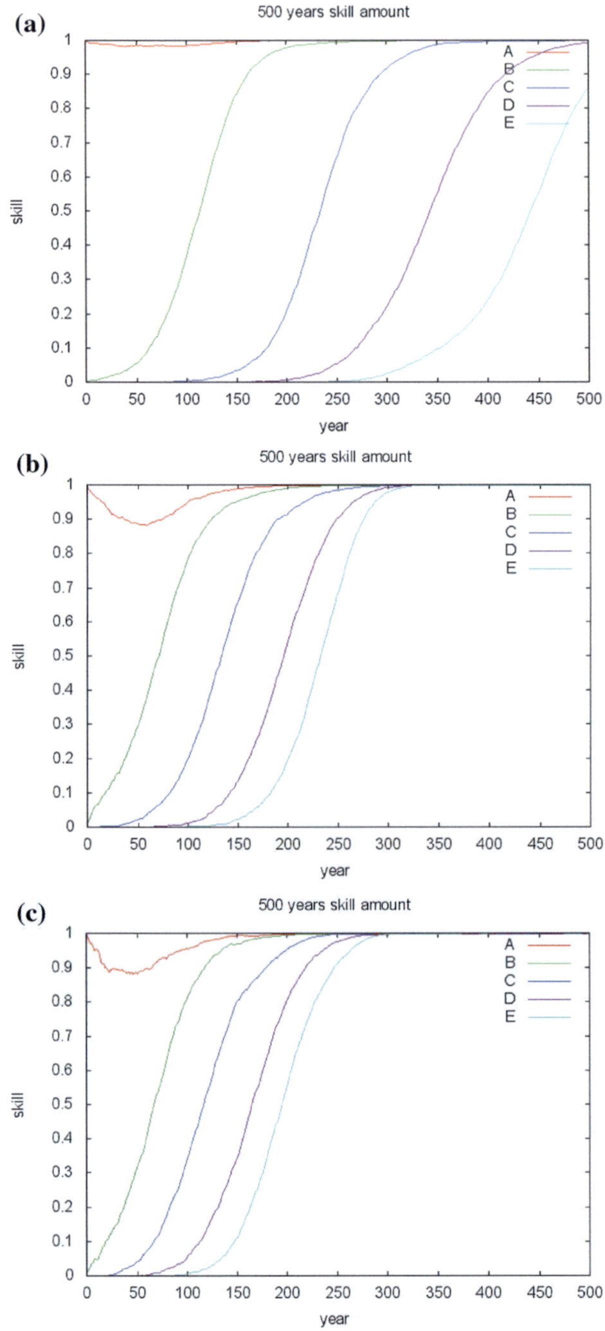

Fig. 11.7 Spread of cultural skill under conditions L2 (transmission of skill from a relative with a positive skill value within two degrees of relationship) and **a** M1 (individual migration with a probability of 0.001 per year), **b** M2 (individual migration with a probability of 0.01 per year), **c** M3 (family migration with a probability of 0.001 per year)

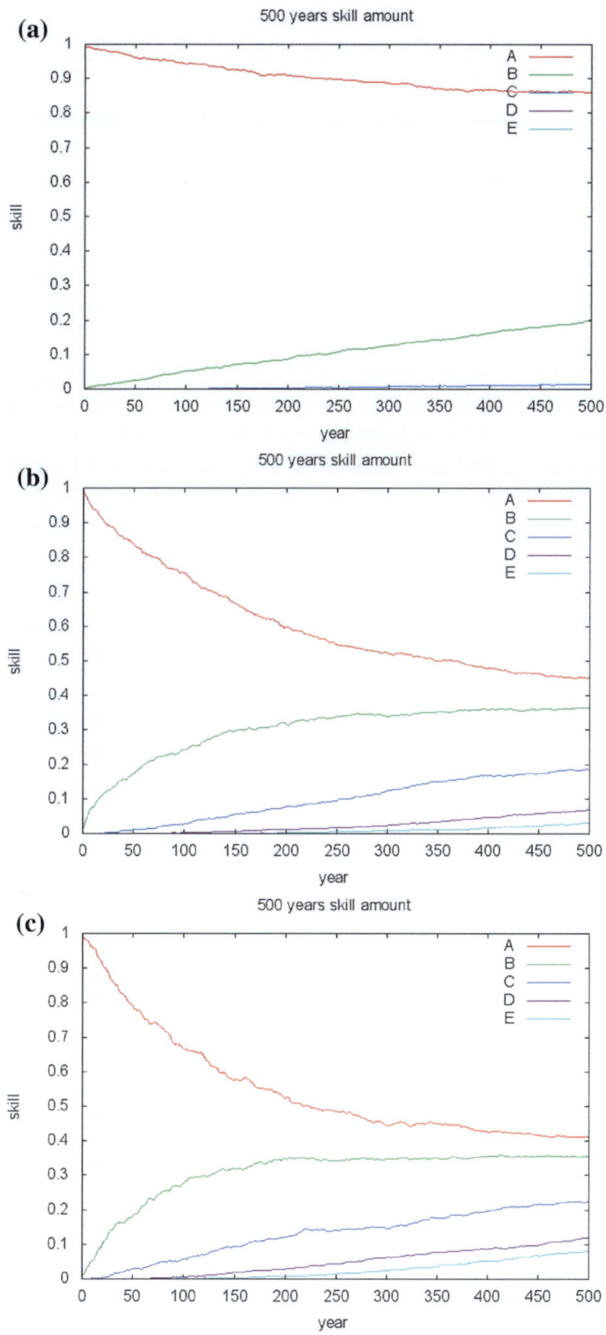

Fig. 11.8 Spread of cultural skill under conditions L3 (random transmission of skill from among relatives within two degree of relationship) and **a** M1 (individual migration with a probability of 0.001 per year), **b** M2 (individual migration with a probability of 0.01 per year), **c** M3 (family migration with a probability of 0.001 per year)

(Fig. 11.7c). This may be because there are more migrating agents in the M3 condition, but the difference between individual (condition M2) and family migration (M3) may be affecting the speed of cultural diffusion, as the number of migrating agents per year does not seem to differ so much during the first 200 years (Fig. 11.3), while a difference in diffusion speed can be observed in this period.

Results with the L3 condition indicate that if there is no preference for cultural skill at all, the resultant pattern of spread is basically the same regardless of the method of master selection (Fig. 11.8). The result would be different if we limit the possible master to parents, as it would resemble the spread of the genetic trait. However, in a society where the average life span is much shorter than that of modern developed societies, it is not uncommon that either one or both parents die before the child becomes old enough to acquire cultural skill. We experimented with a condition restricting the master-apprentice relationship to parent and child, and realized that many children would be left alone without a master and thus cultural skill would be lost eventually. This implies that unlike genetic transmission, strictly vertical transmission cannot be assumed for cultural transmission in most prehistoric societies, and if one can learn from any living relatives, the transmission pattern can be very different from that of genetic transmission. There seems to be a subtle difference between M2 and M3 in the L3 condition as well. As in the case of L1, the ratios of agents with cultural skill in the five areas converge faster in the M3 condition than in M2. Although we are not certain at the moment how family migration contributes to this phenomenon, sporadic group migration may facilitate the spread of cultural skill more than constant individual migration.

The following insights were gained from the analysis.

1. The rate of population increase can vary considerably due to chance factors, while the spread of genetic trait is almost constant as different migration rates were applied.
2. Cultural skill can spread quickly without much loss in the case of biased transmission, even when the migration rate is very low.
3. The spread of cultural skill without significant genetic influence is possible even when cultural transmission is restricted to between relatives.
4. Strictly vertical transmission cannot be assumed for cultural transmission in most prehistoric societies, and if one can learn from any living relative, the transmission pattern can be very different from that of genetic transmission

11.4 Discussion

Kline et al. (2013) examined the relationship between the nature of transmitted skills and how they are learned. Kline et al. classified cultural skill according to difficulty, strength, and importance, and demonstrated with ethnographic research in Fiji that teaching is most common among closely related kin and least common where no genetic relationship exists, although domains requiring greater skill will be associated with higher levels of oblique transmission, where experts may be selected from non-kin as mentors. The L2 condition in our simulation stands for partly vertical and partly oblique transmission, as transmission occurs not only between genetically related agents but also between persons related through marriage.

How to choose a master may vary according to the nature of the cultural skill. For highly visible, easily transmitted types of skill, transmission may not be restricted to kin. In the case of the Jomon–Yayoi transition, a set of complex skills related to wet rice agriculture spreads together with a new style of material culture. Building wet rice fields and managing all the agricultural tasks are a complex, difficult skill, which constitutes an important aspect of daily life. So it would be reasonable to assume that it is likely to be taught by those with a high level of skill who are available in the community. Making a new style of pottery with a newly adopted forming technique is also likely to be learned from the most skilled person available. Here, "available" means that the person is living close to the learner, as learning such skills requires repeated teaching for many years. Apprentices may try to find the most skilled person in the area for acquiring a rare, special skill, but that is unlikely for agricultural and pottery-making skills that belong to important domains in daily life. Thus, the patterns observed with the L2 condition may give us an inspiration for a possible explanatory model for the Jomon–Yayoi transition.

As has been shown in previous sections, indigenous people are considered to have played more major roles in areas farther from northern Kyushu where Yayoi culture was born under the influence of immigrants from the Korean peninsula. The pattern of spread of cultural skill under the L2 condition suggests that if everyone decides to learn a new cultural skill when possible, the new skill spreads reasonably quickly without significant population movement and genetic influence (Figs. 11.3 and 11.8). Although cultural transmission is restricted to relatives within two degrees of relationship, one may learn from a relative by marriage, for example a brother- or sister-in-law, from whom the learner does not inherit any genetic trait. Such a situation seems natural in the prehistoric context. Based on these insights, we may be able to construct a new scenario for the Jomon–Yayoi transition which differs from the typical wave-of-advance model, and may better conform to archaeological evidence. We should further examine the archaeological data with this new possible scenario in mind.

It should also be noted that the marriage rules and conditions for the migration rate adopted in our simulation do not produce results that fit the physical anthropological evidence in northern Kyushu, as has been examined by preceding simulation studies (Nakahashi and Iizuka 1998, 2008; Iizuka and Nakahashi 2002, Sakahira and Terano 2014). A high level of the Yayoi genetic trait in area A cannot be maintained for 500 years under any condition in our simulation. This supports the conclusions of previous studies that differences in reproduction and/or polygamy need to be included in the model of the transition.

11.5 Problems and Prospects

Models should be kept simple to examine particular relationships between factors, but the actual socio-cultural processes are incredibly complex. It should be noted that the migration, birth, and death rates are constant for all agents in the current setting, in order to examine the relationship between variables. The constant rate of migration for 500 years is not realistic for the case of the Jomon–Yayoi transition. We need to examine further the effect of social learning types on the spread of cultural skill, taking the nature of kinship structure and gender into consideration. How polygamy and different rates of reproduction would affect the model should also be investigated. What we regret at this point is that the current study does not make best use of the agent-based simulation. We are hoping to introduce decision-making processes concerning marriage, reproduction, and gender-related differences in cultural transmission to our model and investigate the nature of the Jomon–Yayoi transition further. Although our simulation project is still at a preliminary stage, further examination and comparison with detailed archaeological data promise to produce sounder results.

Acknowledgments We deeply appreciate many valuable suggestions from Joan Anton Barcelo and anonymous reviewers for improving this article. The research was funded by the Grant-in-Aid for Scientific Research (A) in 2008–2014 (Project Number 20320123), Japan Society for the Promotion of Science.

References

Ammerman AJ, Cavalli-Sforza LL (1971) Measuring the rate of spread of early farming in Europe. Man 6:674–688

Ammerman AJ, Cavali-Sforza LL (1973) A population model for the diffusion of early farming in Europe. In: Renfrew C (ed) The explanation of culture change: Models in Prehistory. Duckworth, London, pp 345–357

Ammerman AJ, Cavalli-Sforza LL (1984) The neolithic transition and the genetics of populations in Europe. Princeton University Press, Princeton

Cavalli-Sforza LL, Feldman MW (1981) Cultural transmission and evolution: a quantitative approach. Princeton University Press, Princeton

Cohen MN, Armelagos GJ (eds) (1994) Paleopathology at the origin of agriculture. Academic Press, New York

Fort J (2012) Synthesis between demic and cultural diffusion in the Neolithic transition in Europe. Proc Natl Acad Sci USA 109(46):18669–18673

Fujio S (2003) Yayoi henkakuki no kokogaku (Archaeological study of the Yayoi transitional period). Doseisha, Tokyo

Hanihara K (1987) Estimation of the number of early migrants to Japan: a simulative study. J Anthropol Soc Nippon 95(3):391–403

Harunari H (1990) Yayoi jidai no hajimari (Beginning of the Yayoi period). Tokyo University Press, Tokyo

Henrich J (2001) Cultural transmission and the diffusion of innovations: adoption dynamics indicate that biased cultural transmission is the predominate force in behavioral change. Am Anthropol 103(4):992–1013

Henrich J, McElreath R (2003) The evolution of cultural evolution. Evol Anthropol 12:123–135
Iizuka M, Nakahashi T (2002) A population genetic study on the transition from Jomon people to Yayoi people. Genes Genet Syst 77(5):287–330
Imamura K (1996) Prehistoric Japan: new perspectives on insular East Asia. University of Hawaii Press, Honolulu
Jerardino A, FortJ, Rondelli B (2004) Cultural diffusion was the main driving mechanism of the Neolithic transition in Southern Africa. PLoS ONE 9(12): e113672. doi: 10.1371/journal.pone.0113672
Kanaseki H (ed) (1995) Yayoi bunka no seiritsu: Daihenkaku no shutai wa "Jomonjin" datta (Formation of Yayoi culture: Jomon people were the main agent of a great change). Kadokawa shoten, Tokyo
Katayama K (2000) Jomonjin to "Yayoijin" (Jomon people and "Yayoi people"). Showado, Kyoto
Kline MA, Boyd R, Henrich J (2013) Teaching and the life history of cultural transmission in Fijian villages. Human Nat 24:351–374
Kobayashi S (2013) Jomon to Yayoi (Jomon and Yayoi). In: Intoh M (ed) Jinrui no idoshi (The History of human movement). Rinsen Shoten, Kyoto, pp 155–169
Koyama S (1978) Jomon subsistence and population. Senri Ethnological Studies 2:1–65
Matsumoto N (2000) Ninchi kokogaku no riron to jissenteki kenkyu (Theory and practical application of cognitive archaeology). Kyushu University Press, Fukuoka
Matsumoto N (2002a) Dento to henkaku ni yureru shakai: Ko-banki no Kyushu (Kyushu in the Late and Final Jomon periods: social transformation and tradition). In: Anzai M (ed) Jomon shakai ron (Studies of the Jomon society). Doseisha, Tokyo, pp 103–138
Matsumoto N (2002b) Jomon-Yayoi henkaku to esunishiti (The Jomon-Yayoi transition and ethnicity). Quart Archaeol Stud 49(2):24–41
Matsumoto N, Sasakura M (2015) Jinko simulation ni yoru bunka dotai kenkyu (Study of cultural dynamics with the aid of demographic simulation). In: Proceedings of the 81st annual meeting, Japanese Archaeological Association, Tokyo, p 164–165
Misaka K, Wakabayashi K (2011) The assimilation process in the Yayoi society of western Japan: Was there a coexistence of different cultural groups? In: Matsumoto N, Bessho H, Tomii M (eds) Coexistence and cultural transmission in East Asia. Left Coast Press, Walnut Creek, pp 69–88
Nakahashi T, Iizuka M (1998) Hokubu Kyushu no Jomon-Yayoi ikoki ni kansuru jinruigakuteki kosatsu (1) (Anthropological study of the transition from the Jomon to the Yayoi periods in the northern Kyushu using morphological and palaeodemographical features [1]). Anthropol Sci (Japanese Series) 106(1):31–53
Nakahashi T, Iizuka M (2008) Hokubu Kyushu no Jomon-Yayoi ikoki ni kansuru jinruigakuteki kosatsu (2) (Anthropological study of the transition from the Jomon to the Yayoi periods in the northern Kyushu using morphological and palaeodemographical features [2]). Anthropol Sci (Japanese Series) 116(2):131–143
Nakamura D (2011) The diversity of mortuary practice acceptance at the beginning of the Yayoi Period. In: Matsumoto N, Bessho H, Tomii M (eds) Coexistence and cultural transmission in East Asia. Left Coast Press, Walnut Creek CA, pp 223–256
Nakamura D (2012) Yayoi bunka keisei to Higashi Ajia shakai (Formation of Yayoi culture and East Asian societies). Hanawa shobo, Tokyo
National Museum of Japanese History (2003) Dating of the beginning of Yayoi period: current situation and possibilities of AMS. http://www.rekihaku.ac.jp/kenkyuu/0725/. Accessed 20 May 2014
Obata H, Sasaki Y, Senba Y (2007) Doki akkon kara mita Jomon jidai koubanki ni okeru Kyuushuu no daizu saibai (Impressions on pottery revealed cultivation of Glycine max subsp. max (soybean) in the Late to Latest Jomon periods in Kyusyu island). Shokuseishi Kenkyuu (Japanese Journal of Historical Botany) 15(2):97–114
Sakahira F, Terano T (2014) Yayoi noko bunka no "shutai" wa dare datta ka? Jinruigaku/Kokogaku e no ejento besu shimyureshon no tekiyo (Who played the major role of agricultural culture in Yayoi period? Agent based simulation to anthropological and archaeological problems). Konpyuta Sofutowea (Comput Softw) 31(3):97–108

Shennan S (2011) Descent with modification and the archaeological record. Philos Trans Royal Soc B: Biol Sci 366:1070–1079
Shennan S, Wilkinson J (2001) Ceramic style change and neutral evolution: a case study from Neolithic Europe. Am Antiq 66:577–593
Zvelebil M (1986) Hunters in transition: Mesolithic societies of temperate Eurasia and their transition to farming. Cambridge University Press, Cambridge
Zvelebil M, Lillie M (2000) Transition to agriculture in eastern Europe. In: Price TD (ed) Europe's first farmers. Cambridge University Press, Cambridge, pp 57–92

Chapter 12
Economic Sustainability in Relation to Demographic Decline of Celtic Agglomerations in Central Europe: Multiple-Scenario Approach

Kamila Štekerová and Alžběta Danielisová

12.1 Introduction

On a transition from middle to late Iron Age period we encounter a transformation of the central European society which was represented especially by the new settlement forms—the oppida. They appeared as a part of a socio-economically advanced environment, together with a distinctive intensification of settlement patterns. When they emerged, being understood as "deliberate foundations rather than a gradual evolution" (Collis 2000), they represented complex systems with multiple functions. However, no issue is as variable at the same time as the oppida and range of their activities, functions and social hierarchies (for the discussion on some of them (Collis 2000)).

The central European oppida share the dynamics of their occupation: according to the archaeological record the population density increased from the beginning of the occupation (half of the 2nd century BC), peaked around the end of the 2nd century/beginning of the 1st century BC, and then, within two generations or so, it decreased again. This decrease seems to have been quite rapid and the final population might have been even five times smaller than during its highest density. This massive change in the first half of the 1st century BC was not restricted to the oppida only, but reflected also on settlements in the countryside even in wider European context (Haselgrove and Guichard 2013).

Causes for gradual trend of depopulation can be seen in several factors endogenous and exogenous. However, their greater exploration is obstructed by the

K. Štekerová (✉)
University of Hradec Králové, Hradec Králové, Czech Republic
e-mail: kamila.stekerova@uhk.cz

A. Danielisová
Institute of Archaeology of Academy of Sciences of the Czech Republic, Prague, Czech Republic

J.A. Barceló and F. Del Castillo (eds.), *Simulating Prehistoric and Ancient Worlds*, Computational Social Sciences, DOI 10.1007/978-3-319-31481-5_12

overall lack of detailed archaeological data. In this situation we suggest to use agent-based models. Our aim is especially to ascertain the resilience of the food production system (i.e. carrying capacity) of the oppida under the dynamically changing (increasing/decreasing) population.

In next sections, after summarizing purpose of agent based-modelling and knowledge on economics and society in the Late Iron Age we introduce our models in NetLogo (Fig. 12.1). The first model of the population dynamics generates data on synthetic populations within alternative depopulation scenarios. The following food production and land use model is used for estimating the carrying capacity of the oppidum with respect to alternative agricultural scenarios. The last workforce model is used for studying labor input of agro-pastoral tasks during the harvest season under different weather conditions, overproduction and ratio of non-producers.

Notice here, that when thinking about modelling the Iron Age society and landscape, either we could start with the population data and explore the predicted site catchment or we could use the landscape data and estimate the likely population in the given area. Our approach was to develop the population dynamics model firstly, including alternative depopulation scenarios, and apply population data as input in subsequent models of land use and workforce allocation. Therefore the three models are designed to enable experimenting with alternative scenarios and strategies with the aim

- to test upper limits of self-subsistence (i.e. the highest possible population size, the largest manageable area of fields and maximum acceptable length of the harvest season with respect to available workforce) and
- to verify general theoretical hypotheses related to the functioning of the oppida within particular landscape environment and the ecological and economic rules that were shaping them.

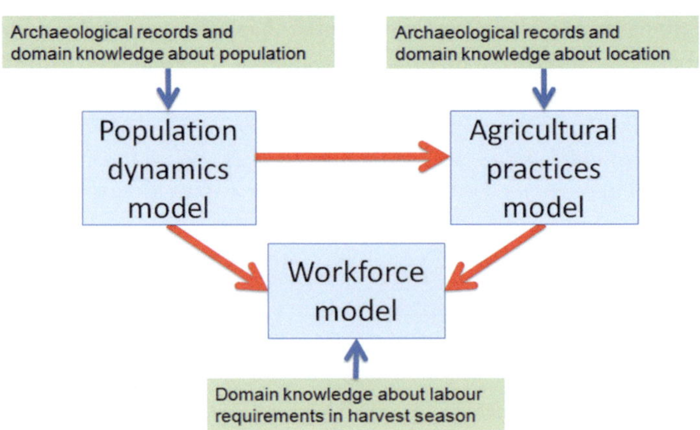

Fig. 12.1 Overview of models

12.2 Theoretical Background

12.2.1 Agent-Based Models in Archaeology

In the scope of archaeological research, agent-based models represent useful tool for testing of hypotheses and building theories through comparison of archaeological evidence with outputs of computational simulations. It is especially the dynamic aspect of models that makes them attractive for archaeologists: using models, it is possible to study spatial and temporal characteristics of development and adaptation of past societies.

Application of the agent-based modelling contributed significantly to the exploration and interpretation of key archaeological questions and topics such as subsistence strategies of hunters and gatherers (Lake 2000; del Castillo and Barceló 2013), spreading of neolitic agriculture to Europe (Conolly et al. 2008; Shennan 2007; van der Vaart et al. 2006), human impact on landscape and natural environment (Axtell et al. 2002; Wainwright 2008; Barton et al. 2010) and socio-economic factors influencing the development and/or collapse of complex societies. Iconic and frequently replicated project was Artificial Anasazi—model of disappearance of Anasazi culture in south-western America (Axtell et al. 2002; Janssen 2009). Other projects were focused e.g. on exploration of political and social structures in ancient Mesopotamia (Altaweel 2007, 2008), where different stress scenarios were applied (e.g. long term dry weather, economic crisis, demographic decline etc.) with the aim to test the resistance and sustainability of society with the given level of social complexity.

Quite often results that were achieved by social simulation and agent-based modelling can challenge traditional theories of economic production, labor input and sustainability of preindustrial society and offer new research directions and archaeological questions. Among these projects, we have to mention also Mesa Verde project which studies the development of population at American middle-west (Kohler and Varien 2012).

As well as in the area of social simulations in general, archaeological computational models are abstract: they work with the idea of past instead of the past itself, and generate data that optionally become source of new hypotheses. Therefore models can serve as behavioral laboratories for experimental ethno-archaeology (Premo 2010). By abstraction we mean the model often operates with artificial variables that have no real equivalents (e.g. attractiveness of the site, potential of the landscape, intensity of interactions) and that cannot be sufficiently and indisputably grounded in empirical data.

12.2.2 Small-Scale Agricultural Production in Late Iron Age

The agricultural economy could be explained partially as a response to environmental conditions and climate. The economic development then can be seen as an adaptive system to the balance of the ecological factor. However, neither the economy nor society is determined solely by the limits of the environment (Erdkamp 2005); social and political factors also play an indispensable role. Therefore, an analysis of the subsistence strategies during the late Iron Age is as much a social and political study as it is an economic one. As such it can eventually help to understand the dynamics of the development in the second half of the 1st century BC.

The whole Iron Age world despite its technological innovations, specialization and economic contacts, or its level of complexity, was still principally a world of the common farmer. The organization of food production and its redistribution is an essential factor for understanding the complexity of the society and for determining its limits. Every type of society has a characteristic way of the flow of resources and commodities through it, and the organization of transforming these resources to products (Fuller and Stevens 2009). The major aspect in the food production is the significance of agriculture as the primary source of subsistence and organization of potential surplus production. For the socio-economic development, the key aspect is the principle of redistribution of surplus between the consumption and investment. In terms of the technological and economic progress, which contributes to social complexity, the surplus needs not be spent, but accumulated for further investment.

When a certain level of complexity within a society is achieved, and seasonal tasks somewhere allow engaging in non-agricultural activities and at the same time a regular supply of necessary foodstuffs from elsewhere is provided, regional differences (in terms of specialization) occur (Klir 2010). Such aspects and their mechanisms in the Iron Age are still being discussed. A traditional argument in these discussions concerning the level of complexity in the late Iron Age society is that the central places were set in their environments as so called "total consumers" (Salač 2006). That generally means that they were too specialized and hence engaged in other activities, so they were not capable of producing any foodstuffs. This fact should have eventually contributed decisively to the collapse of the Iron Age society in the 1st century BC. Some of these settlements surely had to overcome or accept some environmental constrains (imposed for example by higher altitude) or were forced to adapt their subsistence practices (e.g. develop an alternative approach to the exploitation of land). There are several proofs providing support to the notion that the food production was an inseparable part of the oppidum's life. The evidence is in fact abundant: numerous livestock, agricultural tools, storage facilities, botanical and pollen analyses etc.

In the models of social complexity population dynamics and exploitation of natural resources play an important role from which wide range of social phenomena have been explained (Bayliss-Smith 1978). According to historic sources, exceeding the appropriate carrying capacity was not a rare occasion in history (Schreg 2011) even in societies with developed market networks. Intensification of the production led to innovations in the agriculture on one hand but also to a more rapid depletion of the land resources especially where their extent was limited on the other. This prompted behavior, which could have led to more profound social change at the end of the Iron Age in central Europe. Our aim was to test these premises in the socio-cultural milieu of the central European oppida.

12.3 Models of the Staré Hradisko Oppidum

Our case study location is the oppidum of Staré Hradisko in Bohemia (Čižmář 2005). The core concept is the self-subsistence of the oppidum, i.e. the idea of society pursuing agro-pastoral activities within the given temporal and spatial scale which is tested against subsistence, surplus production and carrying capacity factors. We aim to explore the dynamics of the food production and isolate possible crisis factors imposed either by environment or by un-sustainability of the economic strategies pursued. Main three questions are:

- What is the maximum population that can be sustained in a given environment and when is this maximum reached?
- Using what cultivation strategies and labor input can the population most effectively exploit natural resources in order to be self-sufficient?
- What are the dynamics of production with constantly growing or declining population (subsistence—surplus—success rate—diminishing returns)?

To answer these questions, we developed three models: the population dynamics model, subsequent food production and land use model and workforce allocation model.

12.3.1 Population Dynamics Model

12.3.1.1 Objective

This model generates data on synthetic population of the settlement (i.e. numbers of inhabitants with appropriate age/sex structure and related data on energetic requirements and available workforce), including optional population decline and structural changes. Synthetic population corresponds to assumptions based on archaeological evidence.

12.3.1.2 Theoretical Background and Scenarios

The population dynamics is defined by the initial population, its growth rate and death rate. In our case of the oppidum Staré Hradisko, the initial population is estimated to be between 600 and 800 individuals (depends on the spatial structure and the chronology of the site). Although details on structure and size of families are not known, archaeological evidence of settlement features indicates the probable existence of nuclear households of 4–6 members and communities of probably about 20–22 members residing within typical oppidum´s enclosed compounds. There is an archaeological evidence that the initial population grown quite rapidly. According the simplest Malthusian population model, the growth is exponential:

$$P(t) = P_0 e^{rt}$$

(P_{0}—initial population, r—growth rate, t—time)

For establishing the appropriate birth rates and life expectancy during the Iron Age the regional model life-tables created by Coale and Demeny for the ancient Roman population (Saller 1994) are the most relevant source of information. We used the *Model Life Tables Level 3 a 6 West*. To complete missing values in the tables (as they were in 5-year intervals), the Elandt-Johnson estimation method was applied. The constraints to be satisfied are approximately constant ratios of male/female and ratio of age categories. The model outputs are time series of the synthetic population data for the period of 120 years, i.e. time series of numbers of individuals and the consumption of the population in calories representing:

- the energetic requirements of the population,
- the availability of the human workforce, i.e. actual number of people in productive age in particular age/sex categories.

Two main categories were distinguished: "strongforce" (males and young males who can perform heavier task such as ploughing, harvesting with scythes, forest clearance etc.) and "weakforce" (females, older children and elderly, who can pursue other tasks, such as sowing, hoeing, weeding, manuring, milking, various assistance tasks etc.). These categories are important for our later workforce model.

In order to reflect the population decline of the oppidum four (de)population scenarios are formulated:

1. Normal growth of the population (*baseline*) is defined. In this case the population grows by 2 % annual increment up to 2500–3000 individuals. This scenario corresponds to the stable situation without any adverse events.
2. Sudden proportional decline (*sudden depopulation*) is a massive one-time depopulation of 30–60 % of the inhabitants. It is naturally accompanied with the decline of workforce, livestock and food storage. It corresponds to the hypothesis of the emigration of the part of the population in the 1st half of the 1st century BC.
3. Continuous proportional decline (*gradual depopulation*) is less extensive but continuous depopulation of 3 % of the oppidum's inhabitants per year. It corresponds to the hypothesis of continuous emigration beginning in the 1st half of the 1st century BC.
4. Sudden non-proportional decline (*epidemic*) is a massive one-time depopulation of 30–60 % of inhabitants, more conspicuous in certain age groups (suckling, toddlers, children, and elderly). It causes significant workforce decline during the following decades.

Depopulation scenarios have consequences that are subject of our interest in the food production and land allocation model.

12.3.1.3 Model Design

Individuals are represented by agents with two parameters (age, gender). Simulation runs in 120 yearly time-steps. Each step consists of population update, i.e. increasing of agents' age according life tables and adding new agents, representing newborns. Optionally, in case of depopulation scenario, appropriate ratio of agents is removed. Model inputs are:

- initial population size,
- selection list of life tables,
- parameter Q which specifies the probability of woman-agent to give a birth.

Value of Q is applied in formula which was identified experimentally by optimization of two functions. The first function F1 expresses the percentual changes of final population X in relation to original population A.

$$F_1 = \frac{|x - A|}{A}$$

The second function F2 defines average percent change in seven age groups (sucklings, toddlers, small children, older children, young adults, adults, elderly):

$$F_2 = \frac{1}{7} \sum_{i=1}^{7} \frac{|x_i - x_i'|}{x_i'}$$

12.3.1.4 Outputs

This model is not used for experimenting in sense of exploration of spaces of parameters; it only generates population data for alternative depopulation scenarios (Fig. 12.2).

12.3.2 Food Production and Land Use Model

12.3.2.1 Objective

The purpose of the model is to compare agricultural strategies likely to be employed by the oppidum's population in relation to the necessary land-use area and ratio of the population engaged in agricultural work.

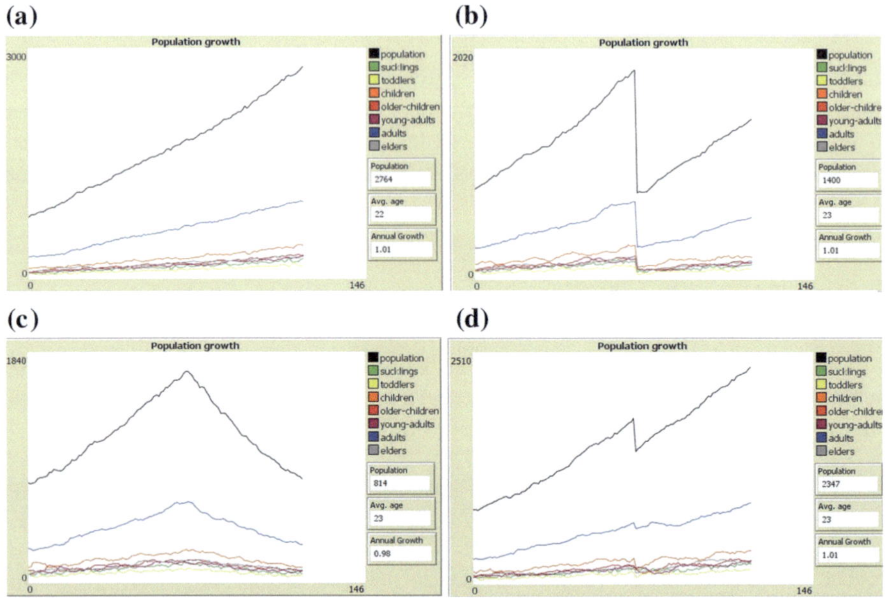

Fig. 12.2 Population dynamics: **a** baseline, **b** sudden decline, **c** gradual decline, **d** epidemics

12.3.2.2 Theoretical Background and Scenarios

The food production model captures the dynamics of agro-pastoral economy process (the oppidum's own agricultural production) in recurrent year-to-year cycles which is tested against subsistence, surplus production and carrying capacity factors. For each year, certain mixture of main land-use strategies (intensive agriculture, extensive agriculture, grazing livestock and deforestation) is applied. The abrupt or profound changes of the food storage make population to adapt to new conditions (to change the land-use strategy).

The food production model can apply population modelling outputs (i.e. time-series of synthetic population and its consumption that were calculated using caloric tables from population dynamics model, and potential workforce calculated from productive age and sex categories) together with authentic archaeological and environmental records of the region. The evidence of agricultural activities carried out by the oppidum inhabitants is indicated by particular artefacts (such as farming implements), archaeobotanical and archaeozoological assemblages, and settlement features (especially storage facilities).

The method of site catchment analysis (Jarman et al. 1972) can be used for the modelling of the oppidum's hinterland. Site catchment analysis approach is based on models of economics and ecological energy expenditure, and provides a framework within which the economic activities of particular site can be related to the resource potential of the surrounding area. We thus need to delimit the easily accessible area in the site's surroundings, which would have encompassed fields/fallows, pastures, meadows and managed forests. Considering the locational rules of the "least effort models" and the variable topography, the area is modelled as cost distance according to walking speed from the centre—the oppidum. This roughly corresponds to a distance of 4–5 km generally considered as a threshold for the travelling on a daily or semi-daily return.

In order to refer more directly to the point of the community's subsistence, demography and organisation of labor in relation to its environment a concept of "ecosystem" (cf. Ebersbach 2002; Schreg 2011) was adopted. The ecosystem consists of all the basic productive aspects of the landscape (extent and quality of arable land, pastures, managed forests, unused resources and reserves) as well of the societal means which exploit them, such as labor, technology, subsistence strategies, land tenure, social and political structure and contacts (Schreg 2011). All these aspects form the spatial layout of the particular ecosystem.

The criteria for the prediction of fields are related to the environmental variables: topography, soils, and climate. The fields in the model have to be placed on fairly moderate slopes—less than 5°, 5–10° and 10–15° respectively. The pastures have to be on slopes less than 30 % and within an accessible distance from the water source. Together with the other variables "soils" (quality, depth, rockiness), "topography", and "wetness" (the topographical tendency of the particular grid cell to be more or less wet) it is put together through the multi-criteria evaluation analysis (Eastman 2006) by which different field suitability categories are created. The plots classified as unsuitable (too wet, too rocky or on slopes too steep) are excluded from the field and pasture suitability model. One of the crucial factors for the prediction of both fields and pastures is the accessibility from the settlement. Therefore most suitable areas are plotted as the most fertile zones located as close as possible to the settlement. A cost penalty was included for more distant fields (Chisholm 1979). This option applies especially for more intensive regimes of land-use; the cost impact is lower for the fields under the extensive practices. Fields within distance zones could have been subjected to different land-use and management—more intensive closer to the oppidum and more extensive further away in terms of infield and outfield management. The terrains which remained can be attributed to forest pastures, forest openings and woodland.

The default presumption for the model is that each household that cultivated the fields used animal traction. The actual area of fields, as well as the labor input per unit area, varies greatly according to the number of inhabitants and different arable farming strategies employed (Halstead 2014). With higher yields during an increasing intensity of cultivation, the area of fields could have decreased and vice versa. High annual harvest fluctuations are apparent in modern agricultural experiments (e.g. (Rothamsed research 2006; Kunzova and Hejcman 2009). Variable annual yields are also being regularly mentioned in the historic records (Erdkamp 2005; Campbell 2007). Therefore, using the mean yield estimation in archaeological modelling would provide only a static indication of production. A relative structure of inter-annual fluctuations in the ancient crop yields from a particular area may be established by extrapolating from modern or historical data, preferably from the same region and without estimating any absolute mean value

(Haltsead and O'Shea 1989). Therefore a general range between 500–3000 kg/ha (mean value 1500 kg/ha for the intensive and 1000 kg/ha for the extensive strategy respectively, can be considered as the suitable variance of general yield variability, derived from the information on local environmental and climate conditions, the reconstructed scale and intensity of farming (by "intensity" it is understood the amount of labour input required to process one unit area of land) and production targets from small subsistence needs to surplus production requirements.

The essential hypothesis supposes the continuous growth of both the population and food production. The following agricultural strategies are assumed to have been possibly practised by the Iron Age population (cf. Halstead 1995):

- *Intensive farming* on small plots: fields were manured namely by stable dung and settlement waste; they were intensively tilled by hand, and weeded. Working animals could be used for ploughing; rotation of crops (cereals, pulses) was practiced. Intensive farming strategy represents the labor demanding option, which tends to be limited in scale or to cover only the subsistence and necessary surplus needs.
- *Extensive farming* on large plots: fields included fallows and were managed less intensively. They were manured especially by grazing animals. The plots could be usually under continuous cropping (i.e. no crops rotation) as the periods of fallow allowed for the sufficient regeneration. An extensive strategy could have been employed especially when the available land was abundant, population pressure low, labor was engaged elsewhere, or it was more preferred than the intensive production. With this strategy the potential for surplus production was higher, but could fluctuate heavily.

Both strategies could be combined in terms of infield and outfield land management in order to balance the work/land requirements. There are different consequences and constraints. Higher cereal consumption requires more intensive growing with ploughing and manuring; intensive manuring requires higher numbers of livestock; more animals require more working hours. Total manpower has to be allocated according to the appropriate sequences of agricultural activities and their timing during the year (seeding, harrowing, ploughing, harvesting or manuring).

Important issue is a livestock. Estimation of sizes of herds can be based on assumptions of sizes of households (Ebersbach 2002; Gregg 1988; Olsson 1991): when we take into account 8–10 cattle (2 ploughing oxen), 20–30 sheep/goats, 4–5 pigs and 1–2 horses per community of 4 families, total livestock can be calculated. The reproducibility of animals differs: for cattles, it is slow—0.5–0.8 calf/cow/year with mortality 20 %, therefore it takes 10–12 years (depends on the number of animals in herd) to double in size. Rates for horses are similar, with longer pregnancy and adolescence and subsequent lower herd growth; natality and mortality rates of sheep, goats and pigs are significantly higher. The culling/year sustainable for maintaining reproducibility is 10 % for horses, 15 % for cattle, 30 % for sheep/goats and 50 % for pigs. For the purpose of our model, there are three livestock scenarios (see also Fig. 12.3).

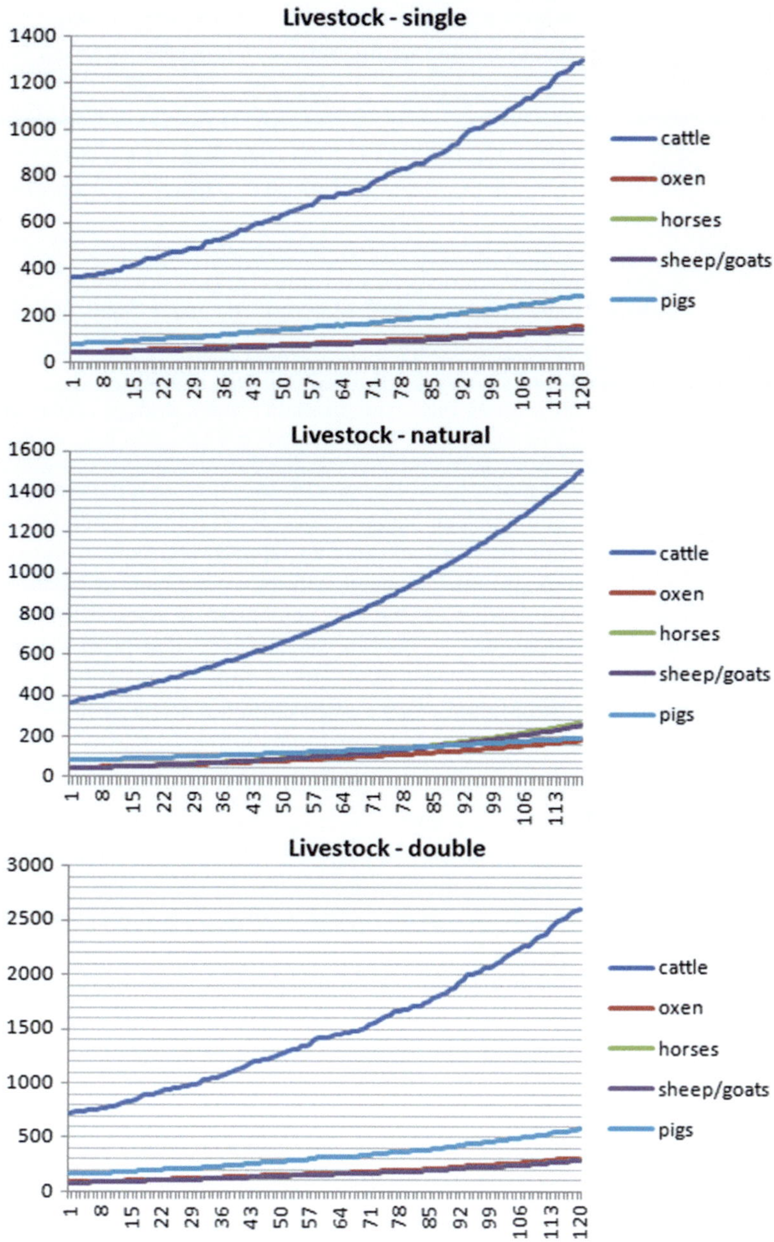

Fig. 12.3 Livestock scenarios for baseline population: single, natural and double numbers

Table 12.1 Minimum size of herds for populations of 800, 2000 and 2500 persons

	Herd per 1 community (20 persons)	800	2000	2500
Cattle	2–4 cows, 2–4 calves, 2 oxen	380–400	950–1000	1187.5–1250
Sheep/Goats	2–2.5	65–70	162.5–175	203.1–218.7
Pigs	4–5	170–180	425–450	531.2–562.5
Horses	1–2	40–50	100–125	125–156.2

- *Minimum numbers* with 0.5 cattle/person (Table. 12.1),
- *Double numbers* with (0.8–1 cattle/person) in case the initial and first-generations oppidum population had enough landscape resources to keep larger herds than originally proposed in the minimum option.
- *Natural numbers* with natural birth and mortality rates and probable slaughtering rates.

Typically, bigger populations have higher consumption requirements, benefit from higher manpower and manage larger areas. If additional land units were required for crop production or livestock grazing, appropriate part of the original woodland has to be cleared and thus changed into the arable land or pastures. The spreading and spatial organization of the site catchment is naturally shaped by accessibility (in model represented by friction surface modelled from local topography). If the limits are achieved, population adapts. Either part of the population leaves, or the food production and/or diet composition has to be changed.

Similarly to the population dynamics model, alternative scenarios were can be taken into account:

- *Sudden event: lost harvest*—the crop is damaged either by floods or droughts. The consumption requirements are not covered sufficiently, therefore the population is expected to adapt to the situation.
- *Sudden event: lost animals*—it can be caused by disease or theft. The meat and milk calories are not available and/or the ploughing oxen cannot be used, the arable land is affected and the agricultural strategy has to be modified.
- *Sudden event: fire*—the crop is destroyed including the storage (reserves from previous one or two years, seed for the next season), the populations is expected to adapt.
- *No event* (*baseline*)—no unexpected events happen, i.e. the food production is not affected by inauspicious weather, fire etc. If the population grows, the food productions grew correspondingly up to the spatial limits.

12.3.2.3 Model Design

The model environment represents Staré Hradisko oppidum (Fig. 12.4) located in a gridded landscape modelled using GIS. Total area is 70 km^2, one cell is 20 × 20 m (400 m^2). The individual cells are described by topographical land-use suitability

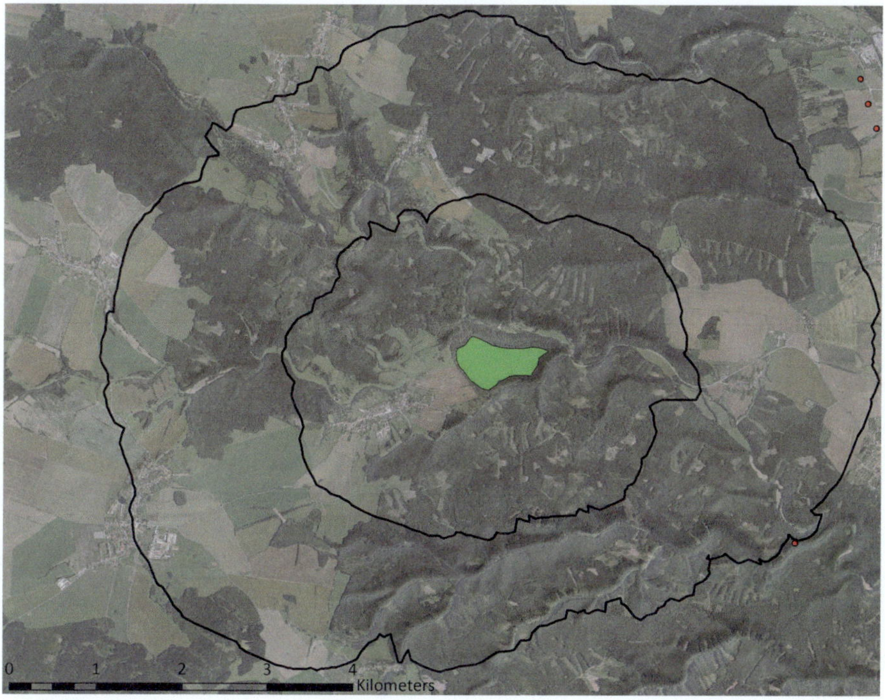

Fig. 12.4 Orthophotomap with the Staré Hradisko oppidum in centre and walking distances of 0.5 and 1 km

and economic variables that are encoded in map layers. Primary maps describe topography, hydrology, geology (soil quality) and potential land cover:

- *Slope* is initial variable for selection of areas to be used as fields and pastures, there are four levels of suitability,
- *Hydrology*: distances from water sources are calculated using gradient from the topography map and the map of fluvial sediments, topographical wetness index expresses tendency of the cell to be saturated by water in relation to values of gradient and surface outflow.
- *Original land cover* before deforesting and transformation into to the agricultural landscape is defined using botanic and pollen data from the oppidum (Neuhaüslová et al. 2001; Přichystal and Opravil 1992). Mixed forests are sources of wood.

Secondary maps define accessibility from the oppidum (*friction*) and suitability of each cell for agricultural activities. Basic walking distance is one hour, the corresponding formula is (Gorenflo and Gale 1990):

$$V = 6 * e^{-3.5(S+0.05)}$$

(S = slope in %)

Except the oppidum and water streams, there are following land use categories: fields and fallows, pastures and meadows, shrubs, managed forest and climax forest. In each of 120 time steps of the simulation, the grid of cells is updated, including transformation of one category into another (fields to fallows or meadows to shrubs). Model inputs are:

- population data,
- GIS data,
- diet specification (e.g. the ratio of cereal vs. proteins to be covered by the agricultural production),
- strategy and work allocation settings (e.g. intensive or extensive agricultural strategy, manpower per land unit and per task).

The food production models apply synthetic population data (i.e. time-series of number of inhabitants and their consumption requirements) together with authentic archaeological and environmental records with the region.

One simulation step corresponds to one agricultural year. The simulation starts with loading biophysical parameters of cells. Each cell updates its state according its current land-use category. At the beginning of the simulation run (year 1), part of the landscapes is already cultivated (initial livestock and fields areas are specified by input parameters). With update of the human population, also livestock populations are updated, including their caloric requirements.

For given parameters (current consumption, surplus, seed, loses) and general agricultural principles (fluctuation of the crop size) the size of field area is calculated. It is possible to simulate changes of areas (size, quality) in time (in single years).

The estimation of the necessary field area is based on the assumption that every year, if there were no unexpected events, the production covers needs of the population including safety margin (Müller-Herold—Sieferle 1997). The field area F is updated using formula:

$$F = \left(\frac{TC \times pCD}{exY \times 3440}\right) \times (1 + r) + \left(\frac{lA \times SR}{exY}\right)$$

(TC—total consumption, exY—expected yield from hectar (in calories), pCD—ratio of cereals in diet, r—reserves, lA—last current area of fields, SR—seed requirement)

The important sub-component of the model is the nitrogen cycle in soil which has impacts the crop production significantly. With the intensive strategy the nitrogen is applied with farmyard manure from animals stabled per nights and during the winter months. Under the extensive strategy the nitrogen is applied by livestock grazing the fallows and biomass decomposition in the grassland pastures. Two strategies were applied in the model—either immediate or gradual releasing of nitrogen affecting the soil fertility for the following harvest.

The yearly production depends on overall tendency in field productivity and current external factors (sudden events, loses). The harvest size is expressed in calories and the amount of the harvest is divided into consumption, seed for the next season, and reserves which can be stored up to three years. From the comparison of reserves and consumption it is possible to estimate the general tendency. The share of cereals in the diet includes current harvest and reserves.

Each kind of domestic animal has its preference regarding pastures; basis is that some species can graze in the forest (cows, pigs) and other cannot (sheep/goats, horses). Overall deforested area is calculated according these preferences. Therefore, the grazed area PA (forest and grassland, including pastures and fallows) in each step is updated according to the formula:

$$\frac{\begin{array}{c}(H\times 2+S\times 0.1+C\times 1.5)+\\(P\times 0.5+(C-(PAS-H\times 2+S\times 0.1))\times 4)\end{array}}{2\pm 0.3}$$

(H—number of horses, S—number of sheep, C—number of cattle, P—number of pigs, PAS—pastures area)

Winter fodder consists of hay, leaf fodder, and surplus of grain production (especially for ploughing oxen) respectively. The area of hay meadows is calculated using formula:

$$MA=\frac{(C\times 5+H\times 6+S)\times 150\pm 30}{3000\pm 500}$$

(H—number of horses, S—number of sheep, C—number of cattle)

Leaf fodder area (LFA) is a forest area required to collect leaf fodder:

$$LFA=\frac{(C\times 6.5+H\times 7.5+S\times 1.5)\times 150\pm 30}{2400}$$

(H—number of horses, S—number of sheep, C—number of cattle)

For each year and each land cell, the land category is optionally updated (transformation of fallows into fields after 3-year rotation, increasing the amount of biomass in meadows and forests or updating the nitrogen rate).

The bank of working hours is maintained, taking into account the current work disposition of the community which is calculated from the time needed for each activity.

12.3.2.4 Outputs

Firstly, we compared intensive and extensive strategy at the beginning (year 1) and at the end (year 120) within baseline population. The objective of the experiment was to estimate the maximum sustainable population and livestock inside the relevant part of the map, i.e. in the area that is manageable with respect to cost distance. In case of intensive strategy, there are two options related to livestock:

- grazing mainly in forests, with minimum areas of meadows for herding,
- maximum deforesting, with most of herds grazing in meadows.

See Fig. 12.5 for results. The initial setting was intensive strategy, mean crop size 1500 kg/ha, hay production 3000 kg/ha, leaf fodder 2400 kg/ha. In this case, the hinterland area is not exhausted and maximum population attacks final values for baseline scenario, i.e. over 3000 persons. With double livestock, which would require more space for grazing, the upper limit for human population is approx. 1500 persons.

In the second experiment, the long-term tendency in crop size, storage size and overall surplus/deficit was examined in relation to weather "events" (storms, rain, drought or frost) which impact on production significantly. The frequency of events was modelled on the basis of historic records from the same region (e.g. Brázdil et al. 2006). To ensure sufficient production to cover the energy consumption of the population of the settlement, including safety margin, the local population creates reserves—cultivating more land and stores surplus.

Our conclusion is that 10 % overproduction was not enough to face sudden events successfully, 50 % overproduction made population self-sufficient and with 100 % overproduction the available surplus (meaning shareable by feasting or market relations) appeared regularly. Version with baseline population scenario and

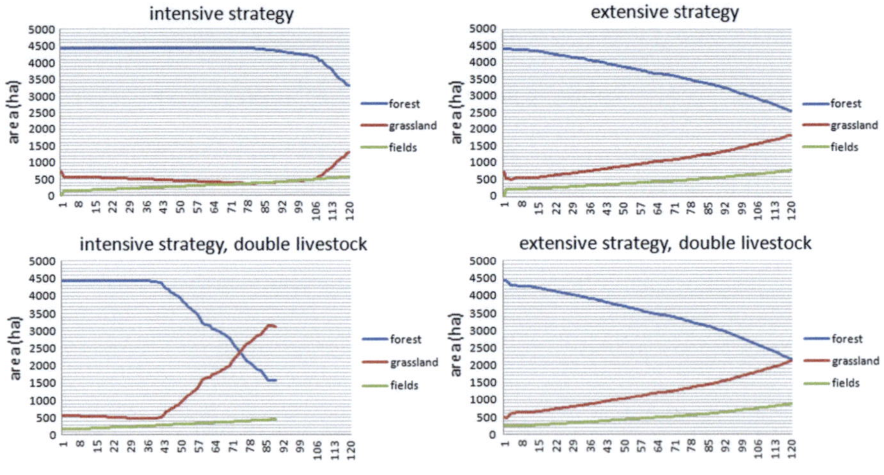

Fig. 12.5 Land use: comparison of intensive and extensive with natural and double livestock

sudden event "animal lost" (half of livestock is lost in year 75) shown that only double size of crop protects the population from deficit. Also, the baseline population scenario was compared with gradual decline scenario with "animal lost" event.

12.3.3 *Workforce Model*

12.3.3.1 Objective

Model enables experimenting with workforce allocation to parallel agricultural activities during the harvest season, which is the bottleneck of the agricultural year (cf. e.g. Halstead 2014). Key issues are the ratio of strong and weak workforce participating in harvest activities, the impact of weather and the ratio of targeted overproduction.

12.3.3.2 Theoretical Background and Scenarios

To achieve self-subsistence, the population has to allocate workforce effectively. For agricultural societies it means managing activities in given periods of the agricultural year and producing food not only to cover current caloric requirements, but also to create reserves, to cover probable loses and to prepare seed for the next season.

In relation to workforce capacities, there are several bottlenecks: spring and autumn periods of ploughing and seeding and especially the summer period of harvest which is relatively short (2–6 weeks) but extremely labor demanding (Halstead 2014). The harvest of cereals and pulses with their gradual ripening time has to be mastered in parallel with hay preparation (winter fodder for livestock) and moreover there are other daily activities such as herding and milking, domestic work or firing wood preparation.

Total working capacity depends on size of population. It is important to differentiate between "strongforce" (given by number adult men who are able to plough with oxen) and "weakforce" (given by the rest of workers). We assume certain ratio of non-working elite as well as some capacities permanently allocated to other than agricultural tasks (crafts, trade).

Labor input is variable during the agricultural year—lower in winter, higher is summer (Fig. 12.6) and differs for strongforce and weakforce (Table 12.2). Our model is focused on harvest season only during which the working capacities are allocated to:

- *standard, repetitive tasks* (housework, herding, milking and other care for livestock, preparing firing wood etc.),

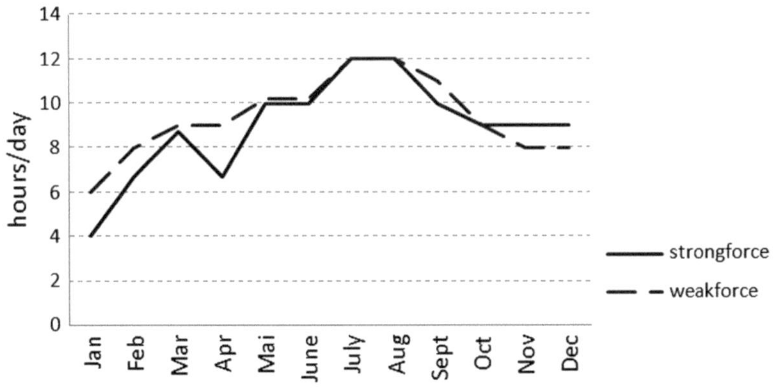

Fig. 12.6 Variable labour input during the year

- *seasonal activities* that form a logical sequence (harvesting and transport, threshing, winnowing and gathering of grain, concurrent hay harvest with drying, transport and storage).

The success of the harvest season depends on weather conditions, which accelerate (or delay) ripening of crops and shorten (or prolong) the period during which the quality of crops is the best (and the yield per hectare is the highest). As for the haymaking (after the rain the grass is wet and cannot be mowed), the number of rainy days represents constraint for the crop harvest process.

12.3.3.3 Model Design

Model runs in daily steps that represent the period from 1st July till the end of the harvest season, maximum length of the season 90 steps. We are interested especially in those settings of the model that would enable finishing the harvest process in three weeks or sooner, because models calculates with the option that after two or three weeks the quality of cereals decreases.

Model has got four input parameters:

- size of population,
- daily labour input of strongforce and weakforce (hours) and the ratio of non-working strongforce,
- average yield (kg/ha)
- probability of rainy weather (total number of rainy days).

Current size of population is used in initial static calculation of current size of livestock and land-use area to be maintained. Both human and animal populations have their caloric requirements that together define overall yearly consumption of cereals (including loses and seed). The main procedure is used to distribute working capacities to parallel tasks (crop harvest, hay harvest, herding and domestic work).

Table 12.2 Labour input during harvest process

Activity	Strongforce	Weakforce
Harvest	90 h/1 ha	225 h/1 ha
Transport	20 h/1500 kg	40 h/1500 kg
Threshing	40 h/1500 kg	–
Winnowing	33 h/1500 kg	–
Gathering, storage	–	11 h/1500 kg

Main output value is number of days that is necessary for completing the harvest process.

12.3.3.4 Outputs

Firstly, we explored the impact of bad weather on prolongation of the harvest process in case of the population of 1000 persons, 12 h long working day, 10 % of non-producers in population and average yield 1500 kg/ha. Under these circumstances and in case of relatively good weather (with probability of rainy weather under 30 %) the harvest process took less than 3 weeks.

Secondly, we assumed the probability of rainy weather between 10 and 30 % and the ratio of non-producers around 20 % and we examined the ability of the population to produce surplus for eventual trade activities. In case of good weather, the population of 1000 inhabitants could cover own needs even if the yield had been very low (around 800 kg/ha). In case of bad weather and very high yield (3200 kg/ha) it is possible to double the production.

Thirdly, we examined the ratio of non-producers (elite). Experimental results show that the maximum share of non-producers is 20 % in case of relatively good weather (probability of rainy weather up to 30 %, according the first experiment).

Depending on the either intensive or extensive strategy chosen, the landscape is covered by the mosaics of fields and pastures gradually verging into the managed forest. With the intensive strategy the livestock has to graze in the forest or, in case of work capacities allocated to forest clearance, on grassland pastures. With the extensive strategy the livestock is mostly left to graze the fallows. Baseline scenario shows clearly the limit of the predicted catchment: by the final years of the simulation the oppidum usually runs out of the area available for pastures. In this case the possible solutions include change of economic strategy, decreasing the number of animals, enlarging the catchment or emigration (Fig. 12.7).

12.4 Conclusion

Our models were created to analyze past socio-economic processes, determine possible crisis factors and understand ecological and cultural changes in Central Europe in late Iron Age. The immediate or gradual impact of the success rate in the

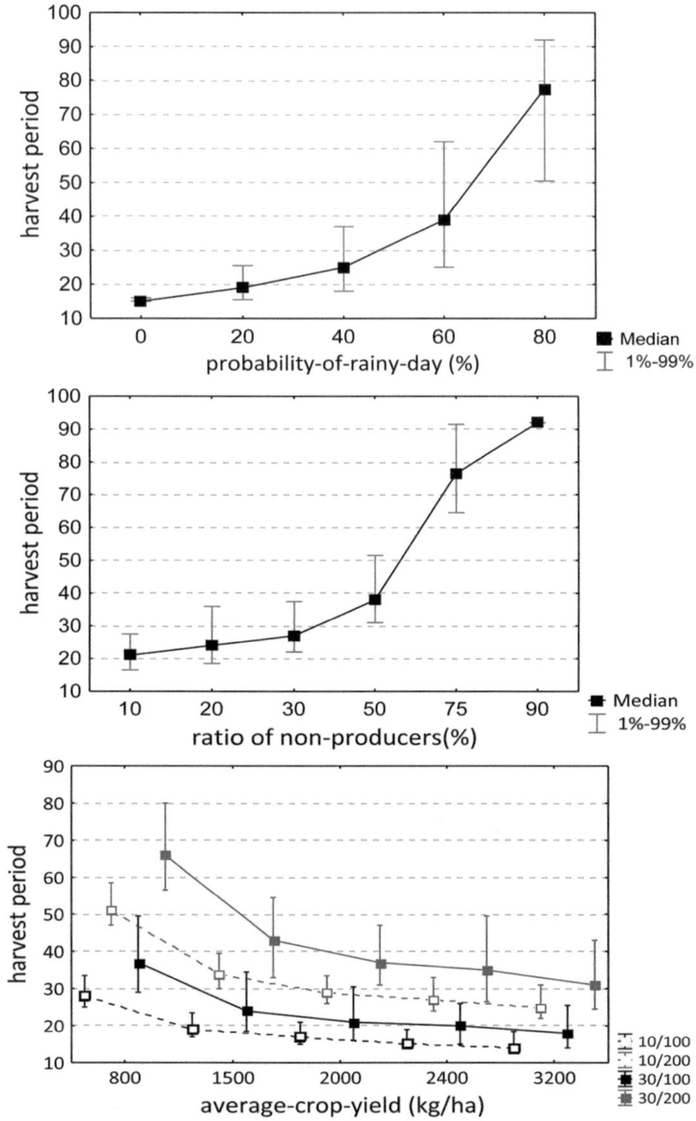

Fig. 12.7 Impact of bad weather, ratio of non-producers and average crop yield on the duration of the harvest process in days

food production and its potential influences on the economic and social processes were also addressed.

Results achieved can be discussed in the light of the framework of available data: according to the archaeological record, the settlement density in the late Iron Age in Central Europe increased over some time and then decreased again rapidly.

The population dynamics model provides realistic time series of energetic requirements, workforce availability and age distributions of population of the oppidum´s agglomeration. The modelling results showed different outcomes of the economic strategies performed by either growing or declining population.

The limits of the land-use strategies returned from the baseline scenario, when the population was expected to react by adjusting their economic strategies, started acting around the population density being around 3000 especially due to the depletion of available hinterland area (i.e. available field, forest and pasture plots) within the predicted catchment.

However, according to the archaeological record the population started decreasing after 70–80 years (sudden decline, gradual decline and epidemic scenarios). With such a demographic profile, the oppidum´s community could in fact practice all land-use strategies without any substantial problems apart from those imposed by natural harvest fluctuations due to weather, accidents (fire, deceasing of the livestock), and other socio-economic (raids, theft) factors.

In our models it has been proven by experiments that not all of the oppidum population had to be engaged in the agricultural work. There is an archaeological evidence of elite members, which, expectably, were not involved in the agricultural production. Increasing and/or decreasing amount of free time represents in fact the level of society´s complexity and its changes reflect decline of this complexity connected to the loss of the production potential. The labor shortage may also point to the necessity of using the external supplies.

Our further research is focused on network analysis and network-based modelling of interactions between the oppidum and open village settlements and between individual settlements (i.e. food and raw resources circulation through social contacts). Network analysis (see e.g. Knappett 2013) is planned to be used for the interpretation of the archaeological data from the sites and for exploration of questions associated with cultural diffusion, settlement hierarchies and regional aspects.

Acknowledgments The support of the Czech Science Foundation under Grant P405/12/0926 “Social modelling as a tool for understanding Celtic society and cultural changes at the end of the Iron Age” is kindly acknowledged.

References

Altaweel M (2007) Addressing the Structures and Dynamics of Modeled Human Ecologies. In: Digital discovery. Exploring new frontiers in human heritage, computer applications and quantitative methods in archaeology. Budapest, p 30–41

Altaweel M (2008) Investigating agricultural sustainability and strategies in northern Mesopotamia: results produced using a socio-ecological modeling approach. J Archaeol Sci 35:821–835

Axtell RL et al (2002) Population growth and collapse in a multi-agent model of the Kayenta Anasazi in Long House Valley. Proc Natl Acad Sci 99(3):7275–7279

Barton CM, Ullah II, Mitasova H (2010) Computational modeling and Neolithic socioecological dynamics: a case study from Southwest Asia. Am Antiq 75:364–386
Bayliss-Smith T (1978) Maximum populations and standard populations: the carrying capacity question. In: Green D, Haselgrove C, Spriggs M (eds.) Social organisation and settlement: contributions from anthropology, archaeology and geography, vol 21, no.1 (supplementary). BAR International Series pp 129–151
Brázdil R, Valášek H, Chromá K (2006) Documentary evidence of an economic character as a source for the study of meteorological and hydrological extremes and their impacts on human activities. Geografiska Annaler 88 A(2):79–86
Campbell BMS (2007) Three centuries of English crops yields. p 1211–1491
Chisholm M (1979) Rural settlement and land use. An essay in location. London
Čižmář M (2005) Keltské oppidum Staré Hradisko. Olomouc
Collis J (2000) "Celtic" Oppida. In: Hansen MH (ed) A comparative study of thirty city-state cultures, an investigation conducted by the Copenhagen Polis Centre, Historisk-filosofiske Skrifter 21. Det Kongelige Danske Videnskabernes Selskab, Copenhagen, pp 229–239
Conolly J, Colledge S, Shennan S (2008) Founder effect, drift, and adaptive change in domestic crop use in early Neolithic Europe. J Archaeol Sci 35:2797–2804
del Castillo F, Barceló JA (2013) Why Hunter and Gatherers did not Die More Often? Simulating Prehistoric Decision Making. Archaeology in the Digital Era. Computer Applications and Quantitative Methods in Archaeology, Southampton, pp 154–163
Eastman JR (2006) IDRISI Andes. Guide to GIS and image processing, Worcester
Ebersbach R (2002)Von Bauern und Rindern. Eine Ökosystemanalyse zur Bedeutung der Rinderhaltung in bäuerlichen Gesellschaften als Grundlage zur Modellbildung im Neolithikum. Basler Beiträge zur Archäologie 15, Basel
Erdkamp P (2005) The grain market in the Roman Empire. A social, political and economic study, Cambridge, Cambridge University Press
Fuller DQ, Stevens J (2009) Agriculture and the development of complex societies: an archaeobotanical agenda. In: Fairbairn N, Weiss E (eds) From foragers to farmers, Gordon C. Oxford, Oxbow Books, Hillman Festschrift, pp 37–57
Gorenflo LJ, Gale N (1990) Mapping regional settlement in information space. J Anthropol Archaeol 9:240–274
Gregg SA (1988) Foragers and farmers. Population interaction and agricultural expansion in prehistoric Europe. Chicago, London
Halstead P (1995) Plough and power: the economic and social significance of cultivation with the ox-drawn ard in the Mediterranean. Bull Summerian Agric 8:11–21
Halstead P (2014) Two oxen ahead. Pre-mechanized farming in the Mediterranean. Chichester
Haselgrove C, Guichard V (2013) Gaulois sont-ils dans la plaine? Reflections on settlement patterns in Gaul in the 1st century BC. In: Krausz S, Colin A, Gruel K, Ralston I, Dechezleprete T (eds) L'Age du Fer en Europe. Melanges offerts a Olivier Buchsenschutz, vol 32. Collection Memoires pp 17–327
Janssen MA (2009) Understanding artificial Anasazi. J Artif Soc Soc Simul 12(4):13
Jarman MR, Vita-Finzi C, Higgs ES (1972) Site Catchment analysis in Archaeology. In: Ucko PJ Tringham R, Dimbleby GW (eds) Man, settlement and urbanism. gloucester, pp 61–66
Klir T (2010) Die BesiedeJung der Gebirgsgegenden Bohmens im Mittelalter und der fruhen Neuzeit—Ausgangspunkte fur eine interdisziplinare Forschung. Archaeologia Historica 35:373–391
Knappett C (2013) Network analysis in archaeology: new approaches to regional interaction. Oxford University Press
Kohler TA, Varien MD (eds.) (2012) Emergence and collapse of early villages. Models of Central Mesa Verde archaeology. University of California Press, Los Angeles
Kunzova E, Hejcman M (2009) Yield development of winter beat over 50 years of FYM, N, P and K fertilizer application on black earth soil in the Czech Republic. Field Crops Res 111:226–234
Lake MW (2000) Computer simulation of mesolithic foraging? Dynamics in human and primate societies: agent-based modeling of social and spatial processes. New York, pp 107–143

Müller-Herold U, Sieferle RP (1997) Surplus and survival: risk, ruin, and luxury in the evolution of early forms of subsistence. Adv Human Ecol 6:201–220

Neuhäuslová Z et al (2001) Mapa potencionální přirozené vegetace České republiky. Praha

Olsson EGA (1991) The agrarian landscape of Viking age farmers at Bjäresjö. The cultural landscape during 6000 years in southern Sweeden. Ecological Buletins 41:190–193

Halstead P, O'Shea J (eds.) (1989) Bad Year Economics: cultural responses to risk and uncertainty. Cambridge University Press, Cambridge

Premo L (2010) Equifinality and explanation: the role of agent-based modeling in postpositivist archaeology. Simulating the change. Archaeology into the twenty-first century. Salt Lake City, pp 28–37

Přichystal A, Opravil E (1992) Poznatky k přírodnímu prostředí keltského oppida Staré Hradisko. Časopis Moravského Muzea LXXVII:115–121

Rothamsted research (2006) Guide to the classical and other long-term experiments, datasets and sample archive. Bury St. Edmund

Salač V (2006) Die keltischen Oppida und ihre Macht. In Krenn- Leeb A (ed) Wirtschaft, Macht und Strategie—Hohensiedlungen und ihre Funktionen in der Ur- und Fruhgeschichte, Archaologie Osterreichs Spezial 1:233–245

Saller R (1994) Patriarchy, property and death in the Roman family. Cambridge

Schreg R (2011) Feeding the village—Reflections on the ecology and resilience of the medieval rural economy. Processing, Storage, Distribution of Food. Food in the Medieval Rural Environment, Ruralia VIII:301–320

Shennan S (2007) The spread of farming into Central Europe ind its consequences: evolutionary models. The Model-Based Archaeology of Socionatural Systems. Santa Fe, New Mexico, pp 141–156

van der Vart E, de Boer B, Hankel A, Verheij B (2006) Agents adopting agriculture, SAB, LNAI 4095. Springer, Berlin, pp 750–761

Wainwright J (2008) Can modelling enable us to understand the rôle of humans in landscape evolution? Geoforum 39:659–674

Chapter 13
ZambeziLand: A Canonical Theory and Agent-Based Model of Polity Cycling in the Zambezi Plateau, Southern Africa

Gary Bogle and Claudio Cioffi-Revilla

13.1 Introduction

The motivation for this model is to explore how the Canonical Theory Cioffi-Revilla (2005), implemented by a computational agent-based model (ABM Cioffi-Revilla 2014, pp. 287–301), generates sociopolitical phase transitions, whereby polities form and dissolve as people migrate to larger, more complex communities. This process of settlement and abandonment exists in the archaeological record of the Zambezi Plateau in present-day Zimbabwe (Fig. 13.1). The process of site abandonment is significant for two reasons: (1) it is key to understanding how the earliest polities in Sub-Saharan Africa originated ("politogenesis") and why they dissolved; and (2) the abandonment and subsequent condition of the Great Zimbabwe polity site is highly significant for ancient and modern Southern African history Fontein (2006, p. 771).

The walled enclosure of Great Zimbabwe supported a capital city for approximately 200 years, from 1275 CE to 1450 CE, based on the presence and absence of imported Chinese ceramics in the archeological record Huffman and Vogel (1991, p. 68). Chinese blue-on-white porcelain, diagnostic of long-distance trade, is not found at Great Zimbabwe after 1450, but it is found at other important centers in Zimbabwe before and after this date. It is important to note that Collett, et al. disagree with Huffman on this point, due to the presence of a large blue-on-white porcelain piece from the Ming Dynasty (1488–1505 CE) that is possibly related to Great Zimbabwe Collett et al. (1992, p. 157). However, Collett, et al. still use the term "abandoned" in reference to Great Zimbabwe Collett et al. (1992, p. 140) (Fig. 13.2).

G. Bogle (✉) · C. Cioffi-Revilla
George Mason University, Fairfax, VA 22030, USA
e-mail: gbogle@gmu.edu

C. Cioffi-Revilla
e-mail: ccioffi@gmu.edu

J.A. Barceló and F. Del Castillo (eds.), *Simulating Prehistoric and Ancient Worlds*,
Computational Social Sciences, DOI 10.1007/978-3-319-31481-5_13

Fig. 13.1 Map of Zimbabwe. *Source* http://www.alightforzimbabwe.org

Great Zimbabwe was not the first or only significant polity in the Zambezi Plateau. Pikirayi notes that prior to Great Zimbabwe, Mapungubwe "attained regional prominence during the thirteenth century, managing the resources of a territory that was equivalent to a state in both political and economic terms" Pikirayi (2001, p. 3). Mapungubwe has been proposed as the first state in southern Africa, based on the most current evidence Huffman (2014). After the fall of Great Zimbabwe—"...marked by the presence of massive stone walls built in a variety of architectural styles" (Fig. 13.3)—the so-called Zimbabwe Culture divided into northern and southwestern regions Pikirayi (2001, p. 2–3).

Kim and Kusimba note that the first agrarian communities of the Zambezi plateau (i.e., chiefdoms) date to the first millennium CE, and that "[t]he landscape ...was dotted with temporary rockshelter settlements, semi-sedentary camps, villages, and permanent settlements" Kim and Kusimba (2008, p. 137) (Fig. 13.2).

Monumental sites in the Zambezi plateau have been the subject of significant archaeological research since the 1930s, following the pioneering excavations of Gertrude Caton-Thompson. However, the research record has lacked a viable theory explaining the pattern of rise, fall, and abandonment (original polity cycling) that is archaeologically recorded for this area. Great Zimbabwe existed as a capital (central place) for a relatively short time period, and its termination by abandonment correlates with the end of imports from China. In fact, from the arrival of the Portuguese, which begins the written historical record, until the beginning of the

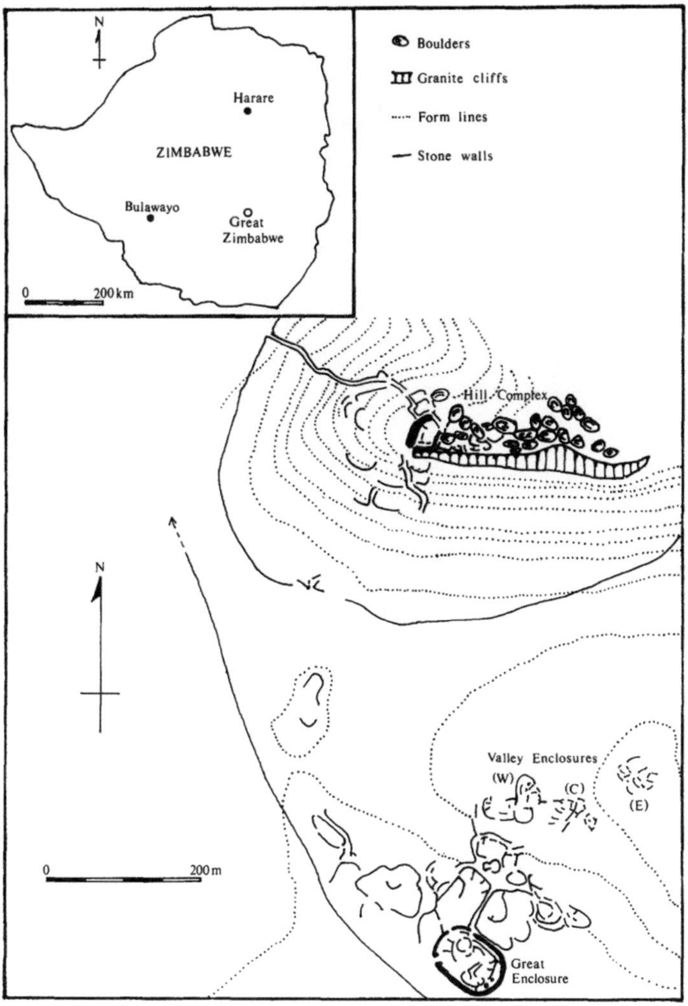

Fig. 13.2 Site map of great Zimbabwe. *Source* Collett et al. (1992, p. 141)

twentieth century, some researchers (notably the archaeologist Randall MacIver in 1906) have questioned whether the site was even created by Africans Collett et al. (1992, p. 140). To this day, the site of Great Zimbabwe is still treated with distant reverence by the local population, as a hallowed but forgotten place Fontein (2006).

This study demonstrates how the Canonical Theory of politogenesis Cioffi-Revilla (2005) provides a viable generative explanation for the process of formation, consolidation, and abandonment of polities in the Zambezi Plateau. The punctuated process of sociopolitical phase transitions, typical of polity cycling (e.g., Marcus 1998, 2012), is explained by modeling the dynamic interplay among leaders and

Fig. 13.3 Great wall enclosure at Great Zimbabwe. *Source* "Zimbabwe wall" by Ulamm. Licensed under public domain via Wikimedia commons

society members (individuals and groups) experiencing fluctuating conditions of leadership and loyalty during recurring times of stress affecting the local community. In this paper, we present an ABM that implements in code the "fast" and "slow" processes of the Canonical Theory to demonstrate how and why a society can evolve from a simple community, such as that which existed in the Zambezi Plateau in the first millennium CE, through the progression of larger and more complex polities shown by archaeology. Larger and more complex polities were generated through a recursive, iterative process of collective action successes and failures by individuals and groups, as explained by the Canonical Theory.

13.2 Methodology

13.2.1 ZambeziLand: An Agent-Based Model (ABM) of Politogenesis by Canonical Processes

The methodology of this study consisted of building and analyzing an organizational agent-based model (ABM) of the region of interest, called ZambeziLand. In particular, ZambeziLand 1.0 implements a causal process for explaining politogenesis (the rise of original social complexity) by applying the Canonical Theory of origins and development of sociopolitical complexity Cioffi-Revilla (2005), Cioffi-Revilla (2014, Chap. 7). The theory uses two time scales. As situational changes recur in a society, a "fast process" punctuated by contingent events begins, including subsequent collective action choices made by society members (leaders and followers). Collective action may succeed or fail, depending on other contingent events. The outcome of each fast process results in the polity generating greater or lesser complexity when examined on a longer time scale Cioffi-Revilla (2005, p. 138) or "slow process." Recursive fast processes Cioffi-Revilla (2005, p. 138) occur relatively quickly as the society succeeds or fails in solving collective action problems that arise in the normal course of its history, with sociopolitical results and effects accumulating over time in the slow process Cioffi-Revilla (2005, p. 138).

The Canonical Theory provides an integrative framework for linking micro-level, short-term political activity by individuals and groups in a given society (fast processes) with macro-level sociopolitical changes experienced over longer periods of time (slow process). All societies experience *numerous* fast processes, each initiated by situational changes, but they realize a *single* slow process resulting from iterations of canonically varying fast processes. The main structure of the fast process is universal and invariant, but the exact branching paths realized vary, depending on contingencies such as a situational change having endogenous or exogenous causes, a society perceiving or not the situational change, collective action occurring or not, success or failure in collective action being realized: hence, the term canonical. The theory explains how and why individual-level choices in the fast process caused by situational changes and associated responses (or lack thereof) can cause the emergent effects evidenced in the archaeological record on the rise and abandonment of sites (slow process) in the Zambezi Plateau.

An ABM was chosen for implementing the Canonical Theory because one of the hallmarks of such formal, computational models is their ability to generate macro-level behaviors caused by micro-level decisions of individual agents characterized by bounded rationality, decision-making autonomy, sociality, and dynamic interactions among them Epstein and Axtell (1996). These are also features assumed in the theory's canonical fast process of situational changes and societal responses that result in the slow process produced by each simulation run.

In the current model (version 1.0), agents represent individual members of society. Each individual can join a group, and each has a level or amount of two attributes: fealty and leadership. Fealty in the ZambeziLand model is a measure of how attached or loyal a person feels towards one's group in general and its leadership in particular. Fealty is a measure of attachment in that if it drops too low for members of a group, they will seek to move to another group with stronger leadership. All members in a group have a leadership score; however, when group decisions or actions need to be made, only the individual with the highest leadership score counts as the group leader.

13.2.2 Model Details

ZambeziLand 1.0 is an ABM consisting of a society comprised of groups of individuals. The model is initialized with 100 groups, each with 50 members, so $N = 5,000$ total population. These features were chosen to represent an egalitarian, undifferentiated society as would have existed prior to the origin of social complexity in the region (i.e., hunter-gatherer tribes). At the start of the simulation, each actor-agent is given an initial value for fealty and leadership. Both are taken from triangular distributions. Fealty randomly is assigned a value between 0 and 100, with a mode of 50. Leadership is assigned a value between 0 and 50 with a mode of 10. Values were chosen to create an initial social situation where strong leadership can exist, but is relatively rare in the population, consistent with social data. Model input parameters set the payoff for an increase or decrease in individual fealty, depending on results from collective action taken by each group.

The model was implemented in Python 2.7.1, which allows for setting fealty and leadership adjustments as input parameters. However, to clarify analysis, all runs are reported here with the same leadership adjustment parameter. Runs of the model were made on a Macbook Pro with four processor cores.

The model takes on average 9 s to run. Four minutes and 30 s were required for executing 30 runs.

13.2.3 Model Action

ZambeziLand 1.0 runs as event loops, where each group of agents has an opportunity to act on one or more of its behaviors at each clock tick. Each event loop starts with a situational change occurring (e.g., drought, attack, or other societal threat or opportunity) and each group deciding if collective action should be undertaken. The situational change is left as generic in the current model version, but can be made specific in subsequent versions. This implements the causal fast process of the Canonical Theory, which links situational changes, societal awareness, collective action, and political results: "[w]hen a society correctly perceives and understands a given situational change, it may or may not be willing and able to undertake collective action …in response to such a change" Cioffi-Revilla (2005, p. 144).

Specifically, a group will undertake collective action if the average fealty score for the group is <50. If the average fealty score is <10, the group will disband and abandon their site, dispersing to eventually form other groups. Collective action is successful with differing probabilities, depending on the quality of the group's leadership: 25 % with good leadership and 10 % with poor leadership. If collective action is successful, each member's fealty is increased by some (differing) amount. If collective action is unsuccessful, fealty for each member is decreased. Furthermore, leadership scores are updated as a result of some (but not all) of the collective action attempts. Importantly, the theory does not assume that collective action will always be undertaken when needed, nor that collective action will always be successful even when undertaken. Therefore, *any emergence of sociopolitical complexity in the resulting long and slow process produced by the model is generative, not deterministically hard-wired or causally pre-determined in any way.*

13.2.4 Model Verification

ZambeziLand 1.0 was verified using four standard model verification procedures: code walk-through, debugging, profiling, and sensitivity analysis Cioffi-Revilla (2014, pp. 235, 297). Although complete sweeps of the entire parameter space were not conducted, numerous parameter settings for initial conditions yielded consistent and replicable results across 30 runs for any given set of initial conditions (parameter settings). All issues encountered were resolved until the model ran as intended.

13.3 Results

The most significant result of the model is the demonstration via computational simulation that an initially egalitarian, homogeneous society can quickly coalesce into a small number of much larger differentiated groups, as shown in Figs. 13.4 and 13.5.

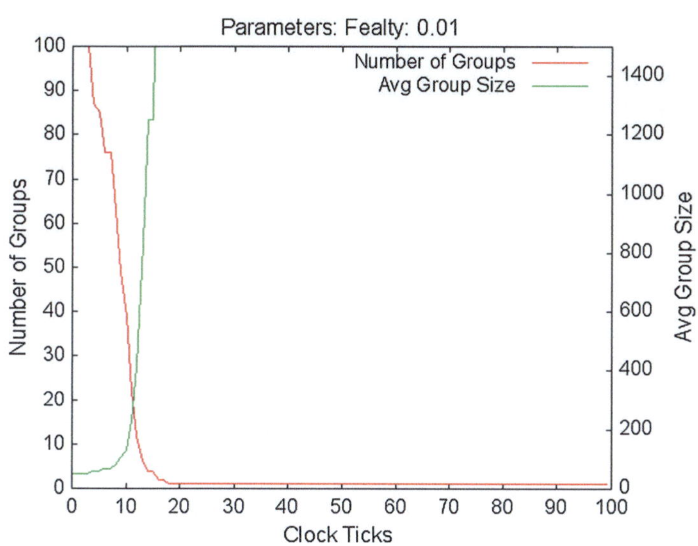

Fig. 13.4 Number of groups (*red*, scaled on the *left*) and mean group size (*green*, scaled on the *right*) for individual fealty payoff = 0.01

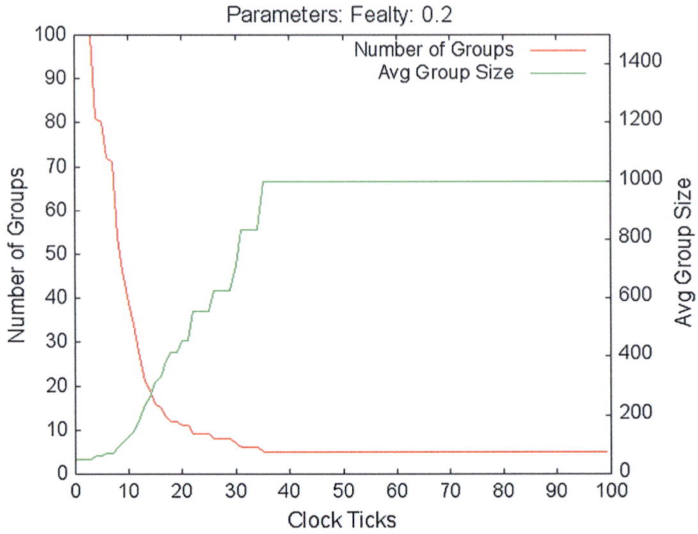

Fig. 13.5 Number of groups (*red*, scaled on the *left*) and mean group size (*green*, scaled on the *right*) for individual fealty payoff = 0.2

Polity emergence (i.e., politogenesis) occurs within the first 18 to 35 clock ticks of a simulation run. After initialization (100 groups, each with 50 members), society rapidly generates between 1 and 13 groups averaging between 384 and 5,000 members. Agents neither die nor are born in this model, so total population remains constant. The speed with which societal change occurs in the model (organizational phase transitions) varies with different input parameters. Interestingly, leadership scores have a positive linear effect on group size, although only the score of the leader is counted; that is, leadership scores are not additive within a group. Also, as the average number of groups increases, average fealty increases for up to between 5 and 6 groups, and average fealty decreases with increasing number of groups.

Additionally, results include a particular qualitative behavior in the trajectory of average fealty levels during model runs. As mentioned earlier, a fealty value is given to each agent at the start of each run, drawn from a triangular distribution between 0 and 100 with a mode of 50. Our results show that fealty quickly drops to relatively low values, becoming unstable, then recovering to a high value that remains stable for the remaining run time. An example of this behavior is shown in Fig. 13.7. This phenomenon occurs under different initial conditions (parameter settings) and occurs at different speeds. But one case behaves differently. Here (see Fig. 13.6), average fealty falls as before, rises to the starting level, but then collapses to a very low value (Table 13.1).

As groups decrease in number, the leadership score of remaining group leaders increases. (Recall that a leadership value is given to each agent at the start of each run, drawn from a triangular distribution between 0 and 100 with a mode of 10.) Few agents begin with high leadership score, by design. However, successful lead-

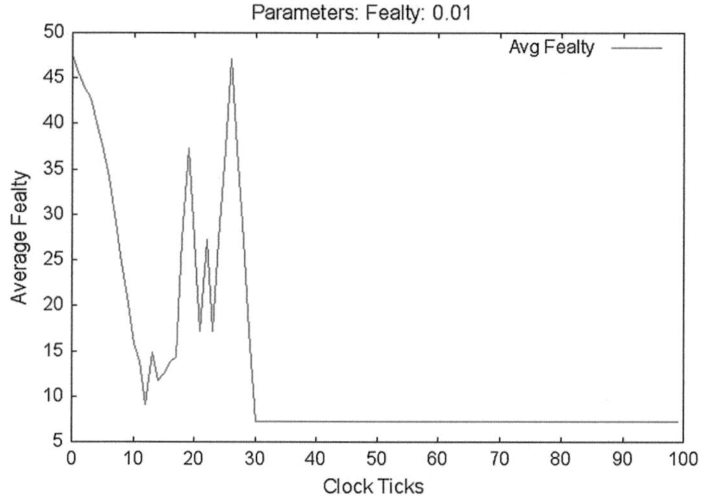

Fig. 13.6 Average group fealty for individual fealty payoff = 0.01

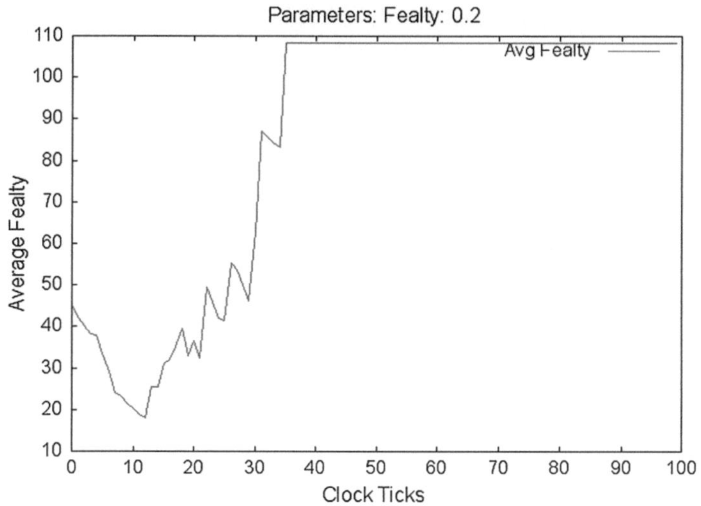

Fig. 13.7 Average group fealty for individual fealty payoff = 0.2

ers end model runs with leadership scores orders of magnitude higher than what they started with, as shown in Figs. 13.8 and 13.9. This result is illustrated by representative graphs of the evolution of leadership in two groups, a successful one (Fig. 13.11) and one that disbanded quickly (Fig. 13.10). These two groups also provide representative examples of change in membership (Figs. 13.12 and 13.13) and group fealty levels (Figs. 13.14 and 13.15).

Table 13.1 Table of model results for representative levels of individual fealty Payoff

Fealty Payoff	Tick	Numb of groups	Avg size	Avg fealty	Leadership score
0.01	18	1	5000	27.285	5079.352
0.1	31	4	1250	77.730	1281.403
0.2	35	5	1000	108.317	1011.797
0.25	33	13	384	64.488	396.870
0.3	32	12	416	78.023	426.149

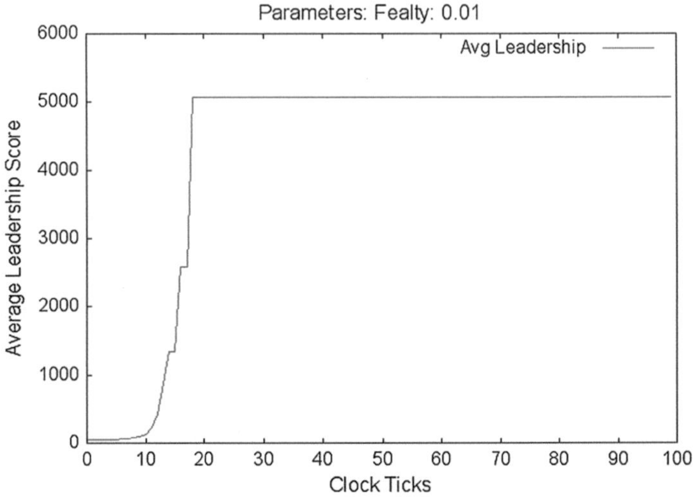

Fig. 13.8 Average leadership score for individual fealty payoff = 0.01

13.4 Discussion

13.4.1 Interpretation of Main Results

ZambeziLand demonstrates how a society of initially small and egalitarian groups could evolve into a complex society with a few large groups in response to changes in how individual members perceive their group and the state of extant leadership. The key in the model's political process—important in societies such as those known to have existed in the Zambezi Plateau—is taking a particular kind of collective action during the fast process: in this case, to abandon a group that is perceived to be unsuccessful and join another, more successful group. Figures 13.4, 13.5, 13.6, 13.7, 13.8, 13.9, 13.11, 13.12, 13.13, and 13.15 show instances of emergent slow processes generated by numerous fast processes iterating by canonical variations during 100 branching processes of collective action attempts in response to situational changes.

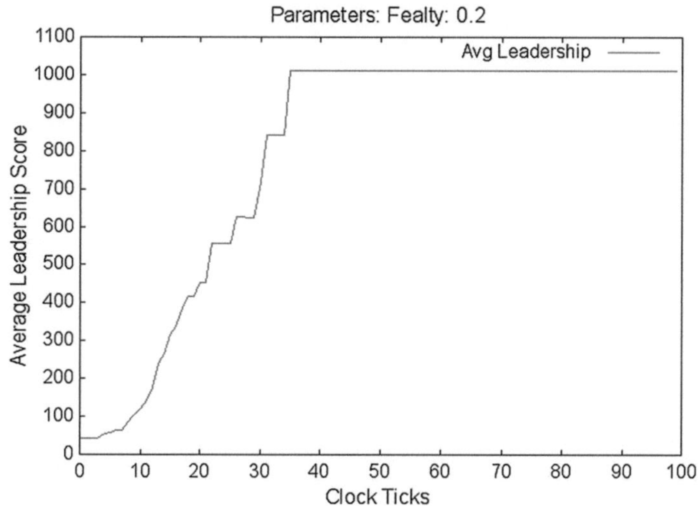

Fig. 13.9 Average leadership score for individual fealty payoff = 0.2

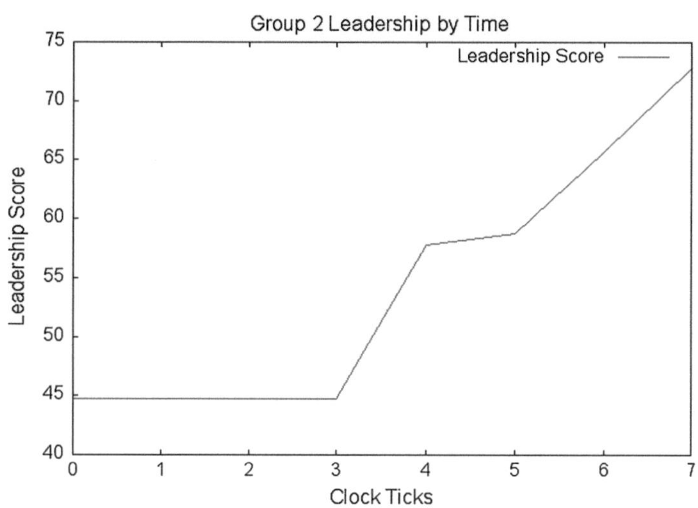

Fig. 13.10 Group 2 leadership score for individual fealty payoff = 0.25

Model runs (i.e., slow processes, in terms of the Canonical Theory) end with a few large groups, in spite of groups and group leadership having more than one chance to improve overall feeling of loyalty to the leadership. Groups must, at each clock tick (fast process), re-assess their need for collective action, and this assessment is largely independent of the group's past history during previous ticks (fast processes). Although this simplifying assumption is more forgiving than the real world, it is still sufficient to cause failure of some groups and the rise of large groups in the slow

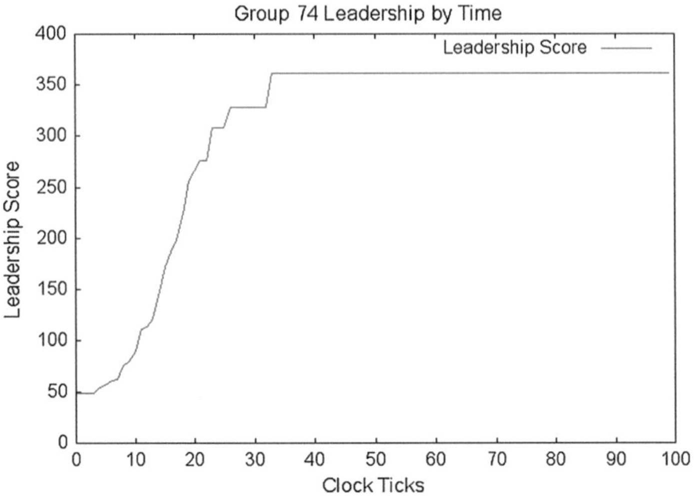

Fig. 13.11 Group 74 leadership score for individual fealty payoff = 0.25

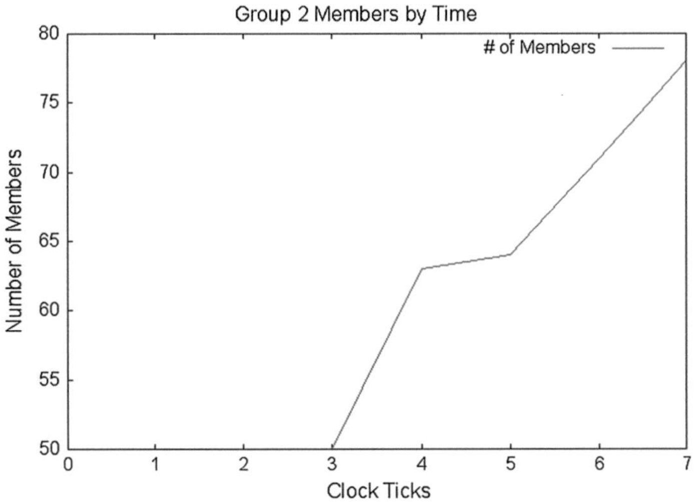

Fig. 13.12 Group 2 membership for individual fealty payoff = 0.25

process. Comparing Fig. 13.14 with Fig. 13.15 results show that one group suffered a significant fall in average feelings of loyalty, but then recovered, due to successful collective actions and addition of members from failed groups.

Some results were expected, given the importance of membership in groups with strong leaders. However, it is surprising how few groups remain in the stable system, and the speed at which the system coalesces is also surprising. This dynamic phenomenon merits further investigation. It may be due to the fact that the model does

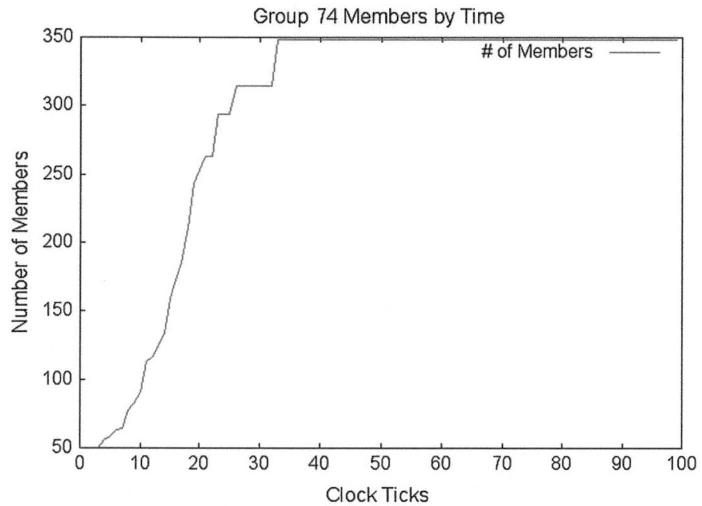

Fig. 13.13 Group 74 membership for individual fealty payoff = 0.25

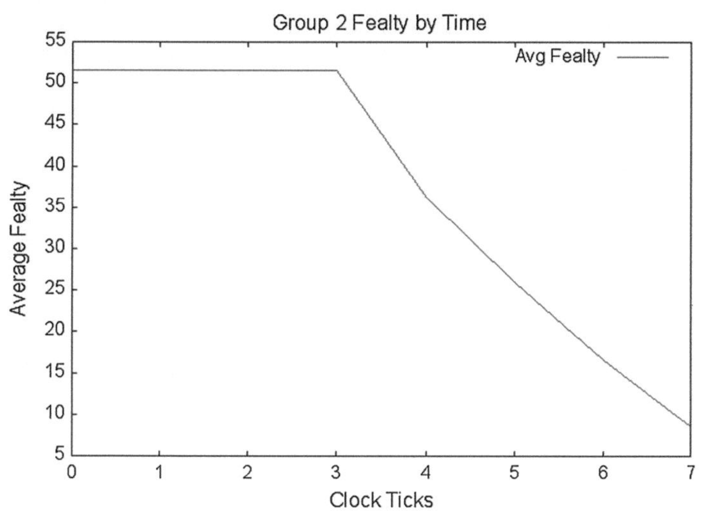

Fig. 13.14 Group 2 average fealty for individual fealty payoff = 0.25

not include dampening effects in regard to communications among group members and among groups. Archaeological and historical records show that long-distance communications take time. Moreover, the model can be extended to add activation and decay effects in the individual decision-making and behavior of agents, an embellishment totally compatible with the Canonical Theory, arguably making the slow process more realistically slow.

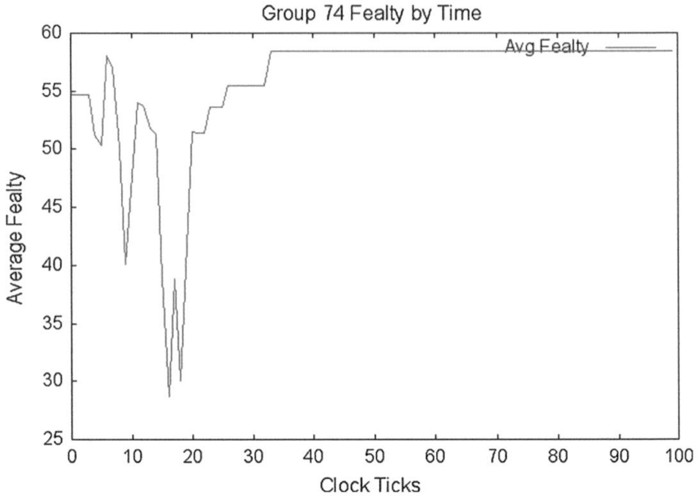

Fig. 13.15 Group 74 average fealty for individual fealty payoff = 0.25

Results also show that leadership is positively and strongly related to group size, but not to average fealty within a group. Preferred group size, by average fealty, is around 1,000 individuals, while average fealty is quite low when everyone is in one large group. Leadership scores continue to rise as groups become larger. This is counterintuitive. Leadership is expected to vary in the same way as average fealty, given the link between leadership and positive group feelings. This is another area that would need to be explored as the model is extended. It may also highlight the possibility of collective action failure, even when leadership seems adequate.

It is interesting that in most model runs, average fealty declines at the beginning of the model run, only to (sometimes) recover and rise. This is due to the fact that collective action succeeds only 25 % of the time with good leadership, and only 10 % of the time with poor leadership. This means that most individual agents and groups will experience failed collective action more often that successful collective action. As groups begin to disband to join stronger groups, group leader scores increase, in turn increasing the overall chance of experiencing successful collective actions.

13.4.2 Further Model Development

ZambeziLand could be developed further to extend the range of research questions and empirical features of the region. In the current version 1.0, the role of environmental factors is not taken into account, although the Canonical Theory includes detailed causal processes explaining how and why exogenous and endogenous types of situational change are generated in each society and environment. These can be

(1) exogenous factors external to and beyond societal control (e.g., attacks by neighbors or natural hazards such as flooding, drought, or epidemics, among others), (2) endogenous factors internal to society (e.g., aggressive individuals, technological failures, miscalculation), or (3) a combination of both. Further, and independent of the type of situational change affecting a society (exogenous, endogenous, or combined), the environment may affect different groups in different ways, consistent with the Canonical Theory. The model can be spatially developed and extended by placing groups that are relatively homogeneous in size in locally distinct environments. This is supported by work by Sinclair and Lundmark on the clustering of farming community sites in the Zimbabwean plateau. As they have noted: "[t]here remains a strong impression that environmental factors of topography, soils, and rainfall play an important role in the localization of southern clusters as a whole, but it seems clear that cluster spacing and internal organization within clusters are much more the result of social and political factors" Sinclair et al. (1993, p. 709). In terms of the Canonical Theory, this is a direct reference to causal anthropogenic triggers of situational change, which can be exogenous or endogenous. ZambeziLand 1.0 is more akin to a dynamic organizational network model, without geographic implementation on a biophysical landscape. However, as is true everywhere, geography plays a significant role in the prehistory of the Zambezi Plateau.

ZambeziLand is an ABM that can be modified and applied to other pleogenic regions—such as Mesoamerica, the American Southwest, Andean Peru, and the Near East, among others—where polity cycling has been established Marcus 1998; 2012, Cioffi-Revilla (2014, Chap. 5). The Canonical Theory also applies to other regions and cases of politogenesis, given appropriate and sufficiently valid and reliable data for individual cultural attributes and features of commonly recurrent local fast processes.

13.5 Summary

The Zambezi Plateau region in Southern Africa experienced the formation and fall of archaeologically visible polities with different levels of sociopolitical complexity during many centuries, before the arrival of Europeans and the beginning of the region's written history. Much archaeological work has been done to recover this past (i.e., the slow process record, in terms of the Canonical Theory), but one of the most important persistent questions has been a theoretically effective explanation for the rise, fall, and abandonment of large polities centered around monumental structures with massive stone walls called *zimbabwes*. Several of these survive to the present day, the largest of which is called Great Zimbabwe, located near present-day Masvingo, Zimbabwe. The Great Zimbabwe period, lasting only 200 years, was preceded by Mapungubwe and succeeded by *zimbabwes* built to the north and southwest of the Great Zimbabwe site. Given the success of these polities, what caused them to decline in such a way that the sites are considered to have experienced not only decline but abandonment?

The agent-based model presented here, called ZambeziLand 1.0, provides support for a theoretically grounded explanation of settlement and abandonment based on the Canonical Theory. In this theory, a succession of opportunities to engage in collective action by individuals and groups in society (iterative fast processes with canonical variations) strengthens or weakens the complexity of their respective polity (the singular slow process of each society). Iterations of this so-called "fast process" over time generate broader institutional changes whereby the effects of collective action within each fast process accumulate through a "slow process" resulting in a polity with variable and seemingly idiosyncratic but explainable levels of complexity over time. These processes exhibit the same cross-cultural universal pattern. This is a novel contribution that advances our understanding of polity cycling in the Zambezi Plateau, arguably extending to other regional applications elsewhere (e.g., as originally observed by Steward and developed more recently by Marcus Marcus 1998, 2012, among others).

The ZambeziLand model provides an explanation of how a society can change its complexity over time through decisions made by group members in fast processes. In the model, groups rose, declined, and disbanded as leadership and feelings of loyalty and group attachment rose and fell. Such feelings were affected by successes and failures in collective action, and the probability of success was dependent in part on the strength of group leaders. Comparable dynamics occur today in all societies.

The main finding presented here is that group dynamics, centered on collective feelings of loyalty to a group, can generate the macro-level behavior observed in the archaeological record of Southern Africa. This computational finding has implications for further investigation into the role of ideologies and imagery, especially on views of group leadership and loyalty among the people that built the monumental *zimbabwes* of Southern Africa.

Acknowledgments An earlier version of this paper was prepared by the first author, who also wrote the original model code, for the Seminar on Origins of Social Complexity, Department of Computational Social Science, George Mason University, Fall 2012, taught by the second author. This version was extensively revised by both authors for presentation at the Conference on Simulating the Past to Understand Human History, Barcelona, Spain, September 3–4, 2014, organized and chaired by Juan Antonio Barceló, Autonomous University of Barcelona. All errors are the responsibility of the authors, who declare no conflicts of interest. Thanks to Jeff Bassett for introducing the authors to ShareLaTeX, the online system used to write and compile this paper while maintaining a single version, and to Henry Oswald and James Allen of the ShareLaTeX team in the UK for enabling this collaborative result (and others to follow).

References

Cioffi-Revilla C (2005) A canonical theory of origins and development of social complexity. J Math Sociol 29(2):133–153

Cioffi-Revilla C (2014) Introduction to computational social science. Springer, London, Heidelberg

Collett D, Vines A, Hughes E (1992) The chronology of the valley enclosures: implications for the interpretation of Great Zimbabwe. Afr Archaeol Rev 10(1):139–161

Epstein J, Axtell R (1996) Growing artificial societies. Brookings Institution and MIT Press, Washington DC and Cambridge MA

Fontein J (2006) Silence, destruction and closure at Great Zimbabwe: local narratives of desecration and alienation. J South Afr Stud 32(4):771–794

Huffman T (2014) Social complexity in Southern Africa. Afr Archaeol Rev 31(4) (Published Online)

Huffman T, Vogel J (1991) The chronology of Great Zimbabwe. South Afr Archaeol Bull 46(154):61–70

Kim N, Kusimba C (2008) Pathways to social complexity and state formation in the Southern Zambezian region. Afr Archaeol Rev 25(3):131–152

Marcus J (1998) The peaks and valleys of ancient states: an extension of the dynamic model. In: Feinman G, Marcus J (eds) Archaic states. School of American Research Press, Santa Fe, NM

Marcus J (2012) Maya political cycling and the story of the Kaan polity. In: Braswell GE (ed) The Ancient Maya of Mexico: reinterpreting the past of the Northern Maya Lowlands. Equinox Press, London, pp 88–116

Pikirayi I (2001) The Zimbabwe culture: origins and decline of Southern Zambezian states, vol 3. AltaMira Press

Sinclair P, Pikirayi I, Pwiti G, Soper R (1993) Urban trajectories on the Zimbabwean Plateau. In: Shaw T, Sinclair P, Andah B, Okpoko A (eds) The archaeology of Africa: food, metals and towns. Routledge, London

Chapter 14
Personalities, Physiology, Institutions and Genetics: Simulating Ancient Societies with Intelligent Virtual Agents

Tomas Trescak, Anton Bogdanovych and Simeon Simoff

14.1 Introduction

Intelligent virtual[1] agents are autonomous computer programs that are represented in[2] a virtual reality environment by human-like (or animal-like) 3-dimensional figures (called avatars) that move around the reconstructed environment and simulate its inhabitants. The use of virtual agents in cultural and historical simulations has become an important way of enriching 3D reconstructions and helping an observer not only to inspect building and artefacts, but also to understand how the reconstructed site has been enacted in the past.

With modern advancement in research and development, we are now reaching the stage when reconstructing a heritage site becomes more affordable. One possible way of reducing the development cost is to automate the design of the reconstructed virtual environment. Such design automation can be achieved with the use of design grammars—a procedural approach to generating historically informed designs of high complexity, allowing for large cities to be created in a matter of days rather than months. One of the well known examples of using this approach in historical reconstructions is the Rome Reborn project (Dylla et al. 2009), where a virtual reconstruction of the entire city of ancient Rome in the period of 320 AD was generated by automatically placing procedurally generated buildings onto a map of the

[1]See the prototype video at: http://youtu.be/ZY_04YY4YRo.
[2]See the prototype video at: https://www.youtube.com/watch?v=-jDsyOLZHN4.

T. Trescak (✉) · A. Bogdanovych · S. Simoff
University of Western Sydney, Penrith, Australia
e-mail: t.trescak@uws.edu.au

A. Bogdanovych
e-mail: a.bogdanovych@uws.edu.au

S. Simoff
e-mail: s.simoff@uws.edu.au

J.A. Barceló and F. Del Castillo (eds.), *Simulating Prehistoric and Ancient Worlds*, Computational Social Sciences, DOI 10.1007/978-3-319-31481-5_14

city produced by archaeologists. However, most historical reconstructions similar to Rome Reborn do not employ virtual agents in their simulations, as the development cost for these agents is high and advanced automation techniques similar to design grammars are not yet readily available for building large populations of virtual agents.

Modern video games are a good illustration in regards to the possibilities that arise with employment of virtual agents in simulating human behaviour. Players of modern games often experience complex human-like interactions with virtual agents and agents themselves become one of the most important aspects of game play and one of the key entertainment factors. Due to problems with automating agent development the cost of developing video games is very high and it is often hard to justify such high spending in non-profit areas of research that usually require cultural and historical simulations. An example that illustrates the magnitude of spending in video games is Crysis 3, a popular game with the estimated cost of developing being in excess of $66 Million (Gauder 2013). It's hard to imagine such level of spending when it comes to historical simulations, so populating a historical environment with virtual agents needs to be automated.

Aiming to achieve cost saving, some researchers model their virtual societies at the level of crowds rather than individual agents. One well known example of using "virtual crowds" in historical simulations is the visualisation of the Roman Colosseum (Gutierrez et al. 2007), where a crowd simulation approach is taken to visualise the spectators in a gladiator fight. While virtual crowds essentially consist of a large number of virtual agents, designing a crowd normally comes down to designing a few individuals and then replicating them a desired number of times with slight modifications so that the crowd appears to be diverse. The state of the art in using agent crowds in historical simulations is outlined in Mam et al. (2007) where a virtual City of Pompeii is populated with a large number of simulated people, who simply walk around the city avoiding collisions. In this work the virtual agents help to give an impression about the appearance of the ancient people who used to populate Pompeii, but these people are not involved in historically authentic interactions. So they play the role of moving decorations and can only extend the atmosphere of the culture simulation, while offering little in regards to understanding everyday life in the simulated society.

A number of crowd simulation and crowd generation approaches appear in the literature but hardly any of them advance beyond having avatars moving around and carrying objects with them. Further in the paper we show how through simulation of physiological needs and motivations together with personality traits we can achieve much more sophisticated simulations of human behaviour. Furthermore, employing genetic methods for inheriting personality traits and appearance characteristics and connecting virtual agents with formalisations of social roles and social norms allows for a similar (or event higher) level of complexity in large agent crowds as seen in commercial video games. In contrast to standard video games, however, the cost of development for such agents can be greatly reduced through a high degree of automation that our approach offers.

The remainder of the paper is structured as follows. Section 14.2 presents motivation for selecting the combination of genetics, social norms, personality and physiology as a way of advancing the state of the art in historical simulations. Section 14.3 presents our methodology to be employed for creating such simulations. Section 14.4 shows how the aforementioned methodology was applied to building a historical simulation of everyday life in the ancient city of Uruk, 3000 B.C. Section 14.5 shows the application of our methodology to an Australian cultural heritage case study, in which we simulate the life of an Aboriginal Darug tribe. In Sect. 14.6 we analyse the results obtained from the case studies. Finally, Sect. 14.7 summarises the contribution and outlines the directions of future work.

14.2 Approach

Simulation of life in 3D reconstructed historical cities is a costly and time-consuming process, comparable in cost and efforts to development of a commercial video game (involving years of development and millions of dollars in funding (Gauder 2013)). Costs and effort can be decreased with automatic generation of population. This is a two-fold process, in which we need to generate the unique appearance and the behaviour of each individual. Unique appearance can be generated by mimicking the biological reproduction, as for example in Trescak et al. (2012). One way of automatisation of behaviour is to represent individuals as autonomous virtual agents that can generate their goals and act upon them (Vosinakis and Panayiotopoulos 2001). To generate such goals, we propose to use motivation, and in particular physiological motivation, such as hunger, thirst, fatigue and comfort. In this case agents generate their goals upon physiological trigger, e.g. getting hungry. If needed, other types of motivation can be employed, such as safety, love, or self-realisation (Maslow et al. 1970; Alderfer 1969).

The problem with classical approaches to agents driven by physiological motivation is that in a historical simulation all such agents would follow the same circadian rhythm (get hungry, thirsty at the same time), what leads to undesired, uniform behaviour. To avoid this, in our methodology, we propose to configure *motivational modifiers*, which affect the decay rate of a given motivation. For example, a hunger modifier affects the pace in which an agent gets hungry. If such modifiers are different for every agent—then every individual follows its own circadian rhythm, executing goals at various time intervals, increasing believability of the simulated population.

In classical Artificial Intelligence (AI), in order to achieve a goal each agent needs a plan. Such plans can be automatically generated using traditional planning techniques (Shehory et al. 1999; Braubach et al. 2005). Such planning techniques normally model perfectly rational behaviour, which is not always suitable for simulating humans as this results in emotionless, "robotic" behaviour. To avoid it, in our methodology, we enrich agents with personalities and emotions, which affect their decisions when creating a plan for a current goal. This approach may even lead to emergent agent behaviour that appears to be closer to human-like reasoning. As an example, imagine a fisherman agent with no personality and emotions, that catches fish when it's hungry. The agent will fish until it succeeds, or until it dies of hunger, unless we manually specify a possible change of plans when hunger level raises to a critical value. In contrast, the same fisherman having personality and emotions may get frustrated when being hungry and unsuccessful. This agent may "decide" to stop fishing when frustration level overwhelms the rational decision for fishing and will search for alternatives to feed, such as begging or stealing food. The decision whether to beg or steal would depend on agent's personality.

In the previous example, fisherman represents a specific *social group* of the simulated population. Social groups combine certain classes of individuals that fulfill their goals in a similar way. Combining individuals into social groups allows us to define and program actions on a group level, rather than having to do this on individual level, reducing effort in defining crowd behaviour.

In human societies, it is not uncommon for members of different social groups to interact with each other and even cooperate in order to fulfill their goals. For example, imagine a fisherman who has to trade fish with a spear-maker in order to replace his broken fishing spear (see Sect. 14.4). A common technique being used in AI to facilitate the kind of interactions between different social groups as in the example above is to employ Organisation-Centred Multi-Agent System (OCMAS). The OCMAS approach is to explicitly formalise social norms of the agent population and connect those norms to the social roles, which represent different population groups. Such social norms capture rules and protocols that drive agent interactions. As a result, agents can use these norms in reasoning to create plans for their current goal. This provides agents the ability to automatically perform their actions depending on their assigned social group.

14.3 Methodology

Following the approach described above, we present our methodology separated into several steps that facilitate automatic generation of intelligent agent crowds, where agents generate goals depending on physiological modifiers and plan their actions depending on their personality and in accordance with social norms.

14.3.1 Step 1: Design the Base Population

Base population represents the initial group of agents used to generate the rest of the crowd. This population has to define the fundamental visual properties of the resulting crowd. Therefore, for each ethnic group that will be generated, there must be at least one couple of avatars, where both individuals maintain the ethnicity-specific visual traits (e.g. asian eyes), while all other non-specific features (e.g. head shape) are varied. Following this approach, during genetic reproduction, ethnicity-specific features are carried on to the following generations (Trescak et al. 2012), while diversity within ethnicity is assured.

This process requires a significant effort, as designers have to define all avatars with distinctive appearance and a library of related textures, clothing and attachments in order to ensure high variety. In order to reduce the effort, we propose to design and use *parametric avatars* (Lewis 2000; Trescak et al. 2012), which are avatars with visual features that can be modified using parametric values. For example, parameter "height" and "body fat" would modify the corresponding parameters of avatar body. Such parameter values of an avatar form genes combined in a chromosome used to reproduce children with diverse appearance.

To better understand how the diversity is achieved—we need to explain the process of genetic reproduction. In this process, an agent's appearance, motivational modifiers (in our case physiological modifiers), and its personality are encoded into "genes". As a result, these three groups of genes form three chromosomes, depicted in Fig. 14.1.

During reproduction, we take two parents and combine each of the three pairs of related parent chromosomes to produce the child's chromosome. We decide how many genes are inherited from the father and how many from the mother using a *father-mother ratio*. A *crossover* operator is responsible for combining chromosomes. Theory of genetic algorithms defines several crossover operators, i.e. split operator, but for our purposes, we define a specific *fuzzy operator*, that imitates the biological crossover using two pairs of chromosomes (Vieira et al. 2010).

Definition 1 Given mother's chromosome c^m consisting of genes $c^m = g_1^m g_2^m \dots g_n^m$, the father's chromosome c^f consisting of genes $c^f = g_1^f g_2^f \dots g_n^f$, the parent *gene selector function* $s^i_{r^{fm}} : 2^G \rightarrow \{0, 1\}$ which for position i, where $0 \leq i \leq n$, selects either mother or father gene depending on probability given by the father-mother ratio r^{fm} and the *fuzzy function* $f : \mathbb{I} \rightarrow \mathbb{R}$ which for gene on position i selects a random value in the interval given by $f(i) = [s(i), (g_i^m - g_i^f)/2]$, we define a **fuzzy** crossover operator $\oslash : C \times C \rightarrow C$ as $c^m \oslash c^f = f(1) \cdot f(2) \dots f(n)$.

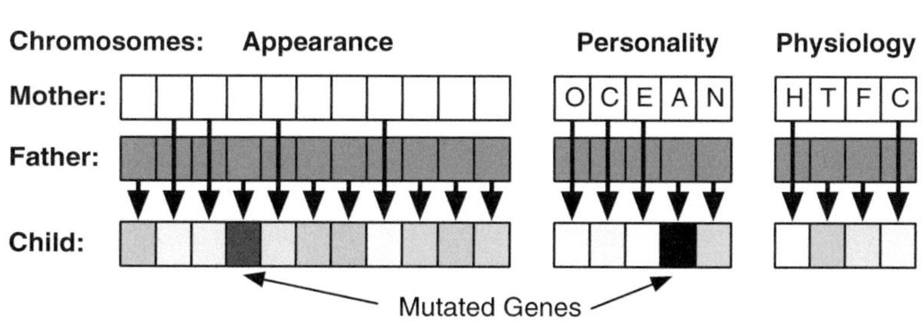

Fig. 14.1 Genetic reproduction using "Fuzzy" operator

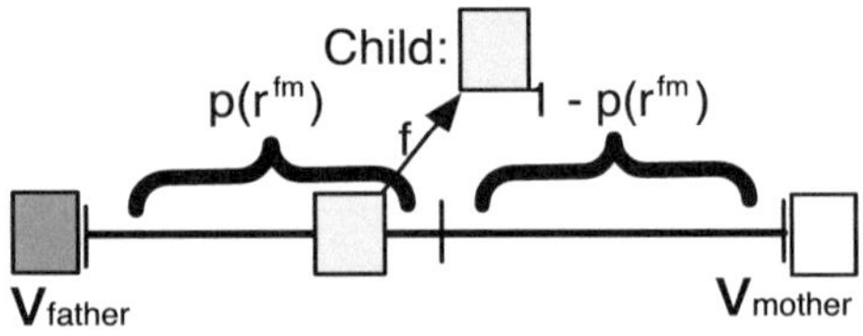

Fig. 14.2 Using genetic operators to form an agent's chromosome

Fuzzy operator creates a new gene value by selecting a random value from the interval defined by the gene values of the parents and depending on the specified father-mother ratio takes this value closer to father or mother gene. This process is depicted in Fig. 14.2, where r^{fm} means father-mother ratio and $p(r^{fm})$ means probability of selecting value from the interval, depending on r^{fm}.

Another important process of the biological reproduction is mutation, which is the driving mechanism of evolution and novelty in species. We mimic the mutation process by modifying the value of pre-defined number of genes to the value from outside of the previously mentioned interval. The result of genetic manipulations is a new chromosome using which we can reconstruct a new child, its appearance, physiological needs and a personality.

Once the appearance of the avatars representing the base population has been specified in a parametric fashion—a diverse crowd of a desired size can be automatically generated following the aforementioned genetic principles. The agents in the crowd will have diverse appearance, while at the same time the important ethnic features of their appearance will be preserved. In order to introduce diversity of their behaviour—further steps of the methodology need to be completed starting with the configuration of motivational modifiers.

14.3.2 Step 2: Configure Motivational Modifiers

Genetic approach is also used to diversify agent behaviour. For this purpose, *motivational modifiers* are encoded into genes of the chromosome. Therefore, in this step, for each member of the base population the *motivational modifiers* are specified. In case of physiological motivation, these modifiers relate to hunger, thirst, fatigue and comfort, and represent the decay rate in which agents are getting hungry, thirsty, tired and sleepy. To avoid an impression that every single agent follows the same day cycle and performs the same set of actions at the same time, these values must be different for every agent from the base population. The more diverse these values are in the base population, the more diversity will be present in the circadian rhythms of the resulting crowd.

14.3.3 Step 3: Specify Personality Traits

While diverse motivational modifiers assure execution of actions at various times, agent personalities determine the kind of actions the agents will execute. In this step, for each member of the base population its personality is specified using the popular OCEAN model (Goldberg 1990), which captures five personality traits: *openness, conscientiousness, extroversion, agreeableness and neuroticism*. Openness relates to imaginative, creative aspect of a person. Consciousness captures the ability to be organised and careful. Extroversion defines, how social and outgoing a person is. Agreeableness relates to ability to cope with people, friendliness and generosity. Neuroticism defines tendency for negative emotions and instability.

Combination of the OCEAN values defines a specific character. Explaining, how to define a specific character is out of scope of this work, therefore we regard interested reader to existing publications (Bartneck 2002; Steunebrink et al. 2009). For the purposes of this methodology, it is important that agents forming the base population have different personality values, so that during genetic reproduction their children will have new, emerging personalities. In Sect. 14.6, we present how the diversity of parent personalities affects their children, and how it determines which actions they select as the result of having a certain personality type.

In order for agents to be able to select an action that is most relevant for their personality, such action has to be annotated by following *personality facets* (Howard and Howard 1995): *temptation, gregariousness, assertiveness, excitement, familiarity, straightforwardness, altruism, compliance, modesty* and *correctness*. Using values of personality facets, the agent selects an action that provides the highest utility for its personality type (Bartneck 2002; Howard and Howard 1995). See Table 14.1 for an example of annotations for *work*, *beg*, *steal* and *search* actions.

Often, actions such as "work" have various meaning in the context of different social groups. Working for fishermen means to catch fish, while for pot makers it means to make pots. Therefore, in the next step of the methodology, the institution is specified, which defines all the social groups, their interactions and also defines the meaning and parameters of specific actions, e.g. determines how quickly a particular object satisfies hunger.

Table 14.1 Personality facets of agent actions

	Tempt.	Gregar.	Assert.	Excitement	Famil.	Altruism	Compliance	Modality.	Corr.
Beg	0	0	−0.5	0	0	0	0.5	0	0.5
Work	0	0	0.5	0	0	0	0	0	1
Search	0.5	0	0.75	0.5	0	−0.25	−0.5	0	−0.5
Steal	1	0	1	1	0	−1	−1	0	−0.75

14.3.4 Step 4: Formalise Social Norms and Roles

To define social groups, their actions and interactions, an Electronic Institutions (EI), a well established Organisation-Centred Multi-Agent System (OCMAS) is specified. EI establishes what agents are permitted and forbidden to do as well as the constraints and the consequences of their actions (Esteva 2003). In general, an EI regulates multiple, distinct, concurrent, interrelated, dialogic activities, each one involving different groups of agents playing different roles. Definition of an EI consists of the following four components:

First, a *dialogical framework* specifies social roles involved in the simulation and their hierarchy. Figure 14.3a depicts the role structure of the simulation of Uruk 3000 B.C and Fig. 14.3b depicts the one of Aboriginal simulation (see Sect. 14.6). Apart from the role structure, the dialogical framework defines ontology, a common language for communication between agents.

Second, a *performative structure* isolates specific activities (also called scenes) that can be performed within an Electronic Institution. It defines how agents can legally move among different scenes (from activity to activity) depending on their role. Furthermore, a performative structure defines when new scene executions start, and if a scene can be multiply executed at run time. A performative structure can be regarded as a graph whose nodes are both scenes and transitions (scene connectives), linked by directed arcs (See Fig. 14.4). The type of transition allows to express choice points (Or transitions) for agents to choose which target scenes to enter, or synchroni-

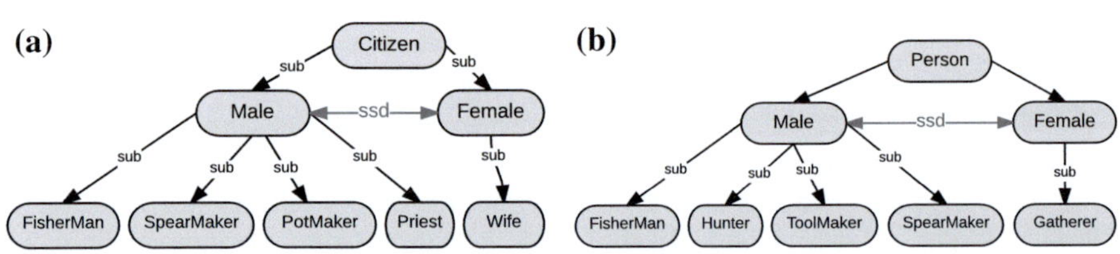

Fig. 14.3 Role hierarchy. **a** Uruk 3000 B.C. **b** Australia

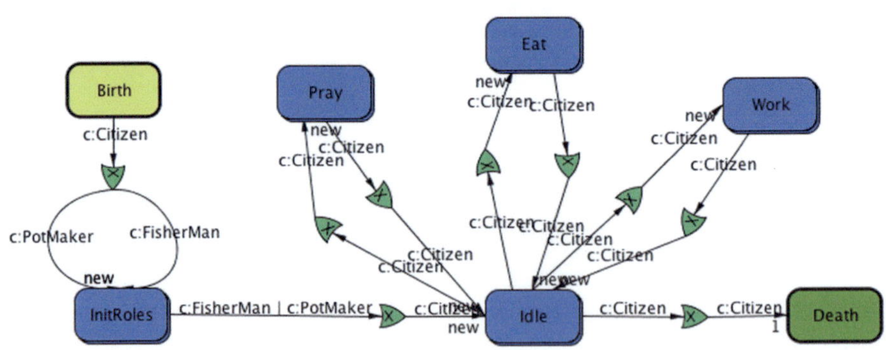

Fig. 14.4 Performative structure

sation/parallelization points (And transitions) that force agents to synchronise before progressing to different scenes in parallel. The labels on the directed arcs determine which agents, depending on their roles, can move between scenes to transitions.

Third, for each activity, interactions between agents are articulated through agent group meetings expresses as *scene protocols*, which follow well-defined interaction protocols, whose participating agents may change over time (agents may enter or leave). A scene protocol is specified by a directed graph whose nodes represent the different states of a dialogic interaction between roles (See Figs. 14.5 and 14.6). Its arcs are labelled with illocution schemes (whose sender, receiver and content may contain variables) or time-outs.

Definition of EI is fundamental to agent reasoning and our dynamic planning algorithm that constructs a list of actions to fulfill the current goal by finding a path (sequence of actions) that make the agent go into the desired scene and reach a desired state within this scene.

An institution provides agents with knowledge about possible actions that can be performed. The next step of the methodology provides means of visualising these actions in the virtual world.

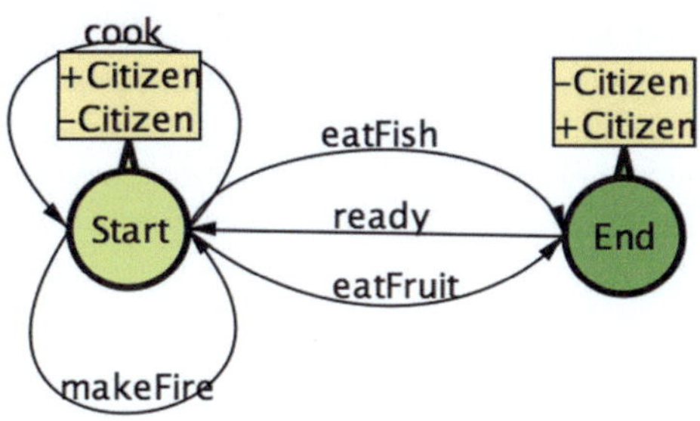

Fig. 14.5 Eat scene protocol

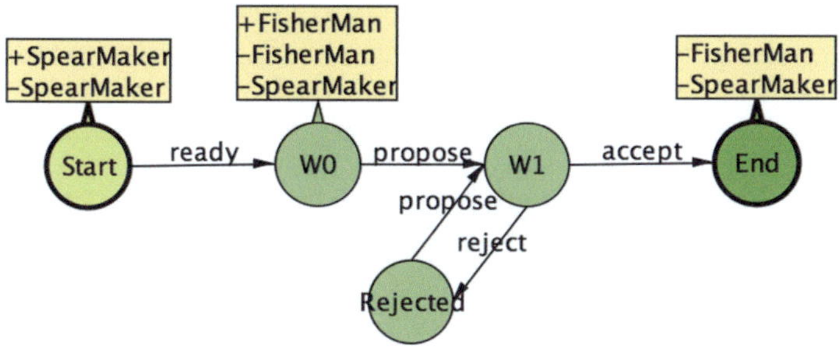

Fig. 14.6 Trade scene protocol

14.3.5 Step 5: Adaptation and Annotation of the Environment

For purposes of visualisation, institutional actions must have corresponding objects, animations and scripts. In this step, objects of the virtual world related to such actions are created and annotated with specific meta-data, so that agents know that a connection between institutional illocutions and objects is established. Agents use annotations in their planning, which is affected by the current state of the environment. Therefore, interactive objects have to contain information on what action they provide and what are the action parameters (Trescak 2012).

Adaptation and annotation of the environment is the last step that requires manual input. In this last step we generate the population of the simulation and make it act within the simulated virtual environment.

14.3.6 Step 6: Generating the Population

Generation of population is a fully automatic process, where the desired number of "children" is generated from the base population using genetic approach described in Sect. 14.3.1. Initially, children are only sets of chromosomes and their appearance has to be reconstructed in a given virtual world. Once connected to the virtual world, they start automatically generate goals and act upon them.

14.4 Case Study: Uruk 3000 B.C

In order to highlight the key aspects of our approach, we have applied it to simulating one of the humanity's first cities—the city of Uruk 3000 B.C. To further address the agility of our approach, we apply our methodology first to Second Life,[3] a well known virtual world platform, and then to Unity 3D,[4] the popular game engine. The Second Life simulation, serves to present the life of Uruk to wide public, using well-know virtual world platform with many existing users. The drawback of Second Life is in its lacking capability of handling large societies of intelligent agents (or non-playable characters, NPCs). On the other hand, Unity 3D facilitates the creation of sophisticated single-user and multi-user 3D games, and also provides the possibility to execute large societies. The size of the society is bounded only by the computational capability of the hardware, on which the game is executed. In this section, we describe how our methodology facilitates deployment of sophisticated historical simulation to both platforms and estimate and compare their work load estimates.

---

[3]http://secondlife.com (last visited 06/2015).

[4]http://unity3d.com (last visited 06/2015).

14.4.1 Preparation: Designing the World

Before we can apply our methodology, we need to design the 3D environment of the simulation. In Second Life, we started with an existing 3D model of the city that included key buildings, plants, animals and terrain. This model was developed by archaeologists and provides some level of historical exactness. For Unity 3D, we have recreated this 3D model in Google Sketchup and Blender. Furthermore, we have modelled historical objects used by various crafts belonging to the epoch. These objects include beds positioned on roofs, various chairs and tables, pots for cooking, market equipment, pottery ring, spears, and spare spear parts, fisherman boats and rows. 3D design requires a lot of effort, and the preparation step took significantly longer then design and execution of the city population. Figure 14.7 portraits the 3D design of the market, executed in Unity 3D, with several, custom designed objects. Figures 14.8 and 14.9 compare the visualisations in both, Second Life and Unity 3D.

With the static 3D design of the environment in place, we can start applying our methodology an populate this environment with autonomous agents.

14.4.2 Step 1: Design the Base Population

When defining the base population is Second Life, we considered only one ethnic group of Uruk citizens. Therefore, we designed only two members of the base population portrayed in Fig. 14.10a, b, using which we have generated the rest of the population.

Fig. 14.7 3D design of the Uruk market with live avatars

Fig. 14.8 Second Life

Fig. 14.9 Unity 3D

Figure 14.10c, depicts a child generated without mutation. This child clearly carries visual traits from both parents, having mother's nose, but father's mouth. Figure 14.10d depicts the child of the same parents, but with high level of mutation. Clearly, some visual traits are still visible (e.g. nose, jaw shape), yet, there are new emergent visual features, such as skin colour.

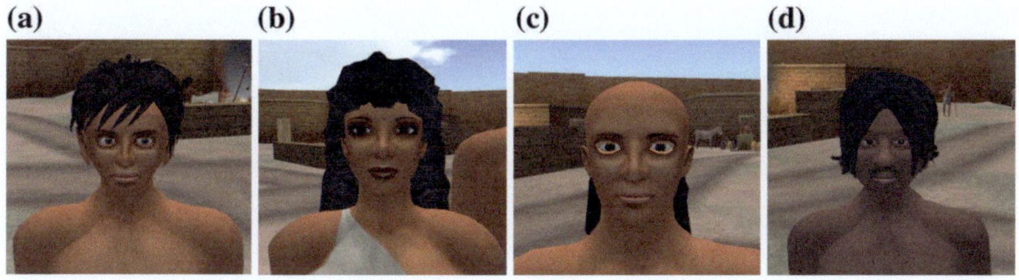

Fig. 14.10 Generating crowd appearance in Second Life. **a** Father. **b** Mother. **c** Child. **d** Mutant

In Unity 3D, we have applied a bit different approach and we have generated the base population using the *genotype rules* (Trescak et al. 2012). Using such rules we can specify a racial or ethnic profile, which limits gene values only to the specific range. For example, we can specify what shades of skin colour can be used, what is the approximate size of the nose, what is the range of person height and so on. Yet, this approach can only generate avatars belonging to the same race/ethnic and does not allow us to generate intra ethnic avatars. Since we are generating avatars belonging to the ancient Uruk ethnic, this is not a problem.

To modify and visualise avatars in Unity 3D, we used the open source Unity Multipurpose Avatars[5] technology for generating random avatars. We have extended the default randomisation mechanism that has only limited control over generated avatars, with our genetic approach allowing to generate avatars belonging to a specific ethnic.

Figure 14.11 depicts the sample of ten avatars generated from the initial population of five avatars. In the base population we have two ethnics, Caucasian (Adam and Bea) and Sumerian (Cyril, Diana and Eva). We have used western names for the sumerian population only for convenience, in order to code them alphabetically by the first letter in their name (A–E). Generated children are named by coded names of their parents, the crossover operator and the mutation level used during generation process. To portrait the preservation of ethnic features we have designed all members of sumerian population with bigger, distinctive noses and darker skin colour, while caucasian population has smaller noses and and lighter skin colour. Child of C + D in the first row and C + E in the second row obviously carry on only the sumerian features, although C + D shows also very distinct features, due to the high level of mutation that has been used. Interesting result is in the second row, where we depict four different children of A + E, each of them visually distinct, yet clearly carrying features from both father and mother. Two children are quite small, with lighter skin or bigger ears as their father, others are taller, or with darker skin and smaller ears as their mother.

[5]http://u3d.as/content/uma-steering-group/uma-unity-multipurpose-avatar/67d (last visited 04/2014).

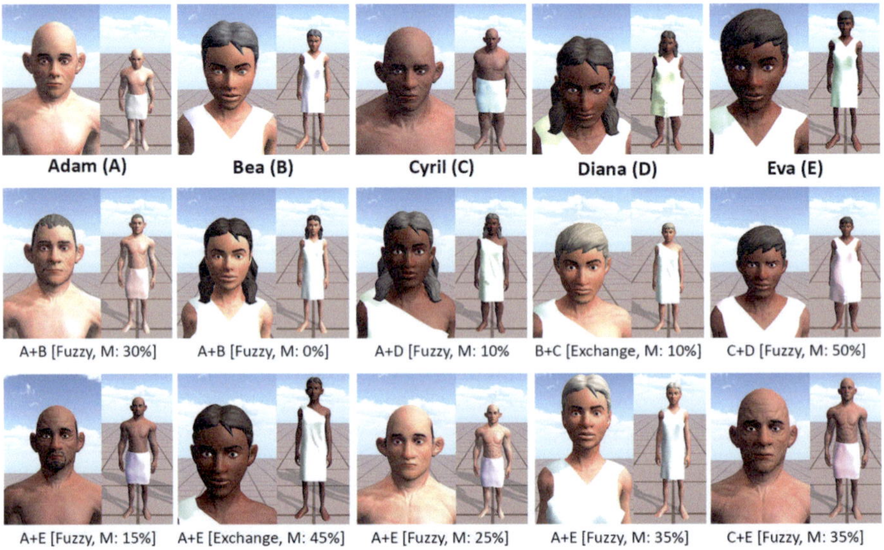

Fig. 14.11 Detail of the crowd generated for Unity 3D

Fig. 14.12 Overview of the crowd generated for Unity 3D

Figure 14.12 depicts the society of 150 avatars, generated from base population belonging to the same ethnic. As a result, none of the generated avatars carries caucasian traits and skin colour. The apparent difference is the overall graphic quality, which is prevailing in Unity 3D.

14.4.3 Step 2: Configure Motivational Modifiers

Base population serves not only to generate avatars with unique appearance, but also with a unique (or non-uniform) behaviour. As a result, in the next step, we defined the physiological modifiers of the base population. We set various decay rates for hunger, thirst, fatigue and comfort for each member of the population. Avatars generated from the base population will obtain varied and mutated values of these modifiers. Since each modifier will have a different value, avatars will become hungry or tired in distinct intervals, executing their actions non-uniformly. Figure 14.13 shows the graphical user interface, that facilitates the specification of physiological properties.

14.4.4 Step 3: Specify Personality Traits

Physiological motivation solves the (when) problem of uniformity, when agents execute their actions at various time frames. On the other hand, having avatars with distinct personalities solves the (what) problem of uniqueness, when agents perform actions matching behavioural profile. As a result, we define personalities for each agent using the OCEAN model. Figure 14.14 shows the graphical user interface, that facilitates the specification of personality properties. In Sect. 14.6 we describe the setups for personalities that were used.

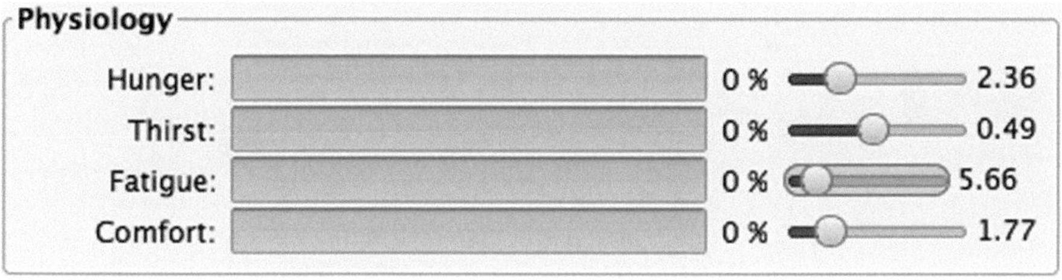

Fig. 14.13 User interface for the definition of physiological properties of an avatar

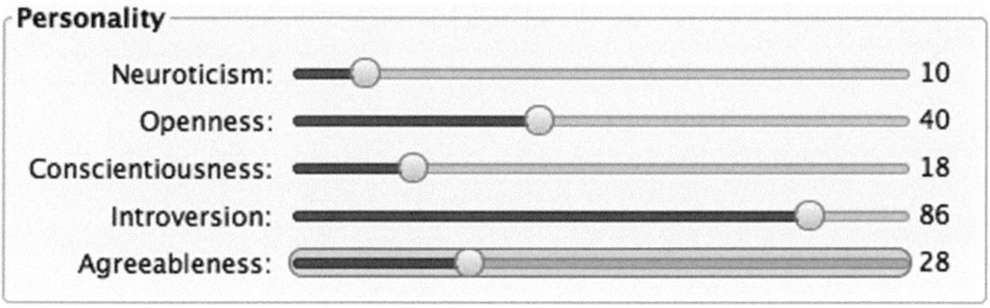

Fig. 14.14 User interface for the definition of personality properties of an avatar

Apart from the definition of agent personalities, we annotated all actions and relate them to a specific personality, using personality facets (see Sect. 14.3.3). Table 14.1 shows four actions that Uruk agents perform to satisfy the goal of "eating". In this table, there are four actions, i.e. beg, work, search and steal, and nine personality facets, e.g. temptation, gregariousness, assertivity with valued ranging from -1 (low) to 1 (high). These facets work as modifiers used to calculate utility of a given action in relation to a specific personality. The higher the utility, the more probable is that the action will be selected. "Stealing" action is defined for agents with more aggressive personalities (very low correctness, low altruism), "begging" for agents with low-confidence (very low assertivity, higher correctness) and "working" and "searching" for more neutral personalities with varying sense of correctness. It is probable, that we will have to adjust these values later on, but for now it sufficed.

14.4.5 Step 4: Formalise Social Norms and Roles

Next, we defined all components of the Electronic Institution, with roles of fisherman, spear-maker, pot-maker, pries, king and wife (see Fig. 14.3). All of these roles are sub-roles of *citizen*, which holds all common properties for all roles, e.g. inventory of owned items.

Then, we defined possible actions of agents in specific scene protocols. For current roles we defined pray, eat, make spear, make pot, trade and fish protocol (Fig. 14.15). Make spear, make pot and fish protocol belong to the scene "Work", and

Fig. 14.15 Working on the land

agents select the correct protocol based on their role. Most of these protocols only command a single agent what actions need to be performed to achieve its goal. The exception is the fishing protocol, which defines collaborative actions for two agents, where one agent has to row a boat, while the other is fishing. Therefore, fisherman always have to agree to go fishing in pairs.

Finally, we grouped scene protocols in a performative structure (see Fig. 14.4), which restricts execution of actions in scenes to specific roles.

14.4.6 Step 5: Adaptation and Annotation of the Environment

For all actions and interactions, we have recorded animations, such as begging or stealing food, using motion capture and copied them in ".BHV" format to Second Life and with the help of Blender 3D, we have converted ".BVH" file to Unity 3D. Recording animations and their subsequent processing in any platform is a very delicate task and usually requires professional crew and equipment. Since we had no such possibility our own acting performance sufficed.

Moreover, since 3D object carry no meta-information on their possible purpose, we have added related objects to the virtual world model and annotated the environment so that agents can use them in their planning. For example, agents use the 3D object camp fire to cook their food. Therefore, we annotate that this 3D object provides action (illocution) "cook" from the scene "Eat" (annotated as action:Eat.cook). As a result, when agent plans its action, it knows that it has to interact with camp fire object to perform the "Eat.cook" action. In another example, we annotated the a pottery ring with "action:Work.PotMaker.makePot", what defines that pottery ring provides action makePot in the scene protocol "PotMaker" from the scene "Work".

14.4.7 Step 6: Generating the Population

In the last step, we generated a population of agents and connected these to Second Life. Each agent had a unique appearance and automatically started fulfilling its goals. Agents were correctly selecting their goals based on their physiology, executing them at various intervals due to different physiological modifiers, planing their actions based on their personality and social norms, and executing them in the simulated environment. Figure 14.16 shows some virtual agents from the resulting simulation.

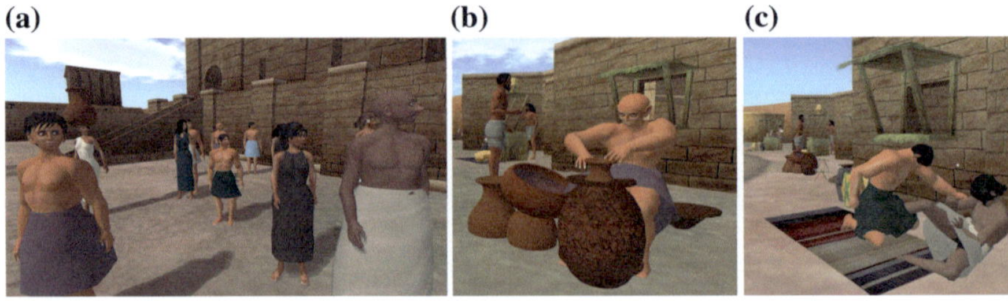

Fig. 14.16 Everyday life in the city of Uruk 3000 B.C. **a** Crwod. **b** Working. **c** Stealing

14.5 Case Study: Darug Clan, Australia

In our second case study, we simulate the life of an Australian Aboriginal clan from the Darug tribe, living in the area of Parramatta, New South Wales, in times before the arrival of first fleet and the establishment of the European settlement. This simulation was built in Unity 3D in the form of an educational video game and a virtual reality experience.

The interactive 3D video game takes the player on a quest to explore the life of an Aboriginal clan in the Parramatta basin. A spiritual mentor and the guardian in the form of an aboriginal elder gradually introduces the participant to the daily life of native clans, the knowledge they possessed, rituals they performed, protocols they kept and their connection to dreamtime. The elder familiarises the player with various clan members as they perform their daily activities such as tool making, painting, fishing or preparing food. During these interactions the player also learns about the aboriginal medicine, arts, as well as ceremonies, such as the smoking ceremony and receives an introduction to their spiritual values.

The virtual reality simulation uses Oculus Rift ([6]) headset to take the user on an immersive journey in historical Australia. The information provided is the same as in the video game, yet the content is not interactive, and user partakes the role of a sole observer listening to the spiritual mentor. In the remainder of this section, we describe how we applied our methodology to deliver this historical simulation and discuss the believability of our approach.

14.5.1 Preparation: Designing the World

The initial step of the 3D simulation creation process was the artistic design of 3D assets that formed the simulation environment. This phase highly depended on the invaluable help from the Elders of the Darug clan, who consulted us on the believability of our simulation. Elders selected the location of the simulation to correspond

[6]https://www.oculus.com/ (last visited (06/2015)).

Fig. 14.17 Environment design. **a** Initial model (sketchup). **b** Final model (Unity)

with grounds, upon which the South Parramatta campus of the University of Western Sydney is located. The initial model of the environment was constructed from the GIS data using Google Sketchup[7] (see Fig. 14.17a). We have modified this initial model in Unity 3D and added local flora and fauna (see Fig. 14.17b). Then, we have implemented the animal behaviour (artificial intelligence), including the flocking behaviour of kangaroos, moving lizards and snakes, flying birds and bats and fish swimming in the river. While bats and lizards follow pre-defined paths, kangaroos show intelligence by fleeing from moving humans and placing bait in the water attracts fish. We implemented the animal behaviour using popular Unity 3D plugins: Playmaker[8] and NodeCanvas.[9] Use of these plugins facilitates the reusability of the developed functionality, and its visual nature helps the non-technical team members actively participate in its specification.

With the static 3D design of the environment in place, we apply our methodology to populate the simulation environment with autonomous agents.

14.5.2 Step 1: Design the Base Population

The population in this simulation consists of a single ethnic group. Therefore, we designed only two members of the base population to generate the rest. While both designed avatars carry typical aboriginal features, such as the wide nose or dark hair, we have also introduced variations of visual properties, such as skin colours or height. Maintaining consistent values (or just a minimal variation) of stereotypical features in all designed avatars, significantly increases the probability of their propagation to descendants, and their exclusion can only be affected by the mutation. On the other hand, features that we wanted to vary, we assigned from both extremes of

[7]http://www.sketchup.com.

[8]http://nodecanvas.com.

[9]http://www.hutonggames.com.

the feasible range. For example, we designed a strong and bulky male and thin and fragile female. Using the fuzzy operator to crossover genes, we obtain avatars with varied body and face builds (Fig. 14.18).

Consequently, consulting aboriginal elders, historic literatures and photographies, we have designed traditional clothing, tools and wearables. Since aboriginal population in the simulated era wore clothing that often did not cover the private parts, in order to target wider audience in which some may be offended by nudity, we decided to use the design of more recent clothes. Figure 14.19 depicts the generated crowd

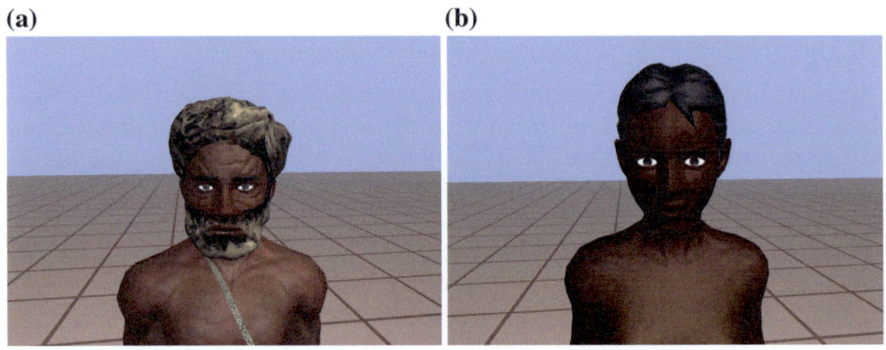

Fig. 14.18 Base population used to generate the Aboriginal population

Fig. 14.19 Aboriginal crowd. **a** Father. **b** Mother

of males and females, wearing traditional hip or neck bags and variations of loin clothes from the kangaroo or possum fur. To assign random clothes to avatars, we have used the popular Unity Multi-Purpose Avatar (UMA) plugin.[10]

14.5.3 Step 2: Configure Motivational Modifiers and Step 3: Specify Personality Traits

Physiological motivation drives agents' proactive goal creation. Motivational modifiers affect the pace in which they get hungry, thirsty or tired. Having varied values assures that agents take decisions at various intervals. Motivational modifiers and personality traits form the part of the chromosome that is used by the genetic reproduction. Since we used only two members of the base population, similarly to visual features, to gain variation in descendants, we have assigned motivational modifier values from both sides of feasible extremes. We created a male that was getting hungry at a high pace, needs to drink often, yet takes a long time to get tired. Female is humble on resources, yet fatigues quickly.

Concerning avatars personalities, we used the very same approach, providing significantly different OCEAN profiles for both avatars, with aggressive, yet timid male and submissive, yet social female.

14.5.4 Step 4: Formalise Social Norms and Roles

In this step, we defined components of the Electronic Institution. The dialogic framework contains roles of fisherman, spear-maker, hunter, tool-maker and gatherer (see Fig. 14.3b). All of these roles are sub-roles of *person*, which holds common properties for all roles, e.g. inventory of owned items.

Please note that this role hierarchy does not correspond to the actual tribe structure. In the real world, tribesmen perform various tasks, where individuals design their spears, create own tools and go hunting with them. This knowledge is incrementally passed onto by elders. We have separated the activities between various roles to isolate effectively agent behaviour and goals. Also, currently there exist only limited means for the dynamic plan creation with a large decision space. By dynamic plan creation we mean a possibility of agents to automatically *generate and adapt* plans that lead to the fulfilment of their goal (e.g. they do not need to re-start the whole plan, but continue from the last feasible point).

During the design of the Electronic Institution, we were able to re-use a large portion of scene protocols from the Uruk project (e.g. eating, gathering, fishing), supporting the usability of our approach. The reason we can reuse EI functionality

---

[10]http://uma.unity3d.com/ (last visited 06/2015).

is that protocols for action execution remained the same, what changed is their visualisation in the 3D environment. For example, in the fishing scene, one fisherman controls the boat while the other is using a spear to catch fish. The process is the same in Uruk as well as with Darug clan, but Darug fishermen no longer sit and stand in the boat, they kneel. Also, not a long paddle but a piece of bark is used to steer and row the boat. As a result, we only needed to record new animations for action execution, their control remained the same.

14.5.5 Step 5: Adaptation and Annotation of the Environment

With the invaluable help from Aboriginal elders who performed as actors, we recorded authentic animations that portray daily chores and activities of the Darug tribesmen. These activities include simple tasks such as eating, drinking, more sophisticated activities such as making tools, spears, creating artwork and also different rituals such as the smoke ceremony, dancing or feasting (Fig. 14.20). These animations trigger upon an agent acquiring a goal that requires accomplishing one or several actions. For example, to make an axe, agents need to find a viable piece of wood, stone or chipped bone. To facilitate this process, agents need to recognise objects and their functionality to consider them in their plans. Therefore, in this step, we placed annotated world objects with the representation understandable by agents. In this project, we have also introduced *dynamic annotations* that change depending on the object state. For example, alive kangaroo is annotated as "spearable", "food source", but when it is killed its annotation changes to "leather", "bone", "food". Agents use these annotations to create plans for accomplishing their goals.

(a) (b)

Fig. 14.20 Simulated activities. **a** Feasting. **b** Tool making

Fig. 14.21 Everyday life in the Darug clan

14.5.6 Step 6: Generating the Population

In the last step of our methodology, we generate the population of agents. Using our approach, the appearance, physiological and personality profile are unique with each generated agent.

For each created agent, a Playmaker script assigns a role and initialises the connection with the Electronic Institution. Agents start the random walk to discover their environment. After an arbitrary period, physiology triggers a feeding request. To feed, agents dynamically create plans based on their role, personality and surrounding objects. For example, the only way for spear-makers to feed is to exchange their produced spears for food with fishermen or hunters. In order to create a spear, they have to use knives, which serve them to work the spear-wood. Another role, Painters, first search for ochre, water and bark and then exchange their pieces with hunters and fishermen. Figure 14.21 shows a scene from the aboriginal simulation showing tool maker and painter at work, as well as men feasting on a kangaroo.

14.6 Evaluation

In this section we analyse our results and estimate the effort (in hours) needed to setup and execute the simulations for both case studies. Then, we describe two experiments, that evaluate the diversity of generated agent behaviour.

14.6.1 Uruk Simulated in Second Life

We estimate that the total time spent on completing the case study from Sect. 14.4 was close to 7 days. The process was relatively fast as we have already had a model of the city and we focused only on generating the population. Step 1, definition of base population took us three days, where most of this time was spent on modelling clothing and attachments for avatars. Second Life provides parametric avatars with possibility to change more than 200 visual features. Therefore designing the body of the avatars took us only a couple hours per avatar. Steps 2 and 3, in our case took only one hour to complete, as the physiological modifiers and personality were defined only focusing on having wide range of values (rather than trying to achieve some pre-determined global personality skew in the resulting population). Step 4, definition of institution took 1 day, during which we designed all scenes and a performative structure and tested agent interactions. Also, we studied how to set-up the personality facets of personality-based actions. Step 5 took a lot of effort and time, in total 4 days. During this time we recorded and tuned all the animations, designed all interactive objects (e.g. pot-making ring) and scripted their behaviour. Step 6 is fully automatic, generation of 100 agents took only a few seconds, visualisation of each avatar in Second Life takes about 30 s per avatar.

14.6.2 Everyday Life of the Darug People Simulated in Unity 3D

We estimate that the total time spent on completing the case study from Sect. 14.5 was close to 31 days. In contrast to the Uruk simulation, the Darug design has not been provided to use, so we needed to spend significantly more time on the initial design. The increase in time is due to the fact, that we needed to re-create manually the 3D design of the terrain and houses in the reconstructed area (7 days) as well as all 3D objects (5 days) and avatar clothing (6 days). Three days were spent on recording animations. Converted animations had to be adjusted and programmed to be used with Unity (i.e. Mecanim). The conversion and animation adjustments took us 2 days. Then, we have annotated the environment with meta-data used by agents during reasoning about possible plans to accomplish their goals. In this case annotation is done directly in Unity 3D, via custom MonoBehaviour objects. With the help of the aboriginal elders we have then designed a simple institution, personality setups for the base population, their daily plans and related cultural information for the institutional roles. As a result it took us only 1 day, to adjust steps 2–6 to Unity 3D.

14.6.3 General Methodology

Using our methodology, in combination with modern game engines and 3D virtual worlds, we significantly cut down the time to populate historical 3D simulations. The drawback of our approach is that we rely on parametric avatars with ability to modify the avatar appearance and clothing using declarative (visual) parameters. But, this is not a major issue, since we already possess the technology for Unity 3D and Second Life, and other game engines offer similar functionality, although in the form of paid plugins.

Having parametric avatars and employing our genetic approach we can generate unique, ethnic avatars in a very little time. Using motion capture, we can easily animate these avatars and believable results depend only on exact historical data and acting skills. Furthermore, using the Electronic Institution technology, we can declaratively specify the social structures and interaction protocols, used by agents to automatically reason about their possible actions. Electronic institution can be tweaked during the simulation runtime, decreasing the debugging efforts in comparison to traditional approach, where simulation has to be restarted after every change.

14.6.4 Generating Children of Parents with Diverse Personalities

To test the validity of generating agents with various behaviour, we performed two experiments. In the first experiment, we set-up diverse personalities of parents, where one parent had very low confidence, while the other was very aggressive (see Fig. 14.22a). When hungry, one parent chooses to beg, the other one to steal. Then, we have generated their 100 children, with father-mother ratio set to 30 % (agents will have 70 % of their genes closer to their mother). Figure 14.22b depicts the highly varying personality profiles of their children. We let generated agents decide what to

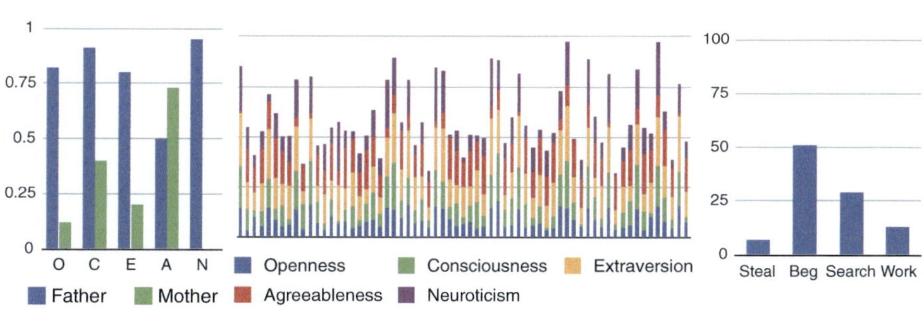

Fig. 14.22 Experiment 1: Children of parents with opposite personalities (no mutation). **a** Parents. **b** Children personalities. **c** Actions

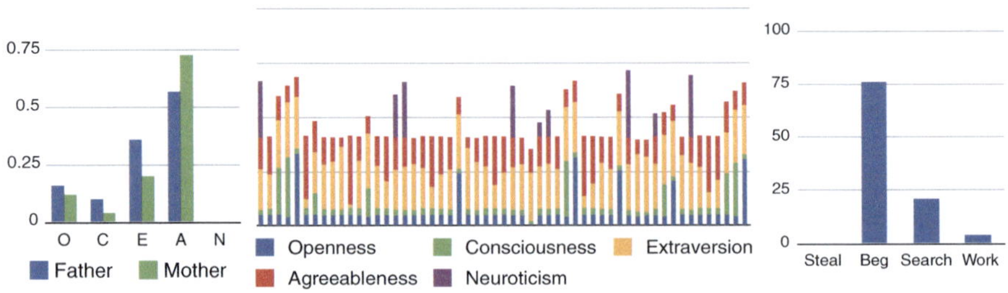

Fig. 14.23 Experiment 2: Children of parents with similar personalities (mutation 25 %). **a** Parents. **b** Children personalities. **c** Actions

do when hungry and observed emerging behaviour of searching for food and working in 40 % of generated children (see Fig. 14.22c). Only a few children decided to steal as the father-mother ratio was in favour of the mother.

14.6.5 Generating Children of Parents with Similar Personalities

In the second experiment we set-up father and mother with similar personalities (see Fig. 14.23a) and during generation applied a high level of mutation (25 %). We observed the children personalities and actions, depicted in Fig. 14.23b. Generated children had very similar personalities, with occasional exceptions, due to mutations. In this experiment father choses to search for food, while mother choses again to beg. Having the same father-mother ratio (30 %), most of children decide to beg, just like their mother (see Fig. 14.23c). Several mutated children decided to work.

The above experiments showed that having a base population with diverse personalities leads to generating children with diverse behaviour. Having parents with similar personalities results in their children having similar personalities and predominantly showing the same behaviour, unless they undergo mutation.

14.7 Conclusions

In this work, we have presented a methodology for generating large and diverse agent populations for the purposes of social simulations. This methodology is using genetic operations to produce individuals with unique appearance and behaviour. We have separated the methodology into six steps. First step is the definition of the base population, which specifies the visual traits of the whole population, although using mutation we may achieve novelty during generation. Second step is the definition of motivational modifiers, where motivation serves as the goal selection mechanism. In our case, we used physiological needs as the main motivation. Third step is the definition of personality traits, where personality affects agents decisions during planning and agents select actions that best match their profile. In the context of social simulations, agents belong to specific social, ethnic or cultural groups and have to obey specific social norms. Therefore, fourth step is the definition of the social system and norms, in our case using Electronic Institutions. The fifth step is the adaptation and annotation of the environment that reflects all actions specified in the electronic institution. Agents are using these annotation to automatically plan their actions and interact with the environment. Following these steps results generating a diverse agent population having a high degree of variety in their appearance and behaviour, while also demonstrating substantially high degree of complexity of actions being performed by the agents.

We have illustrated the application of the methodology proposed in this paper to the development of two case studies. In the first case study virtual agents were used to enrich a historical reconstruction with simulation of everyday life of ancient Sumerians in the city of Uruk, 3000 B.C. In the second case study we have applied our methodology to building a cultural simulation of the Darug tribe in Australia around 1700 A.D. Due to the high degree of automation in the creation of large virtual agent groups that our methodology offers, in both case studies we were able to achieve significant time savings while maintaining a high degree of complexity of the resulting virtual agent behaviour.

References

Alderfer CP (1969) An empirical test of a new theory of human needs. Organ Behav Hum Perform 4(2):142–175

Bartneck C (2002) Integrating the occ model of emotions in embodied characters. In: Workshop on virtual conversational characters. Citeseer

Braubach L, Pokahr A, Moldt D, Lamersdorf W (2005) Goal representation for bdi agent systems. In: Programming multi-agent systems. Springer, pp 44–65

Dylla K, Mueller P, Ulmer A, Haegle S, Fisher b (2009) Rome Reborn 2.0: a case study of virtual city reconstruction using procedural modeling techniques. In: 37th Proceedings of the CAA conference. Archaeopress, Oxford, pp 62–66

Esteva M (2003) Electronic institutions: from specification to development. Ph.D. dissertation, Institut d'Investigació en Intelligència Artificial (IIIA), Spain

Gauder J (2013) Crysis 3 cost $66 million to make, can next gen sustain such budgets? GameChup Video Games News at http://www.gamechup.com/crysis-3-cost-66-million-to-make-can-next-gen-sustain-such-budgets/, 1 Mar 2013

Goldberg LR (1990) An alternative "description of personality": the Big-Five factor structure. J Personal Soc Psychol 59(6):1216–1229. http://psycinfo.apa.org/doi/index.cfm?fuseaction=showUIDAbstractŹuid=1991-09869-001

Gutierrez D, Frischer B, Cerezo E, Gomez A, Seron F (2007) AI and virtual crowds: populating the Colosseum. Cult Heritage 8(2):176–185

Howard PJ, Howard JM (1995) The big five quickstart: an introduction to the five-factor model of personality for human resource professionals

Lewis M (2000) Evolving human figure geometry. Ohio State University, Tech. Rep. OSU-ACCAD-5/00-TR1, ACCAD
Mam J, Haegler S, Yersin B, Muller P, Thalmann D, Van Gool L (2007) Populating Ancient Pompeii with crowds of virtual Romans. In: 8th international symposium on Virtual Reality, Archeology and Cultural Heritage—VAST
Maslow AH, Frager R, Fadiman J (1970) Motivation and personality, vol 2. Harper & Row, New York
Shehory O, Kraus S, Yadgar O (1999) Emergent cooperative goal-satisfaction in large-scale automated-agent systems. Artif Intell 110(1):1–55
Steunebrink BR, Dastani M, Meyer J-JC (2009) The OCC model revisited. In: Reichardt D (ed) Emotion and Computing. Paderborn, Germany
Trescak T (2012) Intelligent generation and control of interactive virtual worlds. Ph.D. dissertation, Autonomous University of Barcelona
Trescak T, Bogdanovych A, Simoff S, Rodriguez I (2012) Generating diverse ethnic groups with genetic algorithms. In: Proceedings of the 18th ACM symposium on virtual reality software and technology, ser. VRST '12. ACM, New York, NY, USA, pp 1–8. http://doi.acm.org/10.1145/2407336.2407338
Vieira RCC, Vidal CA, Neto JBC (2010) Simulation of genetic inheritance in the generation of virtual characters. In: VR, Lok B, Klinker G, Nakatsu R (eds) IEEE, pp 119–126
Vosinakis S, Panayiotopoulos T (2001) Simhuman: a platform for real-time virtual agents with planning capabilities. In: Proceedings of the IVA 2001 Workshop. Springer, pp 210–223